ROMANS

VOLUME 7

THE PREACHER'S OUTLINE & SERMON BIBLE®

ROMANS

VOLUME 7

THE PREACHER'S OUTLINE & SERMON BIBLE®

NEW TESTAMENT

NEW INTERNATIONAL VERSION

Leadership Ministries Worldwide
PO Box 21310
Chattanooga, TN 37424-0310

Publisher & Distributor

DEDICATED:

To all the men and women of the world
who preach and teach the Gospel of our
Lord Jesus Christ and
To the Mercy and Grace of God.

——————— & ———————

• Demonstrated to us in Christ Jesus our Lord.

"In him we have redemption through his blood, the forgiveness
of sins, in accordance with the riches of God's grace." (Eph. 1:7 NIV)

• Out of the mercy and grace of God His Word has flowed.
Let every person know that God will have mercy upon him,
forgiving and using him to fulfill His glorious plan of salvation.

"For God so loved the world, that he gave his one and only Son, that
whosoever believes in him shall not perish, but have eternal life. For
God did not send his Son into the world to condemn the world, but to
save the world through him." (Jn 3:16-17 NIV)

"This is good and pleases God our Saviour; who wants all men to be
saved and to come to the knowledge of the truth." (I Tim. 2:3-4 NIV)

——————— & ———————

The Preacher's Outline and Study Bible®-NIV
is written for God's servants to use in their
study, teaching, and preaching of God's Holy Word.

OUR VISION - PASSION - PURPOSE

● To share the Word of God with the world.
● To help the believer, both minister and layman alike, in his understanding,
preaching, and teaching of God's Word.
● To do everything we possibly can to lead men, women, boys, and girls to
give their hearts and lives to Jesus Christ and to secure the eternal life
which He offers.
● To do all we can to minister to the needy of the world.
● To give Jesus Christ His proper place, the place which the Word gives Him.
Therefore — No work of Leadership Ministries Worldwide will ever be
personalized.

HOW TO USE... The Preacher's Outline & Sermon Bible®

A	*Your Scripture Passage always printed out*	***First***: Glance at the **Subject Heading**. Think about it for a moment. ***Then***: Glance at the **Subject Heading** & the **Major Points** together.
B	*Your Sermon Outline located next to each verse*	
C	*A Wealth of Practical Commentary Material*	***Now***: Glance at both the **Major Points** & **Subpoints** while reading the Scripture. Note how the points are beside the applicable verse—simply stating what the Scripture is saying—in Outline form.
D	*Illustrations and Applications for every audience*	***Finally***: Read the **Commentary**. KEY: Note that the *major point numbers* in the *outline* match those in the *commentary*.
E	*Support Scripture thoroughly researched & written out*	

MATTHEW 6:1-4

CHAPTER 6

K. The Right Motive for Giving,[DS1] **6:1-4**

① **Acts of righteousness— doing good & giving**
 a. Warning: Do not seek recognition
 b. The reason: God will not reward

② **The wrong motive**
 a. Giving for recognition

"**B**e careful not to do your 'acts of righteousness' before men, to be seen by them. If you **A**, you will have no rew**A** from your Father in heaven.
2 "So when you give to the needy, do not announce it with trumpets, as the hy-pocrites do in the syna-gogues and on the streets, to be honored by men. I tell you the truth, they have received their reward in full.
3 But when you give to the needy, do not let your left hand know what your right hand is doing,
4 So that your giving may be in secret. Then your Father, who sees what is done in se-cret, will reward you.

 b. Characteristic of hypocrites
 c. Reward: Recognition by men only

B

3 **The right motive**
 a. Giving unconsciously
 b. Giving quietly—pri-vately—secretly
4 **The reasons**
 a. Father sees in secret
 b. Father rewards openly

DIVISION IV

THE TEACHINGS OF THE MESSIAH TO HIS DISCIPLES: THE GREAT SERMON ON THE MOUNT, 5:1-7:29

K. The Right Motive for Giving, 6:1-4

(6:1-4) Introduction—Motive: what a man does matters greatly to God. God expects men to be kind and to do good in the world: to help others both through personal involve-ment and through giving generously and sacrificially.

But there is something else that God expects, something of critical importance: God expects a man to have *the right motive*. Just why **C** man does good and shows kindness matters greatly to God. It matters so much that a person's eternal fate is determined by his motive. Because of this, Christ warns us about right and wrong motives.

1. Acts of righteousness—doing good and giving (v.1).
2. The wrong motive (v.2).
3. The right motive (v.3-4).
4. The reasons (v.4).

① **(6:1) Righteous Acts—Service—Giving**: there are acts of righteousness—doing good and giving to others. The phrase "acts of righteousness" means giving in order to meet the needs of the poor. To the Jew, acts of righteous-ness and righteousness meant the same thing. Doing right-eous acts was the greatest thing a Jew could do; it was the first act of religion. It was considered to be the very em-bodiment of righteousness, so much so that the two words began to be used synonymously. Giving acts of righteous-ness merited and assured one of righteousness and salva-tion. (See note 5—Mt.5:6.) Christ warned there is great danger in giving and doing acts of righteousness. Take heed and guard yourself. Do not give for recognition, or you will lose your reward.

Thought 1. There are two important lessons in this verse.
1) Man must guard and be alert to the deception of giving and doing good before men. A person's heart can be deceived. The sin creeps up on man; it is insidious and **D** tle. It will keep a person from receiving anything from God.
2) A person must do righteous acts, do good. It is a duty of the Christian. In this passage alone Christ says four times, "Do your acts of righteousness."

② **(6:2) Motive**: there is the wrong motive for doing good. Christ takes for granted that the believer gives and does good. What Christ strikes at is the motive of the human heart for giving and doing good.

1. Giving for recognition is the wrong motive for giv-ing. Recognition is said to be sought by blowing one's own horn in two places: (a) in the synagogue before religious people, and (b) in the streets before the public.

E "Everything they do is done for men to see: They make their phylacteries wide and the tassels on their garments long; (Mat 23:5)

"Beware of the teachers of the law. They like to walk around in flowing robes and love to be greeted in the marketplaces and have the most important seats in the synagogues and the places of honor at ban-quets. (Luke 20:46)

OUTLINE BIBLE RESOURCES

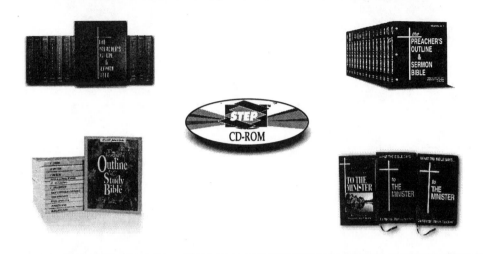

This material, like similar works, has come from imperfect man and is thus susceptible to human error. We are nevertheless grateful to God for both calling us and empowering us through His Holy Spirit to undertake this task. Because of His goodness and grace The Preacher's Outline & Sermon Bible® - New Testament is complete in 14 volumes, and the Old Testament volumes release periodically. **The Minister's Handbook** is available and *OUTLINE* Bible materials are releasing electonically on **POSB-CD** and our **Web site**.

God has given the strength and stamina to bring us this far. Our confidence is that, as we keep our eyes on Him and grounded in the undeniable truths of the Word, we will continue working through the Old Testament volumes and the second series known as **The Teacher's Outline & Study Bible.** The future includes helpful *Outline Bible* books and **Handbook** materials for God's dear servants.

To everyone everywhere who preaches and teaches the Word, we offer this material firstly to Him in whose name we labor and serve, and for whose glory it has been produced.

Our daily prayer is that each volume will lead thousands, millions, yes even billions, into a better understanding of the Holy Scriptures and a fuller knowledge of Jesus Christ the incarnate Word, of whom the Scriptures so faithfully testify.

As you have purchased this volume, you will be pleased to know that a small portion of the price you have paid has gone to underwrite and provide similar volumes in other languages (Russian, Korean, Spanish and others yet to come) — To a preacher, pastor, lay leader, or Bible student somewhere around the world, who will present God's message with clarity, authority, and understanding beyond their own. *Amen*.

For information and prices, kindly contact your *OUTLINE* Bible bookseller or:

LEADERSHIP MINISTRIES WORLDWIDE

P.O. Box 21310, 515 Airport Road, Suite 107
Chattanooga, TN 37424-0310
(423) 855-2181 FAX (423) 855-8616
E-Mail - outlinebible@compuserve.com
www.outlinebible.org — *FREE* download materials

9/98

Currently Available Materials, with New Volumes Releasing Regularly

- **THE PREACHER'S OUTLINE & SERMON BIBLE® — DELUXE EDITION**

  3-Ring, looseleaf binder

  Volume 1 . . . . St. Matthew I (chapters 1-15)
  Volume 2 . . . . St. Matthew II (chapters 16-28)
  Volume 3 . . . . St. Mark
  Volume 4 . . . . St. Luke
  Volume 5 . . . . St. John
  Volume 6 . . . . Acts
  Volume 7 . . . . Romans
  Volume 8 . . . . 1, 2 Corinthians (1 volume)
  Volume 9 . . . . Galatians, Ephesians, Philippians, Colossians (1 volume)
  Volume 10 . . . . 1,2 Thessalonians, 1,2 Timothy, Titus, Philemon (1 volume)
  Volume 11 . . . . Hebrews -James (1 volume)
  Volume 12 . . . . 1,2 Peter, 1,2,3 John, Jude (1 volume)
  Volume 13 . . . . Revelation
  Volume 14 . . . . Master Outline & Subject Index
  FULL SET — 14 Volumes

- **THE PREACHER'S OUTLINE & SERMON BIBLE® — OLD TESTAMENT**

  Volume 1 . . . . Genesis I (chapters 1-11)
  Volume 2 . . . . Genesis II (chapters 12-50)
  Volume 3 . . . . Exodus I (chapters 1-18)
  Volume 4 . . . . Exodus II (chapters 19-40)
  Volume 5 . . . . Leviticus

  New volumes release periodically

- **THE PREACHER'S OUTLINE & SERMON BIBLE® — SOFTBOUND EDITION**
  Identical content as Deluxe above. Lightweight, compact, and affordable for overseas & traveling

- **THE PREACHER'S OUTLINE & SERMON BIBLE® — 3 VOL HARDCOVER w/CD**

- **THE PREACHER'S OUTLINE & SERMON BIBLE® — NIV SOFTBOUND EDITION**

- **The Minister's Personal Handbook - What the Bible Says...to the Minister**
  12 Chapters - 127 Subjects - 400 Verses *OUTLINED* - Paperback, Leatherette, 3-ring

- **THE TEACHER'S OUTLINE & STUDY BIBLE™ • New Testament Books •**
  Complete 45 minute lessons - 4 months of studies/book; 200± pages - Student Journal Guides

- **OUTLINE Bible Studies series: 10 Commandments - The Tabernacle**

- **Practical Word Studies: New Testament - 2,000 Key Words Made Easy**

- **CD-ROM: Preacher, Teacher, and Handbook- (Windows/STEP) - WORDSearch**

- **Translations of Preacher, Teacher, and Minister's Handbook: <u>Limited Quantities</u>**
  Russian — Spanish — Korean *Future: French, Portuguese, Hindi, Chinese*
  — *Contact us for Specific Language Availability and Prices* —

For quantity orders and information, please contact either:

LEADERSHIP MINISTRIES WORLDWIDE   *Your OUTLINE Bible Bookseller*
PO Box 21310
Chattanooga, TN 37424-0310
(423) 855-2181 (9am - 5pm Eastern) • FAX (423) 855-8616 (24 hours)
E•Mail - outlinebible@compuserve.com.
→ FREE Download Sample Pages — www.outlinebible.org

- *Equipping God's Servants Worldwide with OUTLINE Bible Materials* •
LMW is a nonprofit, international, nondenominational mission agency   9/98

ACKNOWLEDGMENTS

Every child of God is precious to the Lord and deeply loved. And every child as a servant of the Lord touches the lives of those who come in contact with him or his ministry. The writing ministry of the following servants have touched this work, and we are grateful that God brought their writings our way. We hereby acknowledge their ministry to us, being fully aware that there are so many others down through the years whose writings have touched our lives and who deserve mention, but the weaknesses of our minds have caused them to fade from memory. May our wonderful Lord continue to bless the ministry of these dear servants, and the ministry of us all as we diligently labor to reach the world for Christ and to meet the desperate needs of those who suffer so much.

THE GREEK SOURCES

1. Expositor's Greek Testament, Edited by W. Robertson Nicoll. Grand Rapids, MI: Eerdmans Publishing Co., 1970

2. Robertson, A.T. Word Pictures in the New Testament. Nashville, TN: Broadman Press, 1930.

3. Thayer, Joseph Henry. Greek-English Lexicon of the New Testament. New York: American Book Co, No date listed.

4. Vincent, Marvin R. Word Studies in the New Testament. Grand Rapids, MI: Eerdmans Publishing Co., 1969.

5. Vine, W.E. Expository Dictionary of New Testament Words. Old Tappan, NJ: Fleming H. Revell Co. No date listed.

6. Wuest, Kenneth S. Word Studies in the Greek New Testament. Grand Rapids, MI: Eerdmans Publishing Co., 1966.

THE REFERENCE WORKS

7. Cruden's Complete Concordance of the Old & New Testament. Philadelphia, PA: The John C. Winston Co., 1930.

8. Josephus' Complete Works. Grand Rapids, MI: Kregel Publications, 1981.

9. Lockyer, Herbert. Series of Books, including his Books on All the Men, Women, Miracles, and Parables of the Bible. Grand Rapids, MI: Zondervan Publishing House, 1958-1967.

10. -Nave's Topical Bible. Nashville, TN: The Southwestern Co., No date listed.

11. The Amplified New Testament. (Scripture Quotations are from the Amplified New Testament, Copyright 1954, 1958, 1987 by the Lockman Foundation. Used by permission.)

12. The Four Translation New Testament (Including King James, New American Standard, Williams - New Testament In the Language of the People, Beck - New Testament In the Language of Today.) Minneapolis, MN: World Wide Publications.

13. The New Compact Bible Dictionary, Edited by T. Alton Bryant. Grand Rapids, MI: Zondervan Publishing House, 1967.

14. The New Thompson Chain Reference Bible. Indianapolis, IN: B.B. Kirkbride Bible Co., 1964,

THE COMMENTARIES

15. Barclay, William. Daily Study Bible Series. Philadelphia, PA: Westminster Press, Began in 1953.

16. Bruce, F.F. The Epistle to the Ephesians. Westwood, NJ: Fleming H. Revell Co., 1968.

17. Bruce, F.F. Epistle to the Hebrews. Grand Rapids, MI: Eerdmans Publishing Co., 1964.

18. Bruce, F.F. The Epistles of John. Old Tappan, NJ: Fleming H. Revell Co., 1970.

19. Criswell, W.A. Expository Sermons on Revelation. Grand Rapids, MI: Zondervan Publishing House, 1962-66.

20. Greene, Oliver. The Epistles of John. Greenville, SC: The Gospel Hour, Inc., 1966.

21. Greene, Oliver. The Epistles of Paul the Apostle to the Hebrews. Greenville, SC: The Gospel Hour, Inc., 1965.

22. Greene, Oliver. The Epistles of Paul the Apostle to Timothy & Titus. Greenville, SC: The Gospel Hour, Inc., 1964.

23. Greene, Oliver. The Revelation Verse by Verse Study. Greenville, SC: The Gospel Hour, Inc., 1963.

24. Henry, Matthew. Commentary on the Whole Bible. Old Tappan, NJ: Fleming H. Revell Co.

25. Hodge, Charles. Exposition on Romans & on Corinthians. Grand Rapids, MI: Eerdmans Publishing Co., 1972-1973.

26. Ladd, George Eldon. A Commentary On the Revelation of John. Grand Rapids, MI: Eerdmans Publishing Co., 1972-1973.

27. Leupold, H.C. Exposition of Daniel. Grand Rapids, MI: Baker Book House, 1969.

28. Morris, Leon. The Gospel According to John. Grand Rapids, MI: Eerdmans Publishing Co., 1971.

29. Newell, William R. Hebrews, Verse by Verse. Chicago, IL: Moody Press, 1947.

30. Strauss, Lehman. Devotional Studies in Galatians & Ephesians. Neptune, NJ: Loizeaux Brothers, 1957.

31. Strauss, Lehman. Devotional Studies in Philippians. Neptune, NJ: Loizeaux Brothers, 1959.

32. Strauss, Lehman. James, Your Brother. Neptune, NJ: Loizeaux Brothers, 1956.

33. Strauss, Lehman. The Book of the Revelation. Neptune, NJ: Loizeaux Brothers, 1964.

34. The New Testament & Wycliffe Bible Commentary, Edited by Charles F. Pfeiffer & Everett F. Harrison. New York: The Iverson Associates, 1971. Produced for Moody Monthly. Chicago Moody Press, 1962.

35. The Pulpit Commentary, Edited by H.D.M. Spence & Joseph S. Exell. Grand Rapids, MI: Eerdmans Publishing Co., 1950.

36. Thomas, W.H. Griffith. Hebrews, A Devotional Commentary. Grand Rapids, MI: Eerdmans Publishing Co., 1970.

37. Thomas, W.H. Griffith. Outline Studies in the Acts of the Apostles. Grand Rapids, MI: Eerdmans Publishing Co., 1956.

38. Thomas, W.H. Griffith. St. Paul's Epistle to the Romans. Grand Rapids, MI: Eerdmans Publishing Co., 1946.

39. Thomas, W.H. Griffith. Studies in Colossians & Philemon. Grand Rapids, MI: Baker Book House, 1973.

40. Tyndale New Testament Commentaries. Grand Rapids, MI: Eerdmans Publishing Co., Began in 1958.

41. Walker, Thomas. Acts of the Apostles. Chicago, IL: Moody Press, 1965.

42. Walvoord, John. The Thessalonian Epistles. Grand Rapids, MI: Zondervan Publishing House, 1973.

MISCELLANEOUS ABBREVIATIONS

&	=	And
Arg.	=	Argument
Bckgrd.	=	Background
Bc.	=	Because
Circ.	=	Circumstance
Concl.	=	Conclusion
Cp.	=	Compare
Ct.	=	Contrast
Dif.	=	Different
e.g.	=	For example
Et.	=	Eternal
F.	=	Following
Govt.	=	Government
Id.	=	Identity or Identification
Illust.	=	Illustration
K.	=	Kingdom, K. of God, K. of Heaven, etc.
No.	=	Number
N.T.	=	New Testament
O.T.	=	Old Testament
Pt.	=	Point
Quest.	=	Question
Rel.	=	Religion
Resp.	=	Responsibility
Rev.	=	Revelation
Rgt.	=	Righteousness
Thru	=	Through
V.	=	Verse
Vs.	=	Verses
Vs.	=	Versus

The Preacher's
Outline
&
Sermon
Bible®

> **"**
> *Woe to me if I do not
> preach the gospel!*
> **"** (I Cor. 9:16 NIV)

ROMANS

INTRODUCTION

AUTHOR: Paul, the Apostle. Paul clearly states that he is the author (Ro.1:1), and the personal references and facts given in Chapter 15 tell us beyond any doubt that Paul is the author.

DATE: A.D. 55-58.

Paul says, "Now, however, I am on my way to Jerusalem in the service of the saint, there." I go unto Jerusalem to minister unto the saints" (Ro.15:25). This journey to Jerusalem was the trip made necessary by the extreme poverty of the believers in the Jerusalem church. Paul had taken a collection from the Gentile churches and felt compelled to deliver the offering himself. This occurred on his third missionary journey.

TO WHOM WRITTEN: "To all in Rome, who are loved by God, and called to be saints."

Several manuscripts have been found with the personal and local touches of chapters 15-16 omitted and the doxology included. This would definitely point to there being several churches. The place of writing seems to be Corinth, for Paul recommended Phoebe to the Romans. Phoebe was a deaconess from Cenchrea, the eastern seaport of Corinth.

PURPOSE: Paul had several reasons for writing.

1. Paul wished to evangelize Spain (Ro.15:25). To do so he needed a local church from which to launch his ministry—a church that would be much closer to Spain than Antioch. Antioch had been his home base up until now. By writing Romans, he was preparing the Roman church for the day when he would reveal his vision to them. He was making them familiar with his name, his mission, and his love.

2. Paul had a personal compulsion to visit and witness in Rome itself. His life-long strategy had been to evangelize the great metropolitan cities along the route that stretched from Jerusalem to Rome. He knew that a route so greatly traveled and cities so actively engaged in commerce would assure the spread of the Gospel. Rome was the capital, the center of the world; it provided the greatest strategic opportunity for world evangelism. A Rome conquered for Christ could mean a world conquered for Christ.

3. Paul was not sure he would ever reach Rome personally. He was going to Jerusalem and knew the danger. There was a chance he might be killed in Jerusalem. He requested the Roman church to pray for him: "I urge you, brothers to join me in my struggles by praying to God for me. Pray that I may be rescued from the unbelievers in Judea" (15:30-31). Yet despite the danger, Paul was a master strategist: he knew the strategic importance of Rome for the spread of the Gospel worldwide. The church had to be rooted and grounded in the faith; therefore he sat down and wrote this great letter. The message of the letter is what Paul would hammer into the believers' hearts if he ever did get to stand before them.

SPECIAL FEATURES:

1. The church at Rome. The church was strong. Five factors show its strength.

First, Rome was a *lay church*. A writer of the fourth century said that some Roman citizens "had embraced the faith of Christ...without any sign of mighty works or any of the apostles" (Ambrosiaster, a Latin Father, in his *Epistle to the Romans*. Quoted by F.F. Bruce. *The Epistle of Paul to the Romans*. "The Tyndale New Testament Commentaries," ed. by RVG Tasker. Grand Rapids, MI: Eerdmans, 1963, p.13). The content of the epistle shows a people of great spiritual depth and maturity. But how did the gospel reach Rome? Who founded the church? The only thing known for sure is that there was a great and flourishing church in the capital. But just when the church was founded is unknown. There are several possibilities.

    a. At Pentecost there were "visitors from Rome, both Jews and converts to Judaism" (Acts 2:10). Were any converted during Pentecost? There is no specific mention of converts among the Romans, but Romans are the only group identified among the European pilgrims.

    b. Many of the members of the Roman church were known by Paul personally. He had met them elsewhere, sometime long ago. The church could have been founded by these. He greets Aquila and Priscilla (16:3; cp. Acts 18:2-3). He also greets some well-known believers whom he says were "in Christ" even before himself: Andronicus and Junia (16:7). Rufus, perhaps the son of Simon of Cyrene who carried the cross of Christ, is also greeted (see note—16:13; cp. Mk.15:21). Paul may have known Rufus and his mother in Antioch.

    c. The lay followers of Christ were probably among the first to carry the gospel to Rome. This was Paul's great strategy as God's chief commander for world evangelization. Paul had penetrated the great cities of the world with the glorious gospel, and he did all he could to establish a strong church in each of the major cities. Each of these cities lay along the world's great roads that led right into the heart of the world's capital, Rome itself. In all the hustle and bustle of business and traveling to and fro, some men, racing throughout the world and carrying on their affairs, were bound to be reached for Christ and to become lay missionaries themselves. It was only inevitable that Rome be penetrated. A church was bound to be founded right in the heart of Rome.

Second, Rome had a *worldwide reputation*. Its faith was strong (1:8). It was spiritually mature, able to digest the *meat* of the Word. Practically every page covers a major doctrine or theological discussion.

Third, Rome was a *Gentile church*. The Gentiles, who comprised a vast majority of the membership, were reminded of the fact that Christianity had come from Jewish roots. Therefore, the Jews were to be deeply respected—even if they were outnumbered (11:18).

Fourth, Rome was a *persecuted church*. The church was severely persecuted seven years after Paul wrote this great letter to the believers. Nero had burned the older section of the great city in a fit of madness, and he blamed the burning of Rome upon the Christians. Believers were also charged with such crimes as cannibalism, immoral practices, and with being enemies of the state. They were actually charged with any other crime that could be connived. However, the blood of the church proved to be its seed (Tertullian, Apology 50. Quoted by F.F. Bruce. *The Epistle of Paul to the Romans.* "The Tyndale New Testament Commentaries," Grand Rapids, MI: Eerdmans Publishing Co., 1958, p.17). Believers, fleeing the persecution, spread all over the world; and wherever they went they shared the glorious news of eternal life in Christ Jesus. In addition, the citizens of Rome grew tired of so much savagery and eventually demanded that the savagery against the Christians stop. The church was left alone and the glorious news of salvation was allowed to be freely proclaimed.

Fifth, Rome was a *triumphant church.* The church was unashamed of its life and witness. It was willing to stand up and be counted by the side of those who suffered. When Paul was being escorted into the city as a Roman prisoner, while still some thirty to forty miles away, the Christian church marched forward to meet and give him a triumphant processional over those thirty to forty miles. The sight of these dear believers filled Paul with a sense of glory seldom experienced by men. (See note—Acts 28:13-15.)

2. Romans is *The Great Epistle of Theology.* It is a statement of what Paul believed, a statement of his theology. Paul was not writing to meet a special problem or danger or error. He was writing primarily to root and ground the Roman believers in the faith as deeply as he could, for they lived in the great strategic center with explosive potential for world evangelization. He was completely free to set forth what he saw to be the essential theology for a living faith.

3. Romans is *The Epistle Written for Every Man.* It is the Gospel of God (1:1). It is a book for the world (1:4-2:16; etc.); a book for the church (see 1:1-7; etc.); a book for theologians (see 3:1-5:21; etc.); a book for philosophers (see 1:1-2:16; etc.); a book for legalists (see 7:1f; etc.); a book for immature believers (see 6:1-8:30); a book for mature believers (see 8:12-14; etc.); a book for sufferers (see 7:1-8:39; etc.); a book for unbelievers (see 1:1-2:16; etc.); a book for religionists (see 2:17-5:21; etc.). Romans is the truth desperately needed by every man, whoever or wherever he may be.

4. Romans is *The Church's Last Testament.* Although one of the driving forces of Paul's heart was to visit the Roman church, he was not sure he would ever get to see them face to face (See Purpose, point 3). Yet, the church's strategic importance necessitated that he do what he could to assure that they use their explosive potential for Christ. Thus, he was forced to write—just in case. And write he did. In the Book of Romans the church has what Paul wished to say to the church—just in case he never got there. In a sense it is *The Church's Last Testament*—just what the church needs to hear. Romans comes closest to being the one written possession a church needs, the most comprehensive statement of Christian truth.

5. Romans is *The Gospel's Main Truth.* This is evident from Special Features, points 1 and 2.

6. Romans is *God's Worldwide Plan for Israel and the Gentiles.* More clearly than any other book, Romans shows God's glorious plan for the ages in Israel and the Gentile nations. A panoramic view of history is given from a Christian perspective. This is quickly grasped by a study of the Outline, chapters 9-11.

OUTLINE OF ROMANS

THE PREACHER'S OUTLINE & SERMON BIBLE® is *unique*. It differs from all other Study Bibles & Sermon Resource Materials in that every Passage and Subject is outlined right beside the Scripture. When you choose any *Subject* below and turn to the reference, you have not only the Scripture, but you discover the Scripture and Subject *already outlined for you—verse by verse.*

For a quick example, choose one of the subjects below and turn to the Scripture, and you will find this marvelous help for faster, easier, and more accurate use.

In addition, every point of the Scripture and Subject is *fully developed in a Commentary with supporting Scripture* at the bottom of the page. Again, this arrangement makes sermon preparation much easier and faster.

Note something else: The Subjects of Romans have titles that are both Biblical and *practical*. The practical titles sometimes have more appeal to people. This *benefit* is clearly seen for use on billboards, bulletins, church newsletters, etc.

A suggestion: For the quickest overview of Romans, first read *all the major titles* (I, II, III, etc.), then come back and read the subtitles.

OUTLINE OF ROMANS

I. **GREETING AND THEME: THE GOSPEL AND GOD'S RIGHTEOUSNESS, 1:1-17**

A. Paul's Credentials: Enslavement to Christ, 1:1-7
B. Paul's Interest in the Church: Enslavement to the Gospel, 1:8-15
C. Paul's Boldness for Christ: Unashamedness of the Gospel, 1:16-17

II. **SIN AND CONDEMNATION: THE WORLD'S NEED TO GET RIGHT WITH GOD, 1:18-3:20**

A. God's Case Against All Godlessness and Wickedness of Men: Why God Shows Wrath, 1:18-23
B. God's Case Against All Godlessness and Wickedness of Men: How God Shows Wrath, 1:24-32
C. God's Case Against the Moralist: Judgment, 2:1-16
D. God's Case Against the Religionist (Jew), 2:17-29
E. The Arguments of the Religionist (Jew) Against a Heart Religion, 3:1-8 (Cp. Romans 2:23-29)
F. God's Case Against All Men, 3:9-20

III. **FAITH AND JUSTIFICATION: THE WAY FOR THE WORLD TO BE RIGHT WITH GOD, 3:21-5:21**

A. Righteousness: The Way to be Right With God, 3:21-26
B. Faith: The Way that Puts an End to Human Boasting and Pride, to Self-Righteousness and Works, 3:27-31
C. Logic: The Evidence that Faith Alone Justifies a Man, 4:1-8
D. Rituals, Rules, and Ordinances: The Wrong Way for a Man to Seek Justification, 4:9-12
E. Law: The Wrong Way for a Man to be Justified, 4:13-16
F. Abraham: The Example of a Man Justified by Faith Alone, 4:17-25
G. God's Unbelievable Love (Part I): The Results of Justification, 5:1-5
H. God's Unbelievable Love (Part II): The Great Depth of Justification, 5:6-11
I. Adam and Christ: The Two Focal Points of History, 5:12-21

IV. **HOLINESS AND SANCTIFICATION: THE WAY FOR THE BELIEVER TO BE FREE FROM SIN, 6:1-23**

A. The Believer is Not to Continue in Sin (Part I): He is to Know His Position in Christ, 6:1-10
B. The Believer is Not to Continue in Sin (Part II): He is to Live Out His Position in Christ, 6:11-13
C. The Believer is Not to Continue in Sin (Part III): He Does Not Have License to Sin, 6:14-23

V. **STRUGGLE AND CONFESSION: THE BELIEVER IS TO BE FREE FROM THE LAW, 7:1-25**

A. The Two Positions of the Law to Man, 7:1-6
B. The Purpose of the Law, 7:7-13
C. The Confessions of a Man's Struggling Soul, 7:14-25

VI. **DELIVERANCE AND REDEMPTION: THE BELIEVER SHALL BE FREED FROM STRUGGLING AND SUFFERING BY THE SPIRIT, 8:1-39**

A. The Man in Christ Jesus is Freed from Condemnation: The Power of the Spirit, 8:1-17
B. The Whole Creation Shall Be Freed from Struggling and Suffering, 8:18-27
C. God Assures Deliverance (Freedom) from Struggling and Suffering, 8:28-39

VII. **ISRAEL AND THE GOSPEL OF RIGHTEOUSNESS, 9:1-11:36**

A. The Privileges of Israel and Their Tragic Failure, 9:1-5
B. The True Israel or Children of God, 9:6-13

3

CHAPTER 1

I. GREETING AND THEME: THE GOSPEL AND GOD'S RIGHTEOUSNESS, 1:1-17

A. Paul's Credentials: Enslavement to Christ,^{DS1} *(omitted — see below)*

1 He was a slave of Christ	**A. Paul's Credentials: Enslavement to Christ,**DS1 **1:1-7**
2 He was an apostle of God	**P**aul, a servant of Christ Jesus, called to be an apostle and set apart for the gospel of God—
3 He was set apart to the gospel of God a. The gospel promised long ago b. The gospel that concerns	2 The gospel he promised beforehand through his prophets in the Holy Scriptures 3 Regarding his Son, who as

to his human nature was a descendant of David,
4 And who through the Spirit of holiness was declared with power to be the Son of God by his resurrection from the dead: Jesus Christ our Lord.
5 Through him and for his name's sake, we received grace and apostleship to call people from among all the Gentiles to the obedience that comes from faith.
6 And you also are among those who are called to belong to Jesus Christ.
7 To all in Rome who are loved by God and called to be saints: Grace and peace to you from God our Father and from the Lord Jesus Christ.

God's Son, Jesus Christ, becoming a Man
c. The gospel that declares Jesus Christ to be the Son of God
1) By Spirit of holiness
2) By the resurrection
4 He had received God's grace & God's mission^{DS2}

5 He acknowledged the enslavement of others
a. They too were called
b. They too were loved
c. They too were saints
d. They too were recipients of grace & peace

DIVISION I

GREETING AND THEME: THE GOSPEL AND GOD'S RIGHTEOUSNESS, 1:1-17

A. Paul's Credentials: Enslavement to Christ, 1:1-7

(1:1-7) **Introduction**: no person is a true follower of Jesus Christ unless he is *enslaved by Christ*. In fact, it is *impossible* for a person to belong to Christ unless he is *enslaved by Christ*. This is the shocking message Paul wants to get across to the believers at Rome.

1. He was a slave of Christ (v.1).
2. He was an apostle of God (v.1).
3. He was set apart to the gospel of God (v.1-4).
4. He had received God's grace and God's mission (v.5).
5. He acknowledged the enslavement of others (v.6-7).

DEEPER STUDY # 1
(1:1-7) **Gospel—Christianity**: in these verses Paul gives the raw outline of the gospel he preached (v.1-4). It is a penetrating look at primitive Christianity. Note the gospel's close agreement with the Apostle's Creed.

1. Paul's view of the Old Testament.
   a. It comes from God.
   b. It is given "through His prophets."
   c. It is "holy" Scripture.
2. Paul's view of the Lord Jesus Christ.
   a. He is God's Son: "regarding His Son."
   b. He is the promised Savior: "Christ," the Messiah.
   c. He is Lord: "our Lord."
   d. He is man: "as to his human nature was a descendant of David"
   e. He is declared to be the very Son of God: "declared with power to be the Son of God."
   f. He is divine or holy: "through the Spirit of holiness."
   g. He is risen from the dead: "by his resurrection from the dead."
3. Paul's view of the gospel.
   a. It is of God: "the Gospel of God" (cp. Ro.1:1, 17; 3:21).
   b. It was prophesied: "he promised...."

c. It agrees with the Old Testament: "promised before...in the Holy Scriptures."
d. It concerns God's very own Son: "regarding His Son."
e. It concerns the divine Savior: Jesus Christ, our Lord:..." who through the Spirit of Holiness was declared with power to be the Son of God by his resurrection from the dead."
f. It concerns the human Savior: "A descendant of David."
g. It concerns the risen Savior: "his resurrection from the dead."

1 (1:1) **Servant—Slave** (doulos): Paul was a "servant" or "slave" of Jesus Christ. The word "servant" or "slave" (doulos) means far more than just a servant. It means a slave totally possessed by the master. It is a *bond-servant* bound by law to a master.

A look at the slave market of Paul's day shows more clearly what Paul meant when he said he was a "slave of Jesus Christ."

1. The slave was owned by his master; he was totally possessed by his master. This is what Paul meant. Paul was purchased and possessed by Christ. Christ had looked upon him and had seen his degraded and needful condition. And when Christ looked, the most wonderful thing happened: Christ loved him and bought him; therefore, he was now the possession of Christ.

2. The slave existed for his master and he had no other reason for existence. He had no personal rights whatsoever. The same was true with Paul: he existed only for Christ. His rights were the rights of Christ only.

3. The slave served his master and he existed only for the purpose of service. He was at the master's disposal any hour of the day or night. So it was with Paul: he lived only to serve Christ—hour by hour, day by day, and night by night.

4. The slave's will belonged to his master. He was allowed no will and no ambition other than the will and ambition of the master. He was completely subservient to the Master and owed total obedience to the will of the master. Paul belonged to Christ. In fact, he said that he fought and struggled to "take captive every thought to make it obedient to Christ."(2 Cor.10:5).

5. There is a fifth and most precious thing that Paul meant by "a slave of Jesus Christ." He meant that he had the highest and most honored and kingly profession in all the world. Men of God, the greatest men of history, have always been called "the servants of God." It was the highest title of honor. The believer's slavery to Jesus Christ is no cringing, cowardly, or shameful subjection. It is the position of honor—the honor that bestows upon a man the privileges and responsibilities of serving the King of kings and Lord of lords.

⇒ Moses was the slave of God (Dt.34:5; Ps.105:26; Mal.4:4).
⇒ Joshua was the slave of God (Josh.24:29).
⇒ David was the slave of God (2 Sam.3:18; Ps.78:70).
⇒ Paul was the slave of Jesus Christ (Ro.1:1; Ph.1:1; Tit.1:1).
⇒ James was the slave of God (Jas.1:1).
⇒ Peter was the slave of Jesus Christ (2 Pt.1:1).
⇒ Jude was the slave of God (Jude 1).
⇒ The prophets were the slaves of God (Amos 3:7; Jer.7:25).
⇒ Christian believers are said to be the slaves of Jesus Christ (Acts 2:18; 1 Cor.7:22; Eph.6:6; Col.4:12; 2 Tim.2:24).

(This point is built upon what William Barclay says. *The Letter to the Romans*. "The Daily Study Bible." Philadelphia, PA: The Westminster Press, 1955, p.2).

Whoever serves me must follow me; and where I am, my servant also will be. My Father will honor the one who serves me. (John 12:26; cp. Ro.12:1; 1 Cor.15:58)

Obey them not only to win their favor when their eye is on you, but like slaves of Christ, doing the will of God from your heart. Serve wholeheartedly, as if you were serving the Lord, not men, (Eph 6:6-7)

Whatever you do, work at it with all your heart, as working for the Lord, not for men, since you know that you will receive an inheritance from the Lord as a reward. It is the Lord Christ you are serving. (Col 3:23-24)

Therefore, since we are receiving a kingdom that cannot be shaken, let us be thankful, and so worship God acceptably with reverence and awe, (Heb 12:28)

Worship the LORD your God, and his blessing will be on your food and water. I will take away sickness from among you, (Exo 23:25)

And now, O Israel, what does the LORD your God ask of you but to fear the LORD your God, to walk in all his ways, to love him, to serve the LORD your God with all your heart and with all your soul, (Deu 10:12)

Serve the LORD with fear and rejoice with trembling. (Psa 2:11)

Worship the LORD with gladness; come before him with joyful songs. (Psa 100:2)

2 (1:1) **Apostle—Paul, Call of**: Paul was an apostle of God. The word "apostle" (apostolos) means either a person who is sent out or a person who is sent forth. An apostle is a representative, an ambassador, a person who is sent out into one country to represent another country. Three things are true of the apostle: (1) he belongs to the One who has sent him out; (2) he is commissioned to be sent out; and (3) he possesses all the authority and power of the One who sends him out.

Note three forceful lessons.

1. Paul said he was "called" to be an apostle. He was not in the ministry because he...
• chose to be.
• had the ability.
• had been encouraged by others to choose the *ministerial profession*.
• enjoyed working with people.

He was an apostle, a minister of the gospel for one reason only: God had called him.

'Now get up and stand on your feet. I have appeared to you to appoint you as a servant and as a witness of what you have seen of me and what I will show you. (Acts 26:16)

I thank Christ Jesus our Lord, who has given me strength, that he considered me faithful, appointing me to his service. (1 Tim 1:12)

The LORD had said to Abram, "Leave your country, your people and your father's household and go to the land I will show you. (Gen 12:1)

So now, go. I am sending you [Moses] to Pharaoh to bring my people the Israelites out of Egypt." (Exo 3:10)

The LORD turned to him [Gideon] and said, "Go in the strength you have and save Israel out of Midian's hand. Am I not sending you?" (Judg 6:14)

Then I [Isaiah] heard the voice of the Lord saying, "Whom shall I send? And who will go for us?" And I said, "Here am I. Send me!" (Isa 6:8)

2. Paul had heard and answered God's call. God did not override Paul's will—He wanted Paul in the ministry, so He called Paul. But note: it was up to Paul to hear and respond.

3. Paul was called to be an apostle, that is, to be a minister. He was not called to occupy a position of authority or to be honored by men.

Thought 1. Every servant of God is called for two primary purposes:
1) To serve and minister.

And whoever wants to be first must be your slave—just as the Son of Man did not come to be served, but to serve, and to give his life as a ransom for many." (Mat 20:27-28)

"Which of these three do you think was a neighbor to the man who fell into the hands of robbers?" The expert in the law replied, "The one who had mercy on him." Jesus told him, "Go and do likewise." (Luke 10:36-37)

Now that I, your Lord and Teacher, have washed your feet, you also should wash one another's feet. (John 13:14)

Carry each other's burdens, and in this way you will fulfill the law of Christ. (Gal 6:2)

Therefore, as we have opportunity, let us do good to all people, especially to those who belong to the family of believers. (Gal 6:10)

2) To go out and bear fruit.

Produce fruit in keeping with repentance. (Mat 3:8)

You did not choose me, but I chose you and appointed you to go and bear fruit—fruit that will last. Then the Father will give you whatever you ask in my name. (John 15:16)

So, my brothers, you also died to the law through the body of Christ, that you might belong to another, to him who was raised from the dead, in order that we might bear fruit to God. (Rom 7:4)

Filled with the fruit of righteousness that comes through Jesus Christ—to the glory and praise of God. (Phil 1:11)

And we pray this in order that you may live a life worthy of the Lord and may please him in every way: bearing fruit in every good work, growing in the knowledge of God, (Col 1:10)

He is like a tree planted by streams of water, which yields its fruit in season and whose leaf does not wither. Whatever he does prospers. (Psa 1:3)

Planted in the house of the LORD, they will flourish in the courts of our God. (Psa 92:13)

3 (1:1-4) **Gospel, Meaning**: Paul was set apart to the gospel of God. This is the reason God called Paul: that Paul might be separated (aphorismenos) or marked and set apart to the gospel of God. The word "gospel" simply means the *good news of God*.

⇒ Paul did not say he was called and set apart to a man-made religion, denomination, or sect; nor was he called primarily to a gospel of social justice and welfare, as important as these calls are.

⇒ Paul said he was set apart to the gospel, the good news of God (cp. 1 Th.2:2-13).

Note what the gospel is.

1. The gospel of the New Testament is the *same good news* of God which was promised in the Old Testament Scriptures. Jesus Christ is the Subject and the Author of the gospel, but the gospel *began long before* the birth of Jesus. The gospel began long, long ago in the *mind and plan* of God, and God foretold the coming of the gospel (His Son) through the prophets of old. Mark says what Paul was to later say: "The beginning of the gospel about Jesus Christ, the Son of God. It is written in Isaiah the prophet: "I will send my messenger ahead of you, who will prepare your way"—"a voice of one calling in the desert, 'Prepare the way for the Lord, make straight paths for him.'" (Mk.1:1-3. See DEEPER STUDY # 1, *Gospel*—Ro.1:1-7. See DEEPER STUDY # 3, *Scripture Fulfilled*—Jn.1:45 for discussion. Also see, *Prophecy*—Master Subject Index.)

You diligently study the Scriptures because you think that by them you possess eternal life. These are the Scriptures that testify about me, (John 5:39)

But I have had God's help to this very day, and so I stand here and testify to small and great alike. I am saying nothing beyond what the prophets and Moses said would happen— (Acts 26:22)

In the past God spoke to our forefathers through the prophets at many times and in various ways, (Heb 1:1)

Concerning this salvation, the prophets, who spoke of the grace that was to come to you, searched intently and with the greatest care, Trying to find out the time and circumstances to which the Spirit of Christ in them was pointing when he predicted the sufferings of Christ and the glories that would follow. (1 Pet 1:10-11)

Above all, you must understand that no prophecy of Scripture came about by the prophet's own interpretation. For prophecy never had its origin in the will of man, but men spoke from God as they were carried along by the Holy Spirit. (2 Pet 1:20-21)

2. The gospel is the incarnation of "The Son of God..., Jesus Christ our Lord" (v.4) (see DEEPER STUDY # 1, *Gospel*—Ro.1:1-7). Note how Paul takes the names and titles of Jesus Christ and stacks them one upon another.

⇒ The Son of God. (See note—Jn.1:34.)
⇒ Jesus. (See DEEPER STUDY # 4—Mt.1:21.)
⇒ Christ. (See DEEPER STUDY # 2—Mt.1:18.)
⇒ Our Lord. (See DEEPER STUDY # 2—Acts 2:36.)

The gospel concerns "The Son of God, Jesus Christ our Lord." He is both the *Subject* and the *Author* of the gospel. By Him and through Him the gospel is created and proclaimed. He brings the *good news* of God to man. He is the very embodiment of the good news of God Himself.

The gospel concerns two glorious truths.

a. The first glorious truth is that God's Son became a man. He was a descendant of David; that is, he was born as a man. David was the greatest ruler of Israel; he was one of the greatest ancestors of Jesus. (See note, Jesus Christ, Davidic Heir—Lk.3:24-31.)

The point is this: God sent His Son into the world in human flesh. The word "was" (genomenou) means to become. God's Son became a man—flesh and blood—just like all other men. He had a human nature, and because He had a human nature...

• He suffered all the *trials of life* which we suffer.

• He is *able to help* us through all the trials of life.

The Word became flesh and made his dwelling among us. We have seen his glory, the glory of the One and Only, who came from the Father, full of grace and truth. (John 1:14)

Since the children have flesh and blood, he too shared in their humanity so that by his death he might destroy him who holds the power of death—that is, the devil—and free those who

7

all their lives were held in slavery by their fear of death. For surely it is not angels he helps, but Abraham's descendants. For this reason he had to be made like his brothers in every way, in order that he might become a merciful and faithful high priest in service to God, and that he might make atonement for the sins of the people. Because he himself suffered when he was tempted, he is able to help those who are being tempted. (Heb 2:14-18)

b. The second glorious truth is both profound and critical, for it proclaims the divine nature of Jesus Christ. Jesus Christ was the Son of God *before He came into the world.* (See notes—Jn.1:1-2; 1:3; Ph.2:6; 2:7 for discussion.) However, since coming, He is declared to be the Son of God by two things.

* The Spirit of holiness that dwelt in Him declares Jesus to be the Son of God. He was the very embodiment of holiness, of purity and morality and justice. His life upon earth proves the fact. He lived as a man for thirty some years and *never sinned.*

God made him who had no sin to be sin for us, so that in him we might become the righteousness of God. (2 Cor 5:21)

For we do not have a high priest who is unable to sympathize with our weaknesses, but we have one who has been tempted in every way, just as we are—yet was without sin. (Heb 4:15)

Such a high priest meets our need—one who is holy, blameless, pure, set apart from sinners, exalted above the heavens. (Heb 7:26)

But with the precious blood of Christ, a lamb without blemish or defect. (1 Pet 1:19)

"He committed no sin, and no deceit was found in his mouth." (1 Pet 2:22; cp. Is.53:9; Jn.8:46.)

* The resurrection from the dead declares that Jesus is the Son of God. All other men are dead and gone. The proof is demonstrated by one simple question: "Where are they? Where are our mothers, our fathers, our sisters, our ancestors?" Once they have left this world, they are gone and the earth never sees them again. But not Christ. He died, but He arose and walked upon the earth again. And today Jesus Christ lives forever in the presence of God. Death could not hold Him because He was the Son of God and possessed the perfect spirit of holiness. (See DEEPER STUDY # 4, *Jesus Christ, Resurrection*—Acts 2:24 for more discussion.)

But God raised him from the dead, freeing him from the agony of death, because it was impossible for death to keep its hold on him. (Acts 2:24)

"Therefore let all Israel be assured of this: God has made this Jesus, whom

you crucified, both Lord and Christ." (Acts 2:36)

The God of our fathers raised Jesus from the dead—whom you had killed by hanging him on a tree. God exalted him to his own right hand as Prince and Savior that he might give repentance and forgiveness of sins to Israel. (Acts 5:30-31)

And who through the Spirit of holiness was declared with power to be the Son of God by his resurrection from the dead: Jesus Christ our Lord. (Rom 1:4)

For this very reason, Christ died and returned to life so that he might be the Lord of both the dead and the living. (Rom 14:9)

[God's power] which he exerted in Christ when he raised him from the dead and seated him at his right hand in the heavenly realms, (Eph 1:20)

And being found in appearance as a man, he humbled himself and became obedient to death— even death on a cross! Therefore God exalted him to the highest place and gave him the name that is above every name, (Phil 2:8-9)

4 (1:5) **Grace—Mission:** Paul had received God's grace and God's mission. Note the word "we." Paul now speaks of all believers, not only of himself.

1. We have received God's glorious grace: His favor, His mercy, His love, His salvation. (See DEEPER STUDY # 1, *Grace*—Tit.2:11-15.) Grace includes all that God has done for us and all the wonderful blessings He showers upon us. Very simply, God's grace includes...

a. His love for us from all eternity past.

Praise be to the God and Father of our Lord Jesus Christ, who has blessed us in the heavenly realms with every spiritual blessing in Christ. For he chose us in him before the creation of the world to be holy and blameless in his sight. In love (Eph 1:3-4)

Who has saved us and called us to a holy life—not because of anything we have done but because of his own purpose and grace. This grace was given us in Christ Jesus before the beginning of time, (2 Tim 1:9)

A faith and knowledge resting on the hope of eternal life, which God, who does not lie, promised before the beginning of time, (Titus 1:2)

b. His saving us freely, without any cost whatsoever.

No! We believe it is through the grace of our Lord Jesus that we are saved, just as they are." (Acts 15:11)

And are justified freely by his grace through the redemption that came by Christ Jesus. (Rom 3:24)

For it is by grace you have been saved, through faith—and this not from yourselves, it is the gift of God—not by works, so that no one can boast. **(Eph 2:8-9)**

For the grace of God that brings salvation has appeared to all men. **(Titus 2:11)**

c. His care and looking after us day by day.

And my God will meet all your needs according to his glorious riches in Christ Jesus. (Phil 4:19)

The grace of our Lord was poured out on me abundantly, along with the faith and love that are in Christ Jesus. (1 Tim 1:14)

d. His glorious promise of eternal redemption: of our being transformed and being made perfect, and being given the glorious privilege of living with Him forever in worship and service.

In him we have redemption through his blood, the forgiveness of sins, in accordance with the riches of God's grace (Eph 1:7)

In order that in the coming ages he might show the incomparable riches of his grace, expressed in his kindness to us in Christ Jesus. (Eph 2:7)

So that, having been justified by his grace, we might become heirs having the hope of eternal life. (Titus 3:7)

2. We have received apostleship, that is, God's mission. The idea is that we have received a special mission, God's very own special task in the world. What is that mission? Paul said it is *"obedience that comes from faith"* (see DEEPER STUDY # 2, *Obedience*—Ro.1:5 for discussion).

DEEPER STUDY # 2
(1:5) Obedience: the Scripture clearly says that God saves us for two specific purposes...
- to obey Him.
- to lead other persons to obey Him—persons from all nations.

What God is after is for mankind to become His family: for men to freely choose to live together with Him and with all other believers in a perfect world. God wants mankind living together in perfect love, joy, peace, worship, praise, and service as the family of God. He wants men living soberly, righteously, and godly before Him. He wants men obeying Him as His dear children.

Therefore, when God saves us, He saves us primarily to obey Him and to carry the glorious message of obedience to a rebellious and corrupt world. God calls us to obey the faith and to proclaim obedience to all the nations.

Note several facts about obedience.
1. There is a massive difference between *forced obedience* and *free obedience*.
  a. Forced obedience has no choice and reveals...
  - fear of rebellion
  - lack of control
  - weakness of purpose
  - selfishness and self-centeredness
  - low self-esteem
  - no sense of godliness

  b. Free obedience has a choice and can choose to obey or not to obey. Therefore, free obedience reveals...

- love and trust
- interest and care
- a sense of godliness
- a sense of brotherhood
- strength of purpose and will
- knowledge of self and confidence in self

2. Scripture says the following about obedience.
  a. Obedience demonstrates several things.

  ⇒ Obedience demonstrates that a person is wise.

  "Therefore everyone who hears these words of mine and puts them into practice is like a wise man who built his house on the rock. (Mat 7:24)

  ⇒ Obedience demonstrates love.

  Whoever has my commands and obeys them, he is the one who loves me. He who loves me will be loved by my Father, and I too will love him and show myself to him." (John 14:21)

  ⇒ Obedience demonstrates that God is worthy.

  Peter and the other apostles replied: "We must obey God rather than men! (Acts 5:29)

  ⇒ Obedience demonstrates that Christ is of God.

  If anyone chooses to do God's will, he will find out whether my teaching comes from God or whether I speak on my own. (John 7:17)

  b. Obedience assures several things.

  ⇒ Obedience assures a prosperous life and success.

  Do not let this Book of the Law depart from your mouth; meditate on it day and night, so that you may be careful to do everything written in it. Then you will be prosperous and successful. (Josh 1:8)

  ⇒ Obedience assures entrance into the kingdom of heaven.

  "Not everyone who says to me, 'Lord, Lord,' will enter the kingdom of heaven, but only he who does the will of my Father who is in heaven. (Mat 7:21; cp. Luke 8:21)

  ⇒ Obedience assures the mercy of God.

  But showing love to a thousand generations of those who love me and keep my commandments. (Exo 20:6)

  ⇒ Obedience assures that a person is a member of God's family.

For whoever does the will of my Father in heaven is my brother and sister and mother." (Mat 12:50; cp. Mk.3:35)

⇒ Obedience assures being blessed.

He replied, "Blessed rather are those who hear the word of God and obey it." (Luke 11:28; cp. Dt.11:27)

⇒ Obedience assures that we know the truth.

If anyone chooses to do God's will, he will find out whether my teaching comes from God or whether I speak on my own. (John 7:17)

⇒ Obedience assures the abiding presence of the Father and of Christ.

Jesus replied, "If anyone loves me, he will obey my teaching. My Father will love him, and we will come to him and make our home with him. (John 14:23)

⇒ Obedience assures deliverance from enemies.

If you listen carefully to what he says and do all that I say, I will be an enemy to your enemies and will oppose those who oppose you. (Exo 23:22)

⇒ Obedience assures that God will be our God and that all things will work out for our good.

But I gave them this command: Obey me, and I will be your God and you will be my people. Walk in all the ways I command you, that it may go well with you. (Jer 7:23)

⇒ Obedience assures being loved by God and by Christ.

If you obey my commands, you will remain in my love, just as I have obeyed my Father's commands and remain in his love. (John 15:10)

⇒ Obedience assures a good and a longer life.

Keep his decrees and commands, which I am giving you today, so that it may go well with you and your children after you and that you may live long in the land the LORD your God gives you for all time. (Deu 4:40)

⇒ Obedience assures being a friend of Christ.

You are my friends if you do what I command. I no longer call you servants, because a servant does not know his master's business. Instead, I have called you friends, for everything that I learned from my Father I have made known to you. (John 15:14-15)

⇒ Obedience assures eating the best from the land.

If you are willing and obedient, you will eat the best from the land; (Isa 1:19)

c. Obedience is better than sacrifice, even the sacrifice of all one has.

But Samuel replied: "Does the LORD delight in burnt offerings and sacrifices as much as in obeying the voice of the LORD? To obey is better than sacrifice, and to heed is better than the fat of rams. (1 Sam 15:22)
Therefore, when Christ came into the world, he said: "Sacrifice and offering you did not desire, but a body you prepared for me; with burnt offerings and sin offerings you were not pleased. Then I said, 'Here I am—it is written about me in the scroll— I have come to do your will, O God.'" (Heb 10:5-7)

5 (1:6-7) **Believers**: Paul acknowledged the enslavement of others. He said four things about believers.

1. Believers are "called to belong to Jesus Christ," called just as Paul was.

⇒ Believers are called to be saved, to "belong to Jesus Christ."

Who wants all men to be saved and to come to a knowledge of the truth. For there is one God and one mediator between God and men, the man Christ Jesus, who gave himself as a ransom for all men—the testimony given in its proper time. (1 Tim 2:4-6)

⇒ Believers are called to the mission and task of Jesus Christ.

Again Jesus said, "Peace be with you! As the Father has sent me, I am sending you." (John 20:21)
Just as the Son of Man did not come to be served, but to serve, and to give his life as a ransom for many." (Mat 20:28)

2. Believers are "loved by God," held ever so close to His heart, counted precious and dear to Him and deeply loved.

The LORD appeared to us in the past, saying: "I have loved you with an everlasting love; I have drawn you with loving-kindness. (Jer 31:3)
"For God so loved the world that he gave his one and only Son, that whoever believes in him shall not perish but have eternal life. (John 3:16)
No, the Father himself loves you because you have loved me and have believed that I came from God. (John 16:27)
But God demonstrates his own love for us in this: While we were still sinners, Christ died for us. (Rom 5:8)

But because of his great love for us, God, who is rich in mercy, made us alive with Christ even when we were dead in transgressions—it is by grace you have been saved. (Eph 2:4-5)

How great is the love the Father has lavished on us, that we should be called children of God! And that is what we are! The reason the world does not know us is that it did not know him. (1 John 3:1)

3. Believers are called to be "saints" (see DEEPER STUDY # 1, *Saint*—1 Pt.1:15-16 for discussion).

4. Believers are recipients of God's grace and peace. (See DEEPER STUDY # 2, *Grace*—Ro.1:5; DEEPER STUDY # 1— Tit.2:11-15; note, *Peace*—Jn.14:27 for discussion.)

But when the kindness and love of God our Savior appeared, he saved us, not because of righteous things we had done, but because of his mercy. He saved us through the washing of rebirth and renewal by the Holy Spirit, whom he poured out on us generously through Jesus Christ our Savior, so that, having been justified by his grace, we might become heirs having the hope of eternal life. (Titus 3:4-7)

But now in Christ Jesus you who once were far away have been brought near through the blood of Christ. For he himself is our peace, who has made the two one and has destroyed the barrier, the dividing wall of hostility, (Eph 2:13-14)

Peace I leave with you; my peace I give you. I do not give to you as the world gives. Do not let your hearts be troubled and do not be afraid. (John 14:27)

"I have told you these things, so that in me you may have peace. In this world you will have trouble. But take heart! I have overcome the world." (John 16:33)

The LORD gives strength to his people; the LORD blesses his people with peace. (Psa 29:11)

	B. Paul's Interest in the Church: Enslavement to the Gospel, 1:8-15	spiritual gift to make you strong—	
1 A great church a. A cause for thanksgiving b. The reason: A world-wide testimony	8 First, I thank my God through Jesus Christ for all of you, because your faith is being reported all over the world.	12 That is, that you and I may be mutually encouraged by each other's faith.	b. To be encouraged together with them
2 The Gospel subjected his spirit, his whole heart, to God's Son^{DS1}	9 God, whom I serve with my whole heart in preaching the gospel of his Son, is my witness how constantly I remember you	13 I do not want you to be unaware, brothers, that I planned many times to come to you (but have been prevented from doing so until now) in order that I might have a harvest among you, just as I have had among the other Gentiles.	c. To bear fruit among them
3 The Gospel stirred him to pray without ceasing **4 The Gospel stirred him to seek people personally**	10 In my prayers at all times; and I pray that now at last by God's will the way may be opened for me to come to you.	14 I am obligated both to Greeks and non-Greeks, both to the wise and the foolish.	**5 The Gospel stirred him with a deep sense of obligation & an eagerness to reach all men** a. His obligation to reach all
a. To impart some spiritual gift to strengthen them	11 I long to see you so that I may impart to you some	15 That is why I am so eager to preach the gospel also to you who are at Rome.	b. His eagerness to reach all

DIVISION I

GREETING AND THEME: THE GOSPEL AND GOD'S RIGHTEOUSNESS, 1:1-17

B. Paul's Interest in the Church: Enslavement to the Gospel, 1:8-15

(1:8-15) **Introduction**: Paul had never visited the Roman church, and he had never seen the believers at Rome; yet here he is writing to them. How could he best reach them and express his purpose for writing them? How could he arouse their interest to such a peak that they would read what he was writing and heed it? This is the subject of the present passage. Paul wanted the Roman believers to know his great interest in them; therefore, to the best of his ability he shared why he was writing to them. Simply stated, he said he was writing because he could do nothing else; he was compelled to share the gospel with the whole world including the capital of the world, Rome itself. In fact he was enslaved by the gospel.

1. A great church (v.8).
2. The gospel subjected his spirit, his whole heart, to God's Son (v.9).
3. The gospel stirred him to pray without ceasing (v.9).
4. The gospel stirred him to seek people personally (v.10-13).
5. The gospel stirred him with a deep sense of obligation and an eagerness to reach all men (v.14-15).

1 (1:8) **Church—Rome—Testimony**: the church at Rome was a great church—so great that Paul thanked God for the church "at all times" (v.9). The phrase "at all times" shows that the church held a very special place in Paul's heart. This is significant, for Paul had never been to the church. He did not know the church personally; he only knew what he had heard about it. But note: the church's testimony for Christ was so strong it was being talked about throughout *the whole world*. It had a phenomenal testimony, and wherever Paul traveled he heard about the strength of the church. What made the church at Rome so strong? Two significant things can be gleaned from Scripture.

1. The believers were living pure lives in the midst of an immoral, base, and unjust society. The citizens of Rome were known for their...

- immorality
- fleshiness
- greed
- selfishness
- drunkenness
- partying
- gluttony
- extravagance
- hoarding
- materialism
- license
- indulgence
- idolatry
- pride
- sin and wickedness

Nevertheless, the believers were standing firm for Christ and living pure lives, proclaiming the gospel of Jesus Christ and the need for morality and justice among men.

2. The believers were serving Christ faithfully and laboring ever so diligently for the Lord. Wherever they were, at home or away traveling, they were sharing Christ and ministering to people—so much so that some of them were known by name all around the world. Paul himself apparently had run across quite a few of them as they were traveling about and ministering. (See outline—Ro.16:3-16 for a list of the believers and a discussion of this point).

Thought 1. The Roman church stands as a testimony for every church.
1) No matter how immoral and base, polluted and corrupt a society is, we are to stand firm for Christ.

Do not conform any longer to the pattern of this world, but be transformed by the renewing of your mind. Then you will be able to test and approve what God's will is—his good, pleasing and perfect will. (Rom 12:2)

"Therefore come out from them and be separate, says the Lord. Touch no unclean thing, and I will receive you." "I will be a Father to you, and you will be my sons and daughters, says the Lord Almighty." (2 Cor 6:17-18)

Do not love the world or anything in the world. If anyone loves the world, the love of the Father is not in him. For everything in the

world—the cravings of sinful man, the lust of his eyes and the boasting of what he has and does—comes not from the Father but from the world. (1 John 2:15-16)

2) No matter where we are, at home or traveling away on business or for pleasure, we are to be witnessing and ministering for Christ.

> But you will receive power when the Holy Spirit comes on you; and you will be my witnesses in Jerusalem, and in all Judea and Samaria, and to the ends of the earth." (Acts 1:8)
> So do not be ashamed to testify about our Lord, or ashamed of me his prisoner. But join with me in suffering for the gospel, by the power of God, (2 Tim 1:8)
> These, then, are the things you should teach. Encourage and rebuke with all authority. Do not let anyone despise you. (Titus 2:15)
> But in your hearts set apart Christ as Lord. Always be prepared to give an answer to everyone who asks you to give the reason for the hope that you have. But do this with gentleness and respect, (1 Pet 3:15)

Thought 2. Every church and every believer should have a strong testimony, a testimony so strong that it is talked about everywhere.

> The brothers at Lystra and Iconium spoke well of him [Timothy]. (Acts 16:2)
> Everyone has heard about your obedience, so I am full of joy over you; but I want you to be wise about what is good, and innocent about what is evil. (Rom 16:19)
> This is what the ancients were commended for [faith]. (Heb 11:2)

2 (1:9) **Gospel—Salvation—Decision:** the gospel subjected Paul's spirit, his whole heart, to God's Son. (See DEEPER STUDY # 1, *Serve*—Ro.1:9 for more discussion.) Every man should subject his spirit to God's Son. Why? Because of the gospel, the glorious salvation that is in Christ Jesus: the deliverance from sin, death, and hell. When a person considers that he is enslaved by sin and that he is actually going to die and have to give an account to God, he is most foolish...

- not to accept the salvation that is in God's Son.
- not to subject his spirit to God's Son.
- not to serve in the gospel of God's Son.

DEEPER STUDY # 1

(1:9) **Serve** (latreuo): labor of hire, service that is bought. Paul says, "I serve with my whole heart in preaching the gospel of His Son." Note three points.

1. The believer's labor and service is bought and paid for by the precious blood of Christ.

> Do you not know that your body is a temple of the Holy Spirit, who is in you, whom you have received from God? You are not your own; you were bought at a price. Therefore honor God with your body. (1 Cor 6:19-20)
> Do not be afraid of those who kill the body but cannot kill the soul. Rather, be

---

afraid of the One who can destroy both soul and body in hell. (Mat 10:28)

> Your attitude should be the same as that of Christ Jesus: Who, being in very nature God, did not consider equality with God something to be grasped, but made himself nothing, taking the very nature of a servant, being made in human likeness. And being found in appearance as a man, he humbled himself and became obedient to death— even death on a cross! (Phil 2:5-8)

2. The believer owes his labor and service to the Lord. Once he has surrendered to the gospel, he has no choice. He is to diligently serve and work for Christ.

> Carry each other's burdens, and in this way you will fulfill the law of Christ. (Gal 6:2)

3. The believer is to serve God in his spirit and in his body. The spirit controls the body. What the spirit does, the body does. Therefore, if the believer is serving God in spirit, he is serving God in body. If a man's spirit is right, then his body will be right. For example, a man may feel bad; he may be down, depressed, and oppressed; but if his spirit is strong, he arises and conquers his feelings. He controls and overcomes the oppressing circumstances, and he lives a victorious day. But if his spirit is weak—whether at work or at play—he often wallows around in self-pity, grumbling and griping, and living a defeated day. And too often the day stretches into weeks and months until a person's life is down more than it is up: all because the spirit is too weak to conquer.

Thought 1. The point is this: the believer is to serve God in his spirit and in his body. He is...
- to keep his spirit strong,
- to conquer his emotions,
- to overcome his weaknesses, the ups and downs of his body.

When a believer does this, then he can serve God to the fullest extent possible.

> Therefore, I urge you, brothers, in view of God's mercy, to offer your bodies as living sacrifices, holy and pleasing to God—this is your spiritual act of worship. Do not conform any longer to the pattern of this world, but be transformed by the renewing of your mind. Then you will be able to test and approve what God's will is—his good, pleasing and perfect will. (Rom 12:1-2)
> And now, O Israel, what does the LORD your God ask of you but to fear the LORD your God, to walk in all his ways, to love him, to serve the LORD your God with all your heart and with all your soul, (Deu 10:12)

3 (1:9) **Prayer:** the gospel stirred Paul to pray without ceasing. Paul was a man of intercessory prayer, a man who always prayed *for others*. Note two points.

1. Paul called upon God to bear witness that he prayed. He did not...
- just talk about praying.
- just tell people he was praying for them as a courtesy.

- just pretend to pray.
- just spend a few minutes in a *religious exercise* of prayer.

Paul really prayed; he took time to ask God to strengthen and help others. (See outline and notes—Eph.3:14-21 for the specifics of what Paul prayed. Also see note and DEEPER STUDY # 1—Mt.6:9-13 for what Christ tells us to pray daily. These two passages taken together tell us what we should be praying every day, both for ourselves and for others.)

> **In the morning, O LORD, you hear my voice; in the morning I lay my requests before you and wait in expectation. (Psa 5:3)**
>
> **Evening, morning and noon I cry out in distress, and he hears my voice. (Psa 55:17)**
>
> **I rise before dawn and cry for help; I have put my hope in your word. (Psa 119:147 cp. Lk.2:36; Acts 10:2; 1 Th.3:10; 1 Tim.5:5).**

2. Paul even prayed for believers and churches whom he did not know. Remember he knew only a few of the believers in the Roman church; he had never met most of them. They were totally unfamiliar and unknown to him, yet he prayed for the church.

Thought 1. Scripture is strong in its charge to us. We are to pray constantly and we are to pray for all believers throughout the world. Our prayers are not to be limited to a few minutes each day nor to our loved ones and close friends.

> **Then Jesus told his disciples a parable to show them that they should always pray and not give up. (Luke 18:1)**
>
> **Until now you have not asked for anything in my name. Ask and you will receive, and your joy will be complete. (John 16:24)**
>
> **And pray in the Spirit on all occasions with all kinds of prayers and requests. With this in mind, be alert and always keep on praying for all the saints. (Eph 6:18)**
>
> **Do not be anxious about anything, but in everything, by prayer and petition, with thanksgiving, present your requests to God. And the peace of God, which transcends all understanding, will guard your hearts and your minds in Christ Jesus. (Phil 4:6-7)**
>
> **Devote yourselves to prayer, being watchful and thankful. And pray for us, too, that God may open a door for our message, so that we may proclaim the mystery of Christ, for which I am in chains. (Col 4:2-3)**
>
> **Pray continually; (1 Th 5:17)**
>
> **I want men everywhere to lift up holy hands in prayer, without anger or disputing. (1 Tim 2:8)**
>
> **Look to the LORD and his strength; seek his face always. (1 Chr 16:11)**

4 (1:10-13) **Gospel—Witnessing—Evangelism—Ministry:** the gospel stirred Paul to seek people personally. He did not leave the ministry and the sharing of the gospel up to others. He became personally involved, so much so that he begged God to give him opportunity after opportunity—even to the point of letting him travel to the capital of the world itself to share Christ with its citizens. Note how deeply he was stirred: he made a request—if by any means, now at last—that he might be allowed to preach the gospel at Rome.

The point is forceful: Paul was stirred to seek people, for he longed to reach people for Christ.

1. Paul wished to *impart some spiritual gift* to the believers. Why? So that they might be more deeply strengthened in the faith. The term spiritual gift (charisma) means a gift of grace. The term often refers to specific gifts given by the Holy Spirit (Ro.12:6-8), but here it means *the truths* of the grace of God, of His spiritual blessings to man revealed in Christ Jesus our Lord. Very simply, Paul longed to share the truths of the gospel with the believers at Rome. God's spiritual blessings were overflowing in his heart, and he was aching to share the gift of God's blessings.

Thought 1. What an indictment against us! How many of us are so full of the gospel that we are aching to share it? How many of us even know the gospel that well, know God's gifts and blessings well enough to be overflowing with them?

> **Praise be to the God and Father of our Lord Jesus Christ, who has blessed us in the heavenly realms with every spiritual blessing in Christ. (Eph 1:3)**
>
> **And the Lord's servant must not quarrel; instead, he must be kind to everyone, able to teach, not resentful. Those who oppose him he must gently instruct, in the hope that God will grant them repentance leading them to a knowledge of the truth, (2 Tim 2:24-25)**
>
> **Be shepherds of God's flock that is under your care, serving as overseers—not because you must, but because you are willing, as God wants you to be; not greedy for money, but eager to serve; not lording it over those entrusted to you, but being examples to the flock. (1 Pet 5:2-3)**

Note that God's spiritual gift strengthens the believer. The word "strengthen" means to fix, set, make fast. Note the descriptive picture behind each word.

2. Paul wished to be *encouraged together* with other believers. The word "encouraged" (sumparakaleo) means to be strengthened and consoled together. Paul expected to be taught and strengthened by the believers as well as to teach and to strengthen them. There was to be a mutual sharing among all. Paul expected all believers to be actively sharing the gospel. He even expected them to share with him so that he might grow and be more firmly rooted in the faith.

Thought 1. How many believers are actively grounded enough in the faith to share with Paul? What an indictment! Yet the *expectation* is that we are to be deeply rooted, ever studying the Word and learning. How much we need to awaken and arise from our slumber.

> **Rooted and built up in him, strengthened in the faith as you were taught, and overflowing with thankfulness. (Col 2:7)**
>
> **Encourage your hearts and strengthen you in every good deed and word. (2 Th 2:17)**

3. Paul wished to bear fruit among them (see Deeper Study # 1, *Bearing Fruit*—Jn.15:1-8 for discussion). Paul wished to bear the fruit of...

- converts (Ro.1:13).
- righteousness (Ro.6:21-23).
- Christian character, the fruit of the Spirit (Gal.5:22-23).

Note Paul's world-wide vision. He wished to bear fruit among the citizens of Rome as well as "among the other Gentiles."

> **Thought 1.** How desperately God needs men, women, boys and girls with a world-wide vision!

> Do you not say, 'Four months more and then the harvest'? I tell you, open your eyes and look at the fields! They are ripe for harvest. (John 4:35)

> Then he said to his disciples, "The harvest is plentiful but the workers are few. (Mat 9:37)

> He told them, "The harvest is plentiful, but the workers are few. Ask the Lord of the harvest, therefore, to send out workers into his harvest field. (Luke 10:2)

> Let us not become weary in doing good, for at the proper time we will reap a harvest if we do not give up. (Gal 6:9)

5 (1:14-15) **Gospel—Preaching—Witnessing—Ministers—Dedication**: the gospel stirred Paul with a deep sense of obligation and an eagerness to reach all men. Note two points.

1. The word "obligated" (opheiletes) means to owe, to be indebted, to be bound by duty. The Greek is impossible to translate into English, for two ideas are being expressed by Paul. He was "obligated"...

- because Christ had done so much for him (saved him).
- because Christ had called him to preach (given him a task to do).

The *obligation* was deeply felt by Paul. The idea is that it was intense, unwavering, unrelentless, powerful. The sense of debt just would not let Paul go. He was compelled to preach the gospel; therefore, he could do nothing else. He was obligated and duty bound to preach it. He actually felt that he owed the gospel to the world; therefore, if he kept quiet, it would be worse than knowing the cure for the most terrible disease of history and refusing to share it.

Note how Paul declared his obligation to the whole world. He made a contrast between the Greeks and the non-Greeks. He meant that he owed the gospel to all nationalities and cultures, to all the peoples of the earth whether civilized or uncivilized, industrialized or primitive, rich or poor. (The Greeks considered everyone a non-Greek who did not speak the Greek language and adopt Greek culture.) He made a contrast between the wise and the foolish. He meant that he owed the gospel to the educated and the uneducated, the learned and the unlearned, the motivated and the unmotivated, the seeking and the complacent.

> **Thought 1.** Paul sensed a *deep obligation* to share the glorious news of salvation with the world. The *answer* to eternal life is now known and must be proclaimed to the whole world. To keep the message

to oneself is the most inexcusable and criminal act in all of human history. The glorious news that death has been conquered and that man can now live eternally must be proclaimed. We who know the wonderful news are *obligated* to get the news out to the world.

> "For God so loved the world that he gave his one and only Son, that whoever believes in him shall not perish but have eternal life. (John 3:16)

> "I tell you the truth, whoever hears my word and believes him who sent me has eternal life and will not be condemned; he has crossed over from death to life. (John 5:24)

> I am obligated both to Greeks and non-Greeks, both to the wise and the foolish. That is why I am so eager to preach the gospel also to you who are at Rome. (Rom 1:14-15)

2. The word "eager" means an *urgent willingness*. Paul experienced both a willingness and an urgency to preach the gospel. Note the words, "That is why I am so eager." Paul wanted to take all that was in him and pour it into people—all the energy and effort, all the truth and knowledge of the gospel. There was nothing that could keep him from sharing the gospel, not if he had a chance to share it. He *allowed* no hindrance to enter his life that would affect his message. He was possessed and obsessed with a readiness to preach the glorious message of the living Lord.

> Yet when I preach the gospel, I cannot boast, for I am compelled to preach. Woe to me if I do not preach the gospel! (1 Cor 9:16)

> As you go, preach this message: 'The kingdom of heaven is near.' (Mat 10:7)

> What I tell you in the dark, speak in the daylight; what is whispered in your ear, proclaim from the roofs. (Mat 10:27)

> He said to them, "Go into all the world and preach the good news to all creation. (Mark 16:15)

> Jesus said to him, "Let the dead bury their own dead, but you go and proclaim the kingdom of God." (Luke 9:60)

> As long as it is day, we must do the work of him who sent me. Night is coming, when no one can work. (John 9:4)

> For we cannot help speaking about what we have seen and heard." (Acts 4:20)

> "Go, stand in the temple courts," he said, "and tell the people the full message of this new life." (Acts 5:20)

> But if I say, "I will not mention him or speak any more in his name," his word is in my heart like a fire, a fire shut up in my bones. I am weary of holding it in; indeed, I cannot. (Jer 20:9)

> The lion has roared— who will not fear? The Sovereign LORD has spoken— who can but prophesy? (Amos 3:8)

> (1:14-16) **Another Outline**: Paul's Three "I Am's."
> 1. I am obligated (v.14).
> 2. I am eager (v.15).
> 3. I am not ashamed (v.16).

	C. Paul's Boldness for Christ: Unashamedness of the Gospel, 1:16-17	lieves: first for the Jew, then for the Gentile. 17 For in the gospel a righteousness from God is revealed, a righteousness that is by faith from first to last, just as it is written: "The righteous will live by faith."	b. All nationalities, both Jew & Gentile

1 It is the "good news" from God Himself
2 It is the power of God to save^{DS1}
  a. All who believe
	16 I am not ashamed of the gospel, because it is the power of God for the salvation of everyone who be-		3 It is the revelation of God's righteousness^{DS2}
			  a. The problem: man's unrighteousness
			  b. The answer: Faith

DIVISION I

GREETING AND THEME: THE GOSPEL AND GOD'S RIGHTEOUSNESS, 1:1-17

C. Paul's Boldness for Christ: Unashamedness of the Gospel, 1:16-17

(1:16-17) **Introduction**: these two verses contain one of the greatest summaries of the gospel ever written. It is a clear declaration of God's power to save all who believe, no matter their nationality or condition. It is a clear explanation of why Paul was never ashamed of the gospel.

1. It is the *good news* from God Himself (v.16).
2. It is the power of God to save (v.16).
3. It is the revelation of God's righteousness (v.17).

(1:16-18) **Another Outline**: The Power or Urgency of the Gospel.

1. It saves (v.16).
2. It reveals the righteousness of God (v.17).
3. It makes possible a life of faith (v.17).
4. It delivers from the wrath of God (v.18).

(1:16-18) **Another Outline**: Paul's Clear Statement about the Gospel.

1. I am not ashamed (v.16).
2. The Gospel is the power of God (v.16).
3. The righteousness of God is revealed (v.17).
4. The wrath of God is revealed (v.18).

1(1:16) **Gospel—Ashamed**: Paul was not ashamed of the gospel, because it was the *good news* from God Himself; that is, the gospel is the news that God has given to the world and wants proclaimed to the world. The fact that the gospel had been given by God Himself made Paul unashamed of the gospel. No man should ever be ashamed of anything concerning the Sovereign Majesty of the universe. (See note—Ro.1:1-4 for discussion.) However, Paul had every reason to be ashamed.

1. Paul's day was a day of moral degeneracy, the hideous days of Nero. Rome was a moral sewer, a cesspool of detestable and inconceivable wickedness. Such a day stood diametrically opposed to the moral righteousness of the gospel.

2. Paul was by nationality a Jew, a race that was thought by many of that day to be a despicable sub-human race, worthy only to be cursed, ill-used, and enslaved. Naturally, Paul would be apprehensive among non-Jews. In the flesh he would be tempted to shy away from them.

3. The gospel Paul preached was almost unbelievable. A male member of the despicable Jewish race was said to be the Savior of the world, and not only was He said to be a Jew, He was said to be a mere man like all other men. But not only that, His death was said to be different from the death of other men. He was said to have died "for all other men," that is, in their place, as a substitute for them. And then to top it all, He was said to have risen from the dead. His resurrection was said to be the proof that He was the very Son of God. Such unbelievable claims made the gos-

pel a contemptible thing in the minds of many. A natural man would shrink from making such phenomenal claims.

4. Paul was often rejected, not by just a few persons, but by whole communities. The authorities imprisoned him in Philippi (Acts 16:19-23). The religionists ran him out of Thessalonica and threatened his life in Berea (Acts 17:5-15). The intellectuals laughed him out of Athens (Acts 17:32; cp. 16-32). His message was considered foolishness to the intellectuals (the Greeks) and a stumbling block to his own people (the Jews). There were several times in Paul's life when he could have given up in shame and fled to some part of the earth to begin life all over again.

Thought 1. Many are ashamed of the gospel. They are ashamed because they fear ridicule, rejection, and loss of recognition, position, and livelihood. They fear two things in particular.

1) There is the fear of intellectual shame. This is the fear that the gospel does not measure up intellectually. It is judged not to be for the scholar or philosopher. Note: this feeling is common to those who do not understand the philosophy of the gospel. No greater philosophy exists; no greater reasoning has ever been worked through. (See all outlines and notes—Romans. As an example, see outlines and notes—Ro.5:1-21; 8:1-39.) A man holds either to the philosophy and thought of the world, or to the philosophy and thought of God's Son, the gospel of Jesus Christ and His redemption. There is no question which philosophy and intellectual thought is greater.

For the foolishness of God is wiser than man's wisdom, and the weakness of God is stronger than man's strength. (1 Cor 1:25; cp. Ro.1:18-31).

It is because of him that you are in Christ Jesus, who has become for us wisdom from God—that is, our righteousness, holiness and redemption. (1 Cor 1:30)

Oh, the depth of the riches of the wisdom and knowledge of God! How unsearchable his judgments, and his paths beyond tracing out! "Who has known the mind of the Lord? Or who has been his counselor?" (Rom 11:33-34)

Do not deceive yourselves. If any one of you thinks he is wise by the standards of this age, he should become a "fool" so that he may become wise. For the wisdom of this world is foolishness in God's sight. As it is written: "He catches the wise in their craftiness"; and again, "The Lord knows

16

that the thoughts of the wise are futile."
(1 Cor 3:18-20)

But the wisdom that comes from heaven is first of all pure; then peace-loving, considerate, submissive, full of mercy and good fruit, impartial and sincere. (James 3:17)

"Do not keep talking so proudly or let your mouth speak such arrogance, for the LORD is a God who knows, and by him deeds are weighed. (1 Sam 2:3)

Do you not know? Have you not heard? The LORD is the everlasting God, the Creator of the ends of the earth. He will not grow tired or weary, and his understanding no one can fathom. (Isa 40:28)

He reveals deep and hidden things; he knows what lies in darkness, and light dwells with him. (Dan 2:22)

2) There is the fear of social shame. Many fear if they accept and proclaim the gospel, they will be...

- ridiculed and mocked
- rejected and ignored
- passed over and cut off
- left without job and livelihood
- left without family and friends
- abused and killed

For God did not give us a spirit of timidity, but a spirit of power, of love and of self-discipline. So do not be ashamed to testify about our Lord, or ashamed of me his prisoner. But join with me in suffering for the gospel, by the power of God, who has saved us and called us to a holy life—not because of anything we have done but because of his own purpose and grace. This grace was given us in Christ Jesus before the beginning of time, (2 Tim 1:7-9)

If you are insulted because of the name of Christ, you are blessed, for the Spirit of glory and of God rests on you. (1 Pet 4:14) Fear of man will prove to be a snare, but whoever trusts in the LORD is kept safe. (Prov 29:25)

"I, even I, am he who comforts you. Who are you that you fear mortal men, the sons of men, who are but grass, (Isa 51:12)

2 (1:16) **Gospel—God, Power of—Salvation**: Paul is not ashamed of the gospel because it is the power of God to save. Note four significant facts.

1. The word "power" (dunamis) means the might, energy, force, and strength that is *within* God. The power is "of God," of His very nature. As God, He is the embodiment of power; He possesses all power, that is, omnipotent power, within His Being. He can do and act as He chooses.

The point is this: God has chosen to use His power in a loving way by sending men the "good news," the gospel of salvation. Being all powerful, God could wipe men off the face of the earth, but instead He has chosen to give men the good news of salvation. This tells us a critical truth: God's nature is love. He is full of compassion and grace. He is the God of salvation; therefore, He sent the gospel of Christ to the world that men might be saved.

2. The word "salvation" must be understood and grasped by every person upon earth. The hope of the world is God's salvation (see note—Ro.1:16 for discussion).

3. God saves all who believe. Belief is the one condition for salvation, *but* we must always remember that a person who really believes *commits himself* to what he believes. If a man does not commit himself he does not believe. True belief is commitment. Therefore, God saves the person who believes, that is, who really commits his life to the gospel of Christ (see notes, *Believe*—Ro.10:16-17; DEEPER STUDY # 2—Jn.2:24 for discussion).

4. God saves all nationalities, both Jew and Greek. Note the word "first." This does not mean favoritism, but *first in time*. God does not have favorites, favoring the Jew over the Gentile. It simply means the gospel was to be carried to the Jew first. They had been the channel through whom God had sent His Word and His prophets and eventually His Son into the world. Therefore, they were to be reached first; then the gospel was to be carried to the Gentiles, that is, to all nationalities. The point is twofold.

a. The gospel is God's power, and it can reach any nationality and any person, no matter who they are.

b. Therefore, no one is to be exempt from the gospel.
⇒ No messenger is to *exempt anyone* from the gospel.
⇒ No person is to *exempt himself* from the gospel. The gospel is for everyone, no matter his race, color, condition, circumstance, or depravity.

On the last and greatest day of the Feast, Jesus stood and said in a loud voice, "If anyone is thirsty, let him come to me and drink. (John 7:37)

For there is no difference between Jew and Gentile—the same Lord is Lord of all and richly blesses all who call on him, for, "Everyone who calls on the name of the Lord will be saved." (Rom 10:12-13)

Who wants all men to be saved and to come to a knowledge of the truth. (1 Tim 2:4)

The Spirit and the bride say, "Come!" And let him who hears say, "Come!" Whoever is thirsty, let him come; and whoever wishes, let him take the free gift of the water of life. (Rev 22:17)

DEEPER STUDY # 1

(1:16) **Salvation** (soteria): means deliverance, made whole, preservation. From what does man need to be saved and delivered and preserved? Scripture paints five descriptive pictures of salvation, showing man's great need. (See DEEPER STUDY # 6, *Salvation*—Mt.1:21 for more discussion.)

1. Salvation means deliverance from being lost. Man is pictured as wandering about in the forest of life trying to go someplace, but unable to find his way. He is lost, and if he continues to stumble about through the forest of life, the underbrush and thorns of the forest will sap his strength and prick him to the point that he lies down and dies. His only hope is for someone to notice that he is lost and to begin seeking for him. This is where the glorious gospel of

salvation comes in. God sees that man is lost and He sends His Son to seek and to save man.

Salvation means that Christ...

- seeks and saves man from his lost condition.
- Sets man on the right road that leads him to eternal life.

> **"What do you think? If a man owns a hundred sheep, and one of them wanders away, will he not leave the ninety-nine on the hills and go to look for the one that wandered off? (Mat 18:12; cp. Lk.15:4).)**
>
> **For the Son of Man came to seek and to save what was lost." (Luke 19:10)**
>
> **Later Jesus found him at the temple and said to him, "See, you are well again. Stop sinning or something worse may happen to you." (John 5:14)**
>
> **I am the gate; whoever enters through me will be saved. He will come in and go out, and find pasture. (John 10:9)**

2. Salvation means deliverance from sin. It means deliverance from mistakes, from corrupt ideas and thoughts, from moral impurity and from a crooked and perverse generation. Sin is like...

- an infection, a disease for which man has no cure.
- A master that enslaves and will not let go.
- a crooked and perverse world that man cannot straighten out.

Man's only hope is for someone to discover a cure, someone with the intelligence and power to do it. This is where God steps in with His glorious salvation. God knows all about man's infection and enslavement by sin, all about his crooked and perverse world; so He sends His Son to save man, to cure him and liberate him and straighten out his world. Salvation means that Christ saves man from the terrible tyranny of sin, from...

- the infection of sin.
- The enslavement of sin.
- the crooked and perverse world of sin.

Salvation also does something else. It frees man from the pricking and burden of guilt and shame, and it plants within man's soul a deep sense of health and peace with God.

> **She will give birth to a son, and you are to give him the name Jesus, because he will save his people from their sins." (Mat 1:21)**
>
> **Jesus said to the woman, "Your faith has saved you; go in peace." (Luke 7:50)**
>
> **For God did not send his Son into the world to condemn the world, but to save the world through him. (John 3:17)**
>
> **Not that I accept human testimony; but I mention it that you may be saved. yet you refuse to come to me to have life. (John 5:34, 40)**
>
> **"As for the person who hears my words but does not keep them, I do not judge him. For I did not come to judge the world, but to save it. (John 12:47)**
>
> **With many other words he warned them; and he pleaded with them, "Save yourselves from this corrupt generation." (Acts 2:40)**
>
> **For it is by grace you have been saved, through faith—and this not from yourselves, it is the gift of God—not by works,**

so that no one can boast. (Eph 2:8-9)

> **And in every sort of evil that deceives those who are perishing. They perish because they refused to love the truth and so be saved. (2 Th 2:10)**
>
> **Who has saved us and called us to a holy life—not because of anything we have done but because of his own purpose and grace. This grace was given us in Christ Jesus before the beginning of time, but it has now been revealed through the appearing of our Savior, Christ Jesus, who has destroyed death and has brought life and immortality to light through the gospel. (2 Tim 1:9-10)**
>
> **He saved us, not because of righteous things we had done, but because of his mercy. He saved us through the washing of rebirth and renewal by the Holy Spirit, (Titus 3:5)**

3. Salvation means deliverance in the future from all evil and corruption: from aging and wasting away, deterioration and decay, death and hell. It is the complete redemption of man's spirit and body at the end of the world. It is salvation from the wrath of God—salvation that saves a man from being separated from God eternally. It is the life and exaltation which believers will receive at the final triumph of Jesus Christ. It is the salvation that will keep a man safe and preserve him both in time and eternity.

Man and his world are pictured as having a *seed of corruption* within their very nature, a seed of corruption that eats away causing them to...

- age and waste away.
- Deteriorate and decay.
- suffer destruction and die.

Again, man is hopeless. He cannot stop himself and his world from death and destruction, but God can. God can save both man and his world; God can deliver them from the terrible fate of death and destruction. This is the message of salvation. God loves man and his world and wants to save them, so He sent His Son into the world to save them. Salvation is...

- the complete redemption of man's body and soul in the future: a redemption that saves man from the process of aging and wasting away, deteriorating and decaying, dying and being condemned to hell.
- The perfect deliverance from the wrath of God: a salvation that saves man from being separated from God eternally.
- the gift of life and exaltation: a salvation that will be given to believers at the final triumph of Jesus Christ.
- The presence of perfect assurance: a salvation of security and preservation both in time and eternity.

> **Not only so, but we ourselves, who have the firstfruits of the Spirit, groan inwardly as we wait eagerly for our adoption as sons, the redemption of our bodies. For in this hope we were saved. But hope that is seen is no hope at all. Who hopes for what he already has? (Rom 8:23-24)**
>
> **For God did not appoint us to suffer wrath but to receive salvation through our Lord Jesus Christ. He died for us so that, whether we are awake or asleep, we may live together with him. (1 Th 5:9-10)**
>
> **The Lord will rescue me from every evil**

attack and will bring me safely to his heavenly kingdom. To him be glory for ever and ever. Amen. (2 Tim 4:18)

Praise be to the God and Father of our Lord Jesus Christ! In his great mercy he has given us new birth into a living hope through the resurrection of Jesus Christ from the dead, and into an inheritance that can never perish, spoil or fade—kept in heaven for you, who through faith are shielded by God's power until the coming of the salvation that is ready to be revealed in the last time. (1 Pet 1:3-5)

For you are receiving the goal of your faith, the salvation of your souls. (1 Pet 1:9)

4. Salvation means deliverance from enemies and dangers. Man is pictured as walking in a world lurking with enemy after enemy and danger after danger. Man has to confront all kinds of enemies and dangers that attack both his body and soul, his mind and spirit. He faces all kinds of problems and difficulties, trials and temptations. No matter how much he may long for peace and security, he is forced to combat...

- a hostile environment
- a savage world of nature
- an unknown universe
- an uncertain future
- unregulated urges
- inevitable aging and dying
- a lust for more and more (possessions, fame, wealth, power)
- an evil pride and ego
- greed and covetousness
- unpreventable accidents
- dreadful diseases

Man is seen as helpless in overcoming all the enemies and dangers that lurk in the shadows of this world. But God is not helpless—God can *save* man; He can gloriously deliver man as he journeys along the road of life. This is exactly what salvation means. God delivers man from the enemies and dangers that war against him. But note the next paragraph, a crucial point.

Salvation does not mean that God delivers man *from* experiencing difficulty and danger, not in this present world. God does not give a life free from the nature and circumstances of this world. What salvation does is deliver one *through* the difficulties and dangers of life.

Salvation means that...
- God gives *security and peace* of soul, no matter what happens.
- God gives *safety* independent of circumstances and environment.
- God gives inward strength and courage to bear the onslaught and attacks of danger.

The disciples went and woke him, saying, "Lord, save us! We're going to drown!" He replied, "You of little faith, why are you so afraid?" Then he got up and rebuked the winds and the waves, and it was completely calm. The men were amazed and asked, "What kind of man is this? Even the winds and the waves obey him!" (Mat 8:25-27)

But when he saw the wind, he was afraid and, beginning to sink, cried out, "Lord, save me!" Immediately Jesus reached out his hand

and caught him. "You of little faith," he said, "why did you doubt?" (Mat 14:30-31)

He has raised up a horn of salvation for us in the house of his servant DavidSalvation from our enemies and from the hand of all who hate us— (Luke 1:69, 71)

Now I urge you to take some food. You need it to survive. Not one of you will lose a single hair from his head." (Acts 27:34)

By faith Noah, when warned about things not yet seen, in holy fear built an ark to save his family. By his faith he condemned the world and became heir of the righteousness that comes by faith. (Heb 11:7)

But the day of the Lord will come like a thief. The heavens will disappear with a roar; the elements will be destroyed by fire, and the earth and everything in it will be laid bare. Since everything will be destroyed in this way, what kind of people ought you to be? You ought to live holy and godly lives as you look forward to the day of God and speed its coming. That day will bring about the destruction of the heavens by fire, and the elements will melt in the heat. But in keeping with his promise we are looking forward to a new heaven and a new earth, the home of righteousness. So then, dear friends, since you are looking forward to this, make every effort to be found spotless, blameless and at peace with him. Bear in mind that our Lord's patience means salvation, just as our dear brother Paul also wrote you with the wisdom that God gave him. (2 Pet 3:10-15)

5. Salvation means to make well, to heal, to restore to health, to make whole both physically and mentally. Man is pictured as a suffering creature, a creature who...
- gets sick
- becomes diseased
- has accidents
- wears out from aging
- suffers infirmities
- struggles against deformities

Salvation declares that Christ is concerned with man's suffering. Christ saves and delivers man, rescues and restores man in body as well as in spirit. He takes a man who suffers and makes him whole.

Just then a woman who had been subject to bleeding for twelve years came up behind him and touched the edge of his cloak. She said to herself, "If I only touch his cloak, I will be healed." Jesus turned and saw her. "Take heart, daughter," he said, "your faith has healed you." And the woman was healed from that moment. (Mat 9:20-22)

"What do you want me to do for you?" Jesus asked him. The blind man said, "Rabbi, I want to see." "Go," said Jesus, "your faith has healed you." Immediately he received his sight and followed Jesus along the road. (Mark 10:51-52)

If we are being called to account today for an act of kindness shown to a cripple and are asked how he was healed, then know this, you and all the people of Israel: It is by the name of Jesus Christ of Nazareth, whom you crucified

> but whom God raised from the dead, that this man stands before you healed. (Acts 4:9-10)
> And the prayer offered in faith will make the sick person well; the Lord will raise him up. If he has sinned, he will be forgiven. (James 5:15)

3 (1:17) **Righteousness**: Paul is not ashamed of the gospel, because it is the revelation of God's righteousness. Note two points.

1. Man has a serious problem—that of thinking he is righteous. The problem is easily seen by picturing the following:

⇒ Man thinks that he is good enough and that he does enough good to be acceptable to God.
⇒ Man thinks he is righteous and that he walks righteously enough to be acceptable to God.

However, there is one problem with man's thinking: man is not perfect. But God is perfect, and He is perfectly righteous. Therefore, He cannot allow an unrighteous and imperfect being to live in His presence, not even man. Man just cannot live with God, not in his imperfect and unrighteous condition, for he would pollute the perfect world of God, the very ground and atmosphere and nature of heaven, of the spiritual world and dimension.

The only way man can live with God is to be made righteous, perfectly righteous. How can man be made perfectly righteous? The gospel gives the answer. The gospel is the revelation of God's righteousness and reveals how man can be made righteous and reconciled to God. (See notes, *Righteousness*—Ro.3:21-22; 4:1-3; Deeper Study # 2—4:22; note—5:1; note 5 and Deeper Study # 5—Mt.5:6 for discussion. These notes should be read for a clear understanding of what the Scripture means by "righteousness" and justification.)

> For I tell you that unless your righteousness surpasses that of the Pharisees and the teachers of the law, you will certainly not enter the kingdom of heaven. (Mat 5:20)
> God made him who had no sin to be sin for us, so that in him we might become the righteousness of God. (2 Cor 5:21)

2. The answer to man's problem is faith. When a person believes the gospel—really believes that Christ saves him—God takes that person's faith and *counts it* for righteousness. The person is not righteous; he is still imperfect, still corruptible, and still short of God's glory as a sinful human being. But he does believe that Jesus Christ saves him. Such belief honors God's Son, and because of that, God accepts and counts that person's faith as righteousness. Therefore, he becomes acceptable to God. This is

justification; this is what is meant by being justified before God.

But note a most critical point: a person must *continue* to believe. A person must continue to live by faith from the very first moment of belief to the last moment of life on this earth, for it is his faith that God takes and counts as righteousness.

What is meant by the two statements…
• "by faith from first to last"
• And, "the righteous will live by faith"?

Very simply, the whole life of the believer is to be a life of faith, from beginning faith to ending faith, by faith from first to last. Therefore, the righteousness of God is revealed *continuously* through all of life, from the beginning of a person's faith to the ending of a person's faith. As Scripture says:

> Abram believed the LORD, and he credited it to him as righteousness. (Gen 15:6)
> Through him everyone who believes is justified from everything you could not be justified from by the law of Moses. (Acts 13:39)
> For in the gospel a righteousness from God is revealed, a righteousness that is by faith from first to last, just as it is written: "The righteous will live by faith." (Rom 1:17)
> For we maintain that a man is justified by faith apart from observing the law. (Rom 3:28)
> What does the Scripture say? "Abraham believed God, and it was credited to him as righteousness." (Rom 4:3)
> The words "it was credited to him" were written not for him alone, but also for us, to whom God will credit righteousness—for us who believe in him who raised Jesus our Lord from the dead. (Rom 4:23-24)
> Therefore, since we have been justified through faith, we have peace with God through our Lord Jesus Christ, (Rom 5:1)
> And that is what some of you were. But you were washed, you were sanctified, you were justified in the name of the Lord Jesus Christ and by the Spirit of our God. (1 Cor 6:11)
> So the law was put in charge to lead us to Christ that we might be justified by faith. (Gal 3:24)
> But he who stands firm to the end will be saved. (Mat 24:13)

DEEPER STUDY # 2
(1:17) **Faith—Justified**: see Deeper Study # 3—Gal.3:11.

		20 For since the creation of the world God's invisible qualities—his eternal power and divine nature—have been clearly seen, being understood from what has been made, so that men are without excuse.	**3 Men reject that "with-out" them: The signs of creation** a. God's eternal power & nature are clearly seen in creation b. Men are without excuse
	II. **SIN AND CONDEMNA-TION: THE WORLD'S NEED TO GET RIGHT WITH GOD, 1:18-3:20** A. **God's Case Against All Godlessness and Wick-edness of Men: Why God Shows Wrath, 1:18-23**		
		21 For although they knew God, they neither glorified him as God nor gave thanks to him, but their thinking be-came futile and their foolish hearts were darkened.	**4 Men do not honor God nor give thanks** a. Result 1: Their imagi-nations become futile (empty) b. Result 2: Their hearts are darkened
1 The subjects of God's wrath[DS1] a. Men: The sinful and the wicked b. Men who suppress the truth **2 Men reject that "within" them: Conscience & thoughts**	18 The wrath of God is being revealed from heaven against all the godlessness and wick-edness of men who suppress the truth by their wickedness, 19 Since what may be known about God is plain to them, because God has made it plain to them.	22 Although they claimed to be wise, they became fools 23 And exchanged the glory of the immortal God for im-ages made to look like mortal man and birds and animals and reptiles.	**5 Men become prideful & turn away from God** a. They imagine & create their own ideas of God b. They exchange the im-mortal God for mortal idols

DIVISION II

SIN AND CONDEMNATION: THE WORLD'S NEED TO GET RIGHT WITH GOD, 1:18-3:20

A. God's Case Against All Godlessness and Wickedness of Men: Why God Shows Wrath, 1:18-23

(1:18-3:20) DIVISION OVERVIEW: the teaching of this whole passage can be summarized into three points.

1. Men who sin bring upon themselves the judgment of God and they need God's righteousness (Ro.1:18-2:16).

2. Men without the law, the heathen, are taught by na-ture and conscience. However, they have sinned by falling short of the standard of righteousness given to them (Ro.1:18-32). Similarly, the moralist and self-righteous who have the law have sinned by falling short of their standard of righteousness, that is, the law (Ro.2:1-3:8).

3. Therefore, all the world becomes guilty before God (Ro.3:19) and needs God's righteousness (Ro.3:9-20).

(1:18-23) Introduction: the message of this passage is per-fectly clear: why God reveals and executes wrath upon men.

1. The subjects of God's wrath (v.18).
2. Men reject that "within" them—conscience and thoughts (v.19).
3. Men reject that "without" them—the signs of creation (v.20).
4. Men do not honor God nor give thanks (v.21).
5. Men become prideful and turn away from God (v.22-23).

1 (1:18) **God's Wrath—Ungodly—Unrighteous:** the subjects of God's wrath. Note three points.

1. The wrath of God is a reality (see DEEPER STUDY # 1, *God's Wrath*—Ro.1:18 for discussion).

2. God's wrath is revealed from heaven. God reveals and shows wrath in four ways. (See note, *God's Wrath*—Ro.1:24-32 for discussion.)

3. The subjects of God's wrath are twofold. God shows His wrath and becomes angry with two classes of men:

  a. Men who are godless and wicked.
    ⇒ The godlessness (asebeia) fail to love and obey God. They are those who do not live as God lives. They are not like God, not holy and righteous and pure. They do not work at developing a godly nature, do not honor God

by word or deed, do not worship and obey God as the only living and true God, do not reverence Him by doing what He says. On the contrary, the sinful are those who do what they want when they want, who may give lip-service to God, but who ignore Him in their day-today lives.
    ⇒ The wicked (adikia) fail to love others. They are those who do not live with men as they should. They act against men: cheating, steal-ing, lying, abusing, enslaving, destroying and taking advantage of them.

    The point is clear: God is angry with such men—men who are ungodly and unrighteous—men who...
    • do not love and obey God.
    • do not love and treat others as they should.

  b. Men who suppress the truth by their wickedness. The word "suppress" (katechonton) means to hold down, repress, stifle, hinder. Men know the truth from three sources:
    ⇒ from nature (cp. Ro.1:20).
    ⇒ from reason and conscience (cp. Ro.1:18; 2:15).
    ⇒ from Scripture (Jn.5:39; 2 Tim.3:16).

    Yet despite having access to the truth, they ignore, neglect, and even push the truth aside, doing all they can to avoid and get rid of it. Why? Because they want to live as *they* wish and not as God says. They want to live wicked lives, to taste and feel and see and have all the stimulating things they want.
    But note what Scripture says: they "suppress the truth by their wickedness;" that is, they know the truth while they go about living in wickedness. They are without ex-cuse.

And in every sort of evil that deceives those who are perishing. They perish because they refused to love the truth and so be saved. (2 Th 2:10)

Again the point is clear: God is angry with men...
• who are godless, who do not love and obey God.
• who are wicked, who do not love and treat others as they should.
• who suppress the truth while they live godless and wicked lives.

For the grace of God that brings salvation has appeared to all men. It teaches us to say "No" to ungodliness and worldly passions, and to live self-controlled, upright and godly lives in this present age, while we wait for the blessed hope—the glorious appearing of our great God and Savior, Jesus Christ, who gave himself for us to redeem us from all wickedness and to purify for himself a people that are his very own, eager to do what is good. (Titus 2:11-14)

DEEPER STUDY # 1
(1:18) **God's Wrath** (orge): anger, not an agitated outburst of violence. It is not the anger that quickly blazes up and just as quickly fades away, not the anger that arises solely from emotion. Rather, it is decisive anger. It is an anger that has arisen from a thoughtful decision, an anger that arises from the mind much more than from the emotions. When used of God, it is always an anger that is *righteous and just and good*. It is an anger that stands against the sin and evil, violence and slaughter, immorality and injustices of men. It is an anger that abhors and hates sin and evil and that dishes out a just revenge and equal justice. However, it is an anger that is *deeply felt*; in fact, it must be felt, for evil and corruption must be opposed and erased from the face of the earth if there is to be a "new heavens and a new earth." And God has promised a new heavens and a new earth where righteousness and perfection dwell forever.
1. There is God's anger in judgment.

But when he saw many of the Pharisees and Sadducees coming to where he was baptizing, he said to them: "You brood of vipers! Who warned you to flee from the coming wrath? (Mat 3:7)
The wrath of God is being revealed from heaven against all the godlessness and wickedness of men who suppress the truth by their wickedness, (Rom 1:18)
But because of your stubbornness and your unrepentant heart, you are storing up wrath against yourself for the day of God's wrath, when his righteous judgment will be revealed. (Rom 2:5)
But for those who are self-seeking and who reject the truth and follow evil, there will be wrath and anger. There will be trouble and distress for every human being who does evil: first for the Jew, then for the Gentile; (Rom 2:8-9)

But if our unrighteousness brings out God's righteousness more clearly, what shall we say? That God is unjust in bringing his wrath on us? (I am using a human argument.) Certainly not! If that were so, how could God judge the world? (Rom 3:5-6)
Since we have now been justified by his blood, how much more shall we be saved from God's wrath through him! (Rom 5:9)
All of us also lived among them at one time, gratifying the cravings of our sinful nature and following its desires and thoughts. Like the rest, we were by nature objects of wrath. (Eph 2:3)
Let no one deceive you with empty words, for because of such things God's wrath comes on those who are disobedient. (Eph 5:6; cp. Col.3:6)
For they themselves report what kind of reception you gave us. They tell how you turned to God from idols to serve the living and true God, and to wait for his Son from heaven, whom he raised from the dead—Jesus, who rescues us from the coming wrath. (1 Th 1:9-10)
For God did not appoint us to suffer wrath but to receive salvation through our Lord Jesus Christ. (1 Th 5:9)
Kiss the Son, lest he be angry and you be destroyed in your way, for his wrath can flare up in a moment. Blessed are all who take refuge in him. (Psa 2:12)

2. There is God's anger with those who disobey the Lord Jesus.

Whoever believes in the Son has eternal life, but whoever rejects the Son will not see life, for God's wrath remains on him." (John 3:36)

3. There was God's anger with Israel in the wilderness.

So I declared on oath in my anger, 'They shall never enter my rest.'" (Heb 3:11)

4. There was the anger of the Lord Jesus at man's stubborn heart.

He looked around at them in anger and, deeply distressed at their stubborn hearts, said to the man, "Stretch out your hand." He stretched it out, and his hand was completely restored. (Mark 3:5)

2 (1:19) **God, Proof of—Mind—Conscience**: God—the only living and true God—shows wrath because men reject that *within them*; that is, they reject their consciences and thoughts and reasoning about God. (Cp. Ro.2:15.) Note three clearly stated facts.
⇒ God can be known. There are *some things* that can be known about God.
⇒ These things are plain (evident, made clear and plain) "*in*" men. Men know about God; they know some things about God *within* their hearts, minds, and consciences.
⇒ How? God has shown or made it plain [made evident and clear] these things to men.

Now note:

1. There is a great deal *about* God that men cannot know (Job 11:7), but there is a great deal that men can know. Men can know enough to be led to God. This is the whole point of this passage: men know about God, but they do not worship Him as God. They have a sense of God, but they suppress the sense, trying to get rid of it.

2. Man's inner sense, or *innate awareness*, and *instinctive knowledge* of God are strong. Man is a very capable creature. He has enormous power and mental capacity. Man can reason and grasp that "God is [exists] and that He rewards those who earnestly seek Him" (Heb.11:6). Man can "know God" (v.19), even the "invisible qualities" of God (v.20); he can know to such a degree that he is "without excuse" (v.20). (See note—Ro.2:11-15 for more discussion.)

However, man chooses not to know God. He even chooses to take the truth that is *within* him and suppress it. Man rejects the knowledge of God that is *within* him. This is the first reason why God reveals and shows His wrath.

3 (1:20) **God, Proof of—Creation—Man, Depravity**: God—the only living and true God—shows wrath because men reject that *without* them—the signs of creation. Creation reveals God. The whole universe, its presence and its nature, declares God.

However, note something often overlooked. Men can look at nature and see *more* than the simple fact that God is the great Creator. Men can see *more* than a Supreme Being behind the creation of the universe. They can see "the invisible qualities" of God. This means at least two things.

1. Man can see the "*eternal power*," the Supreme Intelligence and Force (or Energy), of God. Man can look at the creation of the earth and outer space, of plants and animals, of man and woman; he can look and clearly see their...

- bodies and structure
- variety and beauty
- arrangement and order
- purpose and laws

When man looks at such things and reasons with an *honest spirit*, he sees clearly that the world was made by a Creator. But, as stated above, he sees much more. He sees that the Creator is a God of supreme...

- life & being
- intelligence & knowledge
- energy & power (the Supreme Force)
- purpose & meaning
- design & order (law)
- beauty & majesty
- glory & honor
- value & worth (morality)
- mystery (things not understood; secrets undiscovered)

2. Man can see the "*divine nature*," that is, the deity of God. When he looks at nature and reasons with an *honest spirit*, he sees clearly that the Creator is a God who...

- cares and provides for what He has created.
- gives life and has interest in life.
- regenerates, replenishes, and carries things on.
- deserves worship and obedience (being the Creator of life and purpose, and being the Supreme Person of law and order demands that all his subjects serve and obey Him).

Note what Scripture says: man is without excuse. The point is shocking. Man has every evidence imaginable within creation directing him toward God, yet man rejects the knowledge of God within creation. This is the second reason why God reveals and shows His wrath. Man is without excuse. Man has no defense, no answer, no reason that can justify his rejection of God.

> **Yet he has not left himself without testimony: He has shown kindness by giving you rain from heaven and crops in their seasons; he provides you with plenty of food and fills your hearts with joy." (Acts 14:17)**

> **For since the creation of the world God's invisible qualities—his eternal power and divine nature—have been clearly seen, being understood from what has been made, so that men are without excuse. (Rom 1:20)**

> **For the director of music. A psalm of David. The heavens declare the glory of God; the skies proclaim the work of his hands. (Psa 19:1)**

> **The heavens proclaim his righteousness, and all the peoples see his glory. (Psa 97:6)**

4 (1:21) **God, Sins Against—Unthankful—Dishonor, of God—Man, Depravity**: God—the only living and true God—shows wrath because men do not glorify God nor give Him thanks. Note that Paul shifted to the past tense in this verse. He was speaking of what men had done in the past; and, of course, men still do the same today. Two serious charges are made against men. Men can clearly know God both...

- within themselves: in their own thoughts, reasoning, consciences.
- without themselves: in creation and nature, in the earth and outer space.

They can know that God gives them life and cares and provides for them, and that God runs everything in an orderly and lawful way, giving purpose and meaning to life. Men can see that God is great and good; therefore, God deserves to be glorified and given thanks. But men...

- did not glorify Him: did not worship, obey, or serve Him as God.
- did not give thanks to Him: did not praise, magnify, or express appreciation to Him.

What happens when men reject God is tragic. Two severe things happen when they push God out of their minds.

1. Men's thinking became futile.
   ⇒ The word "thinking" means thoughts, reasoning, deliberations, conclusions, speculations.
   ⇒ The word futile means, empty, unsuccessful, senseless, worthless.

> **Thought 1.** When men push God out of their minds, their minds are void and empty of God. God is not in their thoughts. (Cp. Ps.10:4.) Their minds are ready to be *filled* with some other *god* or *supremacy*.

> **The LORD saw how great man's wickedness on the earth had become, and that every inclination of the thoughts of his heart was only evil all the time. (Gen 6:5)**

> **In his pride the wicked does not seek him; in all his thoughts there is no room for God. (Psa 10:4)**

23

The LORD knows the thoughts of man; he knows that they are futile. (Psa 94:11)

There are six things the LORD hates, seven that are detestable to him: haughty eyes, a lying tongue, hands that shed innocent blood, a heart that devises wicked schemes, feet that are quick to rush into evil, a false witness who pours out lies and a man who stirs up dissension among brothers. (Prov 6:16-19)

The LORD detests the thoughts of the wicked, but those of the pure are pleasing to him. (Prov 15:26)

He said to me, "Son of man, have you seen what the elders of the house of Israel are doing in the darkness, each at the shrine of his own idol? They say, 'The LORD does not see us; the LORD has forsaken the land.'" (Ezek 8:12)

2. Man's "foolish heart is darkened."
⇒ The word "foolish" means senseless, without understanding, unintelligent.
⇒ The word "darkened" means blinded, unable to see.

"They know nothing, they understand nothing. They walk about in darkness; all the foundations of the earth are shaken. (Psa 82:5)

Who leave the straight paths to walk in dark ways, (Prov 2:13)

But the way of the wicked is like deep darkness; they do not know what makes them stumble. (Prov 4:19)

For this people's heart has become calloused; they hardly hear with their ears, and they have closed their eyes. Otherwise they might see with their eyes, hear with their ears, understand with their hearts and turn, and I would heal them.' (Acts 28:27)

The god of this age has blinded the minds of unbelievers, so that they cannot see the light of the gospel of the glory of Christ, who is the image of God. (2 Cor 4:4)

They are darkened in their understanding and separated from the life of God because of the ignorance that is in them due to the hardening of their hearts. (Eph 4:18)

Always learning but never able to acknowledge the truth. (2 Tim 3:7)

Note a critical point. Men suffer empty thoughts and darkened hearts because they...
• do not glorify God.
• do not offer thanks to God.

This is the third reason why God reveals and shows wrath toward men.

But everyone who hears these words of mine and does not put them into practice is like a foolish man who built his house on sand. The rain came down, the streams rose, and the winds blew and beat against that house, and it fell with a great crash." (Mat 7:26-27)

Anyone, then, who knows the good he ought to do and doesn't do it, sins. (James 4:17)

5 (1:22-23) **Man, Depravity—Pride—God, Rejection of:** God—the only living and true God—shows wrath because men become prideful and turn away from God. This scene is one of the greatest tragedies in all of human history, and it is repeated every time a man turns away from God. The scene is man rejecting God and claiming that he is...
• too wise to believe in God.
• too intelligent to depend upon the *fables* of the Bible.
• too capable not to look to self.
• too resourceful not to create his own world and future.
• too masterful not to trust his own *humanistic* ideas.
• too reasonable and rational not to create his own standards and laws to control life.

But note what Scripture says: in denying God, men make two gross mistakes.
1. Men claim to be wise, but in so doing they become fools. Why? For one simple reason.
⇒ God does exist, and He has clearly revealed Himself both within men's thoughts and through creation. Therefore, when men's hearts and minds are emptied of God, men have to fill their hearts and thoughts with something else. They have to have some other god, some other *guiding light* or *principle* to give purpose and meaning and direction to their lives. They have to replace God with something else. They have to have something—some standard, some law, some rule, some person, some god—by which they can guide their lives.

Therefore, when men dethrone and erase God from their lives, they imagine and create their own god within their minds. Men reason and speculate about the ultimate source of life, and whatever they come up with is that to which they give their lives.

Therefore once more I will astound these people with wonder upon wonder; the wisdom of the wise will perish, the intelligence of the intelligent will vanish." (Isa 29:14)

"My people are fools; they do not know me. They are senseless children; they have no understanding. They are skilled in doing evil; they know not how to do good." (Jer 4:22)

Although they claimed to be wise, they became fools (Rom 1:22)

For the message of the cross is foolishness to those who are perishing, but to us who are being saved it is the power of God. For it is written: "I will destroy the wisdom of the wise; the intelligence of the intelligent I will frustrate." (1 Cor 1:18-19)

We do, however, speak a message of wisdom among the mature, but not the wisdom of this age or of the rulers of this age, who are coming to nothing. No, we speak of God's secret wisdom, a wisdom that has been hidden and that God destined for our glory before time began. (1 Cor 2:6-7)

For the wisdom of this world is foolishness in God's sight. As it is written: "He catches the wise in their craftiness"; and again, "The Lord knows that the thoughts of the wise are futile." (1 Cor 3:19-20)

See to it that no one takes you captive through hollow and deceptive philosophy, which depends on human tradition and the basic principles of this world rather than on Christ. Such regulations indeed have an appearance of wisdom, with their self-imposed worship, their false humility and their harsh treatment of the body, but they lack any value in restraining sensual indulgence. (Col 2:8, 23)

2. Men exchange the immortal God for some mortal idol. Note four facts.

a. God is said to be "immortal" (apthartos), which means non-decaying, imperishable, unchanging, and unaging. Immortal means that God is not subject to passing away; He is eternal. God *always has been*, and *always will be*: *God will always exist*.

b. Men swap and exchange God for "mortal man," that is, for the image, the idea, the thought that man is his own god. Men swap God for humanism. They make themselves and mankind...

- the god of life.
- the master of the world.
- the makers of their own destiny.
- the law-givers of their own laws.
- the determiners of their own morality.
- the standard by which their lives are to be governed.

Note that *humanism* makes an idol out of man and worships man as the "god" of his own destiny. This is usually the sin of *scientific and industrialized societies*—societies where a healthy and strong man, both mentally and physically, is es-sential—societies where good self-images and healthy bodies are necessary for the advancement of society.

c. Men swap God for mortal created things. This is usually the worship followed by non-industrialized and non-scientific societies—societies where grotesque images of men and animals are actually constructed out of wood, stone, or metal.

Now note: men create their own humanistic gods, whether mental images and thoughts or some grotesque image, because of pride and conceit. Men want to control their own lives, to do as they wish, to be recognized and honored, and to receive the credit and acknowledgment themselves. Therefore, they turn from God and make their own gods...

- in their own image.
- as they conceive and wish their god to be.

This is the fourth reason why God—the only living and true God—reveals and shows his wrath toward men.

"Therefore since we are God's offspring, we should not think that the divine being is like gold or silver or stone—an image made by man's design and skill. (Acts 17:29)

Dear children, keep yourselves from idols. (1 John 5:21)

See, I am setting before you today a blessing and a curse—the blessing if you obey the commands of the LORD your God that I am giving you today; the curse if you disobey the commands of the LORD your God and turn from the way that I command you today by following other gods, which you have not known. (Deu 11:26-28)

"I am the LORD; that is my name! I will not give my glory to another or my praise to idols. (Isa 42:8)

	B. God's Case Against All Godlessness and Wickedness of Men: How God Shows Wrath, 1:24-32	and received in themselves the due penalty for their perversion.	
1 God gave men over to do as they willed		28 Furthermore, since they did not think it worthwhile to retain the knowledge of God, he gave them over to a depraved mind, to do what ought not to be done.	**4 God gave men over to depraved minds** a. Reason: They rejected God
2 God gave men over to sexual impurity a. Reason: The lusts in their hearts b. Result: Gross idolatry	24 Therefore God gave them over in the sinful desires of their hearts to sexual impurity for the degrading of their bodies with one another. 25 They exchanged the truth of God for a lie, and worshiped and served created things rather than the Creator—who is forever praised. Amen.	29 They have become filled with every kind of wickedness, evil, greed and depravity. They are full of envy, murder, strife, deceit and malice. They are gossips,	b. Result: Depraved, unsuitable behavior*DS1-23*
3 God gave men over to shameful lusts a. Reason: They gave in to unnatural passion & homosexuality b. Result: A burning, passionate bondage 1) Women with women 2) Men with men	26 Because of this, God gave them over to shameful lusts. Even their women exchanged natural relations for unnatural ones. 27 In the same way the men also abandoned natural relations with women and were inflamed with lust for one another. Men committed indecent acts with other men,	30 Slanderers, God-haters, insolent, arrogant and boastful; they invent ways of doing evil; they disobey their parents; 31 They are senseless, faithless, heartless, ruthless. 32 Although they know God's righteous decree that those who do such things deserve death, they not only continue to do these very things but also approve of those who practice them.	**5 God assures final judgment: Death** a. Because men do these things b. Because men approve these things

DIVISION II

SIN AND CONDEMNATION: THE WORLD'S NEED TO GET RIGHT WITH GOD, 1:18-3:20

B. God's Case Against All Godlessness and Wickedness of Men: How God Shows Wrath, 1:24-32

(1:24-32) **Introduction—God's Wrath—Judgment**: Scripture says "the wrath of God is being revealed from heaven" (Ro.1:18). This particular passage discusses the four ways that God reveals and shows His wrath. Note three things.

1. All four ways concern judgments that come upon man. That is, the wrath of God is exercised and falls upon man because of his godlessness and wickedness.

2. All four ways have to do with history, with human experience, with a moral universe. That is, God's wrath is revealed from heaven day by day...
- throughout history.
- in man's experience.
- within a moral universe.

3. Three of the judgments are present judgments; they take place today in the lives of men (v.24-31). The fourth judgment is future and is to be the final judgment upon men (v.32).

How does God reveal and execute His wrath upon man?
1. God gave men over to do as they willed (v.24).
2. God gave men over to sexual impurity (v.24-25).
3. God gave men over to shameful lusts (v.26-27).
4. God gave men over to depraved minds (v.28-31).
5. God assures final judgment: death (v.32).

1 (1:24) **Judgment—Man, Abandoned by God**: God—the only living and true God—gave men over to do as they willed. (See notes—Mt.13:13-15; DEEPER STUDY # 1—Jn.12:39-41 for more discussion.) This is said three times in this passage, and each time was due to a serious sin of man (v.24, 26, 28). Man's sin forced God to give man over and to

abandon him. The scene was terrible and frightening, for to be abandoned and left without God in this world leads to the worst possible life imaginable.

There are two strong reasons why God gives man over, and each issues a loud warning to man.

1. Man chooses sin over God, and when he does, two things happen.
   a. Man becomes enslaved to sin. Sin actually stirs more and more sin. The more a man sins the easier it is for him to sin again. At first he may ponder the wisdom of committing the sin; but later on, after committing the sin over and over, he seldom if ever give the sin a second thought. Sin looks good, tastes good, and feels good. It is attractive and it satisfies the human flesh and urges of man. It satisfies so much that man is naturally attracted to it. By sinning, he steadily makes himself a slave to sin. He becomes addicted. Sin becomes the terrible master and subjects man to its cruel habits and enticements that are almost impossible to break.
   b. Sin *always* lies. This needs to be remembered. Sin entices, claiming to bring pleasure and stimulation and happiness, but in reality it destroys a person's...
   - body
   - family
   - friends
   - soul
   - profession
   - mind
   - will
   - hope
   - values
   - future
   - life

A terrible tragedy that is so often forgotten is this: we are not islands unto ourselves. Our sin involves others; therefore, our sin destroys others—both their lives and their souls. Sin may look, taste, and feel good to us; but it always involves and influences others. It hurts and dooms our children, spouses, friends and society.

2. Man abandons God, actually turns away from God and gives God up. This may be called *spiritual abandonment*: man *spiritually abandons* God. God has given man a free will, and if a man wills to turn away from God, he can. God cannot interfere with that choice. To do so would be to take away man's freedom. So God appeals to man spiritually, through mercy and love and grace, but He does not violate man's choice. He cannot. To do so would be to have a coerced and mechanical universe. Man would become nothing but a robot, coerced to do this and that and to do it exactly as God wills. The result would be tragic: man would never experience love, goodness, care, concern, or feelings. Love is not love if it is coerced. It is mechanical and meaningless. The expression of any affection or virtue is meaningless unless it is freely given. Therefore, when man turns away from God, he himself makes the choice to do so, and God *cannot* interfere. The choice is man's, and man is abandoned—left all alone to himself to do exactly as he has chosen (Hos.4:17; Eph.4:19). Therefore, God has no choice. He must...

- give man over.
- let man go his own way.
- spiritually abandon man.
- leave man to live for that which he has chosen.

So I gave them over to their stubborn hearts to follow their own devices. (Psa 81:12)

But God turned away and gave them over to the worship of the heavenly bodies. This agrees with what is written in the book of the prophets: "'Did you bring me sacrifices and offerings forty years in the desert, O house of Israel? (Acts 7:42)

2 (1:24-25) **Sin—Body—Judgment**: God—the only living and true God—shows wrath by giving men over to sexual impurity. The term "sexual impurity" (akatharsian) means impurity, filthiness, immorality, defilement, dirt, pollution, contamination, infection. When men turn from God—abandon God to live unclean and immoral lives—God leaves men. He abandons them to their choice. God lets men wallow around in their filthiness. Men are judged and condemned to sexual impurity.

1. The *reason* men are condemned to "sexual impurity" is because of the "sinful desires of their hearts." Their hearts are filled with "sinful desires" (epithumiais), that is, passionate cravings, lusts, and urges. They long after things that displease God and that dishonor their bodies. God cares deeply about the human body, and he judges any person who abuses the body. (See outlines and DEEPER STUDY # 6—Mt.6:11; notes—1 Cor.3:16; 3:17; DEEPER STUDY # 1—6:18; notes—6:19; 6:20; cp. 1 Th.4:3-5 for more discussion.)

In the Greek the sinful desires are said to be "*in* [en] their own hearts." Sin takes place in the heart *before* it takes place by act.

He went on: "What comes out of a man is what makes him 'unclean.' For from within, out of men's hearts, come evil thoughts, sexual immorality, theft, murder, adultery, greed, malice, deceit, lewdness, envy, slander, arrogance and folly. All these evils come from inside and make a man 'unclean.'" (Mark 7:20-23)

2. The result of living an impure life is idolatry. Men "exchanged the truth of God for a lie and worshiped and served the created things rather than the Creator." When men live in sexual impurity, they begin to serve and to give their lives to one of two things.
   a. They serve themselves, giving their time and energy to their own desires, pursuits, and lusts.
   b. They serve other "gods," gods that allow them to go ahead and live as they wish. They *imagine* what god is like and they worship him either in their mind or in some graven image molded by their hands. They conceive of a *god* that is...
   - a god of some religion
   - a god of Christianity
   - a god of some part of nature
   - a god of men
   - a god of creation
   - a god of goodness

The point is this. Man abandons the only true and living God and lusts after uncleanness. He lusts and craves so much...
   - that he creates a god in his own mind who allows him to satisfy his lust.
   - that he rationalizes and thinks that his god understands his situation and need, and that his god will not judge him for his impurity and immorality.
   - that he conceives of a god that will allow him to do what he wants.
   - that he matches his god to fit his morals, letting his morals determine the kind of god he is going to worship.
   - that he twists god to fit what he wants.
   - that he allows his morals (sexual impurity) to control his thoughts about God.

Man serves and gives his time and energy to the god he imagines in his mind and to the idols he creates within his imagination and thoughts. He abandons God so that he can live the impure life he craves. Therefore, God judges man and abandons man to live in his sexual impurity.

They have left the straight way and wandered off to follow the way of Balaam son of Beor, who loved the wages of wickedness. (2 Pet 2:15)

Do not love the world or anything in the world. If anyone loves the world, the love of the Father is not in him. For everything in the world—the cravings of sinful man, the lust of his eyes and the boasting of what he has and does—comes not from the Father but from the world. The world and its desires pass away, but the man who does the will of God lives forever. (1 John 2:15-17)

I will pronounce my judgments on my people because of their wickedness in forsaking me, in burning incense to other gods and in worshiping what their hands have made. (Jer 1:16)

"My people have committed two sins: They have forsaken me, the spring of living water, and have dug their own cisterns, broken cisterns that cannot hold water. (Jer 2:13)

You have rejected me," declares the LORD. "You keep on backsliding. So I will lay hands on you and destroy you; I can no longer show compassion. (Jer 15:6)

Do not be like your fathers and brothers, who were unfaithful to the LORD, the God of their fathers, so that he made them an object of horror, as you see. (2 Chr 30:7)

3 (1:26-27) **Sin—Body—Judgment**: God—the only living and true God—shows wrath by giving men over to shameful lusts. The term "shameful lusts" (pathe atimias) means passions, dishonor, disgrace, infamy, vile, and degradation. It means passions that cannot be controlled or governed, that run loose and wild, no matter how much a person tries to control them.

1. The reason God gives men up to shameful lusts is because of their unnatural passion. Men lust and lust, craving the illegitimate and unlawful. They burn in their lust one for another. And note what Scripture is talking about: *unnatural relations*, that is, homosexuality.
⇒ Women burn and lust and exchange the "natural relations for unnatural ones." And note, it is *unnatural*.
⇒ Men burn in their lust one toward another; men with men doing that which is shameful.

Note again that the sin takes place in the heart. Men *burn within*, crave the sin before they commit the act. It is their burning, their lusting, their craving that sets them aflame to pursue the shameful act. Their hearts burn after other men, not after God. Therefore, they stand condemned, and God is forced to judge them.

2. The result of *unnatural* relations is a totally depraved nature. When men choose a life of "shameful lusts," God gives them over to it. It is man's choice, and since it is man's choice, God can do nothing about it. God has to give man over to what he chooses. He does not override man's will.

Note a crucial fact: Scripture says men received in themselves the due penalty for their perversions The judgment for homosexuality is *within*, not *without* man. If a person burns after *unnatural* relationships, he is given over to his burning; he is given over to burn and crave more and more. He is judged and condemned to live in his *unnatural* passion and to feel the shame of it. He is enslaved and held in bondage to it, psychologically and physically. And the judgment is "due," that is, fit, just, exactly what it should be. If men lust and burn after *unnatural* relations, it is only fit that they be given what they so passionately crave. Therefore, God judges men by giving men over to live in their shameful lusts.

That each of you should learn to control his own body in a way that is holy and honorable, not in passionate lust like the heathen, who do not know God; (1 Th 4:4-5)

Marriage should be honored by all, and the marriage bed kept pure, for God will judge the adulterer and all the sexually immoral. (Heb 13:4)

4 (1:28-31) **God, Wrath of—Judgment—Sin**: God—the only living and true God—shows wrath by giving men over to rep, depraved minds. The term "depraved mind" (adokimon noun) means a mind that is rejected, disapproved, degraded, depraved; a mind that cannot stand the test of judgment.

1. The reason God gives men over to depraved minds is because men reject God. They know God, but they do not "like to retain the knowledge of God." They…
• do not like to approve God.
• do not like to recognize God.
• do not like to acknowledge God.

They simply do not want God to have anything to do with their lives; therefore, they push Him out of their minds. They ignore and refuse to accept God's presence.

2. The result is forcibly stated. God gives men over to depraved minds. Men are allowed to do exactly as *they choose*; they are enslaved more and more in their depravity and unsuitable behavior. (See DEEPER STUDY # 1-23—Ro.1:29-31 for the meaning of the terrible sins listed.)

Do not be deceived: God cannot be mocked. A man reaps what he sows. The one who sows to please his sinful nature, from that nature will reap destruction; the one who sows to please the Spirit, from the Spirit will reap eternal life. (Gal 6:7-8)

But because of your stubbornness and your unrepentant heart, you are storing up wrath against yourself for the day of God's wrath, when his righteous judgment will be revealed. (Rom 2:5)

DEEPER STUDY # 1
(1:29) **Wickedness** (adikia): injustice, wrongdoing, evildoing, every kind of evil. It is the opposite of righteousness; therefore, it is…
• mistreating God and man, acting unjustly toward both.
• failing to treat God and man as a person should treat them.

Note the phrase "every kind of wickedness." It is being *filled* with unjust treatment. It is focusing on oneself to the point of making oneself the center of the universe…
• grasping after everything, all the attention and possessions one can secure.
• ignoring and abusing others to get all one can.

DEEPER STUDY #2
(1:29) **Evil** (poneria): to be depraved, to be actively wicked, to do mischief, to trouble others and cause harm, to be malicious, to be dangerous and destructive. It is malice, hatred, and ill-will. It is an active wickedness, a desire within the heart to do harm and to corrupt people. It is a person who actually pursues others to seduce or to injure them.

DEEPER STUDY #3
(1:29) **Greed** (pleonexia): a lust for more and more, an appetite for something, a love of possessing, a cry of "give, give" (2 Pt.2:14). It is a grasping, a craving after and for possessions, pleasure, power, and fame. Covetousness lacks restraint. It lacks the ability to discriminate. It wants to have in order to spend in pleasure and luxury. Covetousness is an insatiable lust and craving of the flesh that cannot be satisfied. It is a lust and craving so deep that a person finds his happiness in things and pleasure instead of God. It is idolatry (Eph.5:5). It is an intense appetite for gain, a passion for the pleasure that things can bring. It is an active, aggressive, grasping covetousness.

DEEPER STUDY #4

(1:29) **Depravity—Hate** (kakia): malice, viciousness, ill-will, spite, a grudge. It means that a man has turned his heart completely over to evil.

⇒ He no longer has any good within—none whatsoever.
⇒ He is full of viciousness and malice.
⇒ He is actively pursuing evil with a vengeance.

DEEPER STUDY #5

(1:29) **Envy** (phthonos): the word goes beyond jealousy. It is the spirit...

- that wants not only the things that another person has, but begrudges the fact that the person has them.
- that wants not only the things to be taken away from the person, but wants him to suffer through the loss of them.

Every thought expresses grief that another person has something, whether honor, recognition, or position.

DEEPER STUDY #6

(1:29) **Murder** (phonos): to kill, to take the life of another. Murder is a sin against the sixth commandment.

DEEPER STUDY #7

(1:29) **Strife** (eridos): discord, contention, fighting, struggling, quarreling, dissension, wrangling. It means that a man fights against another person in order to get something: position, promotion, property, honor, recognition. He fights in a dishonest and evil way.

DEEPER STUDY #8

(1:29) **Deceit** (dolos): to bait, snare, mislead, beguile; to be crafty and deceitful; to mislead or to give a false impression by word, act, or influence. It is a man who connives and twists the truth to get his own way. He plots and deceives, doing whatever has to be done to get what he is after.

DEEPER STUDY #9

(1:29) **Malice** (kakoetheia): evil disposition, evil in nature. It is a spirit full of evil and malice and injury, a character that is as evil as it can be. It is a person who always looks for the worst in other people and always passes on the worst about them. It is the person who so often ruins other people both in reputation and body and in mind and spirit. It is a person so full of evil that he is always ruining others either by word or violence.

DEEPER STUDY # 10

(1:29) **Gossips** (psithuristes): secret gossipers, secret slanderers, backbiters, murmurers. It is a person...

- who whispers behind another person's back, chewing and tearing him up.
- who passes on tales about others, whether true or not.
- who destroys the reputation of others.

DEEPER STUDY # 11

(1:30) **Slanderers** (katalalos): the word differs from the quiet, secret slanderer. It is a loud, open slanderer, a person who broadcasts the tale. Again, whether the tale is true or not does not matter. The backbiting slanderer burns within to tell the gossip to everyone.

DEEPER STUDY # 12

(1:30) **God-Haters** (theostugeis): hating and being hateful to God. It is a person...

- who dislikes the commandments and restraints of God.
- who wants nothing to do with God and His restrictions and laws.
- who wants the license to do exactly as he wishes.
- who wants to be the god of his own life, doing his own thing as he wishes, determining both what he should and should not do.

DEEPER STUDY # 13

(1:30) **Insolent** (hubristes): insulting, and defying. It is a spirit of spite, of attack and assault, verbally or physically. It is despising and attacking, inflicting injury either by word or act. It is a man who...

- lives his own life as he wishes, ignoring both God and men.
- lives as though his rights and affairs are the only rights and affairs which matter.
- stands toe to toe with both God and men, acting as though he needs neither.
- acts so independent in life that he dares God or men to get in his way.
- does what he wants when he wants, even if it hurts or destroys others.

The sin of despite, of being insolent and insulting, is the spirit that hurts and harms others in order to do what one wants.

DEEPER STUDY # 14

(1:30) **Arrogant** (huperephanos): self-exaltation, conceit, arrogant; being haughty; putting oneself above others and looking down upon others; scorn, contempt. It means to show oneself, to lift one's head above another, to hold contempt for another, to compare oneself with others. Pride can be hidden in the heart as well as openly displayed. God resists the proud (Jas.4:6; 1 Pt.5:5; Pr.3:24).

DEEPER STUDY # 15

(1:30) **Boastful** (alazon): braggarts, pretenders, vaunters, swaggerts, boasters. It is a person who...

- boasts in what he has.
- boasts in what he can do.
- pretends to have what he does not have or pretends to have done what he has not done.

Bragging may involve a job, a deal, a possession, an achievement—anything that may impress others. It is a person who feels the need to push himself above others even if it involves *pretension*, *deception*, *make believe*, or *lies*.

DEEPER STUDY # 16

(1:30) **Inventors of evil things** (epheuretes kakon): inventors of new sins, of more sensational forms of excitement and vice. It is a person who is tired of the old forms of sin and who feels the need to seek out new ways and forms of vice.

DEEPER STUDY # 17

(1:30) **Disobedient to parents** (goneusin apeitheis) refusing to do what one's parents say; rebelling against one's parents; showing disrespect to parents; rejecting parental instruction; dishonoring parental example. A child who disobeys his parents is wide open to all forms of evil.

DEEPER STUDY # 18

(1:31) **Senseless** (asunetos): without understanding, foolish, stupid, without conscience. It is a person who...

- ignores experience.
- will not learn no matter who the teacher is.
- refuses to heed the truth.
- closes his mind and eyes to the truth.
- rejects conscience.

DEEPER STUDY # 19

(1:31) **Faithless** (asunthetos): breakers of promises or agreements, untrustworthy, treacherous, untruthful. It is a man who tragically does not keep his word or promise. He is simply untrustworthy and undependable.

DEEPER STUDY # 20

(1:31) **Heartless** (astorgos): abnormal affection and love, without human emotion or love, a lack of feeling for others, abuse of normal affection and love. Others become little more than pawns for a man's own use and benefit, pleasure and purposes, excitement and stimulation. Abnormal affection, sex and perversion prevail.

DEEPER STUDY # 21

(1:31) **Ruthless** (aneleemon): without pity; unwilling to show mercy. It is a person...

- craving to have and to possess others regardless of their welfare.
- craving to use others as one wills regardless of hurt and shame.
- craving to satisfy one's own pleasure even if it means the hurt or death of others.

It is an absence of consideration or feelings for others. What matters is one's own pleasure and rights, not the pleasure and rights of others.

5 (1:32) **Judgment**: God—the only living and true God—assures final judgment which is death, that is, eternal separation from God. There are two reasons why men will be judged and condemned to death.

1. Men will be judged because they sin and approve of others who sin by doing the same things (v.29-31). Men have appetites, desires, and lusts, and they spend their lives seeking to fulfill them. The great tragedy is that they not only *approve of* their own sins, but they *approve of* the sins of others. They *approve of and talk about* their selfishness and exploits and that of their friends. They focus their lives upon...

- extravagant living
- stylish dress
- wealth
- power
- position
- fame
- material possessions
- sexual affairs

1. As a result of such selfishness, the sins listed in the Scripture tear at the world and destroy human life (v.29-31); therefore, the judgment of God is assured. Those who commit such things and *approve of* the sins of others shall die, that is, be separated from God eternally.

> Although they know God's righteous decree that those who do such things deserve death, they not only continue to do these very things but also approve of those who practice them. (Rom 1:32)
> Woe to those who call evil good and good evil, who put darkness for light and light for darkness, who put bitter for sweet and sweet for bitter. (Isa 5:20)
> Because you disheartened the righteous with your lies, when I had brought them no grief, and because you encouraged the wicked not to turn from their evil ways and so save their lives, (Ezek 13:22)
> You have wearied the LORD with your words. "How have we wearied him?" you ask. By saying, "All who do evil are good in the eyes of the LORD, and he is pleased with them" or "Where is the God of justice?" (Mal 2:17)

2. Men will be judged because they are without excuse: they know through an inner sense that the judgment of God is coming upon the world. Men sense that some higher power (God) is going to straighten out the mess in the world: that injustices and inequities will be brought to judgment, condemned and punished. (See outline and notes—Ro.2:1-16 for more discussion.)

> For the wages of sin is death, but the gift of God is eternal life in Christ Jesus our Lord. (Rom 6:23)
> The mind of sinful man is death, but the mind controlled by the Spirit is life and peace; (Rom 8:6)
> Just as man is destined to die once, and after that to face judgment, (Heb 9:27)
> Then, after desire has conceived, it gives birth to sin; and sin, when it is full-grown, gives birth to death. (James 1:15)
> But the cowardly, the unbelieving, the vile, the murderers, the sexually immoral, those who practice magic arts, the idolaters and all liars—their place will be in the fiery lake of burning sulfur. This is the second death." (Rev 21:8)
> The truly righteous man attains life, but he who pursues evil goes to his death. (Prov 11:19)
> For every living soul belongs to me, the father as well as the son—both alike belong to me. The soul who sins is the one who will die. (Ezek 18:4)

CHAPTER 2

C. God's Case Against the Moralist: Judgment, 2:1-16

1 The moralist
a. He judges others
b. He is inexcusable: He condemns himself because he is guilty of the same things

2 The judgment of God is based on truths: Perfect justice

a. The moralist thinks he will escape

b. The moralist thinks God is too good to punish
c. The moralist thinks man is basically good
d. The moralist hardens his heart against the judgment of God
  1) Refuses to repent
  2) Result: Stores up wrath against himself

3 The judgment of God is according to deeds: Eternal reward or punishment
a. The well-doer's reward[DS1,2,3]

b. The evil-doer's severe judgment[DS4-7]

c. Every evil-doer is to be judged[DS8,9]

d. Every well-doer is to be rewarded

4 The judgment of God does not show favoritism: Absolute impartiality
a. The man who sins apart from the law & the man who sins under the law will both be judged
b. The obedient, not the listeners, of the law will be justified

c. The heathen have a threefold witness
  1) Their nature: An instinctive knowledge of right & wrong
  2) Their conscience: Bears witness to what is right & wrong
  3) Their thoughts: Accuse or defend their behavior

5 The judgment of God is to be executed by Jesus Christ & His gospel

You, therefore, have no excuse, you who pass judgment on someone else, for at whatever point you judge the other, you are condemning yourself, because you who pass judgment do the same things. 2 Now we know that God's judgment against those who do such things is based on truth. 3 So when you, a mere man, pass judgment on them and yet do the same things, do you think you will escape God's judgment? 4 Or do you show contempt for the riches of his kindness, tolerance and patience, not realizing that God's kindness leads you toward repentance? 5 But because of your stubbornness and your unrepentant heart, you are storing up wrath against yourself for the day of God's wrath, when his righteous judgment will be revealed. 6 God "will give to each person according to what he has done." 7 To those who by persistence in doing good seek glory, honor and immortality, he will give eternal life. 8 But for those who are self-seeking and who reject the truth and follow evil, there will be wrath and anger 9 There will be trouble and distress for every human being who does evil: first for the Jew, then for the Gentile; 10 But glory, honor and peace for everyone who does good: first for the Jew, then for the Gentile. 11 For God does not show favoritism. 12 All who sin apart from the law will also perish apart from the law, and all who sin under the law will be judged by the law. 13 For it is not those who hear the law who are righteous in God's sight, but it is those who obey the law who will be declared righteous. 14 (Indeed, when Gentiles, who do not have the law, do by nature things required by the law, they are a law for themselves, even though they do not have the law, 15 Since they show that the requirements of the law are written on their hearts, their consciences also bearing witness, and their thoughts now accusing, now even defending them.) 16 This will take place on the day when God will judge men's secrets through Jesus Christ, as my gospel declares.

DIVISION II

SIN AND CONDEMNATION: THE WORLD'S NEED TO GET RIGHT WITH GOD, 1:18-3:20

C. God's Case Against the Moralist: Judgment, 2:1-16

1 (2:1-16) **Introduction**: this is one of the passages that covers several subjects and can be studied from the viewpoint of any one of them. It is an excellent study on judging, criticizing others, the judgment of God, self-righteousness, the moralist, and the legalist. It also deals with the judgment of the heathen, and answers the question so often asked: "What will happen to the heathen, to the person who never hears about Jesus Christ?" (v.11-15). The present study is entitled: "God's Case Against the Moralist."

1. The moralist (v.1).
2. The judgment of God is based on truth: perfect justice (v.2-5).
3. The judgment of God is according to deeds: eternal reward or punishment (v.6-10).
4. The judgment of God does not show favoritism: absolute impartiality (v.11-15).
5. The judgment of God is to be executed by Jesus Christ and His gospel (v.16).

(2:1) **Moralist—Judging Others—Criticism**: the moralist. In the eyes of Scripture a moralist is a person who lives a moral and clean life, but he judges others because they do not live as *he thinks* they should. He is moral, upright, just, good, decent, and honorable. The moralist has strong values, standards, and principles. He is well disciplined and able to control his life. He lives just as everyone thinks he should. He knows right from wrong and he lives it. He knows how to behave and he does it. In the eyes of society he is just what a person should be. He is a good neighbor, an excellent worker and provider, and an ideal citizen. But note three things.

1. The moralist judges others. The words "passes judgment" or "judge" (krino) mean to criticize, to find fault, to condemn. This is the terrible flaw of the moralist.

31

Note: any person becomes a moralist when he sets himself up as a judge of others. Any time we judge another person, we are declaring that we...

- are living by some rule that another person is not living by.
- are more moral than someone else.
- are better than someone else.
- are superior to someone else.
- are more righteous than someone else.
- are more acceptable to God than someone else.

Judging others says, "I am right, and he is not; I succeed, but he fails." Therefore...

- "Look at me, but ignore him."
- "Draw near to me, but shun him."
- "Esteem me, but put him down."
- "Approve me, but condemn him."
- "Be my friend, but withdraw from him."

Very simply, judging others raises self and lowers others, exalts self and debases others; and in the eyes of God this is wrong. It is sin. It is being full of self-righteousness, pride, and arrogance. It sets self up as a moralist, and it makes a person judgmental and critical.

> **"Do not judge, or you too will be judged. (Mat 7:1)**
> **Who are you to judge someone else's servant? To his own master he stands or falls. And he will stand, for the Lord is able to make him stand. (Rom 14:4)**
> **Therefore let us stop passing judgment on one another. Instead, make up your mind not to put any stumbling block or obstacle in your brother's way. (Rom 14:13)**
> **There is only one Lawgiver and Judge, the one who is able to save and destroy. But you—who are you to judge your neighbor? (James 4:12)**

2. The moralist is inexcusable, and he condemns himself because he does the very same things. He fails just as the man whom he judges fails. Scripture says...

> **You, therefore, have no excuse, you who pass judgment on someone else, for at whatever point you judge the other, you are condemning yourself, because you who pass judgment do the same things. (Rom 2:1)**
> **No temptation has seized you except what is common to man. And God is faithful; he will not let you be tempted beyond what you can bear. But when you are tempted, he will also provide a way out so that you can stand up under it. (1 Cor 10:13)**
> **"You have heard that it was said to the people long ago, 'Do not murder, and anyone who murders will be subject to judgment.' But I tell you that anyone who is angry with his brother will be subject to judgment. Again, anyone who says to his brother, 'Raca,' is answerable to the Sanhedrin. But anyone who says, 'You fool!' will be in danger of the fire of hell. (Mat 5:21-22)**
> **"You have heard that it was said, 'Do not commit adultery.' But I tell you that anyone who looks at a woman lustfully has already committed adultery with her in his heart. (Mat 5:27-28)**

In God's eyes, sin is a matter of the heart and mind, not just an act. The thought and desire makes a person just as guilty as the act itself. God knows that many would carry out their thoughts *if they had the courage or opportunity*. God knows the heart, the mind, and the thoughts. Sin, whether thoughts in the mind or acts in public, comes short of God's glory. All stand guilty before God; therefore, the moralist, the person who judges, is as guilty as the one judged. It is for this reason that we are not to judge, criticize, and find fault with others.

> **"Why do you look at the speck of sawdust in your brother's eye and pay no attention to the plank in your own eye? (Mat 7:3)**
> **You, then, who teach others, do you not teach yourself? You who preach against stealing, do you steal? You who say that people should not commit adultery, do you commit adultery? You who abhor idols, do you rob temples? (Rom 2:21-22)**
> **When I saw that they were not acting in line with the truth of the gospel, I said to Peter in front of them all, "You are a Jew, yet you live like a Gentile and not like a Jew. How is it, then, that you force Gentiles to follow Jewish customs? (Gal 2:14)**
> **They claim to know God, but by their actions they deny him. They are detestable, disobedient and unfit for doing anything good. (Titus 1:16)**

Thought 1. This point does not mean that judicial systems of the state are wrong nor that discipline is not to be exercised within families, organizations, and the church. Scripture teaches that both justice and discipline are to be exercised by men. What Scripture means is this: we are not to go around criticizing and finding fault with each other and putting each other down when one of us fails. Instead we are to reach out and try to redeem and help each other. Imagine what a different world this would be if all tongues were stopped! If all criticism and fault-finding ceased! If everyone actually reached out and tried to redeem and save those who failed!

> **Brothers, if someone is caught in a sin, you who are spiritual should restore him gently. But watch yourself, or you also may be tempted. Carry each other's burdens, and in this way you will fulfill the law of Christ. (Gal 6:1-2)**
> **Accept him whose faith is weak, without passing judgment on disputable matters. (Rom 14:1)**
> **We who are strong ought to bear with the failings of the weak and not to please ourselves. (Rom 15:1)**
> **To the weak I became weak, to win the weak. I have become all things to all men so that by all possible means I might save some. (1 Cor 9:22)**
> **And we urge you, brothers, warn those who are idle, encourage the timid, help the weak, be patient with everyone. (1 Th 5:14)**

Suppose a brother or sister is without clothes and daily food. If one of you says to him, "Go, I wish you well; keep warm and well fed," but does nothing about his physical needs, what good is it? (James 2:15-16)

Out of the same mouth come praise and cursing. My brothers, this should not be. (James 3:10)

2 (2:2-5) **Judgment—God, Misconceptions of—Man**: the judgment of God—of the only living and true God—is based on truth. God's judgment will be executed in perfect justice. The word "truth" (aletheian) means true as opposed to false. It means what really is; what actually exists; what exactly takes place. God's judgment is *perfectly* just, exactly what it should be, nothing more and nothing less. His judgment is based upon...
- what really happens.
- what the facts are.
- what actually takes place.
- what a person really is within his heart and what the person actually did.

> **But the LORD said to Samuel, "Do not consider his appearance or his height, for I have rejected him. The LORD does not look at the things man looks at. Man looks at the outward appearance, but the LORD looks at the heart." (1 Sam 16:7)**

God knows the truth, the whole truth and nothing but the truth; therefore, He will judge based on truth. His judgment will be perfect, conforming exactly to our deeds. It will match our deeds perfectly.

Note four points.
1. The moralist thinks he will escape. His offense is much greater, for he is like all other men: sinful and short of God's glory. Yet he criticizes and judges those whose failures are discovered and exposed, and he thinks he will escape. He forgets that God sees the *inner recesses* of the human heart, and that God will judge men not only for their deeds but for their thoughts...
- for the lust of the flesh, the cravings of sinful man.
- for the lust of the eyes.
- for the pride of life, the boasting of what he has and does (1 Jn.2:15-16).

> "You snakes! You brood of vipers! How will you escape being condemned to hell? (Mat 23:33)
> There is nothing concealed that will not be disclosed, or hidden that will not be made known. (Luke 12:2)
> He did not need man's testimony about man, for he knew what was in a man. (John 2:25)
> Therefore judge nothing before the appointed time; wait till the Lord comes. He will bring to light what is hidden in darkness and will expose the motives of men's hearts. At that time each will receive his praise from God. (1 Cor 4:5)
> While people are saying, "Peace and safety," destruction will come on them suddenly, as labor pains on a pregnant woman, and they will not escape. (1 Th 5:3)

> How shall we escape if we ignore such a great salvation? This salvation, which was first announced by the Lord, was confirmed to us by those who heard him. (Heb 2:3)
> "But if you fail to do this, you will be sinning against the LORD; and you may be sure that your sin will find you out. (Num 32:23)
> For God will bring every deed into judgment, including every hidden thing, whether it is good or evil. (Eccl 12:14)

2. The moralist thinks God is too good to punish. When he thinks of God, he thinks of the riches...
- of God's kindness or goodness (chrestotes): His kindness, grace and love.
- of God's tolerance or forbearance (anoche): His refraining, holding back, abstaining and controlling His justice.
- of God's patience and long-suffering: His suffering a long time, being patient and slow in judging sin.

God, of course, is all this and much more. What the moralist fails to see is that God's kindness or goodness...
- is not a blank check for sin.
- does not give license to sin.
- does not condone sin.
- does not indulge sin.
- does not overlook sin.

God's kindness is to lead men to repentance, not to sin. The fact that God *will* forgive sin should stir men to seek forgiveness and to please God. If a man goes out and sins, thinking that God will just overlook and forgive his sin, he is despising God's kindness. He is taking God's kindness and making it a sham, a mockery, a joke, a thing of indulgence. The man who shows contempt for God's kindness—who sins thinking God will just overlook and forgive his sin—is wrong. He is mistaken. God does not just overlook and forgive his sin; He does not condone, indulge, nor give license to his sin. God will judge him and the judgment will be according to the truth.

> **Do you not know that the wicked will not inherit the kingdom of God? Do not be deceived: Neither the sexually immoral nor idolaters nor adulterers nor male prostitutes nor homosexual offenders nor thieves nor the greedy nor drunkards nor slanderers nor swindlers will inherit the kingdom of God. And that is what some of you were. But you were washed, you were sanctified, you were justified in the name of the Lord Jesus Christ and by the Spirit of our God. (1 Cor 6:9-11)**
> Do not be misled: "Bad company corrupts good character. [morals]" Come back to your senses as you ought, and stop sinning; for there are some who are ignorant of God—I say this to your shame. (1 Cor 15:33-34)
> Do not be deceived: God cannot be mocked. A man reaps what he sows. (Gal 6:7)
> Let no one deceive you with empty words, for because of such things God's wrath comes on those who are disobedient. (Eph 5:6)
> Dear children, do not let anyone lead you astray. He who does what is right is righteous, just as he is righteous. He who does what is sinful is of the devil, because

the devil has been sinning from the beginning. The reason the Son of God appeared was to destroy the devil's work. (1 John 3:7-8)

3. The moralist thinks man is basically good. He thinks that man can be good enough for God to accept. He thinks God looks for the good in man and that within each man is *enough good* for God to accept. The moralist thinks that God's goodness accepts man's...

- good works
- good thoughts
- good behavior
- good feelings
- good nature
- good tendencies

God, of course, is pleased with whatever good is in man. But what the moralist fails to see is that *God's goodness is perfect*. It cannot accept...

- any imperfect work
- any foul thoughts
- any evil behavior
- any ugly feelings
- any corruptible nature
- any sinful urges

God can only accept perfection. No man is perfect: not in nature, thought, or behavior. Therefore, all men are unacceptable to God. No man is good enough to be acceptable to God, no matter how good he is. The goodness of God is to lead men to repentance: to turn men to God for righteousness, *not to declare man's self-righteousness*. The fact that God allows men to repent should stir men...

- to confess their imperfection and self-righteousness.
- to seek God's righteousness which is in Christ Jesus the Lord. (See notes—Ro.4:1-3; DEEPER STUDY # 1,2—4:22; 5:1 for more discussion.)

Thought 1. Most people think that God will accept them, that in the final analysis they are good enough for God to accept them. They never dream that God will reject them, not when everything is said and done. What they fail to see is that God's judgment is based upon truth—the truth of what a person's thoughts and motives are, of what is really within a person's mind and heart. God's judgment is based upon the truth of a person's *imperfect nature and behavior*.

For although they knew God, they neither glorified him as God nor gave thanks to him, but their thinking became futile and their foolish hearts were darkened. Although they claimed to be wise, they became fools (Rom 1:21-22)

We do not dare to classify or compare ourselves with some who commend themselves. When they measure themselves by themselves and compare themselves with themselves, they are not wise. (2 Cor 10:12)

If anyone thinks he is something when he is nothing, he deceives himself. (Gal 6:3)

Many a man claims to have unfailing love, but a faithful man who can find? (Prov 20:6)

Do you see a man wise in his own eyes? There is more hope for a fool than for him. (Prov 26:12)

He who trusts in himself is a fool, but he who walks in wisdom is kept safe. (Prov 28:26)

Those who are pure in their own eyes and yet are not cleansed of their filth; (Prov 30:12)

You have trusted in your wickedness and have said, 'No one sees me.' Your wisdom and knowledge mislead you when you say to yourself, 'I am, and there is none besides me.' (Isa 47:10)

The pride of your heart has deceived you, you who live in the clefts of the rocks and make your home on the heights, you who say to yourself, 'Who can bring me down to the ground?' Though you soar like the eagle and make your nest among the stars, from there I will bring you down," declares the LORD. (Oba 1:3-4)

4. The moralist hardens his heart against the judgment of God. He refuses to repent. He just cannot accept the fact...

- that he is not good enough for God to accept.
- that God's kindness and love would ever condemn him.

But note the term "righteous judgment" (dikaiokrisias), which means just, fair, impartial, correct, exact. God's judgment is a judgment that should be, that should and will take place. In fact, God must judge, for God is love. As love, He must straighten out all the injustices on earth. He must right the wrongs and correct all the injustices of men. He must judge men with a perfect and "righteous judgment."

Note also the term "storing up" (thesaurizo), which means to store up, to heap up, to lay up. The man who hardens his heart and refuses to repent stores up more and more wrath against himself in the day of judgment. The fact is clearly seen. Just think how terrible it is for a man to rebel against God's kindness and goodness. He has the glorious privilege of knowing God's goodness, of hearing His kindness proclaimed day by day, week by week, month by month, and year by year. Yet he despises God's goodness, refusing to repent and rejecting God's kindness and goodness time and time again. His rejection is bound to store up wrath against himself. His judgment is bound to be greater than the judgment upon a person who has *never* had the privilege of hearing about the goodness of God.

"I have come to bring fire on the earth, and how I wish it were already kindled! (Luke 12:49)

Whoever believes in the Son has eternal life, but whoever rejects the Son will not see life, for God's wrath remains on him." (John 3:36)

The wrath of God is being revealed from heaven against all the godlessness and wickedness of men who suppress the truth by their wickedness, (Rom 1:18)

But among you there must not be even a hint of sexual immorality, or of any kind of impurity, or of greed, because these are improper for God's holy people. Nor should there be obscenity, foolish talk or coarse joking, which are out of place, but rather thanksgiving. For of this you can be sure: No immoral, impure or greedy person—such a man is an idolater—has any inheritance in the kingdom of Christ and of God. Let no one deceive you with empty words, for because of such things God's wrath comes on those who are disobedient. (Eph 5:3-6)

If this is so, then the Lord knows how to rescue godly men from trials and to hold the unrighteous for the day of judgment, while continuing their punishment. (2 Pet 2:9)

By the same word the present heavens and earth are reserved for fire, being kept for the day of judgment and destruction of ungodly men. (2 Pet 3:7)

A man who remains stiff-necked after many rebukes will suddenly be destroyed—without remedy. (Prov 29:1)

3 (2:6-10) **Judgment**: the judgment of God—of the only living and true God—is according to deeds (Prov.24:12; 2 Tim.4:14; cp. Mt.16:27; Rev.22:12), and it will be universal. Every one will be either eternally rewarded or eternally punished. No one shall be exempt; no one will escape.

Now note: judgment is to be based upon a man's "deeds" (ergon) what a man has "done." This does not mean that *faith* is not necessary. Contrariwise, there is no such thing as...
- faith without works.
- righteous and acceptable works without faith.

God's works—the works that are truly of and for God, that truly please God—are the result of faith. Men believe in and serve and work for many different things in the world. Some believe and work...
- for religion
- for service organizations
- for social clubs
- for humanity

What God demands is that men first believe and work for Him, reaching out to a world lost and gripped in desperate need. When a man truly believes God, he works for God. (Cp. Jas.2:17f.) God is going to either reward or punish every man according to his works, according to what he has done *with and for God*.

1. There shall be the well-doer's wonderful reward. Note three things about the well-doer.
   a. Note what he seeks: glory, honor, and immortality (see DEEPER STUDIES #1-3 on each subject—Ro.2:7).
   b. Note how the well-doer seeks: "by persistence" (hupomone). The word means to be steadfast and constant; to endure, persevere, stick to, and continue. The well-doer is faithful in doing good works.
   ⇒ He does not just start, he finishes.
   ⇒ He does not live an inconsistent, up and down life. He continues and keeps on doing good deeds.
   ⇒ He does not give in to hardships, difficulties, or opposition. He endures and perseveres, always doing good.

   Let us not become weary in doing good, for at the proper time we will reap a harvest if we do not give up. (Gal 6:9)

   But as for you, continue in what you have learned and have become convinced of, because you know those from whom you learned it, (2 Tim 3:14)

   Therefore, since we are surrounded by such a great cloud of witnesses, let us throw off everything that hinders and the sin that so eas-

ily entangles, and let us run with perseverance the race marked out for us. (Heb 12:1)

Therefore, prepare your minds for action; be self-controlled; set your hope fully on the grace to be given you when Jesus Christ is revealed. (1 Pet 1:13)

I am coming soon. Hold on to what you have, so that no one will take your crown. (Rev 3:11)

   c. Note the wonderful reward of the well-doer: eternal life. Eternal life is said to be the inheritance of a world of glory, honor, and peace (v.10; cp. Ro.4:13). (See DEEPER STUDY #2, *Eternal Life*—Jn.1:4; DEEPER STUDY #1—10:10; DEEPER STUDY #1—17:2-3; DEEPER STUDY #1—2 Tim.4:18; also see notes, *Peace*—Ro.5:1; Jn.14:27 for discussion.)

2. There shall be the evil-doer's terrible and severe judgment. The evil-doer is to be judged for three reasons.
   a. He is self-seeking against God (see DEEPER STUDY #4—Ro.2:8). The evil-doer does not like what God says; therefore, he strives against it. He wrangles and wrestles, struggles and fights against God. He refuses to buckle under and surrender to God's will. When dealing with God, the evil-doer is self-seeking.
   b. He rejects the truth. He sees and hears and knows the truth. He even knows the truth is to be done, but he refuses to do it. He refuses to be persuaded and refuses to believe. He rejects both Christ, the Living Truth, and the Word of God, the written truth. He simply goes about his own life, running and controlling it as he wills. He rejects and refuses to believe and to do the truth.
   c. He follows evil (see DEEPER STUDY #5—Ro.2:8 for discussion).

3. Every evil-doer is to be judged, both Jew and Gentile. No evil-doer shall escape. "Every human being who does evil" shall suffer, and the judgment will be severe and terrible. His judgment will involve wrath and anger, trouble and distress (see DEEPER STUDY #6,7—Ro.2:8; DEEPER STUDY #8,9—2:9 for discussion).

   "Then they will go away to eternal punishment, but the righteous to eternal life." (Mat 25:46)

   His winnowing fork is in his hand to clear his threshing floor and to gather the wheat into his barn, but he will burn up the chaff with unquenchable fire." (Luke 3:17)

   "That servant who knows his master's will and does not get ready or does not do what his master wants will be beaten with many blows. (Luke 12:47)

   But for those who are self-seeking and who reject the truth and follow evil, there will be wrath and anger. (Rom 2:8)

   And give relief to you who are troubled, and to us as well. This will happen when the Lord Jesus is revealed from heaven in blazing fire with his powerful angels. He will punish those who do not know God and do not obey the gospel of our Lord Jesus. They will be punished with everlasting destruction and shut out from the presence of the Lord and from the majesty of his power (2 Th 1:74-9)

   How much more severely do you think a man deserves to be punished who has trampled the Son of God under foot, who has treated as an unholy thing the blood of the covenant that sanctified him, and who has insulted the Spirit of grace? (Heb 10:29)

If this is so, then the Lord knows how to rescue godly men from trials and to hold the unrighteous for the day of judgment, while continuing their punishment. (2 Pet 2:9)

If anyone's name was not found written in the book of life, he was thrown into the lake of fire. (Rev 20:15)

On the wicked he will rain fiery coals and burning sulfur; a scorching wind will be their lot. (Psa 11:6)

I will punish the world for its evil, the wicked for their sins. I will put an end to the arrogance of the haughty and will humble the pride of the ruthless. (Isa 13:11)

See, the LORD is coming out of his dwelling to punish the people of the earth for their sins. The earth will disclose the blood shed upon her; she will conceal her slain no longer. (Isa 26:21)

According to what they have done, so will he repay wrath to his enemies and retribution to his foes; he will repay the islands their due. (Isa 59:18)

I will punish you as your deeds deserve, declares the LORD. I will kindle a fire in your forests that will consume everything around you.'" (Jer 21:14)

"Surely the day is coming; it will burn like a furnace. All the arrogant and every evildoer will be stubble, and that day that is coming will set them on fire," says the LORD Almighty. "Not a root or a branch will be left to them. (Mal 4:1)

4. Every well-doer is to be rewarded, both Jew and Gentile. No well-doer shall be exempt or overlooked. "Everyone who does good" shall receive...
- immortality (v.7).
- eternal life (v.7).
- glory (v.7, 10).
- honor (v.7, 10).
- peace (v.10).

DEEPER STUDY # 1
(2:7) **Glory** (doxa): means to possess and to be full of perfect light; to dwell in perfect light, brilliance, splendor, brightness, luster, and magnificence with God.

Then the righteous will shine like the sun in the kingdom of their Father. He who has ears, let him hear. (Mat 13:43)

Now if we are children, then we are heirs—heirs of God and co-heirs with Christ, if indeed we share in his sufferings in order that we may also share in his glory. (Rom 8:17)

Who, by the power that enables him to bring everything under his control, will transform our lowly bodies so that they will be like his glorious body. (Phil 3:21)

When Christ, who is your life, appears, then you also will appear with him in glory. (Col 3:4)

After this I looked and there before me was a great multitude that no one could count, from every nation, tribe, people and language, standing before the throne and in front of the Lamb. They were wearing white robes and were holding palm branches in their hands. (Rev 7:9)

You guide me with your counsel, and afterward you will take me into glory. (Psa 73:24)

I consider that our present sufferings are not worth comparing with the glory that will be revealed in us. (Rom 8:18)

For our light and momentary troubles are achieving for us an eternal glory that far outweighs them all. (2 Cor 4:17)

Therefore I endure everything for the sake of the elect, that they too may obtain the salvation that is in Christ Jesus, with eternal glory. (2 Tim 2:10)

To the elders among you, I appeal as a fellow elder, a witness of Christ's sufferings and one who also will share in the glory to be revealed: (1 Pet 5:1)

DEEPER STUDY # 2
(2:7) **Honor** (time): means to be acknowledged, recognized, approved, accepted, esteemed, and exalted by God. It means to be privileged and exalted to a position of responsibility and service for God.

"'Well done, my good servant!' his master replied. 'Because you have been trustworthy in a very small matter, take charge of ten cities.' (Luke 19:17)

Whoever serves me must follow me; and where I am, my servant also will be. My Father will honor the one who serves me. (John 12:26)

But glory, honor and peace for everyone who does good: first for the Jew, then for the Gentile. (Rom 2:10)

Do you not know that the saints will judge the world? And if you are to judge the world, are you not competent to judge trivial cases? Do you not know that we will judge angels? How much more the things of this life! (1 Cor 6:2-3)

To him who overcomes, I will give the right to sit with me on my throne, just as I overcame and sat down with my Father on his throne. (Rev 3:21)

"Because he loves me," says the LORD, "I will rescue him; I will protect him, for he acknowledges my name. (Psa 91:14)

He who pursues righteousness and love finds life, prosperity and honor. (Prov 21:21)

Humility and the fear of the LORD bring wealth and honor and life. (Prov 22:4)

Those who are wise will shine like the brightness of the heavens, and those who lead many to righteousness, like the stars for ever and ever. (Dan 12:3)

DEEPER STUDY # 3
(2:7) **Immortality** (aphtharsia): means living forever with God; to be incorruptible, perfected, and made permanent and eternal. It means to be free from pain and tears, from being tired and weary, from trials and sin, from defilement, weakness, frailty, sickness, suffering, and death. It means to be free from an imperfect world and to be placed into a perfect world with God—a world that lasts forever and ever.

And they can no longer die; for they are like the angels. They are God's children, since they are children of the resurrection. (Luke 20:36)

I tell you the truth, if anyone keeps my word, he will never see death." (John 8:51)

And whoever lives and believes in me will never die. Do you believe this?" (John 11:26)

To those who by persistence in doing good seek glory, honor and immortality, he will give eternal life. (Rom 2:7)

For the perishable must clothe itself with the imperishable, and the mortal with immortality. (1 Cor 15:53)

Now we know that if the earthly tent we live in is destroyed, we have a building from God, an eternal house in heaven, not built by human hands. (2 Cor 5:1)

After that, we who are still alive and are left will be caught up together with them in the clouds to meet the Lord in the air. And so we will be with the Lord forever. (1 Th 4:17)

But it has now been revealed through the appearing of our Savior, Christ Jesus, who has destroyed death and has brought life and immortality to light through the gospel. (2 Tim 1:10)

But here is the bread that comes down from heaven, which a man may eat and not die. (John 6:50)

For the perishable must clothe itself with the imperishable, and the mortal with immortality. When the perishable has been clothed with the imperishable, and the mortal with immortality, then the saying that is written will come true: "Death has been swallowed up in victory." (1 Cor 15:53-54)

Since the children have flesh and blood, he too shared in their humanity so that by his death he might destroy him who holds the power of death—that is, the devil—and free those who all their lives were held in slavery by their fear of death. (Heb 2:14-15)

He will wipe every tear from their eyes. There will be no more death or mourning or crying or pain, for the old order of things has passed away." (Rev 21:4)

He will swallow up death forever. The Sovereign LORD will wipe away the tears from all faces; he will remove the disgrace of his people from all the earth. The LORD has spoken. (Isa 25:8)

"I will ransom them from the power of the grave ; I will redeem them from death. Where, O death, are your plagues? Where, O grave, is your destruction? "I will have no compassion, (Hosea 13:14)

DEEPER STUDY # 4
(2:8) **Stubborn—Self-Seeking** (eris): means to strive, struggle, fight, quarrel, wrangle, argue, debate; to be divisive, factious, contentious, argumentative, and belligerent.

He sent his servants to those who had been invited to the banquet to tell them to come, but they refused to come. (Mat 22:3)

Yet you refuse to come to me to have life. (John 5:40)

But concerning Israel he says, "All day long I have held out my hands to a disobedient and obstinate people." (Rom 10:21)

Do not be like the horse or the mule, which have no understanding but must be controlled by bit and bridle or they will not come to you. (Psa 32:9)

They would not be like their forefathers— a stubborn and rebellious generation, whose hearts were not loyal to God, whose spirits were not faithful to him. (Psa 78:8)

"But my people would not listen to me; Israel would not submit to me. (Psa 81:11)

But since you rejected me when I called and no one gave heed when I stretched out my hand, since you ignored all my advice and would not accept my rebuke, (Prov 1:24-25)

Listen to me, you stubborn-hearted, you who are far from righteousness. (Isa 46:12)

For I knew how stubborn you were; the sinews of your neck were iron, your forehead was bronze. (Isa 48:4)

My God will reject them because they have not obeyed him; they will be wanderers among the nations. (Hosea 9:17)

If you do not listen, and if you do not set your heart to honor my name," says the LORD Almighty, "I will send a curse upon you, and I will curse your blessings. Yes, I have already cursed them, because you have not set your heart to honor me. (Mal 2:2)

DEEPER STUDY # 5
(2:8) **Evil—Unrighteousness** (adikia): wickedness, iniquity, injustice, wrong-doing, sin, evil, lawlessness, a violation of law.

DEEPER STUDY # 6
(2:8) **Wrath** (thumos): means God's indignation against sin. *Thumos* is an anger that is felt more deeply than the *orge* anger of God; therefore, it arises more quickly. *Thumos* anger is the anger that arises out of deep hurt; therefore, it bursts forth with terrifying judgment. (See DEEPER STUDY # 1, *God's Wrath*—Ro.1:18 for verses.)

DEEPER STUDY # 7
(2:8) **Anger** (orge): means God's anger against sin (see DEEPER STUDY # 1, *God's Wrath*—Ro.1:18 for discussion).

DEEPER STUDY # 8
(2:9) **Trouble** (thlipsis): means distress, oppression, suffering, affliction, pressure; it means being pressed, put in some strait.

DEEPER STUDY # 9
(2:9) **Distress** (stenochoria): means to be put into a narrow place; to be compressed together; to experience extreme pain, sorrow, affliction, and calamity.

4 (2:11-15) **Judgment—Obedience—Doers—Hearers**: the judgment of God—of the only living and true God—does not show favoritism. God's judgment will be executed with absolute impartiality, showing no prejudice whatsoever.

God has no favorites. God does not show partiality; He does not favor the...

- moralist
- religionist
- educated
- wealthy
- benevolent
- famous
- outstanding
- honorable

God favors no one. All men stand on an equal footing before God's judgment. *God loves and cares for all*, but He has no favorites and shows no partiality. Therefore, in the great day of judgment, all will be judged by the same rule and by the same principle.

1. The man who sins apart from the law and the man who sins under the law will both be judged. Again, sin is the basis of judgment. Men will be judged *for sin*.

   a. The man who sins "without law" (anomos) will also perish without law. The word for law is a general word. It refers to the law of God in both the Scriptures and nature. Therefore, the man who does not have the law of Scripture *does have* the law of nature to guide him. If he sins against the law of nature, he will still be judged and perish. He had the opportunity to know through nature itself (see outline and notes—Ro.1:19; 1:20 for more discussion).

   b. The man who sins "under the law" will be judged by the law. His judgment, of course, will be greater, for he had every privilege and opportunity imaginable.

> "Then Peter opened his mouth, and said, Of a truth I perceive that God is no respecter Then Peter began to speak: "I now realize how true it is that God does not show favoritism but accepts men from every nation who fear him and do what is right. (Acts 10:34-35)
>
> He made no distinction between us and them, for he purified their hearts by faith. (Acts 15:9)
>
> For God does not show favoritism. (Rom 2:11)
>
> For there is no difference between Jew and Gentile—the same Lord is Lord of all and richly blesses all who call on him, (Rom 10:12)

2. The obedient and not the hearers of the law will be justified, declared righteous. It is not enough to have the law or the Word of God; it is not enough...

- to hear and see it
- to understand and know it
- to possess and profess it
- to proclaim and teach it

A person must be a doer of the law; he must obey and live the law. The law was not given just to sit on a bookshelf or on a table, not given just to be heard and to secure verbal agreement. The law was given to be obeyed and lived out, to govern and control life so that life could be lived to the fullest. Therefore, those who only hear the law will not be justified, or declared righteous before God, but the obedient—the doers of the law—will be justified.

Thought 1. Possessing, having, hearing, and even proclaiming the law (the Word of God) is not enough to save a person. A person must keep the law; he must live and do the will of God.

> "Not everyone who says to me, 'Lord, Lord,' will enter the kingdom of heaven, but only he who does the will of my Father who is in heaven. (Mat 7:21)
>
> For whoever does the will of my Father in heaven is my brother and sister and mother." (Mat 12:50)
>
> I will show you what he is like who comes to me and hears my words and puts them into practice. He is like a man building a house, who dug down deep and laid the foundation on rock. When a flood came, the torrent struck that house but could not shake it, because it was well built. But the one who hears my words and does not put them into practice is like a man who built a house on the ground without a foundation. The moment the torrent struck that house, it collapsed and its destruction was complete." (Luke 6:47-49)
>
> Now that you know these things, you will be blessed if you do them. (John 13:17)
>
> For it is not those who hear the law who are righteous in God's sight, but it is those who obey the law who will be declared righteous. (Rom 2:13)
>
> Do not merely listen to the word, and so deceive yourselves. Do what it says. (James 1:22)
>
> Brothers, do not slander one another. Anyone who speaks against his brother or judges him speaks against the law and judges it. When you judge the law, you are not keeping it, but sitting in judgment on it. (James 4:11)
>
> The world and its desires pass away, but the man who does the will of God lives forever. (1 John 2:17)
>
> "Blessed are those who wash their robes, that they may have the right to the tree of life and may go through the gates into the city. (Rev 22:14)

3. The heathen have a threefold witness, a witness that is strong enough to lead them to God.

   a. Men have their nature—the nature of man that speaks loudly and clearly—that points toward God. Note exactly what the verse says.

   ⇒ Men may not have the law (the Scriptures)...
   ⇒ But they can do the law *by nature*.
   ⇒ They can become "a law for themselves."

There is that within man, within his nature (physei), that can stir him to do the law. Man has within him an instinctive knowledge of right and wrong. His very nature gives him the opportunity to do what is right.

Something else is meant here as well. Man can look at nature (creation) and see that he is part of it. He can instinctively see by nature the great eternal power and deity of God. (See note—Ro.1:20 for a list of the things nature reveals about God.)

> Since what may be known about God is plain to them, because God has made it plain to them. (Rom 1:19)
>
> For since the creation of the world God's invisible qualities—his eternal power

and divine nature—have been clearly seen, being understood from what has been made, so that men are without excuse. (Rom 1:20)

b. Men have their consciences that bear witness to what is right and wrong. When they do right, they sense approval; when they do wrong, they sense reproach. Man's conscience gives him the opportunity to live righteously and to do good.

> How much more, then, will the blood of Christ, who through the eternal Spirit offered himself unblemished to God, cleanse our consciences from acts that lead to death, so that we may serve the living God! (Heb 9:14)
> Let us draw near to God with a sincere heart in full assurance of faith, having our hearts sprinkled to cleanse us from a guilty conscience and having our bodies washed with pure water. (Heb 10:22)
> Therefore, it is necessary to submit to the authorities, not only because of possible punishment but also because of conscience. (Rom 13:5)

c. Men have their thoughts, their reasoning ability which can approve or disapprove, excuse or accuse them and others. Men's thoughts bear witness to how they should and should not live, whether their behavior is excused (acceptable) or accused (condemned). Now note two critical points.

First, men can learn a great deal about God and about right and wrong through their nature, conscience and thoughts. Men can look at themselves and creation and learn that they are to live...

- by order and law and rules.
- in obedience and respect and peace.
- giving recognition and honor and esteem.
- being clean and pure and moral.
- showing care and concern and love.
- without stealing and lying and cheating.

(See note—Ro.1:19; 1:20 for more discussion.)

Second, men cannot be saved apart from Jesus Christ. No matter how morally they may live—whether they live by law or by nature—they do not live a sinless and perfect life. They sin and come short of God's glory. Therefore, no matter how morally men live, they have to be *perfected* in the "righteousness of God" which is in Christ Jesus Himself (see note, *Justification*—Ro.4:1-3; DEEPER STUDY # 2—4:22; note—5:1 for discussion. Also see note, pt.3—Ro.2:2-5.)

> Jesus answered, "I am the way and the truth and the life. No one comes to the Father except through me. (John 14:6)
> Salvation is found in no one else, for there is no other name under heaven given to men by which we must be saved." (Acts 4:12)
> For there is one God and one mediator between God and men, the man Christ Jesus, (1 Tim 2:5)
> My dear children, I write this to you so that you will not sin. But if anybody does sin, we have one who speaks to the Father in our defense—Jesus Christ, the Righteous One. (1 John 2:1)
> And we have seen and testify that the Father has sent his Son to be the Savior of the world. (1 John 4:14)

5 (2:16) **Judgment**: the judgment of God—of the only living and true God—is to be executed by Jesus Christ and His gospel. Note these facts.

1. A specific day of judgment is coming. It is fixed.

> "When the Son of Man comes in his glory, and all the angels with him, he will sit on his throne in heavenly glory. All the nations will be gathered before him, and he will separate the people one from another as a shepherd separates the sheep from the goats. (Mat 25:31-32)
> Just as man is destined to die once, and after that to face judgment, (Heb 9:27)
> If this is so, then the Lord knows how to rescue godly men from trials and to hold the unrighteous for the day of judgment, while continuing their punishment. (2 Pet 2:9)
> By the same word the present heavens and earth are reserved for fire, being kept for the day of judgment and destruction of ungodly men. (2 Pet 3:7)
> In this way, love is made complete among us so that we will have confidence on the day of judgment, because in this world we are like him. (1 John 4:17)
> Enoch, the seventh from Adam, prophesied about these men: "See, the Lord is coming with thousands upon thousands of his holy ones to judge everyone, and to convict all the ungodly of all the ungodly acts they have done in the ungodly way, and of all the harsh words ungodly sinners have spoken against him." (Jude 1:14-15)

2. In that day "men's secrets" will be judged. All secrets will be exposed, the secret thoughts and deeds done...

- in the dark
- behind closed doors
- off to the side
- silently
- alone
- quietly

> There is nothing concealed that will not be disclosed, or hidden that will not be made known. (Luke 12:2)
> Therefore judge nothing before the appointed time; wait till the Lord comes. He will bring to light what is hidden in darkness and will expose the motives of men's hearts. At that time each will receive his praise from God. (1 Cor 4:5)
> "But if you fail to do this, you will be sinning against the LORD; and you may be sure that your sin will find you out. (Num 32:23)
> For God will bring every deed into judgment, including every hidden thing, whether it is good or evil. (Eccl 12:14)

3. Jesus Christ is the One who will do the judging. He is the One who...

- has earned the right to judge by obeying God perfectly. He is the One who has lived a sinless life and died for men.
- has experienced life on earth in the flesh and can understand and sympathize with men in their infirmities (Heb.2:15-18; 4:15-16).

All the nations will be gathered before him, and he will separate the people one from another as a shepherd separates the sheep from the goats. (Mat 25:32)

Moreover, the Father judges no one, but has entrusted all judgment to the Son, (John 5:22)

He commanded us to preach to the people and to testify that he is the one whom God appointed as judge of the living and the dead. (Acts 10:42)

For he has set a day when he will judge the world with justice by the man he has appointed. He has given proof of this to all men by raising him from the dead." (Acts 17:31)

This will take place on the day when God will judge men's secrets through Jesus Christ, as my gospel declares. (Rom 2:16)

You, then, why do you judge your brother? Or why do you look down on your brother? For we will all stand before God's judgment seat. (Rom 14:10)

In the presence of God and of Christ Jesus, who will judge the living and the dead, and in view of his appearing and his kingdom, I give you this charge: (2 Tim 4:1)

They think it strange that you do not plunge with them into the same flood of dissipation, and they heap abuse on you. But they will have to give account to him who is ready to judge the living and the dead. (1 Pet 4:4-5)

4. The standard or rule by which men shall be judged is the gospel.

There is a judge for the one who rejects me and does not accept my words; that very word which I spoke will condemn him at the last day. (John 12:48)

He who does not love me will not obey my teaching. These words you hear are not my own; they belong to the Father who sent me. (John 14:24)

Now, brothers, I want to remind you of the gospel I preached to you, which you received and on which you have taken your stand. By this gospel you are saved, if you hold firmly to the word I preached to you. Otherwise, you have believed in vain. For what I received I passed on to you as of first importance : that Christ died for our sins according to the Scriptures, that he was buried, that he was raised on the third day according to the Scriptures, (1 Cor 15:1-4)

If anyone teaches false doctrines and does not agree to the sound instruction of our Lord Jesus Christ and to godly teaching, he is conceited and understands nothing. He has an unhealthy interest in controversies and quarrels about words that result in envy, strife, malicious talk, evil suspicions and constant friction between men of corrupt mind, who have been robbed of the truth and who think that godliness is a means to financial gain. (1 Tim 6:3-5)

And this is his command: to believe in the name of his Son, Jesus Christ, and to love one another as he commanded us. (1 John 3:23)

	D. God's Case Against the Religionist (Jew),DS1 **2:17-29**	23 You who brag about the law, do you dishonor God by breaking the law?	b. Result: His hypocrisy causes others to abuse God's name
1 The religionist professes religion a. Rests in the Word b. Professes God c. Knows God's will d. Approves better things e. Is taught God's law f. Is sure he is a guide of the blind g. Is sure he is a light to those in darkness h. Is sure he is an instructor of the foolish i. Is sure he is a teacher of the immature j. Has the law, the embodiment of truth **2 The religionist fails to live what he professes** a. The fact: His life does not match what he says	17 Now you, if you call yourself a Jew; if you rely on the law and brag about your relationship to God; 18 If you know his will and approve of what is superior because you are instructed by the law; 19 If you are convinced that you are a guide for the blind, a light for those who are in the dark, 20 An instructor of the foolish, a teacher of infants, because you have in the law the embodiment of knowledge and truth— 21 You, then, who teach others, do you not teach yourself? You who preach against stealing, do you steal? 22 You who say that people should not commit adultery, do you commit adultery? You who abhor idols, do you rob temples?	24 As it is written: "God's name is blasphemed among the Gentiles because of you." 25 Circumcision has value if you observe the law, but if you break the law, you have become as though you had not been circumcised. 26 If those who are not circumcised keep the law's requirements, will they not be regarded as though they were circumcised? 27 The one who is not circumcised physically and yet obeys the law will condemn you who, even though you have the written code and circumcision, are a lawbreaker. 28 A man is not a Jew if he is only one outwardly, nor is circumcision merely outward and physical. 29 No, a man is a Jew if he is one inwardly; and circumcision is circumcision of the heart, by the Spirit, not by the written code. Such a man's praise is not from men, but from God.	**3 The religionist believes that a ritual (circumcision) is the way to secure God's approval** a. But circ. counts only if a man keeps the law b. The uncircumcised man who keeps the law is counted as circumcised (ritually accepted) c. The uncircumcised man who keeps the law shall judge the religionist who breaks the law **4 The religionist misses the whole point: A true rel. is a man who is righteous inwardly** a. Not an outward thing b. An inward thing—of the heart, by the spirit c. Its praise is not from men (not physical, from the flesh), but from God

DIVISION II

SIN AND CONDEMNATION: THE WORLD'S NEED TO GET RIGHT WITH GOD, 1:18-3:20

D. God's Case Against the Religionist (Jew), 2:17-29

(2:17-29) **Introduction—Religionist—Jew**: this passage is an excellent study of the Christian religionist or church member as well as of the Jew. (See notes, *Religionists—*Lk.15:25-32; 18:9-12 for more discussion.) God's case against the Christian religionist includes four points.

1. The religionist professes religion (v.17-20).
2. The religionist fails to live what he professes (v.21-24).
3. The religionist believes that a ritual (circumcision) is the way to secure God's approval (v.25-27).
4. The religionist misses the whole point: a true religionist is a man who is righteous inwardly (v.28-29).

DEEPER STUDY # 1

(2:17-29) **Religionists**: a religionist is a person who is interested in religion and professes religion. It was because of the Jews' extreme interest in religion that they were looked upon as the epitomy of religionists. However, most people are considered religious and profess some religion regardless of nationality. Therefore, most people can be called religionists. There are two classes of religionists.

1. There are those who feel they are *good enough* for God as they are, that they are doing enough good for God to accept them. They cannot believe that God would reject them when they stand face to face with Him. True, they do wrong, but not that much wrong, not enough for God to reject and condemn them for eternity. These persons go about living as they wish, worshipping God only enough to satisfy

their consciences. The vast, vast majority of people are in this class of self-righteousness. Few men believe they will be rejected by God and refused entrance into heaven. They feel they have *enough goodness* to make them acceptable to God.

> **He saved us, not because of righteous things we had done, but because of his mercy. He saved us through the washing of rebirth and renewal by the Holy Spirit, (Titus 3:5)**
> **Many a man claims to have unfailing love, but a faithful man who can find? (Prov 20:6)**
> **Those who are pure in their own eyes and yet are not cleansed of their filth; (Prov 30:12)**

2. There are those who have a sensitive conscience and feel the need to give themselves to *good works* as much as is humanly possible. They work and do good in order to secure the favor of God. They believe that good works is what it takes to make them righteous and to build them up in the eyes of God. Therefore, they labor all their lives trying to build up virtue and merit before God. They try their best to make themselves acceptable to God.

> **Therefore no one will be declared righteous in his sight by observing the law; rather, through the law we become conscious of sin. (Rom 3:20)**

Know that a man is not justified by observing the law, but by faith in Jesus Christ. So we, too, have put our faith in Christ Jesus that we may be justified by faith in Christ and not by observing the law, because by observing the law no one will be justified. (Gal 2:16)

For it is by grace you have been saved, through faith—and this not from yourselves, it is the gift of God—not by works, so that no one can boast. (Eph 2:8-9)

Note that a genuine believer is not being classified as a religionist. The reason is pointed: the true believer does not follow a religion; he follows Jesus Christ. Jesus Christ is alive; He is living in another world—the spiritual world, the spiritual dimension of being. The believer is in touch with Him daily, communicating through the Holy Spirit and prayer. What the believer does is follow Christ; he lives the life of Jesus Christ, not the rules of a religion. Therefore, the genuine believer is a disciple of Christ, not of religion.

I have been crucified with Christ and I no longer live, but Christ lives in me. The life I live in the body, I live by faith in the Son of God, who loved me and gave himself for me. (Gal 2:20)

And in him [Christ] you too are being built together to become a dwelling in which God lives by his Spirit. (Eph 2:22; cp. 1 Cor.3:16; 6:19)

For to me, to live is Christ and to die is gain. (Phil 1:21)

To them God has chosen to make known among the Gentiles the glorious riches of this mystery, which is Christ in you, the hope of glory. (Col 1:27)

Those who obey his commands live in him, and he in them. And this is how we know that he lives in us: We know it by the Spirit he gave us. (1 John 3:24)

Here I am! I stand at the door and knock. If anyone hears my voice and opens the door, I will come in and eat with him, and he with me. (Rev 3:20)

1 (2:17-20) **Religionists**: the religionist (Jew) professes religion. He accepts the name of his religion whatever it may be, whether Jew, Moslem, or Buddhist; and he shows enough interest in his religion to give him security. Jewish and Christian religionists make ten mistakes.

1. The religionist "relies on; rests in the law," the Word of God (v.17). He possesses the Scriptures (Bible); he...

- has it in his home.
- sometimes reads it.
- carries it with him to church.
- honors it as the Word of God.

Because of this, he feels that he pleases God. He rests upon the fact that he possesses God's Word. By having God's Word, he feels he has God's approval and acceptance. But this is the very mistake of the religionist: God does not accept a person because he happens to have God's Word in his possession. God approves and accepts the person who *does* the Word of God, who lives and obeys the law of God.

What advantage, then, is there in being a Jew, or what value is there in circumcision? Much in every way! First of all, they have been entrusted with the very words of God. (Rom 3:1-2)

2. The religionist professes God. To profess or "brag" (kauchasai) means to boast, to glory, to feel proud about one's profession of God and religion. The idea is that one *openly* professes that he believes in God. He is not ashamed of his belief and religious affiliation. He believes in God and he feels safe and secure in his belief. He confesses God and he feels that God accepts him because of his profession.

However, this is *the mistake* of the religionist. God is not interested in a man's profession but in a man's life. God wants a man living for Him, not just professing and talking about Him.

For I can testify about them that they are zealous for God, but their zeal is not based on knowledge. Since they did not know the righteousness that comes from God and sought to establish their own, they did not submit to God's righteousness. Christ is the end of the law so that there may be righteousness for everyone who believes. (Rom 10:2-4)

3. The religionist knows God's will (v.18). He is familiar with the law and the commandments of God. He knows what God wants done; he knows right from wrong. Therefore, he feels he has God's approval.

However, the religionist fails to see something: knowing God's will is not enough—a man must do God's will.

My people come to you, as they usually do, and sit before you to listen to your words, but they do not put them into practice. With their mouths they express devotion, but their hearts are greedy for unjust gain. Indeed, to them you are nothing more than one who sings love songs with a beautiful voice and plays an instrument well, for they hear your words but do not put them into practice. (Ezek 33:31-32)

4. The religionist approves the superior or excellent things in life (v.18). He not only knows God's will, right from wrong; but he...

- is able to discern the more superior or excellent, the better things to do.
- approves, expresses, and proclaims pleasure in the right things.

Because he supports and pushes and approves the better things in life, the religionist feels he pleases God. But this is his mistake. God is not interested in man's approval of the better things in life. Most men do approve and talk about the better things of life. God wants man living out the better things, living on the level of the more excellent.

Dear children, let us not love with words or tongue but with actions and in truth. (1 John 3:18)

5. The religionist is taught God's law and Word (v.18). He is instructed by family, teacher, preacher, friend. The religionist learns God's Word from someone, and because

he knows God's Word he feels he has a right relationship with God. But again, God's concern is not in what a person knows, but in what a person does. God expects a person to take what he has learned and put it into practice. God expects a person to live as he has been taught.

> **They turned their backs to me and not their faces; though I taught them again and again, they would not listen or respond to discipline. (Jer 32:33)**
>
> **You, however, did not come to know Christ that way. Surely you heard of him and were taught in him in accordance with the truth that is in Jesus. You were taught, with regard to your former way of life, to put off your old self, which is being corrupted by its deceitful desires; (Eph 4:20-22)**

6. The religionist is sure he is a guide to the blind (v.19). The word "convinced" (pepoithas) means persuaded and sure. The religionist is convinced that religion is true, that religion is the way men should live. He believes that a man who does not believe in God and live a religious life is blind and needs to be guided to the truth. By living a religious life, he feels...
- he is an example to men.
- he is a guide to help men find God.
- he can cure men of their blindness to God and religion.

However, being "convinced" that one is a guide of the blind does not mean that one is a true guide. A person must be sure that he himself is following the truth, Jesus Christ (Jn.14:6). There are many guides in the world who are leading people down the wrong road. They are blind guides, the blind leading the blind (Mt.15:14).

> **To some who were confident of their own righteousness and looked down on everybody else, Jesus told this parable: (Luke 18:9)**
>
> **But you have planted wickedness, you have reaped evil, you have eaten the fruit of deception. Because you have depended on your own strength and on your many warriors, (Hosea 10:13)**

7. The religionist is sure he is a light to those in darkness (v.19). The word "dark" (skotei) here pertains to those who stumble about searching for the light, but are unable to find it. The religionist feels he has found the light; therefore, he is a light to those who are searching for it. However, the religionist makes a serious mistake. Religion is not the light of the world—Jesus Christ is. (See DEEPER STUDY # 1—Jn.8:12.)

> **Jesus said, "If you were blind, you would not be guilty of sin; but now that you claim you can see, your guilt remains. (John 9:41)**
>
> **You say, 'I am rich; I have acquired wealth and do not need a thing.' But you do not realize that you are wretched, pitiful, poor, blind and naked. (Rev 3:17)**

8. The religionist is sure he is an instructor of the foolish (v.20). The word "foolish" means thoughtless, senseless, undirected. It refers to people who walk through life giving no thought to life's purpose, as to...
- where they have come from.
- why they are here.
- where they are going.

The religionist is persuaded that religion answers all these questions, the basic questions of life. Therefore, he can help the foolish discover meaning and purpose and significance in life. The critical point for the instructor or the religionist is to make sure that his instruction is true. What he instructs must be the truth or else it is all for naught.

> **So, if you think you are standing firm, be careful that you don't fall! (1 Cor 10:12) He who trusts in himself is a fool, but he who walks in wisdom is kept safe. (Prov 28:26)**

9. The religionist is sure he is a teacher of the immature (v.20). The word "infants" (nepion) means the babes, the immature, the novice, the proselyte, the new church member. The point is the same: a religionist is not mature in God just because he...
- has been baptized and has been a church member for a long time.
- thinks he is mature.
- serves as a teacher.

What makes a person mature and capable of teaching the immature of the world is experience with Christ, having walked and served with Christ for a long time.

> **He replied, "Isaiah was right when he prophesied about you hypocrites; as it is written: "'These people honor me with their lips, but their hearts are far from me. (Mark 7:6)**
>
> **The Lord says: "These people come near to me with their mouth and honor me with their lips, but their hearts are far from me. Their worship of me is made up only of rules taught by men. (Isa 29:13)**

10. The religionist has the law of God, the embodiment of knowledge and of the truth (v.20). The religionist has the Scriptures, the Word of God, at his disposal. He has every opportunity in the world to know the truth. But again, having and knowing and thinking that one can instruct and teach another is not enough. God accepts and uses only those who live the Word, who keep the laws and commandments of God. This is the mistake of the religionist, of the person who professes and does not live.

> **"Woe to you, teachers of the law and Pharisees, you hypocrites! You give a tenth of your spices—mint, dill and cummin. But you have neglected the more important matters of the law—justice, mercy and faithfulness. You should have practiced the latter, without neglecting the former. (Mat 23:23)**
>
> **For this people's heart has become calloused; they hardly hear with their ears, and they have closed their eyes. Otherwise they might see with their eyes, hear with their ears, understand with their hearts and turn, and I would heal them.' (Acts 28:27)**
>
> **Having a form of godliness but denying its power. Have nothing to do with them. (2 Tim 3:5)**

2 (2:21-24) **Religionists—Hypocrisy—False Profession**: the religionist (Jew) fails to live what he professes. This is seen in five pointed questions.

1. "You, then, who teach others, do you not teach yourself?" The question is not only for teachers, but for everyone, because we all teach others. Throughout life we all claim to know some truths about morality and about how people should live and behave. We often share those truths with our children, friends, fellow workers, and others. When we share and teach, do we not listen to the truth? Do we not teach ourselves? What right do we have to tell others how to live if we do not live that way? This is the sin of hypocrisy, a sin committed by so many religionists.

> **In the same way, on the outside you appear to people as righteous but on the inside you are full of hypocrisy and wickedness. (Mat 23:28)**
> **"Why do you call me, 'Lord, Lord,' and do not do what I say? (Luke 6:46)**
> **Dear children, let us not love with words or tongue but with actions and in truth. (1 John 3:18)**

2. "You who preach against stealing, do you steal?" Do you take from others; do you…
- steal money?
- steal from your job?
- steal from your neighbor?
- steal from your family?
- steal while shopping?
- steal while taking tests in school?

If you steal, what right do you have to say that others should not steal—that everyone else should not have the right to take what they want from whom they want? If enough people began to take what they wanted when they wanted, then the world would exist in utter chaos. If you say that men should not steal, why do you steal? This is the sin of too many religionists.

Stealing is a sin that leads to utter chaos. Because of its devastating effect, it is one of the ten commandments, and note: it is so important a commandment, it is repeated time and again.

> **"You shall not steal. (Exo 20:15; Lev.19:11; Dt.5:19; Mt.19:18; Ro.13:9)**
> **He who has been stealing must steal no longer, but must work, doing something useful with his own hands, that he may have something to share with those in need. (Eph 4:28)**

3. "You who say that people should not commit adultery, do you commit adultery?" You who want pure *brides* and spouses, husbands and wives, sons and *daughters*, do you live purely? What are you looking at and watching, reading and hearing? Do you…
- look a second time?
- read pornographic books, magazines, and novels?
- have lustful thoughts?
- harbor sexual thoughts?
- dress in a manner exposing your body?
- watch and support television films that have or suggest scenes of immorality?

Regardless of man's denial, we do what we think; and our thoughts come from what we see and watch, read and hear. Therefore, if we look and watch, read and listen to sexual suggestions, our thoughts center upon fleshly de-

sires, desires of the sinful nature. This is the reason for the breakdown of morals in society. If you say a man should not commit adultery, do you commit adultery? Do you commit it in your mind? This is a major sin among some religionists. Christ knew this; therefore, He said…

> **"You have heard that it was said, 'Do not commit adultery.' But I tell you that anyone who looks at a woman lustfully has already committed adultery with her in his heart. (Mat 5:27-28)**

4. "You who abhor idols, do you rob temples?" The term "rob temples" (hierosuleo) means to violate one's commitment to God and to rob from God. It means to consider something more important than God, something so important that it *requires*…
- the commitment that you owe God.
- the tithes and offerings that you owe God.

You say that you worship God and abhor idols; yet you take what belongs to God—your commitment, your time, your energy, your tithes—and you give it to something else. You make something else more important than God; you make it an idol. This is one of the major sins of the religionists.

> **Be careful, or you will be enticed to turn away and worship other gods and bow down to them. (Deu 11:16)**
> **"I am the LORD; that is my name! I will not give my glory to another or my praise to idols. (Isa 42:8)**
> **Dear children, keep yourselves from idols. (1 John 5:21)**

5. "You who brag about the law [the Bible], do you dishonor God by breaking the law?" The answer is clear.
⇒ We do dishonor God when we talk about His Word yet break His commandments.
⇒ We do dishonor God before men, causing His name to be blasphemed.

When we boast in God's Word yet break His commandments, we give great occasion for the world and its people to take the name of God and…
- blaspheme
- curse
- reproach
- ridicule
- mock
- deny
- insult
- profane

Many a person is doomed because of the hypocrisy of religionists. This is one of the terrible sins of religionists.

> **He replied, "Isaiah was right when he prophesied about you hypocrites; as it is written: "'These people honor me with their lips, but their hearts are far from me. (Mark 7:6)**
> **They claim to know God, but by their actions they deny him. They are detestable, disobedient and unfit for doing anything good. (Titus 1:16)**
> **Out of the same mouth come praise and cursing. My brothers, this should not be. (James 3:10)**

3 (2:25-27) **Religionists**: the religionist believes that *a ritual* is the way to secure God's praise or approval (for example, circumcision, baptism, and church membership).

Just take the word circumcision and substitute whatever ritual a church says is essential for salvation and the meaning of the passage becomes clear. For example, take the ritual of *church membership.*

> "Church membership has value for a man if he keeps the law: but if he breaks the law, his church membership is made or counted as *unchurch* membership."

If a religionist does not keep (prasso, practice) God's law and Word, then his ritual does not count. The man becomes...

- unbaptized
- uncircumcised
- unchurched
- unwhatever

The point is obedience, not ritual. A person is acceptable to God because he lives for God and obeys Him, not because he has undergone some ritual. The next two verses make this pointedly clear (v.26-27).

⇒ "If those who are not circumcised keep the law's requirements, will they not be regarded as ...circumcised [that is, acceptable to God]" (v.26)? A man is not acceptable to God because he has been baptized or joined some church. He becomes acceptable to God because he obeys God, and God's basic commandment is clear, unquestionably so:

> **And this is his command: to believe in the name of his Son, Jesus Christ, and to love one another as he commanded us. (1 John 3:23)**

⇒ The uncircumcised man who keeps the law actually judges the man who has been circumcised and breaks the law (v.27). The basis of judgment is not to be a ritual, whether baptism or church membership; it is to be obedience. No ritual will ever save a man if he transgresses the law, and no ritual will ever cause a man to be lost if he keeps the law. (See outline and notes—Ro.2:11-15 for more discussion.)

> **"Not everyone who says to me, 'Lord, Lord,' will enter the kingdom of heaven, but only he who does the will of my Father who is in heaven. (Mat 7:21)**
> **For whoever does the will of my Father in heaven is my brother and sister and mother." (Mat 12:50)**
> **Now that you know these things, you will be blessed if you do them. (John 13:17)**
> **Do not merely listen to the word, and so deceive yourselves. Do what it says. (James 1:22)**
> **The world and its desires pass away, but the man who does the will of God lives forever. (1 John 2:17)**

4 (2:28-29) **Religionists**: the religionist misses the whole point—a true religionist is a man who is righteous inwardly. This fact is so critical that every one needs to give heed and do something about it. The point is that every man breaks or transgresses the law. Paul has just said:

> **Circumcision has value if you observe the law, but if you break the law, you have**

> **become as though you had not been circumcised. (Rom 2:25)**

Paul will say very shortly:

> **As it is written: "There is no one righteous, not even one; (Rom 3:10)**
> **For all have sinned and fall short of the glory of God, (Rom 3:23)**

No law and no ritual, whether circumcision or baptism (or any other ritual), is able to make man acceptable to God. Being acceptable to God is not an outward thing. It is...

- not the keeping of any ritual or law (Ro.2:21-27).
- not nationality or heritage.
- not being born of any particular race or family, whether Jewish or Christian (Ro.3:1-20; 9:6-13).

True religion—being acceptable to God—is inward. It is of the heart, of the spirit. It is of God. It is being born again of God's Spirit (Jn.3:3-8). It is not of man; therefore, God is to be praised, not man (Ro.2:28-29).

> **I will give you a new heart and put a new spirit in you; I will remove from you your heart of stone and give you a heart of flesh. (Ezek 36:26)**
> **children born not of natural descent, nor of human decision or a husband's will, but born of God. (John 1:13)**
> **In reply Jesus declared, "I tell you the truth, no one can see the kingdom of God unless he is born again." (John 3:3)**
> **Therefore, if anyone is in Christ, he is a new creation; the old has gone, the new has come! (2 Cor 5:17)**
> **He saved us, not because of righteous things we had done, but because of his mercy. He saved us through the washing of rebirth and renewal by the Holy Spirit, (Titus 3:5)**
> **For you have been born again, not of perishable seed, but of imperishable, through the living and enduring word of God. (1 Pet 1:23)**
> **Everyone who believes that Jesus is the Christ is born of God, and everyone who loves the father loves his child as well. (1 John 5:1)**

God's true people are the people who have been circumcised spiritually—in the heart. The real Jews, God's true people, are those who have had the skin of disease (sin) cut out of their heart. They are the people who have been spiritually converted.

> **In him you were also circumcised, in the putting off of the sinful nature, not with a circumcision done by the hands of men but with the circumcision done by Christ, (Col 2:11)**
> **Here there is no Greek or Jew, circumcised or uncircumcised, barbarian, Scythian, slave or free, but Christ is all, and is in all. (Col 3:11)**
> **For it is we who are the circumcision, we who worship by the Spirit of God, who glory in Christ Jesus, and who put no confidence in the flesh— (Phil 3:3)**

The LORD your God will circumcise your hearts and the hearts of your descendants, so that you may love him with all your heart and with all your soul, and live. (Deu 30:6)

Circumcise yourselves to the LORD, circumcise your hearts, you men of Judah and people of Jerusalem, or my wrath will break out and burn like fire because of the evil you have done— burn with no one to quench it. (Jer 4:4)

To whom can I speak and give warning? Who will listen to me? Their ears are closed so they cannot hear. The word of the LORD is offensive to them; they find no pleasure in it. (Jer 6:10)

Awake, awake, O Zion, clothe yourself with strength. Put on your garments of splendor, O Jerusalem, the holy city. The uncircumcised and defiled will not enter you again. (Isa 52:1)

Moses confessed that he was a man of "faltering, uncircumcised lips" (Ex.6:12, 30). Man's "faltering, uncircumcised heart" must be humbled if he wishes God to remember His covenant and give man the promised land of heaven (Lev.26:41-42).

CHAPTER 3

E. The Arguments of the Religionist (Jew) Against a Heart Religion, 3:1-8
(Cp. Ro.2:23-29)

1 What valve is there in being a Jew, a religionist—in being circumcised or baptized?
a. He is privileged
b. He is entrusted with & made responsible for God's Word

2 Does unbelief void God's promises—make God a liar?[DS1]
a. Not at all
b. God's Word stands even if every man is a liar
c. God will prove His Word

What advantage, then, is there in being a Jew, or what value is there in circumcision?
2 Much in every way! First of all, they have been entrusted with the very words of God.
3 What if some did not have faith? Will their lack of faith nullify God's faithfulness?
4 Not at all! Let God be true, and every man a liar. As it is written: "So that you may be proved right when you speak and prevail when you judge."
5 But if our unrighteousness brings out God's righteousness more clearly, what shall we say? That God is unjust in bringing his wrath on us? (I am using a human argument.)
6 Certainly not! If that were so, how could God judge the world?
7 Someone might argue, "If my falsehood enhances God's truthfulness and so increases his glory, why am I still condemned as a sinner?"
8 Why not say—as we are being slanderously reported as saying and as some claim that we say—"Let us do evil that good may result"? Their condemnation is deserved.

d. God will overcome those who judge Him & His Word[DS2]

3 Is God unjust if He punishes the unrighteous?
a. Certainty not!
b. God is moral: He must judge the world
c. The contradiction of such an argument
d. The Condemnation of persons who argue such is deserved

DIVISION II

SIN AND CONDEMNATION: THE WORLD'S NEED TO GET RIGHT WITH GOD, 1:18-3:20

E. The Arguments of the Religionist (Jew) Against a Heart Religion, 3:1-8

(3:1-8) Introduction: Paul has said there is no difference between Jew and Gentile, between a religionist and other men (chapters 1-3). All men stand before God guilty of sin and condemned. Now at this point Paul imagines the religionist seeing exactly what he is saying. The religionist also sees the tremendous weight of Paul's argument; therefore, he strains to counter Paul with three arguments, arguments often made by Christian religionists and church members who profess Christ and attend church only enough to salve their consciences. (See DEEPER STUDY # 1, *Religionists*—Ro.2:17-29; 2:17-20 for a discussion of who the religionist is.)

1. What profit is there in being a religionist—in being circumcised or baptized (v.1-2)?
2. Does unbelief void God's promises—make God a liar (v.3-4)?
3. Is God unjust if He punishes the unrighteous (v.5-8)?

1 (3:1-2) **Religionists—Word of God—Jew**: the question is, "What value is there in being a Jew or a religionist—in being circumcised or baptized or a church member? What do you do with the Jew who is Abraham's seed? The promise of God to Abraham was that his seed (the Jewish nation) would be the children of God (see DEEPER STUDY # 1—Jn.4:22; cp. Gen.12:1-4). If a man is born a Jew (born into a Jewish family) and he professes to be a Jew, a follower of God, is he not acceptable to God (Ro.2:17-29; cp. v.1-29)? If not, then what value is there in being a professing Jew, a follower of God? You are saying there is no advantage in being a Jew or a child of Abraham."

The application of this passage concerns every man. If a man is born a Jew or a Christian (the right nationality), if a man is born into a Jewish or Christian family (the right heritage), if a man claims to be a Jew or a Christian religionist, and he is *still* not acceptable to God, what profit is there in being a religionist?

Paul's answer is simple: the advantages are great. The Jew and Christian are highly privileged, especially in that God has committed His Word to them (Ro.3:2; 9:4-5). They have the privilege…
• of possessing God's Word.
• of reading, hearing, seeing, obeying, and living God's Word.
• of living within a society that has been affected by God's Word.

These are enormous privileges. A man born within a nation and a family that has God's Word has every advantage in coming to God and in living for God. In fact, such a man could have no greater privilege. His privileges are so great that he is left without excuse if he fails to live for God.

> "I tell you the truth, whoever hears my word and believes him who sent me has eternal life and will not be condemned; he has crossed over from death to life. (John 5:24)
> The Spirit gives life; the flesh counts for nothing. The words I have spoken to you are spirit and they are life. (John 6:63)
> Simon Peter answered him, "Lord, to whom shall we go? You have the words of eternal life. (John 6:68)
> I tell you the truth, if anyone keeps my word, he will never see death." (John 8:51)
> You are already clean because of the word I have spoken to you. (John 15:3)
> But these are written that you may believe that Jesus is the Christ, the Son of God, and that by believing you may have life in his name. (John 20:31)
> For everything that was written in the past was written to teach us, so that through endurance and the encouragement of the Scriptures we might have hope. (Rom 15:4)
> To make her holy, cleansing her by the washing with water through the word, (Eph 5:26)

Now that you have purified yourselves by obeying the truth so that you have sincere love for your brothers, love one another deeply, from the heart. (1 Pet 1:22)

I write these things to you who believe in the name of the Son of God so that you may know that you have eternal life. (1 John 5:13)

How can a young man keep his way pure? By living according to your word. (Psa 119:9)

For these commands are a lamp, this teaching is a light, and the corrections of discipline are the way to life, (Prov 6:23)

Righteousness exalts a nation, but sin is a disgrace to any people. (Prov 14:34)

2 (3:3-4) **Unbelief—Religionist—Salvation**: the question is, "If you say some Jews do not believe and are condemned, doesn't that void God's promises and make God a liar?" Or to say it another way, "What if some disbelieve and reject God's Word, will their unbelief cause God to void His Word and promises? God promised the Jews a special place and special privileges through Abraham and his seed (see DEEPER STUDY # 1—Jn.4:22). If some Jews do not believe God's promises and God condemns them, isn't He breaking His promise to Abraham and his seed? Isn't He voiding His Word and Covenant and making Himself a liar? God's Word could not be based on heart religion and on moral character alone. There has to be something else, something outward—a rite (circumcision, baptism, church membership)—that shows we are religious (Jews). If we go through the rite or ritual, then God is bound to accept us. He has promised to so accept us. He is not going to break His Word."

The application of this question concerns every religionist. The thinking religionist poses the same objection and question: "If you say some religionists do not believe and are condemned, doesn't that void God's Word and make God a liar? God's Word promises the religious person special privileges and the hope of eternal life. His Word tells us to believe Christ and to possess His Word, be baptized and join the fellowship of the church. If we do that and God still condemns us, is He not voiding His Word and becoming a liar?"

⇒ Not at all.

⇒ God will be faithful. His Word and promise of salvation will stand even if *every* man lies about believing and lies about giving his heart to serve Jesus.

⇒ God will prove His Word: He will be justified and proven faithful in what He has said. He will still save *any person* who gives his heart to Jesus and obeys Jesus.

⇒ In fact, God will overcome; He will prove His Word another way. He will judge all who make a false profession and who judge Him and His Word, who accuse Him of being unfaithful and voiding His Word. David himself said that God would judge the unfaithful or disobedient man (Ps.51:4). David had sinned greatly, not keeping the commandments of God, so God judged David and charged him with sin. David did the right thing: he confessed his sin and repented and began to live righteously. But David did something else: he declared that God's charge and judgment against him were *just*, that God was perfectly justified. And God was, for God is always just, and He is always justified in what He says and does.

The point is twofold.

1. God is not unfaithful. God never breaks or voids His Word when He rejects the religionist. The religionist who possesses God's Word and belongs to a church but does not obey God's Word is not acceptable to God. It is righteousness God is after, not religion. God is not after an outward religion, but an *inward righteousness*. God wants a heart that will not only possess the Bible, but will keep His commandments. God is after a spiritual rebirth, a new creation, a man who has been truly born again. God wants a heart and life that are focused upon Christ and that keep the commandments of Christ. The only man who is acceptable to God is the man who has given his heart and life to Christ and who lives righteously, trusting God to accept His faith in Christ. (Cp. Ro.2:28-29.)

2. God never voids His Word or promises; He never has and never will be a liar. God has promised salvation and eternal life to men. Even if there should never be a single person who believed God's promise, His promise would still stand. He would still save any person who did what He said.

The problem is in doing what God says, in coming to God as He dictates. God demands that men give their hearts and lives to His Son, Jesus Christ. God demands that men live for Christ, worship and obey Him. But this is too hard for men. They want an *easier* salvation. They want to be able to do something, get it over with, and then be free to live as they wish, giving God some attention here and there. Therefore, men prefer to be saved by being religious: being baptized, joining a church, buying a Bible, and then being free to go about their own lives. But this is *not enough* for God; it is *not doing everything* that God says; it is not giving one's heart and life to live for Jesus Christ by obeying, worshipping, and serving Him. Therefore, God...

• charges the religionist with sin.
• judges and condemns the religionist.

Now note another fact. God fulfills His Word by judging the religionists. God has told men how to live and what would happen if they failed. Therefore, He is justified in His sayings, "proved right" when [He] speaks by following through and by judging the religionists.

⇒ God will not void and break His Word. He will fulfill it all.

⇒ God is justified in fulfilling His Word by doing exactly what He said, that is, in accepting men *only* as He said and in judging men if they do not come to Him as He commands.

DEEPER STUDY # 1

(3:3) **Unbelief—Man, Errors—Faith, Lack of**: this is one of two common but gross deceptions of men—that unbelief makes a thing ineffective and voids it. A man argues: "If I deny something, ignore it, refuse to accept it, push it out of my mind, it will not be, nor will it come to pass." Some even think of God's Word in this way. They think they can deny and reject some part of it and it will not be so. They accept the Scriptures that stress the love of God and allow them to live as they wish, but they reject the Scriptures that stress the supernatural and miraculous power of God and the desperate need of man to be saved from sin, death, and an eternal hell. They reject the Scriptures that demand that man live responsibly.

I tell you the truth, until heaven and earth disappear, not the smallest letter, not the least stroke of a pen, will by any means disappear from the Law until everything is accomplished. (Mat 5:18)

Heaven and earth will pass away, but my words will never pass away. (Luke 21:33)

If we are faithless, he will remain faithful, for he cannot disown himself. (2 Tim 2:13)

The works of his hands are faithful and just; all his precepts are trustworthy. (Psa 111:7)

DEEPER STUDY # 2

(3:4) **Judging—Judgment**: men judge God. They judge Him to be true or false. They judge whether He exists or does not exist. They judge His Word. But in the final hour, God will end up judging men. He will overcome all those who judged Him to be less than He is and less than what He said.

Now we know that God's judgment against those who do such things is based on truth. (Rom 2:2)

But I the LORD will speak what I will, and it shall be fulfilled without delay. For in your days, you rebellious house, I will fulfill whatever I say, declares the Sovereign LORD.'" (Ezek 12:25)

3 (3:5-8) **Love—Justice**: the question is, "Is God unjust if He punishes the unrighteous? If my unbelief and sin give God a chance to overcome (v.4) and to show His justice, then my sin brings greater glory to Him. It gives Him a chance to fulfill His Word. How can He punish me for that? Is He not unjust in inflicting punishment?" The answer is fourfold.

1. Certainly not! (me genoito): away with such a thought! No! Never!

2. God is moral; therefore, He must judge the world. He would not be moral and just if He did not judge the world.

3. Such an argument is contradictory. Think about it. "If my sin and disobedience give God a chance to demonstrate His righteousness, why then am I called a sinner for that? My sin is really a good thing. It gives God a chance to show how good He is. I may sin, yes, but only good has come out of it. When God accepts me as I am, a sinner, God has a chance to show how gloriously merciful He is. You can't condemn me for giving God a chance to show His mercy."

4. The condemnation of persons who argue this point is *just,* deserved; it is not unjust, undeserved. Such arguments are common among every generation of men, but the arguments are gross deceptions. A man exclaims: "A God of love cannot take vengeance. He is too good and loving. He will be denying His very nature of love if He judges me."

What this argument fails to see is that *genuine love is just*. Love expressed unjustly is not love; it is license and indulgence. God's love is perfect, absolutely unbiased and impartial. It is shed upon all (Jn.3:16; 1 Jn.2:2). It is not license and indulgence; neither can it be, not in its perfection. Neither can it allow license and indulgence. God's love is completely and perfectly just. It demands justice. In no respect can it be unjust by failing to judge. Neither can God be accused of being unloving when He executes justice (Ro.2:2-16). God's love is just; God's justice is the demonstration of perfect love. The cross was where God exacted His perfect justice upon His Son, and it is the perfect example of the glorious truth. The cross is the perfect demonstration of both the love and the justice of God.

Thought 1. The cross is the perfect demonstration of God's love and justice.

"For God so loved the world that he gave his one and only Son, that whoever believes in him shall not perish but have eternal life. (John 3:16)

But God demonstrates his own love for us in this: While we were still sinners, Christ died for us. (Rom 5:8)

God made him who had no sin to be sin for us, so that in him we might become the righteousness of God. (2 Cor 5:21)

Christ redeemed us from the curse of the law by becoming a curse for us, for it is written: "Cursed is everyone who is hung on a tree." (Gal 3:13)

And live a life of love, just as Christ loved us and gave himself up for us as a fragrant offering and sacrifice to God. (Eph 5:2)

He himself bore our sins in his body on the tree, so that we might die to sins and live for righteousness; by his wounds you have been healed. (1 Pet 2:24)

For Christ died for sins once for all, the righteous for the unrighteous, to bring you to God. He was put to death in the body but made alive by the Spirit, (1 Pet 3:18)

Thought 2. Men shall be judged and condemned if they have rejected the love and salvation of God provided in His Son, Jesus Christ.

For the Son of Man is going to come in his Father's glory with his angels, and then he will reward each person according to what he has done. (Mat 16:27)

"When the Son of Man comes in his glory, and all the angels with him, he will sit on his throne in heavenly glory. All the nations will be gathered before him, and he will separate the people one from another as a shepherd separates the sheep from the goats. (Mat 25:31-32)

For we must all appear before the judgment seat of Christ, that each one may receive what is due him for the things done while in the body, whether good or bad. (2 Cor 5:10)

Since you call on a Father who judges each man's work impartially, live your lives as strangers here in reverent fear. (1 Pet 1:17)

If this is so, then the Lord knows how to rescue godly men from trials and to hold the unrighteous for the day of judgment, while continuing their punishment. (2 Pet 2:9)

By the same word the present heavens and earth are reserved for fire, being kept for the day of judgment and destruction of ungodly men. (2 Pet 3:7)

Enoch, the seventh from Adam, prophesied about these men: "See, the Lord is coming with thousands upon thousands of his holy ones to judge everyone, and to convict all the ungodly of all the ungodly acts they have done in the ungodly way, and of all the harsh words ungodly sinners have spoken against him." (Jude 1:14-15)

"Behold, I am coming soon! My reward is with me, and I will give to everyone according to what he has done. (Rev 22:12)

	F. God's Case Against All Men, 3:9-20		
1 The charge: All men are under sin	9 What shall we conclude then? Are we any better? Not at all! We have already made the charge that Jews and Gentiles alike are all under sin.	deceit." "The poison of vipers is on their lips." 14 "Their mouths are full of cursing and bitterness." 15 "Their feet are swift to shed blood; 16 Ruin and misery mark their ways, 17 And the way of peace they do not know." 18 "There is no fear of God before their eyes."	b. Deceitful c. Piercing & poisonous d. Cursing & bitterness
2 The case of a sinful nature a. Unrighteous b. Ignorant c. Indifferent—selfish d. Crooked e. Useless f. Evil	10 As it is written: "There is no one righteous, not even one; 11 There is no one who understands, no one who seeks God. 12 All have turned away, they have together become worthless; there is no one who does good, not even one."		**4 The case of sinful acts** a. Murderous b. Oppressive, causing misery c. Restless, disturbed, warring d. Godless, irreverent, disrespectful
		19 Now we know that whatever the law says, it says to those who are under the law, so that every mouth may be silenced and the whole world held accountable to God. 20 Therefore no one will be declared righteous in his sight by observing the law; rather, through the law we become conscious of sin.	**5 The case of the law** a. It speaks to all who are under the law b. It stops all boasting c. It makes all the world accountable, guilty d. It justifies no person, declares no one righteous e. It shows man that he is sinful
3 The case of a sinful tongue a. Foul & corrupt	13 "Their throats are open graves; their tongues practice		

DIVISION II

SIN AND CONDEMNATION: THE WORLD'S NEED TO GET RIGHT WITH GOD, 1:18-3:20

F. God's Case Against All Men, 3:9-20

(3:9-20) **Man, Depravity—Salvation**: in looking at such passages as this, a person must keep in mind the whole point of the passage. The point is not to charge man with sin, nor to berate man; it is not to look upon man with cynical contempt. The point is not to call man to hopelessness and despair, leaving him with a hanged head and low self-esteem. The point is to give man hope: to challenge man to seek a right relationship with God through the Lord Jesus Christ. Man must *never minimize* his sin, lest he ignore or neglect the right way to God. But neither must he minimize the redeeming power of Jesus Christ, lest he hang his head in hopelessness, or wallow in self-pity, or roam the world in despair.

1. The charge: all men are under sin (v.9).
2. The case of a sinful nature (v.10-12).
3. The case of a sinful tongue (v.13-14).
4. The case of sinful acts (v.15-18).
5. The case of the law (v.19-20).

1 (3:9) **Sin—Man, Nature**: all men are under sin. The words "under sin" (hupo hamartian) mean to be subject to the power of or under the authority of. A man outside of Jesus Christ is under the power of sin and he is helpless to escape from it (cp. Gal.3:10, 25; 4:2, 21; 5:18; 1 Tim.6:1).

The religionist (Jew) is "under sin" just as much as other men are "under sin." The Scripture has just declared that being religious does not make men acceptable to God (cp. Ro.2:17-28). Religionists are shocked: "What shall we conclude then! Are we not better—do we not have any advantage over other men? Are we not better if we...

- have the Bible?"
- profess God?"
- know God's will?"
- approve the best things?"
- study the Word of God?"
- guide and teach others?"
- know the truth?"

The answer is a strong exclamation: "No! Not at all! Not in any way are you better than other people. Both Jews and Gentiles, both religionists and non-religionists—you are all under sin."

Now note. This has been the point of all that has been said in Romans...

- God has a case against all godlessness and wickedness of men (Ro.1:18-32).
- God has a case against the moralist (Ro.2:1-16).
- God has a case against the religionist (Jew) (Ro.2:17-3:8).

Scripture shows that God has a case against all men. All men are "under sin." And the fact is clearly seen by any person who will honestly look at man and his world.

> **For all have sinned and fall short of the glory of God, (Rom 3:23)**
> **Therefore, just as sin entered the world through one man, and death through sin, and in this way death came to all men, because all sinned— (Rom 5:12)**
> **But the Scripture declares that the whole world is a prisoner of sin, so that what was promised, being given through faith in Jesus Christ, might be given to those who believe. (Gal 3:22)**
> **If we claim to be without sin, we deceive ourselves and the truth is not in us. (1 John 1:8)**
> **We know that we are children of God, and that the whole world is under the control of the evil one. (1 John 5:19)**
> **The LORD saw how great man's wickedness on the earth had become, and that every inclination of the thoughts of his heart was only evil all the time. (Gen 6:5)**

"When they sin against you—for there is no one who does not sin—and you become angry with them and give them over to the enemy, who takes them captive to his own land, far away or near; (1 Ki 8:46)

If you, O LORD, kept a record of sins, O Lord, who could stand? (Psa 130:3)

Who can say, "I have kept my heart pure; I am clean and without sin"? (Prov 20:9)

There is not a righteous man on earth who does what is right and never sins. (Eccl 7:20)

We all, like sheep, have gone astray, each of us has turned to his own way; and the LORD has laid on him the iniquity of us all. (Isa 53:6)

All of us have become like one who is unclean, and all our righteous acts are like filthy rags; we all shrivel up like a leaf, and like the wind our sins sweep us away. (Isa 64:6)

2 (3:10-12) **Man, Nature—Sin**: there is the case of a sinful nature.

1. A sinful nature is unrighteous (v.10; cp. Ps.14:1): "There is no one righteous, not even, one." Not a single person is righteous, that is, perfect and sinless—not by nature nor by act. No man has ever lived a perfect life, not perfect...

- in every thought
- in every word
- in every act

"There is no one righteous [perfect, sinless] not even one." By nature, man is sinful.

> The world cannot hate you, but it hates me because I testify that what it does is evil. (John 7:7)
>
> The acts of the sinful nature are obvious: sexual immorality, impurity and debauchery; idolatry and witchcraft; hatred, discord, jealousy, fits of rage, selfish ambition, dissensions, factions and envy; drunkenness, orgies, and the like. I warn you, as I did before, that those who live like this will not inherit the kingdom of God. (Gal 5:19-21)

2. A sinful nature is ignorant (v.11; cp. Ps.14:2): "There is no one who understands [sunion]." Not a single person grasps, comprehends, or perceives. The word literally means *to put things together*. It means to look at things and to intelligently discern and comprehend the truth. No man looks at the world and thinks and puts the truth of things together—not perfectly—not about...

- God
- man
- the world
- the origin of all
- the purpose of all
- the destiny of all

No one looks at the world and intelligently discerns the truth of things, not in grasping the truth...

- of where they have come from
- of why they are here
- of where they are going

"There is no one who understands."

For this people's heart has become calloused; they hardly hear with their ears, and they have closed their eyes. Otherwise they might see with their eyes, hear with their ears, understand with their hearts and turn, and I would heal them.' (Acts 28:27)

Always learning but never able to acknowledge the truth. (2 Tim 3:7)

"They know nothing, they understand nothing. They walk about in darkness; all the foundations of the earth are shaken. (Psa 82:5)

But they do not know the thoughts of the LORD; they do not understand his plan, he who gathers them like sheaves to the threshing floor. (Micah 4:12)

3. A sinful nature is indifferent and selfish (v.11; cp. Ps.14:2): "There is no one who seeks God." The word "seeks" (ekzeteo) means to pursue and search for. The idea is that of a diligent, careful, determined seeking and searching. No one searches and seeks after God, not after the only living and true God, not with so careful and determined a spirit. Why? Because men are indifferent and selfish. Men want gods that allow them to do their own thing.

⇒ Some want gods that allow them to glory in self by demonstrating their extreme self-discipline and sacrifice.

⇒ Others want gods who demand less and who allow them to live as they wish, in the pleasures and greed and possessions of this world.

Men do not want a God who is true and living. If He is true and living, it means He is Supreme, the only One who is to be glorified and honored and obeyed. Therefore, in dealing with the only living and true God, men are indifferent and selfish. "There is no one who seeks God." By nature men are sinful, indifferent, and selfish.

> Remember that at that time you were separate from Christ, excluded from citizenship in Israel and foreigners to the covenants of the promise, without hope and without God in the world. (Eph 2:12)
>
> We also know that law is made not for the righteous but for lawbreakers and rebels, the ungodly and sinful, the unholy and irreligious; for those who kill their fathers or mothers, for murderers, for adulterers and perverts, for slave traders and liars and perjurers—and for whatever else is contrary to the sound doctrine (1 Tim 1:9-10)
>
> Who is the liar? It is the man who denies that Jesus is the Christ. Such a man is the antichrist—he denies the Father and the Son. (1 John 2:22)
>
> In his pride the wicked does not seek him; in all his thoughts there is no room for God. (Psa 10:4)
>
> For the director of music. Of David. The fool says in his heart, "There is no God." They are corrupt, their deeds are vile; there is no one who does good. (Psa 14:1)
>
> "You have said, 'It is futile to serve God. What did we gain by carrying out his requirements and going about like mourners before the LORD Almighty? (Mal 3:14)

4. A sinful nature is crooked (v.12; cp. Ps.14:3): "All have turned away." The Greek means that men lean out, turn away, and turn aside…

- from God.
- from the way that leads to God.
- to another way.

Men are crooked; they are not straight with God. They do not follow God nor pursue the right way to God. They take another path, another road, another way.

> The goal of this command is love, which comes from a pure heart and a good conscience and a sincere faith. Some have wandered away from these and turned to meaningless talk. (1 Tim 1:6)
> For you were like sheep going astray, but now you have returned to the Shepherd and Overseer of your souls. (1 Pet 2:25)
> They have left the straight way and wandered off to follow the way of Balaam son of Beor, who loved the wages of wickedness. (2 Pet 2:15)
> They are wild waves of the sea, foaming up their shame; wandering stars, for whom blackest darkness has been reserved forever. (Jude 1:13)
> A man who strays from the path of understanding comes to rest in the company of the dead. (Prov 21:16)
> Like a bird that strays from its nest is a man who strays from his home. (Prov 27:8)
> We all, like sheep, have gone astray, each of us has turned to his own way; and the LORD has laid on him the iniquity of us all. (Isa 53:6)

5. A sinful nature is useless (v.12; cp. Ps.14:3): "They have together become worthless" (achreioo). The word means to become worthless, useless, sour, bad (cp. sour milk). All men without Christ are worthless, useless, sour, bad.

> "You are the salt of the earth. But if the salt loses its saltiness, how can it be made salty again? It is no longer good for anything, except to be thrown out and trampled by men. (Mat 5:13)
> And throw that worthless servant outside, into the darkness, where there will be weeping and gnashing of teeth.' (Mat 25:30)
> What good is it for a man to gain the whole world, and yet lose or forfeit his very self? (Luke 9:25)
> "Salt is good, but if it loses its saltiness, how can it be made salty again? It is fit neither for the soil nor for the manure pile; it is thrown out. "He who has ears to hear, let him hear." (Luke 14:34-35)

6. A sinful nature is evil (v.12; cp. Ps.14:3): "There is no one who does good, not even one." The word "good" (chrestotes) means moral goodness, kindness, graciousness, gentleness, justice. All men fail in being good toward God and their neighbor, in being…

- kind
- gentle
- gracious
- just

Men come short—too often, too much. "There is no one who does good [not always, not perfectly], not even one."

> "Woe to you, teachers of the law and Pharisees, you hypocrites! You are like whitewashed tombs, which look beautiful on the outside but on the inside are full of dead men's bones and everything unclean. (Mat 23:27)
> For from within, out of men's hearts, come evil thoughts, sexual immorality, theft, murder, adultery, greed, malice, deceit, lewdness, envy, slander, arrogance and folly. All these evils come from inside and make a man 'unclean.'" (Mark 7:21-23)

3 (3:13-14) **Tongue—Man, Nature:** there is the case of a sinful tongue.

1. A sinful tongue is foul and corrupt (v.13; cp. Ps.5:9): "Their throats are open graves." An open grave is foul, and it is a symbol of corruption. So is a man with a sinful mouth. His mouth is…

- foul
- detestable
- dirty
- profane
- obscene
- dishonorable
- polluted
- offensive
- filthy

The obscene mouth may range from off-colored humor to dirty jokes, from immoral suggestions to outright propositions. But no matter, a man with a foul mouth stinks just like an open grave; his filthiness causes corruption, the decay of character. The filth from his mouth eats and eats away at his character and at the character of his listeners so much that he becomes as offensive as that of a decayed corpse. The foul, filthy mouth kills character, its attractiveness, trust, faithfulness, morality, honor, and godliness.

> You brood of vipers, how can you who are evil say anything good? For out of the overflow of the heart the mouth speaks. (Mat 12:34)
> The tongue also is a fire, a world of evil among the parts of the body. It corrupts the whole person, sets the whole course of his life on fire, and is itself set on fire by hell. (James 3:6)
> For their hearts plot violence, and their lips talk about making trouble. (Prov 24:2)

2. A sinful tongue is deceitful (v.13; cp. Ps.5:9): "Their tongues practice deceit." The Hebrew says, "They *make* smooth their tongue." A deceitful person has…

- a false tongue
- a lying tongue
- a cheating tongue
- a misleading tongue
- a treacherous tongue
- a beguiling tongue
- a deluding tongue
- a flattering tongue
- a smooth talking tongue

The word "deceit" (edoliousan) is continuous action: "They kept on deceiving." Man is not only guilty of deceiving, but of constantly deceiving. He is *constantly* hiding and camouflaging his true thoughts and feelings and behavior, seeking to protect himself or to get whatever he is after.

> His mouth is full of curses and lies and threats; trouble and evil are under his tongue. (Psa 10:7)
> The words of his mouth are wicked and deceitful; he has ceased to be wise and to do good. (Psa 36:3)
> His speech is smooth as butter, yet war is in his heart; his words are more soothing than oil, yet they are drawn swords. (Psa 55:21)
> And in my dismay I said, "All men are liars." (Psa 116:11)
> Friend deceives friend, and no one speaks the truth. They have taught their tongues to lie; they weary themselves with sinning. (Jer 9:5)
> The heart is deceitful above all things and beyond cure. Who can understand it? (Jer 17:9)
> Her rich men are violent; her people are liars and their tongues speak deceitfully. (Micah 6:12)
> Woe to the city of blood, full of lies, full of plunder, never without victims! (Nahum 3:1)

3. A sinful tongue is piercing and poisonous (v.13; cp. Ps.140:3): "The poison of vipers is on their lips." The viper (aspidon) is the cobra, a deadly snake. God charges men with having tongues that are just as piercing and poisonous as the tongue of the deadly cobra. The idea is that the tongues of some people have a diabolical nature; they are filled with so much malice that they set out to inflict punishment. A poisonous tongue…
- talks and gossips about
- strikes out against
- inserts and spreads venom
- poisons character and reputation
- desires to cause suffering
- lies in wait to strike
- seeks to hurt and destroy

> But now you must rid yourselves of all such things as these: anger, rage, malice, slander, and filthy language from your lips. (Col 3:8)
> Therefore, rid yourselves of all malice and all deceit, hypocrisy, envy, and slander of every kind. (1 Pet 2:1)
> Reckless words pierce like a sword, but the tongue of the wise brings healing. (Prov 12:18)
> They make their tongues as sharp as a serpent's; the poison of vipers is on their lips. Selah (Psa 140:3)

4. A sinful tongue is full of cursing and bitterness (v.14; cp. Ps.10:7): "Their mouths are full of cursing and bitterness." Cursing is sin; a cursing tongue is a sinful tongue. (See outline, note, and DEEPER STUDY # 1,2,3,4—Mt.5:33-37; note and DEEPER STUDY # 5—23:16-22 for more discussion.) Jesus Christ says:

> But I tell you, Do not swear at all: either by heaven, for it is God's throne; Simply let your 'Yes' be 'Yes,' and your

'No,' 'No'; anything beyond this comes from the evil one. (Mat 5:34, 37)

a. Men use profanity; in fact, their mouth is full of cursing and swearing. They curse both God and men. Their cursing may range from what society considers to be a mild word of slang to using God's name in vain. No matter how mild or how acceptable to society, it is sin. God's case against man is that his mouth is full of cursing (cp. Jas.3:8-10).

> But I tell you, Do not swear at all: either by heaven, for it is God's throne; (Mat 5:34)
> But no man can tame the tongue. It is a restless evil, full of deadly poison. With the tongue we praise our Lord and Father, and with it we curse men, who have been made in God's likeness. Out of the same mouth come praise and cursing. My brothers, this should not be. (James 3:8-10)
> Above all, my brothers, do not swear— not by heaven or by earth or by anything else. Let your "Yes" be yes, and your "No," no, or you will be condemned. (James 5:12)
> "You shall not misuse the name of the LORD your God, for the LORD will not hold anyone guiltless who misuses his name. (Exo 20:7)
> "'Do not swear falsely by my name and so profane the name of your God. I am the LORD. (Lev 19:12)
> For the sins of their mouths, for the words of their lips, let them be caught in their pride. For the curses and lies they utter, (Psa 59:12)
> For you know in your heart that many times you yourself have cursed others. (Eccl 7:22)

Note a man's cursing shall fall upon him.

> He loved to pronounce a curse— may it come on him; he found no pleasure in blessing— may it be far from him. He wore cursing as his garment; it entered into his body like water, into his bones like oil. (Psa 109:17-18)

b. Man's mouth is also full of bitterness. His tongue is often…
- sharp
- resentful
- cynical
- cold
- harsh
- stressful
- intense
- relentless
- distasteful
- unpleasant

Any expression involving any of these is sin to God. God desires men to be filled with love and joy and peace and to express such. Anything less than the expression of these is sin. This is God's case against men: a tongue full of cursing and bitterness.

> Get rid of all bitterness, rage and anger, brawling and slander, along with every form of malice. (Eph 4:31)
> See to it that no one misses the grace of God and that no bitter root grows up to cause trouble and defile many. (Heb 12:15)

> But if you harbor bitter envy and selfish ambition in your hearts, do not boast about it or deny the truth. (James 3:14)

4 (3:15-18) **Man, Nature**: there is the case of sinful acts.

1. Sinful acts are murderous acts (v.15; cp. Is.59:7): "Their feet are swift to shed blood." Note the word "swift." Men jump to kill; they are ready to spill and pour out blood...

- out of hurt and shame.
- to have their own way.
- to get what they want.

Men are cruel; they have natures that are prideful and selfish and greedy. They seek and seek to possess, even if it means turning against others and inflicting...

- pain and suffering
- grief and injury
- teasing and tormenting
- killing and slaughtering
- mutilating and mangling

God's case against man is that he is a murderer. His feet are "swift to shed blood."

> "You shall not murder. (Exo 20:13)
> "Which ones?" the man inquired. Jesus replied, "'Do not murder, do not commit adultery, do not steal, do not give false testimony, (Mat 19:18)
> If you suffer, it should not be as a murderer or thief or any other kind of criminal, or even as a meddler. (1 Pet 4:15)
> Anyone who hates his brother is a murderer, and you know that no murderer has eternal life in him. (1 John 3:15)
> For their feet rush into sin, they are swift to shed blood. (Prov 1:16)

2. Sinful acts are oppressive acts that destroy and cause misery (v.16; cp. Is.59:7): "Ruin and misery mark their ways." Man is oppressive; he destroys and causes misery wherever he goes. Because of his pride, selfishness, and greed, man destroys...

- the land (pollution)
- the cities
- the nations
- the country
- the government
- the people
- the shops
- the houses
- the property

He destroys and causes misery wherever he goes, even within his own family, neighborhood, and city. Whether by simple argument within his own family or by war, he is so destructive and full of misery that he brings ruin and misery wherever he goes.

3. Sinful acts are restless, disturbing and warring acts (v.17; cp. Is.59:8): "And the way of peace they do not know." The idea is that men do not experience peace. They do not possess peace within themselves nor among others. They do not know peaceful ways, do not know...

- how to secure peace.
- how to keep peace.

Men are not peaceful within; they are restless. Their own soul is a civil war that experiences constant conflict.

Therefore, men fail to secure peace not only within themselves, but among others. Wherever men are, they disturb and bring faction and war to others. This is God's case against men.

> In the morning you will say, "If only it were evening!" and in the evening, "If only it were morning!"—because of the terror that will fill your hearts and the sights that your eyes will see. (Deu 28:67)
> What does a man get for all the toil and anxious striving with which he labors under the sun? All his days his work is pain and grief; even at night his mind does not rest. This too is meaningless. (Eccl 2:22-23)
> "There is no peace," says the LORD, "for the wicked." (Isa 48:22)
> But the wicked are like the tossing sea, which cannot rest, whose waves cast up mire and mud. (Isa 57:20)
> The way of peace they do not know; there is no justice in their paths. They have turned them into crooked roads; no one who walks in them will know peace. (Isa 59:8)
> Those who pursue us are at our heels; we are weary and find no rest. (Lam 5:5)
> When terror comes, they will seek peace, but there will be none. (Ezek 7:25)

4. Sinful acts are godless, irreverent, disrespectful acts (v.18; cp. Ps.36:1): "There is no fear of God before their eyes." Their eyes and their attention are focused upon other things. They ignore and neglect God, living as though there is no God. They sense little if any responsibility toward God. They do not fear God; they do not fear His anger or wrath or judgment against them. They sense little desire or need to worship God or to study His Word and will. They seldom if ever praise and honor Him or do as He commands. The fear of God is not before their eyes; therefore, this is God's case against men.

> Furthermore, since they did not think it worthwhile to retain the knowledge of God, he gave them over to a depraved mind, to do what ought not to be done. (Rom 1:28)
> (Indeed, when Gentiles, who do not have the law, do by nature things required by the law, they are a law for themselves, even though they do not have the law, (Rom 2:14)
> For he says, 'It profits a man nothing when he tries to please God.' (Job 34:9)
> But no one says, 'Where is God my Maker, who gives songs in the night, (Job 35:10)
> In his pride the wicked does not seek him; in all his thoughts there is no room for God. (Psa 10:4)
> For the director of music. Of David the servant of the LORD. An oracle is within my heart concerning the sinfulness of the wicked: There is no fear of God before his eyes. (Psa 36:1)
> Since they would not accept my advice and spurned my rebuke, (Prov 1:30)

5 (3:19-20) **Law**: there is the case of the law or Scripture. Note five points.

1. The law or Scripture speaks to all. Note the words "we know." Paul means that this is an obvious truth, a clear truth that cannot be missed. All that has just been said has been quoted from Scripture (v.9-18), and Scripture speaks and is intended for everyone. Therefore, all are guilty before God, both Jew and Gentile. Scripture charges everyone with sin, declaring that "all are under sin"—all are subject to its power and authority. No one escapes the charge of God's law. The case of God's law is against everyone, both religionist and heathen.

2. The law or Scripture stops all boasting, every mouth that acts self-sufficient and declares the goodness of men. In light of man's sinful nature and tongue and behavior, who can boast? Who can declare man's goodness and righteousness and capabilities? Who can say anything against God's case against men? Scripture declares that no man is good, leaving only One who could be good, and that is God. God alone is good; God alone deserves praise and honor and glory. Man can boast in God and in God alone. Man is silenced; he has no reason and no right to boast in himself. The law, God's case against man, stops his mouth.

> But now a righteousness from God, apart from law, has been made known, to which the Law and the Prophets testify. (Rom 3:21)
>
> The law was added so that the trespass might increase. But where sin increased, grace increased all the more, (Rom 5:20)
>
> What shall we say, then? Is the law sin? Certainly not! Indeed I would not have known what sin was except through the law. For I would not have known what coveting really was if the law had not said, "Do not covet." (Rom 7:7)
>
> Since they did not know the righteousness that comes from God and sought to establish their own, they did not submit to God's righteousness. (Rom 10:3)
>
> What, then, was the purpose of the law? It was added because of transgressions until the Seed to whom the promise referred had come. The law was put into effect through angels by a mediator. (Gal 3:19)

(See outline and notes—Ro.7:7-13 for more discussion).

3. The law or Scripture makes all the world accountable, guilty before God. God's law declares:

> As it is written: "There is no one righteous, not even one; (Rom 3:10)
>
> All have turned away, they have together become worthless; there is no one who does good, not even one." (Rom 3:12)
>
> All who rely on observing the law are under a curse, for it is written: "Cursed is everyone who does not continue to do everything written in the Book of the Law." (Gal 3:10)
>
> We know that we are children of God, and that the whole world is under the control of the evil one. (1 John 5:19)

No one escapes. All the world stands face to face before God—stands imperfect, stands short of His glory, stands guilty of sin.

4. The law justifies, declares no one righteous. Note carefully what is being said.

⇒ No law and no deed of the law will ever justify or make a man righteous (make him acceptable to God).

⇒ Man cannot be justified or made righteous by keeping any law or work.

⇒ Man cannot be justified or made righteous by any good deed of his own.

⇒ No one, no man, will be justified or made righteous in God's sight, not by the law.

> Therefore no one will be declared righteous in his sight by observing the law; rather, through the law we become conscious of sin. (Rom 3:20)
>
> Clearly no one is justified before God by the law, because, "The righteous will live The law is not based on faith; on the contrary, "The man who does these things will live by them." (Gal 3:11-12)
>
> We also know that law is made not for the righteous but for lawbreakers and rebels, the ungodly and sinful, the unholy and irreligious; for those who kill their fathers or mothers, for murderers, for adulterers and perverts, for slave traders and liars and perjurers—and for whatever else is contrary to the sound doctrine (1 Tim 1:9-10)

5. The law shows man that he is sinful. The purpose of the law is not to justify, not to make righteous, but to point out sin, to tell a man that he is a sinner. The law was given to make a man aware of his sin. Why? So that man would know he is sinful and that he needs to seek God for forgiveness and salvation.

> But now a righteousness from God, apart from law, has been made known, to which the Law and the Prophets testify. This righteousness from God comes through faith in Jesus Christ to all who believe. There is no difference, for all have sinned and fall short of the glory of God, and are justified freely by his grace through the redemption that came by Christ Jesus. (Rom 3:21-24)
>
> For what the law was powerless to do in that it was weakened by the sinful nature, God did by sending his own Son in the likeness of sinful man to be a sin offering. And so he condemned sin in sinful man, (Rom 8:3; cp. Heb 7:19)
>
> Know that a man is not justified by observing the law, but by faith in Jesus Christ. So we, too, have put our faith in Christ Jesus that we may be justified by faith in Christ and not by observing the law, because by observing the law no one will be justified. (Gal 2:16; cp. Gal.3:24-27)
>
> Christ redeemed us from the curse of the law by becoming a curse for us, for it is written: "Cursed is everyone who is hung on a tree." (Gal 3:13)

	III. FAITH AND JUSTIFICATION: THE WAY FOR THE WORLD TO BE RIGHT WITH GOD, 3:21-5:21 A. Righteousness: The Way to Be Right with God, 3:21-26	23 For all have sinned and fall short of the glory of God, 24 And are justified freely by his grace through the redemption that came by Christ Jesus. 25 God presented him as a sacrifice of atonement, through faith in his blood. He did this to demonstrate his justice, because in his forbearance he had left the sins committed beforehand unpunished—	1) All have sinned 2) All fall short of God's glory[DS1]
1 **Righteousness is now revealed** a. The rgt. apart from the law b. The rgt. foretold c. The rgt. through Christ 2 **Rgt. is for everyone** a. All who believe b. All who need: "There is no difference"	21 But now a righteousness from God, apart from law, has been made known, to which the Law and the Prophets testify. 22 This righteousness from God comes through faith in Jesus Christ to all who believe. There is no difference,	26 He did it to demonstrate his justice at the present time, so as to be just and the one who justifies those who have faith in Jesus.	3 **Rgt. is only possible through justification** a. Is free—by grace b. Is through redemption[DS2] 4 **Rgt. is by an act of God alone: By atonement** 5 **Rgt. has one great purpose: To proclaim God's personal righteousness** a. That He forgives sin b. That He is forbearing c. That He is just d. That He is the justifier of believers

DIVISION III

FAITH AND JUSTIFICATION: THE WAY FOR THE WORLD TO BE RIGHT WITH GOD, 3:21-5:21

A. Righteousness: The Way to be Right With God, 3:21-26

(3:21-26) **Introduction—Righteousness**: the "righteousness from God" is used in three ways in Scripture.

1. Righteousness refers to God's character. It means the righteousness, justice, and perfection which God Himself possesses and shows.

2. Righteousness reveals man's lack of godly character. It means the sinful, depraved, unrighteous, unjust, and imperfect nature and behavior of man.

3. Righteousness means the perfection which God provides for man in Christ Jesus. When a man allows the Lord Jesus Christ to take his sins, he is given the righteousness of God. Christ robes the man in the righteousness of God Himself—by faith (2 Cor.5:21; Ph.3:9).

The context is usually clear as to which meaning is meant (see DEEPER STUDY #5, *Righteousness*—Mt.5:6 for more discussion).
1. Righteousness is now revealed (v.21-22).
2. Righteousness is for everyone (v.22-23).
3. Righteousness is only possible through justification (v.24).
4. Righteousness is by an act of God alone: by atonement (v.25).
5. Righteousness has one purpose: to proclaim God's personal righteousness (v.25-26).

1 (3:21-22) **Righteousness—Law**: righteousness is now revealed. God has "now" revealed *how* man is to get right with Him. The word "now" is a cataclysmic breaking point in the message of Romans. It points to a pivotal point in human history. It is saying two things.
⇒ Before, back then, hundreds and hundreds of years ago, God had patience in that He put up with man's attempts at self-righteousness through the law. *But now* the period of God's righteousness has come—the righteousness that is found in God's very own Son.
⇒ Before, back then, man sinned and sinned, learning the impossibility of putting away his own sin. Man's period of time under law showed him the impossibility of securing righteousness on his own.

But now the period of God's righteousness has come—the righteousness that is found in God's very own Son.

1. God's righteousness for man is "apart from the law." Righteousness has to be apart from the law, for the law fails in two critical areas.
   a. The law does not allow disobedience; it requires obedience. Anyone who disobeys the law becomes a lawbreaker, a transgressor. He is guilty and to be condemned.
   b. The law does not have the power to make a person obedient. It does not have the power to prevent a person from disobeying. It only shows a person's disobedience and inadequate strength to be obedient. It only reveals a person's inability to secure any righteousness whatsoever by self-effort. Therefore, if God was to have men living in His presence, He had to provide a righteousness "apart from the law." There had to be a righteousness that had nothing to do with law.

2. God's righteousness for man was foretold by the Old Testament (prophets and law). This is clearly seen in the next chapter in the lives of Abraham and David (Ro.4:1f). (Cp. Jn.5:39, 46; 1 Pt.1:10-11.)

3. God's righteousness is revealed in Jesus Christ. When Jesus Christ came to earth, He came to *reveal* the perfect righteousness of God. Jesus Christ came to live...
   • the Sinless life
   • the Perfect life
   • the Ideal life
   • the Representative life
   • the Pattern life

Jesus Christ is the perfect embodiment of God's righteousness. In fact, Jesus Christ is God's righteousness; or to say it another way, the righteousness of God is Jesus Christ. God's righteousness is now revealed in and through Jesus Christ Himself. (See note—Ro.5:1 for more discussion.)

Christ is the end of the law so that there may be righteousness for everyone who believes. (Rom 10:4)

It is because of him that you are in Christ Jesus, who has become for us wisdom from God—that is, our righteousness, holiness and redemption. (1 Cor 1:30)

And be found in him, not having a righteousness of my own that comes from the law, but that which is through faith in Christ—the righteousness that comes from God and is by faith. (Phil 3:9)

2 (3:22-23) **Righteousness—Sin**: righteousness is for everyone. Scripture is clear in its declaration.

1. Righteousness is for all who believe. Note that righteousness is both *given "to"* the believer and *laid "upon"* the believer.

   a. Righteousness is given *"to"* the believer as a *possession*.

Through these he has given us his very great and precious promises, so that through them you may participate in the divine nature and escape the corruption in the world caused by evil desires. (2 Pet 1:4)

And I will ask the Father, and he will give you another Counselor to be with you forever—the Spirit of truth. The world cannot accept him, because it neither sees him nor knows him. But you know him, for he lives with you and will be in you. (John 14:16-17)

   b. Righteousness is laid *"upon"* the believer as a *covering* or clothing.

God made him who had no sin to be sin for us, so that in him we might become the righteousness of God. (2 Cor 5:21)

And to put on the new self, created to be like God in true righteousness and holiness. (Eph 4:24)

For you died, and your life is now hidden with Christ in God. And have put on the new self, which is being renewed in knowledge in the image of its Creator. (Col 3:3, 10)

2. Righteousness is needed by all. There is no difference and no distinction between men. There are two reasons.

   a. All men are sinners. The word "sinned" (harmartano) is in the Greek aorist tense; that is, it is a once-for-all happening. It looks back to the historical entrance of sin into the world. This means that all men...
- inherited the nature of their sinful fathers and mothers.
- have sinned and are sinners.
- cannot keep from sinning and will sin.

For all have sinned and fall short of the glory of God, (Rom 3:23)

But the Scripture declares that the whole world is a prisoner of sin, so that what was promised, being given through faith in Jesus Christ, might be given to those who believe. (Gal 3:22)

If we claim to be without sin, we deceive ourselves and the truth is not in us. (1 John 1:8)

We know that we are children of God, and that the whole world is under the control of the evil one. (1 John 5:19)

The LORD saw how great man's wickedness on the earth had become, and that every inclination of the thoughts of his heart was only evil all the time. (Gen 6:5)

"When they sin against you—for there is no one who does not sin—and you become angry with them and give them over to the enemy, who takes them captive to his own land, far away or near; (1 Ki 8:46)

Everyone has turned away, they have together become corrupt; there is no one who does good, not even one. (Psa 53:3; cp. Ps.14:3)

Who can say, "I have kept my heart pure; I am clean and without sin"? (Prov 20:9)

There is not a righteous man on earth who does what is right and never sins. (Eccl 7:20)

We all, like sheep, have gone astray, each of us has turned to his own way; and the LORD has laid on him the iniquity of us all. (Isa 53:6)

All of us have become like one who is unclean, and all our righteous acts are like filthy rags; we all shrivel up like a leaf, and like the wind our sins sweep us away. (Isa 64:6)

The godly have been swept from the land; not one upright man remains. All men lie in wait to shed blood; each hunts his brother with a net. (Micah 7:2)

   b. All men "fall short" of God's glory. The tense is present: all men are falling *short*, that is, *continually falling short* of God's glory. Men are in a state or condition of being short of God's glory (see DEEPER STUDY # 1, *Glory*—Ro.3:23 for discussion).

DEEPER STUDY # 1

(3:23) **Glory—God, Glory of**: the "glory of God" is God's standard for man. It means His *moral glory*. It means His excellence, splendor, brilliance, brightness, magnificence, preeminence, dignity, majesty, and grace. It means the absolute perfection of God, the perfection of His person. It is this "glory of God" which demands that man correspond perfectly with God—if man wishes to be at peace with God and to live in His presence.

1. Glory is *light*, perfect light. It is the very highest degree of light: the perfection of splendor, brightness, brilliance, resplendence. This is seen in many passages.

⇒ John saw how bright the glory of God is when he had the vision of the new Jerusalem. (The new Jerusalem will be the center or capital of world government in the new heavens and earth.)

And he carried me away in the Spirit to a mountain great and high, and showed me the Holy City, Jerusalem, coming down out of heaven from God. It shone with the glory of God, and its brilliance was like that of a very precious jewel, like a jasper, clear as crystal. (Rev 21:10-11)

The city does not need the sun or the moon to shine on it, for the glory of God gives it light, and the Lamb is its lamp. (Rev 21:23)

⇒ Jesus experienced the light of God's glory.

There he was transfigured before them. His face shone like the sun, and his clothes became as white as the light. (Mat 17:2)

⇒ Paul experienced the light of God's glory.

"About noon as I came near Damascus, suddenly a bright light from heaven flashed around me. (Acts 22:6, 11; cp. 9:3-9)

⇒ Moses experienced the light of God's glory.

When Moses came down from Mount Sinai with the two tablets of the Testimony in his hands, he was not aware that his face was radiant because he had spoken with the LORD. When Aaron and all the Israelites saw Moses, his face was radiant, and they were afraid to come near him. (Exo 34:29-30; cp. 29-35)

2. Glory is purity, perfect purity. It is the very highest degree of virtue and goodness, of quality and morality. It is the highest excellence of character and the perfection of being.

This is the message we have heard from him and declare to you: God is light; in him there is no darkness at all. (1 John 1:5)

"Why do you ask me about what is good?" Jesus replied. "There is only One who is good. If you want to enter life, obey the commandments." (Mat 19:17)

Be perfect, therefore, as your heavenly Father is perfect. (Mat 5:48)

Who will not fear you, O Lord, and bring glory to your name? For you alone are holy. All nations will come and worship before you, for your righteous acts have been revealed." (Rev 15:4)

3. Glory is majesty, perfect majesty. It is the very highest degree of preeminence and magnificence, of dignity and honor, of meriting worship and praise.

In the year that King Uzziah died, I saw the Lord seated on a throne, high and exalted, and the train of his robe filled the temple. And they were calling to one another: "Holy, holy, holy is the LORD Almighty; the whole earth is full of his glory." (Isa 6:1, 3)

For this is what the high and lofty One says— he who lives forever, whose name is holy: "I live in a high and holy place, but also with him who is contrite and lowly in spirit, to revive the spirit of the lowly and to revive the heart of the contrite. (Isa 57:15)

The LORD reigns, he is robed in majesty; the LORD is robed in majesty and is armed with strength. The world is firmly established; it cannot be moved. (Psa 93:1; cp. 97:1)

4. Glory is being, perfect being. It is the very highest degree of worth, quality and merit, preciousness and value. (See note—Jn.17:2-3.)

"You are worthy, our Lord and God, to receive glory and honor and power, for you created all things, and by your will they were created and have their being." (Rev 4:11)

"You are my witnesses," declares the LORD, "and my servant whom I have chosen, so that you may know and believe me and understand that I am he. Before me no god was formed, nor will there be one after me. (Isa 43:10)

"Why do you ask me about what is good?" Jesus replied. "There is only One who is good. If you want to enter life, obey the commandments." (Mat 19:17)

3 (3:24) **Righteousness—Justification**: righteousness is possible only through justification (see notes, *Justification*—Ro.1:17; DEEPER STUDY #1—4:22; 5:1 for discussion). Note two significant facts.

1. Justification is a free gift of God. Man in no way earns it. Man is justified by God's grace and by God's grace alone. (See notes, *Grace*—Ro.4:16; Tit.2:15 for more discussion.)

2. Justification is only through the redemption that is in Christ Jesus (see DEEPER STUDY #2, *Redemption*—Ro.3:24 for discussion).

DEEPER STUDY # 2

(3:24) **Redemption** (apolutroseos): to redeem, to deliver by paying a price. (See note, *Redemption*—Eph.1:7 for more discussion.) The word is used three ways in the New Testament.

1. It means to redeem (agorazo): to deliver; to set free from the slave market of sin, death, and hell.

You were bought at a price. Therefore honor God with your body. (1 Cor 6:20)

You were bought at a price; do not become slaves of men. (1 Cor 7:23)

But there were also false prophets among the people, just as there will be false teachers among you. They will secretly introduce destructive heresies, even denying the sovereign Lord who bought them—bringing swift destruction on themselves. (2 Pet 2:1)

2. It means to redeem *out of* (exagorazo): to deliver *out of* the enslavement to sin, death, and hell. It means to be delivered *out of* and never returned.

Christ redeemed us from the curse of the law by becoming a curse for us, for it is written: "Cursed is everyone who is hung on a tree." (Gal 3:13)

To redeem those under law, that we might receive the full rights of sons. (Gal 4:5)

3. It means to redeem (lutroo): to deliver by paying a price; to buy.

Who gave himself for us to redeem us from all wickedness and to purify for himself a people that are his very own, eager to do what is good. (Titus 2:14)

For you know that it was not with perishable things such as silver or gold that you were redeemed from the empty way of life handed down to you from your forefathers, (1 Pet 1:18)

Redemption is "in Christ Jesus" (en Christou Iesou), wrought through His death and sufferings. Of this there can be no doubt; the fact is critical to a person's destiny. Redemption is *not* brought about...

- by the life of Christ.
- by the power of Christ.
- by the example of Christ.

Scripture is abundantly clear about this. His cross and His sacrifice in death are what brought about redemption. Redemption is...

accomplished	fulfilled
wrought	a fact
produced	a reality
effected	a truth

...because of the shed blood of Jesus Christ, God's very own Son.

> For the life of a creature is in the blood, and I have given it to you to make atonement for yourselves on the altar; it is the blood that makes atonement for one's life. (Lev 17:11)
> Just as the Son of Man did not come to be served, but to serve, and to give his life as a ransom for many." (Mat 20:28)
> And are justified freely by his grace through the redemption that came by Christ Jesus. (Rom 3:24)
> You were bought at a price. Therefore honor God with your body. (1 Cor 6:20)
> You were bought at a price; do not become slaves of men. (1 Cor 7:23)
> In him we have redemption through his blood, the forgiveness of sins, in accordance with the riches of God's grace (Eph 1:7)
> in whom we have redemption, the forgiveness of sins. (Col 1:14)
> For there is one God and one mediator between God and men, the man Christ Jesus, who gave himself as a ransom for all men—the testimony given in its proper time. (1 Tim 2:5-6)
> For this reason Christ is the mediator of a new covenant, that those who are called may receive the promised eternal inheritance—now that he has died as a ransom to set them free from the sins committed under the first covenant. (Heb 9:15)
> For you know that it was not with perishable things such as silver or gold that you were redeemed from the empty way of life handed down to you from your forefathers, but with the precious blood of Christ, a lamb without blemish or defect. (1 Pet 1:18-19)
> But there were also false prophets among the people, just as there will be false teachers among you. They will secretly introduce destructive heresies, even denying the sovereign Lord who bought them—bringing swift destruction on themselves. (2 Pet 2:1)
> And they sang a new song: "You are worthy to take the scroll and to open its seals, because you were slain, and with your blood you purchased men for God from every tribe and language and people and nation. (Rev 5:9)
> And they sang a new song before the throne and before the four living creatures and the elders. No one could learn the song except the 144,000 who had been redeemed from the earth. These are those who did not defile themselves with women, for they kept themselves pure. They follow the Lamb wherever he goes. They were purchased from among men and offered as firstfruits to God and the Lamb. (Rev 14:3-4)

4 (3:25) **Atonement—Propitiation—Jesus Christ, Blood**: righteousness is by an act of God alone, the act of Atonement, of Propitiation. (See note, *Propitiation—Atonement—1 Jn.2:1-2; DEEPER STUDY #1—2:2* for more discussion). Atonement or propitiation (hilasterion) means to be a sacrifice, a covering, a satisfaction, a payment, an appeasement for sin. Note two very significant points.

1. God is the One who "presented" or "set forth" (proetheto) Christ to be the atonement for man's sins.
   a. God *purposed* to "present" or "set forth" Christ: God determined, resolved, ordained Christ to be the atonement or the sacrifice for man's sins.
   b. God set Christ "before" (pro) the world as the atonement, for the world's sins. The *pro* in the Greek word *pro*etheto presented, set forth indicates this fact.
   ⇒ God set Christ *before Himself*, purposed that He be the atonement, the propitiation or the sacrifice for man's sin.
   ⇒ God set Christ publicly *before the world*, showing that He is definitely the atonement for the world's sins.

2. It is Christ Himself who is the atonement or propitiation for man's sins. But note: it is not His teachings, power, example, or life that make Christ the atonement. It is His blood—His sacrifice, His death, His sufferings, His cross—that causes God to accept Jesus as the atonement or propitiation. It is the blood of Christ that God accepts as...

- the *sacrifice* for our sins.
- the *covering* for our sins.
- the *satisfaction* for our sins.
- the *payment* for the penalty of our sins.
- the *appeasement* of His wrath against sin.

What does the Bible mean by "the blood of Christ?" It means *the willingness* of Christ to die (shed His blood) for man. It means *the supreme sacrifice* Christ paid for man's sins. It means *the terrible sufferings* Christ underwent for man's sins. (See note—Mt.20:19.) It means *the voluntary laying down of His life* for man's sins (Jn.10:17-18).

> For this reason he had to be made like his brothers in every way, in order that he might become a merciful and faithful high priest in service to God, and that he might make atonement for the sins of the people. (Heb 2:17)
> My dear children, I write this to you so that you will not sin. But if anybody does sin, we have one who speaks to the Father in our defense—Jesus Christ, the Righteous One. He is the atoning sacrifice for our

sins, and not only for ours but also for the sins of the whole world. (1 John 2:1-2)

This is love: not that we loved God, but that he loved us and sent his Son as an atoning sacrifice for our sins. (1 John 4:10)

"But the tax collector stood at a distance. He would not even look up to heaven, but beat his breast and said, 'God, have mercy on me, a sinner.' (Luke 18:13)

5 (3:25-26) **Righteousness—Justification**: righteousness has one great purpose—to declare God's personal righteousness and justice. God is righteous and just; therefore, He always does what is right, and He always acts justly toward all persons. This is the reason He has provided a perfect righteousness for man. It was the thing to do: the right thing and the just thing. He is righteous by nature; therefore, he provided righteousness for man. God's righteousness is seen in four glorious facts.

1. God's righteousness is seen in that He forgives sin. Christ died for our sins, and God accepts His death as the propitiation or the sacrifice for our sins. Now note: God did not betray Christ or man; He did not reject Christ's death. He did not act unjustly and unrighteously. On the contrary, God did what was right. He acted righteously and justly. He accepted the death of Christ as the sacrifice for our sins; therefore, His forgiveness of sins declares that He is righteous.

This is my blood of the covenant, which is poured out for many for the forgiveness of sins. (Mat 26:28)

In fact, the law requires that nearly everything be cleansed with blood, and without the shedding of blood there is no forgiveness. (Heb 9:22)

So Christ was sacrificed once to take away the sins of many people; and he will appear a second time, not to bear sin, but to bring salvation to those who are waiting for him. (Heb 9:28)

2. God's righteousness is seen in His forbearance, that is, in His patience and long-suffering with man's sin. Note a most glorious fact: God did not punish man for His sin by destroying all flesh from off the earth; God waited until Christ came before condemning sin *in the flesh or sinful nature of man*. Remember God is perfect righteousness; therefore, He has to provide a perfect righteousness for man "in the flesh or the sinful nature of man."

⇒ There was no man who could embody perfect righteousness.
⇒ Only God's Son could and did embody perfect righteousness.

The fact that God waited until Christ came, that God was forbearing in holding back the punishment of sin, shows that God is righteous. God's righteousness and His justice are declared by His forbearance.

For what the law was powerless to do in that it was weakened by the sinful nature, God did by sending his own Son in the like ness of sinful man to be a sin offering. And so he condemned sin in sinful man, (Rom 8:3)

But when the time had fully come, God sent his Son, born of a woman, born under law, to redeem those under law, that we might receive the full rights of sons. Because you are sons, God sent the Spirit of his Son into our hearts, the Spirit who calls out, "Abba, Father." (Gal 4:4-6)

3. God's righteousness is seen in His justice. He accepted the death of Christ as the substitute for our sins; He exacted the punishment for sin upon Christ. He did the right and just thing. His righteousness is declared by His justice.

Surely he took up our infirmities and carried our sorrows, yet we considered him stricken by God, smitten by him, and afflicted. But he was pierced for our transgressions, he was crushed for our iniquities; the punishment that brought us peace was upon him, and by his wounds we are healed. We all, like sheep, have gone astray, each of us has turned to his own way; and the LORD has laid on him the iniquity of us all. (Isa 53:4-6)

He himself bore our sins in his body on the tree, so that we might die to sins and live for righteousness; by his wounds you have been healed. (1 Pet 2:24)

For Christ died for sins once for all, the righteous for the unrighteous, to bring you to God. He was put to death in the body but made alive by the Spirit, (1 Pet 3:18)

4. God's righteousness is seen in His being the justifier of all who believe. God takes our faith and counts it as righteousness. He takes our faith and judges us acceptable to Him. Now every thinking man knows he is not righteous: not pure, not holy, not sinless. The fact that God accepts the death of Christ as the sacrifice for our sins and justifies us shows a marvelous truth: it shows that God is righteous and just. The fact that God is our Justifier declares His righteousness.

Through him everyone who believes is justified from everything you could not be justified from by the law of Moses. (Acts 13:39)

For we maintain that a man is justified by faith apart from observing the law. (Rom 3:28)

Therefore, since we have been justified through faith, we have peace with God through our Lord Jesus Christ, (Rom 5:1)

And that is what some of you were. But you were washed, you were sanctified, you were justified in the name of the Lord Jesus Christ and by the Spirit of our God. (1 Cor 6:11)

So the law was put in charge to lead us to Christ that we might be justified by faith. (Gal 3:24)

| 1 Faith excludes boasting
a. Works cause boasting in oneself
b. Faith causes boasting in God
2 Faith justifies a man without the works of the law | B. Faith:ᴰˢ¹ The Way that Puts an End to Human Boasting & Pride, to Self-Righteousness & Works, 3:27-31

27 Where, then, is boasting? It is excluded. On what principle? On that of observing the law? No, but on that of faith.
28 For we maintain that a man is justified by faith apart | from observing the law.
29 Is God the God of Jews only? Is he not the God of Gentiles too? Yes, of Gentiles too,
30 Since there is only one God, who will justify the circumcised by faith and the uncircumcised through that same faith.
31 Do we, then, nullify the law by this faith? Not at all! Rather, we uphold the law. | 3 Faith reveals only one God who deals with all equally
a. He created all: He is the God of all
b. He is the only God: All are justified in the *same* way—by faith

4 Faith upholds & establishes the law |

DIVISION III

FAITH AND JUSTIFICATION: THE WAY FOR THE WORLD TO BE RIGHT WITH GOD, 3:21-5:21

B. Faith: The Way that Puts an End to Human Boasting and Pride, to Self-Righteousness and Works, 3:27-31

(3:27-31) **Introduction**: one of the most powerful forces in all the world is faith. This passage discusses the power of faith, revealing four things that faith does.

1. Faith excludes boasting (v.27).
2. Faith justifies a man without the works of the law (v.28).
3. Faith reveals only one God, who deals with all equally (v.29-30).
4. Faith upholds and establishes the law (v.31).

DEEPER STUDY # 1

(3:27-31) **Faith**: see notes—Jn.2:24; Ro.10:16-17; Heb. 10:38.

---

1 (3:27) **Faith—Boasting—Self-righteousness**: faith excludes boasting among men. Boasting is now excluded and eliminated, banished and made impossible. No man can boast in himself before God. No man can boast in his own righteousness, goodness, merit, or virtue.

What is it that keeps man from boasting and glorying in himself? This is puzzling. Think about it, all the advancements of man...

- the scientific and technological advancements.
- the medical and health advancements.
- the commercial and farming advancements.
- the comfort and recreational advancements.

When man is considered, the power of his mind and all that he is able to produce, it is very difficult for some to understand why man cannot boast in himself. What is it, then, that forbids man to boast in himself? What kind of law would prohibit man from glorying in his ability and achievements?

1. It is not the *law of works*. The law of works does not exclude boasting; it promotes boasting. When a man looks at what he has done, at the works of his hands, he is led to boast and to glory in himself. A law of works does not discourage boasting, it encourages it. A law of works encourages a man to be selfish, self-centered, prideful, and self-righteous. It causes a man to stand before God and other men and declare that he...

- is more acceptable than others.
- is more deserving than others.
- has achieved more than others.
- is more sufficient than others.

- is more adequate than others.
- has no need beyond himself and this world.

A law of works causes men to be focused upon self. It causes men to center the world around themselves: to look upon themselves as the power that creates and sustains the world, as the power that gives purpose, meaning, and significance to life. A law of works encourages boasting; it does not exclude it.

> Live in harmony with one another. Do not be proud, but be willing to associate with people of low position. Do not be conceited. (Rom 12:16)
>
> As it is, you boast and brag. All such boasting is evil. (James 4:16)
>
> You say, 'I am rich; I have acquired wealth and do not need a thing.' But you do not realize that you are wretched, pitiful, poor, blind and naked. (Rev 3:17)
>
> He boasts of the cravings of his heart; he blesses the greedy and reviles the LORD. (Psa 10:3)
>
> Those who trust in their wealth and boast of their great riches? No man can redeem the life of another or give to God a ransom for him— (Psa 49:6-7)
>
> Do not be wise in your own eyes; fear the LORD and shun evil. (Prov 3:7)
>
> Like clouds and wind without rain is a man who boasts of gifts he does not give. (Prov 25:14)
>
> Do you see a man wise in his own eyes? There is more hope for a fool than for him. (Prov 26:12)
>
> Do not boast about tomorrow, for you do not know what a day may bring forth. (Prov 27:1)
>
> Woe to those who are wise in their own eyes and clever in their own sight. (Isa 5:21)

2. It is the *law of faith*. The law of faith excludes boasting. Man has to boast in God when man believes what Scripture has just declared (Ro.1:18-3:26)...

- that *God is* (does exist),

- that God is the creator of the universe and can be known by man,
- that man is short of God's glory and righteousness,
- that God has provided righteousness for man *through faith.*

It is God who has created and given man his ability and who has provided righteousness for man. God has provided the way for man to be saved from sin, death, and hell. Therefore, man has to boast in God and not in self, for God is the One who has given man all that he has, both his natural ability and his eternal salvation. It is the law of faith, not the law of works that eliminates boasting.

> But, "Let him who boasts boast in the Lord." (2 Cor 10:17)
> You were bought at a price. Therefore honor God with your body. (1 Cor 6:20)
> We pray this so that the name of our Lord Jesus may be glorified in you, and you in him, according to the grace of our God and the Lord Jesus Christ. (2 Th 1:12)
> You who fear the LORD, praise him! All you descendants of Jacob, honor him! Revere him, all you descendants of Israel! (Psa 22:23)
> In God we make our boast all day long, and we will praise your name forever. Selah (Psa 44:8)
> But in the LORD all the descendants of Israel will be found righteous and will exult. (Isa 45:25)
> But let him who boasts boast about this: that he understands and knows me, that I am the LORD, who exercises kindness, justice and righteousness on earth, for in these I delight," declares the LORD. (Jer 9:24)

2 (3:28) **Faith—Justification**: faith justifies a man without the works of the law. This is of extreme importance. A man is justified by faith and not by the deeds of the law. Boasting shows this. Who is to be praised and set up as the subject of glory? Is man the one in whom to boast? Is man the one who is to be glorified? If man created himself and saved himself from sin and death by his own works and deeds, then he is the one to be glorified. But what man can do these things? Man did not make himself nor can man save himself. When we consider that man is corruptible, and that man can do nothing beyond this life, then boasting is excluded. Therefore man is not justified before God by the deeds of the law; he is justified by faith—by believing in God and His righteousness. (See note, *Justification*—Ro.4:1-3; DEEPER STUDY # 2—4:22; 5:1 for more discussion.)

Thought 1. Despite the great ability and all the marvelous achievements of man, man is still unable to control things morally, unable to live in love, joy, and peace with others. He is unable to control the shame and devastation of selfishness and greed, disease and accident, sin and death. Man's only hope is to come before God...

- not boasting and glorying in self, but bowing in all humility.
- believing in the law of faith: that God saves and justifies man by believing in the righteousness of Jesus Christ.

> Abram believed the LORD, and he credited it to him as righteousness. (Gen 15:6)
> Through him everyone who believes is justified from everything you could not be justified from by the law of Moses. (Acts 13:39)
> For we maintain that a man is justified by faith apart from observing the law. (Rom 3:28)
> Therefore, since we have been justified through faith, we have peace with God through our Lord Jesus Christ, (Rom 5:1)
> And that is what some of you were. But you were washed, you were sanctified, you were justified in the name of the Lord Jesus Christ and by the Spirit of our God. (1 Cor 6:11)
> So the law was put in charge to lead us to Christ that we might be justified by faith. (Gal 3:24)

3 (3:29-30) **God, Nature—Universal Father—Impartial**: faith reveals only one God who deals with all equally. (See note, *God, Nature*—Mk.12:29-31 for more discussion.)

1. God created everyone; therefore, He is the God of all. There is not one God of the Jew (religionist) and another God of the Gentile. There are not different gods of the races and nations of the world, not a different god of Africa and a different god of India, and a different god for Arabs, and a different god for Americans and on and on. Imagine the foolishness of such an idea! Yet how common the idea is! There is only one God who created the universe and only one God who is the God of all mankind.
   a. There is only one God who created all things: "One God, the Father from whom all things came and for whom we live" (1 Cor.8:6).
   b. There is only one God who has made all men alike: "From one man he made every nation of men" (Acts 17:26).
   c. There is only one God "in him we live and move and have our being" (Acts 17:28).

> And do not call anyone on earth 'father,' for you have one Father, and he is in heaven. (Mat 23:9)
> One God and Father of all, who is over all and through all and in all. (Eph 4:6)
> Moreover, we have all had human fathers who disciplined us and we respected them for it. How much more should we submit to the Father of our spirits and live! (Heb 12:9)
> Have we not all one Father? Did not one God create us? Why do we profane the covenant of our fathers by breaking faith with one another? (Mal 2:10)

2. God is the *only* God; therefore, all are justified in the *same* way—by faith. God does not play favorites and show partiality. God does not make it more difficult for some to be saved. God is God; that is, He is perfectly just and equitable in all His dealings.

   a. There "is [only] one God, who will justify the circumcised by faith and the uncircumcision through that same faith" (Ro.3:30).
   b. "There is [only] one God, and one Mediator between God and men, the man Christ Jesus" (1 Tim.2:5).

Then Peter began to speak: "I now realize how true it is that God does not show favoritism (Acts 10:34)

He made no distinction between us and them, for he purified their hearts by faith. (Acts 15:9)

For God does not show favoritism. (Rom 2:11)

For there is no difference between Jew and Gentile—the same Lord is Lord of all and richly blesses all who call on him, for, "Everyone who calls on the name of the Lord will be saved." (Rom 10:12-13)

The point is this. When a man trusts God to save him and to count him righteous in Christ, that man's faith proves...

- that God is, that there is only one true and living God.
- that God treats all men equally; that he, the sinner, is saved just like all other believers.

4 (3:31) **Faith—Law**: faith upholds and establishes the law. This means at least three things.

1. Jesus Christ established the law. Jesus was everything that God said a man should be. He was the ideal of all that God wants man to be. Therefore, Jesus fulfilled the law perfectly.

But there is something more. Jesus not only fulfilled the statutes of the law; He fulfilled the penalty of the law. He took the penalty and the punishment of man upon Himself and died for man. Man is thereby absolved from the penalty and punishment exacted by the law. Therefore, Jesus established the law by fulfilling both the statutes and penalty demanded by the law. (See DEEPER STUDY #2—Mt.5:17; DEEPER STUDY #2—Ro.8:3.)

"Do not think that I have come to abolish the Law or the Prophets; I have not come to abolish them but to fulfill them. (Mat 5:17)

For what the law was powerless to do in that it was weakened by the sinful nature, God did by sending his own Son in the likeness of sinful man to be a sin offering. And so he condemned sin in sinful man, (Rom 8:3)

Christ redeemed us from the curse of the law by becoming a curse for us, for it is written: "Cursed is everyone who is hung on a tree." (Gal 3:13)

2. The believer establishes the law when he admits he is a law breaker or a sinner. In so doing, he admits that the law is good. The law is good because it points out his sin (Ro.3:19-20; 5:20; 7:7; Gal.3:19). It makes him guilty and it leads him to confess his need for help outside of himself.

But the law is also good because it points man to Christ. It makes man cast himself upon Christ *for righteousness*. It forces him to believe in God and to honor God. Therefore, the believer's faith establishes the law.

What, then, was the purpose of the law? It was added because of transgressions until the Seed to whom the promise referred had come. The law was put into effect through angels by a mediator. (Gal 3:19)

But the Scripture declares that the whole world is a prisoner of sin, so that what was promised, being given through faith in Jesus Christ, might be given to those who believe. So the law was put in charge to lead us to Christ that we might be justified by faith. (Gal 3:22, 24)

Christ is the end of the law so that there may be righteousness for everyone who believes. That if you confess with your mouth, "Jesus is Lord," and believe in your heart that God raised him from the dead, you will be saved. For it is with your heart that you believe and are justified, and it is with your mouth that you confess and are saved. (Rom 10:4, 9-10)

3. The believer establishes the law (much more than a legalist) because in seeing what Christ has done for him, he is driven to please God. The believer sees Christ bearing the guilt and punishment for his crimes (sins), and then bows in love and adoration, and arises to work in appreciation for such amazing love. The believer tries to be good, not to earn or to win righteousness, but to serve God. He does not try to put God in debt for salvation, but he thanks God for righteousness, seeing that he owes God whatever service he can do. The genuine believer has come to know above all others that love is a much stronger force than fear.

For Christ's love compels us, because we are convinced that one died for all, and therefore all died. And he died for all, that those who live should no longer live for themselves but for him who died for them and was raised again. (2 Cor 5:14-15)
I have been crucified with Christ and I no longer live, but Christ lives in me. The life I live in the body, I live by faith in the Son of God, who loved me and gave himself for me. (Gal 2:20)
This is how we know what love is: Jesus Christ laid down his life for us. And we ought to lay down our lives for our brothers. (1 John 3:16)

	CHAPTER 4	his wages are not credited to him as a gift, but as an obligation.	**or laborer**
	C. Logic: The Evidence that Faith Alone Justifies a Man,_DS1_ **4:1-8**	5 However, to the man who does not work but trusts God who justifies the wicked, his faith is credited as righteousness.	a. Works mean obligation
			b. Believing in God results in righteousness
1 The logic of Abraham's justification	What then shall we say that Abraham, our forefather, discovered in this matter?	6 David says the same thing when he speaks of the blessedness of the man to whom God credits righteousness apart from works:	
a. He was not justified by works (works cannot qualify one to boast or glory before God)	2 If, in fact, Abraham was justified by works, he had something to boast about—but not before God.	7 "Blessed are they whose transgressions are forgiven, whose sins are covered.	**3 The logic of David's blessed man**
	3 What does the Scripture say? "Abraham believed God, and it was credited to him as righteousness."	8 Blessed is the man whose sin the Lord will never count against him."	a. The blessed man is the man who is counted righteous without works
b. He was justified by believing God			b. The blessed man is the man whose sins are forgiven & covered
2 The logic of the worker	4 Now when a man works,		c. The blessed man is the man whose sins are not counted against him

DIVISION III

FAITH AND JUSTIFICATION: THE WAY FOR THE WORLD TO BE RIGHT WITH GOD, 3:21-5:21

C. Logic: The Evidence that Faith Alone Justifies a Man, 4:1-8

DEEPER STUDY # 1
(4:1-25) **Abraham—Jews, the Seed or Offspring—Justification—Righteousness—New Creation**: Abraham held a unique position in the Jewish nation, for he was the founder of the nation. He was the man whom God had challenged to be a witness to the other nations of the world—a witness to the only living and true God. God had appeared to Abraham and challenged him to leave his home, his friends, his employment, and his country. God made two great promises if Abraham would follow God unquestionably: Abraham would become the father of a new nation, and all nations of the earth would be blessed by his seed or offspring (Gen.12:1-5; 13:14-17; 15:1-7; 17:1-8, 15-19; 22:15-18; 26:2-5, 24; 28:13-15; 35:9-12). (See DEEPER STUDY # 1—Jn.4:22.)

Scripture says Abraham did as God requested. He went out not knowing where he went (Heb.11:8). He completely and unquestionably trusted God and took God at His word.

Now note: it was not Abraham's keeping of the law that pleased God. In fact, the law had not yet been given (Gal.3:17). What pleased God and what caused God to justify Abraham was Abraham doing as God had said. Abraham simply _believed_ the promise of God that God would give him a new life—_in_ a new nation—_with_ a new people. (See DEEPER STUDY # 1—Gal.3:8, 16; notes—Heb.11:8-10; 11:13-16; 11:17-19.)

Note several things.
1. Abraham and his "seed" or "offspring" were the only ones to whom God gave the promises. This is emphatically stated (Ro.4:13-25; Gal.3:6-16, 26, 29).
2. Only a promise was given to Abraham (Ro.4:13-21; Gal.3:14, 18-21, 29). No other information whatsoever was given. God did not identify the country nor tell Abraham where he was to go. Neither did God tell Abraham when his wife (Sarah) would bear the seed (the male child) from whom the promised nation would be born. God made a simple promise, and all Abraham had to go on was that simple promise, that is, the sheer Word of God.
3. Only one condition was attached to the promise. Abraham had to believe God. No works whatsoever were involved.

4. Abraham did believe God (Gen.12:4-5; Ro.4:3, 11-22; Gal.3:6; Heb.11:8f).
5. Abraham was _counted righteous_ because he believed God (Ro.4:3-5, 9-13, 19-22; Gal.3:6; cp. Gen.15:6). God did not count him righteous because of who he was or what he had done. He simply believed God. Therefore, God took his faith and _counted_ his faith as righteousness (see note—Ro.4:1-3; DEEPER STUDY # 2—4:22; note—5:1).
6. The proof that Abraham really believed God was that he did what God had said. His faith _preceded_ his obedience. He believed God and then he obeyed God. If he had not believed God, he would not have left his home or his employment. He would not have left his familiar surroundings and meaningful relationships and personal attachments. The fact that he did as God asked was evidence that he believed the promise of God.
7. The man who believes God is the man who receives the promises of God (Ro.4:5-12, 16-17, 23-25; Gal.3:7-9, 14, 22, 26, 29). Paul argues that neither heritage nor nationality, neither merit nor works, neither the law nor the rules of the law have anything to do with the promises of God (Gal.3:6-7). The true children of Abraham are those who believe God—any person of any nation. In fact, God's promise that a nation would be born to Abraham and "his seed (offspring)" was the promise of an eternal nation. This eternal nation is to be of another world, of another dimension of being: the spiritual dimension, a dimension just as real as the physical dimension. But it is to have one distinction: every citizen is to be a believer—one who has believed God and His Word. This is exactly what this passage is saying: "They who believe are the children of Abraham, the children of God's promise. They are to be blessed along with faithful Abraham. They are to be the citizens of God's Kingdom, of 'the new heavens and the new earth.'" (Cp. Heb.11:8-18; 2 Pt.3:10-14.)

(4:1-8) **Introduction**: most people think they become acceptable to God by doing the best they can. Most actually believe they secure God's approval by being reasonably good: by being a respectable and upright citizen and by occasionally helping others who are less fortunate. But note a startling fact: a man is not justified by works, but by faith. Logic proves the fact.

1. The logic of Abraham's justification (v.1-3).
2. The logic of the worker or laborer (v.4-5).
3. The logic of David's "blessed man" (v.6-8).

1

(4:1-3) **Abraham—Righteousness—Justification—Works vs. Faith**: the logic of Abraham's justification. A person can look at Abraham's life and logically see that a man is not justified by works but by faith.

1. Abraham was not justified by works, for works *cannot qualify* a person to glory before God. Now note this: if Abraham had been justified by works...

- he *would be* qualified to boast or glory before men.
- but he *would not be* qualified to boast or glory before God.

Think about it—the logic, the clarity of the matter. No man is ever qualified to glory before God. No act or work or combination of acts and works could ever elevate man to such a height that he could glory or become qualified before God.

2. Abraham was justified by believing God. What happened was this. Abraham believed God, and God took Abraham's belief and counted his belief as righteousness. It was not Abraham's works, but his faith that God took and counted as righteousness. It was all an act of God; therefore, all glory belonged to God, not to Abraham. Man is saved by faith; that is, God takes a man's faith and counts that man's faith as righteousness. Such has to be the case.

⇒ God is perfect; He is perfectly righteous. No man can achieve perfection; therefore, no man can live in the presence of God.

⇒ However, God is love. So what God does is take a person's faith (any person's faith who is truly sincere) and counts that faith as righteousness, as perfection. Therefore, a man is able to live in God's presence by faith or justification.

> **Many will say to me on that day, 'Lord, Lord, did we not prophesy in your name, and in your name drive out demons and perform many miracles?' Then I will tell them plainly, 'I never knew you. Away from me, you evildoers!' (Mat 7:22-23)**

> **Therefore no one will be declared righteous in his sight by observing the law; rather, through the law we become conscious of sin. (Rom 3:20)**

> **Know that a man is not justified by observing the law, but by faith in Jesus Christ. So we, too, have put our faith in Christ Jesus that we may be justified by faith in Christ and not by observing the law, because by observing the law no one will be justified. (Gal 2:16)**

> **For it is by grace you have been saved, through faith—and this not from yourselves, it is the gift of God—not by works, so that no one can boast. (Eph 2:8-9)**

> **But when the kindness and love of God our Savior appeared, he saved us, not because of righteous things we had done, but because of his mercy. He saved us through the washing of rebirth and renewal by the Holy Spirit, (Titus 3:4-5)**

Thought 1. Why does God justify a man through faith? There are at least two reasons.

First, God loves everyone with a perfect love. God wants everyone to live with Him in a *perfect state of being* throughout all eternity. God is perfect; therefore, He alone can provide the only perfect way for man to live in His presence. Because God is love, He has reached out for man by providing that perfect way through Jesus Christ, His Son.

> **"For God so loved the world that he gave his one and only Son, that whoever believes in him shall not perish but have eternal life. For God did not send his Son into the world to condemn the world, but to save the world through him. (John 3:16-17)**

> **"I tell you the truth, whoever hears my word and believes him who sent me has eternal life and will not be condemned; he has crossed over from death to life. (John 5:24)**

> **But God demonstrates his own love for us in this: While we were still sinners, Christ died for us. (Rom 5:8)**

> **For Christ died for sins once for all, the righteous for the unrighteous, to bring you to God. He was put to death in the body but made alive by the Spirit, (1 Pet 3:18)**

Second, God loves His Son with a perfect love. Any person who honors God's Son by believing in Him is accepted by God. That is, God takes that person's belief and counts it as righteousness. The person receives the right to live in God's presence in a *perfect state of being*. "We were also chosen...*that we might be*" (a state of *being* that is to be eternally lived to the praise of God's glory—Eph.1:11-12).

> **While he was still speaking, a bright cloud enveloped them, and a voice from the cloud said, "This is my Son, whom I love; with him I am well pleased. Listen to him!" (Mat 17:5)**

> **The reason my Father loves me is that I lay down my life—only to take it up again. (John 10:17)**

> **"As the Father has loved me, so have I loved you. Now remain in my love. (John 15:9)**

> **No, the Father himself loves you because you have loved me and have believed that I came from God. (John 16:27)**

> **I in them and you in me. May they be brought to complete unity to let the world know that you sent me and have loved them even as you have loved me. (John 17:23)**

> **I have made you known to them, and will continue to make you known in order that the love you have for me may be in them and that I myself may be in them." (John 17:26)**

> **To the praise of his glorious grace, which he has freely given us in the One he loves. (Eph 1:6)**

For he has rescued us from the dominion of darkness and brought us into the kingdom of the Son he loves, (Col 1:13)

2 (4:4-5) **Works—Righteousness**: the logic of the worker or laborer. A person can look at the day to day laborer and logically see that a man is not justified by works but by faith.

1. Works necessitate *debt or "an obligation."* When a man works, someone owes him something. If a man could work for righteousness, that is, work so that God would owe him righteousness, then God would owe man. But God, being God, is completely self-sufficient; therefore, He cannot be put in debt to any man. He cannot *be made or forced* to do anything.

2. Believing in God results in righteousness. It is the "wicked" who believe who are counted righteous (cp. Ro.5:6). This is because the man who admits he is wicked is the man who rejects self, sensing his need for *godly help* in spiritual matters. He is ready to give himself up and honor and glorify God alone. Therefore, he centers and wraps his whole life around God, depending solely upon God for righteousness.

> **Thought 1.** God can never turn away from a person who senses and confesses his ungodliness and who wishes to recognize and glorify God. God is love, and God's love is bound to be moved by so humble an act and faith.

> **What does the Scripture say? "Abraham believed God, and it was credited to him as righteousness." (Rom 4:3)**
> **Therefore, since we have been justified through faith, we have peace with God through our Lord Jesus Christ, (Rom 5:1) Consider Abraham: "He believed God, and it was credited to him as righteousness." (Gal 3:6)**
> **And be found in him, not having a righteousness of my own that comes from the law, but that which is through faith in Christ—the righteousness that comes from God and is by faith. (Phil 3:9)**

The converse teaching of Scripture needs to be remembered: the man who does not admit he is wicked, who does not reject self and sense the need for godly help is the man declared to be self-sufficient and self-righteous. Therefore, he is pronounced unjustified, not so much because God rejects him as the fact that he has already rejected God.

> **Whoever believes in him is not condemned, but whoever does not believe stands condemned already because he has not believed in the name of God's one and only Son. (John 3:18)**
> **I told you that you would die in your sins; if you do not believe that I am the one I claim to be, you will indeed die in your sins." (John 8:24)**
> **See to it, brothers, that none of you has a sinful, unbelieving heart that turns away from the living God. (Heb 3:12)**
> **Many a man claims to have unfailing love, but a faithful man who can find? (Prov 20:6; cp.. Mt.7:21)**

Those who are pure in their own eyes and yet are not cleansed of their filth; (Prov 30:12)

3 (4:6-8) **Forgiveness—Impute—Credit**: the logic of David's *blessed man*. A person can look at prophecy, at the man described by David and see clearly that justification is not by works but by faith (cp. Ps.32:1-2). Note who the blessed man is.

1. The blessed man is the man who is *counted* righteous without works. Note the word "credit" (logizomai). It means to reckon, to count, to put to one's account, to credit, to deposit. Just think for a moment. If God credits and counts a man righteous "apart from works," then we know something: *Man is not justified by works, but by faith.* (See DEEPER STUDY # 1, *Reckon*—Ro.6:11 for more discussion.)

Pure logic tells us this. Therefore, the blessed man is the man who has righteousness *credited, imputed, counted* to him...

- not because of his works,
- but because he believes God, and God loves him so much that He takes the man's belief and counts it as righteousness.

2. The blessed man is the man whose sins are forgiven and covered. Think for a moment. Lawlessness (sin) exists despite all the works and efforts of men to eliminate it. No matter how hard men try, lawlessness still exists. If lawlessness is to be handled, it has to be handled by God and God alone. He simply has to forgive man's lawlessness (sin).

Now note: logic tells us that if God loves that much, loves enough to simply forgive men for sin, then justification is not by law but by faith.

3. The blessed man is the man whose sins are not imputed, not credited nor counted against him. (See this note, *Credit*—pt.1). Note: it is not the acts of men, but the act of God that justifies men and does not count sin against them. A man cannot justify himself before God. No man can free himself from sin and force God to accept him—not by his own hand. Justification—complete deliverance from sin and condemnation—comes from God and from God alone, not from some act of man. Therefore, logic tells us that it is not works that justifies a man, but faith.

> **Surely it was for my benefit that I suffered such anguish. In your love you kept me from the pit of destruction; you have put all my sins behind your back. (Isa 38:17)**
> **"I, even I, am he who blots out your transgressions, for my own sake, and remembers your sins no more. (Isa 43:25)**
> **I have swept away your offenses like a cloud, your sins like the morning mist. Return to me, for I have redeemed you." (Isa 44:22)**
> **Let the wicked forsake his way and the evil man his thoughts. Let him turn to the LORD, and he will have mercy on him, and to our God, for he will freely pardon. (Isa 55:7)**
> **Yet he was merciful; he forgave their iniquities and did not destroy them. Time after time he restrained his anger and did not stir up his full wrath. (Psa 78:38)**

You forgave the iniquity of your people and covered all their sins. Selah (Psa 85:2)

Who forgives all your sins and heals all your diseases, (Psa 103:3)

As far as the east is from the west, so far has he removed our transgressions from us. (Psa 103:12)

But with you there is forgiveness; therefore you are feared. (Psa 130:4)

Who is a God like you, who pardons sin and forgives the transgression of the remnant of his inheritance? You do not stay angry forever but delight to show mercy. (Micah 7:18)

For what I received I passed on to you as of first importance : that Christ died for our sins according to the Scriptures, (1 Cor 15:3)

Who gave himself for our sins to rescue us from the present evil age, according to the will of our God and Father, (Gal 1:4)

In him we have redemption through his blood, the forgiveness of sins, in accordance with the riches of God's grace (Eph 1:7)

He himself bore our sins in his body on the tree, so that we might die to sins and live for righteousness; by his wounds you have been healed. (1 Pet 2:24)

If we confess our sins, he is faithful and just and will forgive us our sins and purify us from all unrighteousness. (1 John 1:9)

And from Jesus Christ, who is the faithful witness, the firstborn from the dead, and the ruler of the kings of the earth. To him who loves us and has freed us from our sins by his blood, (Rev 1:5)

	D. Rituals, Rules, & Ordinances: The Wrong Way for a Man to Seek Justification, 4:9-12	11 And he received the sign of circumcision, a seal of the righteousness that he had by faith while he was still uncircumcised. So then, he is the father of all who believe but have not been circumcised, in order that righteousness might be credited to them.	4 Abraham received circumcision as a sign or symbol only 5 Abraham was chosen by God for a twofold purpose a. To be the "father" of all believers: Regardless of ritual & ordinance
1 Who receives the blessing of forgiveness? a. The religious only? b. The non-religious also? 2 Abraham was counted righteous when he believed 3 Abraham was counted righteous before the ritual, that is, before circumcision	9 Is this blessedness only for the circumcised, or also for the uncircumcised? We have been saying that Abraham's faith was credited to him as righteousness. 10 Under what circumstances was it credited? Was it after he was circumcised, or before? It was not after, but before!	12 And he is also the father of the circumcised who not only are circumcised but who also walk in the footsteps of the faith that our father Abraham had before he was circumcised.	b. To be the "father" of the circumcised, the religious: Those who follow "in the steps of his faith"

DIVISION III

FAITH AND JUSTIFICATION: THE WAY FOR THE WORLD TO BE RIGHT WITH GOD, 3:21-5:21

D. Rituals, Rules, and Ordinances: The Wrong Way for a Man to Seek Justification, 4:9-12

(4:9-12) **Introduction—Religionists**: most people are religious in the sense that they keep some religious ordinances, rituals, and rules. This is both good and bad: good in the sense that rituals cause a person to think about some higher being, and bad in the sense that rituals are usually thought to be the way a person becomes acceptable to God. The present passage is as clear as can be: ritual is the wrong way for a man to seek acceptance and justification with God.

1. Who receives the blessing of forgiveness (v.9)?
2. Abraham was counted righteous when he believed (v.9).
3. Abraham was counted righteous before circumcision, that is, before the ritual (v.10).
4. Abraham received circumcision as a sign or symbol only (v.11).
5. Abraham was chosen by God for a twofold purpose (v.11-12).

1 (4:9) **Evangelism—Gospel—Forgiveness—Religion**: who receives the blessing of forgiveness? The word "blessedness" or "blessing" refers back to the *blessed man* just discussed (Ro.4:6-8). The blessed man is the man who is justified by faith...

- who is counted righteous without works.
- whose sins are forgiven and covered.
- whose sins are not counted against him.

Such a man is greatly blessed, blessed beyond imagination. But note a critical question. Is the blessing of forgiveness intended...

- for the circumcised only, or for the uncircumcised also?
- for the Jew only, or for the non-Jew (Gentile) also?
- for the religious only, or for the non-religious also?
- for the baptized only, or for the unbaptized also?
- for the saved only, or for the unsaved also?
- for the church member only, or for the unchurched also?
- for the interested only, or for the disinterested also?

Is the blessing of forgiveness—of being justified by faith alone—for only a few people or for all people everywhere? Abraham's experience illustrates the truth for us.

2 (4:9) **Reckoned—Abraham**: Abraham was counted righteous *when he believed*. His *faith* was "credited" for righteousness. The word "credited" (elogisthe) means to count, to reckon, to deposit, to put to one's account, to impute. Abraham's faith was *counted* for righteousness or *credited* as righteousness (see notes, *Justification*—Ro.4:1-3; 4:6-8; DEEPER STUDY #1,2—4:22; 5:1 for more discussion).

Note that Abraham was justified or counted righteous *by faith*; he was not justified...

- by being religious.
- by performing good deeds.
- by doing some good work.
- by being good and virtuous.
- by submitting to a ritual.
- by joining some body of believers.

> **Consider Abraham: "He believed God, and it was credited to him as righteousness." (Gal 3:6)**
> **What does the Scripture say? "Abraham believed God, and it was credited to him as righteousness." (Rom 4:3)**
> **But when the kindness and love of God our Savior appeared, he saved us, not because of righteous things we had done, but because of his mercy. He saved us through the washing of rebirth and renewal by the Holy Spirit, (Titus 3:4-5)**
> **God also testified to it by signs, wonders and various miracles, and gifts of the Holy Spirit distributed according to his will. (Heb 2:4)**

3 (4:10) **Ritual—Justification**: Abraham was counted righteous before the ritual, that is, before circumcision. This is a crucial point and it is clearly seen. Abraham made his decision to follow God at least fourteen years before he was circumcised. The story of Abraham believing the promises of God is a dramatic picture (cp. Gen.15:1-6, esp 5-6). Scripture clearly says, "Abram believed the Lord, and he credited it to him as righteousness" (Gen.15:6). But the story of his circumcision is two chapters and fourteen years later (Gen.17:9f). He was counted righteous long before he underwent any ritual. His righteousness—his being accepted by God—did not depend upon a ritual; it depended upon his faith and his faith alone. God did not count Abraham righteous because of circumcision, not because of...

- a ritual
- a ceremony
- an ordinance
- a good work
- a good deed
- a religious life
- a moral life

God accepted Abraham and counted him righteous because he believed God and His promises.

4 (4:11) **Circumcision—Baptism—Ritual—Faith vs. Works:** Abraham received circumcision as a sign or symbol only. Circumcision was not the road into God's presence; it was not what made Abraham acceptable to God. Circumcision *did not confer* righteousness on him; it only confirmed that he was righteous. Circumcision did not convey righteousness on him; it only bore testimony that he was righteous.

Note that circumcision was both a sign and a seal. (See note, *Circumcision*—Ph.3:3 for more discussion.) Circumcision was...

- a sign of celebration: it was a picture of the joy that the believer experienced in being counted righteous by God.
- a sign of witness: the believer was testifying that he now believed and trusted God.
- a sign of a changed life and a separated life: the believer was proclaiming that he was going to live for God, to live a righteous and pure life that was wholly separated to God.
- a sign of identification: the believer was declaring that he was now joining and becoming one of God's people.
- a sign pointing toward Christ's baptism.

Circumcision was a seal in that it stamped God's justification upon Abraham's mind. Abraham had believed God, and God had counted his faith as righteousness. Circumcision was given as a seal or a stamp upon his body to remind him that God had counted him righteous through belief. Circumcision was a seal in that it...

- confirmed
- assured
- substantiated
- validated
- authenticated
- strengthened
- verified

...what God had done for Abraham. Now note. The Bible never says that rites, rituals, or ordinances bestow anything on anyone. They are merely signs of something that has already taken place. They are merely *shadows*, not the *substance* (Col.2:16-17).

This is not to take away from the importance of rites and rituals. They are extremely important, for they are the *signs and seals* of the Christian believer's faith. To neglect or to reject a rite given by God is to be disobedient, and to be disobedient is a clear sign that one was never sincere in the first place. A person who believes, who truly trusts God, is ready to *obey* God, to follow Him even in the rites, rituals, and ordinances of the church. We must always remember that Abraham was not saved by the ritual

of circumcision, for circumcision had not yet been given by God as a sign.

⇒ But Abraham was *immediately circumcised* after God established circumcision as the sign of "righteousness by faith."

Very simply said, if circumcision had existed when Abraham first believed God, then Abraham would have been circumcised immediately. He would have obeyed God. How do we know this? Because Abraham truly believed God, and when a man believes God, he immediately begins to do what God says.

Thought 1. Circumcision and all other rituals are a matter of the heart, not a matter of being spiritually cleansed by physical and material substances.

> **A man is not a Jew if he is only one outwardly, nor is circumcision merely outward and physical. No, a man is a Jew if he is one inwardly; and circumcision is circumcision of the heart, by the Spirit, not by the written code. Such a man's praise is not from men, but from God. (Rom 2:28-29)**
>
> **In him [Christ] you were also circumcised, in the putting off of the sinful nature, not with a circumcision done by the hands of men but with the circumcision [operation, cutting away] done by Christ, (Col 2:11)**
>
> **Circumcise your hearts, therefore, and do not be stiff-necked any longer. (Deu 10:16)**
>
> **The LORD your God will circumcise your hearts and the hearts of your descendants, so that you may love him with all your heart and with all your soul, and live. (Deu 30:6)**

Thought 2. This is a strong message on baptism for New Testament believers. A true believer should be baptized immediately upon believing. Baptism should be the first step of obedience in the believer's new life in Christ. (See notes, *Baptism*—Lk.3:21; DEEPER STUDY # 1—Acts 2:38 for more discussion.)

> **Jesus replied, "Let it be so now; it is proper for us to do this to fulfill all righteousness." Then John consented. (Mat 3:15)**
>
> **Whoever believes and is baptized will be saved, but whoever does not believe will be condemned. (Mark 16:16)**
>
> **Peter replied, "Repent and be baptized, every one of you, in the name of Jesus Christ for the forgiveness of your sins. And you will receive the gift of the Holy Spirit. (Acts 2:38)**
>
> **Having been buried with him in baptism and raised with him through your faith in the power of God, who raised him from the dead. (Col 2:12)**

5 (4:11-12) **Abraham—Ritual—Salvation—Faith vs. Works:** Abraham was chosen by God for a twofold purpose. Before looking at the purposes, note that Abraham is said to have a unique relationship to the world. He is seen not as a mere private individual, but as a public man, a representative man of the human race, a pivotal figure in human history. He is seen as the "father" of all who believe God, as the head of the household of faith. God chose Abraham for two specific purposes.

1. Abraham was chosen that he might be the "father" of all believers regardless of ritual and ordinance. Abraham was chosen by God to be the father of faith to all—all the ungodly and heathen of the world—who repent and believe Jesus Christ to be their Lord and Savior. No matter how uncircumcised, unbaptized, irreligious, immoral and unclean a person is, he has a father in the faith, a father to follow. Abraham is...

- the pattern
- the picture
- the example
- the standard
- the father

...of faith to all the lost of the world. A person...

- does not have to begin to go to church before God will save him.
- does not have to get religious before God will accept him.
- does not have to be baptized or *ritualized* before God will forgive his sins.

What he *has to do* is believe God and believe God's promises. When he bows in humble faith and believes, two things happen:

⇒ immediately God counts his faith as righteousness.
⇒ immediately he arises and is baptized and begins to keep all the commandments and rituals and ordinances of God.

> Jesus answered them, "It is not the healthy who need a doctor, but the sick. I have not come to call the righteous, but sinners to repentance." (Luke 5:31-32)
> For the Son of Man came to seek and to save what was lost." (Luke 19:10)
> For all have sinned and fall short of the glory of God, and are justified freely by his grace through the redemption that came by Christ Jesus. (Rom 3:23-24)

2. Abraham was chosen that he might be the "father" of the circumcised, of the religious who "follow in the footsteps of Abraham's faith." Note: it is not being...

- circumcised
- baptized
- moral
- ritualized
- religious
- good and virtuous

...that justifies a religious person. It is "walking in the steps" of Abraham's faith that causes God to accept the religious person.

The religionist cannot earn, merit, or work his way into God's presence and righteousness. He can only trust God for the righteousness of Jesus Christ (see note and DEEPER STUDY #2—Ro.3:24; note—3:25; DEEPER STUDY #2—4:22; 5:1 for more discussion).

> Many will say to me on that day, 'Lord, Lord, did we not prophesy in your name, and in your name drive out demons and perform many miracles?' Then I will tell them plainly, 'I never knew you. Away from me, you evildoers!' (Mat 7:22-23)
> Therefore no one will be declared righteous in his sight by observing the law; rather, through the law we become conscious of sin. (Rom 3:20)
> For I can testify about them that they are zealous for God, but their zeal is not based on knowledge. Since they did not know the righteousness that comes from God and sought to establish their own, they did not submit to God's righteousness. Christ is the end of the law so that there may be righteousness for everyone who believes. (Rom 10:2-4)
> For it is with your heart that you believe and are justified, and it is with your mouth that you confess and are saved. (Rom 10:10)
> Know that a man is not justified by observing the law, but by faith in Jesus Christ. So we, too, have put our faith in Christ Jesus that we may be justified by faith in Christ and not by observing the law, because by observing the law no one will be justified. (Gal 2:16)
> For it is by grace you have been saved, through faith—and this not from yourselves, it is the gift of God—not by works, so that no one can boast. (Eph 2:8-9)

		value and the promise is worthless,	a. Law voids faith & erases the hope of the promise
	E. Law: The Wrong Way for a Man to be Justified, 4:13-16	15 Because law brings wrath. And where there is no law there is no transgression.	b. Law brings wrath
			c. Law means transgression
1 The unmistakable statement: The promise is not through the law, but through faith	13 It was not through law that Abraham and his offspring received the promise that he would be heir of the world, but through the righteousness that comes by faith.	16 Therefore, the promise comes by faith, so that it may be by grace and may be guaranteed to all Abraham's offspring—not only to those who are of the law but also to those who are of the faith of Abraham. He is the father of us all.	**3 The argument for faith** a. Faith brings grace b. Faith makes the promise sure, guarantee the promise c. Faith assures the promise for everyone: It is available to all
2 The argument against the law	14 For if those who live by law are heirs, faith has no		

DIVISION III

FAITH AND JUSTIFICATION: THE WAY FOR THE WORLD TO BE RIGHT WITH GOD, 3:21-5:21

E. Law: The Wrong Way for a Man to be Justified, 4:13-16

(4:13-16) Introduction: a man is not justified by the law and its works. The law is the wrong way for a man to seek acceptance and justification by God.

1. The unmistakable statement: the promise is not through the law, but through faith (v.13).
2. The argument against the law (v.14-15).
3. The argument for faith (v.16).

1 (4:13) **Promise, The—Faith vs. Law—Righteousness—Reward**: the unmistakable statement—the promise of the inheritance is not through the law, but through faith. Note several things.

1. The promise involves inheriting the whole world. This is clear from several facts.
   a. Canaan was the *promised land*, a type of heaven and a type of the new heavens and earth God is to recreate for Abraham and his seed or offspring (the believer). (See note, *Promised Land*—Acts 7:2-8 for more discussion.)

   > It was not through law that Abraham and his offspring received the promise that he would be heir of the world, but through the righteousness that comes by faith. For if those who live by law are heirs, faith has no value and the promise is worthless, (Rom 4:13-14)
   > By faith Abraham, when called to go to a place he would later receive as his inheritance, obeyed and went, even though he did not know where he was going. By faith he made his home in the promised land like a stranger in a foreign country; he lived in tents, as did Isaac and Jacob, who were heirs with him of the same promise. For he was looking forward to the city with foundations, whose architect and builder is God. (Heb 11:8-10)
   > All these people were still living by faith when they died. They did not receive the things promised; they only saw them and welcomed them from a distance. And they admitted that they were aliens and strangers on earth. People who say such things show that they are looking for a country of their own. Instead, they were

   > longing for a better country—a heavenly one. Therefore God is not ashamed to be called their God, for he has prepared a city for them. (Heb 11:13, 14, 16)
   > But you have come to Mount Zion, to the heavenly Jerusalem, the city of the living God. You have come to thousands upon thousands of angels in joyful assembly, (Heb 12:22)
   > For here we do not have an enduring city, but we are looking for the city that is to come. (Heb 13:14)
   > But the day of the Lord will come like a thief. The heavens will disappear with a roar; the elements will be destroyed by fire, and the earth and everything in it will be laid bare. Since everything will be destroyed in this way, what kind of people ought you to be? You ought to live holy and godly lives as you look forward to the day of God and speed its coming. That day will bring about the destruction of the heavens by fire, and the elements will melt in the heat. But in keeping with his promise we are looking forward to a new heaven and a new earth, the home of righteousness. (2 Pet 3:10-13)
   > Then I saw a new heaven and a new earth, for the first heaven and the first earth had passed away, and there was no longer any sea. (Rev 21:1)

   b. Abraham was promised that he would be the "father" of many nations. He is said to be the father of all believers from all nations of the earth (v.11-12). He and his offspring (believers) are promised a new world when Christ returns.
   c. Christ is to inherit the world and be exalted as the Sovereign Majesty of the universe, ruling and reigning forever and ever.
   ⇒ Abraham and his offspring (believers) are said to be heirs of God and joint heirs with Christ.

   > The Spirit himself testifies with our spirit that we are God's children. Now if we are children, then we are heirs—

heirs of God and co-heirs with Christ, if indeed we share in his sufferings in order that we may also share in his glory. (Rom 8:16-17)

They shall all reign with Christ through all eternity. (See notes, *Reward*—Mt.19:28; Lk.16:10-12; Rev.14:13; 21:24-27.)

For the Son of Man is going to come in his Father's glory with his angels, and then he will reward each person according to what he has done. (Mat 16:27)
"When the Son of Man comes in his glory, and all the angels with him, he will sit on his throne in heavenly glory. All the nations will be gathered before him, and he will separate the people one from another as a shepherd separates the sheep from the goats. (Mat 25:31-32)
And he will reign over the house of Jacob forever; his kingdom will never end." (Luke 1:33)
For he must reign until he has put all his enemies under his feet. (1 Cor 15:25)
In the presence of God and of Christ Jesus, who will judge the living and the dead, and in view of his appearing and his kingdom, I give you this charge: (2 Tim 4:1)
Then I saw a new heaven and a new earth, for the first heaven and the first earth had passed away, and there was no longer any sea. I saw the Holy City, the new Jerusalem, coming down out of heaven from God, prepared as a bride beautifully dressed for her husband. And I heard a loud voice from the throne saying, "Now the dwelling of God is with men, and he will live with them. They will be his people, and God himself will be with them and be their God. He will wipe every tear from their eyes. There will be no more death or mourning or crying or pain, for the old order of things has passed away." He who was seated on the throne said, "I am making everything new!" Then he said, "Write this down, for these words are trustworthy and true." He said to me: "It is done. I am the Alpha and the Omega, the Beginning and the End. To him who is thirsty I will give to drink without cost from the spring of the water of life. He who overcomes will inherit all this, and I will be his God and he will be my son. (Rev 21:1-7)
Of the increase of his government and peace there will be no end. He will reign on David's throne and over his kingdom, establishing and upholding it with justice and righteousness from that time on and forever. The zeal of the LORD Almighty will accomplish this. (Isa 9:7)
See, a king will reign in righteousness and rulers will rule with justice. (Isa 32:1)
"The days are coming," declares the LORD, "when I will raise up to David a righteous Branch, a King who will reign wisely and do what is just and right in the land. (Jer 23:5)

He was given authority, glory and sovereign power; all peoples, nations and men of every language worshiped him. His dominion is an everlasting dominion that will not pass away, and his kingdom is one that will never be destroyed. (Dan 7:14)

2. The "seed" or "offspring" of Abraham refers to *all believers*. This is clear from the promise that is said to be "guaranteed to all Abraham's offspring" (v.16). Every true believer is an heir of the promise. If a man believes, he receives the most glorious promise: he will inherit the world.

Blessed are the meek, for they will inherit the earth. (Mat 5:5)
If you belong to Christ, then you are Abraham's seed, and heirs according to the promise. (Gal 3:29)

3. God does not give the promise through the law, but through the righteousness of faith.
   a. A man will not receive an inheritance in the *new world* because he...
   • tried to keep the law.
   • did some great works.
   • lived by good deeds.
   • was baptized and joined a church.
   • was moral and very religious.

   b. A man will receive an inheritance in the *new world* because he...
   • believed God for righteousness, and God took his belief and *counted* it for righteousness.

The point is clearly seen, and it is unmistakable:

What does the Scripture say? "Abraham believed God, and it was credited to him as righteousness." (Rom 4:3)
However, to the man who does not work but trusts God who justifies the wicked, his faith is credited as righteousness. (Rom 4:5)
It was not through law that Abraham and his offspring received the promise that he would be heir of the world, but through the righteousness that comes by faith. (Rom 4:13)

2 (4:14-15) **Law—Faith vs. the Law:** the argument against the law. The promise of the inheritance does not come through the law. Three facts about the law show this.

1. Law voids faith; it erases any hope of ever receiving the promise. The reason can be simply stated: law demands perfection; law insists that it be obeyed. Law cries out, "violate and break me and you become guilty and condemned and are to be punished."
No man can live perfectly righteous before God; no man can keep from coming short and breaking the law of God at some point. Therefore every man is a lawbreaker, imperfect and short of God's glory, and is to be condemned and punished.
   a. If the promise of God's inheritance is by law, then no man shall inherit the promise, for the promise is given only to the righteous; and no man is perfectly righteous. This, of course, means something. If the promise is by law, then no man has hope of ever receiving the promise, for he does not and cannot

keep the law. The law erases the promise, makes it of no effect or value whatsoever.

b. If the promise of God's inheritance is by law, then faith is voided and has absolutely nothing to do with securing the promise. A man would have to keep his mind and eyes, and most tragic of all, his heart upon the law, for it would be the law that would determine whether or not the man received the promise. Faith would not be entering the picture; it would be voided, irrelevant, having nothing to with receiving the promise.

> **Now we know that whatever the law says, it says to those who are under the law, so that every mouth may be silenced and the whole world held accountable to God. (Rom 3:19)**
> **For what the law was powerless to do in that it was weakened by the sinful nature, God did by sending his own Son in the likeness of sinful man to be a sin offering. And so he condemned sin in sinful man, (Rom 8:3)**
> **For through the law I died to the law so that I might live for God. (Gal 2:19)**
> **(For the law made nothing perfect), and a better hope is introduced, by which we draw near to God. (Heb 7:19)**

c. This point is often overlooked. If the promise of God's inheritance comes by the law, then receiving the promise would have nothing to do with faith, nothing to do with...
- trusting the love of God.
- learning and knowing the love of God.
- focusing one's mind and thoughts upon God.
- knowing God's Son, the Lord Jesus Christ.

If God accepted us and gave us the promise of inheritance because we kept the law, then we would have to focus our lives upon the law. Believing and loving God and knowing God's Son would have nothing to do with our salvation. The law would force us to seek God by keeping the law. Faith would have nothing to do with the promise. The law would void faith and make useless and ineffective the love of God and the Son of God.

> **We demolish arguments and every pretension that sets itself up against the knowledge of God, and we take captive every thought to make it obedient to Christ. (2 Cor 10:5)**
> **Finally, brothers, whatever is true, whatever is noble, whatever is right, whatever is pure, whatever is lovely, whatever is admirable—if anything is excellent or praiseworthy—think about such things. Whatever you have learned or received or heard from me, or seen in me—put it into practice. And the God of peace will be with you. (Phil 4:8-9)**

2. Law brings or works wrath in three terrible ways.
a. Law shouts out at a man, "Break me and you become guilty, condemned, and are to be punished." Such is antagonistic and stirs and aggravates anger and wrath. When God is seen as a legalistic Per-

son who hovers over us, watching every move we make, there is a tendency to view God as stringent, demanding, condemnatory, upset, angry, vengeful and full of wrath against us. Why? Because we fail and come short ever so often. Therefore if God is legalistic, then He is hovering over us, and not a single one of us is going to inherit the promise. We are guilty and to be judged, and we are not going to be rewarded with an inheritance. Therefore, law works wrath between God and man; it keeps a man from being acceptable to God and from ever receiving the promise of God.

b. Law works wrath in that it keeps a man tied up in knots, under pressure and tension, and in a strain. The man who works to do the law struggles to do the right thing and guards against doing the wrong thing. He fights to avoid all the evil he can, wondering and worrying if he is ever doing enough to be acceptable to God.

Such a life is not full of love and joy and peace. There is no sense of purpose, meaning, and significance, no sense of completeness and fulfillment. Such a life is filled with uneasiness and turmoil, uncertainty and insecurity. Such a life of legalism works wrath: it keeps tension between God and man and establishes and builds a strained and uneasy relationship.

c. Law works wrath in that it causes a man to focus his life upon the law and not upon God. His mind and attention and thoughts are...
- upon keeping the rules, not upon trusting God.
- upon watching where he steps, not upon drawing near God.
- upon avoiding errors, not upon learning the truth of God.
- upon observing certain rituals, not upon fellowshipping with God.
- upon practicing religion, not upon worshipping God.

> **I found that the very commandment that was intended to bring life actually brought death. For sin, seizing the opportunity afforded by the commandment, deceived me, and through the commandment put me to death. (Rom 7:10-11)**
> **All who rely on observing the law are under a curse, for it is written: "Cursed is everyone who does not continue to do everything written in the Book of the Law." (Gal 3:10)**
> **The law is not based on faith; on the contrary, "The man who does these things will live by them." (Gal 3:12)**
> **You who are trying to be justified by law have been alienated from Christ; you have fallen away from grace. (Gal 5:4)**

3. Law means transgression. There are three reasons for this.
a. If no law exists, there is no law to break; therefore, there is no transgression. But if there is a law, then breaking the law begins to exist; transgression becomes a reality, a living fact. Where there is no law, there is no transgression; where there is law, there is transgression. The point is this: the man who seeks God's acceptance by keeping the law lives in a world of transgression,

of breaking the law and coming short of God's glory. The law means transgression, that a man fails and comes short of God's acceptance; therefore, it means that the legalist is guilty and condemned and is not to receive the promise of God.

b. When a law exists, there is an urge within man to stretch it to its limits and to break it. This is one of the paradoxes of human nature. Man has that within himself, an *unregulated urge*...
- not to be regulated
- not to be ordered around
- not to be restricted
- not to be governed
- not to be ruled
- to seek his own desires
- to do as he pleases
- to fill his fleshly passions
- to fulfill his urges
- to see, have, hold, and get more

When a law exists, it *tells* a man he can go this far and no farther. He must not go beyond this limit or he becomes a lawbreaker, a transgressor (cp. a speed sign). The law actually pulls a man to go that far. It is within his nature to go to the limit, to do as much as he can. The urge within his nature even stirs him to stretch the law and to go beyond its limits.
⇒ The grass on the other side looks greener.
⇒ The melon on the other side of the fence is juicier.
⇒ The stolen fruits are sweeter.
⇒ The forbidden is more appealing.
⇒ The unknown is more exciting.

When law exists, there is transgression. Every man becomes guilty and is to be condemned and punished, not rewarded with the promise.

> **For when we were controlled by the sinful nature, the sinful passions aroused by the law were at work in our bodies, so that we bore fruit for death. (Rom 7:5)**
> **But sin, seizing the opportunity afforded by the commandment, produced in me every kind of covetous desire. For apart from law, sin is dead. (Rom 7:8)**

c. When a law exists, it becomes an accuser, an antagonist. It shouts, "Break me and you become a law-breaker and are to be condemned and punished." Now note: the law has no power to keep a person from transgressing; it can only shout: "Transgression!" The law is...
- not a power to save, but a rule to control and condemn.
- not a savior, but a judge.

This is the very problem with the law.
⇒ It can only accuse; it cannot deliver.
⇒ It can only point out sin; it cannot save from sin.
⇒ It can only show a man where he failed; it cannot show him how to keep from failing.
⇒ It can only condemn; it has no power to free.

The man who tries to live by law is left hopeless and helpless, for he transgresses and becomes a law-breaker. He is to be condemned, never receiving the inheritance of God's promise.

> **Therefore no one will be declared righteous in his sight by observing the law; rather, through the law we become conscious of sin. (Rom 3:20)**
> **The law was added so that the trespass might increase. But where sin increased, grace increased all the more, (Rom 5:20)**
> **What shall we say, then? Is the law sin? Certainly not! Indeed I would not have known what sin was except through the law. For I would not have known what coveting really was if the law had not said, "Do not covet." (Rom 7:7)**
> **What, then, was the purpose of the law? It was added because of transgressions until the Seed to whom the promise referred had come. The law was put into effect through angels by a mediator. (Gal 3:19)**
> **So the law was put in charge to lead us to Christ that we might be justified by faith. (Gal 3:24)**
> **We also know that law is made not for the righteous but for lawbreakers and rebels, the ungodly and sinful, the unholy and irreligious; for those who kill their fathers or mothers, for murderers, (1 Tim 1:9)**

3 (4:16) **Faith—Promise—Grace:** the argument for faith. The promise of the inheritance comes through faith. Three facts about faith show this.

1. Faith brings grace. (See DEEPER STUDY # 1, *Grace*—Tit.2:11-15 for more discussion.) Grace (charis) means a gift, a free gift, a gift given without expecting anything in return. It means favor, approval, acceptance, goodwill, assistance, help, kindness—all freely given and given without expecting anything in return.

Picture the scene of a man broken over his sin. He may be a mild sinner or the worst sinner on earth, yet he comes to God. He...
- falls to his knees.
- confesses his sin.
- confesses his inadequacy to save himself.
- cries for God to have mercy and to forgive his sin.
- thanks God that He does forgive sin.
- praises God for answering his prayer and forgiving his sin.

Now, who is the *Savior*, the *Deliverer*, the *Subject* who deserves the praise and the honor and the glory? The answer is obvious: God. God is the center of the picture. This is the very reason salvation and all its promises are by grace through faith. Grace puts God in the center. And when a man makes God the center of his life, casting himself completely upon God and putting all his faith and trust in God, God is bound to hear and answer the man. Why? Because the man is honoring God completely, and the man who honors God is always acceptable and heard by God.

Now note: when a man *really believes* God, his faith brings the grace of God to him. It causes him to focus upon God, to center his life upon the love of God, to see the presence of God, to secure the fellowship and companionship of God, to know the love, joy, peace, care and concern of God. Simply stated, it causes a man to seek a personal relationship with God, a relationship of trust and dependence. Such is the life of grace, the grace that is given to man by faith. It is faith that honors and praises and glorifies God, and because it does, it brings the grace of God to man.

> Not to us, O LORD, not to us but to your name be the glory, because of your love and faithfulness. (Psa 115:1)
> No! We believe it is through the grace of our Lord Jesus that we are saved, just as they are." (Acts 15:11)
> And are justified freely by his grace through the redemption that came by Christ Jesus. (Rom 3:24)
> For it is by grace you have been saved, through faith—and this not from yourselves, it is the gift of God—not by works, so that no one can boast. (Eph 2:8-9; Cp. Ro. 3:24; 5:15; 11:6; Eph. 2:4-10)
> For the grace of God that brings salvation has appeared to all men. (Titus 2:11)

2. Faith makes the promise sure, guarantees the promise. This is seen in the above point. When God is honored and made the center and focus of one's life and trust, that person can rest assured God will accept him and give him the promise of the inheritance. That man will inherit the earth.

> So that, having been justified by his grace, we might become heirs having the hope of eternal life. (Titus 3:7)

3. Faith assures that the promise is for everyone, that it is available to all. The promise is not given to an exclusive club of people, to an exclusive nation or race or class of people. The promise is given to all, to every person on earth. If the promise was by law, then it would be only for those who have the law and are able to keep the law. What then would happen to the heathen who do not have the law and to the handicapped who are unable to do some of the things the law commands? They could never be saved if the promise came by the law. However, when the promise is given by the grace of God through faith, no man is exempt from the inheritance. Every man can be saved and inherit the promise of eternal life in the new heavens and earth, for every man can believe and trust God (the very thing that even a human father wants of his children).

> Heaven and earth will pass away, but my words will never pass away. (Luke 21:33)
> It was not through law that Abraham and his offspring received the promise that he would be heir of the world, but through the righteousness that comes by faith. (Rom 4:13)
> But because of his great love for us, God, who is rich in mercy, made us alive with Christ even when we were dead in transgressions—it is by grace you have been saved. And God raised us up with Christ and seated us with him in the heavenly realms in Christ Jesus, in order that in the coming ages he might show the incomparable riches of his grace, expressed in his kindness to us in Christ Jesus. (Eph 2:4-7)
> For the grace of God that brings salvation has appeared to all men. It teaches us to say "No" to ungodliness and worldly passions, and to live self-controlled, upright and godly lives in this present age, while we wait for the blessed hope—the glorious appearing of our great God and Savior, Jesus Christ, (Titus 2:11-13)
> God did this so that, by two unchangeable things in which it is impossible for God to lie, we who have fled to take hold of the hope offered to us may be greatly encouraged. (Heb 6:18)
> Know therefore that the LORD your God is God; he is the faithful God, keeping his covenant of love to a thousand generations of those who love him and keep his commands. (Deu 7:9)
> The works of his hands are faithful and just; all his precepts are trustworthy. (Psa 111:7)

	F. Abraham: The Example of a Man Justified by Faith Alone, 4:17-25	that Sarah's womb was also dead.	2) He was strong in faith—not wavering but giving glory to God
1 The source of Abraham's faith a. It was God Himself b. It was God who quickened, gives life to the dead c. It was God who created	17 As it is written: "I have made you a father of many nations." He is our father in the sight of God, in whom he believed—the God who gives life to the dead and calls things that are not as though they were.	20 Yet he did not waver through unbelief regarding the promise of God, but was strengthened in his faith and gave glory to God, 21 Being fully persuaded that God had power to do what he had promised.	3) He was convinced of God's ability & God's power b. His faith was credited as righteousness[DS1,2]
2 The strength of Abraham's faith a. His faith was in what God had said: The promise of a seed or offsring, a son 1) He was not weak in faith—despite thinking about his own physical inability	18 Against all hope, Abraham in hope believed and so became the father of many nations, just as it had been said to him, "So shall your offspring be." 19 Without weakening in his faith, he faced the fact that his body was as good as dead—since he was about a hundred years old—and	22 This is why "it was credited to him as righteousness." 23 The words "it was credited to him" were written not for him alone, 24 But also for us, to whom God will credit righteousness—for us who believe in him who raised Jesus our Lord from the dead. 25 He was delivered over to death for our sins and was raised to life for our justification.	**3 The recording of Abraham's faith** a. That men might read b. That men might be counted righteous—by believing 1) That God raised Jesus 2) That Jesus died for our sins & was raised again for our justification[DS3]

DIVISION III

FAITH AND JUSTIFICATION: THE WAY FOR THE WORLD TO BE RIGHT WITH GOD, 3:21-5:21

F. Abraham: The Example of a Man Justified by Faith Alone, 4:17-25

(4:17-25) Introduction: Abraham is the prime example or pattern that a person is justified by faith and by faith alone.
1. The source of Abraham's faith (v.17).
2. The strength of Abraham's faith (v.18-22).
3. The recording of Abraham's faith (v.23-25).

1 (4:17) **Faith, Source**: the source of Abraham's faith was God and God alone. Note three points.

1. It was God Himself whom Abraham believed: "I have made you a father of many nations" (v.17; cp. Gen.17:1-5, esp. 4-5). Abraham had never had a son, not by Sarah. He was now about one hundred years old, and Sarah was close to the same age. They were both well beyond the years of having a son. Just think about it for a moment and the impossibility is clearly realized. If Abraham was ever to have a son, the son would have to come from God. God would have to be the source, for only God could do such an impossible thing. And note: despite the impossibility Abraham *believes God*. The source of Abraham's faith was God.

> **"Have faith in God," Jesus answered. (Mark 11:22)**
>
> **And without faith it is impossible to please God, because anyone who comes to him must believe that he exists and that he rewards those who earnestly seek him. (Heb 11:6)**

2. It was the God who gives life to the dead whom Abraham believed. The source of Abraham's faith was...

- the living and true God: the God who is omnipotent, possessing all power, the power to breathe life into *dead matter*.

The source of Abraham's faith was God: God who has the power to quicken, make alive, revive, animate, rejuvenate and animate what is dead. No matter how impossible

the promise seemed, God was able to fulfill it because *He is God*, the One who possesses all power (omnipotent). God is able to give life and resurrect the dead; therefore, He is able to fulfill His promise.

> **"I tell you the truth, whoever hears my word and believes him who sent me has eternal life and will not be condemned; he has crossed over from death to life. I tell you the truth, a time is coming and has now come when the dead will hear the voice of the Son of God and those who hear will live. (John 5:24-25)**
>
> **For my Father's will is that everyone who looks to the Son and believes in him shall have eternal life, and I will raise him up at the last day." (John 6:40)**
>
> **And I have the same hope in God as these men, that there will be a resurrection of both the righteous and the wicked. (Acts 24:15)**
>
> **For as in Adam all die, so in Christ all will be made alive. (1 Cor 15:22)**
>
> **Because we know that the one who raised the Lord Jesus from the dead will also raise us with Jesus and present us with you in his presence. (2 Cor 4:14)**

3. It was the God who creates who was the source of Abraham's faith. Because God is God, that is, omnipotent, He is able to create. He can make something *out of nothing*. He needs nothing to create. He can speak things into existence just as He did when He created the world (Gen.1:1, 3). Abraham believed this; he believed that if it was necessary God could create life in the organs of his and Sarah's bodies. Abraham trusted and believed the promise of God. God was the source of his faith.

Thought 1. Note a fact often overlooked. Every promise made by God is a promise that only He can fulfill. He is not needed if man can meet and do whatever is needed. Therefore, if a man puts his faith in men, then all the hopes and promises that extend beyond this life will not be met. No man can fulfill the hope and promise of salvation from sin, death, and hell. No man can fulfill the promise that we shall be "the heirs of the world," that we shall receive eternal life in the new heavens and earth (cp. v.13). Only God can fulfill the impossible promise of eternal life.

> For the Lord himself will come down from heaven, with a loud command, with the voice of the archangel and with the trumpet call of God, and the dead in Christ will rise first. (1 Th 4:16)
> Jesus looked at them and said, "With man this is impossible, but with God all things are possible." (Mat 19:26)
> For nothing is impossible with God." (Luke 1:37)
> "I know that you can do all things; no plan of yours can be thwarted. (Job 42:2)

2 (4:18-22) **Faith—Abraham**: the strength of Abraham's faith. Note two very significant lessons.

1. Abraham's faith was in *what God said*, the promise of a descendant or of a son. He had nothing else to go on but God's Word: "just as it had been said to him."

The phrase "against all hope, Abraham in hope believed" means that Abraham was past hope, beyond all human help and any possibility of having a son. His situation was beyond hope, yet he believed God; he placed his hope in God and in what God had said.

a. Abraham was not weak in faith despite thinking about his own physical inability. His body was "good as dead"; he and Sarah were about one hundred years old. The word "dead" is a perfect participle in the Greek which means that his reproductive organs had stopped functioning and were dead forever and could never again function. Abraham could never have a son; it was not humanly possible. He and Sarah were almost one hundred years old, now sexually "dead."

Abraham thought about the matter. The phrase "faced the fact" (katanoeo) means he fixed his thoughts, his mind, his attention upon the matter. But he did not give in to the thoughts. He was not weak in faith.

Thought 1. Just imagine the *personal relationship* Abraham must have had with God! To know God so well—loving and trusting God so strongly—that God could give him an experience so meaningful that Abraham would believe the promise without even staggering in faith.

> "You are my witnesses," declares the LORD, "and my servant whom I have chosen, so that you may know and believe me and understand that I am he. Before me no god was formed, nor will there be one after me. (Isa 43:10)
> Love the LORD your God with all your heart and with all your soul and with all your strength. (Deu 6:5)

> And now, O Israel, what does the LORD your God ask of you but to fear the LORD your God, to walk in all his ways, to love him, to serve the LORD your God with all your heart and with all your soul, and to observe the Lord's commands and decrees that I am giving you today for your own good? (Deu 10:12-13)

b. Abraham was strong in faith—not wavering regarding the promise of God. Instead he walked about glorifying and praising God for His glorious promise. The word "wavering" (diakrino) means he did not stagger, did not vacillate, did not question God's ability to fulfill His promise.
c. Abraham was fully convinced of God's ability and God's power. He knew God could overcome the difficulty of his body being "dead," and he believed God could and would either...
  • quicken and give life to his body, or
  • recreate his reproductive organs (v.17).

He did not know what method God would use, but he knew God was able to do what He had promised. Abraham believed God; he was fully persuaded that the promise would be fulfilled.

> Produce fruit in keeping with repentance. And do not begin to say to yourselves, 'We have Abraham as our father.' For I tell you that out of these stones God can raise up children for Abraham. (Luke 3:8)
> So keep up your courage, men, for I have faith in God that it will happen just as he told me. (Acts 27:25)
> Yet he did not waver through unbelief regarding the promise of God, but was strengthened in his faith and gave glory to God, being fully persuaded that God had power to do what he had promised. (Rom 4:20-21)
> Know therefore that the LORD your God is God; he is the faithful God, keeping his covenant of love to a thousand generations of those who love him and keep his commands. (Deu 7:9)
> "Now write down for yourselves this song and teach it to the Israelites and have them sing it, so that it may be a witness for me against them. (Deu 31:19)
> Commit your way to the LORD; trust in him and he will do this: (Psa 37:5)
> Trust in the LORD with all your heart and lean not on your own understanding; (Prov 3:5)
> You will keep in perfect peace him whose mind is steadfast, because he trusts in you. (Isa 26:3)
> "But blessed is the man who trusts in the LORD, whose confidence is in him. (Jer 17:7)

2. Abraham's faith was credited as righteousness (see DEEPER STUDY #1,2—Ro.4:22 for discussion).

DEEPER STUDY # 1
(4:22) **Credited—Imputed** (elogisthe): means to reckon, to impute, to credit, to count, to compute, to ascribe, to deposit, to put to one's account. Abraham's faith was counted for righteousness. (See DEEPER STUDY # 1, *Reckon*—Ro.6:11 for a fuller discussion.) Abraham deposited his

faith with God, and God credited Abraham's faith as right-eousness.

DEEPER STUDY # 2
(4:22) **Justification—Faith—Righteousness**: in simple terms *justification* means that God takes the believer's faith and counts it as righteousness (Ro.4:3; cp. Gen.15:6; see notes—Ro.4:1-3; DEEPER STUDY # 1—4:1-25; note—5:1. Also see DEEPER STUDY # 4, *Cross*—Jn.12:32 for more discussion.)

When a person *really believes* that Jesus Christ is *his Savior*, God takes that person's faith and counts it for righteousness (Ro.4:3, 5, 9, 11, 22, 24). The person is not righteous; he has no righteousness of his own. He is still imperfect, still sinful, still corruptible, still short of God's glory as a sinful human being. But he does believe that Jesus Christ *is his Savior*. Such belief honors God's Son (whom God loves very much), and because it honors God's Son, God accepts that person's faith for righteous-ness. God counts that person's faith as righteousness. Therefore, that person becomes acceptable to God. (In a discussion of justification, a person's belief—the right kind of belief—is critical. See DEEPER STUDY #2—Jn.2:24; Ro.10:16-17.)

> Abram believed the LORD, and he cred-ited it to him as righteousness. (Gen 15:6)
> Therefore, since we have been justified through faith, we have peace with God through our Lord Jesus Christ, (Rom 5:1)
> Consider Abraham: "He believed God, and it was credited to him as righteous-ness." (Gal 3:6)
> And that is what some of you were. But you were washed, you were sanctified, you were justified in the name of the Lord Jesus Christ and by the Spirit of our God. (1 Cor 6:11)
> And be found in him, not having a righteousness of my own that comes from the law, but that which is through faith in Christ—the righteousness that comes from God and is by faith. (Phil 3:9)

3 (4:23-25) **Faith—Abraham**: the recording of Abra-ham's faith is for two purposes.

1. That men might read the account. It was not recorded just to honor Abraham as a great man. It was written so that we might read and understand how we are to become acceptable to God.

> But these are written that you may be-lieve that Jesus is the Christ, the Son of God, and that by believing you may have life in his name. (John 20:31)
> That which was from the beginning, which we have heard, which we have seen with our eyes, which we have looked at and our hands have touched—this we proclaim concerning the Word of life. The life ap-peared; we have seen it and testify to it, and we proclaim to you the eternal life, which was with the Father and has ap-peared to us. We proclaim to you what we have seen and heard, so that you also may have fellowship with us. And our fellowship is with the Father and with his Son, Jesus Christ. (1 John 1:1-3)
> Therefore, since I myself have carefully investigated everything from the beginning,

it seemed good also to me to write an orderly account for you, most excellent Theophilus, so that you may know the certainty of the things you have been taught. (Luke 1:3-4)

2. That men might be counted righteous by believing. It is necessary to believe two things. (See DEEPER STUDY # 3—Ro.4:25 for discussion.)
   a. That God raised Jesus our Lord from the dead (see DEEPER STUDY # 3, *Jesus Christ, Resurrection*—Ro.4:25; note and DEEPER STUDY # 1—Acts 1:3; DEEPER STUDY # 4—2:24; note—2:25-36 for more discussion).
   b. That Jesus died for our sins and was raised for our justification (see notes—Ro.7:4; DEEPER STUDY # 2—8:3; note and DEEPER STUDY # 1—Acts 1:3; DEEPER STUDY # 3—2:23; note—3:13-15. See Subject Index, *Jesus Christ, Death* for more discussion.)

DEEPER STUDY # 3
(4:25) **Justification—Jesus Christ, Death; Resurrection—Atonement—Propitiation**: Christ was delivered to death for our sins and raised again for our justification. He of-fered Himself as an *atonement* or *propitiation* for our sin. Atonement or propitiation means sacrifice, covering. (See notes—Ro.3:25; 1 Jn.2:1-2.) Christ offered Himself as our sacrifice, as our substitute, as the covering for our sins. God accepted the offering and the sacrifice of His life for us. The resurrection proves it.

1. The resurrection shouts loudly and clearly that God is satisfied with the settlement for sin which Christ made.
2. The resurrection declares the believer justified, free from sin, and righteous in God's eyes. (See DEEPER STUDY #1,2—Ro.4:22; 5:1. Cp.Ro.4:5; 4:1-3; 4:1-25.)

> This man was handed over to you by God's set purpose and foreknowledge; and you, with the help of wicked men, put him to death by nailing him to the cross. But God raised him from the dead, freeing him from the agony of death, because it was impossible for death to keep its hold on him. (Acts 2:23-24)
> Seeing what was ahead, he spoke of the resurrection of the Christ, that he was not abandoned to the grave, nor did his body see decay. God has raised this Jesus to life, and we are all witnesses of the fact. (Acts 2:31-32)
> "We are witnesses of everything he did in the country of the Jews and in Jerusa-lem. They killed him by hanging him on a tree, but God raised him from the dead on the third day and caused him to be seen. He was not seen by all the people, but by witnesses whom God had already chosen—by us who ate and drank with him after he rose from the dead. (Acts 10:39-41)
> But God raised him from the dead, (Acts 13:30)
> And who through the Spirit of holiness was declared with power to be the Son of God by his resurrection from the dead: Je-sus Christ our Lord. (Rom 1:4)
> Which he exerted in Christ when he raised him from the dead and seated him at his right hand in the heavenly realms, far above all rule and authority, power and dominion, and every title that can be given, not only in the present age but also in the one to come. (Eph 1:20-21)

	CHAPTER 5	stand. And we rejoice in the hope of the glory of God.	**4 There is hope for the glory of God**
	G. God's Unbelievable Love (Part I): The Results of Justification, 5:1-5	3 Not only so, but we also rejoice in our sufferings, because we know that suffering produces perseverance.	**5 There is glory in trials & sufferings** a. Trials stir perseverance
1 Justification is by faith **2 There is peace with God**	Therefore, since we have been justified through faith, we have peace with God through our Lord Jesus Christ,	4 Perseverance, character; and character, hope. 5 And hope does not disappoint us, because God	b. Perseverance stirs character c. Character stirs hope d. Hope never disappoints
3 There is access into the grace, the favor & the presence of God	2 Through whom we have gained access by faith into this grace in which we now	has poured out his love into our hearts by the Holy Spirit, whom he has given us.	**6 There is the continuous experience of God's love thru the indwelling Spirit**

DIVISION III

FAITH AND JUSTIFICATION: THE WAY FOR THE WORLD TO BE RIGHT WITH GOD, 3:21-5:21

G. God's Unbelievable Love (Part I): The Results of Justification, 5:1-5

(5:1-5) **Introduction**: man is blessed by God through justification, blessed beyond all imagination. Justification and its results are gloriously covered in this passage of Scripture.
1. Justification is by faith (v.1).
2. There is peace with God (v.1).
3. There is access into the grace, the favor and the presence of God (v.2).
4. There is hope for the glory of God (v.2).
5. There is glory in trials and sufferings (v.3-5).
6. There is the continuous experience of God's love through the indwelling Spirit (v.5).

1 (5:1) **Justification** (diakioun): to count someone righteous. It means to reckon, to credit, to account, to judge, to treat, to look upon as righteous. It does not mean to make a man righteous. All Greek verbs which end in "oun" mean not to make someone something, but merely to count, to judge, to treat someone as something.
There are three major points to note about justification.
1. Why justification is necessary:
  a. Justification is necessary because of the sin and alienation of man. Man has rebelled against God and taken his life into his own hands. Man lives as he desires…
   • fulfilling the cravings of sinful man, the lust of his eyes.
   • clinging to the boasting of what he has and does.
   • clutching to everything in the world.

   Man has become sinful and ungodly, an enemy of God, pushing God out of his life and wanting little if anything to do with God. Man has separated and alienated himself from God.
  b. Justification is necessary because of the anger and wrath of God. "God…expresses his wrath every day" (Ps.7:11). Sin has aroused God's anger and wrath. God is angry over man's…
   • rebellion
   • hostility
   • ungodliness
   • unrighteousness
   • sin
   • desertion

   Man has turned his back upon God, pushing God away and having little to do with Him. Man

has not made God the center of his life; man has broken his relationship with God. Therefore, the greatest need in man's life is to discover the answer to the question: How can the relationship between man and God be restored?
2. Why God justifies a man: God justifies a man because of His Son Jesus Christ. When a man believes in Jesus Christ, God takes that man's faith and counts it as righteousness. The man is not righteous, but God considers and credits the man's faith as righteousness. Why is God willing to do this?
  a. God is willing to justify man because He loves man that much. God loves man so much that He sent His Son into the world and sacrificed Him in order to justify man (Jn.3:16; Ro.5:8).
  b. God is willing to justify man because of what His Son Jesus Christ has done for man.
   ⇒ Jesus Christ has secured the *Ideal* righteousness for man. He came to earth to live a sinless and perfect life. As Man He never broke the law of God; He never went contrary to the will of God, not even once. Therefore, He stood before God and before the world as the Ideal Man, the Perfect Man, the Representative Man, the Perfect Righteousness that could stand for the righteousness of every man.
   ⇒ Jesus Christ came into the world to *die* for man. As the *Ideal Man* He could take all the sins of the world upon Himself and die for every man. His death *could stand* for every man. He exchanged places with man by becoming the sinner (2 Cor.5:19). He bore the wrath of God against sin, bearing the condemnation for every man. Again, He was able to do this because He was the Ideal Man, and as the *Ideal Man* His death could stand for the death of every man.
   ⇒ Jesus Christ came into the world to *arise from the dead* and thereby to conquer death for man. As the *Ideal Man*, His resurrection and exaltation into the presence of God *could stand* for every man's desperate need to conquer death and to be acceptable to God. His resurrected life could stand for the resurrected life of the believer.

Now, as stated above, when a man believes in Jesus Christ—really believes—God takes that man's belief and...

- counts it as the righteousness (perfection) of Christ. The man is counted as *righteous in Christ*.
- counts it as the death of Christ. The man is counted as having already *died in Christ*, as having already paid the penalty for sin *in the death of Christ*.
- counts it as the resurrection of Christ. The man is counted as already having been *resurrected in Christ*.

Very simply, God loves His Son Jesus Christ so much that He honors any man who honors His Son by *believing on Him*. He honors the man by taking the man's faith and counting (crediting) it as righteousness and by giving him the glorious privilege of living with Christ forever in the presence of God.

3. How God justifies a man: the word justify (diakioun) is a legal word taken from the courts. It pictures man on trial before God. Man is seen as having committed the most heinous of crimes; he has rebelled against God and broken his relationship with God. How can he restore that relationship? Within human courts if a man is acquitted, he is declared innocent, but this is not true within the Divine Court. When a man appears before God, he is anything but innocent; he is utterly guilty and condemned accordingly.

But when a man sincerely trusts Christ, then God takes that man's faith and counts it as righteousness. By such God counts the man—judges him, treats him—as if he was innocent. The man is not made innocent; he is guilty. He knows it and God knows it, but God treats him as innocent. "God justifies the wicked"—an incredible mercy, a wondrous grace. (See notes—Ro.4:1-3; Deeper Study # 1—4:1-25; Deeper Study # 2—4:22.)

How do we know this? How can we know for sure that God is like this? Because Jesus said so. He said that God loves us. We are sinners, yes; but Christ said that we are very, very dear to God.

> **Abram believed the LORD, and he credited it to him as righteousness. (Gen 15:6)**
>
> **Through him everyone who believes is justified from everything you could not be justified from by the law of Moses. (Acts 13:39)**
>
> **For all have sinned and fall short of the glory of God, and are justified freely by his grace through the redemption that came by Christ Jesus. (Rom 3:23-24)**
>
> **What does the Scripture say? "Abraham believed God, and it was credited to him as righteousness." (Rom 4:3)**
>
> **Therefore, since we have been justified through faith, we have peace with God through our Lord Jesus Christ, (Rom 5:1)**
>
> **Since we have now been justified by his blood, how much more shall we be saved from God's wrath through him! (Rom 5:9)**
>
> **Because anyone who has died [counted dead, justified] has been freed from sin. (Rom 6:7)**
>
> **Who will bring any charge against those whom God has chosen? It is God who justifies. (Rom 8:33)**
>
> **And that is what some of you were. But you were washed, you were sanctified, you**

> **were justified in the name of the Lord Jesus Christ and by the Spirit of our God. (1 Cor 6:11)**
>
> **Know that a man is not justified by observing the law, but by faith in Jesus Christ. So we, too, have put our faith in Christ Jesus that we may be justified by faith in Christ and not by observing the law, because by observing the law no one will be justified. (Gal 2:16)**
>
> **Consider Abraham: "He believed God, and it was credited to him as righteousness." (Gal 3:6)**
>
> **So the law was put in charge to lead us to Christ that we might be justified by faith. (Gal 3:24)**
>
> **And be found in him, not having a righteousness of my own that comes from the law, but that which is through faith in Christ—the righteousness that comes from God and is by faith. (Phil 3:9)**

2 (5:1) **Peace—Justification**: the first result of justification is peace with God.

1. The meaning of peace with God is striking. Peace with God does not mean escapism, a quiet atmosphere, the absence of trouble, the control of situations by positive thinking, the denial of problems, the ability to keep from facing reality. Peace *with* God means the *sense and knowledge*...

- that one has restored his relationship with God.
- that one is no longer alienated and separated from God.
- that one is now reconciled with God.
- that one is now accepted by God.
- that one is freed from the wrath and judgment of God.
- that one is freed from fearing God's wrath and judgment.
- that one is now pleasing God.
- that one is at peace with God.

2. The source of peace is Jesus Christ. Men can have peace with God only because of Jesus Christ. It is He who reconciles men to God. He has made peace by the blood of His cross (see notes, *Atonement*—Ro.3:25).

> **For he himself is our peace, who has made the two one and has destroyed the barrier, the dividing wall of hostility, by abolishing in his flesh the law with its commandments and regulations. His purpose was to create in himself one new man out of the two, thus making peace, (Eph 2:14-15)**
>
> **And through him to reconcile to himself all things, whether things on earth or things in heaven, by making peace through his blood, shed on the cross. (Col 1:20)**
>
> **But he was pierced for our transgressions, he was crushed for our iniquities; the punishment that brought us peace was upon him, and by his wounds we are healed. (Isa 53:5)**

3. The reason we have peace is the glorious truth of justification (see note, *Justification*—Ro.5:1 for discussion. See Deeper Study #1, *Justification*—Ro.4:1-25; note—4:1-3; Deeper Study #2—4:22 for more discussion).

3 (5:2) **Access—Grace**: the second result of justification is access into the grace of God.

1. Grace (charis) means a gift or a favor, an *unmerited* and undeserved gift or favor (see notes, *Grace*—Ro.4:16; DEEPER STUDY #1—Tit.2:11-15 for more discussion). In the present passage grace is looked upon as a place or a position. Grace is a place to which we are brought, a position into which we are placed. It is the place of God's presence, the position of salvation. The person who is justified...

- stands in God's presence.
- stands before God saved.
- stands in the favor of God.
- stands in the privileges of God.
- stands in the promises of God.

2. Note it is *through Christ* that we have access into this grace. The word "access" (prosagogen) means to bring to, to move to, to introduce, to present. The thought is that of being in a royal court and being presented and introduced to the King of kings. Jesus Christ is the One who throws open the door into God's presence. He is the One who presents us to God, the Sovereign Majesty of the universe.

> **I am the gate; whoever enters through me will be saved. He will come in and go out, and find pasture. (John 10:9)**
> **Through whom we have gained access by faith into this grace in which we now stand. And we rejoice in the hope of the glory of God. (Rom 5:2)**
> **But now in Christ Jesus you who once were far away have been brought near through the blood of Christ. (Eph 2:13)**
> **For through him we both have access to the Father by one Spirit. (Eph 2:18)**
> **In him and through faith in him we may approach God with freedom and confidence. (Eph 3:12)**
> **Therefore, brothers, since we have confidence to enter the Most Holy Place by the blood of Jesus, (Heb 10:19)**
> **For Christ died for sins once for all, the righteous for the unrighteous, to bring you to God. He was put to death in the body but made alive by the Spirit, (1 Pet 3:18)**

Thought 1. Note we "stand" in God's grace, in His presence.
1) We are not bowed down, intimidated, stricken with fear, and humiliated. Christ has justified us, removed our guilt and shame, and given us great confidence before God. Therefore, we take a stand of honor and dignity before Him, standing in the perfect righteousness of the Lord Jesus.
2) We are not sitting or lying down, but we are standing. This pictures our service and labor for God. We are brought into His presence for the purpose of service; therefore, there is not time for sitting and lying around. We stand before Him justified, yes, but we stand to receive our orders from Him (cp. 1 Cor.15:58; 2 Cor.5:18-21).

4 (5:2) **Hope**: the third result of justification is hope, hope for the glory of God (see notes, *Rewards*—Ro.2:6-10; DEEPER STUDY #1, *Glory*—Ro.2:7; DEEPER STUDY # 1—3:23 for discussion and verses). Note that the hope of the believer is for *the glory of God*.

1. When Scripture speaks of the believer's hope, it does not mean what the world means by hope. The hope of the world is a *desire*, a *want*. The world hopes—wants, desires—that something will happen. But this is not the hope of the believer. The hope of the believer is a *surety*: it is perfect assurance, confidence, and knowledge. How can hope be so absolute and assured? By being an *inward possession*. The believer's hope is based upon the presence of God's Spirit who dwells within the believer. In fact, the believer possesses the *hope of glory* only by the Spirit of God who dwells within him (see DEEPER STUDY #1, *Hope*—Ro.8:24-25 for more detailed discussion).

> **And you also were included in Christ when you heard the word of truth, the gospel of your salvation. Having believed, you were marked in him with a seal, the promised Holy Spirit, who is a deposit guaranteeing our inheritance until the redemption of those who are God's possession—to the praise of his glory. (Eph 1:13-14; cp. 2 Cor. 1:21-22; Eph. 4:30; Jn. 14:16-18)**
> **The faith and love that spring from the hope that is stored up for you in heaven and that you have already heard about in the word of truth, the gospel (Col 1:5)**
> **For the grace of God that brings salvation has appeared to all men. It teaches us to say "No" to ungodliness and worldly passions, and to live self-controlled, upright and godly lives in this present age, while we wait for the blessed hope—the glorious appearing of our great God and Savior, Jesus Christ, (Titus 2:11-13)**
> **God did this so that, by two unchangeable things in which it is impossible for God to lie, we who have fled to take hold of the hope offered to us may be greatly encouraged. We have this hope as an anchor for the soul, firm and secure. It enters the inner sanctuary behind the curtain, where Jesus, who went before us, has entered on our behalf. He has become a high priest forever, in the order of Melchizedek. (Heb 6:18-20)**
> **Praise be to the God and Father of our Lord Jesus Christ! In his great mercy he has given us new birth into a living hope through the resurrection of Jesus Christ from the dead, and into an inheritance that can never perish, spoil or fade—kept in heaven for you, (1 Pet 1:3-4)**
> **How great is the love the Father has lavished on us, that we should be called children of God! And that is what we are! The reason the world does not know us is that it did not know him. Dear friends, now we are children of God, and what we will be has not yet been made known. But we know that when he appears, we shall be like him, for we shall see him as he is. Everyone who has this hope in him purifies himself, just as he is pure. (1 John 3:1-3)**

2. The glory hoped for by the believer is to abundantly exceed the most wonderful experience we can ask or think. Glory means to possess and to be full of perfect light; to dwell in the perfect splendor and magnificence of God (see DEEPER STUDY #1, *Glory*—Ro.2:7).

Then the righteous will shine like the sun in the kingdom of their Father. He who has ears, let him hear. (Mat 13:43)

Now if we are children, then we are heirs—heirs of God and co-heirs with Christ, if indeed we share in his sufferings in order that we may also share in his glory. (Rom 8:17)

who, by the power that enables him to bring everything under his control, will transform our lowly bodies so that they will be like his glorious body. (Phil 3:21)

When Christ, who is your life, appears, then you also will appear with him in glory. (Col 3:4)

After this I looked and there before me was a great multitude that no one could count, from every nation, tribe, people and language, standing before the throne and in front of the Lamb. They were wearing white robes and were holding palm branches in their hands. (Rev 7:9)

You guide me with your counsel, and afterward you will take me into glory. (Psa 73:24)

I consider that our present sufferings are not worth comparing with the glory that will be revealed in us. (Rom 8:18)

For our light and momentary troubles are achieving for us an eternal glory that far outweighs them all. (2 Cor 4:17)

Therefore I endure everything for the sake of the elect, that they too may obtain the salvation that is in Christ Jesus, with eternal glory. (2 Tim 2:10)

To the elders among you, I appeal as a fellow elder, a witness of Christ's sufferings and one who also will share in the glory to be revealed: (1 Pet 5:1)

Thought 1. Note how far short we often come. Instead of rejoicing in the glorious hope God has given...

- we moan, groan, and complain, living a discouraged and defeated life.
- we slip back into the ways of the world: the cravings of sinful man, the lust of the eyes and the boasting of what we have and do (cp. 1 Jn.2:15-16).
- we become discouraged and defeated, no longer conscious of the glorious hope for the glory of God.

That he lavished on us with all wisdom and understanding. And he made known to us the mystery of his will according to his good pleasure, which he purposed in Christ, (Eph 1:8-9)

5 (5:3-5) **Trials—Suffering**: the fourth result of justification is glory in trials and sufferings. When a man is truly justified, he is no longer defeated by trials and sufferings. Trials and sufferings no longer discourage and swamp him, no longer cast him down into the dungeon of despair and hopelessness. The very opposite is true. Trials and sufferings become purposeful and meaningful. The *truly* justified man knows...

- that his life and welfare are completely under God's care and watchful eye.
- therefore, whatever events come into his life—whether good or bad—they are allowed by God for a reason. The justified man knows that God will take the trials and sufferings of this world and work them out for good, even if God has to twist and move every event surrounding the believer.

This passage explains the great benefits of trials and sufferings; it shows exactly how the trials and sufferings of life work good for us. The word "trials" or "sufferings" (thlipsis) means pressure, oppression, affliction, and distress. It means to be pressed together ever so tightly. It means all kinds of pressure ranging from the day to day pressures over to the pressure of confronting the most serious afflictions, even that of death itself.

"I have told you these things, so that in me you may have peace. In this world you will have trouble. But take heart! I have overcome the world." (John 16:33)

Strengthening the disciples and encouraging them to remain true to the faith. "We must go through many hardships to enter the kingdom of God," they said. (Acts 14:22)

In fact, when we were with you, we kept telling you that we would be persecuted. And it turned out that way, as you well know. (1 Th 3:4)

I answered, "Sir, you know." And he said, "These are they who have come out of the great tribulation; they have washed their robes and made them white in the blood of the Lamb. (Rev 7:14)

1. Trials stir perseverance (hupomone): endurance, fortitude, steadfastness, constancy, patience. The word is not passive; it is active. It is not the spirit that just sits back and puts up with the trials of life, taking whatever may come. Rather it is the spirit that stands up and faces life's trials, that actively goes about conquering and overcoming them. When trials confront a man who is truly justified, he is stirred to arise and face the trials head on. He immediately sets out to conquer and overcome them. He knows that God is allowing the trials in order to teach him more and more perseverance (endurance).

By standing firm you will gain life. (Luke 21:19)

Be joyful in hope, patient in affliction, faithful in prayer. (Rom 12:12)

You need to persevere so that when you have done the will of God, you will receive what he has promised. (Heb 10:36)

Consider it pure joy, my brothers, whenever you face trials of many kinds, because you know that the testing of your faith develops perseverance. Perseverance must finish its work so that you may be mature and complete, not lacking anything. (James 1:2-4)

Be patient, then, brothers, until the Lord's coming. See how the farmer waits for the land to yield its valuable crop and how patient he is for the autumn and spring rains. (James 5:7)

2. Perseverance stirs character (dokimex): integrity, strength. The idea is that of proven experience, of gaining strength through the trials of life; therefore, the word is more accurately translated character. When a justified man endures trials, he comes out of it stronger than ever before. He is a man of much stronger character and integrity. He knows much more about the presence and strength of God.

> **Praise be to the God and Father of our Lord Jesus Christ, the Father of compassion and the God of all comfort, who comforts us in all our troubles, so that we can comfort those in any trouble with the comfort we ourselves have received from God. (2 Cor 1:3-4)**

> **But he said to me, "My grace is sufficient for you, for my power is made perfect in weakness." Therefore I will boast all the more gladly about my weaknesses, so that Christ's power may rest on me. That is why, for Christ's sake, I delight in weaknesses, in insults, in hardships, in persecutions, in difficulties. For when I am weak, then I am strong. (2 Cor 12:9-10)**

> **I pray that out of his glorious riches he may strengthen you with power through his Spirit in your inner being, (Eph 3:16)**

> **Being strengthened with all power according to his glorious might so that you may have great endurance and patience, and joyfully (Col 1:11)**

> **Who through faith conquered kingdoms, administered justice, and gained what was promised; who shut the mouths of lions, qenched the fury of the flames, and escaped the edge of the sword; whose weakness was turned to strength; and who became powerful in battle and routed foreign armies. (Heb 11:33-34)**

> **But those who hope in the LORD will renew their strength. They will soar on wings like eagles; they will run and not grow weary, they will walk and not be faint. (Isa 40:31)**

> **So do not fear, for I am with you; do not be dismayed, for I am your God. I will strengthen you and help you; I will uphold you with my righteous right hand. (Isa 41:10)**

3. Character stirs hope (elpis): to expect with confidence; to anticipate knowing; to look and long for with surety; to desire with assurance; to rely on with certainty; to trust with the guarantee; to believe with the knowledge. Note that hope is expectation, anticipation, looking and longing for, desiring, relying upon, and trusting. But it is also confidence, knowledge, surety, assurance, certainty, and a guarantee. When a justified man becomes stronger in character, he draws closer to God and the closer he draws to God, the more he hopes for the glory of God. (See note, *Hope*—Ro.5:2 for more discussion and verses.)

4. Hope never disappoints (kataischuno): never makes ashamed, never shames, deludes, deceives, confounds, confuses. The believer, the person who is truly justified, will never be disappointed or shamed. He will see his hope fulfilled. He will live forever in the presence of God inheriting the promises God has given in His Word.

> **As it is written: "See, I lay in Zion a stone that causes men to stumble and a rock that makes them fall, and the one who trusts in him will never be put to shame." (Rom 9:33)**

> **I eagerly expect and hope that I will in no way be ashamed, but will have sufficient courage so that now as always Christ will be exalted in my body, whether by life or by death. (Phil 1:20)**

> **However, if you suffer as a Christian, do not be ashamed, but praise God that you bear that name. (1 Pet 4:16)**

> **And now, dear children, continue in him, so that when he appears we may be confident and unashamed before him at his coming. (1 John 2:28)**

> **They cried to you and were saved; in you they trusted and were not disappointed. (Psa 22:5)**

> **In you, O LORD, I have taken refuge; let me never be put to shame. (Psa 71:1)**

> **Then I would not be put to shame when I consider all your commands. (Psa 119:6)**

> **The prospect of the righteous is joy, but the hopes of the wicked come to nothing. (Prov 10:28; cp. Ps.22:5; 71:1)**

> **Because the Sovereign LORD helps me, I will not be disgraced. Therefore have I set my face like flint, and I know I will not be put to shame. (Isa 50:7)**

> **You will have plenty to eat, until you are full, and you will praise the name of the LORD your God, who has worked wonders for you; never again will my people be shamed. (Joel 2:26)**

6 (5:5) **God, Love of—Holy Spirit, Work of**: there is the continuous experience of God's love through the presence of the Holy Spirit.

1. The love of God is demonstrated in His justifying the man who truly believes in His Son Jesus Christ.

> **"For God so loved the world that he gave his one and only Son, that whoever believes in him shall not perish but have eternal life. (John 3:16)**

> **But God demonstrates his own love for us in this: While we were still sinners, Christ died for us. (Rom 5:8)**

2. The Holy Spirit pours out the love of God in our hearts. He grows and matures us in the love of God, increasing our understanding of what God has done and is doing for us. He helps us learn more and more about our justification and more and more of the glorious salvation He promises.

The Holy Spirit...

- makes us *conscious* and *aware* of God's love, and gives us a *deep* and *intimate* sense of God's love.
- makes us *conscious* and *aware* of God's presence, and of His care and concern for all that is involved in salvation.

It is the sense and intimacy of God's love that is being stressed: a personal manifestation, a personal experience of the presence and love of God, of His justification and care for us as we walk through life moment by moment.

> **Whoever has my commands and obeys them, he is the one who loves me. He who loves me will be loved by my Father, and I too will love him and show myself to him." (John 14:21)**

> **Jesus replied, "If anyone loves me, he will obey my teaching. My Father will love him, and we will come to him and make our home with him. (John 14:23)**

> **But because of his great love for us, God, who is rich in mercy, made us alive with Christ even when we were dead in transgressions—it is by grace you have been saved. (Eph 2:4-5)**

> **How great is the love the Father has lavished on us, that we should be called children of God! And that is what we are! The reason the world does not know us is that it did not know him. (1 John 3:1)**

> **This is how God showed his love among us: He sent his one and only Son into the world that we might live through him. (1 John 4:9)**

> **And so we know and rely on the love God has for us. God is love. Whoever lives in love lives in God, and God in him. (1 John 4:16)**

Note: the Holy Spirit is "given [to] us." He enters our hearts and lives for the very purpose of sealing or guaranteeing us. He seals or guarantees our justification, and He seals the fact that God loves us and cares for and looks after us. It is because of His indwelling presence that we have the continuous and unbroken experience of God's love. But remember: this glorious intimacy with God is a result of justification. *Only the person* who is truly justified experiences the love of God.

Note another fact: the love of God is a gift, a gift deposited in the believer by the Holy Spirit (cp. the divine nature which is *deposited* within us when we truly trust Jesus Christ as our Savior, 2 Pt.1:4).

> **For you did not receive a spirit that makes you a slave again to fear, but you received the Spirit of sonship. And by him we cry, "Abba, Father." The Spirit himself testifies with our spirit that we are God's children. Now if we are children, then we are heirs—heirs of God and co-heirs with Christ, if indeed we share in his sufferings in order that we may also share in his glory. (Rom 8:15-17)**

> **Set his seal of ownership on us, and put his Spirit in our hearts as a deposit, guaranteeing what is to come. (2 Cor 1:22)**

> **And you also were included in Christ when you heard the word of truth, the gospel of your salvation. Having believed, you were marked in him with a seal, the promised Holy Spirit, who is a deposit guaranteeing our inheritance until the redemption of those who are God's possession—to the praise of his glory. (Eph 1:13-14)**

	H. God's Unbelievable Love (Part II): The Great Depth of Justification, 5:6-11	9 Since we have now been justified by his blood, how much more shall we be saved from God's wrath through him!	a. By Christ's death b. By justification c. By saving us from wrath
1 We were ungodly & powerless, yet Christ died for us a. In God's time b. Was an uncommon, unbelievable love	6 You see, at just the right time, when we were still powerless, Christ died for the ungodly. 7 Very rarely will anyone die for a righteous man, though for a good man someone might possibly dare to die.	10 For if, when we were God's enemies, we were reconciled to him through the death of his Son, how much more, having been reconciled, shall we be saved through his life!	**3 We were enemies, yet God reconciled and saved us** a. We are reconciled through Christ's death[DS1] b. We are saved through Christ's life c. We are given joy through Christ's reconciliation
2 We were sinners, yet God demonstrated His love for us	8 But God demonstrates his own love for us in this: While we were still sinners, Christ died for us.	11 Not only is this so, but we also rejoice in God through our Lord Jesus Christ, through whom we have now received reconciliation.	

DIVISION III.

FAITH AND JUSTIFICATION: THE WAY FOR THE WORLD TO BE RIGHT WITH GOD, 3:21-5:21

H. God's Unbelievable Love (Part II): The Great Depth of Justification, 5:6-11

(5:6-11) **Introduction—Love** (agape): this passage discusses God's unbelievable love. It shows the great depth of justification. The passage also gives one of the clearest definitions of *agape love*. It actually shows the meaning of *agape love*. Agape love goes much farther than *phileo love*. Phileo love is brotherly love, a love that gives itself for a brother. But *agape love* is a new kind of love: it is a godly love, a sacrificial love, a love that gives itself for those powerless (Ro.5:6), for the ungodly (Ro.5:6), for sinners (Ro.5:8), and for enemies (Ro.5:10) (see note—Jn.21:15-17).

1. We were ungodly and powerless, yet Christ died for us (v.6-7).
2. We were sinners, yet God demonstrated His love for us (v.8-9).
3. We were enemies, yet God reconciled and saved us (v.10-11).

1 (5:6-7) **Jesus Christ, Death—Man, State of—God, Love of**: we were ungodly and powerless, yet Christ died for us. God's great love is seen in this unbelievable act.

1. We were "powerless" (asthenon): weak, worthless, useless, helpless, hopeless, destitute, without strength. We were spiritually worthless and useless and unable to help ourselves.

> "I loathe my very life; therefore I will give free rein to my complaint and speak out in the bitterness of my soul. (Job 10:1)
> My life is consumed by anguish and my years by groaning; my strength fails because of my affliction, and my bones grow weak. (Psa 31:10)
> My God. My soul is downcast within me; therefore I will remember you from the land of the Jordan, the heights of Hermon—from Mount Mizar. (Psa 42:6)
> I sink in the miry depths, where there is no foothold. I have come into the deep waters; the floods engulf me. (Psa 69:2)
> But as for me, my feet had almost slipped; I had nearly lost my foothold. (Psa 73:2)

> When I tried to understand all this, it was oppressive to me (Psa 73:16)
> Do not run until your feet are bare and your throat is dry. But you said, 'It's no use! I love foreign gods, and I must go after them.' (Jer 2:25)
> Brothers, we do not want you to be ignorant about those who fall asleep, or to grieve like the rest of men, who have no hope. (1 Th 4:13)
> Remember that at that time you were separate from Christ, excluded from citizenship in Israel and foreigners to the covenants of the promise, without hope and without God in the world. (Eph 2:12)

2. We were ungodly (asebon): not like God, different from God, profane, having a different life-style than God. God is godly, that is, perfect; man is ungodly, that is, he is not like God; he is imperfect.

> Furthermore, since they did not think it worthwhile to retain the knowledge of God, he gave them over to a depraved mind, to do what ought not to be done. They have become filled with every kind of wickedness, evil, greed and depravity. They are full of envy, murder, strife, deceit and malice. They are gossips, slanderers, God-haters, insolent, arrogant and boastful; they invent ways of doing evil; they disobey their parents; they are senseless, faithless, heartless, ruthless. Although they know God's righteous decree that those who do such things deserve death, they not only continue to do these very things but also approve of those who practice them. (Rom 1:28-32)
> We also know that law is made not for the righteous but for lawbreakers and rebels, the ungodly and sinful, the unholy and irreligious; for those who kill their fathers or mothers, for murderers, For adulterers and perverts, for slave traders and liars

and perjurers—and for whatever else is contrary to the sound doctrine (1 Tim 1:9-10)

But, dear friends, remember what the apostles of our Lord Jesus Christ foretold. They said to you, "In the last times there will be scoffers who will follow their own ungodly desires." These are the men who divide you, who follow mere natural instincts and do not have the Spirit. (Jude 1:17-19)

3. It was at "just the right time" (kata kairon) that Christ died for us. It was in God's appointed time: His destined time, appropriate time. Men had to be prepared for Christ before God could send Him into the world. Men had to learn that they were without strength and ungodly, that they needed a Savior. (This was the purpose of the Old Testament and the law, to show men that they were sinful. See outline and note—Ro.4:14-15.)

"The time has come," he said. "The kingdom of God is near. Repent and believe the good news!" (Mark 1:15)

But when the time had fully come, God sent his Son, born of a woman, born under law, to redeem those under law, that we might receive the full rights of sons. (Gal 4:4-5)

For there is one God and one mediator between God and men, the man Christ Jesus, who gave himself as a ransom for all men—the testimony given in its proper time. (1 Tim 2:5-6)

A faith and knowledge resting on the hope of eternal life, which God, who does not lie, promised before the beginning of time, and at his appointed season he brought his word to light through the preaching entrusted to me by the command of God our Savior, (Titus 1:2-3)

Then Christ would have had to suffer many times since the creation of the world. But now he has appeared once for all at the end of the ages to do away with sin by the sacrifice of himself. (Heb 9:26)

4. Christ died *for* us. The word "for" (huper) means for our benefit, for our sake, in our behalf, in our stead, as our substitute. (See note and DEEPER STUDY # 4—Mk.10:45.)

a. Christ died as our sacrifice.

Get rid of the old yeast that you may be a new batch without yeast—as you really are. For Christ, our Passover lamb, has been sacrificed. (1 Cor 5:7)

And he died for all, that those who live should no longer live for themselves but for him who died for them and was raised again. (2 Cor 5:15)

God made him who had no sin to be sin for us, so that in him we might become the righteousness of God. (2 Cor 5:21)

And live a life of love, just as Christ loved us and gave himself up for us as a fragrant offering and sacrifice to God. (Eph 5:2)

Such a high priest meets our need—one who is holy, blameless, pure, set apart from sinners, exalted above the heavens.

Unlike the other high priests, he does not need to offer sacrifices day after day, first for his own sins, and then for the sins of the people. He sacrificed for their sins once for all when he offered himself. (Heb 7:26-27)

The blood of goats and bulls and the ashes of a heifer sprinkled on those who are ceremonially unclean sanctify them so that they are outwardly clean. How much more, then, will the blood of Christ, who through the eternal Spirit offered himself unblemished to God, cleanse our consciences from acts that lead to death, so that we may serve the living God! (Heb 9:13-14)

Nor did he enter heaven to offer himself again and again, the way the high priest enters the Most Holy Place every year with blood that is not his own. Then Christ would have had to suffer many times since the creation of the world. But now he has appeared once for all at the end of the ages to do away with sin by the sacrifice of himself. (Heb 9:25-26)

And by that will, we have been made holy through the sacrifice of the body of Jesus Christ once for all. (Heb 10:10)

But when this priest had offered for all time one sacrifice for sins, he sat down at the right hand of God. because by one sacrifice he has made perfect forever those who are being made holy. (Heb 10:12, 14)

He himself bore our sins in his body on the tree, so that we might die to sins and live for righteousness; by his wounds you have been healed. (1 Pet 2:24)

b. Christ died as our ransom (see note—Ro.3:24; Gal.3:13-14).

And are justified freely by his grace through the redemption that came by Christ Jesus. (Rom 3:24)

In whom we have redemption, the forgiveness of sins. (Col 1:14)

Who gave himself for us to redeem us from all wickedness and to purify for himself a people that are his very own, eager to do what is good. (Titus 2:14)

He did not enter by means of the blood of goats and calves; but he entered the Most Holy Place once for all by his own blood, having obtained eternal redemption. (Heb 9:12)

For you know that it was not with perishable things such as silver or gold that you were redeemed from the empty way of life handed down to you from your forefathers, but with the precious blood of Christ, a lamb without blemish or defect. (1 Pet 1:18-19)

And they sang a new song: "You are worthy to take the scroll and to open its seals, because you were slain, and with your blood you purchased men for God from every tribe and language and people and nation. (Rev 5:9)

c. Christ died as our Atonement (see note—Ro.3:25. Cp. 1 Jn.2:1-2).

> **God presented him as a sacrifice of atonement, through faith in his blood. He did this to demonstrate his justice, because in his forbearance he had left the sins committed beforehand unpunished— (Rom 3:25)**
>
> **He is the atoning sacrifice for our sins, and not only for ours but also for the sins of the whole world. (1 John 2:2)**
>
> **This is love: not that we loved God, but that he loved us and sent his Son as an atoning sacrifice for our sins. (1 John 4:10)**

5. God's love is an uncommon and an unbelievable love. Just think about the illustration given. Some persons attempt to save people who are caught in some desperate tragedy, and others offer their lives to represent leaders in their great purpose.

⇒ A few will die for a just and upright man (righteous).

⇒ Some will even *dare* to die for a "good" man.

But this is not what Christ did. Christ did not die for the righteous and godly man, nor for the good and pure man. He went well beyond what men do. Christ...

- died for the ungodly, for those who were the very opposite of righteous and good.
- died for those "powerless": the useless, destitute, worthless, and those without value to society and men.

Christ died for those for whom no man would die, for those who were of no value and of no good. He died for those who were diametrically opposed to God, the very opposite from all that He is. Such is the unbelievable love of God; such is the depth of justification.

2 (5:8-9) **Jesus Christ, Death—Man, State of—God, Love of**: we were sinners, yet God proved His love to us. The word "demonstrates" (sunistemi) means to show, prove, exhibit, demonstrate. It is the present tense: God is always showing and proving His love to us. The word "sinners" (hamartolon) refers to a man who is sinful, the man who sins...

- by disobeying God's Word and will (cp. Ro.1:29-31).
- by living selfishly.
- by ignoring God's commandments.
- by doing his own thing.
- by the cravings of sinful man and the lust of the eyes.
- by boasting of what he has and does.

The point is this: it is *"while* we were still sinners" that God proved His love to us. This is the unbelievable love of God, that He stooped down to save sinners. We would expect Him to save righteous and good men, but it catches us completely off guard when it is stated that He saves sinners. Such is the unbelievable love of God.

Now note how God proved His love.

1. God proved His love by giving up His only Son to die *for* us. Some earthly fathers would be willing to give up their sons for a "good" man or for a great cause. But how many would be willing to give up their sons for a man who committed treason or for a man who murdered one of the greatest men living? Think of the enormous price God paid in proving His love: He gave up His Son to die for the unworthy and useless, the ungodly and sinful, the wicked and depraved—the worst sinners and outcasts imaginable. Just think what God Himself must have gone through: the feelings, the suffering, the hurt, the pain, the terrible emotional strain. Just think what is involved in God giving up His Son:

⇒ God had to send His Son *out of* the spiritual and eternal world (dimension) *into* the physical and corruptible world (dimension).

⇒ God had to humiliate His Son by stripping Him of His eternal glory and insisting that He become clothed with corruptible flesh and die as a man.

⇒ God had to watch His Son walk through life being rejected, denied, cursed, abused, arrested, tortured, and murdered. God had to sit back and watch His Son suffer being murdered by the hands of men; He had to sit back when He knew He could reach out and deliver Him.

⇒ God had to destine His Son to die upon the cross for the sins of men.

⇒ God had to lay all the sins of the world upon His Son and let Him bear them all.

⇒ God had to judge His Son as the sinner and condemn Him to death for sin.

⇒ God had to turn His back upon Christ in death.

⇒ God had to cast His wrath against sin upon Christ.

⇒ God has to bear the pain of His Son's sufferings eternally, for He is eternal and the death of His Son is ever before His face. (Just imagine! It is beyond our comprehension, but the eternal agony is a fact because of the eternal nature of God.)

As stated, God proved His love. He has given up His Son to die for us. We do not deserve it—we never have and we never will—but God loves us with an unbelievable love. Therefore, He has given His Son to die *for* us, as our substitute, in our behalf.

> **But he was pierced for our transgressions, he was crushed for our iniquities; the punishment that brought us peace was upon him, and by his wounds we are healed. (Isa 53:5)**
>
> **"I am the good shepherd. The good shepherd lays down his life for the sheep. (John 10:11)**
>
> **Greater love has no one than this, that he lay down his life for his friends. (John 15:13)**
>
> **For what I received I passed on to you as of first importance : that Christ died for our sins according to the Scriptures, (1 Cor 15:3)**
>
> **But we see Jesus, who was made a little lower than the angels, now crowned with glory and honor because he suffered death, so that by the grace of God he might taste death for everyone. (Heb 2:9)**
>
> **For Christ died for sins once for all, the righteous for the unrighteous, to bring you to God. He was put to death in the body but made alive by the Spirit, (1 Pet 3:18)**

2. God proves His love by justification through the blood of Christ (see notes—Ro.5:1; 3:25 for discussion).

Since we have now been justified by his blood, how much more shall we be saved from God's wrath through him! (Rom 5:9)

And through him to reconcile to himself all things, whether things on earth or things in heaven, by making peace through his blood, shed on the cross. (Col 1:20)

How much more, then, will the blood of Christ, who through the eternal Spirit offered himself unblemished to God, cleanse our consciences from acts that lead to death, so that we may serve the living God! (Heb 9:14)

3. God proves His love by saving us from wrath (see notes and DEEPER STUDY # 1, *God's Wrath*—Ro.1:18. Also see note, pt.1—Ro.5:1 for discussion.)

"For God so loved the world that he gave his one and only Son, that whoever believes in him shall not perish but have eternal life. For God did not send his Son into the world to condemn the world, but to save the world through him. (John 3:16-17)

Whoever believes in the Son has eternal life, but whoever rejects the Son will not see life, for God's wrath remains on him." (John 3:36)

For the wages of sin is death, but the gift of God is eternal life in Christ Jesus our Lord. (Rom 6:23)

Christ redeemed us from the curse of the law by becoming a curse for us, for it is written: "Cursed is everyone who is hung on a tree." (Gal 3:13)

3 (5:10-11) **Reconciliation—Jesus Christ, Death—Man, State of—God, Love of**: we were enemies, yet God has reconciled and saved us. God reconciles and saves us by doing three things.

1. God reconciles us by Christ's death (see DEEPER STUDY #1—Ro.5:10 for discussion).

2. God saves us by Christ's life. "His life" means the life of the *living Lord*. Christ stands before God as our great Intercessor and Mediator. Standing before God, He stands as the Sinless and Righteous Son of God, as the Ideal and Perfect Man. When we believe in Christ, God takes our belief and counts it as righteousness. The Ideal Righteousness of Christ covers us, and God accepts and saves us because we *trust* Christ as the living Lord, as our Intercessor and Mediator before God.

Who is he that condemns? Christ Jesus, who died—more than that, who was raised to life—is at the right hand of God and is also interceding for us. (Rom 8:34)

Therefore he is able to save completely those who come to God through him, because he always lives to intercede for them. (Heb 7:25)

For there is one God and one mediator between God and men, the man Christ Jesus, (1 Tim 2:5)

But the ministry Jesus has received is as superior to theirs as the covenant of which he is mediator is superior to the old one, and it is founded on better promises. (Heb 8:6)

For this reason Christ is the mediator of a new covenant, that those who are called may receive the promised eternal inheritance—now that he has died as a ransom to set them free from the sins committed under the first covenant. (Heb 9:15)

For Christ did not enter a man-made sanctuary that was only a copy of the true one; he entered heaven itself, now to appear for us in God's presence. (Heb 9:24)

To Jesus the mediator of a new covenant, and to the sprinkled blood that speaks a better word than the blood of Abel. (Heb 12:24)

My dear children, I write this to you so that you will not sin. But if anybody does sin, we have one who speaks to the Father in our defense—Jesus Christ, the Righteous One. He is the atoning sacrifice for our sins, and not only for ours but also for the sins of the whole world. (1 John 2:1-2)

3. God gives us joy through the reconciliation of Christ. A person who receives so much from God is bound to be filled with joy and rejoicing (see note, *Joy*—Ph.1:4 for discussion).

I have told you this so that my joy may be in you and that your joy may be complete. (John 15:11)

Until now you have not asked for anything in my name. Ask and you will receive, and your joy will be complete. (John 16:24)

For the kingdom of God is not a matter of eating and drinking, but of righteousness, peace and joy in the Holy Spirit, (Rom 14:17)

Though you have not seen him, you love him; and even though you do not see him now, you believe in him and are filled with an inexpressible and glorious joy, for you are receiving the goal of your faith, the salvation of your souls. (1 Pet 1:8-9)

You have made known to me the path of life; you will fill me with joy in your presence, with eternal pleasures at your right hand. (Psa 16:11)

Our mouths were filled with laughter, our tongues with songs of joy. Then it was said among the nations, "The LORD has done great things for them." (Psa 126:2)

With joy you will draw water from the wells of salvation. (Isa 12:3)

And the ransomed of the LORD will return. They will enter Zion with singing; everlasting joy will crown their heads. Gladness and joy will overtake them, and sorrow and sighing will flee away. (Isa 35:10)

I delight greatly in the LORD; my soul rejoices in my God. For he has clothed me with garments of salvation and arrayed me in a robe of righteousness, as a bridegroom adorns his head like a priest, and as a bride adorns herself with her jewels. (Isa 61:10)

DEEPER STUDY # 1

(5:10) Reconcile—Reconciliation (katallasso): to change, to change thoroughly, to exchange, to change from enmity to friendship, to bring together, to restore. The idea is that two persons who should have been together all along are brought together; two persons who had something between them are restored and reunited.

Three points should be noted about reconciliation.

1. The thing that broke the relationship between God and man was sin. Men are said to be enemies of God (Ro.5:10), and the word "enemies" refers back to the sinners and the ungodly (Ro.5:6, 8). The "enemies" of God are the sinners and ungodly of this world. This simply means that every man is an enemy of God, for every man is a sinner and ungodly. This may seem unkind and harsh, but it is exactly what Scripture is saying. The fact is clearly seen by thinking about the matter for a moment.

The sinner cannot be said to be a friend of God's. He is antagonistic toward God, opposing what God stands for. The sinner is...

- rebelling against God
- rejecting God
- cursing God
- ignoring God
- disobeying God
- fighting against God
- denying God
- refusing

When any of us sin, we work against God and promote evil by word and example.

⇒ When the sinner lives for himself, he becomes an enemy of God. Why? Because God does not live for Himself. God gave Himself up in the most supreme way possible: He gave His only Son to die *for* us.

⇒ When the sinner lives for the world and worldly things, he becomes an enemy of God. Why? Because he chooses the temporal—that which passes away—over God. He chooses it when God has provided eternal life for him through the death of His Son.

This is the point of God's great love or reconciliation. He did not reconcile and save us when we were righteous and good. He reconciled and saved us when we were enemies, ignoring and rejecting Him. As stated above, it is because we are sinners and enemies that we need to be reconciled.

2. The way men are reconciled to God is by the death of His Son, Jesus Christ. Very simply stated, when a man believes that Jesus Christ died for him...

- God accepts the death of Jesus Christ *for* the death of the man.
- God accepts the sins borne by Christ as the sins committed by the man.
- God accepts the condemnation borne by Christ as the condemnation due to the man.

Therefore, the man is freed from his sins and the punishment due his sins. Christ bore both the sins and the punishment for the man. The man who truly believes that God loves that much—enough to give His only begotten Son—becomes acceptable to God, reconciled forever and ever.

3. God is the One who reconciles, not men. Men do not reconcile themselves to God. They cannot do enough work or enough good to become acceptable to God. Reconciliation is entirely the act of God. God is the One who reaches out to men and reconciles them unto Himself. Men *receive* the reconciliation of God.

All this is from God, who reconciled us to himself through Christ and gave us the ministry of reconciliation: (2 Cor 5:18; cp.. v. 19-21)

To the praise of his glorious grace, which he has freely given us in the One he loves. (Eph 1:6)

and in this one body to reconcile both of them to God through the cross, by which he put to death their hostility. (Eph 2:16)

And through him to reconcile to himself all things, whether things on earth or things in heaven, by making peace through his blood, shed on the cross. (Col 1:20)

For this reason he had to be made like his brothers in every way, in order that he might become a merciful and faithful high priest in service to God, and that he might make atonement for the sins of the people. (Heb 2:17)

We love because he first loved us. (1 John 4:19)

	I. Adam and Christ: The Two Focal Points of History, 5:12-21	condemnation, but the gift followed many trespasses and brought justification. 17 For if, by the trespass of the one man, death reigned through that one man, how much more will those who receive God's abundant provision of grace and of the gift of righteousness reign in life through the one man, Jesus Christ.	c. Adam's sin brought the reign of death; God's gift brought the reign of life
1 The entrance of sin & death through Adam[DS1,2] a. Sin came by one man—Adam b. Adam's nature of sin & death passed to all c. The proof: Sin & death existed before the law; sin & death came from & thru Adam d. Adam's real importance: A type of Christ, cp. 1 Cor.15:22, 45-49	12 Therefore, just as sin entered the world through one man, and death through sin, and in this way death came to all men, because all sinned— 13 For before the law was given, sin was in the world. But sin is not taken into account when there is no law. 14 Nevertheless, death reigned from the time of Adam to the time of Moses, even over those who did not sin by breaking a command, as did Adam, who was a pattern of the one to come.	18 Consequently, just as the result of one trespass was condemnation for all men, so also the result of one act of righteousness was justification that brings life for all men. 19 For just as through the disobedience of the one man the many were made sinners, so also through the obedience of the one man the many will be made righteous.	d. Adam's sin brought condemnation to all men; God's gift brought justification & life to all men **3 Conclusion** a. Adam's disobedience made many sinners, but Christ's obedience made many righteous
2 The counteraction—the reversal—of sin & death by Christ a. Adam's sin brought death; God's gift brought righteousness b. Adam's sin brought condemnation; God's gift brought justification	15 But the gift is not like the trespass. For if the many died by the trespass of the one man, how much more did God's grace and the gift that came by the grace of the one man, Jesus Christ, overflow to the many! 16 Again, the gift of God is not like the result of the one man's sin: The judgment followed one sin and brought	20 The law was added so that the trespass might increase. But where sin increased, grace increased all the more, 21 So that, just as sin reigned in death, so also grace might reign through righteousness to bring eternal life through Jesus Christ our Lord.	b. The law was given to point out & magnify sin, but God's grace was so much greater c. Sin reigned in death, but God's grace reigns to eternal life—thru Christ's righteousness

DIVISION III

FAITH AND JUSTIFICATION: THE WAY FOR THE WORLD TO BE RIGHT WITH GOD, 3:21-5:21

I. Adam and Christ: The Two Focal Points of History, 5:12-21

(5:12-21) **Introduction**: this passage deals with two of the focal points of human history. It deals with Adam and Christ, the two chief representatives and figureheads of the human race. It tells how sin and death entered the world and how Jesus Christ counteracted sin and death.

1. The entrance of sin and death through Adam (v.12-14).
2. The counteraction—the reversal—of sin and death by Christ (v.15-18).
3. Conclusion (v.19-21).

1 (5:12-14) **Adam—Sin—Death—History, Pivotal Points**: the entrance of sin and death into the world through Adam.

1. The fact is very simply stated: sin and death entered the world through one man, Adam. God had said:

> But you must not eat from the tree of the knowledge of good and evil, for when you eat of it you will surely die." (Gen 2:17)
> For every living soul belongs to me, the father as well as the son—both alike belong to me. The soul who sins is the one who will die. (Ezek 18:4)
> The soul who sins is the one who will die. The son will not share the guilt of the father, nor will the father share the guilt of

> the son. The righteousness of the righteous man will be credited to him, and the wickedness of the wicked will be charged against him. (Ezek 18:20)

Adam sinned and corrupted himself; therefore, he died.

2. Adam's nature of sin and death was and still is spread and passed on to all men. His corruptible nature was spread and passed on to his children and on down through history to all men. It is a well known fact that the child inherits the nature of his parents. Therefore, if the parent's nature is bent toward sin and is corruptible, so will the child's nature be. Nature is like an *infectious blood line*: whatever the nature is, it is passed on down to the next generation.

Now note a significant fact: a man is not condemned to death because of Adam's sin. Scripture clearly says this: "Death came to all men, because all sinned" (v.12). A man dies because of his own sins, not because of his father's sins. Every man is personally responsible to God.

> For all have sinned and fall short of the glory of God, (Rom 3:23)
> For the wages of sin is death, but the gift of God is eternal life in Christ Jesus our Lord. (Rom 6:23)

But the Scripture declares that the whole world is a prisoner of sin, so that what was promised, being given through faith in Jesus Christ, might be given to those who believe. (Gal 3:22)

If we claim to be without sin, we deceive ourselves and the truth is not in us. (1 John 1:8)

We know that we are children of God, and that the whole world is under the control of the evil one. (1 John 5:19)

"When they sin against you—for there is no one who does not sin—and you become angry with them and give them over to the enemy, who takes them captive to his own land, far away or near; (1 Ki 8:46)

All have turned aside, they have together become corrupt; there is no one who does good, not even one. (Psa 14:3)

Everyone has turned away, they have together become corrupt; there is no one who does good, not even one. (Psa 53:3)

Who can say, "I have kept my heart pure; I am clean and without sin"? (Prov 20:9)

We all, like sheep, have gone astray, each of us has turned to his own way; and the LORD has laid on him the iniquity of us all. (Isa 53:6)

All of us have become like one who is unclean, and all our righteous acts are like filthy rags; we all shrivel up like a leaf, and like the wind our sins sweep us away. (Isa 64:6)

3. The proof that we inherit Adam's nature is that sin and death existed even before the law (v.13). The law of God does charge men with sin; it does show men that they are sinful and condemned to die. But *something* caused men to sin and die before the law was ever given to Moses in a written form. The people before Moses were not charged with sin by the law, for they did not have the law in a permanent and written form. What was it then that was causing the people between Adam and Moses to sin and die? It was nature, the sinful, corruptible nature of man, the nature that every child inherited from his father; and the process began with Adam. Adam was the first man created by God, and he was the first to sin and become corruptible and bear the punishment of death.

By the sweat of your brow you will eat your food until you return to the ground, since from it you were taken; for dust you are and to dust you will return." (Gen 3:19)

Side by side they lie in the dust, and worms cover them both. (Job 21:26)

Those who trust in their wealth and boast of their great riches? No man can redeem the life of another or give to God a ransom for him—the ransom for a life is costly, no payment is ever enough—that he should live on forever and not see decay. (Psa 49:6-9)

When you hide your face, they are terrified; when you take away their breath, they die and return to the dust. (Psa 104:29)

All go to the same place; all come from dust, and to dust all return. (Eccl 3:20)

And the dust returns to the ground it came from, and the spirit returns to God who gave it. (Eccl 12:7)

"Take away the stone," he said. "But, Lord," said Martha, the sister of the dead man, "by this time there is a bad odor, for he has been there four days." (John 11:39)

"For when David had served God's purpose in his own generation, he fell asleep; he was buried with his fathers and his body decayed. (Acts 13:36)

4. The importance of Adam is critical. He was "a pattern [type, picture] of the one to come," that is, of Christ. Adam and Christ are pictured as the two pivotal points of human history, as the two *figureheads or representatives* of the human race (cp. 1 Cor.15:20-28, 45-49). Adam stands at the head of the human race, as *the first* to bring sin and death to man: "Your first father sinned" (Is.43:27). Christ stands at the head of the human race…

- as the first to live a sinless and perfect life, securing a perfect righteousness.
- as the first to conquer death by literally arising from the dead.

Now note the difference between Adam and Christ. Adam became a "living being;" Christ a "quickening, life-giving spirit" (1 Cor.15:45). What man needs and has always needed is a "quickening, life-giving spirit," a spirit that has the power to infuse life into his soul, life that is both abundant and eternal.

Nevertheless, death reigned from the time of Adam to the time of Moses, even over those who did not sin by breaking a command, as did Adam, who was a pattern of the one to come. (Rom 5:14)

Consequently, just as the result of one trespass was condemnation for all men, so also the result of one act of righteousness was justification that brings life for all men. For just as through the disobedience of the one man the many were made sinners, so also through the obedience of the one man the many will be made righteous. (Rom 5:18-19)

For since death came through a man, the resurrection of the dead comes also through a man. For as in Adam all die, so in Christ all will be made alive. (1 Cor 15:21-22)

So it is written: "The first man Adam became a living being;" the last Adam, a life-giving spirit. The spiritual did not come first, but the natural, and after that the spiritual. The first man was of the dust of the earth, the second man from heaven. As was the earthly man, so are those who are of the earth; and as is the man from heaven, so also are those who are of heaven. And just as we have borne the likeness of the earthly man, so shall we bear the likeness of the man from heaven. (1 Cor 15:45-49)

5. Note that sin is *the cause of death*, and that Adam was the cause of sin. He was the author of apostasy. Whatever theories may say, one thing is clear: *Adam was the cause of sin in the very same way in which Christ is the cause of righteousness.*

   a. Note v.13. Since Adam, sin has been universal. But sin was not charged (that is, personal guilt) against a person because there was no law. There has to be a law for there to be a charge.

b. Note v.14. Nevertheless, death was still the judgment and experience of man. Why? Why did man die if he was not charged with personal sin? Because Adam was the figurehead and the representative man for all who would be born with his nature. What does this mean? He sinned, took on a corruptible nature; therefore, he died (Ro.5:12f). So death *was passed on and spread* to all men because all inherited the corruptible nature of Adam (Ro.5:12f).

Some argue that this is unjust—to be condemned to die because the father of the human race, Adam, sinned. But the argument is not familiar with the facts, for the truth is, the way to eternal life is now clearer and much more positive. God has now made a greater provision for life and salvation.

a. This is clearly seen in three facts. A man now has a clearer choice than Adam had. A man can now live forever by simply choosing to take Christ into his life, and the positive choice of choosing Christ is greater and has more pull than Adam's choice. Adam was to remain incorruptible if he did not eat of the fruit of the tree. Note his choice was a negative command and it had no pull and no power to enable him to obey. Man's choice today is positive. Adam was *forbidden to do something*. We are instructed *to do something*—a positive command. These two facts, the fuller and clearer revelation in Christ and the stronger pull of the positive, show that every man has an equal chance at immortality; and in reality, man today has more of a chance than Adam had, more than an equal chance.

b. There is no human life apart from being born to corruptible human beings. It is a matter of being born and privileged with life or not being born and never having the privilege of life. In order to have the privilege of living, a person has to be born of corruptible parents.

c. The way of salvation and the way for man to live forever is now much clearer. Man could never know the love of God apart from being born into a corruptible world and experiencing the love of God demonstrated in Christ Jesus. Therefore, the birth of a person, his entrance into the world, is the greatest imaginable blessing. Being born into this depraved and corruptible world is the only way a person can ever know the love of God and experience eternal life with God.

In order that in the coming ages he might show the incomparable riches of his grace, expressed in his kindness to us in Christ Jesus. (Eph 2:7)
In reply Jesus declared, "I tell you the truth, no one can see the kingdom of God unless he is born again." (John 3:3)
Through these he has given us his very great and precious promises, so that through them you may participate in the divine nature and escape the corruption in the world caused by evil desires. (2 Pet 1:4)

DEEPER STUDY # 1
(5:12) **Sin—Death**: Adam sinned and corrupted himself; therefore, he died. Why is there such an awful penalty for sin? Is not death an awful price to pay for sin? Such questions overlook the awfulness and seriousness of sin. Sin is the most heinous, vulgar, uncouth, abominable, outrageous, shocking, and hateful thing that can exist. Two things show the evil nature of sin.

1. Sin is the ultimate thing that can be done *against God*. Sin is *disobeying God* and *rebelling against God*. Sin acts against God, fights and struggles against God. Sin goes against all that God is. Sin is insurrection against God; it is the crime of high treason against God. To turn away from the Supreme Being of the universe is to commit the *ultimate offense* (disobedience), and the ultimate offense deserves the ultimate judgment: death. (Keep in mind the glorious love of God. The only way to truly see the love of God is to see man committing the ultimate offense against God [disobeying Him] and having to bear the ultimate punishment of death. Seeing this is the only way a man can see how God paid the ultimate price in giving His Son to die *for us*. His love is the supreme love, the love that sacrificed the greatest thing in all the world, that gave His Son to die for sinners. See outline and notes—Ro.5:6-11.)

2. Sin cost God the ultimate price, the supreme sacrifice of His Son. God, being God, is perfect love. As perfect love He is bound to prove His love by providing a way for man to be forgiven his sin and to be saved. And the way chosen to save man had to be the perfect salvation, the perfect expression of His love.

Greater love has no one than this, that he lay down his life for his friends. (John 15:13)

But note, Christ did not give His life just for friends. He went well beyond; He loved perfectly: He gave His life for those who were powerless, for the ungodly, the sinners, the enemies of God (Ro.5:6, 8, 10).

But God demonstrates his own love for us in this: While we were still sinners, Christ died for us. (Rom 5:8)

Sin cost God the ultimate price, the supreme sacrifice, even the death of His own Son.

Sin is the most serious and awful thing a person can do against God. It is the ultimate offense against God and it costs the ultimate price, even the supreme sacrifice of God's dear Son. It is for these two reasons that sin deserves the ultimate penalty of death.

But he was pierced for our transgressions, he was crushed for our iniquities; the punishment that brought us peace was upon him, and by his wounds we are healed. (Isa 53:5)
Therefore I will give him a portion among the great, and he will divide the spoils with the strong, because he poured out his life unto death, and was numbered with the transgressors. For he bore the sin of many, and made intercession for the transgressors. (Isa 53:12)
You see, at just the right time, when we were still powerless, Christ died for the ungodly. (Rom 5:6)
For what I received I passed on to you as of first importance : that Christ died for our sins according to the Scriptures, (1 Cor 15:3)
Meanwhile we groan, longing to be clothed with our heavenly dwelling, (2 Cor 5:2)
And he died for all, that those who live should no longer live for themselves but for

him who died for them and was raised again. (2 Cor 5:15)

I was advancing in Judaism beyond many Jews of my own age and was extremely zealous for the traditions of my fathers. (Gal 1:14)

Who gave himself for us to redeem us from all wickedness and to purify for himself a people that are his very own, eager to do what is good. (Titus 2:14)

So Christ was sacrificed once to take away the sins of many people; and he will appear a second time, not to bear sin, but to bring salvation to those who are waiting for him. (Heb 9:28)

He himself bore our sins in his body on the tree, so that we might die to sins and live for righteousness; by his wounds you have been healed. (1 Pet 2:24)

For Christ died for sins once for all, the righteous for the unrighteous, to bring you to God. He was put to death in the body but made alive by the Spirit, (1 Pet 3:18)

But you know that he appeared so that he might take away our sins. And in him is no sin. (1 John 3:5)

This is how we know what love is: Jesus Christ laid down his life for us. And we ought to lay down our lives for our brothers. (1 John 3:16)

DEEPER STUDY # 2
(5:12) **Sin—Death**: physical, spiritual, and eternal death would be involved here. Sin is universal, so death is universal—all embracing. (See DEEPER STUDY # 1—Heb.9:27.)

---

2 (5:15-18) **Jesus Christ, Works of—Sin—Death**: the counteraction—the reversal—of sin and death by Christ. Jesus Christ has counter acted and reversed what Adam did. He has made it possible for man to live righteously and to conquer death. Note the descriptive contrast between what Adam did and what God did through Christ.

1. Adam's sin brought death; God's gift brought righteousness. The gift is righteousness (cp. v.17). God's gift of righteousness differs entirely from the sin of Adam. Adam sinned and brought sin and death to "many" (to the human race). But Adam was only one man and God is far greater than one mere man, even if that man has influenced the whole human race. God was able to do *"much more"* good than Adam was able to do bad. In fact, God *has done* "much more." He has counteracted and reversed all the bad Adam did.
   a. God has showered the grace of God, His glorious favor and care and love, upon man. (See DEEPER STUDY # 1, *Grace*—Tit.2:11-15).

   But because of his great love for us, God, who is rich in mercy, made us alive with Christ even when we were dead in transgressions—it is by grace you have been saved. And God raised us up with Christ and seated us with him in the heavenly realms in Christ Jesus, in order that in the coming ages he might show the incompa-

rable riches of his grace, expressed in his kindness to us in Christ Jesus. For it is by grace you have been saved, through faith—and this not from yourselves, it is the gift of God—not by works, so that no one can boast. (Eph 2:4-9)

So that, having been justified by his grace, we might become heirs having the hope of eternal life. (Titus 3:7)

   b. God has made the gift of God (righteousness) available to man. (See note, *Righteousnesss—Ro.1:17*.)

   But also for us, to whom God will credit righteousness—for us who believe in him who raised Jesus our Lord from the dead. He was delivered over to death for our sins and was raised to life for our justification. (Rom 4:24-25)

   God made him who had no sin to be sin for us, so that in him we might become the righteousness of God. (2 Cor 5:21)

God's grace and gift have overflowed to many. But note: it all comes through One Man, Jesus Christ, God's very own Son.

   But when the kindness and love of God our Savior appeared, he saved us, not because of righteous things we had done, but because of his mercy. He saved us through the washing of rebirth and renewal by the Holy Spirit, whom he poured out on us generously through Jesus Christ our Savior, (Titus 3:4-6)

2. Adam's sin brought condemnation; God's gift brought justification. God's gift differs entirely from what Adam did. Adam doomed the human race, but God's gift justifies the human race. And note how glorious God's justification is: when Adam sinned, his one sin was judged and brought condemnation to men; but what God did is so glorious, it explodes the human mind.
   ⇒ God's gift not only dealt with Adams's trespasses and condemnation, it dealt with *"many"* trespasses. God's gift of righteousness justifies us from *all our trespasses*, not only from Adam's one trespass. God's gift justifies us from all the corruption we have inherited from our fathers and from all the corruption of human nature—all the sins we have committed with our own hands.

The man who truly trusts Christ is justified from all things, from all sin and corruption and condemnation...
   • inherited from our fathers (Adam).
   • committed and caused by our own sinful behavior.

   Through him everyone who believes is justified from everything you could not be justified from by the law of Moses. (Acts 13:39)

   Therefore, since we have been justified through faith, we have peace with God through our Lord Jesus Christ, (Rom 5:1)

   Consider Abraham: "He believed God, and it was credited to him as righteousness." (Gal 3:6)

93

3. Adam's sin brought the reign of death; God's gift brought the reign of life. Adam sinned and brought the reign of death upon all men. But Adam was only one man, one mere man. No matter what he did, God was able to counteract it and do more, for He is greater; and He is able to do anything.

God has done more, much more. They who "receive" God's grace and God's gift of righteousness "will" reign in life." The term "reign in life" means to dwell and rule in eternal life. But note, the source of righteousness is Jesus Christ (see DEEPER STUDY # 2, *Justification*—Ro.4:22; note—5:1).

Thought 1. Note two glorious truths.
1) Believers "reign in life" while on this earth. They receive the abundance of God's grace.
   a) There is the gift of a full abundant life.

> **The thief comes only to steal and kill and destroy; I have come that they may have life, and have it to the full. (John 10:10)**

   b) There is having all you need, all sufficiency in all things.

> **And God is able to make all grace abound to you, so that in all things at all times, having all that you need, you will abound in every good work. (2 Cor 9:8)**

   c) There is great power.

> **Now to him who is able to do immeasurably more than all we ask or imagine, according to his power that is at work within us, (Eph 3:20)**

   d) There is the supply of all needs.

> **And my God will meet all your needs according to his glorious riches in Christ Jesus. (Phil 4:19)**

   e) There is a rich welcome, an abundant entrance into heaven.

> **And you will receive a rich welcome into the eternal kingdom of our Lord and Savior Jesus Christ. (2 Pet 1:11)**

   f) There is abundant satisfaction.

> **They feast on the abundance of your house; you give them drink from your river of delights. (Psa 36:8)**

2) Believers will "reign in life" throughout all eternity.

> **"For God so loved the world that he gave his one and only Son, that whoever believes in him shall not perish but have eternal life. (John 3:16)**
> **"I tell you the truth, whoever hears my word and believes him who sent me has eter-**

nal life and will not be condemned; he has crossed over from death to life. (John 5:24)
> **"'Well done, my good servant!' his master replied. 'Because you have been trustworthy in a very small matter, take charge of ten cities.' (Luke 19:17)**
> **You are those who have stood by me in my trials. And I confer on you a kingdom, just as my Father conferred one on me, (Luke 22:28-29)**
> **Do you not know that the saints will judge [govern, rule, manage] the world? And if you are to judge the world, are you not competent to judge trivial cases? Do you not know that we will judge angels? How much more the things of this life! (1 Cor 6:2-3)**

4. Adam's sin brought condemnation to all men; God's gift brought justification of life upon all men. This is simply a summary of what has already been said.
   ⇒ "The result of one trespass [Adam] was condemnation for all men."
   ⇒ "The result of one act of righteousness [Jesus Christ] was justification that brings life for all men."

> **For the wages of sin is death, but the gift of God is eternal life in Christ Jesus our Lord. (Rom 6:23)**
> **He who did not spare his own Son, but gave him up for us all—how will he not also, along with him, graciously give us all things? (Rom 8:32)**
> **Thanks be to God for his indescribable gift! (2 Cor 9:15)**
> **For it is by grace you have been saved, through faith—and this not from yourselves, it is the gift of God— (Eph 2:8)**

3 (5:19-21) **Justification—Righteousness—Law:** the conclusion is one of the most instructive and striking passages in all of Scripture. It includes three points.

1. Adam's disobedience made many (all men, v.12, 18) sinners, but Christ's obedience made many righteous. Jesus Christ lived a sinless life; He never sinned, never displeased God—not even once. He was perfectly righteous, *securing the Ideal Righteousness.*

Since His righteousness is *the Ideal Righteousness*, it can stand for the righteousness of all men, and that is exactly what happens. When a man believes in Jesus Christ, God takes that man's belief and counts it as righteousness. God lets the *Ideal Righteousness* of Jesus Christ cover the man because the man *believes and honors* His Son, Jesus Christ.

Any man who will so honor God's Son by believing and trusting Him, God will honor by counting his faith as the righteousness of Christ. It is that simple and that profound: "By the obedience of Jesus Christ many will be made righteous." But note, a person must truly believe—he must have the kind of belief that really trusts Jesus Christ, that really casts his life upon Christ, that casts all that he is and has upon Christ and His keeping.

> **In bringing many sons to glory, it was fitting that God, for whom and through whom everything exists, should make the**

author of their salvation perfect through suffering. (Heb 2:10)

And, once made perfect, he became the source of eternal salvation for all who obey him (Heb 5:9)

Therefore he is able to save completely those who come to God through him, because he always lives to intercede for them. Such a high priest meets our need—one who is holy, blameless, pure, set apart from sinners, exalted above the heavens. (Heb 7:25-26)

2. The law was given to point out and magnify sin, but God's grace was so much greater. If righteousness is by Jesus Christ, then why did God give us the law? What is the purpose of the law? Very simply. "The law was added [to the world] so that the trespass might increase." The law was given...

- to point out and magnify sin.
- to make men more aware of sin.
- to give men a greater knowledge of sin.
- to stir more conviction over sin.
- to increase the fact and awareness of sin more and more.
- to make men more responsible for their sin.

Therefore no one will be declared righteous in his sight by observing the law; rather, through the law we become conscious of sin. (Rom 3:20)

What, then, was the purpose of the law? It was added because of transgressions until the Seed to whom the promise referred had come. The law was put into effect through angels by a mediator. (Gal 3:19)

So the law was put in charge to lead us to Christ that we might be justified by faith. (Gal 3:24)

But note the glorious truth about the grace of God: wherever sin increases, the grace of God increases even more. God's grace is far more effective and powerful than any sin or sins, no matter how magnified. God's grace can forgive any man, no matter how great a sinner.

In him we have redemption through his blood, the forgiveness of sins, in accordance with the riches of God's grace (Eph 1:7)

In order that in the coming ages he might show the incomparable riches of his grace, expressed in his kindness to us in Christ Jesus. (Eph 2:7)

The grace of our Lord was poured out on me abundantly, along with the faith and love that are in Christ Jesus. Here is a trustworthy saying that deserves full acceptance: Christ Jesus came into the world to

save sinners—of whom I am the worst. (1 Tim 1:14-15)

3. Sin reigned in death, but God's grace reigns to eternal life.

a. By Adam, sin *reigns*, triumphs, holds authority and leads to death.

Therefore, just as sin entered the world through one man, and death through sin, and in this way death came to all men, because all sinned— (Rom 5:12)

The truly righteous man attains life, but he who pursues evil goes to his death. (Prov 11:19)

For every living soul belongs to me, the father as well as the son—both alike belong to me. The soul who sins is the one who will die. (Ezek 18:4)

The soul who sins is the one who will die. The son will not share the guilt of the father, nor will the father share the guilt of the son. The righteousness of the righteous man will be credited to him, and the wickedness of the wicked will be charged against him. (Ezek 18:20)

b. By God, grace reigns, triumphs, holds authority, and leads to eternal life. (See DEEPER STUDY #2, *Life*—Jn.1:4; DEEPER STUDY #1—10:10; DEEPER STUDY #1—17:2-3.)

In him was life, and that life was the light of men. (John 1:4)

Jesus said to her, "I am the resurrection and the life. He who believes in me will live, even though he dies; and whoever lives and believes in me will never die. Do you believe this?" (John 11:25-26)

Jesus answered, "I am the way and the truth and the life. No one comes to the Father except through me. (John 14:6)

But it has now been revealed through the appearing of our Savior, Christ Jesus, who has destroyed death and has brought life and immortality to light through the gospel. (2 Tim 1:10)

The life appeared; we have seen it and testify to it, and we proclaim to you the eternal life, which was with the Father and has appeared to us. (1 John 1:2)

He who has the Son has life; he who does not have the Son of God does not have life. (1 John 5:12)

But note the source: eternal life comes only through the righteousness of "Jesus Christ our Lord."

CHAPTER 6

IV. HOLINESS AND SANCTIFICATION: THE WAY FOR THE BELIEVER TO BE FREE FROM SIN, 6:1-23

A. The Believer is Not to Continue in Sin (Part I): He is to Know His Position in Christ, 6:1-10

1 The believer & the question of license
   a. Does grace give a person a free reign to sin?
   b. By no means!
   c. The bel. is dead to sin
2 Know 1st: By position, the believer is immersed, placed into Christ[DS1]
   a. Immersed, identified with Christ in death
   b. Immersed, identified with Christ in resurrection
     1) Raised through God's

What shall we say, then? Shall we go on sinning so that grace may increase?
2 By no means! We died to sin; how can we live in it any longer?
3 Or don't you know that all of us who were baptized into Christ Jesus were baptized into his death?
4 We were therefore buried with him through baptism into death in order that, just as Christ was raised from the dead through the glory of the Father, we too may live a new life.
5 If we have been united with him like this in his death, we will certainly also be united with him in his resurrection.
6 For we know that our old self was crucified with him so that the body of sin might be done away with, that we should no longer be slaves to sin—
7 Because anyone who has died has been freed from sin.
8 Now if we died with Christ, we believe that we will also live with him.
9 For we know that since Christ was raised from the dead, he cannot die again; death no longer has mastery over him.
10 The death he died, he died to sin once for all; but the life he lives, he lives to God.

glory
     2) Purpose: That we should live a new life
   c. Immersed, identified with the most glorious hope: The believer will be raised just as Jesus was raised
3 Know 2nd: By position, the believer's old self was crucified with Christ
   a. To destroy the body of sin
   b. To enable man to renounce sin
   c. Illust.: A dead man

4 Know 3rd: By position, the believer lives with Christ—now & forever
   a. Christ has conquered death—once for all

   b. Christ now lives forever to God[DS2]

DIVISION IV

HOLINESS AND SANCTIFICATION: THE WAY FOR THE BELIEVER TO BE FREE FROM SIN, 6:1-23

A. The Believer is Not to Continue in Sin (Part I): He is to Know His Position in Christ, 6:1-10

(6:1-10) **Introduction—Holiness**: the believer who is justified (whose faith is counted as righteousness, Ro.3:21-5:21) is to let his righteousness work holiness (Ro.6:19). The believer is to live a holy life and become a servant of righteousness. A genuinely saved person cannot abuse the mercy of God. He cannot walk in sin; he cannot make a habit of sinning. To do so is to tread upon the mercy of God and make a mockery of God's grace. It is to say that God's grace gives a person the license to sin, and such is a contradiction of terms—as much a contradiction as to say that a dead man is alive. (See notes—Ro.6:14-15; Gal.5:13.)

The way for a man to break the habit of sin is for him to know the glorious position he can have in Christ. One thing is certain: every believer should definitely know the position he holds in Christ. It will revolutionize his life.

Now for the point of the passage. The believer is to know his real position in Christ. Knowledge of his position will help keep him from sin. Note the word "*know*" is used three times (Ro.6:3, 6, 9).

1. The believer and the question of license (v.1-2).
2. Know 1st: by position, the believer is immersed, placed into Christ (v.3-5).
3. Know 2nd: by position, the believer's old self, his old man, was crucified with Christ (v.6-7).
4. Know 3rd: by position, the believer lives with Christ—now and forever (v.8-10).

1 (6:1-2) **License—Grace vs. Law—Sin**: the believer and the question of license. Note three points.

1. Does the grace of God give a person a free reign to sin? Can a person just go ahead and do what he wants ex-

pecting God to forgive him? Grace means God's undeserved and unmerited favor. It means that God freely accepts and forgives a person's sins; that He freely justifies a person by faith. (See DEEPER STUDY # 1,2—Ro.4:22; 5:1 for more discussion.) Two things bother a lot of people about the teaching of salvation by grace and grace alone.

   a. Grace seems to give free reign to sin, to put no restraint upon sin. These are often the thoughts of the common man, even believers. There is the feeling that if we are forgiven by grace and not by law and doing good, then sin does not matter that much. We do not have to worry too much about the law of God and righteousness, just so we do a fair amount of good. We can pretty much do what we want, for God is going to forgive us anyway. God is gracious and loving and good; therefore, He is going to forgive our sins no matter what we do. Christ died for our sins. All we have to do is ask Him and He will forgive us.

   b. Grace seems to encourage sin. Paul had just said that grace is stronger than sin (Ro.5:15-21, esp. 20-21). God's grace is so strong it can forgive any sin, no matter how terrible. In fact, the greater the sin, the more magnified God's grace becomes. When a *great sinner* is forgiven, God's grace is much more magnified than when a morally good person repents and is forgiven. As stated, the greater the sin or sinner, the more God's grace is magnified and glorified.

   Now note: some theologians and philosophers, in particular those who stress the law, carry this argument even farther in their position against grace. No doubt Paul was asked this question time and again by the legalists who hounded and fought against him and just did not understand the wonderful grace of God. They argued that if forgiveness is by grace, then is sin not a good thing? Should we not continue in sin so that God will have more opportunity to prove His grace and become more magnified and glorified?

2. Paul's answer is the answer of righteous indignation: "By no means!" Away with such a thought! Far be it that we ever think such a thing, especially as believers.

3. The *believer's position* in Christ shows the utter impossibility of a true believer *continuing, going on in sin*. The words "going on" or "continuing" mean to practice or to habitually yield to sin. A true believer no longer practices sin and no longer yields to sin. He cannot live *without sin*, not totally, but he no longer lives *in sin*. A true believer is dead to sin, and a dead man cannot do anything: he cannot think, speak, or move. How can a dead man live any longer in sin? It is utterly impossible! It is totally against nature! *Positionally*, the true believer has died to self and has been *placed* into Christ to live for Him. He now possesses the *divine nature*, God's very own nature (2 Pt.1:4). He is *placed* and *positioned* in Christ which means he is dead to self and alive to God. How can he dare think that he can go ahead and sin because God will forgive him anyway?

Note another fact: when a man turns *to* God, he turns *away from* sin. It is a contradiction to say that when a man turns to God he turns to more and more sin. God's grace does not bring a man to God so that he can be *free to sin* more; God's grace brings a man to God so that he can be *free from sin* and its guilt and judgment. Grace does not give license to sin any more than a dead man is able to move about and sin. (See note, *License*—Ro.6:14-15 for more discussion.)

2 (6:3-5) **Jesus Christ, Death—Believer, Position in Christ**: first, the believer has been *immersed or placed into Jesus Christ*. This is the first thing the believer should know about his position in Christ. This is one of the most glorious truths in all of Scripture, yet so much controversy has raged over what is meant by baptism that the glorious meaning has often been bypassed. The meaning of baptism is discussed in another note. In the present note the glorious truth of these verses is being concentrated upon. Christians everywhere agree that baptism is a picture of the death, burial, and resurrection of Jesus Christ. When a true believer is immersed, he is proclaiming to the world that he is being identified with Christ:

⇒ by being placed under the water, he is proclaiming that he has died and been buried with Christ.
⇒ by being raised up from the water, he is proclaiming that he has been raised from the dead with Christ to live a new life.

Now note three glorious points.

1. The believer is immersed, placed into, or identified with Christ *in* death. This is the believer's position in Christ. Very simply, if the believer really died when Christ died, then he has died to sin and is freed from sin and its penalty and punishment. What a glorious gift from God! What a glorious position to receive from God's wonderful grace!

What happens is this. When a person really believes in Christ, then God takes that person's faith and counts it as the death of Christ. That is, God counts the person as having died in Christ. God takes the person's faith (and baptism as stated in this passage) and counts the person as

participating in Christ's death. God counts and considers the person...

- to have died in Christ's death.
- to be placed into Christ's death.
- to be identified with Christ's death.
- to be a partaker of Christ' death.
- to be in union with Christ's death.
- to be bound with Christ in death.

When a person truly honors God's Son by trusting Him, God honors that person by spiritually placing him into the death of Christ. What is it that causes God to do so much for the believer? Very simply, His love for His Son. God loves His Son so much that He will do anything for anyone who honors His Son by believing and trusting Him.

Now note the point: if the believer is *counted* by God as having been immersed into the death of Christ, then the believer...

- has died to sin
- has died to the penalty of sin
- has died to the judgment of sin
- is freed from sin
- is freed from the penalty of sin
- is freed from the judgment of sin

This means that the rule and reign and the habits and desires of sin no longer have control over us. Sin *ceases* to have a place or a position in our lives. We are free from sin, free from...

- sin's habits
- sin's control
- sin's bondage
- sin's enslavement
- sin's rule and reign
- sin's guilt

It means that we no longer live "in" sin, in the *position and place of sin*. We cannot live without sin, not perfectly, but we are *free* from living "in" sin. We no longer practice and desire sin. We desire and practice righteousness, seeking to please God in all that we do. And as glorious as this is, it means that we are freed from the condemnation of sin, the terrible punishment that shall be measured out in the awful day of judgment.

This is the believer's position in Christ. He is immersed, buried, placed into, and identified with Christ in death. And having died, the believer never has to be under the rule and reign of sin and its judgment again. He is a partaker of Christ's death, bound and united to Christ in death; therefore, he is dead to sin and all its effects.

However, note a critical point. A true believer is a person who *really believes*. This simply means he repents, confesses, obeys, and is baptized. It is this person whom God credits as having died in Christ. This is the glorious position of the true believer.

> **Or don't you know that all of us who were baptized into Christ Jesus were baptized into his death? (Rom 6:3)**
>
> **For we know that our old self was crucified with him so that the body of sin might be done away with, that we should no longer be slaves to sin— (Rom 6:6)**
>
> **For we were all baptized by one Spirit into one body—whether Jews or Greeks, slave or free—and we were all given the one Spirit to drink. (1 Cor 12:13)**

For we who are alive are always being given over to death for Jesus' sake, so that his life may be revealed in our mortal body. (2 Cor 4:11)

I have been crucified with Christ and I no longer live, but Christ lives in me. The life I live in the body, I live by faith in the Son of God, who loved me and gave himself for me. (Gal 2:20)

For all of you who were baptized into Christ have clothed yourselves with Christ. (Gal 3:27)

2. The believer is immersed, placed into, or identified with Christ in His resurrection. The same picture of baptism is used again to strike home this glorious truth. God counts the true baptized believer as having been raised in Christ. God takes the believer's faith (and baptism as stated in this passage) and counts the person as participating in Christ's resurrection. He counts and considers the person...

- to be raised in Christ's resurrection.
- to be placed into Christ's resurrection.
- to be identified with Christ's resurrection.
- to be a partaker of Christ's resurrection.
- to be in union with Christ's resurrection.
- to be bound with Christ in His resurrection.

Note two significant points.

a. Christ was raised up from the dead through the glory of the Father. This tells how our glorious position in Christ happened. It happened by the glory and the power of God. The "glory" (doxa) of God means all the excellence of God; all that He is in His might and power, love and grace, compassion and mercy. It means all His attributes: His omnipotence (all power), omniscience (all knowing), omnipresence (being everywhere), and sovereignty. In this particular passage it refers primarily to His glorious power. It was the glory of His might and power that raised up Jesus from the dead, and it is by the glory of His might and power that he *places and positions* us in Christ.

By his power God raised the Lord from the dead, and he will raise us also. (1 Cor 6:14)

For to be sure, he was crucified in weakness, yet he lives by God's power. Likewise, we are weak in him, yet by God's power we will live with him to serve you. (2 Cor 13:4)

b. God's purpose for raising us up with Christ is dynamic and meaningful. It involves living in a whole new life. The word "live" or "walk" (peripateo) means to walk about, to walk step by step, to control and order our behavior, to constantly and habitually walk in "a new life."

Think about it for a moment. When Christ died, he laid aside His old life and left it behind Him. Therefore, when He arose, He took on a totally new life, a changed life, a resurrected life. It is His new life, His changed and resurrected life that is given to us. In the Bible the word "new" often carries the idea of purity, righteousness, holiness, godliness. The believer...

- receives a "new birth" (1 Pt.1:23; 2:2).
- receives a "new heart" (Ezk.11:19; 18:31).

- becomes a "new creation" (2 Cor.5:17; Gal.6:15).
- puts on the "new self" or "new man" (Eph.4:24; Col.3:10).

God's very purpose for *placing* us in the resurrected life of Jesus Christ is that we might walk in Christ, walk soberly, righteously and godly in this present world. The true believer puts off the "old self" or "old man" of sin and puts on the new self of righteousness and godliness. He lives a pure, clean, and holy life.

Having been buried with him in baptism and raised with him through your faith in the power of God, who raised him from the dead. (Col 2:12)

And his incomparably great power for us who believe. That power is like the working of his mighty strength, which he exerted in Christ when he raised him from the dead and seated him at his right hand in the heavenly realms, (Eph 1:19-20)

So I say, live by the Spirit, and you will not gratify the desires of the sinful nature. (Gal 5:16)

As a prisoner for the Lord, then, I urge you to live a life worthy of the calling you have received. (Eph 4:1)

So then, just as you received Christ Jesus as Lord, continue to live in him, (Col 2:6)

3. The believer is immersed, placed into, or identified with the most glorious hope: that he shall be planted (immersed) in the very likeness of Jesus' resurrection. This simply means that...

- as Jesus was raised to a *new life*, so shall the believer be.

Made us alive with Christ even when we were dead in transgressions—it is by grace you have been saved. And God raised us up with Christ and seated us with him in the heavenly realms in Christ Jesus, (Eph 2:5-6)

Since, then, you have been raised with Christ, set your hearts on things above, where Christ is seated at the right hand of God. (Col 3:1)

- as Jesus was raised to *live with God*, so shall the believer be.

In my Father's house are many rooms; if it were not so, I would have told you. I am going there to prepare a place for you. And if I go and prepare a place for you, I will come back and take you to be with me that you also may be where I am. (John 14:2-3)

For the Lord himself will come down from heaven, with a loud command, with the voice of the archangel and with the trumpet call of God, and the dead in Christ will rise first. After that, we who are still alive and are left will be caught up together with them in the clouds to meet the Lord in the air. And so we will be with the Lord forever. (1 Th 4:16-17)

Here is a trustworthy saying: If we died with him [identified with His death], we will also live with him; (2 Tim 2:11)

(See Deeper Study #1, *Believer, Position In Christ*—Ro.8:1 for more discussion.)

DEEPER STUDY # 1

(6:3-5) **Baptism**: this note is being placed as the last note under verse 10 as Deeper Study # 2 because of its length, and because it is a specialized note dealing with the meaning of "baptism" as used in this passage. It is suggested that the note be studied last because of its length, feeling that the reader can be helped more by going ahead and studying the notes on the major points of the outline to keep from losing the continuity of thought.

---

3 (6:6-7) **Old Self—Body of Sin—Believer, Crucified with Christ**: second, the believer's old self or old man was crucified with Christ. This is the second thing the believer should know about his position in Christ. The Greek definitely uses the past tense: "Our old self *was* crucified with Christ." It was a *once-for-all act* that Christ Himself effected. He took our "old self" to the cross with Him when He died. The "old self" means…

- our old man
- our old life
- our sinful self
- our sinful life
- our corrupt nature
- our depraved nature
- our unregenerate nature
- our sinful nature

Our "old self" means our old life without God, the old sinful life that is immersed or identified with Christ in death. Now note three points.

1. The old self was crucified so that "the body of sin" might be destroyed or done away with. The "body of sin" is not plural (sins) but singular (sin). Sin is seen as a *body*, a *whole package*. The human body is seen as the *seat* of sin and as the *instrument* of sin. It is seen as containing and embodying and packaging all sin within itself. The idea is that all sin within a believer is destroyed, conquered, forgiven, and crucified with Christ. The believer is freed from sin. He starts anew, and he *stays* clean and free from sin by walking in constant confession and fellowship before God. (1 Jn.1:9).

> Then he said to them all: "If anyone would come after me, he must deny himself and take up his cross daily and follow me. (Luke 9:23)

> For we know that our old self was crucified with him so that the body of sin might be done away with, that we should no longer be slaves to sin— (Rom 6:6)

> As it is written: "For your sake we face death all day long; we are considered as sheep to be slaughtered." (Rom 8:36)

> For we who are alive are always being given over to death for Jesus' sake, so that his life may be revealed in our mortal body. (2 Cor 4:11)

> I have been crucified with Christ and I no longer live, but Christ lives in me. The life I live in the body, I live by faith in the Son of God, who loved me and gave himself for me. (Gal 2:20)

Here is a trustworthy saying: If we died with him, we will also live with him; (2 Tim 2:11)

2. The old self was crucified to *enable* and to *empower* the believer to renounce sin. The believer is not to serve sin; he is to renounce it, knowing that it has been crucified and put to death in Christ. By the power of the cross, sin is not to be served; it is…

- to be renounced
- to be refused
- to be repudiated
- to be rejected
- to be denied
- to be conquered

> For we know that our old self was crucified with him so that the body of sin might be done away with, that we should no longer be slaves to sin— (Rom 6:6)

> In the same way, count yourselves dead to sin but alive to God in Christ Jesus. (Rom 6:11)

> Those who belong to Christ Jesus have crucified the sinful nature with its passions and desires. (Gal 5:24)

> For you died, and your life is now hidden with Christ in God.…Put to death, therefore, whatever belongs to your earthly nature: sexual immorality, impurity, lust, evil desires and greed, which is idolatry. (Col 3:3, 5)

> He himself bore our sins in his body on the tree, so that we might die to sins and live for righteousness; by his wounds you have been healed. (1 Pet 2:24)

> Therefore, since Christ suffered in his body, arm yourselves also with the same attitude, because he who has suffered in his body is done with sin. As a result, he does not live the rest of his earthly life for evil human desires, but rather for the will of God. (1 Pet 4:1-2)

3. The clearest of all illustrations is given to show the believer's position in Christ. He is not to serve sin because he is dead; he has been crucified with Christ. And a dead man is freed from sin. When we believe that Jesus died for our sins, our belief is counted as righteousness; our belief makes us acceptable to God once for all. And it does something else just as wonderful: it gives us constant access into God's presence as we walk about day by day. This means that as we pick up the pollutions of this world and fail here and there, we can constantly come before God and ask forgiveness; and when we ask, He forgives. This is the way we are freed from sin: by constantly walking in *open confession* before God, praying all day long for His forgiveness. And just as He promises, He always forgives us (1 Jn.1:9). Why does He do such a glorious thing as freeing us from sin eternally?

⇒ Because we honor His Son by trusting Christ's death to free us from sin.

⇒ Because He loves His Son and will honor any man who so trusts His Son. He will honor the man by doing exactly what the man believes. If the man honors Christ by *believing* that he is freed from sin by the death of Christ, then God counts the man as being freed from sin.

> In him we have redemption through his blood, the forgiveness of sins, in accordance with the riches of God's grace (Eph 1:7)

If we confess our sins, he is faithful and just and will forgive us our sins and purify us from all unrighteousness. (1 John 1:9)

My dear children, I write this to you so that you will not sin. But if anybody does sin, we have one who speaks to the Father in our defense—Jesus Christ, the Righteous One. He is the atoning sacrifice for our sins, and not only for ours but also for the sins of the whole world. (1 John 2:1-2)

So then, just as you received Christ Jesus as Lord [by faith], continue to live in him, (Col 2:6)

For in the gospel a righteousness from God is revealed, a righteousness that is by faith from first to last, just as it is written: "The righteous will live by faith." (Rom 1:17)

This is the glorious position of the believer in Christ: his old self "was crucified" with Christ in order to free him from sin. Note the most glorious and striking truth: it is all through the *death of Christ*. Our salvation is *through the death of God's dear Son*.

4 (6:8-10) **Believer, Position in Christ—Hope—Jesus Christ, Resurrection**: third, the believer *shall live with Christ both now and forever*. This is the third thing the believer should know about his position in Christ. We know and possess absolute assurance and confidence that "we will...live with Christ." The idea is that we will live eternally with Him. What gives us such belief and absolute assurance?

1. Christ has conquered death—once-for-all. Think about it. Christ has already died. Now we are to *know*...
   * "Since Christ was raised from the dead, He cannot die again."
   * "Since He was raised "death no longer has mastery over him."
   * Since Christ was raised He is freed from death.

But [God'it has now been revealed through the appearing of our Savior, Christ Jesus, who has destroyed death and has brought life and immortality to light through the gospel. (2 Tim 1:10)

Since the children have flesh and blood, he too shared in their humanity so that by his death he might destroy him who holds the power of death—that is, the devil—and free those who all their lives were held in slavery by their fear of death. (Heb 2:14-15)

For Christ died for sins once for all, the righteous for the unrighteous, to bring you to God. He was put to death in the body but made alive by the Spirit, (1 Pet 3:18)

2. Christ now lives forever to God. We are to know...
   * that Christ died to sin once for all.
   * that Christ now lives in the presence of God forever.
   * that Christ lives to God; that is, He lives in an unbroken devotion and service to God.

The believer is to live to God through all eternity, beginning right now, from the moment of his conversion. Death has no more dominion over him. He is immersed or placed into the resurrected life of Christ. He is an eternal

person *now*; therefore, he is to live to God beginning right now, even as he will live unto God through all eternity.

I came from the Father and entered the world; now I am leaving the world and going back to the Father." (John 16:28)

I will remain in the world no longer, but they are still in the world, and I am coming to you. Holy Father, protect them by the power of your name—the name you gave me—so that they may be one as we are one. (John 17:11)

After the Lord Jesus had spoken to them, he was taken up into heaven and he sat at the right hand of God. (Mark 16:19)

But from now on, the Son of Man will be seated at the right hand of the mighty God." (Luke 22:69)

Which he exerted in Christ when he raised him from the dead and seated him at his right hand in the heavenly realms, (Eph 1:20)

And being found in appearance as a man, he humbled himself and became obedient to death— even death on a cross! Therefore God exalted him to the highest place and gave him the name that is above every name, (Phil 2:8-9)

But when this priest had offered for all time one sacrifice for sins, he sat down at the right hand of God. (Heb 10:12)

Thought 1. This, of course, means that we too shall be living on and on in an unbroken devotion and service to God—forever.

"For God so loved the world that he gave his one and only Son, that whoever believes in him shall not perish but have eternal life. (John 3:16)

"I tell you the truth, whoever hears my word and believes him who sent me has eternal life and will not be condemned; he has crossed over from death to life. (John 5:24)

"Father, I want those you have given me to be with me where I am, and to see my glory, the glory you have given me because you loved me before the creation of the world. (John 17:24)

For Christ's love compels us, because we are convinced that one died for all, and therefore all died. And he died for all, that those who live should no longer live for themselves but for him who died for them and was raised again. (2 Cor 5:14-15)

DEEPER STUDY # 2
(6:3-5) **Baptism**: remember this note is not out of place. It is being placed as the last note of this outline because of its length and its dealing with a specialized subject. Men have dissected and argued over how a person is "saved" so much that the preciousness, and in too many cases, the truth of the experience has been lost. The result is a confused public. Many people think if they have been baptized and do half-way right, then they are saved and God will never reject them. Others, who are highly disciplined and have reformed their lives, think they are as acceptable to God as anyone else because they do live moral and decent lives. A confused public, including both those within and

without the church, is basing their eternal fate upon one or more of the following. They think they are saved...

- by baptism.
- by doing good deeds.
- by being as good as they can.
- by church membership.
- by faith.
- by repentance.

Much of the confusion has been caused by men *over-stressing or misunderstanding* one of the truths of Scripture. Too often too many of us have been guilty of abusing Scripture; and once we have taken a strong position, we have been unwilling to back off or to give balance to the whole truth, even when we realized we had gone too far. It is time for us to totally commit our lives to the Lord, to lay aside our *bandwagons* and exhaustively labor to proclaim the whole truth both to the church and to the world. Again, it is time for the truth to be proclaimed, the whole balance of Scripture—time for us to help straighten out the confusion of the public, for many within the church are deceived and are without Christ; and the world cannot come to Christ with a genuine experience until they come as *Scripture dictates*.

In the passage before us an argument rages over the word baptism (v.3-4). Does "baptism" mean the actual baptism experience of a person, or is it being used in a symbolic or spiritual sense? Those who hold to baptism being essential for salvation say it means the actual baptism experience; whereas those who hold to salvation by faith tend to say it is speaking symbolically and spiritually. And the battle rages on. The great tragedy is...

- many within and without the church have become confused.
- many have never had a true experience of salvation because they have never heard the truth of Scripture.
- many have never heard nor understand the truth of Scripture.
- many have mocked the divisiveness and irrelevance of church positions.

And all with whom we have failed to share the truth are doomed, and we are responsible. Now, note several points.

1. Scripture speaks strongly in unmistakable terms on the subject of salvation—on just how we are saved—and to an *honest and thoughtful mind* it speaks clearly.

   a. We are saved by *faith*.

   For it is by grace you have been saved, through faith—and this not from yourselves, it is the gift of God—not by works, so that no one can boast. (Eph 2:8-9; cp. Jn.1:12; 3:16; Ro.10:9-10)

   b. We are saved by *obedience*.

   And, once made perfect, he became the source of eternal salvation for all who obey him (Heb 5:9; cp. Mt.7:21; Jn.15:10; Rev 22:14)

   c. We are saved by *repentance*.

   I have not come to call the righteous, but sinners to repentance." (Luke 5:32; cp. Acts 11:18)

   d. We are saved by *confession*.

"Whoever acknowledges me before men, I will also acknowledge him before my Father in heaven. But whoever disowns me before men, I will disown him before my Father in heaven. (Mat 10:32-33; cp. Ro.10:9-10; 1 Jn.4:15)

   e. We are saved by *baptism*.

   Peter replied, "Repent and be baptized, every one of you, in the name of Jesus Christ for the forgiveness of your sins. And you will receive the gift of the Holy Spirit. (Acts 2:38)

Now, in all honesty, what does this show? Is it not that the true experience of salvation is a *whole* experience, a *comprehensive* experience, an experience that involves the *whole life* of a believer? Is salvation not a past and a present and a future experience? (See DEEPER STUDY # 1, *Salvation*—1 Cor.1:18 for discussion.)

What Scripture declares is that salvation is looked upon as the *whole* experience of a truly *born again* person. When Scripture speaks...

- of believing in Christ, it means a person who repents, confesses, obeys, and is baptized.
- of obedience to Christ, it means a person who believes, repents, confesses, and is baptized.
- of repentance toward Christ, it means a person who believes, confesses, obeys, and is baptized.
- of baptism in Christ, it means a person who believes, repents, confesses, and obeys.
- of confession to Christ, it means a person who believes, repents, obeys, and is baptized.

Now note a most critical point: just because a person professes and does some of these things does not mean the person is saved. Just because a person...

- professes faith,
- lives a moral and good life,
- is baptized,
- claims to live as Jesus taught,

...does not mean he is saved. The power of salvation is not in these things, not in profession and moral goodness and baptism and the teachings of Jesus. The power to save is *in Jesus Christ Himself*, in believing that He is the crucified Savior, the Son of God Himself who has the power to save.

The point is this: Scripture speaks of the true believer in different ways at different times, anyone of which means that he is saved. Scripture says that a *true believer* is a person...

- who believes.
- who obeys.
- who repents.
- who confesses.
- who is baptized.

Each of these terms is *inclusive*, that is, sometimes Scripture uses each term to include the others. The present passage says that believers who "were baptized into Christ Jesus were baptized into his death." Paul is using the symbolic meaning of our baptism experience to picture our "death" and "resurrection" with Christ. He is not saying that baptism is the "substance" that has the power to "place" us into Christ. Only God has that power. Paul is saying that the baptized person (as a person who believes, repents, obeys, and confesses) is the person who is *placed* into the death of Christ. Our baptism experience is being used as an inclusive term, not as an exclusive term or in an exclusive sense.

2. Among the believers in the New Testament, faith and baptism were not so much two experiences as two parts of one experience (F.F. Bruce. *The Epistle of Paul to the Romans.* "The Tyndale New Testament Commentaries," p.136). A person who genuinely believed *was baptized*, and a person who was baptized *was to be a genuine believer*. To be "baptized into Jesus Christ" did not mean "to be baptized *without faith*" and to "believe in Jesus Christ" did not mean to believe *without being baptized*. Scripture definitely indicates this. Therefore, *when Scripture speaks of baptism*, it means that baptism is for a genuine believer: a genuine believer is baptized, and a baptized person is to be a genuine believer. There just was no such thing as a *genuine believer* who was not baptized unless he was providentially prohibited, and there was no such thing as a *genuinely baptized* person who was not to be a true believer.

3. Scripture definitely teaches that the power to make a person acceptable to God, to place a person into Christ is not in the water of baptism, but *in Christ*. For example, this is the whole point of Romans up to this point, the whole teaching of justification. If the power to save is in water, then what do we do with the thousands who have been baptized and live like the devil himself, the thousands who show no changed life at all?

The power is definitely in Christ; Christ is the One who saves. And He saves the person who believes, not the person who is baptized. This is clearly evident from the *unholy lives lived by so many who have been baptized.*

However, as mentioned in point one, the person who truly believes does repent and he does turn from his old life to follow Christ. He does what Christ says, and the first commandment is to follow Him in baptism. Baptism is the very first act, the very first proof that a person believes and repents.

There is another way to see the connection between faith and baptism or between our union with Christ and baptism. The power to save—to make a person acceptable to God—is not in the waters of baptism, but in Christ; therefore...

- not everyone who is baptized is saved. Their unbelieving and unholy lives prove the fact.
- Everyone who is saved will be baptized immediately as an *act of belief and obedience* in Christ. The person will be baptized unless he is physically unable.

4. The physical symbol is never the truth itself; it is a picture of the truth. No physical substance has the power to bring about anything spiritual. The whole physical world and everything in it passes away, including water. Physical substances can symbolize spiritual truth, but they cannot be the cause or the power to bring about the spiritual reality. If a physical substance such as water baptism had such power, it would mean that the spiritual reality had its basis in the physical and material which passes away. And if the basis passes away (water baptism), then the substance (spiritual salvation) itself would also pass away.

Another way to say the same thing is this: the physical can never penetrate nor create the spiritual; it is the spiritual that must penetrate and create the physical. Philosophi-cally, we must always remember this or else we doom ourselves and cause thinking men in the world to mock us. Why? Because the philosophical and thinking men of the world know that if we are saved by water (the physical and material), then we are doomed; for no physical substance can impart something it does not have, an eternal quality (eternal life, salvation, forgiveness of sins). Only the spiritual—only God and His power—can impart the spiritual quality of eternal life and salvation and forgiveness of sins. God can impart spiritual salvation and then say, "Immersion in water is a picture of what I do for you. And if you really believe in Me, then the very first evidence of your faith is for you to be baptized."

5. Practical experience tells us that belief and baptism are *separate acts* involved in salvation, yet they are both involved. They are both involved in the sense that baptism is an immediate act of obedience and repentance. A true believer should be baptized, and no true believer will fail to be baptized unless he is providentially stopped.

⇒ Example one: a believer flying across country leads a person to truly trust Christ to save him. The plane crashes and the new believer is killed before he can be baptized. He is not doomed to hell. Scripture teaches no such thing. To say he is doomed is to say that the power of salvation is in the waters of baptism and not in God's Son. In fact, to say such is to dishonor God's Son, to take the love and power and grace that belongs to Him and to ascribe it to a physical substance. If the new believer truly believes within his heart, truly honors God's Son by trusting Jesus to save him, God accepts that man. God accepts the man because he honors God's Son, and God will do anything for any man who honors His Son. The man is thereby accepted by God, accepted because he honors God's Son by believing and committing his life to Him.

However, the man who reaches the ground and is not baptized as soon as he can make arrangements is not genuine. His faith is suspect, for he is not putting God first in his life. He has not turned to Christ *ready* to obey and live for Him. The man who truly believes is the man who is not only ready to obey Christ, he *does* obey and live for Christ.

⇒ Note another example. There are masses of people who live in arrid and desert countries where thousands are starving and dying of thirst. What about them and baptism? What if a missionary leads some to Christ. Are they to be immersed when there is so little water and multitudes are dying of thirst? The point is clear, not only in the teaching of Scripture, but in the love of God and in practical terms. A person is justified *by faith*, but he is to be baptized immediately, as soon as he possibly can. Why? Because he is genuine, he does believe in the Lord Jesus, loving Him and wishing to obey Him in all things and thereby fulfilling all righteousness. However, his salvation does not depend upon baptism; it depends upon God's dear Son, our Lord and Savior, Jesus Christ.

	B. The Believer is Not to Continue in Sin (Part II): He is to Live Out His Position in Christ, 6:11-13	that you obey its evil desires. 13 Do not offer the parts of your body to sin, as instruments of wickedness,	a. Does not let it reign b. Does not obey its lusts 3 He does not yield the parts of his body to sin[DS2]
1 He counts himself dead to sin, but alive to God[DS1] a. Dead to sin b. Alive to God c. Source: Thru Christ 2 He resists sin	11 In the same way, count yourselves dead to sin but alive to God in Christ Jesus. 12 Therefore do not let sin reign in your mortal body so	but rather offer yourselves to God, as those who have been brought from death to life; and offer the parts of your body to him as instruments of righteousness.	a. He yields himself to God b. He yields the parts of his body to be instruments of righteousness

DIVISION IV

HOLINESS AND SANCTIFICATION: THE WAY FOR THE BELIEVER TO BE FREE FROM SIN, 6:1-23

B. The Believer is Not to Continue in Sin (Part II): He is to Live Out His Position in Christ, 6:11-13

(6:11-13) **Introduction**: the true believer does not continue in sin; he does not live in sin. He conquers and triumphs over sin. In very clear terms this passage tells exactly what the believer must do to live in victory over sin.

1. He counts himself dead to sin, but alive to God (v.11).
2. He resists sin (v.12).
3. He does not yield the parts of his body to sin (v.13).

1 (6:11) **Sin—Life, Victorious**: the believer must count himself dead to sin, but alive to God (see DEEPER STUDY # 1, *Reckon*—Ro.6:11 for discussion). How does the believer keep from walking in sin?

1. The believer must count himself *dead to sin*. If a person is a true believer, then he has *died* with Christ. God has taken his belief and counted him as having died in Christ, and a dead man can do nothing; he cannot sin. He is freed from sin.

What happens is this: when a believer truly believes in Christ, God takes his faith and counts him *dead in Christ*. God frees him from sin and its power as well as from its consequences and penalty. Therefore, the believer is to…

- count himself
- treat himself
- consider himself
- regard himself
- reckon himself
- credit himself

…as *dead in Christ*, as being free from sin and its power. He is to *receive* this truth into his heart and life, become totally *convicted and convinced* of it.

(Note a crucial point: the true believer is not left only to the power of his own mind or thoughts to convince himself of this glorious truth. It is not only a matter of *human thought and reasoning* or of mental control. God has given the Holy Spirit to stir and build confidence of the glorious truth within the believer. The Holy Spirit is our "seal," our guarantee, of salvation. But this is the subject of another discussion, of chapter eight. The present chapter concerns *our part* in overcoming sin. God does help us overcome sin through the Holy Spirit, but we also have a part. And it is our part that is presently being considered.)

> Then he said to them all: "If anyone would come after me, he must deny himself and take up his cross daily and follow me. (Luke 9:23)

> By no means! We died to sin; how can we live in it any longer? For we know that our old self was crucified with him so that the body of sin might be done away with,

that we should no longer be slaves to sin—because anyone who has died has been freed from sin. (Rom 6:2, 6-7)

> I have been crucified with Christ and I no longer live, but Christ lives in me. The life I live in the body, I live by faith in the Son of God, who loved me and gave himself for me. (Gal 2:20)

> Those who belong to Christ Jesus have crucified the sinful nature with its passions and desires. (Gal 5:24)

> For you died, and your life is now hidden with Christ in God. (Col 3:3)

> Here is a trustworthy saying: If we died with him, we will also live with him; (2 Tim 2:11)

> He himself bore our sins in his body on the tree, so that we might die to sins and live for righteousness; by his wounds you have been healed. (1 Pet 2:24)

2. The believer must count himself *alive to God*. The true believer is not only identified with Christ in death, he is identified with Christ in resurrection. God not only counts the believer's faith as *death in Christ*, He counts his faith as *life in Christ*. The believer is counted to have risen in Christ's resurrection. The resurrection of the Lord Jesus counts as the resurrection of the believer. As Jesus Christ was raised to a new life, so the believer is raised to a new life. As Jesus Christ was raised to live in the presence of God and to serve Him forever, so the believer is raised to live in the presence of God and to serve Him forever.

The point is this: let the believer receive into his heart and life the truth of *his resurrected life*. Let the believer now *live unto God*. Let the believer now *serve God and not sin*. Let the believer *walk before God* in his new, resurrected life; let him walk soberly, righteously, and godly in this present world. Let him walk…

- counting himself
- treating himself
- considering himself
- regarding himself

…as alive to God, now and forever serving God.

> He is not the God of the dead, but of the living, for to him all are alive." (Luke 20:38)

> In the same way, count yourselves dead to sin but alive to God in Christ Jesus. (Rom 6:11)

If we live, we live to the Lord; and if we die, we die to the Lord. So, whether we live or die, we belong to the Lord. (Rom 14:8)

And he died for all, that those who live should no longer live for themselves but for him who died for them and was raised again. (2 Cor 5:15)

3. Note the most glorious truth. The believer's life is due to Christ and Christ alone. All that the believer knows—his glorious deliverance from sin and the wonderful victory of eternal life—is due to Christ's death and resurrection. And note: it is the believer who really *keeps his mind* upon the death and resurrection of Christ that *walks above sin*. It is he who walks free from sin who conquers it every step of the way and glorifies God by the victory of his righteous life.

In conclusion, the believer's first step in conquering sin is to count himself dead to sin, but alive to God. The believer must *know and live out* his position, the glorious life God has given him in the death and resurrection of Jesus Christ our Lord. The believer who keeps his mind and thoughts upon *his position* in Christ's death and resurrection will conquer sin—every time.

DEEPER STUDY # 1

(6:11) **Reckon—Count—Impute** (logizethe): to credit; to set to one's account; to lay to one's charge; to judge; to consider; to treat; to compute; to ascribe. It is an accounting word; it implies something put to a man's credit. It is used many times throughout Romans, about eleven times in chapter four of Romans alone. It is an extremely important idea in Scripture.

1. Scripture says that righteousness is imputed, counted, or reckoned to the genuine believer by God.

This is why "it was credited to him as righteousness." The words "it was credited to him" were written not for him alone, but also for us, to whom God will credit righteousness—for us who believe in him who raised Jesus our Lord from the dead. He was delivered over to death for our sins and was raised to life for our justification. (Rom 4:22-25)

2. Scripture says that the genuine believer is immersed, imputed, counted, or reckoned as dead in Christ's death; that is, his "old self" is imputed or reckoned as crucified in Christ's death .

Or don't you know that all of us who were baptized into Christ Jesus were baptized into his death? We were therefore buried with him through baptism into death in order that, just as Christ was raised from the dead through the glory of the Father, we too may live a new life. (Rom 6:3-4)

For we know that our old self was crucified with him so that the body of sin might be done away with, that we should no longer be slaves to sin—(Rom 6:6. See note. Sin—Ro.6:11 for more discussion and verses)

3. Scripture says that a new life, a resurrected life is imputed, counted, reckoned or put to the account of the believer through Christ's resurrection.

If we have been united with him like this in his death, we will certainly also be united with him in his resurrection. (Rom 6:5)

Now if we died with Christ, we believe that we will also live with him. For we know that since Christ was raised from the dead, he cannot die again; death no longer has mastery over him. The death he died, he died to sin once for all; but the life he lives, he lives to God. (Rom 6:8-10)

Very simply stated, God counts the believer righteous because of what Christ has done. Christ is seen to be "the Lord our righteousness," and His righteousness is said to be put to a man's account through faith (cp. Phile.18).

---

2 (6:12) **Sin—Life, Victorious:** the believer must resist sin. This is an imperative—a forceful command. It is up to the believer to resist sin; he is responsible for resisting it.

1. He must not let sin reign (basileueto): have authority, rule, control, occupy, hold sway, prevail over him. The present tense is used, so the idea is a continuous attitude and behavior. The believer is always to keep his mind off sin. He is to keep his mind under control by keeping his mind off...

- wealth and material things
- position and power
- recognition and fame
- the lust of the eyes
- the lust of the flesh
- the pride of life
- parties and sex
- appearance and clothes

The believer is not to let sin dominate, control, and reign in his mortal body. Sin is not to dominate his thoughts and life. He is to resist sin by standing against it and by rebuking and fighting against it. He is to oppose sin with all his might.

Later Jesus found him at the temple and said to him, "See, you are well again. Stop sinning or something worse may happen to you." (John 5:14)

Therefore do not let sin reign in your mortal body so that you obey its evil desires. (Rom 6:12)

Come back to your senses as you ought, and stop sinning; for there are some who are ignorant of God—I say this to your shame. (1 Cor 15:34)

My dear children, I write this to you so that you will not sin. But if anybody does sin, we have one who speaks to the Father in our defense—Jesus Christ, the Righteous One. (1 John 2:1)

2. He must not obey sin in its lusts and evil desires (epithumiais). The word means strong desire or craving and passion. The pull of sin is sometimes strong, very strong. All men know what it is to lust after things, after more and more, whether it be money, property, security, position, pleasure, fun, or fleshly stimulation. The true believer must not *yield* to these pulls. He must not let the lusts of his eyes and flesh rule and regulate his mind and behavior. He must not let lust *order* his life. He must not

obey sin in its lusts, in its cravings and desires and passions. He must resist the lusts of his "mortal body."

> If your right eye causes you to sin, gouge it out and throw it away. It is better for you to lose one part of your body than for your whole body to be thrown into hell. (Mat 5:29)

> For if you live according to the sinful nature, you will die; but if by the Spirit you put to death the misdeeds of the body, you will live, (Rom 8:13)

> Rather, clothe yourselves with the Lord Jesus Christ, and do not think about how to gratify the desires of the sinful nature. (Rom 13:14)

> Put to death, therefore, whatever belongs to your earthly nature: sexual immorality, impurity, lust, evil desires and greed, which is idolatry. (Col 3:5)

> Dear friends, I urge you, as aliens and strangers in the world, to abstain from sinful desires, which war against your soul. (1 Pet 2:11)

> As a result, he does not live the rest of his earthly life for evil human desires, but rather for the will of God. (1 Pet 4:2)

3 (6:13) **Sin**: three things need to be said about sin at this point in Romans. (1) Sin is an offense and a disease in chapters 1-4. In chapter 6 it is a master or a ruling power. (2) Sin is not done away with or "destroyed" in the believer. It is still active and can still injure. The believer is to fight against its pull. (3) The body is not the source of sin, but the Bible says and man's experience proves that the body is the *instrument* of sin, the *organ* which sin uses to manifest and satisfy itself. The body is under the *heavy influence* and *severe power* of sin and corruption—so much so that the sensual appetites of the body tend to enslave the soul and lead men to sin, even against his better judgment. Therefore, the believer is strongly exhorted, resist—"do not let sin reign in your mortal body" (Ro.6:12).

DEEPER STUDY # 2
(6:13) **Sin—Life, Victorious**: the believer must not yield the parts of his body to sin. The word "yield" or "offer" (paristemi) means to put at the disposal of; to give; to grant; to turn over to. The believer *is not* to yield the parts of his body to be instruments or tools of unrighteousness. If he takes a part of his body and uses it as an instrument or tool of unrighteousness, he sins. The parts of a person's body refer to all the parts of the body: the eyes, ears, mouth, tongue, hands, feet, mind, or any of the covered and dressed parts. No believer is to offer or give any part of his body over to unrighteousness. To do so is to sin. The tense is present action, so the believer is to be constantly on guard against allowing any parts of his body to be yielded to sin. Note: the word "yield" has the idea of struggling. It is a struggle to fight against sin and to control and protect the parts of our body.

1. The believer is to yield himself to God. Note a significant fact: in the Greek this is not written in the present tense, but in the aorist tense. This simply means the believer is to make a *one-time* decision for God, a *once-for-all* dedication of his life to God. The presentation of his life to God is to be sincere and genuine—a one time decision. He is to yield himself—his body, his life, all that he is—to God; and his decision is to be a permanent, one time decision.

Note just how complete this dedication is to be. It is to be as deep a commitment as the dedication of those who are alive from the dead. And just think how deeply committed to God the believers are who have gone on to be with Him!

2. The believer is to yield the parts of his body as instruments of righteousness *unto* God. The believer is to *turn* the parts of his body over to God: his eyes, ears, mouth, tongue, hands, feet, mind—all his members. Every part of his body is to be given over as an instrument or tool to do righteousness. Every part of the believer's body is to be given over to God for the purpose of working righteousness.

> If your right eye causes you to sin, gouge it out and throw it away. It is better for you to lose one part of your body than for your whole body to be thrown into hell. And if your right hand causes you to sin, cut it off and throw it away. It is better for you to lose one part of your body than for your whole body to go into hell. (Mat 5:29-30; cp. Mt.18:8-9)

> Do not offer the parts of your body to sin, as instruments of wickedness, but rather offer yourselves to God, as those who have been brought from death to life; and offer the parts of your body to him as instruments of righteousness. (Rom 6:13)

> Therefore, I urge you, brothers, in view of God's mercy, to offer your bodies as living sacrifices, holy and pleasing to God—this is your spiritual act of worship. Do not conform any longer to the pattern of this world, but be transformed by the renewing of your mind. Then you will be able to test and approve what God's will is—his good, pleasing and perfect will. (Rom 12:1-2)

> Therefore put on the full armor of God, so that when the day of evil comes, you may be able to stand your ground, and after you have done everything, to stand. (Eph 6:13)

> Submit yourselves, then, to God. Resist the devil, and he will flee from you. (James 4:7)

> Therefore, dear friends, since you already know this, be on your guard so that you may not be carried away by the error of lawless men and fall from your secure position. (2 Pet 3:17)

	C. The Believer is Not to Continue in Sin (Part III): He Does Not Have License to Sin, 6:14-23	from sin and have become slaves to righteousness.	b. Result: Set free from sin, the despotic master
1 Learn something: Sin shall not dominate the true believer a. Bc. he is not under law, but under grace b. Shall he continue to sin? Take license to sin?	14 For sin shall not be your master, because you are not under law, but under grace. 15 What then? Shall we sin because we are not under law but under grace? By no means!	19 I put this in human terms because you are weak in your natural selves. Just as you used to offer the parts of your body in slavery to impurity and to ever-increasing wick-edness, so now offer them in slavery to righteousness leading to holiness. 20 When you were slaves to sin, you were free from the control of righteousness.	**4 Do something: Serve God with the same fervor that you served sin** a. Your sin furthered more sin—resulted in more & more sin b. Now let your righteousness work holiness c. You never had such opportunity before
2 Know something: You can serve only one master, sin or God a. Do you serve sin? You shall die b. Do you serve God? You shall live	16 Don't you know that when you offer yourselves to someone to obey him as slaves, you are slaves to the one whom you obey—whether you are slaves to sin, which leads to death, or to obedience, which leads to righteousness?	21 What benefit did you reap at that time from the things you are now ashamed of? Those things result in death! 22 But now that you have been set free from sin and have become slaves to God, the benefit you reap leads to holiness, and the result is eternal life.	**5 Question something: What benefit is there in sin?**
3 Remember something: Remember your decision—you chose righteousness a. Fact: "You used to be... [but you] obeyed"	17 But thanks be to God that, though you used to be slaves to sin, you wholeheartedly obeyed the form of teaching to which you were entrusted. 18 You have been set free	23 For the wages of sin is death, but the gift of God is eternal life in Christ Jesus our Lord.	**6 Consider something: The wages of sin vs. the gift of God, of eternal life**

DIVISION IV

HOLINESS AND SANCTIFICATION: THE WAY FOR THE BELIEVER TO BE FREE FROM SIN, 6:1-23

C. The Believer is Not to Continue in Sin (Part III): He Does Not Have License to Sin, 6:14-23

(6:14-23) **Introduction**: a believer is not to continue in sin, for he does not have license to sin.
1. Learn something: sin shall not dominate the true believer (v.14-15).
2. Know something: you can serve only one master, sin or God (v.16).
3. Remember something: remember your decision—you chose righteousness (v.17-18).
4. Do something: serve God with the same fervor that you served sin (v.19-20).
5. Question something: what benefit is there in sin (v.21-22)?
6. Consider something: the wages of sin vs. the gift of God, of eternal life (v.23).

(6:14-23) **Another Outline**: The Believer Does Not Have License to Sin.
1. He is not to be dominated by sin (v.14).
   a. He is not under law, but grace.
   b. This does not give license to sin (v.15).
2. He can choose only one master—an illustration (v.16).
   a. There are two masters: Sin or obedience to God (cp. v.22).
   b. Sin leads to death; obedience to righteousness.
3. He has been emancipated—become a new man, a slave of righteousness (v.17; cp. v.22).
   a. The emancipation: "You used to be...[but you] obeyed"
   b. By obeying God's form of doctrine.
   c. By being set free from sin, that despotic master (v.18).
   d. By yielding his bodily parts to righteousness (v.19).

4. He is now ashamed of his former behavior (sin) (v.20).
   a. Because he was not free to do righteousness.
   b. Because the end of those things (sin) is death (v.21).
5. He now has a new life and a new end (v.22).
   a. A life of fruit: holiness.
   b. An end of hope: everlasting life.
6. Conclusion: The laborer's wages (v.23; cp. v.16).

1 (6:14-15) **Grace vs. Law—God, Father—License**: learn something, sin shall not dominate the genuine believer. There is a strong reason for this: the believer is under grace and not under the law.
   1. The person under law is always struggling to keep the law, yet he is constantly aware that he fails and comes short of the law. The law is ever before his face. He struggles and strives, wrestles and grapples, works and labors to obey; but his experience is full of tension and pressure, disappointment and discouragement. The person under law never lives a victorious life, for he is constantly coming short of God's glory and perfection. When he fails, he goes through periods of self-accusation, of reproaching and censoring himself for having failed. He accuses and downs himself, feeling unworthy and undeserving, wretched and vile before God. He is constantly feeling unacceptable to God, as though he no longer has the right to approach God; and he often does not approach God for long periods of time, living a defeated life, always bearing the burden of his sin and failure. (See note, *Spiritual Struggle*—Ro.7:24 for more discussion.)

There will be trouble and distress for every human being who does evil: first for the Jew, then for the Gentile; (Rom 2:9)

You will live in constant suspense, filled with dread both night and day, never sure of your life. In the morning you will say, "If only it were evening!" and in the evening, "If only it were morning!"—because of the terror that will fill your hearts and the sights that your eyes will see. (Deu 28:66-67)

Even if I were innocent, my mouth would condemn me; if I were blameless, it would pronounce me guilty. (Job 9:20)

All his days the wicked man suffers torment, the ruthless through all the years stored up for him. (Job 15:20)

My guilt has overwhelmed me like a burden too heavy to bear. (Psa 38:4)

For troubles without number surround me; my sins have overtaken me, and I cannot see. They are more than the hairs of my head, and my heart fails within me. (Psa 40:12)

For I know my transgressions, and my sin is always before me. (Psa 51:3)

Some became fools through their rebellious ways and suffered affliction because of their iniquities. (Psa 107:17)

Good understanding wins favor, but the way of the unfaithful is hard. (Prov 13:15)

2. The true believer is under grace, not under law. God is not a legal judge hovering over the believer to punish him every time he sins by breaking a particular law. The believer is not under such frightening dominion: he is not under law,

but under grace. What does this mean?

    a. It means that the believer accepts the grace of God demonstrated in Jesus Christ. That is, the believer accepts the righteousness, the sinless perfection of Christ as his own righteousness. The believer identifies his life with the life of Christ, and God takes the believer's acceptance of Christ and counts his acceptance as righteousness. (See outline and DEEPER STUDY # 1,2—Ro.4:22; 5:1; 6:1-10 for more discussion.) Very simply stated, God credits righteousness to the believer when the believer accepts the righteousness of Christ. God counts the faith of the believer as the righteousness of Jesus Christ. Such is the *great love of God*. But note, this is the *position of grace*, that is, the believer is counted righteous and placed in the *position of righteousness* when he believes in Christ. He is *placed into Christ* and *positioned in Christ* once-for-all when he truly believes. Such is the *righteous position* of the believer.

    However, what about the *righteous life* of the believer? Very practically, how does the believer keep from serving sin and from living under sin and from displeasing God? How can he honestly live *under* grace day by day? How can he live under God's favor all of the time? How can he go about pleasing God and receiving His approval and acceptance?

    b. The genuine believer *must constantly* keep before his face the glorious truth: he is *under* God's grace. God is the believer's Father, and the believer has become a true child of God's. There-

fore, the true believer is favored and accepted by his Father. What the child has to do is stay in that favor. He must keep his Father's favor and approval. When he sins, he needs to go to His Father in all sincerity and ask forgiveness and repent of his sin. If he keeps an open relationship with His Father—always approaching Him and asking His forgiveness and repenting—he is forgiven. The slate is wiped clean—sin does not have dominion over him. There is nothing between the child and his Father. All has been discussed and forgiven. The offense is gone, resolved, put away forever. Therefore, sin does not dominate and rule over the child.

Now, note the point: God is a gracious and loving Father. He cares and suffers long with growing children. When His child falls into sin, God is long-suffering, ever willing to forgive His erring child—if the child will only come and ask forgiveness and turn from his sin (Lk.17:3-4; 1 Jn.1:9). Just how patient, how long-suffering is God? "His love endures forever;" His mercy covers every sin and all sin (Ps.106:1; 107:1; 118:1-4).

It would be better for him to be thrown into the sea with a millstone tied around his neck than for him to cause one of these little ones to sin. So watch yourselves. "If your brother sins, rebuke him, and if he repents, forgive him. (Luke 17:2-3)

In him we have redemption through his blood, the forgiveness of sins, in accordance with the riches of God's grace (Eph 1:7)

If we confess our sins, he is faithful and just and will forgive us our sins and purify us from all unrighteousness. (1 John 1:9)

Give thanks to the LORD, for he is good. His love endures forever. (Psa 136:1)

The LORD will fulfill his purpose for me; your love, O LORD, endures forever—do not abandon the works of your hands. (Psa 138:8)

3. In light of so wondrous a relationship, a question needs to be asked. Is the child of God allowed to continue in sin? Can he sin and sin expecting God to forgive and forgive him? Scripture shouts: By no means! Then Scripture argues that a true child of God must not continue in sin. (See note—Ro.6:1-2; Introduction, Purpose—Colossians.) He does not set God aside for a night or two and sin. He does not rationalize that he can go ahead and sin because God is going to forgive him anyway. Why does the true child of God not do this? Why does he keep away from sin?

    ⇒ Because his Father (God) loves him and he loves his Father. A true child of God does not want to hurt and displease his Father, and his Father is displeased with sin. Consequently, the true child of God strives not to sin (Ro.2:23-24; Heb.6:6). He fights against it, for sin is contrary to the nature of his Father and cuts the heart of his Father beyond all else. Therefore, he does all he can to keep away from sin.

If they fall away, to be brought back to repentance, because to their loss they are crucifying the Son of God all over again and subjecting him to public disgrace. (Heb 6:6)

For the LORD your God detests anyone who does these things, anyone who deals dishonestly. (Deu 25:16)
You are not a God who takes pleasure in evil; with you the wicked cannot dwell. (Psa 5:4)

⇒ Because he turned to God in order to get away from sin and its shame and destruction. He did not turn to God in order to have the freedom to sin, but to be set free from the enslavement and habits of sin, to break the bondage and consequences of sin (see note, *License*—Ro.6:1-2 for more discussion).

What benefit did you reap at that time from the things you are now ashamed of? Those things result in death! (Rom 6:21)
For the wages of sin is death, but the gift of God is eternal life in Christ Jesus our Lord. (Rom 6:23)

In summary of what is said above, the believer must learn something: sin will not dominate the true believer. There are three reasons.

1. God is not a legal judge hovering over the child to punish him every time he sins by breaking a particular law. The child is not under such frightening dominion.

2. God is a gracious and loving Father. He cares and suffers long with growing children. When His child falls into sin, God is long-suffering, ever willing to forgive His erring child—if the child will only come and ask forgiveness and turn from his sin (Lk.17:3-4; 1 Jn.1:9).

3. God is a teaching Father who disciplines. He exhorts His child not to fall into the dominating trap of sin (cp. Heb.12:5-11; 1 Jn.2:1-2).

The emphasis of this chapter, however, is of supreme importance. A believer who is genuine—who really belongs to Christ—shows his genuineness by obeying Christ as Master. He does not consistently practice sin. (See note—Ro.6:1-2.)

2 (6:16) **Sin, Results—Sin, Deliverance From**: know something—you can serve only one master, sin or God. A person is either the slave of sin or of God, and there is a very simple test to tell which master a person serves.
⇒ Do you yield to sin, that is, serve sin?
⇒ Do you yield to God, that is, serve God?

If you yield to sin, you will die. If you yield to God and obey Him, you will be counted righteous and live.
Now note a crucial point. Either sin is your master or God is your Master. You either yield to sin or you yield to God. This does not mean that you become sinless and perfect, but that...
• you do not plan to sin.
• you hate sin and fight against it.
• you struggle to please God by not sinning.
• you diligently seek to make God the Master of your life by obeying Him.
• you study God's Word so that you will know His commandments and can obey Him.
• you immediately seek God's forgiveness when you do sin and you repent—you turn away from the sin (1 Jn.1:9; 2:1-2).
• you walk in open confession before God, talking to Him all day long, ever gaining an unbroken fellowship with Him as the Master of your life.

Again, note the results, for *whom* we serve determines our destiny. If we yield to sin, we will die; but if we yield to God, we will be counted righteous and live eternally.

"No one can serve two masters. Either he will hate the one and love the other, or he will be devoted to the one and despise the other. You cannot serve both God and Money. (Mat 6:24)
Jesus replied, "I tell you the truth, everyone who sins is a slave to sin. (John 8:34)
Don't you know that when you offer yourselves to someone to obey him as slaves, you are slaves to the one whom you obey—whether you are slaves to sin, which leads to death, or to obedience, which leads to righteousness? (Rom 6:16)
For in my inner being I delight in God's law; but I see another law at work in the members of my body, waging war against the law of my mind and making me a prisoner of the law of sin at work within my members. (Rom 7:22-23)
You cannot drink the cup of the Lord and the cup of demons too; you cannot have a part in both the Lord's table and the table of demons. (1 Cor 10:21)
he is a double-minded man, unstable in all he does. (James 1:8)
They promise them freedom, while they themselves are slaves of depravity—for a man is a slave to whatever has mastered him. (2 Pet 2:19)
The evil deeds of a wicked man ensnare him; the cords of his sin hold him fast. (Prov 5:22)

3 (6:17-18) **Decision—Sin, Penalty—Sin, Deliverance From**: remember something, remember your decision. You chose righteousness.

1. Note the stated fact: believers "used to be slaves to sin." The word "slaves" (doulos) means bond slaves, persons bound to a master. Believers used to yield to sin, all kinds of sin ranging from...
⇒ simple off-colored jokes to using God's name in vain.
⇒ immoral thoughts to adultery.
⇒ simple thoughts of pride to drunkenness.
⇒ simple acts of selfishness to stealing.
⇒ wanting more to actually indulging.
⇒ seeking position and power to hurting and crushing people.

But *now* believers have obeyed the teaching of God, that is, the gospel of justification. Note the word "obeyed." They obeyed the gospel of God, doing exactly what God commanded.
They obeyed God's commandment. They "believed" in the name of God's Son, Jesus Christ; therefore, God took their faith and counted (credited) it as righteousness. They chose God and righteousness, and because they did, God accepted them as righteous.

And this is his command: to believe in the name of his Son, Jesus Christ, and to love one another as he commanded us. (1 John 3:23)

"Not everyone who says to me, 'Lord, Lord,' will enter the kingdom of heaven, but only he who does the will of my Father who is in heaven. (Mat 7:21)

The world and its desires pass away, but the man who does the will of God lives forever. (1 John 2:17)

2. Note the stated result: believers are set free from sin. They are counted righteous by God, *not sinful*. God sees believers as righteous people, not as sinners. Therefore, believers are set free from sin and its consequences. God does not charge believers with sin; He does not lay sin against them. Believers are set free from the accusation of sin, and they shall never be charged with sin. God has set them free from sin through His Son, the Lord Jesus Christ (cp. Ro.8:33-34).

Now this means something significant, very significant. The believer becomes the slave of righteousness. There is no way he could ever serve sin again, not if he has really been justified, not if he has really come to know God's love revealed in the Lord Jesus Christ. Once he truly knows God's glorious love, he is driven to serve God in appreciation for what God has done for him in Christ Jesus. He is driven to be the servant of God by living righteously and godly in this present world.

Thought 1. The degree to which a believer grasps the love of God in justification is the degree to which he is driven to serve God and to live righteously.

Who will bring any charge against those whom God has chosen? It is God who justifies. Who is he that condemns? Christ Jesus, who died—more than that, who was raised to life—is at the right hand of God and is also interceding for us. (Rom 8:33-34)

For Christ's love compels us, because we are convinced that one died for all, and therefore all died. And he died for all, that those who live should no longer live for themselves but for him who died for them and was raised again. (2 Cor 5:14-15)

Therefore, if anyone is in Christ, he is a new creation; the old has gone, the new has come! God made him who had no sin to be sin for us, so that in him we might become the righteousness of God. (2 Cor 5:17, 21)

And to put on the new self, created to be like God in true righteousness and holiness. (Eph 4:24)

4 (6:19-20) **Dedication—Sin, Enslavement to**: do something—serve God with the same fervor that you served sin.

1. Your sin did further sin; it resulted in more and more sin, an ever increasing wickedness. The word "parts" means the parts of a person's body: the eyes, ears, mouth, tongue, hands, feet, mind, or any of the covered and dressed parts. Before a person obeyed the gospel, truly believed in Jesus Christ, he yielded parts of his body to serve uncleanness and to work sin upon sin. He sinned and found that *sin worked sin*, just increased and increased, grew and grew. He found that sin enslaved him, became a bondage, a habit that he could not easily break. Sin simply led to more sin, no matter what the sin was...

- smoking
- drinking
- grumbling
- cursing

- immorality
- overeating
- greed
- lust
- gossip
- criticism
- selfishness
- popularity
- recognition
- power
- fame

The point is this. The believer had found that his sin worked more sin and that he could not break the power of sin, not the power of *all* sin. Therefore, he had turned to the only hope he had, God Himself.

For when we were controlled by the sinful nature, the sinful passions aroused by the law were at work in our bodies, so that we bore fruit for death. (Rom 7:5)

You were taught, with regard to your former way of life, to put off your old self, which is being corrupted by its deceitful desires; (Eph 4:22)

For you have spent enough time in the past doing what pagans choose to do—living in debauchery, lust, drunkenness, orgies, carousing and detestable idolatry. (1 Pet 4:3)

But each one is tempted when, by his own evil desire, he is dragged away and enticed. Then, after desire has conceived, it gives birth to sin; and sin, when it is fullgrown, gives birth to death. (James 1:14-15)

2. Now the believer is to let righteousness work holiness (hagiasmon). The word means sanctification or holy. The believer is to yield the parts of his body to serve righteousness, and he is to let righteousness sanctify him more and more. He is to live righteously and become more and more holy like God. (See Deeper Study #1, *Holy*—1 Pt.1:15-16 for more discussion.)

3. The believer never had the opportunity to work righteousness before he was justified. Before believing in Christ, the believer was not counted righteous, not by God. God never credits a person with righteousness unless the person honors His Son by believing in His Son's glorious name. Only those who believe are counted righteous. Therefore, the message is loud and clear: "When you were slaves to sin, you were free from righteousness: you were not credited with righteousness. You did not have the opportunity to live righteously before God. *But now* you have obeyed God; you have believed. Now you have the opportunity to live righteously, so begin to serve God with the same fervor and energy with which you were serving sin. Let righteousness enslave you and become the bondage and habit of your life."

Do not offer the parts of your body to sin, as instruments of wickedness, but rather offer yourselves to God, as those who have been brought from death to life; and offer the parts of your body to him as instruments of righteousness. (Rom 6:13)

Rather, clothe yourselves with the Lord Jesus Christ, and do not think about how to gratify the desires of the sinful nature. (Rom 13:14)

So I say, live by the Spirit, and you will not gratify the desires of the sinful nature. (Gal 5:16)

Those who belong to Christ Jesus have crucified the sinful nature with its passions and desires. (Gal 5:24)

Set your minds on things above, not on earthly things. For you died, and your life is now hidden with Christ in God. When Christ, who is your life, appears, then you also will appear with him in glory. Put to death, therefore, whatever belongs to your earthly nature: sexual immorality, impurity, lust, evil desires and greed, which is idolatry. (Col 3:2-5)

Dear friends, I urge you, as aliens and strangers in the world, to abstain from sinful desires, which war against your soul. (1 Pet 2:11)

As a result, he does not live the rest of his earthly life for evil human desires, but rather for the will of God. (1 Pet 4:2)

5 (6:21-22) **Sin**: question something—what benefit is there in sin? Note several clear facts.

1. The true believer is ashamed of his past sin.

He answered, "I heard you in the garden, and I was afraid because I was naked; so I hid." (Gen 3:10)

And prayed: "O my God, I am too ashamed and disgraced to lift up my face to you, my God, because our sins are higher than our heads and our guilt has reached to the heavens. (Ezra 9:6)

My disgrace is before me all day long, and my face is covered with shame (Psa 44:15)

2. The fruit of sin is death (see DEEPER STUDY # 1, *Death*—Ro.6:23; DEEPER STUDY # 1—Heb.9:27). The fruit of sin is not good; there is nothing good about it. Sin corrupts, destroys, and dooms all who seek its fruits. This should always be remembered by men.

3. Believers are "set free" from sin by justification, that is, through the glorious love of God. Therefore, they have become slaves to God...

• bearing the benefit of holiness.

Then you will know the truth, and the truth will set you free." (John 8:32)

"I am the vine; you are the branches. If a man remains in me and I in him, he will bear much fruit; apart from me you can do nothing. (John 15:5)

You have been set free from sin and have become slaves to righteousness. (Rom 6:18)

But now that you have been set free from sin and have become slaves to God, the benefit you reap leads to holiness, and the result is eternal life. (Rom 6:22)

Because through Christ Jesus the law of the Spirit of life set me free from the law of sin and death. (Rom 8:2)

To rescue us from the hand of our enemies, and to enable us to serve him without fear in holiness and righteousness before him all our days. (Luke 1:74-75)

Since we have these promises, dear friends, let us purify ourselves from everything that contaminates body and spirit, perfecting holiness out of reverence for God. (2 Cor 7:1)

May the Lord make your love increase and overflow for each other and for everyone else, just as ours does for you. May he strengthen your hearts so that you will be blameless and holy in the presence of our God and Father when our Lord Jesus comes with all his holy ones. (1 Th 3:12-13)

Make every effort to live in peace with all men and to be holy; without holiness no one will see the Lord. (Heb 12:14)

For it is written: "Be holy, because I am holy." (1 Pet 1:16)

Since everything will be destroyed in this way, what kind of people ought you to be? You ought to live holy and godly lives (2 Pet 3:11)

• bearing the glorious hope and result of eternal life.

Whoever believes in the Son has eternal life, but whoever rejects the Son will not see life, for God's wrath remains on him." (John 3:36)

Even now the reaper draws his wages, even now he harvests the crop for eternal life, so that the sower and the reaper may be glad together. (John 4:36)

"I tell you the truth, whoever hears my word and believes him who sent me has eternal life and will not be condemned; he has crossed over from death to life. (John 5:24)

The man who loves his life will lose it, while the man who hates his life in this world will keep it for eternal life. (John 12:25)

Now this is eternal life: that they may know you, the only true God, and Jesus Christ, whom you have sent. (John 17:3)

The one who sows to please his sinful nature, from that nature will reap destruction; the one who sows to please the Spirit, from the Spirit will reap eternal life. (Gal 6:8)

6 (6:23) **Sin, Wages of—Death**: consider something, the wages of sin vs. the gift of God.

1. The wages of sin is death. (See DEEPER STUDY # 1, *Death*—Heb.9:27 for more discussion.) Sin deserves death for two very clear reasons.

a. Sin is acting against God, acting against His very nature. Sin strikes out against God, attempts to tear down God's nature...
   • of purity and morality.
   • of holiness and glory.
   • of justice and righteousness.
   • of love and grace.

b. Sin is rebellion against God. It is rejecting God, ignoring God, disobeying God, denying God, and refusing to live for God. (See note—Ro.5:10 for more discussion.)

The point is this. True justice demands that sin receive its payment or its wages. Since sin is so opposed to God's nature and is actually rebellion against God, it deserves to die...
   • to be cast far, far away from God.
   • to have no part of God.

- to be banished from God's sight.
- to be separated from God's presence forever.
- to be condemned and punished for having dishonored and cursed God so much.

As a laborer receives his wages, so sin shall receive its wages. Just as it would be unjust not to pay the laborer, it would be unjust not to pay sin for its work. In fact, if sin did not receive its just punishment, it would be the most gross injustice of eternity. Why? Because sin is against the Sovereign Majesty of the universe, against God Himself. Sin must receive its just wages. Sin must die; it must be banished forever from the presence of God.

Therefore, just as sin entered the world through one man, and death through sin, and in this way death came to all men, because all sinned— (Rom 5:12)

For the wages of sin is death, but the gift of God is eternal life in Christ Jesus our Lord. (Rom 6:23)

Then, after desire has conceived, it gives birth to sin; and sin, when it is full-grown, gives birth to death. (James 1:15)

But the cowardly, the unbelieving, the vile, the murderers, the sexually immoral, those who practice magic arts, the idolaters and all liars—their place will be in the fiery lake of burning sulfur. This is the second death." (Rev 21:8)

But you must not eat from the tree of the knowledge of good and evil, for when you eat of it you will surely die." (Gen 2:17)

The truly righteous man attains life, but he who pursues evil goes to his death. (Prov 11:19)

The soul who sins is the one who will die. The son will not share the guilt of the father, nor will the father share the guilt of the son. The righteousness of the righteous man will be credited to him, and the wickedness of the wicked will be charged against him. (Ezek 18:20)

2. The gift of God is eternal life. Note that eternal life *is not* the payment of wages. A man cannot work for and earn eternal life. It is the gift of God, and it is only through Jesus Christ our Lord (see outlines and notes—Ro.6:14-15; 5:1; 6:1-10).

"For God so loved the world that he gave his one and only Son, that whoever believes in him shall not perish but have eternal life. (John 3:16)

He saved us, not because of righteous things we had done, but because of his mercy. He saved us through the washing of rebirth and renewal by the Holy Spirit, whom he poured out on us generously through Jesus Christ our Savior, so that, having been justified by his grace, we might become heirs having the hope of eternal life. (Titus 3:5-7)

CHAPTER 7

V. STRUGGLE AND CONFESSION: THE BELIEVER IS TO BE FREE FROM THE LAW, 7:1-25

A. The Two Positions of the Law to Man, 7:1-6

1 The law dominates man only as long as he lives

a. The two positions are illustrated by marriage
1) The law is alive & active for the living
2) The law is dead & inactive through death
b. The conclusion
1) The law condemns

Do you not know, brothers—for I am speaking to men who know the law—that the law has authority over a man only as long as he lives?
2 For example, by law a married woman is bound to her husband as long as he is alive, but if her husband dies, she is released from the law of marriage.
3 So then, if she marries another man while her husband is still alive, she is called an adulteress. But if her husband dies, she is released from that law and is not an adulteress, even though she marries another man.
4 So, my brothers, you also died to the law through the body of Christ, that you might belong to another, to him who was raised from the dead, in order that we might bear fruit to God.
5 For when we were controlled by the sinful nature, the sinful passions aroused by the law were at work in our bodies, so that we bore fruit for death.
6 But now, by dying to what once bound us, we have been released from the law so that we serve in the new way of the Spirit, and not in the old way of the written code.

the living who violate its demands
2) Death frees a person from the law

2 Position 1: The law is dead to believers
a. How: By Christ's death
b. The purpose for the believer's death
1) To unite him to Christ
2) To bear fruit

3 Position 2: The law is alive to those controlled by the sinful nature
a. How: By arousing sin
b. Result: Death

4 The law is inactivated by conversion
a. How: By death "in" Christ
b. Purpose: To serve in the new way of the Spirit

DIVISION V

STRUGGLE AND CONFESSION: THE BELIEVER IS TO BE FREE FROM THE LAW, 7:1-25

A. The Two Positions of the Law to Man, 7:1-6

(7:1-6) **Introduction**: the law of God stands before man. It stands in two positions that must be understood if man wishes to secure peace in this life.
1. The law dominates man *only* as long as he lives (v.1-3).
2. Position 1: the law is dead to believers (v.4).
3. Position 2: the law is alive to those "controlled by the sinful nature" (v.5).
4. The law is inactivated by conversion (v.6).

(7:1-6) **Another Outline**: The Two Marriages Illustrating the Law and Man.
1. Marriage 1: married to the law (v.1-3).
2. Marriage 2: married to Christ (v.4).
3. The divorce from the law (v.5-6).

1 (7:1-3) **Law**: the law dominates and rules over a man *only* as long as he lives. The law applies only to the living; it has no bearing whatsoever upon the dead. A dead man is freed from the law; it has no jurisdiction or power over a dead man.
1. Note the two positions of the law illustrated by the law of marriage (v.2).
   a. The law is alive or active to the living (Cp. the husband and wife who are living and the law of marriage and divorce).
   b. The law is dead or inactive when death enters the picture (Cp. the wife who is loosed or freed from the law when her husband dies).
2. Note the conclusion of the illustration (v.3).
   a. The law condemns the living who violate its demands. (Cp. the woman who marries another man while her husband lives).
   b. Death frees a person from the law (Cp. the wife who is free from the law when her husband dies).

The point is clear. When death enters the picture, a person is *no longer under* the law and he can *no longer be condemned* by the law. Death forever frees a person from the law, from its demands, guilt, and condemnation.

2 (7:4) **The Law—Jesus Christ, Redemption**: the first position of the law is a glorious truth—the law is dead to "brothers" (believers). Note: Scripture says that believers have "died to the law," whereas the outline states that the law is dead to believers. Both are true and are saying the same thing.
⇒ Believers have "died to the law;" therefore the law is bound to be dead and inactive to believers.

The law has no jurisdiction, power, rule, authority, or dominion over the true believer. The law is a dead issue to the believer; it has nothing to do with the believer. The believer is dead to the law and the law is dead to the believer. The law simply does not exist for the believer. This is a shock to most people, but it is exactly what Scripture is declaring. The believer is no longer under the law and its accusing finger, no longer under its...
• guilt and shame
• condemnation and punishment
• discouragement and frustration
• tension and pressure
• sense of failure and unworthiness
• sense of disappointment

1. Note how the glorious truth becomes a reality in the life of a person. The believer is dead to the law by the [crucified] body of Christ. The believer is slain or put to death *in Christ*. The law has nothing to say to a dead man. The believer's death in Christ is a *vicarious death*: he does

not literally die himself, but he participates in the death of Christ—*spiritually*. When a man believes in Christ's death, God takes that man's belief and counts him as having died in Christ. That is, God counts the death of Christ *for* the death of the believer; God considers the believer to have been in Christ when Christ died. Why does God do this? Because Christ died in man's behalf, in man's stead, taking the penalty and punishment of the law upon Himself. Therefore, the believer—being dead in Christ—is freed from the law, from its demands and guilt and punishment.

The believer is freed "through the body of Christ," that is, by His slain body or by His death. Christ redeemed the believer from the law...

*   by being a curse.

    All who rely on observing the law are under a curse, for it is written: "Cursed is everyone who does not continue to do everything written in the Book of the Law." Christ redeemed us from the curse of the law by becoming a curse for us, for it is written: "Cursed is everyone who is hung on a tree." (Gal 3:10, 13)

*   by His blood.

    In him we have redemption through his blood, the forgiveness of sins, in accordance with the riches of God's grace (Eph 1:7)
    But now in Christ Jesus you who once were far away have been brought near through the blood of Christ. (Eph 2:13)

*   by His flesh.

    By abolishing in his flesh the law with its commandments and regulations. His purpose was to create in himself one new man out of the two, thus making peace, (Eph 2:15)

*   by the cross.

    And in this one body to reconcile both of them to God through the cross, by which he put to death their hostility. (Eph 2:16)

*   by His physical body.

    But now he has reconciled you by Christ's physical body through death to present you holy in his sight, without blemish and free from accusation— (Col 1:22)

These are equivalent expressions. They teach the same truth: Christ bore our sins in His own body upon the tree (1 Pt.2:24). His sufferings satisfied justice. His death makes us acceptable to God and delivers us from the penalty of the law; therefore the believer is free from the law.

He himself bore our sins in his body on the tree, so that we might die to sins and live for righteousness; by his wounds you have been healed. (1 Pet 2:24)
For Christ died for sins once for all, the righteous for the unrighteous, to bring you to God. He was put to death in the body but made alive by the Spirit, (1 Pet 3:18)

2. Note the glorious purpose for the believer's death to the law.
    a. The believer dies to the law so that he can be united to Christ, the risen and living Lord. Note the picture of marriage is used again. Before coming to Christ, the believer was married and united to the law; he was under its rule and authority. But now, since coming to Christ, he is married and united to Christ; he is under His rule and authority. The believer no longer lives as the law says, but as Christ lived and commanded. (Note: Christ came to fulfill the law; therefore He and His commandments include not only the law, but much more. See note—Mt.5:17-18 for more discussion.) Note that believers are married to Christ, the risen and living Lord. The marriage is not a dead or an inactive marriage, but a living, active marriage.

        So, my brothers, you also died to the law through the body of Christ, that you might belong to another, to him who was raised from the dead, in order that we might bear fruit to God. (Rom 7:4)
        Do you not know that your bodies are members of Christ himself? Shall I then take the members of Christ and unite them with a prostitute? Never! (1 Cor 6:15)
        I am jealous for you with a godly jealousy. I promised you to one husband, to Christ, so that I might present you as a pure virgin to him. (2 Cor 11:2)
        For we are members of his body. (Eph 5:30)
        See that what you have heard from the beginning remains in you. If it does, you also will remain in the Son and in the Father. (1 John 2:24)

    b. The believer dies to the law so that he can bring forth fruit unto God. Bearing fruit would mean...
        *   to bear righteousness (Ro.6:21-23; Ph.1:11).
        *   to bear converts (Ro.1:13; Jn.15:16).
        *   to bear Christian character, the fruit of the Spirit (Gal.5:22-23; Col.1:10).

3 (7:5) **The Law—Lust—Sin:** the second position of the law is a warning—the law is alive to those in the flesh, "controlled by the sinful nature." A man "controlled by the sinful nature" is the natural man: the man without Christ, the unsaved, the unjustified, the unregenerate man. To be "controlled by the sinful nature" means that a man is still "under the law," that he must keep its demands and suffer its guilt and bear its punishment. (See DEEPER STUDY #1, *Flesh*—Jn.1:14; DEEPER STUDY # 1—1 Cor.3:1-4 for more discussion.) Note two significant points.

1. The law is alive and active to the man without Christ.
    a. It is alive and active in that it points out sin and arouses guilt within a man when he violates the law. (See note, *Grace vs. Law*—Ro.6:14-15 for more discussion and verses on guilty feelings.)

        Therefore no one will be declared righteous in his sight by observing the law;

rather, through the law we become conscious of sin. (Rom 3:20)

The law was added so that the trespass might increase. But where sin increased, grace increased all the more, (Rom 5:20)

What shall we say, then? Is the law sin? Certainly not! Indeed I would not have known what sin was except through the law. For I would not have known what coveting really was if the law had not said, "Do not covet." (Rom 7:7)

What, then, was the purpose of the law? It was added because of transgressions until the Seed to whom the promise referred had come. The law was put into effect through angels by a mediator. (Gal 3:19)

So the law was put in charge to lead us to Christ that we might be justified by faith. (Gal 3:24)

We also know that law is made not for the righteous but for lawbreakers and rebels, the ungodly and sinful, the unholy and irreligious; for those who kill their fathers or mothers, for murderers, (1 Tim 1:9)

b. It is alive and active in that it arouses sinful passions or "the passions of sins" (ta pathemata ton hamartion). The law not only points out sin, it actually arouses feelings and stirs the emotions to do the forbidden. Sinful feelings are actually "aroused" (energeito) by the law in our bodies. When the law prohibits and forbids something, it actually creates within us…

- an interest
- an attraction
- an excitement
- an appeal
- a tug or pull
- a fascination
- a seduction
- an arousal

There is within man something that makes him want to do what he is forbidden to do. When he is restricted or fenced in, he wants to break through the restriction or fence. He wants to go beyond where he is allowed, to take control of his own life as he wishes and wills. (See note—Ro.7:8 for more discussion).

For when we were controlled by the sinful nature, the sinful passions aroused by the law were at work in our bodies, so that we bore fruit for death. (Rom 7:5)

But sin, seizing the opportunity afforded by the commandment, produced in me every kind of covetous desire. For apart from law, sin is dead. (Rom 7:8)

But each one is tempted when, by his own evil desire, he is dragged away and enticed. Then, after desire has conceived, it gives birth to sin; and sin, when it is full-grown, gives birth to death. (James 1:14-15)

What causes fights and quarrels among you? Don't they come from your desires that battle within you? You want something but don't get it. You kill and covet, but you cannot have what you want. You quarrel and fight. You do not have, because you do not ask God. (James 4:1-2)

For the sinful nature desires what is contrary to the Spirit, and the Spirit what

is contrary to the sinful nature. They are in conflict with each other, so that you do not do what you want. (Gal 5:17)

2. The result of combating the law—of refusing to obey the law—is that one bears the fruit of sin. When a man violates the law, he bears transgression and sin, and sin leads to death. In fact, sin deserves death (see note—Ro.6:23 for more discussion).

Therefore, just as sin entered the world through one man, and death through sin, and in this way death came to all men, because all sinned— (Rom 5:12)

For the wages of sin is death, but the gift of God is eternal life in Christ Jesus our Lord. (Rom 6:23)

The mind of sinful man is death, but the mind controlled by the Spirit is life and peace; (Rom 8:6)

Then, after desire has conceived, it gives birth to sin; and sin, when it is full-grown, gives birth to death. (James 1:15)

But the cowardly, the unbelieving, the vile, the murderers, the sexually immoral, those who practice magic arts, the idolaters and all liars—their place will be in the fiery lake of burning sulfur. This is the second death." (Rev 21:8)

But you must not eat from the tree of the knowledge of good and evil, for when you eat of it you will surely die." (Gen 2:17)

The truly righteous man attains life, but he who pursues evil goes to his death. (Prov 11:19)

The soul who sins is the one who will die. The son will not share the guilt of the father, nor will the father share the guilt of the son. The righteousness of the righteous man will be credited to him, and the wickedness of the wicked will be charged against him. (Ezek 18:20)

4 (7:6) **Law—New Life**: the law is inactivated by conversion. Believers "have been delivered, released" (katergethemen), that is, have been *discharged* from the law. How? By their death "in" Christ (see note, *Jesus Christ, Redemption*—Ro.7:4 for discussion).

The believer is freed from the law so that he might serve in "the new way of the Spirit," and not in the "old way of the written code."

⇒ The "old way of the written code" refers to the law. It is the *written* law which a man tries to keep in order to please God. But note: the law was the *old way* for man to live; it is no longer the way for a man to approach God.

⇒ The "the new way of the Spirit" can refer to either the Holy Spirit or to the believer's new spirit. The Holy Spirit is the One who brings new life to the believer and bears fruit within the believer (cp. Ro.8:13-17; Gal.5:22-23. See outline and notes—Ro.8:1-17).

The believer's new spirit is also focused upon God and upon his relationship with God. The believer is now a child of God, a true member of God's family who has open access into God's presence anytime and under any condition.

The believer seeks to serve God knowing that if he fails, God will forgive him and allow him to continue on—to continue on as if nothing had ever happened. The believer no longer serves God in a legal and slavish spirit that dooms him to discouragement and defeat; but he serves God in "the new spirit" of love, joy, peace, forgiveness, and acceptance.

For if you live according to the sinful nature, you will die; but if by the Spirit you put to death the misdeeds of the body, you will live, because those who are led by the Spirit of God are sons of God. For you did not receive a spirit that makes you a slave again to fear, but you received the Spirit of sonship. And by him we cry, "Abba, Father." The Spirit himself testifies with our spirit that we are God's children. Now if we are children, then we are heirs—heirs of God and co-heirs with Christ, if indeed we share in his sufferings in order that we may also share in his glory. (Rom 8:13-17)

For Christ's love compels us, because we are convinced that one died for all, and therefore all died. And he died for all, that those who live should no longer live for themselves but for him who died for them and was raised again. (2 Cor 5:14-15)

Therefore, if anyone is in Christ, he is a new creation; the old has gone, the new has come! (2 Cor 5:17)

Neither circumcision nor uncircumcision means anything; what counts is a new creation. (Gal 6:15)

In him we have redemption through his blood, the forgiveness of sins, in accordance with the riches of God's grace (Eph 1:7)

And to put on the new self, created to be like God in true righteousness and holiness. (Eph 4:24)

And have put on the new self, which is being renewed in knowledge in the image of its Creator. (Col 3:10)

If we confess our sins, he is faithful and just and will forgive us our sins and purify us from all unrighteousness. (1 John 1:9)

My dear children, I write this to you so that you will not sin. But if anybody does sin, we have one who speaks to the Father in our defense—Jesus Christ, the Righteous One. He is the atoning sacrifice for our sins, and not only for ours but also for the sins of the whole world. (1 John 2:1-2)

	B. The Purpose of the Law, 7:7-13	10 I found that the very commandment that was intended to bring life actually brought death.	
1 Is the law sin, that is, evil?	7 What shall we say, then? Is the law sin? Certainly not! Indeed I would not have known what sin was except through the law. For I would not have known what coveting really was if the law had not said, "Do not covet."	11 For sin, seizing the opportunity afforded by the commandment, deceived me, and through the commandment put me to death.	**5 The law reveals the deceitfulness of sin**
2 The law reveals the fact of sin		12 So then, the law is holy, and the commandment is holy, righteous and good.	**6 The law reveals the way of God: Holiness, righteousness, & goodness**
3 The law gives sin the opportunity to be aroused & to work every kind of evil	8 But sin, seizing the opportunity afforded by the commandment, produced in me every kind of covetous desire. For apart from law, sin is dead.	13 Did that which is good, then, become death to me? By no means! But in order that sin might be recognized as sin, it produced death in me through what was good, so that through the commandment sin might become utterly sinful.	**7 The law shows that sin is utterly sinful and that it is the cause of death**
4 The law reveals the fact of condemnation & death	9 Once I was alive apart from law; but when the commandment came, sin sprang to life and I died.		

DIVISION V

STRUGGLE AND CONFESSION: THE BELIEVER IS TO BE FREE FROM THE LAW, 7:1-25

B. The Purpose of the Law, 7:7-13

(7:7-13) **Introduction**: the purpose of the law is clearly pointed out in this passage. It is a passage that needs to be carefully studied by both the world and believers. It is a passage that needs to be proclaimed from the housetops, for the law was given by God to show man his desperate need for a Savior.

1. Is the law sin, that is, evil? (v.7).
2. The law reveals the fact of sin (v.7).
3. The law gives sin the opportunity to be aroused and to work every kind of evil (v.8).
4. The law reveals the fact of condemnation and death (v.9-10).
5. The law reveals the deceitfulness of sin (v.11).
6. The law reveals the way of God: holiness, righteousness, and goodness (v.12).
7. The law shows that sin is utterly sinful and that it is the cause of death (v.13).

1 (7:7) **The Law**: Is the law sin, that is, evil? This is a legitimate question because of what Romans has declared about the law.

1. The law judges and condemns men: all who sin under the law will be judged by the law (Rom 2:12).
2. The law and ritual do not make a person a Christian: "No, a man is a Jew [Christian] if he is one inwardly; and circumcision [a ritual] is circumcision of the heart, by the Spirit, not by the written code [law]. Such a man's praise is not from men, but from God" (Rom 2:29).
3. The law cannot make a man righteous and acceptable to God: "Therefore no one will be declared righteous in his sight by observing the law; rather, through the law we become conscious of sin" (Rom 3:20; cp. Ro.3:27).
4. The purpose of the law is not to save man but to bear witness that man desperately needs the righteousness of God: "But now a righteousness from God, apart from law, has been made known, to which the Law and the Prophets testify. This righteousness from God comes through faith in Jesus Christ to all who believe. There is no difference" (Rom 3:21-22).
5. The law leads man to boast in himself—in his own works and self-righteousness—not in God: "Where, then, is boasting? It is excluded. On what principle? On that of observing the law? No, but on that of faith" (Rom 3:27; cp. Ro.4:2, 4; 2:29).
6. The law does not justify a person: "If, in fact, Abraham was justified by works, he had something to boast about--but not before God". What does the Scripture say? "Abraham believed God, and it was credited to him as righteousness." Now when a man works, his wages are not credited to him as a gift, but as an obligation. However, to the man who does not work but trusts God who justifies the wicked, his faith is credited as righteousness (Rom 4:2-5).
7. The law is not the way a person receives the promise of God: "It was not through law that Abraham and his offspring received the promise that he would be heir of the world, but through the righteousness that comes by faith" (Rom 4:13).
8. The law works wrath in that it accuses man of sin and condemns him: "Because law brings wrath. And where there is no law there is no transgression" (Rom 4:15).
9. The law causes sin to increase and multiply: "the law was added so that the trespass might increase. But where sin increased, grace increased all the more" (Rom 5:20).
10. The law enslaves and brings men into bondage: "For sin shall not be your master, because you are not under law, but under grace" (Rom 6:14; cp. Ro.7:1).
11. The law arouses men to sin: "For when we were controlled by the sinful nature, the sinful passions aroused by the law were at work in our bodies, so that we bore fruit for death" (Rom 7:5).

Such facts as these can naturally cause a person to question the value of God's law. If the law lays such a burden of sin upon man, what good is it? Is it not evil? Scripture declares loudly and clearly: "Certainly not!" Let it never be! Such a thought is far from the truth!

2 (7:7) **The Law**: the law of God reveals the fact of sin. Apart from the law, man would be aware that some acts are wrong, such as stealing and killing. However, there would be much that man could not know if he did not have the law, much that he would desperately need to know in order to live a full and peaceful life.

The law reveals the fact of sin, the fact...

- that men are not in a right relationship with God.
- that men are not in a right relationship with other men.
- that men are living selfishly, thereby dooming themselves.
- that men are coveting and lusting, thereby destroying their world and their future.
- that men are displeasing God and have become unacceptable to Him.

The point is this: when a man sees the fact of sin, the fact that he is a sinner, he can *correct it* and *do something* about it. The knowledge of sin is a great and glorious thing, for we can take our knowledge and use it to *correct the wrong*. Without the law, we would roam in ignorance, not knowing what was wrong and what was right, what was dooming us and what was freeing us. If there was no restraint, that is, no law, every man would be doing what he wanted when he wanted; he would be doing his own thing—fulfilling his own desires—regardless of the fallout and the hurt inflicted upon others.

Now note: the law reveals sin; it awakens man to three facts about sin.

1. The law reveals the fact of sin, that sin actually exists. The law awakens man to the reality and truth of sin. Man knows that coveting is wrong because the law says, "You shall not covet." He knows that some things are good and other things are bad because the law tells him. He knows that certain things please and other things displease God because the law says so. In simple and clear language, the law tells a man...

- what the nature and will of God is.
- what he must do to be acceptable to God.

2. The law reveals the fact of man's own sin, that man is unquestionably a sinner. The law awakens man to the reality that he himself is a sinner. The law shows man...

- that he does not always do the will of God.
- that he cannot keep the law of God, not perfectly.
- that he is guilty of acting contrary to the nature of God.
- that he is imperfect, guilty of violating God's law.
- that being imperfect, he comes short of God's glory.
- that being short of God's glory, he is unacceptable to God.

3. The law reveals the fact of man's sinful nature, that man is actually aroused to do some of the things that are forbidden. The law shows man that he has a sinful, depraved, polluted, and corrupted nature. The law shows man that he covets and lusts, enjoys and is aroused...

- to take the second helping of food.
- to take the melons on the other side of the fence.
- to secure the same things owned by his neighbor.
- to go after the excitement and stimulation of the forbidden.
- to fulfill the lust of the flesh, the cravings of sinful man.
- to feed the lust of the eyes.
- to satisfy the pride of life, the boasting of what he has and does.

The purpose of the law is to reveal sin so that man can correct his behavior and save himself and his world. Apart from God's law, he would not know that he needed to be saved.

> **Therefore no one will be declared righteous in his sight by observing the law; rather, through the law we become conscious of sin. (Rom 3:20)**
>
> **The law was added so that the trespass might increase. But where sin increased, grace increased all the more, (Rom 5:20)**
>
> **What shall we say, then? Is the law sin? Certainly not! Indeed I would not have known what sin was except through the law. For I would not have known what coveting really was if the law had not said, "Do not covet." (Rom 7:7)**
>
> **What, then, was the purpose of the law? It was added because of transgressions until the Seed to whom the promise referred had come. The law was put into effect through angels by a mediator. (Gal 3:19)**
>
> **So the law was put in charge to lead us to Christ that we might be justified by faith. (Gal 3:24)**
>
> **We also know that law is made not for the righteous but for lawbreakers and rebels, the ungodly and sinful, the unholy and irreligious; for those who kill their fathers or mothers, for murderers, (1 Tim 1:9)**

3 (7:8) **The Law—Lust—Sin**: the law gives sin the opportunity to be aroused, working every kind of evil. Note the exact words of the Scripture: "Sin, seizing the opportunity afforded by the commandment, produced in me every kind of covetous desire" that is, sin uses the commandment. Sin is *not within* the commandment; it is *separate* from it. The commandment or law is not sinful. Sin is within man, not within the law. Man's aging, deteriorating, and corrupt nature has within it...

- the principle of sin
- the tendency to sin
- the fondness for sin
- the urge to sin
- a diseased flesh
- a selfish appetite
- a self-centered mind
- a dead spirit

Note three points.

1. It is the law that gives sin the opportunity to be aroused. The law actually stirs, awakens, and arouses sin to work all manner of evil. When a man is told not to do something, there is something within him that is stirred and wants to do it. Sometimes the desire to do the forbidden is so strong it becomes a rage, inflamed to such a point that the person just has to do it. (See note—Ro.7:5 for more discussion.)

2. It is man that takes and misuses the law; it is not the law that takes and misuses man. The law does not violate man; man violates the law. It is not the law that *takes* man and forces him to sin. It is man that *takes* the law and breaks it, that deliberately goes against what it says. It is sin within man that takes and misuses the law to work all manner of sin. Therefore, it is not the law that is evil; it is man who is evil.

3. Without the law, *sin was dead*; that is, it was not alive and active. It was not guiding and directing man; it was not able to fulfill its function which was so desperately needed: showing man his critical need for deliverance from sin and its condemnation of death.

Without the law, *sin is dead*, but with the law sin becomes alive. Man is able to look at the law and his true condition, that he is a sinner who must be saved if he is to become acceptable to God and live eternally. The law is not evil but good, gloriously good, for it shows us our desperate need for salvation.

> **For when we were controlled by the sinful nature, the sinful passions aroused by the law were at work in our bodies, so that we bore fruit for death. (Rom 7:5)**
>
> **But sin, seizing the opportunity afforded by the commandment, produced in me every kind of covetous desire. For apart from law, sin is dead. (Rom 7:8)**
>
> **But each one is tempted when, by his own evil desire, he is dragged away and enticed. Then, after desire has conceived, it gives birth to sin; and sin, when it is full-grown, gives birth to death. (James 1:14-15)**
>
> **What causes fights and quarrels among you? Don't they come from your desires that battle within you? You want something but don't get it. You kill and covet, but you cannot have what you want. You quarrel and fight. You do not have, because you do not ask God. (James 4:1-2)**
>
> **For the sinful nature desires what is contrary to the Spirit, and the Spirit what is contrary to the sinful nature. They are in conflict with each other, so that you do not do what you want. (Gal 5:17)**

4 (7:9-10) **The Law:** the law reveals the fact of condemnation and death. This is a major purpose of the law. Note three points.

1. A man who does not know or pay attention to the law feels alive. He is just not aware of the law; therefore, he does not pay attention to sin. He is not aware that he is a sinner and short of God's glory, violating God's will and going contrary to God's nature. He is ignorant of God's law; he pays little attention to right and wrong. When he does wrong and fails to do right, he is not aware of it. Therefore he feels...

- no consciousness of sin
- no guilt
- no dread of punishment
- no sense of judgment

He feels alive, safe, secure, confident, and assured that he is pleasing to God and will be approved and accepted by God. He feels alive despite the reality of his sinful state and condition. Without the law he does not know the truth, that he is a sinner, condemned and unclean and ever so short of God's glory and acceptance.

2. A man who does know God's law and pays attention to it sees sin come alive. By knowing the law the man becomes *acutely aware* of sin when he breaks the law. It is the law that gives him...

- a painful awareness of sin
- a sense of guilt
- a sense of judgment to come
- a dread of punishment and of death

It is the law that causes his spirit to die, that destroys his confidence and assurance, comfort and security. It is the law that shows him the true state and condition of man: that he is a sinner who is to face condemnation and death; that he desperately needs to be delivered from sin and death; that he desperately needs a Savior who can make him acceptable to God.

3. The point is this: the law is ordained to bring life, but not in the way men think. Men think that the law was given to be kept, and that by keeping the commandment they can earn the acceptance of God and work their way into heaven. However, this is not the way the law brings life to man. The law brings life to man...

- by destroying his self-centeredness and self-righteousness.
- by revealing the truth to him, his true state and condition.
- by showing him that he is a corrupt, sinful being.
- by demonstrating that he desperately needs to be delivered from sin and death.
- by proving that he desperately needs a Savior, One who can make him acceptable to God.

When a man really looks at the law of God, he learns his true condition: he is corrupt and destined to face condemnation and death. In learning this fact, he is driven to seek the salvation of God. Therefore, the law is not evil; it is good.

> **For in my inner being I delight in God's law; but I see another law at work in the members of my body, waging war against the law of my mind and making me a prisoner of the law of sin at work within my members. What a wretched man I am! Who will rescue me from this body of death? (Rom 7:22-24)**
>
> **So the law was put in charge to lead us to Christ that we might be justified by faith. (Gal 3:24)**
>
> **In the way of righteousness there is life; along that path is immortality. (Prov 12:28)**
>
> **And if a wicked man turns away from his wickedness and does what is just and right, he will live by doing so. (Ezek 33:19)**

5 (7:11) **The Law:** the law reveals the deceitfulness of sin. Note again: it is sin that takes the law and misuses it; it takes the law and deceives us. How? There are at least two ways.

1. Sin misuses the law and deceives a person by making him feel safe and secure. Sin, that is, self-righteousness, says obey the law and you shall live. But this is deception, for no man can keep the law perfectly. Down deep, the thinking and honest man knows he can never achieve perfection by keeping God's law; but his sin, his self-righteousness, drives him onward to try and try; and he is forever deceived and doomed. The point is this: the law reveals the deceitfulness of sin or of self-righteousness. The law proves that man is not perfect, that he cannot live without sinning, that he sins and sins and cannot keep from sinning. When a man honestly looks at the law, the law destroys the deceitfulness of sin.

2. Sin misuses the law and deceives a person by discouraging him and making him feel helpless and hopeless. Sin deceives men into thinking that the law has been given

to bring life to man. Therefore, when a man continues to break the law, he is keenly aware that he is condemned and unable to achieve the righteousness of the law. He knows that he has displeased God and senses that he is unacceptable to God. Feelings of helplessness and hopelessness swarm over him and he becomes defeated and down and out. Sin simply takes the law and uses man's failure to discourage him. Sin uses the law, so to speak, to whip man, to make him feel unworthy and helpless and hopeless, to drive him deeper and deeper into despair.

> **For sin, seizing the opportunity afforded by the commandment, deceived me, and through the commandment put me to death. (Rom 7:11)**
>
> **At one time we too were foolish, disobedient, deceived and enslaved by all kinds of passions and pleasures. We lived in malice and envy, being hated and hating one another. (Titus 3:3)**
>
> **But encourage one another daily, as long as it is called Today, so that none of you may be hardened by sin's deceitfulness. (Heb 3:13)**
>
> **The integrity of the upright guides them, but the unfaithful are destroyed by their duplicity. (Prov 11:3)**
>
> **The truly righteous man attains life, but he who pursues evil goes to his death. (Prov 11:19)**

Now note: such an attitude toward the law is the attitude of sin. The law was never given to drive men to despair, and in truth, it cannot. It is sin *within* men that drives them to despair. Twisted minds and ungodly thoughts drive men into a state of hopelessness. The law was given to reveal sin to men, to take the sin that already exists and to reveal its shame and consequences to men. When the law was first given, man was already in a state of sin and death: he was sinning and he was dying. God gave the law to man because He loved man, because He knew that men needed to be pointed toward Christ and needed to be shown their terrible condition and desperate need for a Savior. Such is the glorious purpose of the law, a purpose which is far from being evil.

6 (7:12) **The Law**: the law reveals the way of God, the way of holiness and righteousness and goodness.

1. The law is holy: set apart and full of purity, majesty, and glory—set apart in that it reveals God's nature and will—set apart in that it exposes sin, all that is contrary to God's nature and will. The law is holy in that it is different and set apart from everything else on earth. The law is God's way of holiness, the way to live a life of holiness, the way that is so different and so set apart that no man can reach its purity.

2. The law is righteous: just, fair, impartial, equitable, straight. The law treats a man exactly like he should be treated; it shows no partiality to anyone. It also reveals how a man should treat others. The law is just in that it reveals exactly how a man should live. It shows him how to live in relation to God and to his fellow man, and it judges him fairly and impartially.

3. The law is good: it shows man how to live and tells him when he fails to live that way. It exposes his sin and demonstrates his desperate need for a Savior. The law tells man the truth about the nature of man in a most explicit

way, and it points him toward the need for *outside* help in order to be saved.

> **The law of the LORD is perfect, reviving the soul. The statutes of the LORD are trustworthy, making wise the simple. (Psa 19:7)**
>
> **Your righteousness is everlasting and your law is true. (Psa 119:142)**
>
> **So then, the law is holy, and the commandment is holy, righteous and good. (Rom 7:12)**
>
> **We know that the law is spiritual; but I am unspiritual, sold as a slave to sin. (Rom 7:14)**
>
> **We know that the law is good if one uses it properly. (1 Tim 1:8)**

7 (7:13) **The Law—Sin**: the law shows that sin is utterly sinful and that it is the cause of death. Note three points.

1. The law is good; it is not the cause of death. "By no means! Such is impossible!"

2. The law was given to expose sin and to make men deeply aware of its presence and consequences. Men needed to know just how utterly sinful sin is. Men needed to know that sin...
- is the worst possible affront to God.
- is the worst imaginable rebellion against God.
- is against all that God represents.

The law proves that sin is against God: against all that He is, against all of His nature and will. Sin is selfish, destructive, dirty, ugly, and impure. The law is the very opposite. The law was given to show how utterly sinful sin is, to show just how terrible it is. Take any sin and stand it up against the law that prohibits it and the great contrast is seen. For example, take murder and stand it beside the commandment "You shall not murder." Look at the great contrast.
- ⇒ The commandment protected man's life, but sin took his life away.
- ⇒ The commandment protected man's presence with loved ones, but sin took his presence away.
- ⇒ The commandment protected man's existence upon earth, but sin took his existence away.
- ⇒ The commandment protected man's contribution to society, but sin took his contribution away.
- ⇒ The commandment said that man could live, but sin said "no," and killed him.

So it is with every sin, whether adultery, stealing, or taking God's name in vain. The law was given to show how utterly sinful sin is. It was given to make men think of their sinful state and condition and of their desperate need for deliverance and salvation.

3. The law was given to make men think about death, to make men aware that they die because they violate the will and nature of God. Men died *before* the law was ever given. They died because they did not live holy and righteous lives, did not live according to the nature and will of God. God gave the law so that sin and its condemnation of death would be *exposed* more than ever before. Men had to be shown that they were great sinners and that they died because they sinned. The law shows men clearer than ever before and in no uncertain terms...
- that they do sin
- that they are not perfect
- that they are condemned to die

Therefore, they need a Savior who will deliver them from sin and its terrible consequence of death. The law shows man his desperate need to be saved from sin, death, and judgment.

> **As it is written: "There is no one righteous, not even one; there is no one who understands, no one who seeks God. All have turned away, they have together become worthless; there is no one who does good, not even one." Now we know that whatever the law says, it says to those who are under the law, so that every mouth may be silenced and the whole world held accountable to God. (Rom 3:10-12, 19; cp. v.9-19)**
>
> **For the wages of sin is death, but the gift of God is eternal life in Christ Jesus our Lord. (Rom 6:23)**

		b. The conclusion: he has a sinful, depraved, & corrupt nature
1 The law is spiritual **2 Confession 1: He is un-spiritual, carnal, a slave to sin** a. An unspiritual life is a helpless, unceasing struggle b. An unspirital life demon-strates that human nature & knowledge are inade-quate c. The conclusion: man has a sinful, depraved, & corrupt nature **3 Confession 2: He is empty of anything good** a. He wills & resolves but it is all inadequate	**C. The Confessions of a Man's Struggling Soul, 7:14-25** 14 We know that the law is spiritual; but I am unspiritual, sold as a slave to sin. 15 I do not understand what I do. For what I want to do I do not do, but what I hate I do. 16 And if I do what I do not want to do, I agree that the law is good. 17 As it is, it is no longer I myself who do it, but it is sin living in me. 18 I know that nothing good lives in me, that is, in my sinful nature. For I have the desire to do what is good, but I cannot carry it out. 19 For what I do is not the good I want to do; no, the evil I do not want to do—this I keep on doing.	20 Now if I do what I do not want to do, it is no longer I who do it, but it is sin living in me that does it. 21 So I find this law at work: When I want to do good, evil is right there with me. 22 For in my inner being I delight in God's law; 23 But I see another law at work in the members of my body, waging war against the law of my mind and making me a prisoner of the law of sin at work within my mem-bers. 24 What a wretched man I am! Who will rescue me from this body of death? 25 Thanks be to God—through Jesus Christ our Lord! So then, I myself in my mind am a slave to God's law, but in the sinful nature a slave to the law of sin.	**4 Confession 3: He finds two laws or forces within** a. The law of God works in him b. The law of sin wages war against the law of his mind **5 Confession 4: He is a desperate, wretched man who needs a Deliverer** **6 Confession 5: The Deliv-erer is Jesus Christ**

DIVISION V

STRUGGLE AND CONFESSION: THE BELIEVER IS TO BE FREE FROM THE LAW, 7:1-25

C. The Confessions of a Man's Struggling Soul, 7:14-25

(7:14-25) **Introduction**: this is a great passage of Scripture in that it portrays the struggling soul of the believer as he ploughs through life. It is a rare picture of the life of Paul, of what he sensed and learned and experienced as he struggled to please God and to become conformed to the glorious image of the Lord Jesus. It is the confession of a man's soul as he struggles through life.

1. The law is spiritual (v.14).
2. Confession 1: he is unspiritual, carnal, a slave to sin (v.14-17).
3. Confession 2: he is empty of anything good (v.18-20).
4. Confession 3: he finds two laws or forces within (v.21-23).
5. Confession 4: he is a desperate, wretched man who needs a Deliverer (v.24).
6. Confession 5: the Deliverer is Jesus Christ (v.25).

1 (7:14) **Law**: the law is spiritual. It is spiritual in at least three senses.

1. The law was given to man by the Spirit of God (pneumatikos). The Greek word used is the very name of the Holy Spirit. The Holy Spirit is the source of the law.

2. The law is the expression of the will and nature of God. The law is spiritual because it describes the will of God and tells man just what God is like. The rules of the law reveal both the mind and nature of God.

3. The law is spiritual because of its purposes (see note, *Law, Purpose*—Ro.7:12 for discussion. Also cp. outline and notes—Ro.7:7-13 for more discussion.)

2 (7:14-17) **Carnal—Unspiritual—Flesh—Man, Nature**: the first confession of Paul is that he is unspiritual, carnal, a slave to sin. The word "unspiritual" or "carnal"

(sarkinos) means to be made of flesh; to consist of flesh; to have a body of flesh and blood. It means the flesh with which a man is born, the fleshly, sinful nature one inherits from his parents when he is born.

The word unspiritual or carnal also means to be given up to the fleshly, sinful nature that is, to live a sinful nature, sensual life; to be given over to animal appetites; to be con-trolled by one's sinful nature (see DEEPER STUDY #1, *Carnal*—1 Cor.3:1-4 for more discussion).

Paul says that he is "sold as a slave to sin." He simply means that as a creature of the sinful nature, that is, as a man, he is...

- a slave to sin.
- under sin's influence.
- subject to sin.
- capable of sinning.
- guilty of sinning.
- cannot free himself from being short of God's glory.
- cannot keep from sinning—not perfectly.
- cannot erase sin's presence—not completely.
- cannot cast sin out of his life—not totally.
- cannot get rid of sin—not permanently.

> **The evil deeds of a wicked man ensnare him; the cords of his sin hold him fast. (Prov 5:22)**
>
> **Jesus replied, "I tell you the truth, eve-ryone who sins is a slave to sin. (John 8:34)**
>
> **For I see that you are full of bitterness and captive to sin." (Acts 8:23)**
>
> **Do not offer the parts of your body to sin, as instruments of wickedness, but rather offer yourselves to God, as those who have been brought from death to life;**

and offer the parts of your body to him as instruments of righteousness. (Rom 6:13)

And that they [the carnal] will come to their senses and escape from the trap of the devil, who has taken them captive to do his will. (2 Tim 2:26)

They promise them freedom, while they themselves are slaves of depravity—for a man is a slave to whatever has mastered him. (2 Pet 2:19)

Paul makes three points about his being unspiritual, a slave to sin.

1. He says that an unspiritual or a carnal life is a helpless, unceasing struggle.

   a. "I do not understand what I do:" the word "understand" (ginosko) means to recognize, to know, to perceive. An unspiritual man finds himself doing things, and he cannot understand why he is doing them. He fights and struggles against them, but before he knows it, he has sinned and come short. The sin was upon him before he even recognized and saw it. If he had known that the behavior was sin, he would have never done it, but he did not recognize it as coming short of God's glory and God's will for his life.

   b. "What I want to do I do not do." Paul says that he wanted to do right and to please God as he walked throughout life day by day. He wanted to be conformed to the image of Christ and to become all that God wanted him to be. But despite his desire and expectation, before he knew it, he found himself coming short of God's glory and will.

   c. "What I hate, I do." Paul hated sin and hated coming short of God's glory. He struggled against failing and displeasing God; he hated everything that hurt and cut the heart of God, and he fought to erase it completely from his life. But no matter how much he hated and struggled against coming short, he still found himself failing.

For the sinful nature desires what is contrary to the Spirit, and the Spirit what is contrary to the sinful nature. They are in conflict with each other, so that you do not do what you want. (Gal 5:17)

2. An unspiritual, carnal life demonstrates that human nature and knowledge is inadequate. An unspiritual, carnal man fails to live for God like he should. No matter how much he tries to please God and to be conformed to the image of Christ, he comes short.

Now note: it is the law that tells man that he comes short. The law tells him that despite all his efforts to please God, he is short and not acceptable to God. He may know the law and he may try to keep the law, but his desire to know and to seek God will not save him. His nature and knowledge are not enough; they fail. What he needs is a Savior, One outside his own flesh who can forgive his sins and impart eternal life to him.

Note another fact: an unspiritual, carnal life proves the law is good. The word "agree" (sumphemi) means to agree, to say the same thing, to speak right along with the law, to prove and demonstrate and show that the law is right. The law proves and demonstrates that a man cannot live a perfectly righteous life. An unspiritual man proves the very same thing. He sins, finding himself doing exactly what the law says not to do and what he himself prefers not to do.

The point is this: when an unspiritual, carnal man sins, the law points out his sin. The law tells the unspiritual man the truth: he is a sinner doomed to die. Knowing this, the unspiritual man is able to seek the Lord and His forgiveness. Therefore, the unspiritual man agrees with the law; the law is very good, for it tells him that he must seek the Savior and His forgiveness. He may not actually follow through and seek the Lord, but the law has at least fulfilled its function and shown the unspiritual man what he needs to do.

The way of peace they do not know; there is no justice in their paths. They have turned them into crooked roads; no one who walks in them will know peace. (Isa 59:8)

"My people are fools; they do not know me. They are senseless children; they have no understanding. They are skilled in doing evil; they know not how to do good." (Jer 4:22)

I thought, "These are only the poor; they are foolish, for they do not know the way of the LORD, the requirements of their God. (Jer 5:4)

But they do not know the thoughts of the LORD; they do not understand his plan, he who gathers them like sheaves to the threshing floor. (Micah 4:12)

Since they did not know the righteousness that comes from God and sought to establish their own, they did not submit to God's righteousness. (Rom 10:3)

They are darkened in their understanding and separated from the life of God because of the ignorance that is in them due to the hardening of their hearts. (Eph 4:18)

3. Paul's conclusion is that man has a sinful, depraved, and corrupt nature. What causes him to conclude this? As a man who was a genuine believer, he did not want to sin; he actually willed not to sin. However, he found that he could not keep from sinning. He continually came short of the glory of God and failed to be consistently conformed to the image of Christ. Why?

⇒ Not because he failed to exercise his will.
⇒ Not because his mind was not focused upon Christ.
⇒ Not because he did not know God's will.
⇒ Not because he did not seek to do God's will.
⇒ Not because he did not call upon every faculty and power of his being.

He came short and failed because of *sin that lives and dwells in him*, because of *sin within* his sinful nature. The unspiritual, carnal man finds a principle, a law of sin *within* his sinful nature that tugs and pulls him to sin. He finds that no matter what he does, he sins...

• by living for himself before he lives for God and for others.
• by putting himself before the laws concerning God and the laws concerning man. (This refers to the ten commandments where the first laws govern our relationship to God and the last laws govern our relationship to man.)

No matter what resources and faculties man uses and no matter how diligently he tries, he is unable to control sin and to keep from sinning. Sin is *within* his sinful nature; it lives and *dwells in* him. In fact, man is corrupt and dies for

122

this very reason. He was never made to be corruptible nor to die; he was not created with the *seed of corruption* that causes him to age and deteriorate and decay (Ro.5:12). The *seed of corruption* was planted in his sinful nature, in his body and life when he sinned. The unspiritual, carnal life proves that man cannot keep from sinning, that man is diseased with the *seed of corruption*, the seed of a sinful and a depraved nature.

> Jesus answered, "I tell you the truth, you are looking for me, not because you saw miraculous signs but because you ate the loaves and had your fill. (John 6:26)
> For in my inner being I delight in God's law; but I see another law at work in the members of my body, waging war against the law of my mind and making me a prisoner of the law of sin at work within my members. What a wretched man I am! Who will rescue me from this body of death? (Rom 7:22-24)
> The sinful mind is hostile to God. It does not submit to God's law, nor can it do so. Those controlled by the sinful nature cannot please God. (Rom 8:7-8)
> So I tell you this, and insist on it in the Lord, that you must no longer live as the Gentiles do, in the futility of their thinking. (Eph 4:17)
> To the pure, all things are pure, but to those who are corrupted and do not believe, nothing is pure. In fact, both their minds and consciences are corrupted. (Titus 1:15)

3 (7:18-20) **Flesh—Sin—Man, Nature**: the second confession of Paul is that he is empty of anything good. By "sinful nature" (sarki) Paul means the human, depraved, and corrupt nature of man. (See note, *Unspiritual, Carnal*—Ro.7:14-17 for more discussion). Paul declares: that "nothing good" lives in him. This does not mean that he never did any good thing or work. It means that his sinful nature, his flesh...

- is unable to please the goodness of God.
- is unable to be as good as it should be.
- is unable to be perfectly good.
- is unable to conquer the tendency and push toward sin.
- is unable to be conformed to the image of Christ.
- is corrupted and short of God's glory.
- is contaminated and diseased by sin.
- is incapable of reaching God on its own and by itself.
- is aging and deteriorating, dying and decaying.
- is condemned to face the judgment of God.

1. Note why Paul says that his sinful nature is empty. He wills and resolves not to sin, but it is all to no avail. No matter how much he wills and resolves, he fails and comes short. Note that *he desires to do what is good*. The word "desires" means that it is constantly before his face. He is *always* willing to do good and to please God. There is no lack of will in him. It is not the weakness of will nor of his resolve that causes him to come short of God's glory and will. How does he know this?
⇒ Because what he wills to do, he fails to do.
⇒ Because the evil he tries not to do, he does.

2. Paul's conclusion is the same as that of point one. He is empty of anything good because he has a sinful, depraved, and corrupt nature. He is held in spiritual bondage (see note, pt.3—Ro.7:14-17 for discussion and verses).

4 (7:21-23) **Sin, Law of—Mind, Law of—Inward Man—Inner being**: the third confession of Paul is that he finds two laws or two forces *within* him. Very simply, as soon as Paul wills to do good, he is immediately confronted...
- by a law of evil (v.21).
- by the law of sin (v.23).

The law of sin and evil battles *the law of the inner being, the inward man* (v.22), *the law of his mind* (v.23).
1. The *law of evil* or the *law of sin* means that sin is a law, a rule, a force, a principle, a disposition, an urge, a tendency, a pull, a tug, a corruption, a depravity within man's nature or inner being. It is called a law...
- because of its regularity; it rises up and rules all the time.
- because of its permanent and controlling power.because it is impossible to break its rule and to keep from sinning.
- because it has captivated and enslaved the nature of man (Ro.7:14f).
- because it is not passive but active, constantly struggling to gain the ascendancy over the law of the mind.

Any man who allows the law of sin to rule in his life is a miserable and helpless victim of sin.
2. The *law of the inner being, the inward man* or *the law of the mind* means...
- the divine nature of God implanted within the believer.

> Through these he has given us his very great and precious promises, so that through them you may participate in the divine nature and escape the corruption in the world caused by evil desires. (2 Pet 1:4)

- the "new self," or "new man" created when a believer is born again.

> To be made new in the attitude of your minds; and to put on the new self, created to be like God in true righteousness and holiness. (Eph 4:23-24)
> And have put on the new self, which is being renewed in knowledge in the image of its Creator. (Col 3:10)

- the abiding presence of Christ in the believer's life.

> I will not leave you as orphans; I will come to you. On that day you will realize that I am in my Father, and you are in me, and I am in you. (John 14:18, 20)
> I have been crucified with Christ and I no longer live, but Christ lives in me. The life I live in the body, I live by faith in the Son of God, who loved me and gave himself for me. (Gal 2:20)

- the indwelling presence of the Holy Spirit.

> **And I will ask the Father, and he will give you another Counselor to be with you forever—the Spirit of truth. The world cannot accept him, because it neither sees him nor knows him. But you know him, for he lives with you and will be in you. But the Counselor, the Holy Spirit, whom the Father will send in my name, will teach you all things and will remind you of everything I have said to you. (John 14:16-17, 26)**
>
> **Do you not know that your body is a temple of the Holy Spirit, who is in you, whom you have received from God? You are not your own; you were bought at a price. Therefore honor God with your body. (1 Cor 6:19-20)**

- the "hidden man of the heart, of the inner self."

> **Instead, it [one appearance] should be that of your inner self, the unfading beauty of a gentle and quiet spirit, which is of great worth in God's sight. (1 Pet 3:4)**

Very simply stated, the *law of the inner being, of the inward man* is the law, rule, disposition, urge, tendency, pull, and tug of the Holy Spirit to please God and to delight in doing His will.

The confession of Paul is striking. He declares that the law of sin wars against the law of his mind and that it gains the ascendancy. The law of sin captivates and enslaves him.

5 (7:24) **Spiritual Struggle—Sanctification—Paul**: the fourth confession of Paul is that he is a desperate, wretched man who needs a Deliverer. There is a sense in which man is a walking civil war. He has the ability to see what is good, but he is unable to do it. He can see what is wrong, but he cannot keep from doing it. Paul says he was pulled in two directions, pulled so much that he was almost like two men in the same body. He knew *the right*, yet he did *the wrong*. He knew what was wrong, yet he was unable to stay away from it.

There is no believer, no matter how advanced in holiness, who cannot use the same language used by the Apostle. There is a bondage, a power of sin, within the believer's nature that he cannot totally resist. True, he may and does struggle against the power, and he desires to be free from it; but despite all his efforts, he still finds himself under its influence. This is precisely the bondage of sin, of coming short of the glory of God. Too often he finds himself distrusting God, being hard of heart, loving the world and self, being too prideful, too cold, too slothful—disapproving what he knows to be right and approving what he hates. He groans under the weight of sin, of being short of God's glory and of failing to be conformed to the image of Christ. He aches to walk in humility and gentleness and to be filled with the fruit of love, joy, and peace. But day by day he finds the force of sin reasserting its power over him. He struggles and struggles against it, but he finds that he cannot find the power to free himself. The believer senses an utter helplessness and longs and desires for God to free him. He is a slave looking and longing for liberty. As one has said, this conflict between the flesh and spirit, the struggle that is waged because of the *sinful nature*,

"continues in us so long as we live, in some more, and in others less, according as the one or the other principle is the stronger. Yet, the whole man is both flesh and spirit, and contends with himself until he is completely spiritual" (Martin Luther as quoted by Charles Hodge. *Commentary on the Epistle to the Romans.* Grand Rapids, MI: Eerdmans, 1950, p.236).

It is this consciousness that drives the believer to the awareness that deliverance is found only through Jesus Christ our Lord. (See note—Gal.5:16-18.)

> **If they fall away, to be brought back to repentance, because to their loss they are crucifying the Son of God all over again and subjecting him to public disgrace. (Heb 6:6)**
>
> **For the LORD your God detests anyone who does these things, anyone who deals dishonestly. (Deu 25:16)**
>
> **You are not a God who takes pleasure in evil; with you the wicked cannot dwell. (Psa 5:4)**

6 (7:25) **Spiritual Struggle—Sanctification—Deliverance—Life, Victorious**: the fifth confession of Paul is that the great Deliverer is the Lord Jesus Christ. This is an exclamation! Paul bursts forth with praise to God, for there is a glorious deliverance from sin! But note: the deliverance does not come through...

- some man-made law
- some man-possessed power
- some man-possessed ability
- some superior quality and faculty
- some great spiritual force

1. The deliverance comes through the great Deliverer Himself, Jesus Christ our Lord. He is the Deliverer from sin; He alone can deliver from sin. He is perfectly clear about this.

> **Jesus answered, "I am the way and the truth and the life. No one comes to the Father except through me. (John 14:6)**
>
> **Some men brought to him a paralytic, lying on a mat. When Jesus saw their faith, he said to the paralytic, "Take heart, son; your sins are forgiven." (Mat 9:2)**
>
> **This is my blood of the covenant, which is poured out for many for the forgiveness of sins. (Mat 26:28)**
>
> **Peter replied, "Repent and be baptized, every one of you, in the name of Jesus Christ for the forgiveness of your sins. And you will receive the gift of the Holy Spirit. (Acts 2:38)**
>
> **Because through Christ Jesus the law of the Spirit of life set me free from the law of sin and death. (Rom 8:2)**
>
> **In him we have redemption through his blood, the forgiveness of sins, in accordance with the riches of God's grace (Eph 1:7)**
>
> **This is good, and pleases God our Savior, who wants all men to be saved and to come to a knowledge of the truth. For there is one God and one mediator between God and men, the man Christ Jesus, who gave himself as a ransom for all men—the testimony given in its proper time. (1 Tim 2:3-6)**

Jesus Christ delivers the believer from sin in two ways.

   a. Jesus Christ justifies the believer (see note, *Grace vs. Law*, pts.1, 2—Ro.6:14-15 for discussion).

   b. Jesus Christ places the believer under God's grace (see note, pt.2f—Ro.6:14-15 for discussion).

2. Paul's conclusion is that he serves the law of God with his mind, that is, with his *renewed mind*. The believer who truly *knows* that his deliverance is through Jesus Christ our Lord learns something. He learns that his *mind* is *transformed* and *renewed* by Jesus Christ; he learns that his "mind" is born again and experiences a new birth just as his "old self" does. He learns that his *old mind* becomes the *new mind* and that his "old self" becomes the "new self." (See note, *Mind*—Ro.12:2 for more discussion and verses.)

> **Do not conform any longer to the pattern of this world, but be transformed by the renewing of your mind. Then you will be able to test and approve what God's will is—his good, pleasing and perfect will. (Rom 12:2)**
>
> **For Christ's love compels us, because we are convinced that one died for all, and therefore all died. And he died for all, that those who live should no longer live for themselves but for him who died for them and was raised again. (2 Cor 5:14-15)**
>
> **You were taught, with regard to your former way of life, to put off your old self, which is being corrupted by its deceitful desires; to be made new in the attitude of your minds; and to put on the new self, created to be like God in true righteousness and holiness. (Eph 4:22-24)**
>
> **Therefore, prepare your minds for action; be self-controlled; set your hope fully on the grace to be given you when Jesus Christ is revealed. (1 Pet 1:13)**

Because of Jesus Christ, the believer takes his *new mind* and does all he can to serve the law of God. When he fails—when his flesh or sinful nature caves in to sin—he knows that it is the law or force of sin that has caused it, not the law of his *new mind*. He knows that he is still flesh as well as spirit, that he is still indwelt by two laws, two forces that struggle for allegiance; therefore, he does all he can to focus his mind upon the law of God. He simply serves God—His will and His nature (that is, His law)—trying to please God in all that he does. He dedicates himself not to come short of God's glory but to be conformed to the image of Christ. He knows that he is delivered from the law (force) of sin through Jesus Christ; therefore, the believer keeps justification and God's grace ever before his face. The believer knows that when his flesh serves the law of sin by failing, he has open access into God's presence to ask forgiveness. Therefore, he "girds up the loins of his mind" and comes before God for forgiveness. And once receiving a fresh surge of God's forgiveness and grace, he starts all over again. The believer begins to sense the law of God with renewed fervor, the fervor of his renewed mind.

It should be noted that most commentators see the latter part of this verse as reverting back to what Paul had been saying, as a summary statement of what the carnal man or believer experiences. However, it seems much more natural to see Paul building upon his confession of Jesus Christ as the great Deliverer from sin. After coming to know Jesus Christ as the great Deliverer, it is not reasonable for him to be reverting back to the fleshly struggle of the unspiritual, carnal man. It is much more reasonable to see the mind as the *renewed mind* of the "new self." However, if one prefers the summary interpretation, then the meaning would be as follows.

⇒ The unspiritual, carnal man uses his mind, his human, fleshly reasoning to serve the law of God. He tries and tries with all his might to honor and to keep the law of God.

⇒ However, he is flesh and he is unspiritual; therefore, he is subject to sin. No matter how much he tries to struggle against sin, his flesh, his sinful nature gives in to the law of sin and comes short of God's glory

CHAPTER 8

VI. DELIVERANCE AND REDEMPTION: THE BELIEVER SHALL BE FREED FROM STRUGGLING AND SUFFERING BY THE SPIRIT, 8:1-39

A. The Man in Christ Jesus is Freed from Condemnation: The Power of the Spirit, 8:1-17

1 **Now since Christ has come**
   a. The bel.is not condemned
   b. Why: He is "in" Christ[DS1]
2 **The Spirit gives life**
   a. By freeing the believer from sin & death
   b. By doing what the law was powerless to do

   c. By Christ condemning sin in sinful man[DS2]
   d. By Christ providing righteousness: For all who do not follow the sinful nature, but the Spirit

3 **The Spirit pulls the mind to spiritual things**
   a. The sinful, carnal mind vs. the spiritual mind
   b. The fate of both minds: Death vs. life & peace

   c. The reason the sinful, carnal mind dwells in death

Therefore, there is now no condemnation for those who are in Christ Jesus,
2 Because through Christ Jesus the law of the Spirit of life set me free from the law of sin and death.
3 For what the law was powerless to do in that it was weakened by the sinful nature, God did by sending his own Son in the likeness of sinful man to be a sin offering. And so he condemned sin in sinful man,
4 In order that the righteous requirements of the law might be fully met in us, who do not live according to the sinful nature but according to the Spirit.
5 Those who live according to the sinful nature have their minds set on what that nature desires; but those who live in accordance with the Spirit have their minds set on what the Spirit desires.
6 The mind of sinful man is death, but the mind controlled by the Spirit is life and peace;
7 The sinful mind is hostile to God. It does not submit to God's law, nor can it do so.
8 Those controlled by the sinful nature cannot please God.
9 You, however, are controlled not by the sinful nature but by the Spirit, if the Spirit of God lives in you. And if anyone does not have the Spirit of Christ, he does not belong to Christ.
10 But if Christ is in you, your body is dead because of sin, yet your spirit is alive because of righteousness.
11 And if the Spirit of him who raised Jesus from the dead is living in you, he who raised Christ from the dead will also give life to your mortal bodies through his Spirit, who lives in you.
12 Therefore, brothers, we have an obligation—but it is not to the sinful nature, to live according to it.
13 For if you live according to the sinful nature, you will die; but if by the Spirit you put to death the misdeeds of the body, you will live,
14 Because those who are led by the Spirit of God are sons of God.
15 For you did not receive a spirit that makes you a slave again to fear, but you received the Spirit of sonship. And by him we cry, "Abba, Father."
16 The Spirit himself testifies with our spirit that we are God's children.
17 Now if we are children, then we are heirs—heirs of God and co-heirs with Christ, if indeed we share in his sufferings in order that we may also share in his glory.

   1) It is bitterly set against God
   2) It cannot please God

4 **The Spirit dwells within the believer**
   a. He removes him from being controlled by the flesh, by the sinful nature
   b. He identifies him as being "in" Christ
5 **The Spirit gives life to the spirit of the believer**
   a. He gives life *now*

   b. He quickens, gives life to the mortal body[DS3]

6 **The Spirit gives the power to put to death evil deeds**
   a. Believers are obligated to the Spirit
   b. Believers determine their own fate: Death or life

7 **The Spirit leads the believer, identifying him as a son of God**
8 **The Spirit adopts**
   a. He delivers from the slavery of fear
   b. He gives access to God

9 **The Spirit testifies, bears witness with our spirit**
   a. We are God's children
   b. We are heirs of God
   c. We are equal heirs with Christ[DS4]
   d. We are conquerors over suffering

DIVISION VI

DELIVERANCE AND REDEMPTION: THE BELIEVER SHALL BE FREED FROM STRUGGLING AND SUFFERING BY THE SPIRIT, 8:1-39

A. The Man in Christ Jesus is Freed from Condemnation: The Power of the Spirit, 8:1-17

(8:1-17) **Introduction**: this is one of the most important passages in all of Scripture. Its subject cannot be overemphasized: the power of God's Spirit in the life of the believer. If the believer needs anything, he needs the power of God's Spirit. Forcefully, Scripture spells out point by point what the power of the Holy Spirit is.
   1. Now since Christ has come (v.1).
   2. The Spirit gives life (v.2-4).
   3. The Spirit pulls the mind to spiritual things (v.5-8).
   4. The Spirit dwells within the believer (v.9).
   5. The Spirit gives life to the spirit of the believer (v.10-11).

   6. The Spirit gives the power to put to death evil deeds (v.12-13).
   7. The Spirit leads the believer, identifying him as a son of God (v.14).
   8. The Spirit adopts (v.15).
   9. The Spirit testifies, bears witness with our spirit (v.16-17).

1 (8:1) **Condemnation—Deliverance From**: since Christ has come (Ro.3:21-22), a most wonderful thing has happened. The people who believe *in* Christ are not condemned.

1. "No condemnation" (ouden katakrima) means that the believer is not doomed and damned, but is freed from the penalty and condemnation of sin; he is not judged as a sinner, but is delivered from the condemnation of death and hell; he is not judged to be unrighteous, but is counted to be righteous.

Very simply stated, the person who is *in* Christ is safe and secure from condemnation now and forever. He will not be judged as a sinner; he will not face condemnation. He is beyond condemnation; he shall never be condemned for sin; he shall never be separated from the love of God which is *in* Christ Jesus our Lord (cp. Jn.3:16; Ro.8:33-39). (But remember: the believer is to be judged for his faithfulness to Christ. He will be judged for how responsible he is—for how well he uses his "spiritual gifts" for Christ—for how diligently he serves Christ in the work of God. The judgment of the believer will take place at the great *judgment seat of Christ.*)

2. Now note the most crucial point: only the believer who is *in* Christ Jesus will not be condemned. All non-believers will face condemnation for sin. A genuine believer is a person who does not "live according to the sinful nature but according to the Spirit." Note what it means to be *in* Christ Jesus (see DEEPER STUDY # 1, *Believer*—Ro.8:1 for discussion).

DEEPER STUDY # 1

(8:1) **Believer, Position In Christ**: What do the words "in Christ" mean? What does it mean for a person to be *in* Christ?

1. In the simplest of terms, to be *in* Christ means that a person's faith in Christ *places* him *in* Christ. Positionally, the person is placed in all that Christ is. Christ lived and died and arose, so to be *in* Christ means that a person lives, dies, and arises *in* Christ. Christ is the person's Representative, his Agent, his Substitute, his Mediator in life and death and resurrection. The person who believes *in* Jesus Christ is *identified* with Christ: counted and considered to be "in" Christ; reckoned and credited as "in" Christ.

Spelled out in a little more detail, when a person believes *in* Christ, God *places and positions* the believer "in" Christ. The believer's faith actually causes God to identify the believer *with Christ*, to count the believer...

- as having lived *in* Christ when Christ lived upon earth; therefore, the believer is counted sinless and righteous because Christ was sinless and righteous.
- as having died *in* Christ; therefore, the believer never has to die (Jn.3:16). The penalty and condemnation of his sins are already paid for in the death of Christ.
- as having been raised "in" Christ; therefore, the believer has received the "*new life*" of Christ. Just as Christ had a new life after His resurrection, even so the believer receives the "new life" of Christ when he believes in Christ. (See outline and notes—Ro.6:3-5. Also see DEEPER STUDY # 1,2—Ro.4:22; notes—5:1; 6:14-15.)

2. To be *in* Christ means that a believer walks and lives *in* Christ day by day. A true believer lives and moves and has his being *in* Christ. He is in union with Christ. To truly believe is to walk and to truly walk is to believe. A true believer...

- lays his life—his past sins, his present behavior, all that he is—upon Christ.
- entrusts his present welfare and destiny—all that he is or ever will be—into the hands of Christ.

A person who truly *lays* his life upon Christ and *entrusts* all he is to Christ is a person...

- who truly believes.
- who lives and walks *in* Christ.

Now, to live and walk *in* Christ means that we do not "live according to the sinful nature but according to the Spirit" (Ro.8:4). It means for "us to say 'No' to ungodliness and worldly passions, and to live self-controlled, upright and godly lives in this present age." (Tit.2:12). It means that we bear the fruit of the Spirit (Gal.5:22-23). It means that we abide *in* Christ, that we become as connected and attached to Christ...

- as the members of the body are connected and attached to each other (1 Cor.12:12-27).
- as the branch is connected and attached to the vine (Jn.15:4-7).

This is what it means for a person to be "in" Christ. A person simply *believes* in Christ, putting all he is and has into the hands and keeping of Christ. The person honestly believes that Christ will take care of his past sins, present welfare, and future destiny. Therefore, the believer simply places and positions himself—his faith and welfare—*in* Christ; and God in turn identifies the person with Christ, with all that Christ is. God counts and considers the person to be *in* Christ. (See note, *Believer, Position In Christ*—Ro.6:3-5 for more discussion.)

2 (8:2-4) **Holy Spirit—Life—Believer**: the Spirit gives life. The term "the law of the *Spirit* of life" means two things. It means...

- the *law* of the Holy Spirit.
- the *Spirit of life* which is in Christ Jesus.

Within the universe there is a law so important that it has become the law of the Holy Spirit. It is called "*the law of the Spirit of life.*" What is meant by this law? Very simply, life is in Jesus Christ and in Him alone. Whatever life is—energy, being, spirit, love, joy, peace—it is all in Jesus Christ and nowhere else. Within Christ, within His very being is the *Spirit of life*, the very energy and being of life. This fact is important, so important that God has written it into the laws of the universe. It is titled "the law of *the Spirit of life*," which is in Christ Jesus and in Him alone. The Spirit of life for which we long and ache is available *in* Christ Jesus.

> **In him was life, and that life was the light of men. (John 1:4)**
> **The thief comes only to steal and kill and destroy; I have come that they may have life, and have it to the full. (John 10:10)**
> **Jesus said to her, "I am the resurrection and the life. He who believes in me will live, even though he dies; and whoever lives and believes in me will never die. Do you believe this?" (John 11:25-26)**
> **Jesus answered, "I am the way and the truth and the life. No one comes to the Father except through me. (John 14:6)**
> **"I tell you the truth, whoever hears my word and believes him who sent me has eternal life and will not be condemned; he has crossed over from death to life. (John 5:24)**

He who has the Son has life; he who does not have the Son of God does not have life. (1 John 5:12)

Now for the critical question. How does the Spirit give life? How does a person go about securing "the Spirit of life" so that he may not die but live forever?

1. The Spirit gives life by freeing the believer from sin and death, that is, from the "law of sin and death." The "law of sin and death" simply means the rule and reign of death. Every man dies: death rules and reigns over every man. But the Spirit of God frees a man from the rule and reign of death. This is natural and understandable; it is common sense, for it is a rule of the universe. If a person has the Spirit of life, then he naturally does not have the spirit of sin and death. He is not sinning and dying; he is living righteously and eternally. This is exactly what the Spirit of life does for the believer:

⇒ He frees the believer from sin and death: from the law or the energy and the power of sin and death.

⇒ He frees the believer to live righteously and eternally: to live in the Spirit of life or in the energy and power of life.

Stated another way, the Spirit of life frees the believer from both sin and death. The Holy Spirit frees the believer to live as Christ lived, to actually live out the life which Christ lived. The *active energy* of life, the dynamic force and being of life—all that is in Christ Jesus—is given to the believer. The believer actually lives *in* Christ Jesus. And the Spirit of life which is in Christ frees the believer from the fate (law) of sin and death. This simply means that the believer lives in a consciousness of being free. He breathes and senses a depth of life, a richness, a fullness of life that is indescribable. He lives with power—power over the pressure and strain, impediments and bondages of life— even the bondages of sin and death. He lives now and shall live forever. He senses this and knows this. Life to him is a *spirit, a breath, a consciousness* of being set free through Christ. Even when he sins and guilt sets in, there is a tug, a power (Holy Spirit) that draws him back to God. He asks forgiveness and removal of the guilt (1 Jn.1:9), and immediately upon asking, the same power (the Holy Spirit) instills an instantaneous assurance of cleansing. The spirit of life, the consciousness of living instantaneously takes up its abode within him once again. He feels free again, and he feels full of life in all its liberating power and freedom. He bubbles over with all the depth of the richness and fullness of life itself. He is full of the "Spirit of life." Life itself becomes once again *a spirit, a consciousness of living.* He lives now and forever.

Now the Lord is the Spirit, and where the Spirit of the Lord is, there is freedom. (2 Cor 3:17)

But the fruit of the Spirit is love, joy, peace, patience, kindness, goodness, faithfulness, gentleness and self-control. Against such things there is no law. (Gal 5:22-23)

You have made known to me the path of life; you will fill me with joy in your presence, with eternal pleasures at your right hand. (Psa 16:11)

2. The Spirit gives life by doing what the law could not do. The law could not make man righteous because man's flesh is too weak to keep the law. No man has ever been able to keep the law of God, not to perfection or even close to perfection. All flesh has miserably failed—come far short of God's glory and law. Consequently, all flesh dies physically and spiritually. Therefore, righteousness and life just cannot come by the law. *But* what the law could not do, the Spirit is able to do. He can provide righteousness and life.

3. The Spirit gives life by Christ condemning sin in the sinful man (see Deeper Study # 3, *Christ, Fulfills Law—* Ro.8:3 for discussion).

4. The Spirit gives life by Christ providing righteousness for us. He provides righteousness for all who do not follow the sinful nature, but follows the Spirit. This is a most marvelous statement, a glorious truth.

a. The Spirit "meets the righteous requirements of the law in us." He credits righteousness as being *in* us. When?

⇒ When we believe that Jesus Christ is our righteousness, the sinless and perfect Son of God.

⇒ When we believe that Jesus Christ is our Savior, the One who died *for* us.

When we believe in Jesus Christ, the Spirit of God fulfills righteousness in us; that is, He takes the righteousness of Jesus Christ (which is the righteousness of the law) and credits it to us. He actually places within us the perfect righteousness of Jesus Christ. He places the Divine nature (righteousness) of God *in* us (2 Pt.1:4).

It is critical to see this fact, for the Spirit fulfills righteousness *in us, not by us.* He alone meets the righteous requirements of the law *in* us. We do not and cannot even come close to keeping the law perfectly, but Christ did (see Deeper Study #3— Ro.8:3). If His righteousness cannot be credited and fulfilled *in* us, then we are hopeless and doomed.

God made him who had no sin to be sin for us, so that in him we might become the righteousness of God. (2 Cor 5:21)
Abram believed the LORD, and he credited it to him as righteousness. (Gen 15:6)
Through him everyone who believes is justified from everything you could not be justified from by the law of Moses. (Acts 13:39)
The words "it was credited to him" were written not for him alone, but also for us, to whom God will credit righteousness— for us who believe in him who raised Jesus our Lord from the dead. He was delivered over to death for our sins and was raised to life for our justification. (Rom 4:23-25)
Filled with the fruit of righteousness that comes through Jesus Christ—to the glory and praise of God. (Phil 1:11)

b. Now note: righteousness is not fulfilled or credited *in* everyone. It is only fulfilled in those...

• who *do not* "live according to the sinful nature"
• who *do* "live according to the Spirit"

You can tell who is righteous and who is not; you can actually see who is fulfilling righteousness and who is not. All we have to do is look and see:

⇒ Is a man living according to the sinful nature?
⇒ Is a man living according to the Spirit?

The point is this: the Spirit gives life to men, but He gives life only to those who forsake the sinful nature and live according to the Spirit. The spiritual man, the man who lives according to the Spirit, loves Christ and wants to honor Christ *in all that he does*. Therefore, he strives to follow Christ and His example. Such love and honor of Christ pleases God to no end, for God loves His Son with a perfect love. He loves His Son so much that He will take whatever honor a man gives His Son and match it for the man. Whatever recognition and honor a man heaps upon Christ, God matches it for the man.

⇒ If a man trusts Christ for righteousness, then God gives that man righteousness.
⇒ If a man trusts Christ for meaning, purpose, and significance, then God gives the man meaning, purpose, and significance.
⇒ If a man trusts Christ to lead him through some trial or need, then God leads him through the trial or need.
⇒ If a man trusts Christ for healing, then God gives the man healing.

Whatever the man sows in Christ, he reaps: God matches it. Whatever a man measures out to Christ, the same is measured back to the man: God matches it. In fact, Scripture says that God will even go beyond and do much more than we ask or think (cp. Eph.3:20).

Therefore, the man who lives according to the "Spirit of life" which is in Christ Jesus is given the Spirit of life. The Holy Spirit fulfills and credits him with the righteousness of the law, with the right to live eternally.

We were therefore buried with him through baptism into death in order that, just as Christ was raised from the dead through the glory of the Father, we too may live a new life. (Rom 6:4)

Therefore, there is now no condemnation for those who are in Christ Jesus, (Rom 8:1)

For if you live according to the sinful nature, you will die; but if by the Spirit you put to death the misdeeds of the body, you will live, because those who are led by the Spirit of God are sons of God. (Rom 8:13-14)

So I say, live by the Spirit, and you will not gratify the desires of the sinful nature. (Gal 5:16)

As a prisoner for the Lord, then, I urge you to live a life worthy of the calling you have received. (Eph 4:1)

And live a life of love, just as Christ loved us and gave himself up for us as a fragrant offering and sacrifice to God. (Eph 5:2)

So then, just as you received Christ Jesus as Lord, continue to live in him, (Col 2:6)

But if we walk in the light, as he is in the light, we have fellowship with one another, and the blood of Jesus, his Son, purifies us from all sin. (1 John 1:7)

Whoever claims to live in him must walk as Jesus did. (1 John 2:6)

DEEPER STUDY # 2
(8:3) Christ, Fulfills Law—Sin: Christ condemned sin in the sinful man, the flesh in by three acts.

1. Christ pointed to sin and condemned it as being evil. The very fact that He never sinned points out that sin is contrary to God and to God's nature. Christ rejected sin, and by rejecting it He showed that it was evil, that it was not to be touched. He condemned it as evil and unworthy of God and man.

2. Christ secured righteousness for all men. When He came into the world, He came with the same human nature, the same flesh that all men are born with—the same human nature, the same flesh with all its desires, passions, and potential for evil. However, He never sinned, not once. Therefore, He secured a perfect righteousness; and because His righteousness is perfect and ideal, it becomes the model and pattern for all men. It stands for and covers the unrighteousness of all men. His perfect righteousness overcomes sin and its penalty—it condemns sin. It is to be noted that He condemned sin "in sinful man, in his flesh;" therefore, all flesh finds its perfection and ideal in His righteousness and perfection. All flesh finds its power to condemn sin "in Christ," in His ideal righteousness.

Can any of you prove me guilty of sin? If I am telling the truth, why don't you believe me? (John 8:46)

God made him who had no sin to be sin for us, so that in him we might become the righteousness of God. (2 Cor 5:21)

For we do not have a high priest who is unable to sympathize with our weaknesses, but we have one who has been tempted in every way, just as we are—yet was without sin. (Heb 4:15)

Such a high priest meets our need—one who is holy, blameless, pure, set apart from sinners, exalted above the heavens. (Heb 7:26)

How much more, then, will the blood of Christ, who through the eternal Spirit offered himself unblemished to God, cleanse our consciences from acts that lead to death, so that we may serve the living God! (Heb 9:14)

But with the precious blood of Christ, a lamb without blemish or defect. (1 Pet 1:19)

"He committed no sin, and no deceit was found in his mouth." (1 Pet 2:22)

But you know that he appeared so that he might take away our sins. And in him is no sin. (1 John 3:5)

3. Christ allowed the law of sin and death to be enacted upon Him instead of upon the sinner. Man has sinned, so the natural consequence is corruption and death. However, Christ approached God and made two requests. First, He asked God to accept His *Ideal righteousness* for the unrighteousness of man. Second, He asked God to lay man's sin and death upon Himself. He asked God to let Him bear the law of sin and death for man and to experience hell for man. He asked God to let Him condemn sin and death "in His body on the tree" (1 Pt.2:24). He was the perfect, ideal Man. Therefore, He could bear all the violations of the law and all the experiences of death for *all* men. God so purposed, and God bore the awful price of having to condemn sin and death in the death of His very own Son. Sin and its power have been made powerless. Death has been con

quered (1 Cor.15:1-58, esp. vs.54-57), and he who had the power of death has been destroyed, that is, Satan. (See DEEPER STUDY #1—Jn.16:11. Cp. Heb.2:14.) (See note—Mt. 5:17-18.)

> You see, at just the right time, when we were still powerless, Christ died for the ungodly. (Rom 5:6)
>
> But God demonstrates his own love for us in this: While we were still sinners, Christ died for us. (Rom 5:8)
>
> For what I received I passed on to you as of first importance : that Christ died for our sins according to the Scriptures, (1 Cor 15:3)
>
> And he died for all, that those who live should no longer live for themselves but for him who died for them and was raised again. (2 Cor 5:15)
>
> Christ redeemed us from the curse of the law by becoming a curse for us, for it is written: "Cursed is everyone who is hung on a tree." (Gal 3:13)
>
> Who gave himself for us to redeem us from all wickedness and to purify for himself a people that are his very own, eager to do what is good. (Titus 2:14)
>
> But we see Jesus, who was made a little lower than the angels, now crowned with glory and honor because he suffered death, so that by the grace of God he might taste death for everyone. (Heb 2:9)
>
> So Christ was sacrificed once to take away the sins of many people; and he will appear a second time, not to bear sin, but to bring salvation to those who are waiting for him. (Heb 9:28)
>
> He himself bore our sins in his body on the tree, so that we might die to sins and live for righteousness; by his wounds you have been healed. (1 Pet 2:24)
>
> For Christ died for sins once for all, the righteous for the unrighteous, to bring you to God. He was put to death in the body but made alive by the Spirit, (1 Pet 3:18)
>
> This is how we know what love is: Jesus Christ laid down his life for us. And we ought to lay down our lives for our brothers. (1 John 3:16)

3 (8:5-8) **Mind, The—Carnal—Flesh—Sinful Nature—Spiritual Mind**: the Spirit pulls the mind to spiritual things. This is one of the most important passages in all of Scripture, for it discusses the human mind: "he is the kind of man who is always thinking about the cost" (Pr.23:7). Where a man keeps his mind and what he thinks about determine who he is and what he does. If a man keeps his mind and thoughts in the gutter, he becomes part of the filth in the gutter. If he keeps his mind upon the *good*, he becomes good. If he focuses upon achievement and success, he achieves and succeeds. If his mind is filled with religious thoughts, he becomes religious. If his thoughts are focused upon God and righteousness, he becomes godly and righteous. A man becomes and does what he thinks. It is the law of the mind. Scripture says three things about the power of the Spirit and of the human mind.

1. There is the unspiritual, carnal mind vs. the spiritual mind. The unspiritual, carnal mind is the mind of man's flesh or body. The phrase "controlled by the sinful nature" (to phronema tes sarkos, v.6) means the *mind of the flesh.* It is the mind with which man is born, the fleshly mind which he inherits from his parents.

The unspiritual, carnal mind also means something else, something that must be heeded. It means the mind that is given over to the sinful nature; that focuses upon the sinful nature and its worldly urges and desires; that gives its attention and pursuits over to the sinful nature; that savors tasting and partaking of the sinful nature; that is controlled by one's sinful nature.

The unspiritual, carnal mind focuses upon three areas of life, or to word it another way, there are three directions of thought the carnal mind takes:

a. The unspiritual, carnal mind may focus upon the base, the immoral, the violent, the material, and the physical. This is usually the life-style most people think about when an unspiritual person is mentioned. The minds of some are consumed with the lust for sex, power, money, houses, lands, furnishings, recognition, position—concerned and filled with the earthly and the worldly.

b. The unspiritual, carnal mind may focus upon the moral, upright, and cultured life. Some minds are centered upon the welfare and comfort of themselves and of their society. They want themselves and their society to be as refined and educated, as moral and upright as possible, so they focus their minds upon such *commendable* ends. And they are commendable purposes, but a person can be refined and well educated and live as independently and as separate from God as the base and immoral person. Most cultured people depend upon their *good works* and service to make them acceptable to God. Most just think that God will accept them because their lives and efforts have been focused upon building a good life and better society for all. What they fail to see is that God is interested in building a God-centered society and not a world-centered society. God wants the needs of every man to be met, but He wants it to be done from a spiritual basis, not from a human basis. He wants men led to Christ—their minds and lives focused upon God—so that they may have life, life that is both *abundant* and *eternal.* Just taking care of the physical needs of man does not meet the spiritual needs of man. It leaves a gaping hole in man's life; for the *spirit* of man determines how a man lives, either defeated or victorious, either with or apart from God (see note—Eph.1:3).

c. The unspiritual, carnal mind may also focus upon religion: upon living a religious life of benevolence and good works, of ceremony and ritual. However, note again: a person can be a strict religionist and still live separate from God. He can have his mind *set on religion* and its welfare instead of God. He can be living for religion instead of for God, carrying out the function of *institutional religion* instead of the mission of God. He can be depending upon his commitment to religion to make him acceptable to God instead of believing and trusting God's Son, Jesus Christ our Lord. In all of this, note where the religionist's mind is—note where his thoughts are. There is little if any stress upon a *personal relationship* with God; little stress upon knowing God—really knowing, believing, and understanding Him—little stress upon walking and living in Him. The stress of the unspiritual religionist is his religion and its rituals and ceremonies, its welfare and projects. Such a focus is fleshly and unspiritual. It is of the earth, attached to the physical and material *institution* which passes away and dies.

The point is this: a carnal mind does not necessarily mean that a man's thoughts are upon the base, immoral, and vicious. An unspiritual, carnal mind means any mind that does not find its basis in God, any mind that is not focused upon God first. A carnal mind may focus upon a moral, upright, and cultured life and still ignore, neglect, and exempt God. An unspiritual mind may also focus upon religion and still exempt God. An unspiritual mind is a mind that finds its basis in this world, that focuses its thoughts upon the physical and material instead of God.

> **Furthermore, since they did not think it worthwhile to retain the knowledge of God, he gave them over to a depraved mind, to do what ought not to be done. (Rom 1:28)**
>
> **The sinful mind is hostile to God. It does not submit to God's law, nor can it do so. (Rom 8:7)**
>
> **So I tell you this, and insist on it in the Lord, that you must no longer live as the Gentiles do, in the futility of their thinking. (Eph 4:17)**
>
> **Do not let anyone who delights in false humility and the worship of angels disqualify you for the prize. Such a person goes into great detail about what he has seen, and his unspiritual mind puffs him up with idle notions. (Col 2:18)**
>
> **To the pure, all things are pure, but to those who are corrupted and do not believe, nothing is pure. In fact, both their minds and consciences are corrupted. (Titus 1:15)**

2. There is the spiritual mind. It is the natural mind of man that has been *renewed by the Spirit of God* (see notes, pt.2—Ro.7:21-23; 7:25 for more discussion).

> **Do not conform any longer to the pattern of this world, but be transformed by the renewing of your mind. Then you will be able to test and approve what God's will is—his good, pleasing and perfect will. (Rom 12:2)**
>
> **You were taught, with regard to your former way of life, to put off your old self, which is being corrupted by its deceitful desires; to be made new in the attitude of your minds; and to put on the new self, created to be like God in true righteousness and holiness. (Eph 4:22-24)**

The words "the mind controlled by the Spirit" (to phronema tou pneumatos) mean to be possessed by the Spirit or to be controlled and dominated by the Spirit. It means that the man who "lives according to the Spirit sets his mind on what the Spirit" desires day by day. And note: it is the Spirit of God who draws the believer's mind to focus upon spiritual things. The Spirit of God lives within the believer. He is there to work within the believer, both to will and to do God's pleasure; He is there to keep the mind and thoughts of the believer focused upon spiritual things.

a. The believer *keeps* his mind upon developing spiritual character and fruit.

> **But the fruit of the Spirit is love, joy, peace, patience, kindness, goodness, faithfulness, gentleness and self-control. Against such things there is no law. (Gal 5:22-23)**

b. The believer *keeps* his mind upon carrying out the ministry and mission of Christ.

> **Just as the Son of Man did not come to be served, but to serve, and to give his life as a ransom for many." (Mat 20:28)**
>
> **For the Son of Man came to seek and to save what was lost." (Luke 19:10)**
>
> **Again Jesus said, "Peace be with you! As the Father has sent me, I am sending you." (John 20:21)**
>
> **Therefore go and make disciples of all nations, baptizing them in the name of the Father and of the Son and of the Holy Spirit, and teaching them to obey everything I have commanded you. And surely I am with you always, to the very end of the age." (Mat 28:19-20)**
>
> **He said to them, "Go into all the world and preach the good news to all creation. (Mark 16:15)**
>
> **But you will receive power when the Holy Spirit comes on you; and you will be my witnesses in Jerusalem, and in all Judea and Samaria, and to the ends of the earth." (Acts 1:8)**
>
> **We are therefore Christ's ambassadors, as though God were making his appeal through us. We implore you on Christ's behalf: Be reconciled to God. (2 Cor 5:20)**
>
> **And the things you have heard me say in the presence of many witnesses entrust to reliable men who will also be qualified to teach others. (2 Tim 2:2)**
>
> **But in your hearts set apart Christ as Lord. Always be prepared to give an answer to everyone who asks you to give the reason for the hope that you have. But do this with gentleness and respect, (1 Pet 3:15)**

c. The believer *keeps* his mind upon knowing, believing, and understanding God.

> **"You are my witnesses," declares the LORD, "and my servant whom I have chosen, so that you may know and believe me and understand that I am he. Before me no god was formed, nor will there be one after me. (Isa 43:10)**
>
> **Now this is eternal life: that they may know you, the only true God, and Jesus Christ, whom you have sent. (John 17:3)**
>
> **I want to know Christ and the power of his resurrection and the fellowship of sharing in his sufferings, becoming like him in his death, (Phil 3:10)**

d. The believer *keeps* his mind upon being conformed more and more to the image of Christ.

For those God foreknew he also predestined to be conformed to the likeness of his Son, that he might be the firstborn among many brothers. (Rom 8:29)

And we, who with unveiled faces all reflect the Lord's glory, are being transformed into his likeness with ever-increasing glory, which comes from the Lord, who is the Spirit. (2 Cor 3:18)

But our citizenship is in heaven. And we eagerly await a Savior from there, the Lord Jesus Christ, Who, by the power that enables him to bring everything under his control, will transform our lowly bodies so that they will be like his glorious body. (Phil 3:20-21)

And have put on the new self, which is being renewed in knowledge in the image of its Creator. (Col 3:10)

Dear friends, now we are children of God, and what we will be has not yet been made known. But we know that when he appears, we shall be like him, for we shall see him as he is. (1 John 3:2)

e. The believer *keeps* his mind upon casting down imaginations, demolishing arguments and making *every thought* obedient to Christ.

We demolish arguments and every pretension that sets itself up against the knowledge of God, and we take captive every thought to make it obedient to Christ. (2 Cor 10:5)

Finally, brothers, whatever is true, whatever is noble, whatever is right, whatever is pure, whatever is lovely, whatever is admirable—if anything is excellent or praiseworthy—think about such things. (Phil 4:8)

3. There is the fate of both minds. The unspiritual, carnal mind is strongly warned, whereas the spiritual mind is assured and comforted.

a. The fate of the unspiritual, carnal mind is death. By death is meant spiritual death, being separated and cut off from God eternally. It means the soul is dead *now*, while the man lives on this earth; and it means that the soul remains dead (separated and cut off from God) even when the man enters the next world. The unspiritual, carnal mind...

- cannot ignore God now and expect to have thoughts of God in the next world.
- cannot focus upon the flesh now and expect to focus upon God in the next world.
- cannot think as it wills now and expect to think as God wills in the next world.
- cannot have a worldly mind now and expect to have a spiritual mind in the next world.
- cannot choose the sinful nature now and expect to be saved from the sinful nature in the next world.
- cannot reject God now and expect to be accepted by God in the next world.

Very simply stated, whatever the mind chooses will continue on and on. If the mind chooses the sinful nature instead of God, then the choice is made. The mind will continue on without

God from now on, forever and ever. The mind is allowed to do as it chooses. If it chooses to be separated and cut off from God so that it can dwell upon the sinful nature, then the soul *shall* have the sinful nature; it shall be separated and cut off from God. God loves man; God will not violate man's mind and force man to choose Him. The choice is man's: he may choose God, or he may choose the sinful nature and death (to be separated and cut off from God).

A man who strays from the path of understanding comes to rest in the company of the dead. (Prov 21:16)

Jesus said to them, "I tell you the truth, unless you eat the flesh of the Son of Man and drink his blood, you have no life in you. (John 6:53)

For the wages of sin is death, but the gift of God is eternal life in Christ Jesus our Lord. (Rom 6:23)

For Christ's love compels us, because we are convinced that one died for all, and therefore all died. (2 Cor 5:14)

As for you, you were dead in your transgressions and sins, (Eph 2:1)

For it is light that makes everything visible. This is why it is said: "Wake up, O sleeper, rise from the dead, and Christ will shine on you." (Eph 5:14)

Then, after desire has conceived, it gives birth to sin; and sin, when it is full-grown, gives birth to death. (James 1:15)

"To the angel of the church in Sardis write: These are the words of him who holds the seven spirits of God and the seven stars. I know your deeds; you have a reputation of being alive, but you are dead. (Rev 3:1)

But the cowardly, the unbelieving, the vile, the murderers, the sexually immoral, those who practice magic arts, the idolaters and all liars—their place will be in the fiery lake of burning sulfur. This is the second death." (Rev 21:8)

b. The fate of the spiritual mind is life and peace. It is the very opposite of death. The spiritual mind is a state of mind, a mind that is filled with life and peace, with thoughts of life and peace. The spiritual mind dwells in life; it lives all that life was intended to be and lives it eternally. The spiritual mind is full...

- of meaning, purpose, and significance.
- of assurance and confidence.
- of joy and rejoicing.
- of knowing, believing, and understanding God.
- of spiritual fruit, the fruit of love, joy, and peace (Gal.5:22-23).

The spiritual mind is also full of peace. The man who is spiritually minded is at *peace with God*: he has peace with God because he knows beyond question that his sins are forgiven and that he is now acceptable to God. He also dwells in the *peace of God*: he has the *peace of God* because he experiences the day by day care and guidance of God in his life. He actually walks through life in the peace of God, knowing that God is looking after him and working all things out for his good. He knows his eternity is taken care of, that he shall be given the glorious privilege of living eternally and serving God in some glorious responsibility. Note something else as well: the man who is spiritually minded is at peace with all other men. He loves and cares for all men, no matter who they are, just as Jesus loves and cares for them.

The spiritual mind, the mind that focuses upon the things of the spirit, knows and experiences life and peace. Life and peace are its destiny forever and ever. Such is the promise of God and the testimony of His saints who have gone on before. To be spiritually minded reaps its reward, and its reward is eternal life and peace.

> **"I tell you the truth, whoever hears my word and believes him who sent me has eternal life and will not be condemned; he has crossed over from death to life. (John 5:24)**
>
> **"I have told you these things, so that in me you may have peace. In this world you will have trouble. But take heart! I have overcome the world." (John 16:33)**
>
> **For the kingdom of God is not a matter of eating and drinking, but of righteousness, peace and joy in the Holy Spirit, (Rom 14:17)**
>
> **But the fruit of the Spirit is love, joy, peace, patience, kindness, goodness, faithfulness, gentleness and self-control. Against such things there is no law. (Gal 5:22-23)**
>
> **Great peace have they who love your law, and nothing can make them stumble. (Psa 119:165)**
>
> **In the way of righteousness there is life; along that path is immortality. (Prov 12:28)**
>
> **You will keep in perfect peace him whose mind is steadfast, because he trusts in you. (Isa 26:3)**

4. There is the reason the unspiritual, carnal mind dwells in death. The unspiritual mind dwells in death because it is at odds with God. This is simply seen.

⇒ God is holy, righteous, and pure; whereas the unspiritual mind is impure, immoral, and polluted. The unspiritual or fleshly mind is opposed to God by its very nature.

⇒ God acts only in morality and justice and goodness; whereas the unspiritual, carnal mind behaves immorally, unjustly, and selfishly. The unspiritual or fleshly mind is opposed to God by its very behavior.

⇒ God is eternal, from everlasting to everlasting; whereas the unspiritual, carnal mind ages, deteriorates, dies, and decays. The carnal or fleshly mind is opposed to God by its very destiny, death.

The unspiritual, carnal mind is opposed to God, to all that He is. It is not pure or lasting; it is sinful and full of corruption, and it dwells in death. The unspiritual or fleshly mind is bitterly opposed to all that God is. Therefore, the unspiritual mind dwells in death, and it shall dwell in death eternally.

Now note: all this is saying one simple thing: the unspiritual, carnal mind "does not submit to God's law nor can it do so." The unspiritual mind cannot be subject to God's law because it is not "like" God: not by nature, not by behavior, not by destiny. An unspiritual mind has no interest in the law of God nor in trying to live as God wishes. The unspiritual mind wants to live as it wishes and do its own thing. The unspiritual man wants to indulge his flesh, his sinful nature, whether by food, sex, pride, power, position, money, recognition, fame, or self-righteousness.

The fate of the unspiritual, carnal mind is clearly stated, a fate that is strongly warned.

> **Those controlled by the sinful nature cannot please God. (Rom 8:8)**
>
> **But the widow who lives for pleasure is dead even while she lives. (1 Tim 5:6)**
>
> **So Christ was sacrificed once to take away the sins of many people; and he will appear a second time, not to bear sin, but to bring salvation to those who are waiting for him. (Heb 9:28)**
>
> **"Then he will say to those on his left, 'Depart from me, you who are cursed, into the eternal fire prepared for the devil and his angels. (Mat 25:41)**

However, the glorious truth is this. The Spirit of God can transform the mind of man. The Spirit of God can pull the mind to spiritual things (cp. Ro.12:2; Eph.4:22-24. See notes, pt.2—Ro.7:21-23; 7:25 for more discussion).

> **Thought 1.** Most sinful minds are influenced heavily by their environment and those around them. If their friends are materialistic or immoral, they focus upon the same. If their environment offers films and literature, they fill their minds with such, whether X-rated or educational and philosophic. Few unspiritual minds ever break away from their environment and friends. Only the Spirit of God can penetrate the human mind and set it free from the sinful nature and its fleshly, carnal passions.

4 (8:9) **Indwelling Presence—Holy Spirit, Power of**: the Spirit dwells within the believer, putting the Spirit of Christ within him. There is so much in these two verses that cannot be outlined beside the verses. There just is not enough space.

1. The power of the Spirit is seen in the word "lives" (oikeo). The word "lives" is the picture of a home (oikos). The Holy Spirit lives in the believer: He makes His home, takes up residence, and lives in the believer just as we live in our homes.

2. The power of the Spirit creates the glorious truth of the *indwelling presence* of God within the believer and of the believer within God.

⇒ The believer is said to be "controlled by the [Holy] Spirit" (v.9).

⇒ The Spirit of *God* is said to "live" in the believer (v.9).

⇒ The believer is said to have "the Spirit of Christ" (v.9).

⇒ Christ is said to be in the believer (v.10).

> **And I will ask the Father, and he will give you another Counselor to be with you forever—the Spirit of truth. The world**

cannot accept him, because it neither sees him nor knows him. But you know him, for he lives with you and will be in you. (John 14:16-17)

On that day you will realize that I am in my Father, and you are in me, and I am in you. Jesus replied, "If anyone loves me, he will obey my teaching. My Father will love him, and we will come to him and make our home with him. (John 14:20, 23)

You, however, are controlled not by the sinful nature but by the Spirit, if the Spirit of God lives in you. And if anyone does not have the Spirit of Christ, he does not belong to Christ. (Rom 8:9)

Don't you know that you yourselves are God's temple and that God's Spirit lives in you? (1 Cor 3:16)

Do you not know that your body is a temple of the Holy Spirit, who is in you, whom you have received from God? You are not your own; (1 Cor 6:19)

Guard the good deposit that was entrusted to you—guard it with the help of the Holy Spirit who lives in us. (2 Tim 1:14)

As for you, the anointing [Holy Spirit] you received from him remains in you, and you do not need anyone to teach you. But as his anointing teaches you about all things and as that anointing is real, not counterfeit—just as it has taught you, remain in him. (1 John 2:27)

And I will put my Spirit in you and move you to follow my decrees and be careful to keep my laws. (Ezek 36:27)

Note how the deity of Christ is being proclaimed. The "Spirit of Christ" is said to live in the believer the same as the "Spirit of God." Both are said to be equally within the believer. (Cp. Gal.4:6; Ph.1:10; 2 Cor.3:18; 1 Pt.1:11.)

3. The power of the Spirit removes the believer from being controlled by the sinful nature and places him within *Himself*, within the Spirit of God. Very simply...

• the believer is no longer *positioned* "in" the sinful nature: not in God's eyes and not in God's accounting. The believer no longer lives "in" the sinful nature: he no longer makes his home in the sinful nature nor lives in the sinful nature. He is no longer at home, that is, no longer comfortable with the things of the sinful nature.

• the believer is *positioned* "in" the Spirit of God. God sees and counts the believer as being placed and positioned in His Spirit; therefore, the believer lives "in" the Holy Spirit. He makes his home in the Spirit, and he takes up his residence and lives "in" the Spirit. He is at home and comfortable only with the things of the Spirit.

4. The power of the Spirit identifies the believer as being "in" Christ. This is easily seen. Whatever spirit lives in a man, it is *that spirit* to whom man belongs. If he has the spirit of selfishness within, he belongs to the spirit of selfishness and is known as being selfish. If he has the spirit of complaining, he belongs to the spirit of complaining and is known as being a complainer. If he has the spirit of evil, he belongs to evil and is known as an evil person. If he has the spirit of caring, he belongs to the spirit of caring, and he is known as a caring person. If he has the Spirit of Christ, he belongs to Christ and is known as a follower of Christ.

I will not leave you as orphans; I will come to you. (John 14:18)

I have been crucified with Christ and I no longer live, but Christ lives in me. The life I live in the body, I live by faith in the Son of God, who loved me and gave himself for me. (Gal 2:20)

So that Christ may dwell in your hearts through faith. And I pray that you, being rooted and established in love, (Eph 3:17)

To them God has chosen to make known among the Gentiles the glorious riches of this mystery, which is Christ in you, the hope of glory. (Col 1:27)

Those who obey his commands live in him, and he in them. And this is how we know that he lives in us: We know it by the Spirit he gave us. (1 John 3:24)

Here I am! I stand at the door and knock. If anyone hears my voice and opens the door, I will come in and eat with him, and he with me. (Rev 3:20)

A person is *spirited*, driven to live according to the spirit that is within him. The Holy Spirit has the power to drive the believer to live as Christ lived. We can look at the spirit of a person and tell if he has the Spirit of Christ. If he does, then he bears the fruit of Christ's Spirit. The Spirit and His fruit are seen in the life of the believer. The true believer *proves* that he is "in" Christ, that he is placed and positioned "in" Christ by the life which he lives.

5 (8:10-11) **Holy Spirit—Resurrection, Believers**: the Spirit gives life to the *spirit* of the believer. The idea of the Greek makes this verse clear: "If Christ be in you, *although* the body is to die because of sin, the spirit shall live because of righteousness." Very simply stated, the body of man does die, but his spirit can live forever if Christ is "in" him. Note two points.

1. The Spirit of Christ gives life to the *spirit of man* now, the very moment a person believes. Man's body is to die because of sin: the body is corruptible, aging, deteriorating, decaying, and dying. It is in a process of dying—in such a rapid movement toward death—that it can actually be said to be *dead*. The body is dying; therefore, its death is inevitable. However, it is in the midst of death that the Spirit of Christ enters. He enters and converts the spirit of man from death to life. How?

a. The spirit of man lives because of the righteousness and death of Jesus Christ (see DEEPER STUDY #1, "*In Christ*"—Ro.8:1; cp. Ro.4:22; 5:1).

That if you confess with your mouth, "Jesus is Lord," and believe in your heart that God raised him from the dead, you will be saved. For it is with your heart that you be-lieve and are justified, and it is with your mouth that you confess and are saved. (Rom 10:9-10)

God made him who had no sin to be sin for us, so that in him we might become the righteousness of God. (2 Cor 5:21)

He himself bore our sins in his body on the tree, so that we might die to sins and live for righteousness; by his wounds you have been healed. (1 Pet 2:24)

b. The spirit of man lives by living a righteous and godly life (see notes—Ro.6:14-15; 6:17-18; 6:19-20).

"Not everyone who says to me, 'Lord, Lord,' will enter the kingdom of heaven, but only he who does the will of my Father who is in heaven. (Mat 7:21)

But thanks be to God that, though you used to be slaves to sin, you wholeheartedly obeyed the form of teaching to which you were entrusted. You have been set free from sin and have become slaves to righteousness. (Rom 6:17-18)

Therefore, there is now no condemnation for those who are in Christ Jesus, (Rom 8:1)

2. The Spirit of Christ quickens, gives life to the mortal body *in the future*, in the great day of redemption. Note two things.
   a. The words "gives life" (zoopoiesei) mean to make alive, to give life, to cause to live, to renew and remake life.
   b. The "mortal body" shall be quickened, given life and made alive.
   ⇒ The mortal body is the same body that died. The person is the very same person.
   ⇒ The mortal body is given a totally new life; its elements are recreated and remade into a perfect and eternal body. The new body is to be given the power and energy of eternal elements, eternal molecules and atoms or whatever the most minute elements are. All will be arranged so that the mortal body becomes an immortal body.

For my Father's will is that everyone who looks to the Son and believes in him shall have eternal life, and I will raise him up at the last day." (John 6:40)

Jesus said to her, "I am the resurrection and the life. He who believes in me will live, even though he dies; (John 11:25)

And I have the same hope in God as these men, that there will be a resurrection of both the righteous and the wicked. (Acts 24:15)

So will it be with the resurrection of the dead. The body that is sown is perishable, it is raised imperishable; it is sown in dishonor, it is raised in glory; it is sown in weakness, it is raised in power; it is sown a natural body, it is raised a spiritual body. If there is a natural body, there is also a spiritual body. (1 Cor 15:42-44)

I declare to you, brothers, that flesh and blood cannot inherit the kingdom of God, nor does the perishable inherit the imperishable. Listen, I tell you a mystery: We will not all sleep, but we will all be changed—in a flash, in the twinkling of an eye, at the last trumpet. For the trumpet will sound, the dead will be raised imperishable, and we will be changed. For the perishable must clothe itself with the imperishable, and the mortal with immortality. (1 Cor 15:50-53)

Because we know that the one who raised the Lord Jesus from the dead will also raise us with Jesus and present us with you in his presence. (2 Cor 4:14)

For the Lord himself will come down from heaven, with a loud command, with the voice of the archangel and with the trumpet call of God, and the dead in Christ will rise first. (1 Th 4:16)

Praise be to the God and Father of our Lord Jesus Christ! In his great mercy he has given us new birth into a living hope through the resurrection of Jesus Christ from the dead, and into an inheritance that can never perish, spoil or fade—kept in heaven for you, (1 Pet 1:3-4)

c. There are two great assurances of the believer's resurrection.
   ⇒ The assurance of Jesus' resurrection (see DEEPER STUDY #3, *Resurrection, of Believers*—Ro.8:11 for discussion. Also see outline and notes—1 Cor.15:12-19; 15:20-23.)
   ⇒ The assurance of the Holy Spirit, of Him who lives in the believer. The very same Spirit who raised up Christ shall raise up the believer (2 Cor.4:14). He is the power and energy of life, and He dwells within the believer. Therefore, He shall raise up the believer (see note, *Spirit of Life*—Ro.8:2-4 for more discussion).

And who through the Spirit of holiness was declared with power to be the Son of God by his resurrection from the dead: Jesus Christ our Lord. (Rom 1:4)

Because we know that the one who raised the Lord Jesus from the dead will also raise us with Jesus and present us with you in his presence. (2 Cor 4:14)

DEEPER STUDY # 3

(8:11) **Resurrection, of Believers—Jesus Christ, Resurrection of**: the resurrection of Jesus Christ assures the believer that he too shall be raised from the dead.

1. The resurrection of Christ proves that *God is*: that He does exist and care for the earth. There is no power on earth that can raise a man from the dead. Only a Supreme, Eternal Power and Person can do that. Only God can give life to dead matter and to the dust of the earth. The very fact that Jesus Christ was raised from the dead proves that God exists and cares for this earth.

2. The resurrection of Christ proves that Jesus Christ is who He claimed to be, the Son of God Himself. It proves that Jesus Christ was sent to earth to secure the Ideal righteousness for man and to die and to arise from the dead for man (see note, *Justification*—Ro.5:1 for more discussion).

And who through the Spirit of holiness was declared with power to be the Son of God by his resurrection from the dead: Jesus Christ our Lord. (Rom 1:4)

Which he exerted in Christ when he raised him from the dead and seated him at his right hand in the heavenly realms, (Eph 1:20)

3. The resurrection of Christ proves that Jesus Christ is the Savior of the world. It proves that Christ is the very One whom God sent to earth to save men from death and to give them life (see DEEPER STUDY # 2—Ro.6:3-5 for discussion).

> He was delivered over to death for our sins and was raised to life for our justification. (Rom 4:25)
> That if you confess with your mouth, "Jesus is Lord," and believe in your heart that God raised him from the dead, you will be saved. (Rom 10:9)
> By this gospel you are saved, if you hold firmly to the word I preached to you. Otherwise, you have believed in vain. For what I received I passed on to you as of first importance : that Christ died for our sins according to the Scriptures, that he was buried, that he was raised on the third day according to the Scriptures, (1 Cor 15:2-4)

4. The resurrection of Christ proves that He is "the Spirit of life." It proves that Christ is the very Energy and Force of life, the very Power and Being of life, and that He can give the same "Spirit of life" to men. He can raise men from the dead, even as He arose from the dead (see note—Ro.8:2-4 for more discussion. Also see outline and notes—1 Cor.15:12-19; 15:20-23).

> And if the Spirit of him who raised Jesus from the dead is living in you, he who raised Christ from the dead will also give life to your mortal bodies through his Spirit, who lives in you. (Rom 8:11)
> We believe that Jesus died and rose again and so we believe that God will bring with Jesus those who have fallen asleep in him. (1 Th 4:14)
> Praise be to the God and Father of our Lord Jesus Christ! In his great mercy he has given us new birth into a living hope through the resurrection of Jesus Christ from the dead, and into an inheritance that can never perish, spoil or fade—kept in heaven for you, (1 Pet 1:3-4)
> For Christ died for sins once for all, the righteous for the unrighteous, to bring you to God. He was put to death in the body but made alive by the Spirit, (1 Pet 3:18)

6 (8:12-13) **Holy Spirit**: the Spirit gives the power to put to death evil deeds. Note two points.

1. Believers are in debt to the Spirit, not to the sinful nature, not to the flesh. The word "obligation" (opheiletes) means to be obligated, to owe, to be bound by some duty.
 a. Believers are not in "obligated" to the sinful nature. The sinful nature has done nothing for man, nothing of real value. Note what the sinful nature has done for man.
  ⇒ It is sinful nature, contaminated by sin (v.3).
  ⇒ It is unspiritual or fleshly minded (v.5).
  ⇒ It causes man to die (v.6, 13).
  ⇒ It is the opposite of life and peace (v.6).
  ⇒ It has a mind that is at odds with God (v.7).
  ⇒ It cannot please God (v.8).

> A man owes the sinful nature nothing. He is not in debt or obligated to the sinful nature, for the

sinful nature brings nothing but misery and suffering to man.

Thought 1. A man is a fool to focus his life upon such a weak thing as the flesh; a fool to live as though he is in debt and obligated to something that *caves in...*
• to sickness and disease so often.
• to sin and shame so often.
• to death much too quickly.

> I know that nothing good lives in me, that is, in my sinful nature. For I have the desire to do what is good, but I cannot carry it out. (Rom 7:18)
> The mind of sinful man is death, but the mind controlled by the Spirit is life and peace; (Rom 8:6)
> Those controlled by the sinful nature cannot please God. (Rom 8:8)
> For if you live according to the sinful nature, you will die; but if by the Spirit you put to death the misdeeds of the body, you will live, (Rom 8:13)
> For the sinful nature desires what is contrary to the Spirit, and the Spirit what is contrary to the sinful nature. They are in conflict with each other, so that you do not do what you want. (Gal 5:17)
> The one who sows to please his sinful nature, from that nature will reap destruction; the one who sows to please the Spirit, from the Spirit will reap eternal life. (Gal 6:8)
> Do not love the world or anything in the world. If anyone loves the world, the love of the Father is not in him. For everything in the world—the cravings of sinful man, the lust of his eyes and the boasting of what he has and does—comes not from the Father but from the world. (1 John 2:15-16)

 b. Believers are obligated to the Spirit. It is the Spirit who has done so much for man, the Spirit to whom we are so indebted. The Spirit of God...
• is the "Spirit of life" (v.2).
• has freed us from sin and death (v.2).
• fulfills righteousness "in" us (v.4).
• pulls our minds to spiritual things (v.5).
• gives us life and peace (v.6).
• lives and dwells in us, removing us from the sinful nature and identifying us as being "in" Christ (v.9).
• gives life to our spirits now and assures us that He will give life to our mortal bodies in the great day of redemption (v.10-11).

> It is the Spirit who has done so much for us; it is the Spirit to whom we are in debt and "obligated."

2. Believers determine their own fate. The point is clearly seen: if a man lives after the sinful nature, he shall die because the flesh dies. The flesh is doomed; it dies, and there has never been an exception. Therefore, if a man chooses to live after the flesh, that is, to follow after the flesh, then in following the flesh he experiences what the flesh experiences. If the flesh stumbles and falls, the man stumbles and falls, for he is following after the sinful nature of the flesh. If the flesh kills itself, then the man dies

with the flesh, for he is following the flesh. Scripture clearly teaches this.

> **For the wages of sin is death, but the gift of God is eternal life in Christ Jesus our Lord. (Rom 6:23)**
> **The mind of sinful man is death, but the mind controlled by the Spirit is life and peace; (Rom 8:6)**
> **For if you live according to the sinful nature, you will die; but if by the Spirit you put to death the misdeeds of the body, you will live, (Rom 8:13)**
> **Then, after desire has conceived, it gives birth to sin; and sin, when it is full-grown, gives birth to death. (James 1:15)**
> **The soul who sins is the one who will die. The son will not share the guilt of the father, nor will the father share the guilt of the son. The righteousness of the righteous man will be credited to him, and the wickedness of the wicked will be charged against him. (Ezek 18:20)**

However, if a man puts to death the misdeeds of his body, he shall live. Note four facts.

a. "The misdeeds of the body" mean the evil deeds, the evil lusts and passions, the desires and urges that lead to sin and shame, destruction and death.

b. The Greek word *thanatoute* means to "put to death." The idea is that of denying, subjecting, subduing, deadening, destroying the strength of.

c. The power to put to death the evil misdeeds of the body comes "through the Spirit." However, note this: we deny the evil deeds, and then the Spirit gives the strength to *deaden* and to *subdue* their strength. We are involved just as the Spirit is involved. He cannot destroy the strength of sin unless we exercise our will and work to destroy it ourselves, and we cannot will and work at it apart from Him. Both the Spirit and ourselves have to be involved, each doing his part if we wish the evil misdeeds of the body to be put to death. To repeat the point above: we exercise our will to deny the evil misdeeds, and then the Spirit immediately steps in to *deaden* the pull and strength of the evil misdeed. If we do not want the evil misdeeds of our body destroyed, if we want to continue living in the sins of the sinful nature, if we want nothing to do with the Spirit—then the Spirit can do nothing for us. God loves us too much to force us; He will not override our choice. But if we honestly will to follow the Spirit and honestly desire to destroy the evil misdeeds of our body, the Spirit will step in and give the power to do so. He will break the power of sin: He will deaden and subdue the strength of it.

⇒ Our part is to *will* to follow the Spirit: to put to death the evil misdeeds and begin to deny them. (See note and DEEPER STUDY # 1—Lk.9:23 for more discussion.)

⇒ The Spirit's part is to deaden and subdue and eventually to destroy the strength of evil misdeeds.

Now note: the conquest of evil misdeeds is not an immediate, once-for-all thing. It is a continuous struggle as long as we live in the sinful nature. This is actually brought out in the tense of the verb "live." The tense is a continuous and habitual action. We must *continue* to follow the Spirit and *continue* to put to death the evil misdeeds of the body. It is a day by day experience just as living is a day by day experience. We are to *live* by developing the habit of living in the Spirit and conquering the evil misdeeds of the body. The believer *cannot destroy* his sinful nature while on earth, but he *can break* the strength of evil misdeeds in his sinful nature. He can destroy evil misdeeds in his body.

d. The person who puts the evil misdeeds of his body to death shall live. A man dies because of evil, and he lives because of righteousness. If he destroys the evil misdeeds and follows the Spirit of righteousness, he will not die. He will live.

> **If your right eye causes you to sin, gouge it out and throw it away. It is better for you to lose one part of your body than for your whole body to be thrown into hell. (Mat 5:29; cp. Mt 18:8)**
> **For we know that our old self was crucified with him so that the body of sin might be done away with, that we should no longer be slaves to sin— (Rom 6:6)**
> **For if you live according to the sinful nature, you will die; but if by the Spirit you put to death the misdeeds of the body, you will live, (Rom 8:13)**
> **Rather, clothe yourselves with the Lord Jesus Christ, and do not think about how to gratify the desires of the sinful nature. (Rom 13:14)**
> **So I say, live by the Spirit, and you will not gratify the desires of the sinful nature. (Gal 5:16)**
> **Those who belong to Christ Jesus have crucified the sinful nature with its passions and desires. (Gal 5:24)**
> **Put to death, therefore, whatever belongs to your earthly nature: sexual immorality, impurity, lust, evil desires and greed, which is idolatry. (Col 3:5)**
> **Dear friends, I urge you, as aliens and strangers in the world, to abstain from sinful desires, which war against your soul. (1 Pet 2:11)**
> **As a result, he does not live the rest of his earthly life for evil human desires, but rather for the will of God. (1 Pet 4:2)**

7 (8:14) **Believers, Duty**: the Spirit leads the believer. There are several ideas in the Greek word *lead* or *led* (ago).

⇒ There is the idea of *carrying and bearing along*. The Spirit leads the believer and carries him through the trials of this life. He bears the believer up, carrying him over the corruption's of this world.

⇒ There is the idea of *leading and guiding along*. The Spirit leads and guides the believer along the way of righteousness and truth. He guides the believer by moving in advance and going ahead of him. He blazes the path, making sure the believer knows where to walk (cp. Jn.16:13; cp. Gal.5:18; 2 Pt.1:21).

⇒ There is the idea of *directing on a course and of bringing along to an end.* The Spirit directs the believer here to go and how to get there, and He actually brings the believer to his destined end. The Spirit actually becomes involved in the life of the believer, directing him to live righteously and conforming him to the image of Christ. He actually brings the believer to his destined end, that is, to heaven, to live eternally in the presence of God Himself.

This is one of the great powers of the Holy Spirit, the power to lead the believer and to become involved in his life.

Now note a crucial point. The evidence or proof that a person is a son of God is just this: Is the person led by the Spirit of God?

⇒ Is the person being carried through the trials of life victoriously, acknowledging God and rejoicing in His strength and eternal security?

⇒ Is the person being led along the way of righteousness and truth?

⇒ Is the person being directed and brought along on the course to heaven, to spend eternity with God?

Very simply, is the person living for God and talking about the things of God? The person who is truly led by the Spirit is wrapped up in the things of God, for he is a son of God. He rejoices in his Father and seeks to please His Father in all that he does.

> But when he, the Spirit of truth, comes, he will guide you into all truth. He will not speak on his own; he will speak only what he hears, and he will tell you what is yet to come. (John 16:13)

> This is what we speak, not in words taught us by human wisdom but in words taught by the Spirit, expressing spiritual truths in spiritual words. The man without the Spirit does not accept the things that come from the Spirit of God, for they are foolishness to him, and he cannot understand them, because they are spiritually discerned. (1 Cor 2:13-14)

> But the fruit of the Spirit is love, joy, peace, patience, kindness, goodness, faithfulness, gentleness and self-control. Against such things there is no law. (Gal 5:22-23)

> As for you, the anointing you received from him remains in you, and you do not need anyone to teach you. But as his anointing teaches you about all things and as that anointing is real, not counterfeit—just as it has taught you, remain in him. (1 John 2:27)

> For this God is our God for ever and ever; he will be our guide even to the end. (Psa 48:14)

> You guide me with your counsel, and afterward you will take me into glory. (Psa 73:24)

> Whether you turn to the right or to the left, your ears will hear a voice behind you, saying, "This is the way; walk in it." (Isa 30:21)

8 (8:15) **Adoption—Sonship**: the Spirit adopts the believer. Note two very significant points.

1. The Spirit delivers man from a terrible spirit—"a spirit that makes you a slave....to fear." Note what the slavery is: it is fear. Man is gripped by the bondage of fear, usually experiencing some apprehension, anxiety, tension, dread, alarm, danger, terror. Man is usually sensing some subjection, some enslavement to some form of fear. The one spirit with which all men are familiar is the *spirit of fear.* Men are enslaved and held in bondage by fear. What causes fear? Almost everything and anything can arouse fear: a list could go on and on. A few of the more prominent things are...

- suffering
- disease
- unemployment
- loss of livelihood
- not measuring up
- failure
- disapproval
- blame
- death
- traumatic trials
- loss of position
- loss of spouse
- falling short
- punishment
- condemnation
- rejection

The point is this: the Holy Spirit delivers the believer from the bondage of fear. How? By adoption, by actually adopting the believer as a son of God.

> Yet to all who received him, to those who believed in his name, he gave the right to become children of God— (John 1:12)

> For you did not receive a spirit that makes you a slave again to fear, but you received the Spirit of sonship. And by him we cry, "Abba, Father." (Rom 8:15)

> "Therefore come out from them and be separate, says the Lord. Touch no unclean thing, and I will receive you." "I will be a Father to you, and you will be my sons and daughters, says the Lord Almighty." (2 Cor 6:17-18)

> But when the time had fully come, God sent his Son, born of a woman, born under law, to redeem those under law, that we might receive the full rights of sons. Because you are sons, God sent the Spirit of his Son into our hearts, the Spirit who calls out, "Abba, Father." (Gal 4:4-6)

> For you are a people holy to the LORD your God. Out of all the peoples on the face of the earth, the LORD has chosen you to be his treasured possession. (Deu 14:2)

> But you are our Father, though Abraham does not know us or Israel acknowledge us; you, O LORD, are our Father, our Redeemer from of old is your name. (Isa 63:16)

2. The Spirit gives access into God's presence. The believer has access to God because he has been adopted as a son of God. Note: the Spirit is called "the Spirit of sonship" or perhaps better worded, *the spirit of adoption.* Adoption is such a significant work of the Holy Spirit that it is called "the Spirit of sonship." The believer actually receives the "Spirit of sonship" and the sense—the consciousness, the awareness, the knowledge—that he is a son of God. The believer is a son of God with all the privileges of sonship, especially the privilege of access—of entering God's presence anytime and anyplace. It is this wonderful privilege that enables the believer to break the bondage of fear and to conquer the spirit of fear.

No matter what faces the believer, the believer is able...

- to enter the presence of God.
- to lay his fear before God.
- to cry out, "Father, Father—help me!"
- to know that God will help him, for God loves him as His adopted son.

I am the gate; whoever enters through me will be saved. He will come in and go out, and find pasture. (John 10:9)

Therefore, since we have been justified through faith, we have peace with God through our Lord Jesus Christ, through whom we have gained access by faith into this grace in which we now stand. And we rejoice in the hope of the glory of God. (Rom 5:1-2)

For through him we both have access to the Father by one Spirit. (Eph 2:18)

In him and through faith in him we may approach God with freedom and confidence. (Eph 3:12)

Therefore, since we have a great high priest who has gone through the heavens, Jesus the Son of God, let us hold firmly to the faith we profess. For we do not have a high priest who is unable to sympathize with our weaknesses, but we have one who has been tempted in every way, just as we are—yet was without sin. Let us then approach the throne of grace with confidence, so that we may receive mercy and find grace to help us in our time of need. (Heb 4:14-16)

Therefore, brothers, since we have confidence to enter the Most Holy Place by the blood of Jesus, (Heb 10:19)

For the eyes of the Lord are on the righteous and his ears are attentive to their prayer, but the face of the Lord is against those who do evil." (1 Pet 3:12)

Every *genuine believer* knows what it is to fear in this life, and he knows what it is to experience God delivering him through the fear. He knows what it is to have the "Spirit of adoption" surge through his being, giving assurance and confidence that God is in control and looking after him. He knows what it is to be a true son of God, a son whom God loves so much that He will move the world in order to meet the need of His dear child. God's love for His adopted child is as great as God's sovereign power. God will do anything for the believer who is His adopted son. (One of the great powers of the Spirit is the power of sonship. See DEEPER STUDY #2, Sonship—Adoption—Gal.4:5-6 for more discussion).

And we know that in all things God works for the good of those who love him, who have been called according to his purpose. (Rom 8:28)

9 (8:16-17) **Adoption—Sonship**: another power of the Spirit is the power to testify or to bear witness with our spirit. He testifies or bear witness to four glorious truths.

1. The Holy Spirit testifies that we are the children of God. Very simply stated, the Holy Spirit quickens; makes alive our hearts with the perfect knowledge and the complete confidence that we are children of God.

Note how clearly Scripture proclaims this glorious truth, the truth which every believer longs for the world to know.

a. The Spirit pours out the love of God in our hearts. He spreads the knowledge that God loves us and spreads it all through our being.

And hope does not disappoint us, because God has poured out his love into our hearts by the Holy Spirit, whom he has given us. (Rom 5:5)

b. The Spirit is the deposit or the guarantee that we are children of God.

Set his seal of ownership on us, and put his Spirit in our hearts as a deposit, guaranteeing what is to come. (2 Cor 1:22)

Now it is God who has made us for this very purpose and has given us the Spirit as a deposit, guaranteeing what is to come. (2 Cor 5:5)

c. The Spirit is the seal or the guarantee that we are children of God.

And you also were included in Christ when you heard the word of truth, the gospel of your salvation. Having believed, you were marked in him with a seal, the promised Holy Spirit, (Eph 1:13)

And do not grieve the Holy Spirit of God, with whom you were sealed for the day of redemption. (Eph 4:30)

2. The Holy Spirit testifies that we are the heirs of God. If God is truly our Father, then we inherit what He possesses.

a. We are heirs of eternal life.

So that, having been justified by his grace, we might become heirs having the hope of eternal life. (Titus 3:7)

b. We are heirs of salvation.

Are not all angels ministering spirits sent to serve those who will inherit salvation? (Heb 1:14)

c. We are heirs of the promises made to Abraham, that is, the promises to inherit the world and to become the citizens of a great nation of people. The heirs of God shall inherit a great kingdom, that is, the new heavens and earth.

It was not through law that Abraham and his offspring received the promise that he would be heir of the world, but through the righteousness that comes by faith. (Rom 4:13)

If you belong to Christ, then you are Abraham's seed, and heirs according to the promise. (Gal 3:29)

This mystery is that through the gospel the Gentiles are heirs together with Israel, members together of one body, and sharers together in the promise in Christ Jesus. (Eph 3:6)

For of this you can be sure: No immoral, impure or greedy person—such a man is an idolater—has any inheritance in the kingdom of Christ and of God. (Eph 5:5. See note—Ro.4:13 for more discussion)

By faith he made his home in the promised land like a stranger in a foreign

139

country; he lived in tents, as did Isaac and Jacob, who were heirs with him of the same promise. For he was looking forward to the city with foundations, whose architect and builder is God. (Heb 11:9-10)

All these people were still living by faith when they died. They did not receive the things promised; they only saw them and welcomed them from a distance. And they admitted that they were aliens and strangers on earth. People who say such things show that they are looking for a country of their own. If they had been thinking of the country they had left, they would have had opportunity to return. Instead, they were longing for a better country—a heavenly one. Therefore God is not ashamed to be called their God, for he has prepared a city for them. (Heb 11:13-16)

But the day of the Lord will come like a thief. The heavens will disappear with a roar; the elements will be destroyed by fire, and the earth and everything in it will be laid bare. Since everything will be destroyed in this way, what kind of people ought you to be? You ought to live holy and godly lives as you look forward to the day of God and speed its coming. That day will bring about the destruction of the heavens by fire, and the elements will melt in the heat. But in keeping with his promise we are looking forward to a new heaven and a new earth, the home of righteousness. (2 Pet 3:10-13)

d. We are heirs of glory.

Now if we are children, then we are heirs—heirs of God and co-heirs with Christ, if indeed we share in his sufferings in order that we may also share in his glory. (Rom 8:17)

I pray also that the eyes of your heart may be enlightened in order that you may know the hope to which he has called you, the riches of his glorious inheritance in the saints, (Eph 1:18)

Giving thanks to the Father, who has qualified you to share in the inheritance of the saints in the kingdom of light. (Col 1:12)

e. We are heirs of righteousness.

By faith Noah, when warned about things not yet seen, in holy fear built an ark to save his family. By his faith he condemned the world and became heir of the righteousness that comes by faith. (Heb 11:7)

f. We are heirs of the grace of life.

Husbands, in the same way be considerate as you live with your wives, and treat them with respect as the weaker partner and as heirs with you of the gracious gift of life, so that nothing will hinder your prayers. (1 Pet 3:7)

The point is that the Holy Spirit is the One who seals the truth to our hearts. He is "a deposit guaranteeing our in-

heritance" (Eph.1:14). There is much more that we inherit as children of God (see note—Lk.16:10-12; DEEPER STUDY #4—Ro.8:17).

3. The Holy Spirit testifies that we are joint-heirs or "co-heirs" with Christ. However, this does not mean that we will receive an equal amount or quantity with Christ. (See DEEPER STUDY #4, *Inheritance*—Ro.8:17 for discussion.)

4. The Holy Spirit testifies that we are conquerors over suffering. All men suffer: as long as a man lives in a sinful and corrupt world, he will suffer and he will be unable to escape suffering. Sin and corruption take their toll upon his body and spirit and pull him ever onward toward the grave. However, this is not the suffering being spoken about in this passage. There is a suffering that is distinct to the true Christian believer, a suffering that can be called *godly persecution*. *Godly persecution* means more than being persecuted for some great cause or purpose. Many men in the world suffer persecution by some of their fellow citizens because of their dedication to some great purpose. However, not all men within the world oppose them. It is this that makes *godly persecution* different and distinctive. Every person in the world who is not godly opposes the *genuine* Christian believer. The world and its citizens oppose the believer by their very nature. The believer stands for and proclaims righteousness and self-denial, the sacrifice of all one is and has. The world opposes such a life and message, and they desire to stamp it out (see note, *Persecuted*—Mt.5:10-12 for more discussion).

It is suffering for the Kingdom of God and His righteousness that is the point of the Scripture. If we suffer with Christ in the great cause of God and His righteousness, then we will be glorified with Him eternally.

The point is clearly seen. The person who is a true follower of Christ proclaims and stands for Christ; therefore, he suffers the persecution of the world even as Christ did. And because he does suffer with Christ, he will share in the glory of Christ as well.

"Blessed are you when people insult you, persecute you and falsely say all kinds of evil against you because of me. (Mat 5:11)

All men will hate you because of me, but he who stands firm to the end will be saved. (Mat 10:22)

And everyone who has left houses or brothers or sisters or father or mother or children or fields for my sake will receive a hundred times as much and will inherit eternal life. (Mat 19:29)

As it is written: "For your sake we face death all day long; we are considered as sheep to be slaughtered." (Rom 8:36)

And our hope for you is firm, because we know that just as you share in our sufferings, so also you share in our comfort. (2 Cor 1:7)

For we who are alive are always being given over to death for Jesus' sake, so that his life may be revealed in our mortal body. (2 Cor 4:11)

If we endure, we will also reign with him. If we disown him, he will also disown us; (2 Tim 2:12)

For it has been granted to you on behalf of Christ not only to believe on him, but also to suffer for him, (Phil 1:29)

I want to know Christ and the power of his resurrection and the fellowship of sharing in his sufferings, becoming like him in his death, (Phil 3:10)

He chose to be mistreated along with the people of God rather than to enjoy the pleasures of sin for a short time. (Heb 11:25)

But how is it to your credit if you receive a beating for doing wrong and endure it? But if you suffer for doing good and you endure it, this is commendable before God. (1 Pet 2:20)

But even if you should suffer for what is right, you are blessed. "Do not fear what they fear ; do not be frightened." (1 Pet 3:14)

However, if you suffer as a Christian, do not be ashamed, but praise God that you bear that name. (1 Pet 4:16)

And the God of all grace, who called you to his eternal glory in Christ, after you have suffered a little while, will himself restore you and make you strong, firm and steadfast. (1 Pet 5:10)

DEEPER STUDY # 4

(8:17) **Inheritance**: the believer is a co-heir or joint-heir with Christ. This is an astounding truth and promise. We shall inherit all that God has and all that Christ is and has. We will be given the privilege of sharing in all things with the Son of God Himself.

However note this: to be a joint-heir with Christ does not mean that believers will receive an equal amount of the inheritance with Christ. Rather, it means that believers are fellow-heirs with Christ; that is, believers will share in the inheritance of Christ; they will *share* Christ's inheritance with Him.

Being a fellow-heir with Christ means at least three glorious things: it means that we will share in the *nature*, *position*, and *responsibility* of Christ. The following chart shows this with a quick glance.

FELLOW HEIRS BY NATURE

Christ is the Son of God, the very being
and energy of life and perfection. Therefore,
we share in the inheritance of His nature.
We receive...

- the adoption as a son of God (Gal.4:4-7; 1 Jn.3:1).
- the sinless nature of being blameless (Ph.2:15).
- eternal life (Jn.1:4; 10:10; 17:2-3; Jn.3:16; 1 Tim. 6:19).
- lasting possessions (Heb.10:34).
- a glorious body (Ph.3:21; 1 Cor.15:42-44).
- eternal glory and honor and peace (Ro.2:10).
- eternal rest and peace (Heb.4:9; Rev.14:13).
- a crown that will last forever, an incorruptible body

(1 Pt 1:3-4; 1 Cor.9:25, 15:42).
- a righteous being (2 Tim.4:8).

FELLOW HEIRS BY POSITION

Christ is the exalted Lord, the Sovereign
Majesty of the universe, the Lord of lords
and King of kings. Therefore, we share in
the inheritance of His position. We receive...

- the position of exalted beings (Rev.7:9-12).
- a citizenship in the Kingdom of God (Jas.2:5; Mt.25:34).
- enormous treasures in heaven (Mt.19:21; Lk.12:33).
- unsearchable riches (Eph.3:8).
- the right to surround the throne of God (Rev.7:9-13; 20:4).
- the position of a king (Rev.1:5; 5:10).
- the position of a priest (Rev.1:5; 5:10; 20:6).
- the position of glory (1 Pt.5:4).

FELLOW HEIRS BY RESPONSIBILITY

Christ is the Sovereign Majesty of the Universe,
the One who is ordained to rule and oversee all.
Therefore, we share in the inheritance of His responsibility. We receive...

- the rulership over many things (Mt.25:23).
- the right to rule and hold authority (Lk.12:42-44; 22:28-29).
- eternal responsibility and joy (Mt.25:21, 23).
- rule and authority over cities (Lk.19:17, 19).
- thrones and the privilege of reigning forever (Rev.20:4; 22:5).

These passages will give some idea of what Scripture teaches when it speaks of the believer being a *fellow-heir* with Christ. There are a large number of Scriptures that could be added to these. As Paul declares:

However, as it is written: "No eye has seen, no ear has heard, no mind has conceived what God has prepared for those who love him"— (1 Cor 2:9)

Oh, the depth of the riches of the wisdom and knowledge of God! How unsearchable his judgments, and his paths beyond tracing out! "Who has known the mind of the Lord? Or who has been his counselor?" "Who has ever given to God, that God should repay him?" For from him and through him and to him are all things. To him be the glory forever! Amen. (Rom 11:33-36)

| 1 In this life
a. The believer suffers & struggles
b. The future glory will be worth the agony

2 The creation suffers & struggles for deliverance from corruption

a. Creation is subject to corruption

b. Creation will be delivered

c. Creation groans in labor for deliverance | **B. The Whole Creation Shall Be Freed from Struggling and Suffering, 8:18-27**

18 I consider that our present sufferings are not worth comparing with the glory that will be revealed in us.
19 The creation waits in eager expectation for the sons of God to be revealed.
20 For the creation was subjected to frustration, not by its own choice, but by the will of the one who subjected it, in hope
21 That the creation itself will be liberated from its bondage to decay and brought into the glorious freedom of the children of God.
22 We know that the whole creation has been groaning as | in the pains of childbirth right up to the present time.
23 Not only so, but we ourselves, who have the firstfruits of the Spirit, groan inwardly as we wait eagerly for our adoption as sons, the redemption of our bodies.
24 For in this hope we were saved. But hope that is seen is no hope at all. Who hopes for what he already has?
25 But if we hope for what we do not yet have, we wait for it patiently.
26 In the same way, the Spirit helps us in our weakness. We do not know what we ought to pray for, but the Spirit himself intercedes for us with groans that words cannot express.
27 And he who searches our hearts knows the mind of the Spirit, because the Spirit intercedes for the saints in accordance with God's will. | 3 The believer suffers & struggles for deliverance from corruption
a. The first-fruits of the Spirit deliver & save him
b. Hope delivers & saves him[DS1]

c. Prayer & the Spirit deliver & save him

d. God delivers & saves him |

DIVISION VI

DELIVERANCE AND REDEMPTION: THE BELIEVER SHALL BE FREED FROM STRUGGLING AND SUFFERING BY THE SPIRIT, 8:1-39

B. The Whole Creation Shall Be Freed from Struggling and Suffering, 8:18-27

(8:18-27) **Introduction**: this is one of the most glorious promises in all of Scripture. God is going to free *all creation* from struggling and suffering.

1. In this life (v.18).
   a. The believer suffers and struggles.
   b. The future glory will be worth the agony.
2. The creation suffers and struggles for deliverance from corruption (v.19-22).
3. The believer suffers and struggles for deliverance from corruption (v.23-27).

1 (8:18) **Suffering—Spiritual Warfare, Struggle**: in this life the believer suffers and struggles. The word "suffering" means all the forms of suffering which the believer experiences throughout life. It means...

- the suffering that comes from persecution.
- the suffering that comes from the struggle of his spirit to overcome the sinful nature and the world.

Very simply, suffering means the struggle waged by our spirits to overcome all that is experienced in this life, all that is involved in the sinful nature and the world (See note—Gal.5:16-18 for more discussion). It is the spiritual struggle discussed in Romans Chapters 5-8, and so descriptively illustrated in Chapter 7. It is the weight and agony of fighting to overcome...

- sin and corruption.
- disease and pain.
- abuse and persecution.
- unregulated urges and desires.
- weaknesses and shortcomings.
- aging and loss.
- deterioration and decay.

The genuine believer struggles against everything that keeps him from living abundantly and eternally. His sole passion is to bring everything under the control of Christ and to be conformed to the image of Christ. Therefore, he struggles to overcome the flesh and the world with their aging and corruption, sin and death. No matter what suffering is required, the believer bears it in order to overcome and gain the victory of eternal life and its glory.

Note that the believer is to suffer with Christ "in order that" (ina—Greek) he may be glorified with Christ (Ro.8:17). Suffering prepares the believer to participate in the glory of Christ. It is the necessary condition for exaltation. Suffering and struggling are a refining process through which the believer must pass (1 Pt.1:6-7). It refines the believer by forcing him to expand his trust in God more and more. Suffering drives a believer to cast himself more and more upon the care of God; therefore, the believer moves closer and closer to that perfect trust and care in God. He will never achieve the perfect trust and care in God, but he will come to know it when God transports him into the very Kingdom of Heaven itself. Suffering enlarges, purifies, expands, and ennobles the believer. It makes him more and more like what he will be when he actually lives face to face with God. This future glory *transcends immeasurably* the suffering and struggling of this present world.

a. The future glory shall be revealed "in" us; it shall become part of our very nature and being. Glory shall radiate and shine forth from our resurrected bodies.

I consider that our present sufferings are not worth comparing with the glory that will be revealed in us. (Rom 8:18)

When Christ, who is your life, appears, then you also will appear with him in glory. (Col 3:4)

I pray also that the eyes of your heart may be enlightened in order that you may know the hope to which he has called you, the riches of his glorious inheritance in the saints, (Eph 1:18)

Therefore I endure everything for the sake of the elect, that they too may obtain the salvation that is in Christ Jesus, with eternal glory. (2 Tim 2:10)

To the elders among you, I appeal as a fellow elder, a witness of Christ's sufferings and one who also will share in the glory to be revealed: (1 Pet 5:1)

b. The future glory shall be an *eternal* glory that outweighs them all (just imagine such a weight, a weight beyond all measure, surpassing all measurements and calculations).

For our light and momentary troubles are achieving for us an eternal glory that far outweighs them all. So we fix our eyes not on what is seen, but on what is unseen. For what is seen is temporary, but what is unseen is eternal. (2 Cor 4:17-18)

c. The future glory shall far exceed anything we have seen or heard or longed for in our hearts.

However, as it is written: "No eye has seen, no ear has heard, no mind has conceived what God has prepared for those who love him"— (1 Cor 2:9)

And when the Chief Shepherd appears, you will receive the crown of glory that will never fade away. (1 Pet 5:4)

d. The future glory shall be so glorious it will reflect through us to others, making us *ministers* of glory.

As for Titus, he is my partner and fellow worker among you; as for our brothers, they are representatives of the churches and an honor to Christ. (2 Cor 8:23)

His intent was that now, through the church, the manifold wisdom of God should be made known to the rulers and authorities in the heavenly realms, (Eph 3:10)

e. The future glory shall make us just like Jesus in all that He is.

Dear friends, now we are children of God, and what we will be has not yet been made known. But we know that when he appears, we shall be like him, for we shall see him as he is. (1 John 3:2)

But our citizenship is in heaven. And we eagerly await a Savior from there, the Lord Jesus Christ, who, by the power that enables him to bring everything under his control, will transform our lowly bodies so that they will be like his glorious body. (Phil 3:20-21)

2 (8:19-22) **Creation**: the creation suffers and struggles for deliverance from corruption. The word "creation" refers to everything *under* man: animal, plant, and mineral. All creation is pictured as living and waiting expectantly for the day when the sons of God shall be glorified. The words "eager expectation" (apokaradokia) mean to watch with the neck outstretched and the head erect. It is a persistent, unswerving expectation, an expectation that does not give up but keeps looking until the event happens. Note three facts revealed about the universe in which man lives.

1. Creation is subject to corruption. This is clearly seen by men; and what men see is constantly confirmed by such authorities as the botanist, zoologist, geologist, and astronomers of the world. All of creation, whether mineral, plant, or animal, suffers just as men do. All creation suffers hurt, damage, loss, deterioration, erosion, death, and decay—all creation struggles for life. It is full of "frustration" (mataios), that is, condemned to futility and frustration, unable to realize its purpose, subject to corruption. Note the two things said about creation in this verse (v.20).

a. Creation was condemned to frustration—futility and a feeling of disappointment—by God. Creation did not willingly choose to be condemned to corruption. The world was made to be the home of man, the place where he lived. Therefore, when man sinned, his world was doomed to suffer the consequences of sin with him. Man's world was cursed right along with him.

To Adam he said, "Because you listened to your wife and ate from the tree about which I commanded you, 'You must not eat of it,' "Cursed is the ground because of you; through painful toil you will eat of it all the days of your life. (Gen 3:17)

The earth dries up and withers [for], the world languishes and withers, the exalted of the earth languish. The earth is defiled by its people; they have disobeyed the laws, violated the statutes and broken the everlasting covenant. Therefore a curse consumes the earth; its people must bear their guilt. Therefore earth's inhabitants are burned up, and very few are left. (Isa 24:4-6)

How long will the land lie parched and the grass in every field be withered? Because those who live in it are wicked, the animals and birds have perished. Moreover, the people are saying, "He will not see what happens to us." (Jer 12:4)

Thought 1. Just picture the enormous hurt and damage and decay that takes place in our world. Think about...

* the disease and savagery of the animal world.
* the hurt and damage that so easily happens in the plant world.
* the destruction and deterioration that takes place in the mineral world.

Think about the earthquakes, tornadoes, storms, diseases, starvation, attacks, and struggles for survival that take place. And these are only a few of the myriad happenings that show the corruption of the world.

b. Creation has been subjected to corruption "in hope." The news of Scripture is glorious: the situation of the world is neither hopeless nor final. Creation has the same *hope of redemption and of renovation* as man. The world was made for man, therefore all creation shall be ultimately delivered from corruption just as man shall be delivered from corruption.

2. Creation shall be delivered from corruption. This is the wonderful news of the glorious gospel. Note a most significant point: whatever happens to man is bound to happen to his world. Man is the summit of God's creation; therefore, all that is under man is intertwined, interwoven, and interrelated to him. Man and his world are one and the same; they are dependent upon each other. This is enormously significant: since man and his world are interrelated, it means that the world will experience whatever man experiences. When man fell, his world was bound to fall with him. But this is the glorious news as well. When man is liberated from corruption, his world shall be liberated as well. God had to subject man's world to man's fate, but God also had to subject man's world "in" hope. Creation will experience the glorious hope of *living forever* with man, of being completely and perfectly renovated. There will be a "new heavens and a new earth" (cp. Ps.96:11-13; 98:7-9; Is.11:6-9; Rev.5:13).

> But the day of the Lord will come like a thief. The heavens will disappear with a roar; the elements will be destroyed by fire, and the earth and everything in it will be laid bare. Since everything will be destroyed in this way, what kind of people ought you to be? You ought to live holy and godly lives as you look forward to the day of God and speed its coming. That day will bring about the destruction of the heavens by fire, and the elements will melt in the heat. But in keeping with his promise we are looking forward to a new heaven and a new earth, the home of righteousness. (2 Pet 3:10-13)
>
> Then I saw a new heaven and a new earth, for the first heaven and the first earth had passed away, and there was no longer any sea. (Rev 21:1 cp. Heb.12:26-27)
>
> "Behold, I will create new heavens and a new earth. The former things will not be remembered, nor will they come to mind. (Isa 65:17)
>
> "As the new heavens and the new earth that I make will endure before me," declares the LORD, "so will your name and descendants endure. (Isa 66:22)

3. Creation groans in labor for deliverance. Note that all creation suffers together: all creation is interrelated, intertwined, and interconnected. The whole universe is dependent upon its various parts for survival. The earth could not survive without the heavens, and the heavens would have no purpose apart from God's creation of man and his earth. This does not mean that man is to be egocentric or egotistical. It simply means that man and his earth are the focal point of God's unbelievable creation, of His eternal plan and purpose. Being the center of creation *before God* is not a truth to make man proud, but to make him humble—a truth to cause him to bow in worship and praise, appreciation and thankfulness. Being the summit of God's creation

is not a gift of privilege, not presently, but of enormous responsibility.

Note the word "groaning." The picture is that of a woman giving birth. Creation experiences "birth pains of childbirth" under its struggle to survive. And note: it has been experiencing the "birth pains of childbirth" *until now*, that is, from the fall of man up until this present moment.

In conclusion, the whole scene of these four verses is that creation awaits a renovated world. Creation resents evil and struggles against decay and death. It fights for survival. It struggles against the bondage of being slaughtered or changed.

The idea expressed is that creation awaits the Day of Redemption: anxiously, expectantly, longingly, and eagerly awaits for its deliverance from corruption. Creation moans and groans and cries for the unveiling of the Son of God.

> That the creation itself will be liberated from its bondage to decay and brought into the glorious freedom of the children of God. (Rom 8:21)
>
> But in keeping with his promise we are looking forward to a new heaven and a new earth, the home of righteousness. (2 Pet 3:13)
>
> No longer will there be any curse. The throne of God and of the Lamb will be in the city, and his servants will serve him. They will see his face, and his name will be on their foreheads. There will be no more night. They will not need the light of a lamp or the light of the sun, for the Lord God will give them light. And they will reign for ever and ever. (Rev 22:3-5)

3 (8:23-27) **Corruption, Deliverance from**: the believer suffers and struggles for deliverance from corruption. Note four facts.

1. It is the first-fruit of the Holy Spirit that delivers and saves man. The term first-fruit means either the presence of the Holy Spirit or the fruit of the Holy Spirit: life, love, joy, peace (Gal.5:22-23). When a believer is truly saved, he possesses the Holy Spirit and bears the fruit of the Spirit. He actually begins to live abundantly and eternally, and he experiences the fullness of God's Spirit: His love, joy, and peace. Experiencing these causes the believer to groan and ache...

- for the perfection of the Spirit's presence and fruit.
- for the day of adoption, the day when he will actually move into the perfect presence of God.
- for the redemption of his body.

The believer is stirred by the taste of the Spirit and of His first-fruits, stirred to groan for their perfection. He groans and aches to be delivered from the sufferings of this world and released into the glorious *liberty of perfection* with God.

> It is sown a natural body, it is raised a spiritual body. If there is a natural body, there is also a spiritual body. (1 Cor 15:44)
>
> And just as we have borne the likeness of the earthly man, so shall we bear the likeness of the man from heaven. (1 Cor 15:49)
>
> I declare to you, brothers, that flesh and blood cannot inherit the kingdom of God, nor does the perishable inherit the imperishable. For the perishable must clothe itself with the imperishable, and the mortal

with immortality. When the perishable has been clothed with the imperishable, and the mortal with immortality, then the saying that is written will come true: "Death has been swallowed up in victory." (1 Cor 15:50, 53-54)

Meanwhile we groan, longing to be clothed with our heavenly dwelling, (2 Cor 5:2)

He will wipe every tear from their eyes. There will be no more death or mourning or crying or pain, for the old order of things has passed away." He who was seated on the throne said, "I am making everything new!" Then he said, "Write this down, for these words are trustworthy and true." (Rev 21:4-5)

2. It is hope that delivers and saves man. Hope saves us, for it is hope that keeps us seeking after God and His redemption. We hope for redemption; therefore, "we wait for it patiently" (see DEEPER STUDY # 1, *Hope*—Ro.8:24-25 for discussion).

3. It is prayer and the Holy Spirit that delivers and saves a man. As the believer faces the sufferings of this life he has the greatest resource imaginable: prayer. He has the right to approach God whenever needed, and to ask God for the strength to walk through and to conquer the suffering. That is what prayer is all about.

Two significant things are said about prayer.
　a. Believers do not know how to pray *as they should*. Note the word "we." Paul includes himself in this, which is to say no believer knows how to pray. By nature we are weak, lacking the power...
　　• for prolonged concentration.
　　• to avoid distractions.
　　• to stop all wandering thoughts.
　　• to prevent emotional changes.
　　• to govern varying affections.
　　• to know what lies in the future, even one hour from now.
　　• to know what is *really* best for us and our growth in any given situation.

　b. The Holy Spirit helps our weaknesses. It is true that He helps us in *all* our weaknesses, but the point of the present passage deals only with prayer. Note: it is assumed that we are praying in this verse. The Spirit is not going to force us to pray. It is our responsibility to pray: to take the time to get alone and pray. When we do this the Spirit begins to act both *upon* and *for* us.
　　Note this also: the Spirit helps us in our weakness. Whatever our particular weakness is, it is that weakness which He helps. If we are truly sincere and are wrestling to pray, then the Spirit helps us to control concentration, distractions, wandering thoughts, emotional changes, and affections. How? As we struggle to pray by controlling our sinful nature and its weakness, the Holy Spirit takes our mind and emotions and...
　　• quiets and silences them
　　• stirs and excites them
　　• draws and pulls them
　　• directs and guides them

　　He leads us to pray as we should, controlling and subjecting the sinful nature and concentrating upon the prayer.

Note another fact: the Holy Spirit Himself "prays for us with groanings that cannot be expressed in words." Sometimes the struggles and sufferings of life become so heavy we just cannot bear them. At other times, matters of such importance grip our hearts to such an extent that words are impossible. Emotions become too much for words. We become lost in the presence of God. Every genuine believer knows what it is to be speechless before God and left groaning in the Spirit. Every believer has experienced...
⇒ God's indescribable gift.

Thanks be to God for his indescribable gift! (2 Cor 9:15)

⇒ joy inexpressible and glorious.

Though you have not seen him, you love him; and even though you do not see him now, you believe in him and are filled with an inexpressible and glorious joy, (1 Pet 1:8)

⇒ words which are inexpressible.

Was caught up to paradise. He heard inexpressible things, things that man is not permitted to tell. (2 Cor 12:4)

The point to note is that the Holy Spirit takes these great moments of prayer and helps us in our "groans" before the Lord. We are not able to utter words; therefore, the Spirit intercedes for us with groans that cannot be uttered.

And pray in the Spirit on all occasions with all kinds of prayers and requests. With this in mind, be alert and always keep on praying for all the saints. (Eph 6:18)

Thought 1. The believer's great need is to come before God—and to come often—in such intense prayer.

Look to the LORD and his strength; seek his face always. (1 Chr 16:11)
"Ask and it will be given to you; seek and you will find; knock and the door will be opened to you. (Mat 7:7)
Then Jesus told his disciples a parable to show them that they should always pray and not give up. (Luke 18:1)

4. It is God who delivers and saves a man. Note the three things said in this verse.
　a. God searches the heart of us all. There is no exception. He knows exactly what is within our hearts. He can read and understand what our groans and needs are. Not a need will be missed.

"And you, my son Solomon, acknowledge the God of your father, and serve him with wholehearted devotion and with a willing mind, for the LORD searches every heart and understands every motive behind the thoughts. If you seek him, he will be found by you; but if you forsake him, he will reject you forever. (1 Chr 28:9)

Would not God have discovered it, since he knows the secrets of the heart? (Psa 44:21)

"I the LORD search the heart and examine the mind, to reward a man according to his conduct, according to what his deeds deserve." (Jer 17:10)

b. God knows the mind of the Holy Spirit. The Holy Spirit prays for us according to the will of God; therefore, God knows exactly what the Spirit is requesting for us. There is perfect agreement between the Holy Spirit and God the Father.

But when he, the Spirit of truth, comes, he will guide you into all truth. He will not speak on his own; he will speak only what he hears, and he will tell you what is yet to come. (John 16:13)

c. God will answer our prayer and meet our need. He will deliver and save us, causing the very best thing to happen.

You did not choose me, but I chose you and appointed you to go and bear fruit—fruit that will last. Then the Father will give you whatever you ask in my name. (John 15:16)

In that day you will no longer ask me anything. I tell you the truth, my Father will give you whatever you ask in my name. Until now you have not asked for anything in my name. Ask and you will receive, and your joy will be complete. (John 16:23-24)

In that day you will ask in my name. I am not saying that I will ask the Father on your behalf. No, the Father himself loves you because you have loved me and have believed that I came from God. (John 16:26-27)

And we know that in all things God works for the good of those who love him, who have been called according to his purpose. (Rom 8:28)

DEEPER STUDY # 1

(8:24-25) **Hope** (elpis): assured expectation, confident knowledge, inward possession, spiritual surety. Note the statements of definition again, for they are packed full of meaning. The believer's hope cannot be defined as the world defines hope. The believer's hope is entirely different from the world's hope or desire or wish. The world desires and wishes for what it can see, and they may or may not be able to get what they long for.

The believer's hope is entirely different in that it deals with spiritual things and the believer will unquestionably get what he hopes for. The believer's hope is based on the *inward experience and witness of God's Spirit*. The believer knows that God's Spirit lives within him, and he actually experiences the things of the Spirit *now*. Granted, his experience is but a taste; the things of the Spirit are *not yet perfected* in his life, *but they do exist*, and they are present in his body. He already possesses the things of God while in the human body. His hope of salvation is a present experience—he is saved now—he already has a taste of salvation. The believer's hope to be saved is a living reality now; therefore,

his hope is a *sure* hope. To the genuine believer, hope is the absolute assurance of things promised, but not yet seen.

He has absolute assurance because he already experiences the things of God. They are already an *inward possession*, a *spiritual surety*, an *assured expectation*, a *confident knowledge*. Note four facts about hope.

1. God has chosen for us to be saved by hope and not by sight. If we were saved by sight, we would not hope in God. If we could actually see and experience perfect redemption and salvation now, then there would be nothing more for which to hope. The result would be catastrophic: we would not be drawing close to God, believing and trusting Him, nor looking to Him to provide a perfect salvation for us. There would be *no liberty and freedom between God and man*, *no love and trust established*. There just would be no relationship and no fellowship between God and man, not based on a *free moral love, trust, and belief*.

2. God is after one thing: our being patient in hope, that is, our persevering in hope. Why? The more we *hope* for salvation and redemption, the closer we draw to God. And, above all else, God wants us to draw near Him: fellowshipping, believing, trusting, loving, and hoping in Him.

3. The path of hope is the only way God could choose for salvation. For only as a man hopes in God will he draw near to God; and in reality, the more a man hopes in God, the closer he draws to God. The more he hopes, the more he will trust, believe, love, and depend upon God. And this is exactly what God is after; it is His plan and purpose for man and his world.

4. The believer's hope is expressed in several glorious ways. Note that God Himself is called "the God of hope" (Ro.15:13).
   a. The hope of "the resurrection of the dead" (Acts 23:6).
   b. The hope of the promise (Acts 26:6-7).
   c. The hope of Israel (Acts 28:20).
   d. The hope that is the object of faith (Ro.4:18; cp. Acts 26:6-7).
   e. The hope of the glory of God (Ro.5:2; Col.1:27; Tit.2:13).
   f. The hope that saves us (Ro.8:24).
   g. The hope that causes believers to endure afflictions (Ro.8:25; 1 Th.1:3).
   h. The hope of believers that comes through the Scripture (Ro.15:4).
   i. The hope which is a gift of the Holy Spirit (Ro.15:13).
   j. The hope that is one of the three essential traits of the believer (1 Cor.13:13).
   k. The hope in Christ (1 Cor.15:10; 1 Tim.1:1).
   l. The hope of righteousness (Gal.5:5).
   m. The hope of God's calling (Eph.1:18; 4:4).
   n. The hope which the lost do not have (Eph.2:12).
   o. The hope of the gospel (Col.1:23).
   p. The hope of salvation (1 Th.5:8).
   q. The "good hope" which God gives (2 Th.2:16).
   r. The hope of eternal life (Tit.1:2; 3:7; cp. Acts 2:26).
   s. The "blessed hope" of the Lord's return (Tit.2:13).
   t. The hope that stirs diligence and gives full assurance (Heb.6:11).
   u. The hope set before believers (Heb.6:18).
   v. The hope which anchors the believer's soul (Heb.6:19).
   w. The hope that stirs belief (Heb.11:1).
   x. The "living hope" of the believer (1 Pt.1:3).
   y. The hope that stirs believers to purify themselves (1 Jn.3:3).

1 Assurance 1: God works things out for those who love Him **2 Assurance 2: God has determined to fulfill His purpose for the believer** a. To conform him to Christ b. To honor Christ **3 Assurance 3: God has set the glorification of the believer—once-for-all** **4 Assurance 4: God has acted for the believer, not against him** a. He is our Savior b. He is our Provider c. He is our Justifier	**C. God Assures Deliverance (Freedom) from Struggling and Suffering, 8:28-39** 28 And we know that in all things God works for the good of those who love him, who have been called according to his purpose. 29 For those God foreknew he also predestined to be conformed to the likeness of his Son, that he might be the firstborn among many brothers. 30 And those he predestined, he also called; those he called, he also justified; those he justified, he also glorified. 31 What, then, shall we say in response to this? If God is for us, who can be against us? 32 He who did not spare his own Son, but gave him up for us all—how will he not also, along with him, graciously give us all things? 33 Who will bring any charge against those whom	God has chosen? It is God who justifies. 34 Who is he that condemns? Christ Jesus, who died—more than that, who was raised to life—is at the right hand of God and is also interceding for us. 35 Who shall separate us from the love of Christ? Shall trouble or hardship or persecution or famine or nakedness or danger or sword? 36 As it is written: "For your sake we face death all day long; we are considered as sheep to be slaughtered." 37 No, in all these things we are more than conquerors through him who loved us. 38 For I am convinced that neither death nor life, neither angels nor demons, neither the present nor the future, nor any powers, 39 Neither height nor depth, nor anything else in all creation, will be able to separate us from the love of God that is in Christ Jesus our Lord.	**5 Assurance 5: Christ does not condemn the believer** a. He died for us b. He arose for us c. He was exalted for us d. He intercedes for us **6 Assurance 6: Christ protects the believer from the severest circumstances** **7 Assurance 7: Christ protects the believer from the most extreme experiences & forces**

DIVISION VI

DELIVERANCE AND REDEMPTION: THE BELIEVER SHALL BE FREED FROM STRUGGLING AND SUFFERING BY THE SPIRIT, 8:1-39

C. God Assures Deliverance (Freedom) from Struggling and Suffering, 8:28-39

(8:28-39) **Introduction—Predestination—Man, Struggles—Suffering**: the glorious message of Romans is that God assures deliverance (freedom) from struggling and suffering—through Christ. This is the whole point of all that has been written before. Man desperately struggles against the pressures and forces both within himself and alien to himself. He struggles against the weight and discouragement of trials; against the pollution and corruption of life; against the relentless accusations and bombardments of conscience and law; against the pain and decay of his body; against the striking fear and hopelessness of an eternal judgment hereafter. He struggles against the unknown and against pain, hurt, sorrow, loneliness, alienation, aging, death, and hell (cp. Gal.5:17). And somehow, through his suffering and struggle throughout life, he feels that his suffering and struggling are *due to a wrong relationship with God*.

Therefore, man views his many problems as *really* being one supreme problem: how to get right with God. If he can establish the right relationship with God, he feels sure God will help him through his trials and take care of his future hereafter.

This is the very message of Romans. Man needs to get right with God, for he is under the condemnation and wrath of God (Ro.1:18-3:20). Man needs a right relationship with God; he needs to be justified, that is, declared righteous by God (Ro.3:21-5:21). Man needs to be freed from the struggle of sin, for sin corrupts and leads to death (Ro.6:1-23). Man needs to be freed from the bondage of law (spiritual le-

galism); for the law enslaves, accuses, condemns, and strikes hopelessness within the heart (Ro.7:1-25).

> **What a wretched man I am! Who will rescue me from this body of death? (Rom 7:24)**
> **Thanks be to God—through Jesus Christ our Lord! So then, I myself in my mind am a slave to God's law, but in the sinful nature a slave to the law of sin. (Rom 7:25a; cp.Ro.8:1-39).**

All the discussion in Chapter 8 up to this point has now moved to the summit. Those who love God and are called by Him will definitely be freed from the bondages and corruptions of this life and ushered into glory. God assures this. Nothing, absolutely nothing, shall prevent God's settled plan and purpose from coming about in the life of the believer. God's settled plan and purpose for the universe shall be consummated. He has determined two supreme things (Ro.8:29).

⇒ Believers shall be conformed to the image of His dear Son (v.29).
⇒ His Son shall have many brothers, among whom He is to be honored as the first (the most preeminent) Person (v.29).

1. Assurance 1: God works things out for those who love Him (v.28).
2. Assurance 2: God has determined to fulfill His purpose for the believer (v.29).

3. Assurance 3: God has set the glorification of the believer—once-for-all (v.30).
4. Assurance 4: God has acted for the believer, not against him (v.31-33).
5. Assurance 5: Christ does not condemn the believer (v.34).
6. Assurance 6: Christ protects the believer from the severest circumstances (v.35-37).
7. Assurance 7: Christ protects the believer from the most extreme experiences and forces (v.38-39).

1 (8:28) **Assurance—Call—Man, Struggles—Salvation**: God works all things out for those who love Him. This is the first assurance of deliverance. What a comforting declaration! Scripture actually declares that "in all things God works for the good" for the believer. Think about it: nothing could assure the believer any more than God working all things out for his good. Note four things.

1. The word "work" go well beyond the great events of the world. God does control the events of the world, but He controls much more. He rules over "all things"—all the events and happenings that occur in the life of the believer. He works "all things" out for good in behalf of His dear child.

2. The word "work" (sunergei) means to create and eliminate, place and replace, connect and group, interrelate and intermingle, shape and forge, press and stretch, move and operate, control and guide, arrange and influence. The word "work" is also present action which means that God is *continually* working all things together for good. God is in control of the believer's life. Daily, moment by moment, God is arranging and re-arranging all things for the believer's good.

3. The word "good" (agathon) means for the ultimate good. We cannot see the future; we cannot take a single event and see all the lines and ramifications that run from it. We cannot see all the things that result from one single event, much less see the results of every event. But God does; therefore, God takes all the events of our lives and works them out for our ultimate good.

4. There is, however, a limitation on this glorious promise, a limitation that desperately needs to be noted. God works all things out for good *only* to those who *love God* and are *called* according to His purpose.

   a. This fact is graphically seen in the Greek. The clause "of those who love Him" is placed first in the sentence: "But we know that to those who love God all things work together for good." Scripture makes sure the point is not missed. God *only* looks after the affairs of the person who loves Him.

Thought 1. Think about it for a moment, for it is the only reasonable conclusion. If a man does not love God—does not place his life into the hands of God—how can God take care of Him? If the man turns his back and walks away from God, how can God look after him? God is not going to force His care upon any of us. He is not going to make mechanical robots out of us, forcing us to live at His beck and call. Such is not love; it is only mechanical behavior. What God wants is love that flows from a heart that *chooses* to love Him. The choice is ours: we either turn our lives over to Him in love, or we continue to take our lives into our own hands.

   b. Note the words, "called according to his purpose." The believer's deliverance is purposed by God. God calls him for the glorious purpose of

being saved from the struggle and sufferings of this life.

Note a significant fact. The believer's *position* and *behavior* are both involved in the call of God.

⇒ *Positionally*, God chooses the believer by setting him apart through the Holy Spirit and through belief of the truth.

> But we ought always to thank God for you, brothers loved by the Lord, because from the beginning God chose you to be saved through the sanctifying work of the Spirit and through belief in the truth. He called you to this through our gospel, that you might share in the glory of our Lord Jesus Christ. (2 Th 2:13-14)

⇒ *In behavior*, God calls the believer to a life of purity and holiness.

> For God did not call us to be impure, but to live a holy life. (1 Th 4:7)

The point is this: God delivers the person who is positioned in Christ and who lives a pure and holy life. The person who truly *loves God* and is living a godly life is the person who experiences all things being worked out for his good. It is the godly person who loves God that will be delivered from the struggling and suffering of this corrupt world.

> No temptation has seized you except what is common to man. And God is faithful; he will not let you be tempted beyond what you can bear. But when you are tempted, he will also provide a way out so that you can stand up under it. (1 Cor 10:13)
> A righteous man may have many troubles, but the LORD delivers him from them all; (Psa 34:19)
> So do not fear, for I am with you; do not be dismayed, for I am your God. I will strengthen you and help you; I will uphold you with my righteous right hand. (Isa 41:10)
> When you pass through the waters, I will be with you; and when you pass through the rivers, they will not sweep over you. When you walk through the fire, you will not be burned; the flames will not set you ablaze. (Isa 43:2)

Thought 1. Contrast the unspiritual, carnal attitude of Jacob and the spiritual attitude of Paul.

⇒ Jacob said, "Everything is against me!" (Gen.42:36).
⇒ Paul said, "In all things God works for the good of those who love him" (Ro.8:28).

2 (8:29) **Assurance—Foreknowledge—Predestination—Conformed—Image—Salvation**: God has determined to fulfill His purpose for the believer. This is the second assurance of deliverance. Note three significant points.

1. This passage is often abused and misused. It is not dealing so much with theology or philosophy, but more with the spiritual experience of the Christian believer. If

the pure logic of philosophy and theology are applied, then the passage says that God chooses some for heaven and others for a terrible hell. But this is simply not the meaning God intends for the passage. What God wants believers to do is to take heart, for He has assured their salvation.

God knows the suffering that believers go through daily (cp. Ro.8:28-39). God "foreknew" even before the foundation of the world (v.29). But no matter how great the suffering, no matter how great the opposition, no matter how great the struggle, God is going to complete His purpose for believers. God has "predestined [believers] to be conformed to the likeness of His Son," and absolutely nothing can change that. Why? "That Christ might be the first-born [have the preeminence] among many brothers" (Ro.8:29).

God loves His Son in the most supreme way possible. God has ordained that His Son shall have many brothers (adopted brothers) who will love and serve Him as the first-born, that is, as the first Person or the most preeminent Person of the universe. God has ordained that Jesus Christ shall hold the highest rank and position: that He be the exalted Head of all creation and the One to whom all men look (cp. Col.1:15, 18). Therefore, God is going to allow nothing to permanently defeat believers. God is going to allow no fallen child of His to ever remain down permanently. God is going to fulfill His purpose in every child of His, and nothing can stop His purpose. Jesus Christ, His Son, will have a *multitude of brothers and sisters* who worship and serve Him throughout eternity.

2. Believers will be conformed to the likeness of God's dear Son. The words "conformed to the likeness" (summorphous tes eikonos) mean both an inward and an outward likeness.

   a. "Conformed" (summorphous) means the very same form or likeness as Christ. Within our nature—our being, our person—we shall be made just like Christ. As He is perfect and eternal—without disease and pain, sin and death—so we shall be perfected just like Him. We shall be transformed into His very likeness.

   b. "Likeness" (eikonos) means a derived or a given image. The image of Christ is not something which believers merit or for which they work; it is not a likeness that comes from their own nature or character. No man can earn or produce the perfection and eternal life possessed by Christ. The likeness of Christ, His perfection and life, is a gift of God. To be conformed to the likeness of God's Son means...

- to become a participant in the divine nature (2 Pt.1:4).
- to be adopted as a son of God (Eph.1:5).
- to be holy and blameless in His sight (Eph.1:4; 4:24).
- to bear the image of the heavenly: which is an imperishable, immortal body (1 Cor.15:49-54; cp. 1 Cor.15:42-44).
- to have one's body transformed just like His glorious body (Ph.3:21).
- to be changed (transformed) into the same likeness of the Lord (2 Cor.3:18).
- to be recreated just like Him (1 Jn.3:2-3).

3. Note what it is that assures the believer's deliverance from the suffering and struggling of this world. It is two things.

   a. The foreknowledge of God. The word "foreknew" (proginosko) is used three different ways in Scripture. It means...

- to know something beforehand, ahead of time.
- to know something intimately by loving and accepting and approving it.
- to elect, foreordain, and predetermine something.

The present passage is interpreted differently by scholars. Note that the second and third meanings are much the same. When a person is loved and approved, selection or election is involved. The person becomes a very special or select person.

Again, the point to see is not the pure logic of the theological or philosophical argument. This is not God's purpose in this passage. God's purpose is to assure the believer: the believer is going to be conformed to the likeness of Christ, and nothing can stop the glorious process. God foreknew the fact, saw it even before the world was ever founded. He has always loved and approved the believer, electing and ordaining him from the very beginning (see DEEPER STUDY #3, Foreknowledge—Acts 2:23 for more detailed discussion).

That have been known for ages. (Acts 15:18)

For those God foreknew he also predestined to be conformed to the likeness of his Son, that he might be the firstborn among many brothers. (Rom 8:29)

God did not reject his people [Israel], whom he foreknew. (Rom 11:2)

For you know that it was not with perishable things such as silver or gold that you were redeemed from the empty way of life handed down to you from your forefathers, but with the precious blood of Christ, a lamb without blemish or defect. He was chosen before the creation of the world, but was revealed in these last times for your sake. (1 Pet 1:18-20)

Nevertheless, God's solid foundation stands firm, sealed with this inscription: "The Lord knows those who are his," and, "Everyone who confesses the name of the Lord must turn away from wickedness." (2 Tim 2:19)

Who have been chosen according to the foreknowledge of God the Father, through the sanctifying work of the Spirit, for obedience to Jesus Christ and sprinkling by his blood: Grace and peace be yours in abundance. (1 Pet 1:2)

   b. The predestination of God. The word predestination (proorisen) means to destine or appoint before, to foreordain, to predetermine. The basic Greek word (proorizo) means to *mark off or to set off* the boundaries of something. The idea is a glorious picture of what God is doing for the believer. The boundary is marked and set off for the believer: the boundary of being conformed to the likeness of God's dear Son. The believer shall be made just like Christ, conformed to His very likeness. Nothing can stop God's purpose for the believer. It is predestined, set, and marked off. The believer may struggle and suffer through the sin and shame of this world; he may even stumble and fall or become discouraged and downhearted. But if he is a genuine child of God, he will not be defeated, not totally. He will soon arise from his fall and begin to follow Christ again. He is predestined to be a brother of Christ, to worship and serve Christ throughout all eternity. And Christ will not be disappointed. God loves His Son too much to allow Him to be disappointed by losing a single brother. Jesus Christ will have His joy fulfilled; He will see every brother of His face to face, conformed perfectly to His image. He will have the worship and service of every brother chosen to be His by God the Father. The believer's eternal destiny, that of being an adopted brother to the Lord Jesus Christ, is determined. The believer can rest assured of this glorious truth. God has predestined him to be delivered from the suffering and struggling of this sinful world. (See notes, *Predestination*—Jn.6:37; 6:39; 6:44-46 for God's part and man's part in salvation. See DEEPER STUDY # 3—Acts 2:23; DEEPER STUDY #1—Ro.9:10-13; note—9:14-33 for more discussion.)

> For he chose us in him before the creation of the world to be holy and blameless in his sight. In love he predestined us to be adopted as his sons through Jesus Christ, in accordance with his pleasure and will— (Eph 1:4-5)
> According to his eternal purpose which he accomplished in Christ Jesus our Lord. In him and through faith in him we may approach God with freedom and confidence. (Eph 3:11-12)

3 (8:30) **Glory of Believer**: God has set the glorification of the believer once-for-all. This is the third assurance of deliverance. It must be remembered throughout this passage that Scripture is talking about the genuine believer. A genuine believer is a person who sincerely believes in Jesus Christ and diligently seeks to please Him by living soberly, righteously, and godly in this present world (Tit.2:11-13). It is the genuine believer whose glorification is predestined, set forever and ever by God. The true believer can rest in this glorious truth, for God has done three wonderful things for him. God has *called, justified, and glorified him*. Note that all three steps are in the past tense; all three steps are something already accomplished. The believer's glorification has already taken place in the plan and mind of God. God already sees believers glorified; He already sees believers in His presence. It is assured and predestined—already written down in the annals of heaven, never to be erased.

Again, does this mean that some are destined to hell and some to heaven? No, a thousand times, no! This is not the purpose of this Scripture. God's purpose is to give enormous assurance to the true believer: he shall be delivered from the struggling and suffering of this sinful world. He is going to be freed—if he is a true believer—freed from all the sin and shame, failure and shortcoming, pain and death. He is going to be glorified right along with God's dear Son, the Lord Jesus Christ.

1. God has *called* the true believer. Some time ago the Spirit called and stirred the heart of the true believer to come to Christ. The believer responded to the call. Scripture definitely teaches that the believer had a choice. He could have chosen to respond or not to respond. (Cp. Rev.22:17.) Thank God he responded and came to Christ. Therefore, the call was *effective*; the call worked. The be-

liever did respond to Christ. (See note, *Draw*—Jn.6:44-46 for God's part and man's part in salvation.)

> "Come to me, all you who are weary and burdened, and I will give you rest. (Mat 11:28)
> We are therefore Christ's ambassadors, as though God were making his appeal through us. We implore you on Christ's behalf: Be reconciled to God. (2 Cor 5:20)
> Here I am! I stand at the door and knock. If anyone hears my voice and opens the door, I will come in and eat with him, and he with me. (Rev 3:20)
> The Spirit and the bride say, "Come!" And let him who hears say, "Come!" Whoever is thirsty, let him come; and whoever wishes, let him take the free gift of the water of life. (Rev 22:17)
> "Come now, let us reason together," says the LORD. "Though your sins are like scarlet, they shall be as white as snow; though they are red as crimson, they shall be like wool. (Isa 1:18)
> "Come, all you who are thirsty, come to the waters; and you who have no money, come, buy and eat! Come, buy wine and milk without money and without cost. (Isa 55:1)

2. God has justified the believer. Again, note the past tense. Justification has *already taken place* for the true believer (see note, *Justification*—Ro.5:1).

Thought 1. The point is clear. If the believer has been truly *called*, if he has been truly saved, then his deliverance from struggling and suffering is assured. His deliverance is a past fact and it is set eternally by God. No matter how deeply the believer senses his shortcoming and failure, his struggle with the sin and suffering of this world, he is a child of God. Every time he comes short or stumbles and falls, he needs to get up and begin all over again. He must not become discouraged and defeated, self-accusing and incriminating, feeling unworthy and undeserving, unwanted and rejected. Such a state of mind is one the most useful strategies of the devil—a strategy which he uses to defeat believers by the multitudes. God *has called* the believer, so he must arise and begin to diligently follow Christ once again. Every believer who is walking about defeated—no matter how great his fall—should arise right now and turn back to Christ. This is our call, our duty.

> And that is what some of you were. But you were washed, you were sanctified, you were justified in the name of the Lord Jesus Christ and by the Spirit of our God. (1 Cor 6:11)
> My dear children, I write this to you so that you will not sin. But if anybody does sin, we have one who speaks to the Father in our defense—Jesus Christ, the Righteous One. He is the atoning sacrifice for our sins, and not only for ours but also for the sins of the whole world. (1 John 2:1-2)

Paul the apostle, who was a converted murderer, is a dynamic example of this victorious attitude, the very attitude needed so desperately by all believers.

> **Brothers, I do not consider myself yet to have taken hold of it. But one thing I do: Forgetting what is behind and straining toward what is ahead, I press on toward the goal to win the prize for which God has called me heavenward in Christ Jesus. (Phil 3:13-14; cp. Job 17:9; Ps.84:7; Pr.4:18; Heb.12:4).)**

3. God has glorified the believer. This, too, is past tense: the glorification of the believer is an accomplished fact, a fact that has already taken place in God's mind and plan. God already sees and counts the believer as *glorified* in His presence for eternity (see DEEPER STUDY #1,2,3—Ro.2:7; DEEPER STUDY # 1—3:23; DEEPER STUDY #1—Jn.17:22 for what the believer's glorification involves).

> **I consider that our present sufferings are not worth comparing with the glory that will be revealed in us. (Rom 8:18)**
> **For our light and momentary troubles are achieving for us an eternal glory that far outweighs them all. (2 Cor 4:17)**
> **I pray also that the eyes of your heart may be enlightened in order that you may know the hope to which he has called you, the riches of his glorious inheritance in the saints, (Eph 1:18)**
> **Who, by the power that enables him to bring everything under his control, will transform our lowly bodies so that they will be like his glorious body. (Phil 3:21)**
> **When Christ, who is your life, appears, then you also will appear with him in glory. (Col 3:4)**
> **Therefore I endure everything for the sake of the elect, that they too may obtain the salvation that is in Christ Jesus, with eternal glory. (2 Tim 2:10)**
> **To the elders among you, I appeal as a fellow elder, a witness of Christ's sufferings and one who also will share in the glory to be revealed: (1 Pet 5:1)**
> **There will be no more night. They will not need the light of a lamp or the light of the sun, for the Lord God will give them light. And they will reign for ever and ever. (Rev 22:5)**
> **You guide me with your counsel, and afterward you will take me into glory. (Psa 73:24)**

4 (8:31-33) **God, Work of—Assurance—Jesus Christ, Death**: God has acted for the believer, not against him. This is the fourth assurance of deliverance. This is the greatest truth in all the world. God did not have to act for man, but He did. God loves every man, no matter his condition or sin and shame. Therefore, believers can rest assured that nothing, absolutely nothing shall ever separate them from the plan and purpose of God. God's love is absolute. It is perfect. And God shall have His perfect love expressed by completing His perfect plan and purpose for each life. The believer can have absolute assurance that God will work all things out for his good, even things that fail and are painful to the heart. God shall deliver the believer from the struggling and suffering of this world. The

true believer shall be conformed to the likeness of Christ and glorified with Him (v.29-30).

The point is this: God Himself is the believer's assurance. God Himself has acted for the believer; He has done everything necessary and then more: "If God is for us, who can be against us?"

1. God is our Savior. It was God who "did not spare His own Son, but gave Him up for us all" (v.32). The words "did not spare" (ouk epheisato) mean that God did not hold back or refrain from giving His Son; He did not refuse or even hesitate to give His Son. The picture is that of God weighing man's eternal separation from Him against the sacrifice of His Son. He had a choice to make and He made it; He deliberately chose to sacrifice His Son for us. God knew exactly what He was doing. He wanted man delivered from this struggling and suffering world, and there was only one way for man to be saved:

⇒ Someone had to bear man's penalty for transgression and sin, which was the judgment of death.

Therefore, God handed His own Son over to die *for* us—in our behalf, in our stead, in our place, as our substitute. God *did not spare* His own Son; He gave Christ Jesus up for us all. What a glorious, marvelous, wonderful love! And just how wonderful His love is can be clearly seen in this: it was while we were sinners, acting and rebelling against God, that He gave His Son to die for us.

> **But God demonstrates his own love for us in this: While we were still sinners, Christ died for us. (Rom 5:8)**
> **You see, at just the right time, when we were still powerless, Christ died for the ungodly. (Rom 5:6)**
> **"For God so loved the world that he gave his one and only Son, that whoever believes in him shall not perish but have eternal life. (John 3:16)**
> **Who gave himself for our sins to rescue us from the present evil age, according to the will of our God and Father, (Gal 1:4)**
> **We all, like sheep, have gone astray, each of us has turned to his own way; and the LORD has laid on him the iniquity of us all. (Isa 53:6)**

(See notes, *Jesus Christ, Death*—Jn.3:16; DEEPER STUDY #2—Acts 2:23 for more discussion. Cp. 1 Pt.2:24; 3:18.)

2. God is our Provider. Since God has done such a great and glorious thing, how shall He not also give us all things? Giving His own Son for us was the greatest gift in all the world; therefore, He is bound to give us everything else. Nothing could ever cost God anything close to the price He has paid in giving up His Son; therefore, God shall give us everything else. Note three points.

a. God's provision includes spiritual, eternal, and material gifts.

⇒ The spiritual provision is the fruit of the Spirit (See note—Eph.1:3.)

> **But the fruit of the Spirit is love, joy, peace, patience, kindness, goodness, faithfulness, gentleness and self-control. Against such things there is no law. (Gal 5:22-23)**
> **Praise be to the God and Father of our Lord Jesus Christ, who has blessed**

us in the heavenly realms with every spiritual blessing in Christ. (Eph 1:3)

⇒ The eternal provision is deliverance from the struggling and suffering of this sinful world. It is the gift of eternal life, of living gloriously conformed to the image of His dear Son, Jesus Christ (see note, pt.2—Ro.8:29 for just what this means).

In order that in the coming ages he might show the incomparable riches of his grace, expressed in his kindness to us in Christ Jesus. (Eph 2:7)

⇒ The material gifts are the necessities of life (see outline and notes—Mt.6:25-34).

So do not worry, saying, 'What shall we eat?' or 'What shall we drink?' or 'What shall we wear?' But seek first his kingdom and his righteousness, and all these things will be given to you as well. (Mat 6:31, 33)
And my God will meet all your needs according to his glorious riches in Christ Jesus. (Phil 4:19)

b. The provision is *freely* given. God's gift of His Son was freely given; therefore, all that God provides for man is freely given. No man can merit or earn God's provision. God provides and meets the need of the believer because He loves the believer.

For it is by grace you have been saved, through faith—and this not from yourselves, it is the gift of God—not by works, so that no one can boast. (Eph 2:8-9)

c. The provision of God comes through Christ and through Him alone. Note the words "with Him." It is *with Christ* that God gives us all things. If we are *with Christ*, then all things are given to us. We shall be delivered from struggling and suffering. Believers can rest assured of this. No matter how much we struggle and suffer through the sin and shame of this world, God will see us through it all. He is going to conform us to the glorious likeness of His Son.

Jesus answered her, "If you knew the gift of God and who it is that asks you for a drink, you would have asked him and he would have given you living water." (John 4:10)
For the wages of sin is death, but the gift of God is eternal life in Christ Jesus our Lord. (Rom 6:23)
Thanks be to God for his indescribable gift! (2 Cor 9:15)

3. God is our Justifier. This is the most glorious truth: God does not charge us with sin. In fact, He does not bring any charge against us. He justifies us (see DEEPER STUDY # 1,2, *Justification*—Ro.4:22; 5:1 for more discussion).
Note the question: Who shall bring any charge against God's elect? It is God; only God can charge us with sin and shame. But note: if we have truly trusted Jesus Christ as our Savior, if we are one of God's elect, he does not charge us with sin. He justifies us. He forgives our sin and

counts us righteous in Christ Jesus. If we are God's child, no one can charge us with anything. We are God's; we belong to God. No one can charge, count, or doom us to be...

- a failure
- a detriment
- a shame
- a sinner
- an embarrassment
- hopeless
- helpless
- defeated
- lost
- unusable
- unworthy
- of no value

Man is not our judge; therefore, man cannot judge these things to be true of us—only God can. God is our Judge, and this is the glorious truth: God does not judge His elect. He does not lay sin and shame against His children; He justifies His children. No matter how much we have struggled and suffered through the sin and shame of this world, God delivers us. No matter how far we have fallen, no matter how discouraged we have become, if we are truly God's child, He picks us up and justifies us in Christ Jesus and continues to conform us to the likeness or image of His dear Son. God does not leave us down and defeated, nor does He go around charging us with sin and shame. God justifies us and continues His work of forgiveness and grace in our lives. (See note, *Grace*—Ro.6:14-15 for more discussion. Also see note, *Foreknowledge and Predestination*—Ro.8:29 for a discussion of the elect.)

Do you not know that the wicked will not inherit the kingdom of God? Do not be deceived: Neither the sexually immoral nor idolaters nor adulterers nor male prostitutes nor homosexual offenders Nor thieves nor the greedy nor drunkards nor slanderers nor swindlers will inherit the kingdom of God. And that is what some of you were. But you were washed, you were sanctified, you were justified in the name of the Lord Jesus Christ and by the Spirit of our God. (1 Cor 6:9-11)
Being confident of this, that he who began a good work in you will carry it on to completion until the day of Christ Jesus. (Phil 1:6)
Who are you to judge someone else's servant? To his own master he stands or falls. And he will stand, for the Lord is able to make him stand. (Rom 14:4)
So we say with confidence, "The Lord is my helper; I will not be afraid. What can man do to me?" (Heb 13:6)
He will have no fear of bad news; his heart is steadfast, trusting in the LORD. (Psa 112:7)
But whoever listens to me will live in safety and be at ease, without fear of harm." (Prov 1:33)

5 (8:34) **Jesus Christ, Work of—Salvation:** Christ does not condemn the believer. This is the fifth assurance of deliverance. Note how direct and forceful the question is: "Who is he that condemns?" It is Christ; only Christ can condemn us for our sin and shame. But the glorious news is that Christ does not condemn us. On the contrary, the very opposite is true. Christ does four wonderful things for us.

1. Christ has died for us. Christ is our glorious Savior. When we *honestly* come to Him, He does not condemn us

152

for our sin and shame; He forgives us. He is able to forgive us because He died for us.

⇒ Our sins are a shame, for sin is rebellion against God. Sin acts against God, fights and struggles against God. Sin goes against all that God stands for. Sin is insurrection against God; it is the crime of high treason against God. Sin is the most terrible act that can be done against God.

Therefore, we deserve to be condemned by God and put to death for sin. But we do not have to face condemnation. Christ has already paid the penalty for sin. Christ has already been condemned and executed for our transgression against God. This is the glorious love of Christ. He has already died *for us*: in our place, in our stead, as our substitute. Therefore when we sincerely come to Christ, He does not condemn us; He loves us and forgives our sin and shame. This is the very purpose of His death—to free us from sin, from its penalty and condemnation.

> You see, at just the right time, when we were still powerless, Christ died for the ungodly. (Rom 5:6)
> But God demonstrates his own love for us in this: While we were still sinners, Christ died for us. (Rom 5:8)
> For if, when we were God's enemies, we were reconciled to him through the death of his Son, how much more, having been reconciled, shall we be saved through his life! (Rom 5:10)
> He himself bore our sins in his body on the tree, so that we might die to sins and live for righteousness; by his wounds you have been healed. (1 Pet 2:24)
> For Christ died for sins once for all, the righteous for the unrighteous, to bring you to God. He was put to death in the body but made alive by the Spirit, (1 Pet 3:18)
> But you know that he appeared so that he might take away our sins. And in him is no sin. (1 John 3:5)
> We all, like sheep, have gone astray, each of us has turned to his own way; and the LORD has laid on him the iniquity of us all. (Isa 53:6)

2. Christ has risen from the dead for us. Christ is our risen Lord. His resurrection does two marvelous things for the believer.

a. The resurrection of the Lord proves that God was perfectly *satisfied* with the death of Jesus Christ. What Christ did—His dying for our sins—was *acceptable* to God; therefore, God has *accepted* Jesus' death *for us*. God has *approved* His dying *for us*. God's divine justice was perfectly satisfied with Christ dying for us. This is clearly seen in the resurrection of Jesus Christ: if God had not been satisfied, He would have left Jesus in the grave. But thank God, God was satisfied, so He raised up Jesus to live forever as the Sovereign Savior of the world.

> And who through the Spirit of holiness was declared with power to be the Son of God by his resurrection from the dead: Jesus Christ our Lord. (Rom 1:4)

> He was delivered over to death for our sins and was raised to life for our justification. (Rom 4:25)
> For he has set a day when he will judge the world with justice by the man he has appointed. He has given proof of this to all men by raising him from the dead." (Acts 17:31)
> And if Christ has not been raised, your faith is futile; you are still in your sins. (1 Cor 15:17)

b. The resurrection of the Lord gives the believer a new life, making the believer a *new creation* and a *new man* (see note, pt.2—Ro.6:3-5 for discussion).

> We were therefore buried with him through baptism into death in order that, just as Christ was raised from the dead through the glory of the Father, we too may live a new life. (Rom 6:4)
> The death he died, he died to sin once for all; but the life he lives, he lives to God. In the same way, count yourselves dead to sin but alive to God in Christ Jesus. (Rom 6:10-11)
> For we who are alive are always being given over to death for Jesus' sake, so that his life may be revealed in our mortal body. (2 Cor 4:11)
> And he died for all, that those who live should no longer live for themselves but for him who died for them and was raised again. Therefore, if anyone is in Christ, he is a new creation; the old has gone, the new has come! (2 Cor 5:15, 17)
> And his incomparably great power for us who believe. That power is like the working of his mighty strength, which he exerted in Christ when he raised him from the dead and seated him at his right hand in the heavenly realms, (Eph 1:19-20)
> Having been buried with him in baptism and raised with him through your faith in the power of God, who raised him from the dead. (Col 2:12)
> Since, then, you have been raised with Christ, set your hearts on things above, where Christ is seated at the right hand of God. (Col 3:1)

3. Christ has been exalted for us. He is our exalted Lord. He sits face to face with God at His right hand. This gives two assurances to the believer.

a. The believer shall also be exalted into the presence of God. Just as Christ lives face to face with God, the believer shall also live face to face with God throughout all eternity. (See note, pt.2—Ro.8:29 for discussion. See DEEPER STUDY #1—Ro.3:23 for more discussion.)

> If we have been united with him like this in his death, we will certainly also be united with him in his resurrection. (Rom 6:5)
> Now if we died with Christ, we believe that we will also live with him. For we know that since Christ was raised from the dead, he cannot die again; death no longer

has mastery over him. The death he died, he died to sin once for all; but the life he lives, he lives to God. (Rom 6:8-10)

And if the Spirit of him who raised Jesus from the dead is living in you, he who raised Christ from the dead will also give life to your mortal bodies through his Spirit, who lives in you. (Rom 8:11)

The Spirit himself testifies with our spirit that we are God's children. Now if we are children, then we are heirs—heirs of God and co-heirs with Christ, if indeed we share in his sufferings in order that we may also share in his glory. (Rom 8:16-17)

In my Father's house are many rooms; if it were not so, I would have told you. I am going there to prepare a place for you. And if I go and prepare a place for you, I will come back and take you to be with me that you also may be where I am. (John 14:2-3)

"Father, I want those you have given me to be with me where I am, and to see my glory, the glory you have given me because you loved me before the creation of the world. (John 17:24)

When Christ, who is your life, appears, then you also will appear with him in glory. (Col 3:4)

b. The Lord Jesus Christ is exalted as the Sovereign and majestic Lord of the universe. He is the Ruler who reigns and rules over all, who possesses all might and power and is full of all wisdom and truth. He is the One who is going to destroy and utterly eliminate sin and evil in the world. He is the One who is going to establish a kingdom of righteousness and justice, love and truth in the new heavens and earth.

Which he exerted in Christ when he raised him from the dead and seated him at his right hand in the heavenly realms, far above all rule and authority, power and dominion, and every title that can be given, not only in the present age but also in the one to come. (Eph 1:20-21)

Therefore God exalted him to the highest place and gave him the name that is above every name, that at the name of Jesus every knee should bow, in heaven and on earth and under the earth, and every tongue confess that Jesus Christ is Lord, to the glory of God the Father. (Phil 2:9-11)

The Son is the radiance of God's glory and the exact representation of his being, sustaining all things by his powerful word. After he had provided purification for sins, he sat down at the right hand of the Majesty in heaven. (Heb 1:3)

Who has gone into heaven and is at God's right hand—with angels, authorities and powers in submission to him. (1 Pet 3:22)

But the day of the Lord will come like a thief. The heavens will disappear with a roar; the elements will be destroyed by fire, and the earth and everything in it will be laid bare. Since everything will be de-stroyed in this way, what kind of people ought you to be? You ought to live holy and godly lives as you look forward to the day of God and speed its coming. That day will bring about the destruction of the heavens by fire, and the elements will melt in the heat. But in keeping with his promise we are looking forward to a new heaven and a new earth, the home of righteousness. (2 Pet 3:10-13)

To him who overcomes, I will give the right to sit with me on my throne, just as I overcame and sat down with my Father on his throne. (Rev 3:21)

Note: it is Jesus Christ (and not another) who rules and reigns over the universe. This stirs enormous assurance in the hearts of genuine believers. Why? Because Jesus Christ has demonstrated His glorious love and care for the world. He not only can, but He will look after us and work all things out for good until He returns (v.28). The *control of evil* in the world and our lives are under His care. He is working all things out for good to those of us who truly love Him and are called according to His purpose (v.28).

So do not worry, saying, 'What shall we eat?' or 'What shall we drink?' or 'What shall we wear?' But seek first his kingdom and his righteousness, and all these things will be given to you as well. (Mat 6:31, 33)

And teaching them to obey everything I have commanded you. And surely I am with you always, to the very end of the age." (Mat 28:20)

Indeed, the very hairs of your head are all numbered. Don't be afraid; you are worth more than many sparrows. (Luke 12:7)

I give them eternal life, and they shall never perish; no one can snatch them out of my hand. (John 10:28)

And we know that in all things God works for the good of those who love him, who have been called according to his purpose. (Rom 8:28)

Keep your lives free from the love of money and be content with what you have, because God has said, "Never will I leave you; never will I forsake you." (Heb 13:5)

Cast all your anxiety on him because he cares for you. (1 Pet 5:7)

To him who is able to keep you from falling and to present you before his glorious presence without fault and with great joy— (Jude 1:24)

I am with you and will watch over you wherever you go, and I will bring you back to this land. I will not leave you until I have done what I have promised you." (Gen 28:15)

Indeed, he who watches over Israel will neither slumber nor sleep. (Psa 121:4)

When you pass through the waters, I will be with you; and when you pass through the rivers, they will not sweep over you. When you walk through the fire, you will not be burned; the flames will not set you ablaze. (Isa 43:2)

4. Christ intercedes for us before the throne of God. He is our great Intercessor, our Mediator and Advocate who stands between God and man. It is Christ Jesus who brings us to God and who makes redemption, even the forgiveness of our sins, possible (Eph.1:7).

⇒ It is His advocacy, the advocacy of His death and resurrection for us, that forgives our sins.

> **My dear children, I write this to you so that you will not sin. But if anybody does sin, we have one who speaks to the Father in our defense—Jesus Christ, the Righteous One. He is the atoning sacrifice for our sins, and not only for ours but also for the sins of the whole world. (1 John 2:1-2)**

⇒ It is His intercession, the intercession of His death and resurrection for us, that saves us.

> **He was delivered over to death for our sins and was raised to life for our justification. (Rom 4:25)**

⇒ It is His presence in heaven and His plea, the *plea* of His death and resurrection *for us*, that opens the door of heaven to us.

> **For Christ did not enter a man-made sanctuary that was only a copy of the true one; he entered heaven itself, now to appear for us in God's presence. (Heb 9:24)**

The point is this. The believer has the greatest assurance imaginable: he shall be delivered from the struggling and suffering of this world. No matter the sin and shame of his life, if he truly comes to Christ, he is not condemned. He is not judged for sin, no matter how terrible or how far he has fallen. If he will only come to Christ, Christ will deliver him. Christ will not leave him down and discouraged and defeated. Christ will not even scold or reproach him. Christ will receive His dear child with open arms.

> **In him we have redemption through his blood, the forgiveness of sins, in accordance with the riches of God's grace (Eph 1:7)**
> **If we confess our sins, he is faithful and just and will forgive us our sins and purify us from all unrighteousness. (1 John 1:9)**
> **"Come to me, all you who are weary and burdened, and I will give you rest. (Mat 11:28)**

6 (8:35-37) **Trials, Deliverance from—Salvation—God, Love of:** Christ protects the believer from the severest circumstances. This is the sixth assurance of deliverance, and it is the most wonderful assurance imaginable. "Who [or what] shall separate us from the love of Christ?" Too many people, even believers, feel that God does not love them, that He just could not love them. They feel unworthy of His love, for they come too short, are too disobedient, and fail too often. How could God possibly love them when they go against His will so much? The results of such feelings are...

- a sense of unworthiness
- a downing of oneself
- a sense of discouragement
- an accusing of oneself
- a low self-esteem
- a defeated life

Note a crucial point: such feelings totally contradict Scripture. Look at the verse: "Who [or what] shall separate us from the love of Christ?" There is no circumstance, no situation, no event that can cause Christ to turn away from us. No matter how terrible or severe the situation, it cannot separate the true believer from the love of Christ. Christ loves the believer regardless of the circumstance, and He longs to be reconciled to the believer. No more severe circumstance can be imagined than the ones given:

⇒ Trouble: to undergo struggle, trials, temptation, suffering, or affliction.
⇒ Hardship: to suffer anguish, trouble, strain, agony; not knowing which way to turn or what to do.
⇒ Persecution: to be abused, mocked, ridiculed, shamed, mistreated, ignored, neglected, harrassed, attacked, or injured.
⇒ Famine: to have no food, to be starving and have no way to secure food.
⇒ Nakedness: to be stripped of all clothes and earthly comforts; to be bare, having all earthly possessions taken away.
⇒ Danger: to be exposed to the most severe risks; to be confronted with the most terrible dangers to one's body, mind, soul, property, family, and loved ones.
⇒ Sword: to be killed; to suffer martyrdom.

Imagine a person experiencing all this. What would his thoughts be? Would he feel that he had been forsaken by God? In the midst of so much dark trouble, would he believe that God loved him?

Scripture declares loudly and clearly that God does love him. There is absolutely nothing—no matter how dark and depressing, no matter how severe—that can separate the believer from the love of Christ. Circumstances are not evidence that God does not love us. God loves us no matter what the circumstances may be.

But believers must always remember: they are going to suffer while they are in this world. In fact, the world is going to count them as sheep for the slaughter, rejecting and persecuting them (Ps.44:22). The world is going to persecute believers as long as believers continue to live for Christ. Their lives of godliness convict the world, and the world rejects godliness (see note, *Persecution*—Mt.5:10-12 for why believers are persecuted).

However, note what is said. No matter the circumstances, we are more than conquerors through Christ who has loved us (v.37). No matter the circumstances and their severity, Christ will carry us through all, strengthening and encouraging us. We cannot lose, no matter the severity of the situation. Christ loves us and is going to look after and take care of us. The believer can rest assured, Christ protects him from the severest circumstances:

⇒ Christ meets all the material necessities of life.

> **So do not worry, saying, 'What shall we eat?' or 'What shall we drink?' or 'What shall we wear?' But seek first his kingdom and his righteousness, and all these things will be given to you as well. (Mat 6:31, 33)**

⇒ Christ gives us rest.

> "Come to me, all you who are weary and burdened, and I will give you rest. (Mat 11:28)

⇒ Christ gives us peace.

> Peace I leave with you; my peace I give you. I do not give to you as the world gives. Do not let your hearts be troubled and do not be afraid. (John 14:27)
> "I have told you these things, so that in me you may have peace. In this world you will have trouble. But take heart! I have overcome the world." (John 16:33)

⇒ Christ provides an escape from temptation.

> No temptation has seized you except what is common to man. And God is faithful; he will not let you be tempted beyond what you can bear. But when you are tempted, he will also provide a way out so that you can stand up under it. (1 Cor 10:13)

⇒ Christ comforts us through all trials.

> Praise be to the God and Father of our Lord Jesus Christ, the Father of compassion and the God of all comfort, who comforts us in all our troubles, so that we can comfort those in any trouble with the comfort we ourselves have received from God. (2 Cor 1:3-4)

⇒ Christ supplies all our needs.

> I can do everything through him who gives me strength. (Phil 4:13)

⇒ Christ delivers us through persecution.

> Consider him who endured such opposition from sinful men, so that you will not grow weary and lose heart. (Heb 12:3)
> Dear friends, do not be surprised at the painful trial you are suffering, as though something strange were happening to you. But rejoice that you participate in the sufferings of Christ, so that you may be overjoyed when his glory is revealed. (1 Pet 4:12-13)

⇒ Christ delivers us into His very presence, giving us eternal life if we are martyred.

> The Lord will rescue me from every evil attack and will bring me safely to his heavenly kingdom. To him be glory for ever and ever. Amen. (2 Tim 4:18)
> To him who overcomes, I will give the right to sit with me on my throne, just as I overcame and sat down with my Father on his throne. (Rev 3:21)

⇒ Christ cares for us no matter the situation.

> Cast all your anxiety on him because he cares for you. (1 Pet 5:7)

⇒ Christ enables us to overcome the world.

> For everyone born of God overcomes the world. This is the victory that has overcome the world, even our faith. (1 John 5:4)

⇒ Christ strengthens those whose hearts are fully committed to Him.

> For the eyes of the LORD range throughout the earth to strengthen those whose hearts are fully committed to him. You have done a foolish thing, and from now on you will be at war." (2 Chr 16:9)

⇒ Christ delivers us from fear.

> So do not fear, for I am with you; do not be dismayed, for I am your God. I will strengthen you and help you; I will uphold you with my righteous right hand. (Isa 41:10)

⇒ Christ sustains and supports the aged believer.

> Even to your old age and gray hairs I am he, I am he who will sustain you. I have made you and I will carry you; I will sustain you and I will rescue you. (Isa 46:4)

7 (8:38-39) **Trials, Deliverance from—Salvation—God, Love of**: Christ protects believers from the most extreme experiences and forces. This is the seventh assurance of deliverance. There is nothing in the universe that can separate the believer from the love of God which is in Christ Jesus our Lord. The believer can be fully persuaded of this glorious fact. Just consider the experiences and forces mentioned by Scripture:

⇒ Not death: confronting death and leaving this world cannot separate us from Christ and His love (Jn.5:24).

⇒ Not life: no trial or pleasure or comfort of life, not any person nor any thing in this life can separate us from Christ and His love.

⇒ Not angels, nor demons: no heavenly or spiritual creature, no being from any other dimension can separate us from Christ and His love.

⇒ Not the present nor the future: neither present events, beings or things, nor future events, beings, or things—absolutely nothing in existence or any thing in future existence—can cut us off from Christ and His love.

⇒ Not height or depth: nothing from outer space or from the depths of the earth can separate us from Christ and His love.

Note the *grand finale*: if there be any other creature than the ones named, that creature cannot separate us from "the love of God, that is in Christ Jesus our Lord."

> The LORD your God is with you, he is mighty to save. He will take great delight in you, he will quiet you with his love, he will rejoice over you with singing." (Zep 3:17)

"For God so loved the world that he gave his one and only Son, that whoever believes in him shall not perish but have eternal life. (John 3:16)

In that day [after Jesus' ascension) you will ask in my name. I am not saying that I will ask the Father on your behalf. No, the Father himself loves you because you have loved me and have believed that I came from God. (John 16:26-27)

But God demonstrates his own love for us in this: While we were still sinners, Christ died for us. (Rom 5:8)

But because of his great love for us, God, who is rich in mercy, made us alive with Christ even when we were dead in transgressions—it is by grace you have been saved. (Eph 2:4-5)

How great is the love the Father has lavished on us, that we should be called children of God! And that is what we are! The reason the world does not know us is that it did not know him. (1 John 3:1)

This is how God showed his love among us: He sent his one and only Son into the world that we might live through him. (1 John 4:9)

The LORD appeared to us in the past, saying: "I have loved you with an everlasting love; I have drawn you with loving-kindness. (Jer 31:3)

| | | 3 For I could wish that I myself were cursed and cut off from Christ for the sake of my brothers, those of my own race, | c. The unbelievable willingness of a man to be sacrificed for his people |

CHAPTER 9

VII. ISRAEL AND THE GOSPEL OF RIGHTEOUSNESS, 9:1-11:36

A. The Privileges of Israel and Their Tragic Failure, 9:1-5

1 A man's great love for his people
a. The plea of a distressed man to be trusted
b. The heart of a distressed man

I speak the truth in Christ—I am not lying, my conscience confirms it in the Holy Spirit—
2 I have great sorrow and unceasing anguish in my heart.

3 For I could wish that I myself were cursed and cut off from Christ for the sake of my brothers, those of my own race,
4 The people of Israel. Theirs is the adoption as sons; theirs the divine glory, the covenants, the receiving of the law, the temple worship and the promises.
5 Theirs are the patriarchs, and from them is traced the human ancestry of Christ, who is God over all, forever praised! Amen.

c. The unbelievable willingness of a man to be sacrificed for his people

2 A man's great respect for his people
a. Were Israelites[DS1]
b. Had the adoption[DS2]
c. Had the glory[DS3]
d. Had the covenants[DS4]
e. Had the law[DS5]
f. Had the true worship[DS6]
g. Had the promises[DS7]
h. Had the ancestors (fathers)[DS8]
i. Had the Messiah[DS9]

DIVISION VII

ISRAEL AND THE GOSPEL OF RIGHTEOUSNESS, 9:1-11:36

A. The Privileges of Israel and Their Tragic Failure, 9:1-5

(9:1-11:36) **DIVISION OVERVIEW: Israel**: the change from Chapter 8 is abrupt and striking. Chapters 9-11 have to do with the place of the Jews in world history. The church faces this bewildering problem because the Jews were God's chosen people with a unique and special place in God's purposes. However, when God sent His Son into the world, the Jews rejected Him. How can this tragic and terrible paradox be explained? Why would God's people choose to reject and crucify God's very own Son? This is the problem that Paul begins to deal with in these chapters.

Two things need to be noted throughout this section.

First, the Jews were the special chosen people of God. Paul never questioned this. The Jews had a very special place in God's plan for the salvation of man down through human history. (See notes also DEEPER STUDY #1—Jn.4:22; DEEPER STUDY #1—Ro.4:1-25.)

Second, the real chosen people, the real Israel, always lay in a righteous remnant, not in the whole nation (cp. Ro.9:25, esp. 27f).

(9:1-5) **Introduction**: Paul bears his heart in this passage, revealing a deep evangelistic fervor for his people, the Jews. It is a rare glimpse of the burning compassion that every servant of God should possess for his own loved ones and kinsmen.
1. A man's great love for his people (v.1-3).
2. A man's great respect for his people (v.4-5).

1 (9:1-3) **Evangelism—Witnessing—Compassion—Great Commission**: this is the picture of a man's great love and concern for his people, a love and concern for their salvation.

1. Paul pleads for his people to trust him. The Jews called Paul a false prophet and a liar. Why? He was now proclaiming God's love and salvation for all men instead of just for the Jews. Man no longer had to become a proselyte of Jewish religion in order to know God (cp. Ro.10:12-13). To the traditional Jew, Paul was a heretic. He was a man who was to be utterly distrusted. They hated and despised him and wanted to kill him and do away with his message (see notes—Acts 21:27-30; 24:1-9. Cp. Acts 22:22; 1 Cor.4:13).

2. Note how distressed Paul's heart is. Despite the rejection and ill treatment from the Jews, Paul still loved his kinsmen, and he sensed a deep urgency for them to grasp the truth. Their salvation was of such concern that he swore his concern by three things: Christ, his conscience, and the Holy Spirit. Paul was forcibly saying, "I am not lying...
• "I speak the truth *in Christ*...
• "*my conscience* confirms it...
• "my conscience confirms it in the *Holy Spirit*...
"I do have a great concern and love for my kinsmen. But my concern is not that their sinful ways be approved, but that they come to know the truth; for without the truth, they will be lost and doomed."

Just how deeply Paul's heart was distressed over his kinsmen is clearly seen in the description of his heart.
⇒ "I have great sorrow" (lupe): pain, grief, mourning.
⇒ "I have...unceasing anguish" (odune): intense pain, sorrow, torment. And note: it is continuous and unceasing. Paul was always bearing pain for the salvation of his kinsmen. The depth of Paul's love and concern is graphically seen in what he said.

3. Paul is the picture of a man who had an unbelievable willingness to be sacrificed for his people. He could wish to be cursed (anathema), that is, separated from Christ if it would save his people. He could be willing to swap his salvation for their doom if it would lead to their salvation. Paul felt the deepest emotion and love and concern for his people.

Note: the words of Paul must not be stretched too far. Paul was speaking from an evangelistic fervor, not from a theological view. He was immersed in emotion, just as so many of God's people sometimes become over loved ones who are lost. Many have been so immersed in emotion that they have offered to swap their salvation for a loved one. Sometimes the Spirit of God works in the hearts of God's people to strain and suffer through intense prayer for the salvation of lost souls, and sometimes the strain and intensity of prayer is so deep that a believer could wish one extreme (his own salvation) for the other extreme (the salvation of loved ones).

Thought 1. The point is forceful: God's people should be willing to suffer the ultimate pain for the salvation of souls.

Do you not say, 'Four months more and then the harvest'? I tell you, open your eyes and look at the fields! They are ripe for harvest. (John 4:35)

Brothers, my heart's desire and prayer to God for the Israelites is that they may be saved. (Rom 10:1)

To the weak I became weak, to win the weak. I have become all things to all men so that by all possible means I might save some. (1 Cor 9:22)

We are therefore Christ's ambassadors, as though God were making his appeal through us. We implore you on Christ's behalf: Be reconciled to God. (2 Cor 5:20)

This is how we know what love is: Jesus Christ laid down his life for us. And we ought to lay down our lives for our brothers. (1 John 3:16)

Keep yourselves in God's love as you wait for the mercy of our Lord Jesus Christ to bring you to eternal life. Be merciful to those who doubt; snatch others from the fire and save them; to others show mercy, mixed with fear—hating even the clothing stained by corrupted flesh. (Jude 1:21-23)

2 (9:3-5) **Israel, Privileges of—Glory**: a man's great respect for his people. Paul had just declared his great love for Israel; now he assures them of his respect. He did not deny their place in the plan and purposes of God. He knew they were a greatly privileged people, a people who had been highly favored by God. (See DEEPER STUDY # 1-9—Ro.9:4-5 for discussion. Also see DEEPER STUDY # 8, Israel—Mt.21:43 for an overview of Israel.)

DEEPER STUDY # 1
(9:4) **Israel—Israelites**: the Jews were Israelites. Their very name, Israel, meant *a prince with God* or *one who rules with God* or *one who contends with God*. And their name had been given them from the very founding of their nation. It had come from Jacob, whose name had been changed by God to Israel. The name was later adopted by the descendants of Jacob (Gen.32:28; 34:7; Jn.1:47).

Thought 1. In the providence of God, believers have been highly privileged just as Israel was. Believers have been given the name of God's own Son, *Christian*, which means *a follower* or *a disciple of Jesus Christ*. What we must guard against is bringing shame to the Lord's name. Too many profess His name, but do not really follow Him.

"Not everyone who says to me, 'Lord, Lord,' will enter the kingdom of heaven, but only he who does the will of my Father who is in heaven. (Mat 7:21)

"'These people honor me with their lips, but their hearts are far from me. (Mat 15:8; cp. Is.29:13)

They claim to know God, but by their actions they deny him. They are detestable, disobedient and unfit for doing anything good. (Titus 1:16)

DEEPER STUDY # 2
(9:4) **Adoption**: the Jews had the privilege of being adopted by God. They were chosen in a very special sense to be the children of God (see DEEPER STUDY # 1—Jn.4:22; DEEPER STUDY #8—Mt.21:43 for more discussion).

You are the children of the LORD your God. Do not cut yourselves or shave the front of your heads for the dead, (Deu 14:1)

Then say to Pharaoh, 'This is what the LORD says: Israel is my firstborn son, (Exo 4:22)

"When Israel was a child, I loved him, and out of Egypt I called my son. (Hosea 11:1)

Note a crucial point: this does not mean that the whole nation of Israel was saved. Not all citizens of Israel *believed* God, and being adopted into God's family has always been by genuine faith. In order to be a true child of God it has always been necessary for a *person* to believe in God, entrusting his whole being into God's keeping. (Cp. Ro.9:6-8, 27, 29; 2:28-29; 4:13. See DEEPER STUDY # 8—*Israel*, pt.3—Mt.21:43 for more discussion.)

Thought 1. Believers, too, have the glorious privilege of being adopted by God through faith (see notes, *Adoption*—Ro.8:15; 8:16-17; DEEPER STUDY # 2—Gal.4:5-6 for discussion and application).

Yet to all who received him, to those who believed in his name, he gave the right to become children of God— (John 1:12)

For you did not receive a spirit that makes you a slave again to fear, but you received the Spirit of sonship. And by him we cry, "Abba, Father." (Rom 8:15)

"Therefore come out from them and be separate, says the Lord. Touch no unclean thing, and I will receive you." "I will be a Father to you, and you will be my sons and daughters, says the Lord Almighty." (2 Cor 6:17-18)

To redeem those under law, that we might receive the full rights of sons. Because you are sons, God sent the Spirit of his Son into our hearts, the Spirit who calls out, "Abba, Father." (Gal 4:5-6)

DEEPER STUDY #3
(9:4) **Shekinah Glory**: the Jews had the privilege of the glory of God, that is, the Shekinah Glory. The Shekinah Glory was the brilliant light which descended into the midst of God's people when God was visiting His people. It symbolized God's glorious presence and was revealed in the form of a cloud. The cloud of God's glory and presence was revealed in two very special ways.

1. It was the glorious presence of God in the cloud that led Israel through the desert wanderings.

By day the LORD went ahead of them in a pillar of cloud to guide them on their way and by night in a pillar of fire to give them light, so that they could travel by day or night. (Exo 13:21)

While Aaron was speaking to the whole Israelite community, they looked toward the desert, and there was the glory of the LORD appearing in the cloud. (Exo 16:10)

On the morning of the third day there was thunder and lightning, with a thick cloud over the mountain, and a very loud trumpet blast. Everyone in the camp trembled. Mount Sinai was covered with smoke, because the LORD descended on it in fire. The smoke billowed up from it like smoke from a furnace, the whole mountain trembled violently, The LORD descended to the top of Mount Sinai and called Moses to the top of the mountain. So Moses went up (Exo 19:16, 18, 20)

2. It was the glorious presence of God in the cloud that filled the tabernacle and came to rest over the ark.

Then the cloud covered the Tent of Meeting, and the glory of the LORD filled the tabernacle. (Exo 40:34)

There also I will meet with the Israelites, and the place will be consecrated by my glory. (Exo 29:43)

I appear in the cloud over the atonement cover. (Lev 16:2)

For the glory of the LORD filled his temple. (1 Ki 8:11)

Thought 1. Believers have seen "the glory of God in the face of Christ" (2 Cor.4:6); believers are the light of the world (Mt.5:14). This means two significant things.
1) It is a terrible thing to possess the light and the glory of God and not to share it with those in darkness (see note—Mt.5:14-15 for more discussion).

In the same way, let your light shine before men, that they may see your good deeds and praise your Father in heaven. (Mat 5:16)

Therefore I endure everything for the sake of the elect, that they too may obtain the salvation that is in Christ Jesus, with eternal glory. (2 Tim 2:10)

To the elders among you, I appeal as a fellow elder, a witness of Christ's sufferings and one who also will share in the glory to be revealed: (1 Pet 5:1)

2) It is a terrible thing to be in darkness and to see light off in the distance and not follow after it. There is absolutely no excuse for seeing the glory of God and failing to follow it.

Put your trust in the light while you have it, so that you may become sons of light." When he had finished speaking, Jesus left and hid himself from them. (John 12:36)

DEEPER STUDY # 4
(9:4) **Covenants**: the Jews had the privilege of the covenants. A covenant is an agreement made between two parties; a contract drawn up between two or more people; a

special relationship set up and established between persons. Note the plural is used: covenants. God made several covenants with Israel. There was...
- the covenant with Noah after the flood (Gen.9:9f).
- the covenant with Abraham (Gen.12:1f; 15:18; 17:4f).
- the covenant of law made at Mount Sinai (Ex.19:5; 24:8; 34:10; Dt.29:1f).
- the covenant with David (2 Sam.7:16).
- the covenant of grace (Heb.8:8-13).

The point to note is the great love of God. He did not reach out for man only once and then leave man to his doom. God reached out to man time and again. God sought man at every opportunity, seeking to establish a relationship with him.

The LORD appeared to us in the past, saying: "I have loved you with an everlasting love; I have drawn you with lovingkindness. (Jer 31:3)

Continue your love to those who know you, your righteousness to the upright in heart. (Psa 36:10)

Here I am! I stand at the door and knock. If anyone hears my voice and opens the door, I will come in and eat with him, and he with me. (Rev 3:20)

DEEPER STUDY # 5
(9:4) **Law**: the Jews had the privilege of the law. They did not just have the ten commandments given to Moses on Mount Sinai, but they had the whole law of God. By law is simply meant the will of God written down. Through the centuries God simply had Moses and His messengers write out His will so that man would always know exactly how to live.

Thought 1. One of the great tragedies of human life is for a person to know that something is right and not do it. Yet, this is the daily life of man. It may be a simple matter of consuming something that damages his body or the more serious matter of cursing God's name. No matter what the transgression is, man stands guilty. He is inexcusable, for he has the law of God, and he has had God's law for centuries. Man knows how to live in love and justice. No greater indictment could exist than the charge: "There is no one righteous, not even one" (Ro.3:10; cp. Ro.3:9-18).

"That servant who knows his master's will and does not get ready or does not do what his master wants will be beaten with many blows. (Luke 12:47)

Elijah was a man just like us. He prayed earnestly that it would not rain, and it did not rain on the land for three and a half years. (James 5:17)

"A curse on him who is lax in doing the Lord's work! (Jer 48:10)

DEEPER STUDY # 6
(9:4) **Worship—Witnessing**: the Jews had the privilege of true worship and of the true service of God. They had...
- the true temple.
- the true ordinances of God.

- the true priests, prophets, and messengers of God.
- the true approach to God.
- The Jews had been given every opportunity and privilege to approach God, and even more, to understand and grasp the person of God Himself. The Jews were greatly privileged. While other people stumbled and wandered about in the darkness of false worship, creating *gods* within their own imaginations, the Jews had access to God Himself, access to the only true and living God. They had the opportunity to establish a personal relationship with God.

Thought 1. What an indictment! To have the opportunity to know God personally, but to turn one's back and walk away. However, there is an even greater offense than this. How much greater is the offense when a person knows the true approach to God and does not share it.

Believers know the truth; they know the way to God. Therefore, they must share the glorious message of the only living and true God. Note two significant facts.
1) Many know the truth; they know the true approach to God, yet they refuse to enter His presence. The tragic fact is this: God does not close the door to them; they shut the door upon themselves.

> For this people's heart has become calloused; they hardly hear with their ears, and they have closed their eyes. Otherwise they might see with their eyes, hear with their ears, understand with their hearts and turn, and I would heal them.' (Acts 28:27)

2) The blood of the lost is upon the hands of the believer. Why? Because the way to God and the means to proclaim the message to the world has existed for some time. Yet, we have failed to go into the world and share the life-saving news. There is no one to blame but us. Note the severe warning of God to His people:

> But if the watchman sees the sword coming and does not blow the trumpet to warn the people and the sword comes and takes the life of one of them, that man will be taken away because of his sin, but I will hold the watchman accountable for his blood.' "Son of man, I have made you a watchman for the house of Israel; so hear the word I speak and give them warning from me. When I say to the wicked, 'O wicked man, you will surely die,' and you do not speak out to dissuade him from his ways, that wicked man will die for his sin, and I will hold you accountable for his blood. (Ezek 33:6-8)

The only way for us to be freed from the judgment is to share the message of God and warn men.

DEEPER STUDY # 7
(9:4) **Promises**: the Jews had the promises of God. God had shared with them all of His blessings and He had given them the hope for which a man's soul craves. He had shared with them the plan and destiny for which He had created man. When man sinned and turned away from God, it was to the Jews that God gave...

- the promise of the Savior. (See notes—Lk.3:24-31; DEEPER STUDY # 3—Jn.1:45 for most of the prophecies concerning the first coming of Jesus Christ.)
- the promise of the world as an inheritance (cp. Acts 13:23, 32-33. See notes—Ro.4:13; DEEPER STUDY # 4—8:17; note—Acts 7:2-8 for more detailed discussion.)
- all the glorious promises stretching from Genesis to Revelation.

Thought 1. Three things are essential when dealing with the promises of God, three things which so many within Israel failed to do.
1) We must not stagger or waver at the promises of God.

> Yet he did not waver through unbelief regarding the promise of God, but was strengthened in his faith and gave glory to God, (Rom 4:20)
> And without faith it is impossible to please God, because anyone who comes to him must believe that he exists and that he rewards those who earnestly seek him. (Heb 11:6)

2) We must be careful to not fall short of His promises.

> Therefore, since the promise of entering his rest still stands, let us be careful that none of you be found to have fallen short of it. (Heb 4:1)
> We must pay more careful attention, therefore, to what we have heard, so that we do not drift away. For if the message spoken by angels was binding, and every violation and disobedience received its just punishment, how shall we escape if we ignore such a great salvation? This salvation, which was first announced by the Lord, was confirmed to us by those who heard him. (Heb 2:1-3)

3) We must steadfastly look for the promise of the new heavens and earth.

> First of all, you must understand that in the last days scoffers will come, scoffing and following their own evil desires. They will say, "Where is this 'coming' he promised? Ever since our fathers died, everything goes on as it has since the beginning of creation." But the day of the Lord will come like a thief. The heavens will disappear with a roar; the elements will be destroyed by fire, and the earth and everything in it will be laid bare. Since everything will be destroyed in this way, what kind of people ought you to be? You ought to live holy and godly lives as you look forward to the day of God and speed its coming. That day will bring about the destruction of the heavens by fire, and the elements will melt in the heat. But in keeping with his promise we are looking forward to a new heaven and a new earth, the home of righteousness. (2 Pet 3:3-4, 10-13)

DEEPER STUDY # 8
(9:5) **Heritage—Backsliding**: the Jews had the privilege of the fathers and their heritage. Their ancestors had been the primary recipients of the promises between God and man. They had the tradition and the history. (See DEEPER STUDY # 1—Jn.4:22 for the four primary reasons God chose Israel.)

Thought 1. It is a sad thing for a person to have a godly heritage (parents, friends, teachers, schooling, etc.) and go astray. The Bible is full of examples.
⇒ There were the two who began denying the resurrection (2 Tim.2:16-19).
⇒ There was Demas, who turned back to the world (2 Tim.4:10).
⇒ There was Judas, who forsook Christ (Mt.26:14-16).

It is impossible for those who have once been enlightened, who have tasted the heavenly gift, who have shared in the Holy Spirit, who have tasted the goodness of the word of God and the powers of the coming age, if they fall away, to be brought back to repentance, because to their loss they are crucifying the Son of God all over again and subjecting him to public disgrace. (Heb 6:4-6)

If we deliberately keep on sinning after we have received the knowledge of the truth, no sacrifice for sins is left, but only a fearful expectation of judgment and of raging fire that will consume the enemies of God. (Heb 10:26-27)

DEEPER STUDY # 9
(9:5) **Israel—Messiah**: the Jews had the privilege of the Messiah coming from their roots. This was the most glorious privilege of the Jews. It involved being the very people…
• through whom God was to send His Son.
• through whom God was to bless the world.

Note that Paul declares both the humanity and deity of Jesus Christ. He came as a man, but He "is God over all, forever praised"

Thought 1. A person's attitude and response toward Jesus Christ determine his eternal destiny.

"Whoever acknowledges me before men, I will also acknowledge him before my Father in heaven. But whoever disowns me before men, I will disown him before my Father in heaven. (Mat 10:32-33)

If anyone is ashamed of me and my words in this adulterous and sinful generation, the Son of Man will be ashamed of him when he comes in his Father's glory with the holy angels." (Mark 8:38)

"I tell you, whoever acknowledges me before men, the Son of Man will also acknowledge him before the angels of God. (Luke 12:8)

That if you confess with your mouth, "Jesus is Lord," and believe in your heart that God raised him from the dead, you will be saved. (Rom 10:9)

if we endure, we will also reign with him. If we disown him, he will also disown us; (2 Tim 2:12)

But there were also false prophets among the people, just as there will be false teachers among you. They will secretly introduce destructive heresies, even denying the sovereign Lord who bought them—bringing swift destruction on themselves. (2 Pet 2:1)

Who is the liar? It is the man who denies that Jesus is the Christ. Such a man is the antichrist—he denies the Father and the Son. No one who denies the Son has the Father; whoever acknowledges the Son has the Father also. (1 John 2:22-23)

If anyone acknowledges that Jesus is the Son of God, God lives in him and he in God. (1 John 4:15)

	B. The True Israel or Children of God, 9:6-13	9 For this was how the promise was stated: "At the appointed time I will return, and Sarah will have a son."	
1 God's Word, His promise, has not failed	6 It is not as though God's word had failed. For not all who are descended from Israel are Israel.	10 Not only that, but Rebekah's children had one and the same father, our father Isaac.	b. Proof 2: Scripture— God's Word & God's promise to Isaac*DS1*
2 They are not members of a race or institution	7 Nor because they are his descendants are they all Abraham's children. On the contrary, "It is through Isaac that your offspring will be reckoned."	11 Yet, before the twins were born or had done anything good or bad—in order that God's purpose in election might stand:	1) The promise was before the children's birth
3 They are not of any particular parentage or heritage		12 Not by works but by him who calls—she was told, "The older will serve the younger."	
4 They are the believers of God's promise	8 In other words, it is not the natural children who are God's children, but it is the children of the promise who are regarded as Abraham's offspring.	13 Just as it is written: "Jacob I loved, but Esau I hated."	2) The promise was by election, not by the goodness of the children*DS2*
a. Proof 1: Scripture— God's Word & God's promise to Abraham			

DIVISION VII

ISRAEL AND THE GOSPEL OF RIGHTEOUSNESS, 9:1-11:36

B. The True Israel or Children of God, 9:6-13

(9:6-13) **Introduction**: this is a startling passage, a passage that should awaken many a person to their true relationship with God. In no uncertain terms this passage declares just who the children of God are.

1. God's Word, His promise, has not failed (v.6).
2. The children of God are not members of a race or institution (v.6).
3. The children of God are not of any particular parent age or heritage (v.7).
4. The children of God are the believers of God's promise (v.7-13).

1 (9:6) **Word of God—Promises—Israel vs. Gentiles**: God's Word, His promise, has not failed. God made a glorious promise to Abraham, a promise that had two major points. If Abraham would follow God…

- then God would give him a seed, a descendant, a son through whom a great nation would be born. He would become the father of a great host of people.
- then God would cause all nations to be blessed through his seed, his descendant.

Scripture says that Abraham did exactly as God said. He believed God with all his heart and followed God not knowing where God would lead him (Heb.11:8. Think how this is true of every follower of God.) (See DEEPER STUDY # 1—Ro.4:1-25; note and DEEPER STUDY # 1—Jn.4:22 for more detailed discussion.)

Note a significant point: all the promises in Scripture are based upon this single promise to Abraham; that is, if the promise made to Abraham is voided and done away with, then all the promises of God's Word are invalid. God's Word and His promises will have failed. In light of this there are two things that make some people think the Word of God has failed.

1. Israel rejected God's Son, Jesus Christ, when God sent Him to earth. Ever since that day, very few Jews have turned and followed Christ. Where is the nation that God promised Abraham?

2. The Gentiles are the ones who are following God through His Son Jesus Christ, not the Jews. Therefore, it looks like God has turned from Israel to the Gentiles.

These two facts cannot be denied. They are a fact of history. How then can God's Word and promise to Abraham ever be fulfilled? Has God's Word and promise failed? Is God's Word now invalid?

Forcefully, Paul declares that God's Word has not failed. God's Word and the promises of it are effective and still valid. God is fulfilling His promise to Abraham: a nation is being born to Abraham, a nation which is the true Israel and the true children of God.

> **The grass withers and the flowers fall, but the word of our God stands forever."** (Isa 40:8)
> **I tell you the truth, until heaven and earth disappear, not the smallest letter, not the least stroke of a pen, will by any means disappear from the Law until everything is accomplished. (Mat 5:18)**
> **Heaven and earth will pass away, but my words will never pass away. (Luke 21:33)**
> **Therefore, the promise comes by faith, so that it may be by grace and may be guaranteed to all Abraham's offspring—not only to those who are of the law but also to those who are of the faith of Abraham. He is the father of us all. (Rom 4:16)**

2 (9:6) **Salvation**: the true children of God are not members of a race or institution: "Not all who are descended from Israel are Israel." Many Jews believed they were children of God because they were…

- born in the nation of Israel as an Israelite.
- reared in the Jewish religion.

The Jewish people reverenced God and His law and were known as a God-fearing and religious people. Therefore, a Jew felt he was a child of God by being a citizen of Israel and a circumcised member of Judaism. Many Jews felt that God's promise to Abraham meant that every citizen of the nation of Israel was a child of God as long as he was circumcised and half-way practiced the religion of Judaism.

Thought 1. The same thoughts have always prevailed among peoples of the world. Many believe they are Christians because they are citizens of a so-called Christian nation or Christian institution. They think they are acceptable to God because they profess belief in God and have been baptized, becoming a full fledged member of some church. Such, of course, is just not so. A person *does not* become a child of God by being...
- a citizen of a particular nation, no matter what nation it is nor how good and benevolent the nation is.
- a member of a particular religion or institution, no matter how true and godly the religion or institution may be.

Thought 2. Being a citizen of a great Christian nation and being a member of a great church does not make a person a child of God. It is not an earthly nation or a material church that makes a person acceptable to God.

> Yet to all who received him, to those who believed in his name, he gave the right to become children of God—children born not of natural descent, nor of human decision or a husband's will, but born of God. (John 1:12-13)
>
> He replied, "Isaiah was right when he prophesied about you hypocrites; as it is written: "'These people honor me with their lips, but their hearts are far from me. (Mark 7:6)
>
> They claim to know God, but by their actions they deny him. They are detestable, disobedient and unfit for doing anything good. (Titus 1:16)
>
> My people come to you, as they usually do, and sit before you to listen to your words, but they do not put them into practice. With their mouths they express devotion, but their hearts are greedy for unjust gain. (Ezek 33:31)

3 (9:7) **Salvation:** the true children of God are not of any particular parentage or heritage: "Nor because they are his descendants are they all Abraham's children." As stated, many Jews felt they were children of God because they were children of Abraham, one of the great servants of God (cp. Mt.3:9; Jn.8:38-39). They rested...
- in the godliness of Abraham, feeling that his godliness would cover them.
- in the promises made to Abraham, thinking that the promises made to him would include them.

Many Jews believed that they were children of God because of their godly heritage. They trusted in the fact that their parents and so many others in their roots (genealogies) worshipped the God of Judaism. They considered themselves to be children of godly forefathers; therefore, they professed to believe in God no matter what kind of lives they lived.

Thought 1. Some are trusting their godly heritage to save them. Too many are trusting godliness to rub off on them—to rub off from...
- their godly parents
- their godly brothers & sisters
- the godly minister
- their godly spouse
- their godly friends

Few think that God will really reject them. They think that in *the final analysis* God will accept them. They think that enough godliness will rub off on them from some godly heritage, person, or institution for God to accept them.

> "Not everyone who says to me, 'Lord, Lord,' will enter the kingdom of heaven, but only he who does the will of my Father who is in heaven. (Mat 7:21)
>
> Produce fruit in keeping with repentance. And do not begin to say to yourselves, 'We have Abraham as our father.' For I tell you that out of these stones God can raise up children for Abraham. (Luke 3:8)
>
> A man is not a Jew if he is only one outwardly, nor is circumcision merely outward and physical. No, a man is a Jew if he is one inwardly; and circumcision is circumcision of the heart, by the Spirit, not by the written code. Such a man's praise is not from men, but from God. (Rom 2:28-29)
>
> Who can bring what is pure from the impure? No one! (Job 14:4)
>
> Many a man claims to have unfailing love, but a faithful man who can find? (Prov 20:6)
>
> Those who are pure in their own eyes and yet are not cleansed of their filth; (Prov 30:12)

4 (9:7-13) **Salvation—Promise—Abraham—Isaac—Ishmael—Hagar:** the children of God are the *believers of God's promise*. Note two proofs.

1. There is the proof of Scripture, of God's Word and promise to Abraham: "through Isaac...your offspring will be reckoned" (v.7; cp. Gen.21:12). When God gave this promise to Abraham, Abraham had two sons, Ishmael and Isaac. Ishmael had been born through a slave-girl, Hagar. For decades Abraham's wife, Sarah, had been unable to bear a child. Sometime after her child-bearing years had passed, Sarah insisted Abraham attempt to have a son for her through her personal slave, Hagar. It was from this physical union that Ishmael was born. However, it was only a few years later that God appeared to Abraham and told him that Sarah was to bear the child of promise, the very child whom God had promised to Abraham when He first called Abraham (cp. Gen.18:1f).

The point is twofold.
   a. The natural children are not the children of God's promise. The birth of Ishmael was due to man's effort. He was born because Sarah and Abraham were trying to secure the "promise" by their own works. Ishmael was entirely the product of natural, human, carnal, fleshly, and unspiritual plans. Abraham and Sarah were trying to bring about the promise of God by their own efforts and works. God had absolutely nothing to do with Ishmael's birth.

Thought 1. Ishmael represents all who seek the promise of God—that is, to become children of God—by their own unspiritual, and fleshly works and efforts.

> **Yet to all who received him, to those who believed in his name, he gave the right to become children of God—Children born not of natural descent, nor of human decision or a husband's will, but born of God. (John 1:12-13)**
>
> **He saved us, not because of righteous things we had done, but because of his mercy. He saved us through the washing of rebirth and renewal by the Holy Spirit, (Titus 3:5)**
>
> **For it is by grace you have been saved, through faith—and this not from yourselves, it is the gift of God—not by works, so that no one can boast. (Eph 2:8-9)**

b. The children of the promise are counted for the seed, regarded as Abraham's offspring. Isaac was the child whom God had promised to Abraham (v.8-9). This means three things.
  ⇒ The promised child is the "seed," the "offspring," through whom the promise was to be fulfilled.
  ⇒ The promised child was born miraculously by the grace of God. Abraham and Sarah were about one hundred years old, well beyond child-bearing years, when Isaac was born (Ro.4:19).
  ⇒ The child of promise was born through faith (Heb.11:11).

Thought 1. A person becomes a child of God through faith in the promises of God. A child of the promise is a person who believes the promise of God, a person who...
  • does not seek to secure the promise by his own efforts and works.
  • follows through on his belief, waiting upon God to fulfill His promise.

> **You are all sons of God through faith in Christ Jesus, for all of you who were baptized into Christ have clothed yourselves with Christ. There is neither Jew nor Greek, slave nor free, male nor female, for you are all one in Christ Jesus. If you belong to Christ, then you are Abraham's seed, and heirs according to the promise. (Gal 3:26-29)**
>
> **And without faith it is impossible to please God, because anyone who comes to him must believe that he exists and that he rewards [fulfills His promise] those who earnestly seek him. (Heb 11:6)**
>
> **To those who by persistence in doing good seek glory, honor and immortality, he will give eternal life. (Rom 2:7)**
>
> **Be patient, then, brothers, until the Lord's coming. See how the farmer waits for the land to yield its valuable crop and how patient he is for the autumn and spring rains. You too, be patient and stand firm, because the Lord's coming is near. (James 5:7-8)**

2. There is the proof of Scripture, of God's Word and promise to Rebecca: "The older will serve the younger" (Gen.25:23). (See DEEPER STUDY # 1,2—Ro.9:10-13 for discussion.)

DEEPER STUDY # 1

(9:10-13) Election—Predestination—God, Grace of—Jacob—Esau: a striking and decisive proof of God's election is seen in the choice of Jacob over Esau. Also, a striking proof that salvation is solely by the grace of God and not by the works and goodness of men is seen in the two sons. Note three facts.

1. The promise to Rebecca was given before Jacob and Esau were born. Jacob's character, behavior, ability, works, and parents had nothing to do with God choosing him. God and God alone chose Jacob to be the child of promise. Jacob's choice was not by his own personal efforts but by the grace of God.

2. The promise was by election, not because of "anything good or bad" the children had done (v.11). Unquestionably, when we accept Scripture for what it says, our minds stagger at this argument. But there is one great truth that must always be remembered: neither Jacob nor Esau *deserved* mercy. Neither one *deserved* being chosen by God for anything. No man *deserves* mercy or purpose from God. God does not have mercy on a man because a man deserves or merits mercy nor because a man wills or runs after God (cp. Jn.1:12; Ro.9:16). God has mercy upon a man because He is a merciful God.

3. Election, being children of the promise, is *not of works, but of God who calls men to salvation*. The point is this. Paul is using the two children to get across the same point he stressed with Isaac: a true child of God is not a person who...
  • belongs to a particular race or institution.
  • belongs to a particular family or heritage.
  • works to secure the promise through his own plans and efforts.

God is merciful and He is love—absolutely so. Therefore, God has predestined a line of people to receive His promise of glory. Back in antiquity God chose Jacob, showing His mercy to Jacob. He chose Jacob to continue the line through whom He could send the Savior into the world and through whom He could fulfill all the promises of God to man. The fact that God chose Jacob for the line does not mean in any sense of the word that He condemned Esau for hell.

> **"For God so loved the world that he gave his one and only Son, that whoever believes in him shall not perish but have eternal life. (John 3:16)**
>
> **"I tell you the truth, whoever hears my word and believes him who sent me has eternal life and will not be condemned; he has crossed over from death to life. (John 5:24)**
>
> **Jesus answered, "The work of God is this: to believe in the one he has sent." (John 6:29)**
>
> **But these are written that you may believe that Jesus is the Christ, the Son of God, and that by believing you may have life in his name. (John 20:31)**
>
> **That if you confess with your mouth, "Jesus is Lord," and believe in your heart that God raised him from the dead, you will be saved. For it is with your heart that you believe and are justified, and it is with**

your mouth that you confess and are saved. (Rom 10:9-10)

Everyone who believes that Jesus is the Christ is born of God, and everyone who loves the father loves his child as well. (1 John 5:1)

DEEPER STUDY # 2
(9:11-13) **God—Purpose—Predestination**: "Esau I hated." This does not mean to hate in the sense of despising. It is merely a deliberate decision on the part of God for Jacob to be the child of promise instead of Esau. There is *no personal feeling* involved. Esau had done no wrong to merit God's disapproval. Neither had Jacob done any good to merit God's approval. It is merely the right of God to choose Jacob over Esau. It is critical to note that God was always choosing the younger son over the oldest son throughout the Old Testament. He did so for a specific purpose: God was illustrating that man was to receive His promises by grace. Man's law and efforts gave the inheritance to the oldest son; therefore, God chose the younger son over the oldest. God overruled man's law and efforts by giving the promise and inheritance to the younger son, for the younger son was not appointed by men to receive it nor did he deserve it. He received the promise and the inheritance *only by the mercy and grace of God*. Note this also: God's choice of Jacob was not a question of personal salvation, but of *God's purpose* being settled before they were born (cp. Mal.1:2-3. Also cp. Gen.29:33; Mt.6:24; Lk.14:26; Jn.12:25.)

	C. The Rejection of Israel: God's Right to Show Mercy and Justice as He Wills, 9:14-33	mercy, whom he prepared in advance for glory—	2) To prepare some for glory 3) The subjects of His glory: Both Jews & Gentiles
1 Is God righteous, that is, just? **2 God has the right to be merciful & just** a. He shows mercy as He wills	14 What then shall we say? Is God unjust? Not at all! 15 For he says to Moses, "I will have mercy on whom I have mercy, and I will have compassion on whom I have compassion." 16 It does not, therefore, depend on man's desire or effort, but on God's mercy.	24 Even us, whom he also called, not only from the Jews but also from the Gentiles? 25 As he says in Hosea: "I will call them 'my people' who are not my people; and I will call her 'my loved one' who is not my loved one," 26 And, "It will happen that in the very place where it was said to them, 'You are not my people,' they will be called 'sons of the living God.'"	**5 God has identified the chosen long ago in prophecy** a. They are from other nations as well as from Israel
b. He shows justice as He wills	17 For the Scripture says to Pharaoh: "I raised you up for this very purpose, that I might display my power in you and that my name might be proclaimed in all the earth." 18 Therefore God has mercy on whom he wants to have mercy, and he hardens whom he wants to harden.	27 Isaiah cries out concerning Israel: "Though the number of the Israelites be like the sand by the sea, only the remnant will be saved. 28 For the Lord will carry out his sentence on earth with speed and finality."	b. They are the small remnant of Israel 1) God will finish the work—fulfill His promise to Israel
3 God has the right to do as He wills a. Man has no right to talk back to God b. God's right is as the potter's right over clay	19 One of you will say to me: "Then why does God still blame us? For who resists his will?" 20 But who are you, O man, to talk back to God? "Shall what is formed say to him who formed it, 'Why did you make me like this?'" 21 Does not the potter have the right to make out of the same lump of clay some pottery for noble purposes and some for common use?	29 It is just as Isaiah said previously: "Unless the Lord Almighty had left us descendants, we would have become like Sodom, we would have been like Gomorrah." 30 What then shall we say? That the Gentiles, who did not pursue righteousness, have obtained it, a righteousness that is by faith;	2) God will leave believing descendants in Israel c. They are the pursuers of righteousness by faith
4 God has the right to put up with evil (unbel.) men in order to share His glory with some (bel.) men a. God is willing to be very patient with evil b. God's purpose 1) To make known His glory	22 What if God, choosing to show his wrath and make his power known, bore with great patience the objects of his wrath—prepared for destruction? 23 What if he did this to make the riches of his glory known to the objects of his	31 But Israel, who pursued a law of righteousness, has not attained it. 32 Why not? Because they pursued it not by faith but as if it were by works. They stumbled over the "stumbling stone." 33 As it is written: "See, I lay in Zion a stone that causes men to stumble and a rock that makes them fall, and the one who trusts in him will never be put to shame."	d. They are not the pursuers of righteousness by the works of the law—as Israel was e. They are not those who stumble over the Stone (Jesus Christ) as Israel did f. They are the persons who believe in Christ

DIVISION VII

ISRAEL AND THE GOSPEL OF RIGHTEOUSNESS, 9:1-11:36

C. The Rejection of Israel: God's Right to Show Mercy and Justice as He Wills, 9:14-33

(9:14-33) **Introduction**: this passage discusses two major questions: Is God righteous (v.14-24), and why has Israel been rejected by God as His primary mission force to the world (v.25-33)?

1. Is God righteous, that is, just (v.14)?
2. God has the right to be merciful and just (v.15-18).
3. God has the right to do as He wills (v.19-21).
4. God has the right to put up with evil (unbelieving) men in order to share His glory with some (believing) men (v.22-24).
5. God has identified the chosen long ago in prophecy (v.25-33).

1 (9:14) **God, Nature**: Is God righteous, that is, just? Paul's question is shocking: Is there unrighteousness with God? Remember what it was that caused this question. God went against all the laws of men in the ancient world, the laws governing the inheritance left to children. According to man's law, the oldest son was to receive the inheritance; however, in dealing with Isaac's children, God announced that the oldest son, Esau, would serve the younger son, Jacob. Jacob was God's choice to inherit the promise made to Abraham and Isaac, and note: God choose Jacob even before the children were born (Ro.9:10-13).

The question is this: Can God elect men, favor and disfavor men, and still be righteous and just? Can God choose and reject men even before they are born and still be righteous and just? Is there unrighteousness with God?

Not at all! It could never be! It is utterly impossible for God to be unrighteous and unjust. *Glance quickly* at the five points of the outline and the answer to the question is immediately seen.

2 (9:15-18) **God, Election**: God has the right to be merciful and just.

1. God shows mercy as He wills. He has mercy and compassion upon whom He wills. Therefore, if God chooses to show mercy to men, He has the right to do so, even when men do not deserve it. Again, if God chooses to show compassion to men, He has the right to do so even when men do not deserve it.

Note when it was that God spoke these words to Moses (Ex.33:19). Israel had just been worshipping the golden calf, committing the most serious offense, that of idolatry; and Moses had just interceded for Israel, asking God to forgive their sin (Ex.32:32). The people did not deserve God's forgiveness. They deserved annihilation in the face of God's holiness. A quick glance at the idolatrous and licentious event will show why. The event demonstrates just how depraved the heart of men can be (Ex.32:1-6). God answered Moses by saying He would not destroy the people, but He would have mercy and compassion. He is God; therefore, if He chooses to be merciful He can be merciful.

> **For he says to Moses, "I will have mercy on whom I have mercy, and I will have compassion on whom I have compassion." (Rom 9:15)**

Now note: God had mercy and compassion upon Israel *not* because they...
- willed to receive His mercy (human resolve).
- ran after God (human works, effort, energy).
- deserved God's mercy.

Israel received the forgiveness and mercy of God because God willed to be merciful to them. The point is clear: God is not unrighteous if He has mercy upon men. Men do not deserve mercy; they deserve judgment. Therefore, when God gives the unrighteous a gift, it is not unjust or unrighteous; it is being merciful and compassionate.

2. God shows justice as He wills. The historical event of Pharaoh is an example. Note five points.

a. Scripture says that God "raised up" (exegeiro) Pharaoh. This means that God allowed Pharaoh to appear, brought him forth upon the scene of world history. We must always remember the teaching of Scripture:

> **Everyone must submit himself to the governing authorities, for there is no authority except that which God has established. The authorities that exist have been established by God. (Rom 13:1)**

b. Pharaoh was evil, very evil. He was an unbeliever: a harsh, stubborn, obstinate man who stood against and cursed God as though face to face. Scripture declares that God does not tempt men with evil (Jas.1:13). Therefore, Pharaoh would have been evil, stubborn, harsh, and unbelieving even if he had been a small town vendor in south-

ern Egypt. God did not make Pharaoh sinful and evil. Pharaoh would have been sinful and evil no matter where he had lived.

c. Pharaoh had a unique opportunity; he had something many never receive: Pharaoh heard the truth from one of God's greatest servants, Moses. He had opportunity after opportunity to repent, but he refused. Scripture says time and again that Pharaoh himself hardened his heart (Ex.8:15, 32; 9:34).

d. Scripture also says that God hardened Pharaoh's heart (Ex.4:21; 7:3; 9:12; 10:20, 27; 11:10). What does this mean? On the basis of Scripture...
- it does not mean that God caused Pharaoh to sin and to be stubborn. God never tempts men to sin (Jas.1:13).
- it means that God judged Pharaoh the same as He judges all men. Pharaoh hardened his heart; therefore, he was judged and condemned to have a hardened heart. Pharaoh "sowed" a hardened heart; therefore, he "reaped" a hardened heart (Gal.6:7-8); Pharaoh "measured" out a hardened heart; therefore, he was "measured" out a hardened heart (Mt.7:2).

Very simply stated, God's law and nature of justice, of judicial equity took effect upon Pharaoh just as it does upon all men. Pharaoh reaped exactly what he sowed. (See notes—Mt.13:13-15; Deeper Study # 1—Jn.12:39-41; note—Ro.1:24 for detailed discussion.)

e. God overruled Pharaoh's evil and used it for the good of His people (Ro.8:28). God used Pharaoh's evil to demonstrate His sovereign power and to declare the name of God throughout all the earth.

The point is this: Pharaoh was a very sinful and evil man; therefore, God demonstrated His justice in Pharaoh. God acted righteously toward Pharaoh. Just as men execute justice upon evil men, God executed justice upon Pharaoh because of his evil. God is God; therefore, He has the right to execute justice as He wills.

The conclusion is clearly stated:

> **Therefore God has mercy on whom he wants to have mercy, and he hardens whom he wants to harden. (Rom 9:18)**

Thought 1. A man desperately needs to do two things.

1) A man needs to seek the face of God for mercy.

> **Let the wicked forsake his way and the evil man his thoughts. Let him turn to the LORD, and he will have mercy on him, and to our God, for he will freely pardon. (Isa 55:7)**

> **Because of the Lord's great love we are not consumed, for his compassions never fail. (Lam 3:22)**

> **Who is a God like you, who pardons sin and forgives the transgression of the remnant of his inheritance? You do not stay angry forever but delight to show mercy. (Micah 7:18)**

> **But because of his great love for us, God, who is rich in mercy, Made us alive with Christ even when we were dead in**

transgressions—it is by grace you have been saved. (Eph 2:4-5)

He saved us, not because of righteous things we had done, but because of his mercy. He saved us through the washing of rebirth and renewal by the Holy Spirit, (Titus 3:5)

For I will forgive their wickedness and will remember their sins no more." (Heb 8:12)

2) A man needs to guard ever so diligently against becoming hard toward God.

Do not harden your hearts as you did at Meribah, as you did that day at Massah in the desert, (Psa 95:8)

A man who remains stiff-necked after many rebukes will suddenly be destroyed—without remedy. (Prov 29:1)

But because of your stubbornness and your unrepentant heart, you are storing up wrath against yourself for the day of God's wrath, when his righteous judgment will be revealed. (Rom 2:5)

But encourage one another daily, as long as it is called Today, so that none of you may be hardened by sin's deceitfulness. (Heb 3:13)

3 (9:19-21) **Election—God, Sovereignty**: God has the right to do as He wills. Men object to God's sovereignty, to His right to run the world as He wills. The reason men object to God's right to rule and reign is clearly stated. Men want the right to determine their own fate, to live as they wish while on earth and still be assured of a good life in the next world. They do not want God or anyone else determining their fate. It is this spirit of self-centeredness and pride that causes men to object to God's sovereignty. Note how the present objection is worded. If God has mercy upon some and hardens others…

- why does He find fault and blame the sinner?
- who has resisted His will? For God is choosing to forgive some and choosing not to forgive others.

Paul gives three answers to this objection, answers that establish the sovereignty of God beyond question. Note that the third answer is set off by itself as a major point because of its significance to the whole subject (pt.4, v.22-24).

1. Man has no right to talk back to God, no right to accuse God of being unrighteous and unjust. Any man who replies against God has too low a view of God and too high a view of man. How can a creature who has been formed by God say to God, why have You made me like this? How can a creature question God, a creature…

- who owes his life, all that he is and has to God?
- who is so frail and so easily subject to destruction?
- who knows so little of the universe and its truth?
- who is so morally undisciplined and sinful?
- who is so limited to the material world and the physical dimension of being?
- who lives only for a few short years?

How can man dare question the Supreme Being who made the universe and all that is therein? Who is man that he thinks he can accuse the God of the universe with being unrighteous and unjust? Who does man think he is in accus-

ing God with being immoral and with showing partiality and favoritism?

The point is this: God is God; therefore, He can do as He wills. As God, He sees the overall view; therefore, He knows what should be done, and He does it. Man is foolish to question and charge God with wickedness, with being unrighteous and unjust. In fact, when man questions and charges God, man only shows…

- how *finite and foolish* he really is.
- how *wicked and depraved* he really is.

2. God's right over man is as the potter's right over clay. Now note a crucial point that must not be missed if we are to correctly understand this passage.

- The clay already exists. This passage is not dealing with creation, but with God's government and rule over creation. God is not creating the clay; He is taking a lump that is already existing and using it for His purposes.

Paul is not speaking of God creating some men to be sinners. God does not purpose to condemn men to hell. The fact is, God wills no man to perish; He longs for every man to be saved (2 Pt.3:9). What, then, is this verse saying?

Very simply, God uses the clay as He finds it. He takes the clay (man) and molds it, using it for His purposes. All men are sinful, being born into a sinful and depraved world. God knows the hearts of all men even when they are born. He knows a heart is subject to be an honorable vessel or to be a dishonorable vessel.

⇒ All hearts that are subject to honor, God takes and moulds into vessels of honor.
⇒ All hearts that are subject to dishonor, God takes and moulds into vessels of dishonor.

God is God; therefore, He knows the heart of every man. He knows if the heart is subject to be tender, loving, and responsive to Him. If the heart is responsive to the things of God, then God gets the gospel to that person and gives life to the person's heart, saving him and beginning the process of making him a vessel of honor.

God also knows if a person's heart is subject to hardness, selfishness, and rejection of God. This person is made into a vessel of dishonor; that is, God uses even the sinner and his rejection to His glory. How the sinner's rejection is used to glorify God is seen in the next major point (see note, pt.6—Ro.9:22).

The point is this: God has the *right* to make and use both honorable and dishonorable men to work all things out for good. He has the right to use both good and evil men to work out His purposes, purposes which are always good. His right is no different than the potter's.

And we know that in all things God works for the good of those who love him, who have been called according to his purpose. For those God foreknew he also predestined to be conformed to the likeness of his Son, that he might be the firstborn among many brothers. (Rom 8:28-29)

For he chose us in him before the creation of the world to be holy and blameless in his sight. In love he predestined us to be adopted as his sons through Jesus Christ, in accordance with his pleasure and will— (Eph 1:4-5)

Therefore God exalted him to the highest place and gave him the name that is above every name, that at the name of Jesus every knee should bow, in heaven and on earth and under the earth, and every tongue confess that Jesus Christ is Lord, to the glory of God the Father. (Phil 2:9-11)

Who has saved us and called us to a holy life—not because of anything we have done but because of his own purpose and grace. This grace was given us in Christ Jesus before the beginning of time, (2 Tim 1:9)

A faith and knowledge resting on the hope of eternal life, which God, who does not lie, promised before the beginning of time, (Titus 1:2)

And has made us to be a kingdom and priests to serve his God and Father—to him be glory and power for ever and ever! Amen. (Rev 1:6)

"You are worthy, our Lord and God, to receive glory and honor and power, for you created all things, and by your will they were created and have their being." (Rev 4:11)

All inhabitants of the earth will worship the beast—all whose names have not been written in the book of life belonging to the Lamb that was slain from the creation of the world. (Rev 13:8)

Then I heard what sounded like a great multitude, like the roar of rushing waters and like loud peals of thunder, shouting: "Hallelujah! For our Lord God Almighty reigns. (Rev 19:6)

4 (9:22-24) **Election—Predestination—God, Sovereignty—Grace:** God has the right to put up with evil and unbelieving men in order to share His glory with some believing men. The outline gives an overview of what is said.

God is willing to suffer (tolerate, put up with, endure) evil men for a long time. Why? Why does God not go ahead and do away with evil and with evil men? There is one very powerful reason: God is fulfilling His purpose in the world.

⇒ God is making known the riches of His glory upon believers, the subjects of mercy.

⇒ God is preparing still others for glory (cp. 2 Pt.3:9).

⇒ The ones being prepared for glory include both Jews and Gentiles. (Note how even this fact points toward God showing no partiality toward any people or person, Jew or Gentile. God does not pick some for sin and hell and some for righteousness and heaven.)

Several significant things need to be noted in these verses.

1. Note the difference about what is said. The objects of wrath or judgment are "prepared" for destruction, but the objects of mercy are "prepared in advance" for glory. The agent that "prepared" the vessels for wrath *is not identified*. Scripture simply says that they are "prepared" for destruction. This allows the interpretation that they "prepared" or "fitted" themselves for destruction; whereas God is said to *prepare* the vessels of mercy for glory.

Thought 1. Scripture is clear about this fact. Men *prepare and fit* themselves for wrath; God does not tempt or lead men into sin (Jas.1:13). The very opposite is true. God saves men and wants all men to be

saved; and He prepares all those who come to Him for glory.

"For God so loved the world that he gave his one and only Son, that whoever believes in him shall not perish but have eternal life. For God did not send his Son into the world to condemn the world, but to save the world through him. Whoever believes in him is not condemned, but whoever does not believe stands condemned already because he has not believed in the name of God's one and only Son. (John 3:16-18)

On the last and greatest day of the Feast, Jesus stood and said in a loud voice, "If anyone is thirsty, let him come to me and drink. (John 7:37)

For there is no difference between Jew and Gentile—the same Lord is Lord of all and richly blesses all who call on him, (Rom 10:12)

Who wants all men to be saved and to come to a knowledge of the truth. (1 Tim 2:4)

The Lord is not slow in keeping his promise, as some understand slowness. He is patient with you, not wanting anyone to perish, but everyone to come to repentance. (2 Pet 3:9)

He is the atoning sacrifice for our sins, and not only for ours but also for the sins of the whole world. (1 John 2:2)

The Spirit and the bride say, "Come!" And let him who hears say, "Come!" Whoever is thirsty, let him come; and whoever wishes, let him take the free gift of the water of life. (Rev 22:17)

"Turn to me and be saved, all you ends of the earth; for I am God, and there is no other. (Isa 45:22)

"Come, all you who are thirsty, come to the waters; and you who have no money, come, buy and eat! Come, buy wine and milk without money and without cost. (Isa 55:1)

2. Note the whole passage has to do with proving that God is just and righteous. If God actually created men to be sinful so that He could condemn them to wrath, He would not be righteous and just. Even in our finite world, to make something evil is considered unrighteous and unjust. How much more is this so in the infinite world of heaven? God does not *prepare* men for destruction; men *prepare* themselves for destruction.

3. The whole world is sinful and depraved. "There is no one righteous, not even one" (Ro.3:10). "All have sinned and fall short of the glory of God" (Ro.3:23. Cp. Ro.10:9-18 for a descriptive picture of man's sinful condition.) God knows the heart of every man, even before he is born. He even knows who will be saved and who will not be saved. Why, then, does He not stop the world instead of letting it go on, when He knows some men are going to doom themselves? There is one primary reason: if God stopped the world then there would be...

• no more objects of mercy, no more believers.

• no more believers to be brought and offered as brothers and sisters to Christ (Ro.8:29).

• no more people upon whom God could demonstrate His glorious mercy and love (Ro.9:23; Eph.2:7).

Note what Scripture says, for it clearly states why God does not end the world and keep any more evil men from being doomed: God is willing to put up with evil men in order to shower "the riches of His glory" upon those who believe on His Son (v.23; cp. v.33). God has only one Son, and He loves His Son so much that He wants Him to be glorified and honored beyond imagination.

4. The one thing to be remembered is this: there is nothing inconsistent with God showing mercy to some while condemning others. God punishes the *wicked* only for their sins. Human experience as well as the Bible prove beyond doubt that all men are sinful. None deserve mercy. No man deserves to be chosen by God for anything (see DEEPER STUDY # 1, *Election*—Ro.9:10-13). All men stand under the wrath of God. Therefore, there is no injustice done to a wicked man if God chooses to show mercy to another. One thing will happen, however. The object of mercy will fall upon his face in utter adoration and praise, and he will become a willing servant, willingly owned and possessed by his Savior (Ro.9:22-23; cp. Ro.11:33-36).

Thought 1. When we truly realize that God has had mercy upon us, it causes us to fall upon our face before Him. He has loved us, truly loved us to the point of forgiving our sins through the Lord Jesus Christ. Seeing His love for us breaks us in humble adoration and worship. It is the love of Christ for us that constrains us to love God.

> **For Christ's love compels us, because we are convinced that one died for all, and therefore all died. And he died for all, that those who live should no longer live for themselves but for him who died for them and was raised again. (2 Cor 5:14-15)**
>
> **We love because he first loved us. (1 John 4:19)**
>
> **Keep yourselves in God's love as you wait for the mercy of our Lord Jesus Christ to bring you to eternal life. (Jude 1:21)**

5. Another point brought out in this passage is this: the "riches of God's glory" are more clearly seen in the lives of the chosen because of the wickedness of all others. The highest good is said to be accomplished in both the wicked and the chosen objects. The glory of God's love is much more clearly seen by the contrast of a fallen and depraved universe (cp. v.22-23).

6. Still another point to be kept foremost in mind is this: there is nothing inconsistent or unjust if God looks at two undeserving men and chooses to have mercy upon one. There is no injustice done to a wicked man if God chooses to forgive another.

Some people say this: there must be something in a man or something done by a man to cause God to choose him. But this just is not so, for it says that man earns salvation. Such says that salvation is by works, and this is totally against the teaching of Scripture. Salvation is by God's grace alone; it is "not by works, so that no one can boast" (Eph.2:8-9). Therefore, as is taught by this passage, God chooses the objects of mercy out of the depth of His own justice and mercy.

The mind staggers at this whole passage. We can only ponder it and stand in amazement at the depth of the riches both of the wisdom and knowledge of God!

> **Oh, the depth of the riches of the wisdom and knowledge of God! How un-**

searchable his judgments, and his paths beyond tracing out! "Who has known the mind of the Lord? Or who has been his counselor?" (Rom 11:33-34)

> **Now to the King eternal, immortal, invisible, the only God, be honor and glory for ever and ever. Amen. (1 Tim 1:17)**

We will understand God's providence and our freedom of choice in the Day of Redemption. Until then, we can only accept the doctrine as two parallel lines that will find their union and explanation in Him. In that day, He will explain them to us face to face. (What a glorious day that will be!)

A final point of paramount importance is the conclusion drawn in verses 25-33. Paul's point is to give weight to this fact: God has judged the rejection of Israel as a nation by choosing persons from the Gentile nations as well. God's people are persons from *all nations* who pursue His righteousness as found in Christ (see DEEPER STUDY # 1—Jn.4:22). The conclusion of the whole passage is, "anyone who trusts in him [Christ] will never be put to shame" (Ro.10:11). This conclusion, that the one who believes is the one truly saved, gives balance to the whole argument.

5 (9:25-33) **Chosen, The—Election—Israel vs. Gentiles**: God has identified *the chosen* long ago in prophecy. "Salvation is from the Jews" (Jn.4:22). Israel was the chosen people of God, chosen to be God's witnesses to carry the message of salvation to the world (see note—Jn.4:22 for the reasons that God chose Israel). However, Israel failed and kept the message to itself and excluded all other peoples. Israel even took the lead in killing God's Son, Jesus Christ. This is the whole point of these verses, to point out how *the chosen* people of God come from all nations of the earth. This fact is clearly seen even in the Jewish prophets. "The chosen" are identified in six different statements which are irrefutable to the open and honest mind. (See DEEPER STUDY # 8, *Israel*—Mt.21:43 for more discussion of this point.)

1. The chosen people of God are from other nations as well as from Israel. The Jewish prophet Hosea predicted this fact. Note the three things Hosea said about the Gentiles. The Gentiles...

- will be called "God's people." They are the very ones who were not called God's "people" (Hos.2:23).
- will be called "My loved one." They are the very ones who were not called "My loved one" (Hos.2:23).
- were in a place where it was said that they were not God's people. The Gentiles were in the very place where they were to be called the children of God (Hos.1:10).

Thought 1. History has always proven that the Gentiles are as morally depraved and self-righteous as people can be. But despite all, God in His glorious mercy has thrown open the door of salvation to the Gentiles as well as to the Jews. No matter how self-righteous or morally evil a person has been, God reaches out to that person. Neither the most depraved corruption nor the most humanistic self-righteousness can keep God from forgiving a person if that person truly believes in His Son, the Lord Jesus Christ (v.33).

> **All the prophets testify about him that everyone who believes in him receives for-**

giveness of sins through his name." (Acts 10:43)

I am not ashamed of the gospel, because it is the power of God for the salvation of everyone who believes: first for the Jew, then for the Gentile. (Rom 1:16)

For, "Everyone who calls on the name of the Lord will be saved." (Rom 10:13)

You are all sons of God through faith in Christ Jesus, For all of you who were baptized into Christ have clothed yourselves with Christ. There is neither Jew nor Greek, slave nor free, male nor female, for you are all one in Christ Jesus. (Gal 3:26-28)

Everyone who believes that Jesus is the Christ is born of God, and everyone who loves the father loves his child as well. (1 John 5:1)

2. The chosen are the small remnant of Israel. The great prophet Isaiah predicted this.
   a. Isaiah predicted that only a few among Israel would truly believe and love God supremely. The nation would be a great people whose numbers would be as the sand of the sea, but only a *remnant* would be saved (v.27). Note that God would have to fulfill His Word by cutting short His dealings with Israel. That is, so many in Israel would be so sinful, they would be a threat to destroying everyone. Therefore, God would have to cut His work short in dealing with Israel in order to assure a remnant of believers and to fulfill His word to Abraham (cp. Is.10:22-23).
   b. Isaiah also predicted that God would leave a seed, a small remnant of believing descendants, in Israel (Is.1:9). Note that Israel's wickedness is compared to Sodom and Gomorrah. Israel has suffered a fate just as terrible as Sodom and Gomorrah, perhaps worse because the nation's sufferings have been the epitomy of severity down through the centuries. But note: God has saved a remnant through it all. There are Jews who have trusted God's Son, even Jesus Christ of Nazareth (cp. Ro.11:27-29).

I ask then: Did God reject his people? By no means! I am an Israelite myself, a descendant of Abraham, from the tribe of Benjamin. And what was God's answer to him? "I have reserved for myself seven thousand who have not bowed the knee to Baal." (Rom 11:1, 4)

3. The chosen are the pursuers of righteousness by faith (see note, *Righteousness*—Ro.1:17). Note the contrast between this point and the next. The most unlikely thing happened.
   ⇒ The Gentiles who have always been so base and self-righteous have all of a sudden turned to God for righteousness, even the righteousness of faith.
   ⇒ The Jews who have always been so God-centered and religious have missed God's righteousness, even the righteousness of faith in Christ.

He replied, "Isaiah was right when he prophesied about you hypocrites; as it is written: "'These people honor me with their lips, but their hearts are far from me. (Mark 7:6)

Since they did not know the righteousness that comes from God and sought to establish their own, they did not submit to God's righteousness. Christ is the end of the law so that there may be righteousness for everyone who believes. (Rom 10:3-4)

It is because of him that you are in Christ Jesus, who has become for us wisdom from God—that is, our righteousness, holiness and redemption. (1 Cor 1:30)

God made him who had no sin to be sin for us, so that in him we might become the righteousness of God. (2 Cor 5:21)

And be found in him, not having a righteousness of my own that comes from the law, but that which is through faith in Christ—the righteousness that comes from God and is by faith. (Phil 3:9)

Having a form of godliness but denying its power. Have nothing to do with them. (2 Tim 3:5)

4. The chosen are not pursuers of righteousness by the works of the law—as Israel was (v.31-32). Note that this begins to answer why God had to turn away from Israel as the primary mission force of His grace. Israel was zealous to secure righteousness, but failed because she sought righteousness by the law.

Many will say to me on that day, 'Lord, Lord, did we not prophesy in your name, and in your name drive out demons and perform many miracles?' Then I will tell them plainly, 'I never knew you. Away from me, you evildoers!' (Mat 7:22-23)

Therefore no one will be declared righteous in his sight by observing the law; rather, through the law we become conscious of sin. (Rom 3:20)

Know that a man is not justified by observing the law, but by faith in Jesus Christ. So we, too, have put our faith in Christ Jesus that we may be justified by faith in Christ and not by observing the law, because by observing the law no one will be justified. (Gal 2:16)

For it is by grace you have been saved, through faith—and this not from yourselves, it is the gift of God—not by works, so that no one can boast. (Eph 2:8-9)

But when the kindness and love of God our Savior appeared, he saved us, not because of righteous things we had done, but because of his mercy. He saved us through the washing of rebirth and renewal by the Holy Spirit, (Titus 3:4-5)

5. The chosen are not those who stumble over the Stone, Christ Himself, as Israel has done (cp. Is.8:14; 28:16). (See DEEPER STUDY # 7, *Jesus Christ, Cornerstone*—Mt.21:42 for discussion.)

Blessed is the man who does not fall away on account of me." (Mat 11:6)

But we preach Christ crucified: a stumbling block to Jews and foolishness to Gentiles, (1 Cor 1:23)

Now to you who believe, this stone is precious. But to those who do not believe, "The stone the builders rejected has become the capstone," and, "A stone that causes men to stumble and a rock that makes them fall." They stumble because they disobey the message—which is also what they were destined for. (1 Pet 2:7-8)

6. The chosen are the persons who believe in Christ. (See note, *Believe*—Ro.10:16-17 for discussion.)

That everyone who believes in him may have eternal life. (John 3:15)

"I tell you the truth, whoever hears my word and believes him who sent me has eternal life and will not be condemned; he has crossed over from death to life. (John 5:24)

Jesus said to her, "I am the resurrection and the life. He who believes in me will live, even though he dies; (John 11:25)

I have come into the world as a light, so that no one who believes in me should stay in darkness. (John 12:46)

But these are written that you may believe that Jesus is the Christ, the Son of God, and that by believing you may have life in his name. (John 20:31)

That if you confess with your mouth, "Jesus is Lord," and believe in your heart that God raised him from the dead, you will be saved. For it is with your heart that you believe and are justified, and it is with your mouth that you confess and are saved. (Rom 10:9-10)

CHAPTER 10

D. The Tragic Mistake of Israel: Missing God's Righteousness, 10:1-11

1 Paul's desire & Israel's mistake
   a. Paul's desire for Israel's salvation
   b. Israel's mistake: They have zeal, but it is not based on correct knowledge
      1) They seek their own righteousness
      2) They do not submit to God's righteousness

2 God's righteousness is Jesus Christ

3 God's righteousness is opposed to man's righteousness, to man's way for reaching God

Brothers, my heart's desire and prayer to God for the Israelites is that they may be saved. 2 For I can testify about them that they are zealous for God, but their zeal is not based on knowledge. 3 Since they did not know the righteousness that comes from God and sought to establish their own, they did not submit to God's righteousness. 4 Christ is the end of the law so that there may be righteousness for everyone who believes. 5 Moses describes in this way the righteousness that is by the law: "The man who does these things will live by them.

6 "But the righteousness that is by faith says: "Do not say in your heart, 'Who will ascend into heaven?' " (that is, to bring Christ down) 7 "Or 'Who will descend into the deep?' " (that is, to bring Christ up from the dead). 8 But what does it say? "The word is near you; it is in your mouth and in your heart," that is, the word of faith we are proclaiming: 9 That if you confess with your mouth, "Jesus is Lord," and believe in your heart that God raised him from the dead, you will be saved. 10 For it is with your heart that you believe and are justified, and it is with your mouth that you confess and are saved. 11 As the Scripture says, "Anyone who trusts in him will never be put to shame."

4 God's righteousness does not have to seek out a Messiah or a Deliverer (utopia)
   a. Rgt. is not trying to climb up to heaven
   b. Rgt. is not by descending into the depths to conquer death & hell

5 God's righteousness & salvation are right before a person
   a. By confessing Jesus to be the Lord (from heaven, cp. v.6)
   b. By believing God raised Jesus from the dead (from the depths, cp. v.7)
   c. By believing with the heart & confessing with the mouth

6 God's righteousness & salvation deliver a person from shame

DIVISION VII.

ISRAEL AND THE GOSPEL OF RIGHTEOUSNESS, 9:1-11:36

D. The Tragic Mistake of Israel: Missing God's Righteousness, 10:1-11

(10:1-11) **Introduction**: this passage has two powerful points. It shows the tragic mistake of Israel, and it proclaims the great danger of missing God's righteousness. It is an excellent study on God's righteousness. It shows man exactly what has to be done in order to receive his utopia upon earth, exactly what has to be done to make all things right. It reveals how a man can receive righteousness and be saved from death and judgment and live forever.

1. Paul's desire and Israel's mistake (v.1-3).
2. God's righteousness is Jesus Christ (v.4).
3. God's righteousness is opposed to man's righteousness, to man's way for reaching God (v.5).
4. God's righteousness does not have to seek out a Messiah or a Deliverer (utopia) (v.6-7)
5. God's righteousness and salvation are right before a person (v.8-10).
6. God's righteousness and salvation deliver a person from shame (v.11).

1 (10:1-3) **Israel, Errors of**: Paul's desire and Israel's mistake. Paul had a burning desire for Israel's salvation. He loved his people and loved them deeply.
   ⇒ The word "desire" (eudokia) means longing, willing, yearning, craving. He craved and yearned to see the salvation of his people. If he saw their salvation, his desire would be fulfilled.
   ⇒ Note that Paul prayed for Israel's salvation. They could be saved; their rejection of Christ was not hopeless. The door of salvation is open to all men, the Jew as well as the Gentile.

Thought 1. The fact that Paul prayed for the salvation of the Jews is a lesson to all believers. We, too, need to be praying for the salvation of the Jews. Why? Because so much of the world's heritage that is good and decent has come from the Jews:
   ⇒ morality
   ⇒ law
   ⇒ the Bible
   ⇒ the Prophets
   ⇒ the Son of God, Jesus Christ
   ⇒ the true religion

You Samaritans worship what you do not know; we worship what we do know, for salvation is from the Jews. (John 4:22)

Now note Israel's great mistake: they had a zeal for God, but it was not based on correct knowledge.
   ⇒ The Jews had knowledge (gnosis) about God, and knew a great deal about Him (Ro.2:17f).
   ⇒ But the Jews did not have the correct knowledge of God. The word knowledge (epignosis) means correct, right, full, complete. It means an *experiential knowledge* of the truth.

The point is, the Jews knew some things about God, but their knowledge was only partial. What they knew was incomplete; it was not enough. Therefore, their knowledge was incorrect. As a result they did not know God personally.

Why did Israel have an incomplete and incorrect knowledge of God? There are three reasons.

1. Israel was ignorant of God's righteousness. They failed to understand…
- God's true nature: His holiness and perfection, and the utter necessity to be perfect in order to be acceptable to Him and given the right to live in His presence.
- Man's true nature: his sin and desperate need for *perfect* righteousness in order to be acceptable to God and given the right to live in God's presence.
- God's love: His love in sending His Son to save man by providing a perfect righteousness for him.

Very simply, Israel was ignorant of God's method of justification, ignorant as to how a man really becomes acceptable to God.

> **They are darkened in their understanding and separated from the life of God because of the ignorance that is in them due to the hardening of their hearts. (Eph 4:18)**

> **I thought, "These are only the poor; they are foolish, for they do not know the way of the LORD, the requirements of their God. (Jer 5:4)**

> **But they do not know the thoughts of the LORD; they do not understand his plan, he who gathers them like sheaves to the threshing floor. (Micah 4:12)**

2. Israel went about establishing its own way of righteousness. They sought to make themselves acceptable to God through…
- rituals
- ceremonies
- laws
- works

They sought to save themselves by being as religious as they could. They felt God would never reject them if they did the best they could. Therefore, they drew up every rule and regulation they could to make themselves *religiously good* and acceptable, and they worked and worked to follow the rules and regulations. They sought to build their own way and route to God.

> **He replied, "Isaiah was right when he prophesied about you hypocrites; as it is written: "'These people honor me with their lips, but their hearts are far from me. (Mark 7:6)**

> **We do not dare to classify or compare ourselves with some who commend themselves. When they measure themselves by themselves and compare themselves with themselves, they are not wise. (2 Cor 10:12)**

> **Even if I were innocent, my mouth would condemn me; if I were blameless, it would pronounce me guilty. (Job 9:20)**

> **Many a man claims to have unfailing love, but a faithful man who can find? (Prov 20:6)**

> **Those who are pure in their own eyes and yet are not cleansed of their filth; (Prov 30:12)**

3. Israel refused to submit themselves to the righteousness of God. Very simply, they refused to accept Jesus Christ, who is God's righteousness.

Thought 1. Note a crucial point. Zeal and sincerity are not enough in seeking God. No person or group of people could be any more zealous or sincere in seeking God than the Jews. But something else is always needed; zeal and sincerity always require one other ingredient: accurate, and complete knowledge. Zeal and sincerity by themselves cannot reach a destination. A person can be as zealous and sincere as possible and still be on the wrong road and never reach his destination. To reach his destination, he must know the right road.

> **Who wants all men to be saved and to come to a knowledge of the truth. For there is one God and one mediator between God and men, the man Christ Jesus, (1 Tim 2:4-5)**

2 (10:4) **Righteousness—Jesus Christ, The Righteousness of God**: God's righteousness is Jesus Christ. Jesus Christ is the One who puts an end (telos) to man having to seek righteousness through the law. Man no longer has to work and work to be acceptable to God, to work and work knowing full well that he is coming up ever so short of God's glory and demand. Man no longer has to live under the enslaving power of sin, under its guilt and shame and punishment. Man no longer has to live under the weight and pressure of failing and of being ever so unworthy and hopeless, lonely and alienated. Man can now be set free and know full well that he is acceptable to God. Man can now have a heart that swells with assurance and confidence, the perfect knowledge that he is God's and God is his. Man can know that he is accepted as righteous before God. How? Through the righteousness of Jesus Christ. "Christ is the end of the law so that there may be righteousness for everyone who believes." This means at least three things.

1. Christ *ended* the law in that He is the object toward which the law pointed. All the ceremonies, sacrifices, offerings, and purifications—they all led and pointed toward Christ.
⇒ The law was the supervisor, the schoolmaster to bring us to Christ.

> **So the law was put in charge to lead us to Christ that we might be justified by faith. Now that faith has come, we are no longer under the supervision of the law. (Gal 3:24-25)**

Very simply, the law was never intended to be the way to become righteous and acceptable to God. The law was given to point and lead men to Christ, who is the righteousness of God.
⇒ The law was but a shadow of the real substance that was to come.

> **These are a shadow of the things that were to come; the reality, however, is found in Christ. (Col 2:17; cp. Heb.9:9)**

2. Christ *ended* the law in that He fulfilled and completed the law perfectly. He lived under the law and kept it perfectly. He was sinless, obeying every rule and require-

ment of the law. By fulfilling the law, Jesus Christ has become...

- the Ideal Man
- the Perfect Man
- the Representative Man

The law finds its perfection in Jesus Christ. He is the very embodiment of all that God wants man to be. Therefore, man no longer looks to the law for his righteousness. Man no longer looks to the law as the way to reach God and to secure God's favor. Man now looks to Jesus Christ and approaches God through Jesus Christ.

> **God made him who had no sin to be sin for us, so that in him we might become the righteousness of God. (2 Cor 5:21)**
> **For you know that it was not with perishable things such as silver or gold that you were redeemed from the empty way of life handed down to you from your forefathers, but with the precious blood of Christ, a lamb without blemish or defect. (1 Pet 1:18-19)**

3. Christ *ended* the law in that he destroyed the penalty and condemnation of the law against man. Christ took the sin of man upon Himself and bore the condemnation for man. Christ died for man; He bore the execution of being separated from God for man.

> **By abolishing in his flesh the law with its commandments and regulations. His purpose was to create in himself one new man out of the two, thus making peace, (Eph 2:15)**
> **Having canceled the written code, with its regulations, that was against us and that stood opposed to us; he took it away, nailing it to the cross. (Col 2:14)**

However, note a critical point: Christ ends the law for righteousness *only to those who believe*. A man is justified, that is, counted righteous by God, only if he truly believes that Jesus Christ is the righteousness of God. (See notes—Ro.5:1; Deeper Study # 2—Mt.5:17. Also see outline and notes—Ro.3:21-22; 8:2-4; Deeper Study # 2—8:3.)

Thought 1. Jesus Christ is the righteousness of God; He is the very embodiment of God's righteousness.

> **Christ is the end of the law so that there may be righteousness for everyone who believes. (Rom 10:4)**
> **It is because of him that you are in Christ Jesus, who has become for us wisdom from God—that is, our righteousness, holiness and redemption. (1 Cor 1:30)**
> **And be found in him, not having a righteousness of my own that comes from the law, but that which is through faith in Christ—the righteousness that comes from God and is by faith. (Phil 3:9)**

3 (10:5) **Righteousness**: God's righteousness is opposed to man's righteousness, that is, opposed to man's way for reaching God. Man tries to reach God by law and works, by simply doing the very best he can. However, there is a terrible flaw in this approach. Moses was the first to point

out the flaw: the man who lives by the law must keep the law, and keep it perfectly (cp. Lev.18:5).

> **Moses describes in this way the righteousness that is by the law: "The man who does these things will live by them." (Rom 10:5)**
> **All who rely on observing the law are under a curse, for it is written: "Cursed is everyone who does not continue to do everything written in the Book of the Law." (Gal 3:10)**
> **The law is not based on faith; on the contrary, "The man who does these things will live by them." (Gal 3:12)**

The point is this. There are only two ways to become righteous. A person can become righteous...

- by keeping the law perfectly, by never sinning in act, word, or thought. If a person could keep the law perfectly—never sinning even once—he could be declared righteous.
- by trusting in the righteousness of a Person who has lived a sinless life and who stands before us as the Ideal Man, the Ideal Man who can represent us before God. (See note, *Justification*—Ro.5:1 for more discussion.)

4 (10:6-7) **Righteousness—Utopia**: God's righteousness does not have to seek out a Messiah or a Deliverer (utopia). Note the contrast between heaven and the deep or abyss. This is a picture of the summit and the pit, of the very best and the very worst. Men search...

- for the height of heaven: for life and joy and pleasure, for the very best, for their utopia.
- for the answer to death and hell: for the release and freedom from death and the sense of judgment—for their utopia.

Another way to say the same thing is this: men search for righteousness, that is, for everything to be right. If they can achieve righteousness and make everything right, then they will have their utopia.

The point is this. Man's search for life or for utopia is *really* a search for a deliverer who can do two things: ascend into heaven to bring utopia down to earth and descend into the depths to conquer sin, death, and hell (cp. Dt.30:11-13. Cp. Ps.139:6-9; Pr.24:7; Amos 9:2.) Men are really searching for a true Messiah, for Christ Himself.

Thought 1. A person does not have to scale heaven nor fathom the deep to be saved. If he did, he would be lost eternally, for no man can penetrate heaven to secure righteousness or go into the depths to conquer death and hell. No man can work hard enough to climb up into heaven or labor enough to conquer death and hell. No man or combination of men can penetrate the spiritual world and dimension or transform man into a perfect being so that he never has to die and face judgment. Righteousness—man being right and perfect—is beyond the grasp of man's efforts.

> **Who has gone up to heaven and come down? Who has gathered up the wind in the hollow of his hands? Who has wrapped up the waters in his cloak? Who has established all the ends of the earth? What is his**

name, and the name of his son? Tell me if you know! (Prov 30:4)

No one has ever gone into heaven except the one who came from heaven—the Son of Man. (John 3:13)

5 (10:8-10) **Righteousness**: God's righteousness and salvation (utopia) are right before a person (cp. Dt.30:14). Jesus Christ is the Deliverer who has ascended into heaven and brought utopia down to man, and He is the Savior who has descended into the depths to conquer death and hell (Ro.10:9).

This is why it says: "When he ascended on high, he led captives in his train and gave gifts to men." (What does "he ascended" mean except that he also descended to the lower, earthly regions ? He who descended is the very one who ascended higher than all the heavens, in order to fill the whole universe.) (Eph 4:8-10)

Since Christ has come, the gospel does not require man to scale the heavens nor to fathom the great abyss. Such requirements would be impossible. The gospel only demands faith and open confession that Christ has done both. Why would God commission His Son to go to such limits for man? Simply because God loves man that much (Jn.3:16; Ro.5:8).

All that a man desires—righteousness, salvation, and utopia—are found within man's mouth and heart. Man has to do three simple things to be counted righteous and acceptable by God. He has to do three simple things to be saved from sin, death, and hell, and to receive utopia:

1. Man must confess with his mouth *that Jesus is Lord*. He must confess that Jesus Christ is the *Lord from heaven* (cp. v.6. See DEEPER STUDY # 1, *"From Above"*—Jn.3:31.)

No one has ever gone into heaven except the one who came from heaven—the Son of Man. (John 3:13)

"The one who comes from above is above all; the one who is from the earth belongs to the earth, and speaks as one from the earth. The one who comes from heaven is above all. (John 3:31)

For the bread of God is he who comes down from heaven and gives life to the world." (John 6:33)

But here is the bread that comes down from heaven, which a man may eat and not die. I am the living bread that came down from heaven. If anyone eats of this bread, he will live forever. This bread is my flesh, which I will give for the life of the world." (John 6:50-51)

What if you see the Son of Man ascend to where he was before! (John 6:62)

Jesus said to them, "If God were your Father, you would love me, for I came from God and now am here. I have not come on my own; but he sent me. (John 8:42)

And now, Father, glorify me in your presence with the glory I had with you before the world began. (John 17:5)

2. Man must believe that God raised Jesus from the dead. He must believe that Jesus Christ...
- died for man.
- was raised up from the dead because He perfectly satisfied God's demand for justice.

God's holiness and justice were perfectly satisfied with the death of Jesus Christ. God was perfectly satisfied with Christ taking man's sin upon Himself and bearing the punishment of sin for man. God was perfectly satisfied with Christ dying for man; therefore, God raised up Jesus Christ from the dead.

He was delivered over to death for our sins and was raised to life for our justification. (Rom 4:25)

And who through the Spirit of holiness was declared with power to be the Son of God by his resurrection from the dead: Jesus Christ our Lord. (Rom 1:4)

"We tell you the good news: What God promised our fathers he has fulfilled for us, their children, by raising up Jesus. As it is written in the second Psalm: "'You are my Son; today I have become your Father.' (Acts 13:32-33)

For he has set a day when he will judge the world with justice by the man he has appointed. He has given proof of this to all men by raising him from the dead." (Acts 17:31)

Praise be to the God and Father of our Lord Jesus Christ! In his great mercy he has given us new birth into a living hope through the resurrection of Jesus Christ from the dead, and into an inheritance that can never perish, spoil or fade—kept in heaven for you, (1 Pet 1:3-4)

3. Man must believe with the heart and then confess with the mouth. A man believes unto righteousness; that is, a man believes in Jesus Christ, and God takes that man's faith and counts it *as righteousness*. Then the man confesses Christ *to salvation*; that is, he is saved by openly confessing Christ. No man can deny God's Son and expect God to save him.

"Whoever acknowledges me before men, I will also acknowledge him before my Father in heaven. But whoever disowns me before men, I will disown him before my Father in heaven. (Mat 10:32-33)

"I tell you, whoever acknowledges me before men, the Son of Man will also acknowledge him before the angels of God. (Luke 12:8)

That if you confess with your mouth, "Jesus is Lord," and believe in your heart that God raised him from the dead, you will be saved. (Rom 10:9)

No one who denies the Son has the Father; whoever acknowledges the Son has the Father also. (1 John 2:23)

If anyone acknowledges that Jesus is the Son of God, God lives in him and he in God. (1 John 4:15)

6 (10:11) **Righteousness:** God's righteousness and salvation deliver a person from shame (cp. Is.28:16). Note two points.

1. Whoever believes in Christ is saved. The gospel is available to all, both Jew and Gentile. The gospel is the message of God's righteousness and salvation to the whole world. The gospel is universal.

> On the last and greatest day of the Feast, Jesus stood and said in a loud voice, "If anyone is thirsty, let him come to me and drink. (John 7:37)
>
> Who wants all men to be saved and to come to a knowledge of the truth. (1 Tim 2:4)
>
> Everyone who believes that Jesus is the Christ is born of God, and everyone who loves the father loves his child as well. (1 John 5:1)
>
> The Spirit and the bride say, "Come!" And let him who hears say, "Come!" Whoever is thirsty, let him come; and whoever wishes, let him take the free gift of the water of life. (Rev 22:17)
>
> "Turn to me and be saved, all you ends of the earth; for I am God, and there is no other. (Isa 45:22)
>
> "Come, all you who are thirsty, come to the waters; and you who have no money, come, buy and eat! Come, buy wine and milk without money and without cost. (Isa 55:1)

2. The true believer is not ashamed.
   a. He is not ashamed to face God, for he is covered with the righteousness of Christ.

> Rather, clothe yourselves with the Lord Jesus Christ, and do not think about how to gratify the desires of the sinful nature. (Rom 13:14)
>
> For all of you who were baptized into Christ have clothed yourselves with Christ. (Gal 3:27)
>
> And to put on the new self, created to be like God in true righteousness and holiness. (Eph 4:24)
>
> And have put on the new self, which is being renewed in knowledge in the image of its Creator. (Col 3:10)

   b. He is not ashamed to confess Christ before men. He readily confesses the glorious life and assurance God has given him in Christ Jesus the Lord.

> But you will receive power when the Holy Spirit comes on you; and you will be my witnesses in Jerusalem, and in all Judea and Samaria, and to the ends of the earth." (Acts 1:8)
>
> So do not be ashamed to testify about our Lord, or ashamed of me his prisoner. But join with me in suffering for the gospel, by the power of God, (2 Tim 1:8)
>
> But in your hearts set apart Christ as Lord. Always be prepared to give an answer to everyone who asks you to give the reason for the hope that you have. But do this with gentleness and respect, (1 Pet 3:15)

	E. The Gospel (Righteousness by Faith) is Not for Israel Alone—It is Universal, 10:12-21	Isaiah says, "Lord, who has believed our message?" 17 Consequently, faith comes from hearing the message, and the message is heard through the word of Christ.	a. Proves some Jews did not believe b. Proves "believing the message" is the method of salvation for all
1 Proof 1: The Lord treats all men just alike a. He makes no distinction between men b. He richly blesses all	12 For there is no difference between Jew and Gentile— the same Lord is Lord of all and richly blesses all who call on him,	18 But I ask: Did they not hear? Of course they did: "Their voice has gone out into all the earth, their words to the ends of the world."	5 Proof 5: Israel's disobedience proves the gospel is universal a. Not because they did not hear, cp. Ps.19:4 b. Not because they did not know, cp. Dt.32:21; Is.65:1
2 Proof 2: All men are saved by the same promise	13 For, "Everyone who calls on the name of the Lord will be saved."	19 Again I ask: Did Israel not understand? First, Moses says, "I will make you envious by those who are not a nation; I will make you angry by a nation that has no understanding."	
3 Proof 3: The world cannot be saved apart from the gospel a. The world cannot call, nor believe, nor hear without a preacher, cp. Is.52:7	14 How, then, can they call on the one they have not believed in? And how can they believe in the one of whom they have not heard? And how can they hear without someone preaching to them?	20 And Isaiah boldly says, "I was found by those who did not seek me; I revealed myself to those who did not ask for me."	
b. The preacher cannot preach unless he is sent	15 And how can they preach unless they are sent? As it is written, "How beautiful are the feet of those who bring good news!"	21 But concerning Israel he says, "All day long I have held out my hands to a disobedient and obstinate people."	c. Because they were disobedient & obstinate (unbelieving), cp. Ro.9:33; Is.65:2
4 Proof 4: Scripture says the gospel is universal[DS1]	16 But not all the Israelites accepted the good news. For		

DIVISION VII

ISRAEL AND THE GOSPEL OF RIGHTEOUSNESS, 9:1-11:36

E. The Gospel (Righteousness by Faith) is Not for Israel Alone—It is Universal, 10:12-21

(10:12-21) **Introduction**: God loves the whole world and every person in the world. His love is not limited to any one nation or people or type of person. The gospel is universal; it is for the world.

1. Proof 1: the Lord treats all men just alike (v.12).
2. Proof 2: all men are saved by the same promise (v.13).
3. Proof 3: the world cannot be saved apart from the gospel (v.14-15).
4. Proof 4: Scripture says the gospel is universal (v.16-17).
5. Proof 5: Israel's disobedience proves the gospel is universal (v.18-21).

1 (10:12) **Partiality—Israel vs. Gentiles**: the gospel is universal—the Lord God treats all men just alike.

1. There is no distinction between men, not in God's eyes. All men are related to God in the very same way. In God's eyes, all men...
   • are His creatures.
   • are sinful and alienated from Him.
   • are loved by Him.
   • are saved only through the righteousness provided by His Son.

God does not save one man a certain way and another man some other way; neither does God reject a man because he is a Jew or a Greek. God does not show partiality; He has no favorites. No person is favored over another person in being saved or condemned.

> **Now we know that God's judgment against those who do such things is based on truth. (Rom 2:2)**

> **Then Peter began to speak: "I now realize how true it is that God does not show favoritism but accepts men from every nation who fear him and do what is right. (Acts 10:34-35)**

> **Is he not the One who says to kings, 'You are worthless,' and to nobles, 'You are wicked,' who shows no partiality to princes and does not favor the rich over the poor, for they are all the work of his hands? (Job 34:18-19)**

2. The Lord God "richly blesses all who call on him." Scripture clearly declares:

> **And he passed in front of Moses, proclaiming, "The LORD, the LORD, the compassionate and gracious God, slow to anger, abounding in love and faithfulness, (Exo 34:6; cp. 2 Chron.30:9; Ps.103:8; 116:5; 145:8; Joel 2:13)**

The Lord God is rich in mercy and grace and in all else that is good and beneficial. He is so wealthy that every good gift and every perfect gift that exists in the world has flowed from His mercy and grace (Jas.1:17). Note two significant points.

   a. God has enough supply to richly bless all who call upon Him. There is no limit to the riches of His grace.

> **In him we have redemption through his blood, the forgiveness of sins, in accor-**

179

dance with the riches of God's grace (Eph 1:7)

I pray also that the eyes of your heart may be enlightened in order that you may know the hope to which he has called you, the riches of his glorious inheritance in the saints, (Eph 1:18)

But because of his great love for us, God, who is rich in mercy, made us alive with Christ even when we were dead in transgressions—it is by grace you have been saved. And God raised us up with Christ and seated us with him in the heavenly realms in Christ Jesus, in order that in the coming ages he might show the incomparable riches of his grace, expressed in his kindness to us in Christ Jesus. (Eph 2:4-7)

And my God will meet all your needs according to his glorious riches in Christ Jesus. (Phil 4:19)

b. A man must call upon God to receive the riches of God's mercy and grace. (See note—Ro.10:13 for discussion.)

2 (10:13) **Salvation**: all men are saved by the same promise. Note that this promise was foretold in the Old Testament (Joel 2:32). This verse is one of the great promises of God. God loves every person, no matter his nationality or race. God is not willing that any person should perish; He wants every person to be saved (2 Pt.3:9). In fact, God promises salvation to every man if the man will do but one thing: "Call on the name of the Lord." Note what God says.

1. "*Everyone* who calls on the name of the Lord will be saved." The word "everyone" means anyone, whoever, no matter who they are.

⇒ It means any person, any nationality, any race, any color.
⇒ It means any person from any environment, condition, background, country, government, or family.
⇒ It means any person, whether immoral or moral, unjust or just, bad or good, poor or wealthy, mean or nice, lonely or befriended, unpopular or popular, deformed or attractive, diseased or healthy, needful or without need.

"Everyone" means that any person can be saved, no matter who he is. No matter how terrible a person and his circumstances may be, he can be saved. He may be in the depths of the inner city or in the depths of the jungle, and he may be enslaved by the most terrible spirit of sin and evil imaginable—God will still save him.

On the last and greatest day of the Feast, Jesus stood and said in a loud voice, "If anyone is thirsty, let him come to me and drink. (John 7:37)

Who wants all men to be saved and to come to a knowledge of the truth. (1 Tim 2:4)

Everyone who believes that Jesus is the Christ is born of God, and everyone who loves the father loves his child as well. (1 John 5:1)

The Spirit and the bride say, "Come!"

And let him who hears say, "Come!" Whoever is thirsty, let him come; and whoever wishes, let him take the free gift of the water of life. (Rev 22:17)

"Turn to me and be saved, all you ends of the earth; for I am God, and there is no other. (Isa 45:22)

"Come, all you who are thirsty, come to the waters; and you who have no money, come, buy and eat! Come, buy wine and milk without money and without cost. (Isa 55:1)

2. "Everyone who *calls on the name of the Lord* will be saved. To "call on the name of the Lord" means at least two things.

a. It means that a person *calls* on the name of Lord Jesus Christ: he believes Jesus Christ can and will savehim. It means that the person looks upon and believes that Jesus Christ is the Savior of the world, that He is the Son of God who came to earth to save men. Very simply, it means that a person believes the message of John 3:16.

"For God so loved the world that he gave his one and only Son, that whoever believes in him shall not perish but have eternal life. (John 3:16)

"I tell you the truth, whoever hears my word and believes him who sent me has eternal life and will not be condemned; he has crossed over from death to life. (John 5:24)

b. It means that a person calls Jesus Christ *Lord*, that he looks upon Jesus as the Lord God of the universe and upon himself as His servant. It means that a person surrenders and dedicates himself to serve Jesus Christ throughout life—in everything and through everything, no matter the cost. To "call on the name of the *Lord*" means total surrender and dedication of all one is and has. (See note and DEEPER STUDY # 1—Lk.9:23; DEEPER STUDY # 2—Acts 2:36 for more discussion.)

Then he said to them all: "If anyone would come after me, he must deny himself and take up his cross daily and follow me. (Luke 9:23)

Therefore, I urge you, brothers, in view of God's mercy, to offer your bodies as living sacrifices, holy and pleasing to God—this is your spiritual act of worship. Do not conform any longer to the pattern of this world, but be transformed by the renewing of your mind. Then you will be able to test and approve what God's will is—his good, pleasing and perfect will. (Rom 12:1-2)

And every tongue confess that Jesus Christ is Lord, to the glory of God the Father. (Phil 2:11)

If anyone acknowledges that Jesus is the Son of God, God lives in him and he in God. (1 John 4:15)

3. "Everyone who calls...will be saved." (See DEEPER STUDY # 1, *Salvation*—Ro.1:16 for discussion.)

3 (10:14-15) **Gospel—Missions**: the world cannot be saved apart from the gospel. Remember what has just been said: "*Everyone* who calls on the name of the Lord will be saved "Everyone" refers to the whole world. But note the critical point: a person has to "call" in order to be saved. A person cannot "call on the name of the Lord" unless he has heard about the Lord. Therefore, the gospel has to be carried to the whole world. This is the point of the present two verses.

1. The world cannot call or believe or hear without a preacher. To prove the point, Scripture reverses the order of what actually happens.

   a. How can a person call on Jesus Christ if he has not believed in Him? It is impossible. Even in dealing with secular purposes, a person has to really believe in the purpose before he will give his life to it. Imagine giving all one is and has! No person is going to do that unless he really believes in something. The same is true in dealing with the Lord. No person is going to call upon the *Lord* to save him, nor is any person going to surrender and dedicate all he is and has to the Lord, unless he truly believes in the Lord.

   b. How can a person believe in Christ if he has not heard about Christ? How can a person know that Jesus Christ came to earth and died for his sins, and that Jesus Christ arose from the dead conquering death so that he might live eternally? Is a person born with the knowledge about Jesus Christ?

   ⇒ Picture the native in the depths of the jungle. Does he know that God's Son died for his sins? Was he born with knowledge of Jesus Christ? The answer is obvious: No! The native in the depths of the jungle has to hear before he can believe and call upon the Lord to save him.

   ⇒ Picture the man in the depths of the inner city, the city dweller who has never been exposed to the gospel, who has interest only in the things of the city and the world. Does he know that God's Son died for his sins? The answer is obvious: No! Not if he has never heard. The city dweller has to hear before he can believe and call upon the Lord to save him.

   ⇒ Picture the religionist in the depths of religion, the religionist who has never been exposed to the clear-cut presentation of the gospel, who has only heard about the life of Jesus and the form, ceremony, and ritual of religion. Does the religionist know that God's Son died to set him free from sin, death, and hell so that he might not serve sin any more? The answer is obvious: No! Not if he has never heard a clear-cut presentation of the gospel. Even the religionist has to hear before he can truly believe and truly call upon the Lord to save him. (What an indictment and warning to Christian ministers and teachers—a warning to present the gospel in simple, clear-cut terms.)

   c. How can a person hear without a preacher? How can a person hear that Jesus Christ died for him if a preacher or some Christian does not tell him? To hear anything requires a person who either speaks or writes. To receive communication requires a communicator. To hear a message requires a messenger. The message of the Lord Jesus Christ must be carried to the world, but in order to be carried, a messenger is needed. Christian believers must preach the message if people are to hear the message.

2. Now note that the basis of missions and evangelism is the preacher or witness himself. In the present context the "preacher" means any believer who bears witness to the Lord Jesus Christ. It takes a preacher to proclaim the message of the Lord Jesus so that people can hear and believe and call upon Him. However, note what this verse says: the preacher cannot preach unless he is sent.

   a. God is the One who sends forth preachers and witnesses of the Lord Jesus Christ. God is the One who commissions, qualifies, and instructs the preachers and witnesses of the gospel.

   > **You did not choose me, but I chose you and appointed you to go and bear fruit—fruit that will last. Then the Father will give you whatever you ask in my name. (John 15:16)**
   > **We are therefore Christ's ambassadors, as though God were making his appeal through us. We implore you on Christ's behalf: Be reconciled to God. (2 Cor 5:20)**
   > **I became a servant of this gospel by the gift of God's grace given me through the working of his power. (Eph 3:7)**
   > **I thank Christ Jesus our Lord, who has given me strength, that he considered me faithful, appointing me to his service. (1 Tim 1:12)**
   > **And of this gospel I was appointed a herald and an apostle and a teacher. (2 Tim 1:11)**
   > **Be shepherds of God's flock that is under your care, serving as overseers—not because you must, but because you are willing, as God wants you to be; not greedy for money, but eager to serve; not lording it over those entrusted to you, but being examples to the flock. (1 Pet 5:2-3)**

   b. Christian believers have a part in sending forth laborers as well as God. We are to pray for diligent workers (Mt.9:37).

   ⇒ We are to go forth ourselves.

   > **Therefore go and make disciples of all nations, baptizing them in the name of the Father and of the Son and of the Holy Spirit, and teaching them to obey everything I have commanded you. And surely I am with you always, to the very end of the age." (Mat 28:19-20)**
   > **He said to them, "Go into all the world and preach the good news to all creation. (Mark 16:15)**

   ⇒ We are to pray for laborers, for diligent workers.

   > **Then he said to his disciples, "The harvest is plentiful but the workers are few. Ask the Lord of the harvest, therefore, to send out workers into his harvest field." (Mat 9:37-38)**

c. We are to give to meet the needs of the world.

> But just as you excel in everything—in faith, in speech, in knowledge, in complete earnestness and in your love for us —see that you also excel in this grace of giving. (2 Cor 8:7)
>
> Remember this: Whoever sows sparingly will also reap sparingly, and whoever sows generously will also reap generously. (2 Cor 9:6)
>
> He who has been stealing must steal no longer, but must work, doing something useful with his own hands, that he may have something to share with those in need. (Eph 4:28)
>
> If anyone has material possessions and sees his brother in need but has no pity on him, how can the love of God be in him? (1 John 3:17)

3. The gospel is the message of peace and good news, the glad tidings of good things. Note three points.
   a. The message of the gospel is peace (see notes, *Peace*—Ro.5:1; Jn.14:27 for discussion).

> Peace I leave with you; my peace I give you. I do not give to you as the world gives. Do not let your hearts be troubled and do not be afraid. (John 14:27)
>
> "I have told you these things, so that in me you may have peace. In this world you will have trouble. But take heart! I have overcome the world." (John 16:33)

   b. The message of the gospel is good news (see note, *Inheritance*—Ro.8:17. Also see DEEPER STUDY #1, *Salvation*—Ro.1:16; outlines and notes—Ro.8:1-39 for discussion.)

> "I tell you the truth, whoever hears my word and believes him who sent me has eternal life and will not be condemned; he has crossed over from death to life. (John 5:24)
>
> The thief comes only to steal and kill and destroy; I have come that they may have life, and have it to the full. (John 10:10)
>
> But the fruit of the Spirit is love, joy, peace, patience, kindness, goodness, faithfulness, gentleness and self-control. Against such things there is no law. (Gal 5:22-23)
>
> Praise be to the God and Father of our Lord Jesus Christ! In his great mercy he has given us new birth into a living hope through the resurrection of Jesus Christ from the dead, and into an inheritance that can never perish, spoil or fade—kept in heaven for you, (1 Pet 1:3-4)

   c. The feet of the preacher and witness are beautiful; that is, they are a welcome sight to the world. The world desperately needs the message of peace and good news. (Note: this verse is a quotation from Is.52:7.)

4 (10:16-17) **Salvation—Belief—Hearing**: Scripture says the gospel is universal. Isaiah says that many Jews did not "believe the message of God" (cp. Is.53:1). Therefore, they prove that salvation is not by race, heritage, tradition, religion, institution, nor by works established by the Jewish nation or any other people.

Note a second thing: Isaiah used the phrase, "believing our message." Isaiah was saying that *believing the message* is the way of salvation. The message was to stir faith.

There are three steps involved in faith. (See DEEPER STUDY # 2—Jn.2:24.)

1. The step of hearing. A man must be willing to listen to the message of Christ.

> But blessed are your eyes because they see, and your ears because they hear. (Mat 13:16)
>
> But the one who received the seed that fell on good soil is the man who hears the word and understands it. He produces a crop, yielding a hundred, sixty or thirty times what was sown." (Mat 13:23)
>
> She had a sister called Mary, who sat at the Lord's feet listening to what he said. (Luke 10:39)
>
> People were also bringing babies to Jesus to have him touch them. When the disciples saw this, they rebuked them. (Luke 18:15)
>
> Yet to all who received him, to those who believed in his name, he gave the right to become children of God— (John 1:12)
>
> Now the Bereans were of more noble character than the Thessalonians, for they received the message with great eagerness and examined the Scriptures every day to see if what Paul said was true. (Acts 17:11)
>
> And we also thank God continually because, when you received the word of God, which you heard from us, you accepted it not as the word of men, but as it actually is, the word of God, which is at work in you who believe. (1 Th 2:13)
>
> My dear brothers, take note of this: Everyone should be quick to listen, slow to speak and slow to become angry, (James 1:19)
>
> Blessed is the man who listens to me, watching daily at my doors, waiting at my doorway. (Prov 8:34)
>
> He who listens to a life-giving rebuke will be at home among the wise. (Prov 15:31)
>
> The heart of the discerning acquires knowledge; the ears of the wise seek it out. (Prov 18:15)

2. The step of mental assent. A man must agree that the message is true, that the facts of the case are thus and so. But this is not enough. Mere agreement does not lead to action. Many a person knows that something is true, but he does not change his behavior to match his knowledge. For example, a man knows that eating too much harms his body, but he may continue to eat too much. He is a double-minded man: he agrees to the truth and knows the truth, but he does nothing about it. This man still does not have faith, not the kind of faith that the Bible talks about.

He chose to give us birth through the word of truth, that we might be a kind of firstfruits of all he created. (James 1:18)

Come near to God and he will come near to you. Wash your hands, you sinners, and purify your hearts, you double-minded. (James 4:8)

And if you have not been trustworthy with someone else's property, who will give you property of your own? (Luke 16:12)

You cannot drink the cup of the Lord and the cup of demons too; you cannot have a part in both the Lord's table and the table of demons. (1 Cor 10:21)

Their heart is deceitful, and now they must bear their guilt. The LORD will demolish their altars and destroy their sacred stones. (Hosea 10:2)

3. The step of commitment. When the New Testament speaks of faith, it speaks of *commitment*, a personal commitment to the truth. A man hears the truth and agrees that it is true and does something about it. He commits and yields his life to the truth. The truth becomes a part of his very being, a part of his behavior and life.

Saving faith is believing in the name of Jesus Christ and committing one's life to Him. It is trusting Jesus Christ, completely putting one's trust in Him, who He is and what He has done. It is casting one's life into His hands, believing He will take care of one's past (sins), present (looking after), and future (delivering from death unto life eternal).

That everyone who believes in him may have eternal life. (John 3:15)

Whoever believes in the Son has eternal life, but whoever rejects the Son will not see life, for God's wrath remains on him." (John 3:36)

"I tell you the truth, whoever hears my word and believes him who sent me has eternal life and will not be condemned; he has crossed over from death to life. (John 5:24)

Then they asked him, "What must we do to do the works God requires?" Jesus answered, "The work of God is this: to believe in the one he has sent." (John 6:28-29)

Jesus said to her, "I am the resurrection and the life. He who believes in me will live, even though he dies; (John 11:25)

But these are written that you may believe that Jesus is the Christ, the Son of God, and that by believing you may have life in his name. (John 20:31)

All the prophets testify about him that everyone who believes in him receives forgiveness of sins through his name." (Acts 10:43)

Through him everyone who believes is justified from everything you could not be justified from by the law of Moses. (Acts 13:39)

They replied, "Believe in the Lord Jesus, and you will be saved—you and your household." (Acts 16:31)

That if you confess with your mouth, "Jesus is Lord," and believe in your heart

that God raised him from the dead, you will be saved. (Rom 10:9)

In the same way, faith by itself, if it is not accompanied by action, is dead. (James 2:17)

DEEPER STUDY # 1
(10:16) **Faith—Obedience**: note that the gospel is to be obeyed. Obedience and belief are synonymous terms when dealing with the gospel. To believe in Christ is to obey Him, and to obey Him is to believe Him. A person who truly believes in Jesus Christ will obey Him. (See DEEPER STUDY # 2, *Believe*—Jn.2:24 for more discussion.) There is no such thing...
- as belief without obedience.
- as believing in Jesus Christ and not following Him.
- as believing Jesus Christ has forgiven one's sin and living in sin.
- as believing the gospel and living like the world.

"Therefore come out from them and be separate, says the Lord. Touch no unclean thing, and I will receive you." "I will be a Father to you, and you will be my sons and daughters, says the Lord Almighty." (2 Cor 6:17-18)

And, once made perfect, he became the source of eternal salvation for all who obey him (Heb 5:9)

5 (10:18-21) **Israel vs. Gentiles**: Israel's disobedience proves the gospel is universal. Why did Israel not obey the gospel?

1. Israel's disobedience was not because they did not hear the Word of God (v.18). The very opposite is true. Israel was the very custodian of the Scriptures, the very people whom God had chosen to bring salvation to the world (see note—Jn.4:2 for discussion). No matter where the Jewish people were scattered, they had the Word of God and heard it. (Note that Paul quotes Ps.19:4 as Scriptural proof of what he says.)

2. Israel's disobedience was not because the people did not know the truth (v.19). They knew the truth, and they had a dynamic example and demonstration of the truth. They had the example of the Gentiles who turned to the gospel in great numbers.

Note how Scripture words this: "I will make you envious." Israel had the stirrings of jealousy and envy to help them turn to the gospel. They heard and knew. Their disobedience to the gospel was not because they were ignorant of the gospel. The gospel was actually lived out before their faces in the person of Jesus Christ and in the Gentiles turning to Christ for salvation. (Again, Paul supports his point from the Old Testament, Dt.32:21; Is.65:1.)

3. Israel's rejection was because they were a disobedient and obstinate people. Note how good God had been to Israel.
   a. God "held out His hands": inviting, offering forgiveness and peace and reconciliation, pleading and begging for Israel to return to Him.
   b. "All day long": being patient and longsuffering and forebearing, bearing for a long time, waiting until the last moment to turn away.

Say to them, 'As surely as I live, declares the Sovereign LORD, I take no pleasure in the death of the wicked, but rather that they turn from their ways and live. Turn! Turn from your evil ways! Why will you die, O house of Israel?' (Ezek 33:11)

"Come, let us return to the LORD. He has torn us to pieces but he will heal us; he has injured us but he will bind up our wounds. (Hosea 6:1)

We are therefore Christ's ambassadors, as though God were making his appeal through us. We implore you on Christ's behalf: Be reconciled to God. (2 Cor 5:20)

Here I am! I stand at the door and knock. If anyone hears my voice and opens the door, I will come in and eat with him, and he with me. (Rev 3:20)

However, Israel refused and rejected God's gracious invitations. Israel chose to remain disobedient and obstinate. They closed their minds despite the clear evidence and refused to consider the truth of Christ as the true Savior of the world (see DEEPER STUDY # 3,4—Mt.12:24; 21:33-46; 22:1-14 for discussion).

Do not harden your hearts as you did at Meribah, as you did that day at Massah in the desert, (Psa 95:8)

Blessed is the man who always fears the LORD, but he who hardens his heart falls into trouble. (Prov 28:14)

A man who remains stiff-necked after many rebukes will suddenly be destroyed—without remedy. (Prov 29:1)

But because of your stubbornness and your unrepentant heart, you are storing up wrath against yourself for the day of God's wrath, when his righteous judgment will be revealed. (Rom 2:5)

But encourage one another daily, as long as it is called Today, so that none of you may be hardened by sin's deceitfulness. (Heb 3:13)

CHAPTER 11

F. The Callous on Israel's Heart is Not Total—There is a Remnant, 11:1-10

1 Israel was disobedient (10:21) a. Is all Israel rejected? b. By no means!	I ask then: Did God reject his people? By no means! I am an Israelite myself, a descendant of Abraham, from the tribe of Benjamin.
2 Proof 1: Paul himself was part of the remnant	2 God did not reject his people, whom he foreknew. Don't you know what the Scripture says in the passage about Elijah—how he appealed to God against Israel:
3 Proof 2: God's foreknowledge guarantees a remnant	
4 Proof 3: Elijah foresaw the remnant[DS1]	3 "Lord, they have killed your prophets and torn down your altars; I am the only one left, and they are trying to kill me"?
a. Elijah's mistake: He felt he was the only faithful believer in all Israel	
b. God's assurance to Elijah: There is a godly	4 And what was God's answer to him? "I have reserved

for myself seven thousand who have not bowed the knee to Baal."	remnant	
5 So too, at the present time there is a remnant chosen by grace.	**5 Proof 4: There is a remnant at this present time—a strong assertion**	
6 And if by grace, then it is no longer by works; if it were, grace would no longer be grace.	**6 Proof 5: God's grace assures a remnant**	
7 What then? What Israel sought so earnestly it did not obtain, but the elect did. The others were hardened,	a. Israel did not obtain righteousness, but the chosen few did[DS2]	
8 As it is written: "God gave them a spirit of stupor, eyes so that they could not see and ears so that they could not hear, to this very day."	b. Israel is accused by Scripture 1) Of being drowsy	
9 And David says: "May their table become a snare and a trap, a stumbling block and a retribution for them.	2) Of being worthy of judgment	
10 May their eyes be darkened so they cannot see, and their backs be bent forever."	3) Of being blinded	

DIVISION VII

ISRAEL AND THE GOSPEL OF RIGHTEOUSNESS, 9:1-11:36

F. The Callous on Israel's Heart is Not Total—There is a Remnant, 11:1-10

(11:1-10) **Introduction**: there is a glorious hope both for Israel and for the world. God's promises are always fulfilled. The callous on *Israel's heart* is not total—there is a remnant. The callous on *any people's heart* is not total—there can be a remnant. God will have His witnesses among all people. People everywhere can be saved if they will turn to God's Son, Jesus Christ.

1. Israel was disobedient (v.1).
2. Proof 1: Paul himself was part of the remnant (v.1).
3. Proof 2: God's foreknowledge guarantees a remnant (v.2).
4. Proof 3: Elijah foresaw the remnant (v.2-4).
5. Proof 4: there is a remnant at this present time—a strong assertion (v.5).
6. Proof 5: God's grace assures a remnant (v.6-10).

1 (11:1) **Israel, Remnant**: Israel was disobedient to God, gripped by an obstinate unbelief (cp. Ro.10:21). The nation as a whole did not believe or obey God. They even rejected God's own Son (Jn.1:11). How can this fact be reconciled with the fact that Israel is *God's people*? Note that even in this verse they are called "His people" (v.1).

⇒ God had given birth to Israel through Abraham and had made some great promises to the nation through Abraham (see notes—Ro.9:6; DEEPER STUDY # 1—4:1-25 for discussion).

⇒ God had even promised that He would never reject nor cast off His people: "For the LORD will not reject his people, he will never forsake his inheritance" (Ps.94:14).

In light of this, is it not inconsistent and is it not denying God's Word to teach that Israel is not saved, that Israel is no longer the people of God? To ask the question as Paul words it: "Did God reject His people?" The word "reject"

(a posato) means to push away, to thrust away, to repel, to repudiate. The idea is to *utterly and totally and finally* cast away. Has God utterly rejected the Jews? Paul shouts: "By no means" (me genoito). It is impossible! It must never be! It can never be! God has not broken and violated His Word to Israel. God's promises to Israel did not mean that all Jews were *locked in* to salvation no matter how sinful and disobedient they were. It did not mean that an unbelieving and disobedient Jew was acceptable to God simply because he had been *born* a Jew. God's promises were intended for those who *believed and obeyed Him*. The people who believed and obeyed Him have always been "His people." Paul gives five proofs to show that God has not rejected every Jew. God accepts and fulfills His promises to all those who believe and obey Him.

2 (11:1) **Israel, Remnant**: proof one is that Paul himself was part of God's remnant. God had not totally rejected Israel. There was a remnant of godly and obedient believers in Israel. Paul himself is proof of the glorious fact.

1. Paul was a pure Jew, a true descendant of Abraham, not a mere proselyte; and he was of the elite, of the Benjaminite aristocracy.

2. Paul was part of the remnant of God. He was claiming to be a true child of God, a true son of Abraham, one of the sons whom God had not rejected. Therefore, he himself was proof that God had not rejected His people. (Cp. Acts 9:1-19; 22:1-6; 26:12-18 for Paul's conversion.)

"Who are you, Lord?" Saul asked. "I am Jesus, whom you are persecuting," he replied. "Now get up and go into the city, and you will be told what you must do." (Acts 9:5-6)

But whatever was to my profit I now consider loss for the sake of Christ. What is more, I consider everything a loss compared to the surpassing greatness of knowing Christ Jesus my Lord, for whose sake I have lost all things. I consider them rubbish, that I may gain Christ and be found in him, not having a righteousness of my own that comes from the law, but that which is through faith in Christ—the righteousness that comes from God and is by faith. (Phil 3:7-9; cp. v.3-16)

3 (11:2) **Israel, Remnant—God, Foreknowledge**: proof two is that God's foreknowledge guarantees a remnant (see note, *Foreknowledge*, pt.3—Ro.8:29 for discussion. Also see DEEPER STUDY # 3—Acts 2:23 for more detailed discussion.) Very simply stated, God Himself guarantees a remnant; He saves those whom He foreknows.

That have been known for ages. (Acts 15:18)

For those God foreknew he also predestined to be conformed to the likeness of his Son, that he might be the firstborn among many brothers. (Rom 8:29)

God did not reject his people [Israel], whom he foreknew. Don't you know what the Scripture says in the passage about Elijah—how he appealed to God against Israel: (Rom 11:2)

For you know that it was not with perishable things such as silver or gold that you were redeemed from the empty way of life handed down to you from your forefathers, but with the precious blood of Christ, a lamb without blemish or defect. He was chosen before the creation of the world, but was revealed in these last times for your sake. (1 Pet 1:18-20)

Nevertheless, God's solid foundation stands firm, sealed with this inscription: "The Lord knows those who are his," and, "Everyone who confesses the name of the Lord must turn away from wickedness." (2 Tim 2:19)

Who have been chosen according to the foreknowledge of God the Father, through the sanctifying work of the Spirit, for obedience to Jesus Christ and sprinkling by his blood: Grace and peace be yours in abundance. (1 Pet 1:2)

4 (11:2-4) **Israel, Remnant**: proof three is that Elijah foresaw the remnant (1 Ki.19:9-18). This is proof from the very highest authority among men, the authority of Scripture itself. From the very beginning Scripture very clearly says that not all Israel was saved, but only a remnant truly followed God. This is clearly seen in Elijah's experience. His day was a terrible day of sin and apostasy, and he himself was being marked for death because he refused to stop his preaching of righteousness. In a moment of extreme pressure and uncertainty, he cried out to God in prayer wondering if he was the only godly person left in Israel. God assured Elijah by telling him there were still seven thousand godly believers in the nation. The point is this. In Elijah's day the vast majority of people were as they are

today: disobedient and disloyal to God, rejecting and denying God, controlling their own lives and following after the man-made and humanistic gods of this earth. But there *was* a remnant, a few who were loyal and obedient to God. There were only seven thousand; nevertheless there was a remnant, a few who were trusting God to fulfill His promises to them.

Thought 1. Note two revealing facts:
⇒ how many stray away from God and reject Him—how many within a nation, a state, a city, a neighborhood, a family, a religious body!
⇒ how God always has His few, His promised remnant who do obey and remain loyal to Him!

Therefore, since we are surrounded by such a great cloud of witnesses, let us throw off everything that hinders and the sin that so easily entangles, and let us run with perseverance the race marked out for us. (Heb 12:1)

Therefore, prepare your minds for action; be self-controlled; set your hope fully on the grace to be given you when Jesus Christ is revealed. (1 Pet 1:13)

Yet you have a few people in Sardis who have not soiled their clothes. They will walk with me, dressed in white, for they are worthy. (Rev 3:4)

I am coming soon. Hold on to what you have, so that no one will take your crown. (Rev 3:11)

True instruction was in his mouth and nothing false was found on his lips. He walked with me in peace and uprightness, and turned many from sin. (Mal 2:6)

Thought 2. Note how the image of a nation is determined by the life-style of the majority. The wickedness of the majority in Israel overshadowed the godliness of the few. Even Elijah, the great prophet of God, was unaware of the seven thousand godly scattered throughout the nation. Yet they were there. God will never leave Himself without a witness, nor will He ever leave His people without fellow laborers throughout the world. We may not know about each other, but we can rest assured there are other witnesses scattered around, witnesses who are bearing testimony for the Lord Jesus. God has His remnant, His faithful few.

Righteousness exalts a nation, but sin is a disgrace to any people. (Prov 14:34)

DEEPER STUDY # 1
(11:2) **Israel, Remnant**: Elijah foresaw the remnant in 1 Ki.19:9-18. Other prophets also saw the remnant: Isaiah (Is.1:9; 4:3; 11:16; 37:4), Jeremiah (Jer.6:9; 23:3; 3:7), Ezekiel (Ezk.14:14, 20, 22), Amos (Amos 9:8-12), Micah (Mic.2:12; 5:3), Zephaniah (Zeph.2:9; 3:12-13).

5 (11:5) **Israel, Remnant**: proof four is that there is a remnant at this present time. This is a strong assertion: "There is a remnant." There is no question about the fact. Note why: because of the they are "chosen by grace." If there was a remnant in Israel in the day of Elijah, there is bound to be a remnant of believers today. Why? Because of grace: the grace of God in Jesus Christ has now come to earth, and the Spirit of God is actively at work making God's grace known.

> For the grace of God that brings salvation has appeared to all men. It teaches us to say "No" to ungodliness and worldly passions, and to live self-controlled, upright and godly lives in this present age, while we wait for the blessed hope—the glorious appearing of our great God and Savior, Jesus Christ, who gave himself for us to redeem us from all wickedness and to purify for himself a people that are his very own, eager to do what is good. (Titus 2:11-14)

> Isaiah cries out concerning Israel: "Though the number of the Israelites be like the sand by the sea, only the remnant will be saved. (Rom 9:27)

6 (11:6-10) **Israel, Remnant—God, Grace of**: proof five is that God's grace assures a remnant. A person is not saved because he merits or works for salvation. No man deserves God's grace. No one deserves being chosen by God for anything. God does not bestow His grace upon a man because a man deserves or earns grace. A man does not secure God's acceptance because he wills or runs after God (Jn.1:12). God has mercy upon a man because He is a gracious God. If a man was saved because of works, then salvation...

- would not be by grace (of God) but by works (of man).
- would remove grace (God) from the picture and put works (man) in the forefront.

Very simply, God would no longer be necessary, for man would be saving himself. If by some figment of the imagination and scientific work man could save himself by figuring out how to live eternally, then God Himself would not be needed. In fact, neither grace nor work would be necessary, for man would have reached perfection. (The absurdity of such a possibility is clearly seen in the thought.) (See DEEPER STUDY # 1, *Election*—Ro.9:10-13 for more discussion.)

The point is this: it is God's grace that saves men. Therefore, God will see to it that there is always a remnant of believers in Israel. The vast majority of Jews stumbled and fell at the snare of works (v.6), but the callous on Israel's heart is not total. There is a remnant. Note two points.

1. The vast majority of Israel did not obtain righteousness, but the chosen few did.
   ⇒ Most sought after righteousness, but they failed to secure it because they sought it by works (see note, *Israel*—Ro.10:1-3 for more discussion).
   ⇒ However, the elect have obtained righteousness (see note—Ro.10:4 for more discussion).

2. Israel is accused and condemned by Scripture of three terrible things.
   ⇒ Of being drowsy and condemned to drowsiness (Is.29:10; 6:9).
   ⇒ Of being worthy of judgment and condemned to judgment (Ps.69:22).
   ⇒ Of being blind and condemned to blindness (Ps.69:23).

The picture is that of men sitting and feasting comfortably at a banquet table. They are at ease, secure, and pos-sessed with a sense of safety. In fact they are so comfortable that their safety becomes their ruin. The enemy sneaks upon them unaware.

Note this: God is said to be the One who made Israel drowsy and blind and worthy of judgment. This is Scripture's way of stressing what can be called the *judicial blindness and rejection of men* (see DEEPER STUDY # 2—Ro.11:7-10 for discussion).

DEEPER STUDY # 2

(11:7-10) **Judgement—Judicial Blindness and Rejection—Spiritual Abandonment**: note the words were "made unresponsive" and "God gave them a spirit of stupor" (cp. Is.39:10; 6:9; Ps.69:22-23). The idea is that God is the One who made Israel unresponsive. However, Scripture clearly says that God does not tempt men, much less cause them to sin and be unresponsive (Jas.1:13). What does this mean then? It means at least two things.

1. The unbeliever's rejection is willful, always deliberate. The unbeliever does see and hear, yet he refuses to really open his eyes and ears. He refuses to understand. But why does a person act so illogically by rebelling and refusing to understand? Christ answers this question by saying, "This people's heart has become calloused [hardened]" (Mt.13:15). The Greek is "this people's heart has grown fat [overweight]." Being fat indicates sensuality and senselessness. To eat and eat, adding weight upon weight, is living after the sinful nature; and living after the sinful nature makes no sense at all. It is sensual and senseless. Christ is therefore saying that the unbeliever has become so sensual and senseless that he rebels and refuses to understand the gospel of God.
   ⇒ His sensuality is due to worldliness and the lust for the things of the world.

> Those who live according to the sinful nature have their minds set on what that nature desires; but those who live in accordance with the Spirit have their minds set on what the Spirit desires. The mind of sinful man is death, but the mind controlled by the Spirit is life and peace; the sinful mind is hostile to God. It does not submit to God's law, nor can it do so. Those controlled by the sinful nature cannot please God. (Rom 8:5-8)

> Do not love the world or anything in the world. If anyone loves the world, the love of the Father is not in him. For everything in the world—the cravings of sinful man, the lust of his eyes and the boasting of what he has and does—comes not from the Father but from the world. (1 John 2:15-16)

   ⇒ His senselessness is due to being deceived by the evil one.

> And even if our gospel is veiled, it is veiled to those who are perishing. The god of this age has blinded the minds of unbelievers, so that they cannot see the light of the gospel of the glory of Christ, who is the image of God. (2 Cor 4:3-4)

2. The unbeliever experiences a judicial blindness and rejection by God. A person who *deliberately chooses* to be blind to the gospel and to reject Christ is given over to a *just punishment*. God offers His love and salvation of eter-

nal life to a man, but a man has to choose to receive God's offer.

⇒ Man's unbelief is allowed to roam in the sphere of unbelief and to become obstinate unbelief—if the man continues to blind himself to the truth. God will not violate the will of a man.

⇒ Man's sin is allowed to roam in the sphere of sin and to become constant sin—if the man continues to blind himself to the truth. God does not violate the will of a man.

A person's rejection leads to *judicial blindness* and to being rejected by God. (See notes—Ro.1:24; DEEPER STUDY # 1—Jn.12:39-41 for more discussion.)

> For in the same way you judge others, you will be judged, and with the measure you use, it will be measured to you. (Mat 7:2)
>
> Therefore God gave them over in the sinful desires of their hearts to sexual impurity for the degrading of their bodies with one another....Because of this, God gave them over to shameful lusts. Even their women exchanged natural relations for unnatural ones....Furthermore, since they did not think it worthwhile to retain the knowledge of God, he gave them over

to a depraved mind, to do what ought not to be done. (Rom 1:24, 26, 28)

> But because of your stubbornness and your unrepentant heart, you are storing up wrath against yourself for the day of God's wrath, when his righteous judgment will be revealed. God "will give to each person according to what he has done." (Rom 2:5-6)
>
> Do not be deceived: God cannot be mocked. A man reaps what he sows. The one who sows to please his sinful nature, from that nature will reap destruction; the one who sows to please the Spirit, from the Spirit will reap eternal life. (Gal 6:7-8)
>
> Then the LORD said, "My Spirit will not contend with man forever, for he is mortal ; his days will be a hundred and twenty years." (Gen 6:3)
>
> "But my people would not listen to me; Israel would not submit to me. So I gave them over to their stubborn hearts to follow their own devices. (Psa 81:11-12)
>
> A man who remains stiff-necked after many rebukes will suddenly be destroyed—without remedy. (Prov 29:1)
>
> Ephraim is joined to idols; leave him alone! (Hosea 4:17)

1 Proof 1: God has overruled Israel's stumbling over Christ a. God opens salvation to the Gentiles b. God stirs the Jews to be restored c. God assures the glorious restoration of Israel & a rich blessing for the whole earth	**G. The Callous on Israel's Heart is Not Final—There is to be a Restoration, 11:11-16** 11 Again I ask: Did they stumble so as to fall beyond recovery? Not at all! Rather, because of their transgression, salvation has come to the Gentiles to make Israel envious. 12 But if their transgression means riches for the world, and their loss means riches for the Gentiles, how much greater riches will their fullness bring!	13 I am talking to you Gentiles. Inasmuch as I am the apostle to the Gentiles, I make much of my ministry 14 In the hope that I may somehow arouse my own people to envy and save some of them. 15 For if their rejection is the reconciliation of the world, what will their acceptance be but life from the dead? 16 If the part of the dough offered as firstfruits is holy, then the whole batch is holy; if the root is holy, so are the branches.	**2 Proof 2: Paul tries to stir the Jews to be saved** a. By magnifying his ministry to the Gentiles b. Paul's purpose 1) To stir some to be saved 2) To bring about the restoration, the great climax of history **3 Proof 3: The forefathers, that is, the patriarchs, give a heritage of holiness**

DIVISION VII

ISRAEL AND THE GOSPEL OF RIGHTEOUSNESS, 9:1-11:36

G. The Callous on Israel's Heart is Not Final—There is to be a Restoration, 11:11-16

(11:11-16) **Introduction**: the callous on a man's heart does not have to be final. Every man can repent and turn to Christ and be restored to God. This is the message of this passage. The callous on Israel's heart is not final. There is to be a restoration of Israel. Many in Israel are going to return to God and accept the Lord Jesus Christ as their Savior.

1. Proof 1: God has overruled Israel's stumbling over Christ (v.11-12).
2. Proof 2: Paul tries to stir the Jews to be saved (v.13-15).
3. Proof 3: the forefathers, that is, the patriarchs, give a heritage of holiness (v.16).

1 (11:11-12) **Israel, Restoration—God, Sovereignty**: proof one is that God has overruled Israel's stumbling over Christ.

⇒ Israel has stumbled over Christ (see DEEPER STUDY #9,10—Mt.21:44 for discussion).
⇒ Has Israel stumbled that they should fall?

The contrast between stumble and fall is devastating. The idea is that of a permanent and final fall—spiritually. Is Israel's problem with Christ permanent and final? Will Israel never accept God's Son, Jesus Christ, as the true Messiah? Is the spiritual fall of Israel to be forever?

Paul's response is forceful: God forbid! Not at all! Perish the thought! Let it never be! Such a thing is impossible in God's plan for the world. God has overruled Israel's stumble over Christ in three glorious ways.

1. God has opened the door of salvation to the whole world. The Lord's messengers went to Israel first, but Israel did not want to hear that Jesus Christ is the Messiah, the Son of God Himself. Very few received the gospel. In fact, so many rejected the message that it can be said that Israel, the nation as a whole, has stumbled over Christ. Israel, the Jews...

- have shut their eyes, lest they should see Christ (v.8).
- have closed their ears, lest they should hear Christ (v.8).
- have set themselves to bitterly oppose Christ (1 Th.2:15-16).

God had no other choice but to do the logical thing. The glorious message of His love and of His Son was at stake; therefore, God sent His messengers throughout the world (the Gentile world) in search of any person who would receive the message of His Son. God did what the Jews had always failed to do: God threw open the door of salvation to the whole world. (See DEEPER STUDY # 8, *Israel*—Mt.21:43 for more detailed discussion.)

Then Paul and Barnabas answered them boldly: "We had to speak the word of God to you first. Since you reject it and do not consider yourselves worthy of eternal life, we now turn to the Gentiles. (Acts 13:46)

For this people's heart has become calloused; they hardly hear with their ears, and they have closed their eyes. Otherwise they might see with their eyes, hear with their ears, understand with their hearts and turn, and I would heal them.' "Therefore I want you to know that God's salvation has been sent to the Gentiles, and they will listen!" (Acts 28:27-28)

"Then he said to his servants, 'The wedding banquet is ready, but those I invited did not deserve to come. Go to the street corners and invite to the banquet anyone you find.' (Mat 22:8-9)

"The servant came back and reported this to his master. Then the owner of the house became angry and ordered his servant, 'Go out quickly into the streets and alleys of the town and bring in the poor, the crippled, the blind and the lame.' "'Sir,' the servant said, 'what you ordered has been done, but there is still room.' "Then the master told his servant, 'Go out to the roads and country lanes and make them come in, so that my house will be full. I tell you, not one of those men who were invited will get a taste of my banquet.'" (Luke 14:21-24)

Thought 1. Note two provoking thoughts.
1) Think how wonderful it would have been if the Jews had accepted Jesus Christ and had become God's missionary force to carry the message of Christ to the world! Would the world have been reached by now? It has been two thousand years since Christ came to earth, and the world still has not been reached with the gospel. If the Jews had accepted Christ, would the task now be complete? How many more people would have been saved?
2) Think how wonderful it would be if more of us (the Gentiles) would accept Christ! If we would dedicate our lives more sacrificially to carry God's message of salvation to the world, how many more people would be saved and delivered from death?

Thought 2. Note how God "works for the good of the world." He took Israel's rejection of His Son and *enriched* the world. Why? Because God has determined that His Son Jesus Christ shall have many *brothers* who will worship and serve Him throughout all eternity. Therefore, if a people rejects the message of His Son, God will work it out to send the message to another people (cp. Ro.8:28-29).

2. God stirs the Jews to be restored. God has not forsaken the Jews. The door of salvation is open to them as well as to the Gentiles. The Jews can look at true Christian believers and see the holiness, love, joy, and peace of their lives; and the Jews can be stirred to receive Christ. In fact, this is the very point of the present passage. God sees to it that some Jews are "made envious," that is, stirred to receive Christ and the glorious life of salvation which He offers.

> But I tell you the truth: It is for your good that I am going away. Unless I go away, the Counselor will not come to you; but if I go, I will send him to you. When he comes, he will convict the world of guilt in regard to sin and righteousness and judgment: in regard to sin, because men do not believe in me; in regard to righteousness, because I am going to the Father, where you can see me no longer; and in regard to judgment, because the prince of this world now stands condemned. (John 16:7-11)
> And repentance and forgiveness of sins will be preached in his name to all nations, beginning at Jerusalem. (Luke 24:47)
> I am not ashamed of the gospel, because it is the power of God for the salvation of everyone who believes: first for the Jew, then for the Gentile. (Rom 1:16)
> For all of you who were baptized into Christ have clothed yourselves with Christ. There is neither Jew nor Greek, slave nor free, male nor female, for you are all one in Christ Jesus. (Gal 3:27-28)

3. God assures the glorious restoration of Israel and a rich period for the whole earth. Note the sharp contrast...
• between "falling beyond recovery" and "riches."
• between "loss" and "riches."

The word "loss" (hettema) means utter loss, defeat and injury. It means that Israel became impoverished spiritually. Israel was spiritually injured and defeated; the Jewish people lost the blessings of salvation. Now...
• if the spiritual fall of Israel led to the riches of salvation being carried to the world...
• if the spiritual loss of Israel led to the riches of salvation being carried to the Gentiles...

...how much more shall the fullness (the restoration of Israel) bring the blessings of God to earth?

Note the word "fullness" (pleroma), which means completion or that which is filled. The idea is that the day is coming when God's plan and purpose for Israel will be completed and perfectly fulfilled. That day, the day of Israel's restoration, will cause even a greater blessing to spread out across the world.

Thought 1. The spread of the gospel has had an enormous impact upon the world.
⇒ It has liberated millions from sin and shame.
⇒ It has saved millions from death and hell.
⇒ It has assured millions of life eternal with God.
⇒ It has liberated women and children from slavery.
⇒ It has proclaimed morality and purity worldwide.
⇒ It has stirred justice and the enactment of just laws among men.

However, when Israel is restored and large numbers of Jews begin to turn to Christ, then the world will experience unprecedented blessings from the hand of God. God promises such blessings to the world.
The point is clear: God has overruled and is going to continue overruling Israel's stumble and fall over Christ.
⇒ More and more Gentiles are going to be saved. The uttermost part of the earth is going to hear the gospel.

> And this gospel of the kingdom will be preached in the whole world as a testimony to all nations, and then the end will come. (Mat 24:14)

⇒ More and more Jews are going to be stirred to accept Christ and to be restored to God.
⇒ A glorious restoration of Israel is going to take place. Jews by the teeming thousands are going to turn to Christ someday out in the future. So many will turn to Christ that it can be said that the nation Israel has been restored. And when that day comes, the whole earth will be greatly blessed, blessed more fully than ever before.

> I do not want you to be ignorant of this mystery, brothers, so that you may not be conceited: Israel has experienced a hardening in part until the full number of the Gentiles has come in. And so all Israel will be saved, as it is written: "The deliverer will come from Zion; he will turn godlessness away from Jacob. (Rom 11:25-26)
> I will give them a heart to know me, that I am the LORD. They will be my people, and I will be their God, for they will return to me with all their heart. (Jer 24:7)

ROMANS 11:11-16

2 (11:13-15) **Israel, Restoration—Paul, Love for His People**: proof two is Paul's attempt to stir the Jews to be saved. Paul was God's primary minister to the Gentiles in the first century. Paul magnified the ministry and gloried in God's call, and he stressed the fact every chance he could. Why? Paul had two purposes.

1. He wanted to arouse the Jews to envy; that is, he wanted to stir them to look at Christ, and to see what Christ had done for the Gentiles. He wanted to stir men to look at the lives of believers and to see the wonderful change Christ had wrought. Thereby, Paul hoped that some Jews would be saved.

2. Paul wanted to hasten the day for Israel's restoration. He knew there was to be a restoration; therefore, he knew that every time he was able to reach a Jew for Christ, the callous on Israel's heart would soften a little more. The more he could soften the callous, the sooner the restoration would take place. Note the question of Paul:

> For if their rejection is the reconciliation of the world, what will their acceptance be but life from the dead? (Rom 11:15)

a. The *reconciliation* of the world has a twofold meaning. It means...
- that *all* men, both Jew and Gentile can now be reconciled to God. All men can now have *peace with God* and possess the *peace of God* (see notes, *Peace*—Ro.5:1; DEEPER STUDY # 1—5:10; Jn.14:27).

> For if, when we were God's enemies, we were reconciled to him through the death of his Son, how much more, having been reconciled, shall we be saved through his life! (Rom 5:10)
> Therefore, if anyone is in Christ, he is a new creation; the old has gone, the new has come! All this is from God, who reconciled us to himself through Christ and gave us the ministry of reconciliation: (2 Cor 5:17-18)
> And through him to reconcile to himself all things, whether things on earth or things in heaven, by making peace through his blood, shed on the cross. (Col 1:20)

- that all men, both Jew and Gentile, can now be reconciled to each other (see outline and notes—Eph.2:13-18 for discussion).

> And in this one body to reconcile both of them to God through the cross, by which he put to death their hostility. (Eph 2:16)

b. Paul believed strongly in the restoration of Israel. The very fact that he asked the question indicates his belief. He firmly expected Israel to be restored, and he expected their restoration to bring such a great revival to earth that it would be like the world moving to "life from the dead."

c. The phrase "life from the dead" is interpreted several ways.
- Some say it refers to the resurrection of the dead, to the climax of human history when Jesus Christ shall return to deliver the whole creation from corruption and to rule and reign over the world (cp. Ro.8:21). This, of course, would mean that believers are not resurrected until the restoration of the Jews to God.
- Others say it is merely figurative language. When the Jews are restored, it will be like a resurrection, like gaining life from the dead.

Whatever the interpretation, the restoration of Israel will be a most glorious event, an event so glorious that it will be like a true resurrection. It will lead to a new world, a world of righteousness that will benefit all involved. The scene is that the most glorious blessings will be poured out upon the whole world and everyone in it.

> I will give them a heart to know me, that I am the LORD. They will be my people, and I will be their God, for they will return to me with all their heart. (Jer 24:7)
> So I prophesied as he commanded me, and breath entered them; they came to life and stood up on their feet—a vast army. (Ezek 37:10)
> For this son of mine was dead and is alive again; he was lost and is found.' So they began to celebrate. (Luke 15:24)
> And if the Spirit of him who raised Jesus from the dead is living in you, he who raised Christ from the dead will also give life to your mortal bodies through his Spirit, who lives in you. (Rom 8:11)
> I pray also that the eyes of your heart may be enlightened in order that you may know the hope to which he has called you, the riches of his glorious inheritance in the saints, (Eph 1:18)
> But because of his great love for us, God, who is rich in mercy, made us alive with Christ even when we were dead in transgressions—it is by grace you have been saved. And God raised us up with Christ and seated us with him in the heavenly realms in Christ Jesus, in order that in the coming ages he might show the incomparable riches of his grace, expressed in his kindness to us in Christ Jesus. (Eph 2:4-7)
> The grace of our Lord was poured out on me abundantly, along with the faith and love that are in Christ Jesus. (1 Tim 1:14)

3 (11:16) **Israel, Restoration—Remnant—Parents**: proof three is that Israel's forefathers, that is, the patriarchs, give a heritage of holiness. This is an extremely important verse in dealing with the restoration of Israel. God gives two pictures to show that Israel can never be totally or finally rejected. Both pictures have to do with the first-fruits.
- The Jew always dedicated the first fruit of his harvest to God. He gave the first part to God and by giving the first part, the man was saying to God that he was dedicating all of his food to God. It was not necessary to offer every mouthful to God. The offering of the first part sanctified the whole.
- The second picture is that of a little tree being planted and the sapling being offered to God. Every branch thereafter was looked upon as being sacred to God. It was not necessary to dedicate each branch separately.

191

What Paul is saying is that the root, the first part, refers to the patriarchs, that is, the fathers of Israel. Israel by merit of their patriarchs, their fathers, holds a very special place in God's heart. The whole nation benefits from the dedicated lives of Abraham and the other godly fathers. The whole nation (masses of them) will be restored and saved, brought back to God because of the godliness of their forefathers and because of God's promise to the forefathers (cp. v.25).

Note this: to call Israel a holy nation does not mean that the Jewish people live holy lives in the sight of God. Scripture is not talking about practical, day-to-day holiness. There have been few Jews—just as there have always been few Gentiles—who have lived holy lives. But Israel was *initially* chosen by God to be His witness upon earth: chosen to be His *federal nation* or His *representative nation* to bear testimony for Him. The first fathers of the nation believed God and lived lives of faith, and a few Jews have continued to follow God down through the generations of every century. God very clearly says that because of the holiness of these few, He cares for the nation as a whole—for the whole lump. What this means is this: because of the holy lives of the few, God looks with favor upon the nation. It does not mean that He saves everyone in the nation; but rather, He blesses the nation , all those who live around the followers of God. Those who live holy lives bring godly blessings upon all who surround them and who succeed from them. Many of Israel will be blessed by God and restored because of the nation's godly patriarchs.

Thought 1. Note the influence of godly parents, forefathers, and nations upon children and succeeding generations. It is important for every parent and generation to live godly lives.

> And he passed in front of Moses, proclaiming, "The LORD, the LORD, the compassionate and gracious God, slow to anger, abounding in love and faithfulness, maintaining love to thousands, and forgiving wickedness, rebellion and sin. Yet he does not leave the guilty unpunished; he punishes the children and their children for the sin of the fathers to the third and fourth generation." (Exo 34:6-7; cp. Lev.14:18)

> They rejected his decrees and the covenant he had made with their fathers and the warnings he had given them. They followed worthless idols and themselves became worthless. They imitated the nations around them although the LORD had ordered them, "Do not do as they do," and they did the things the LORD had forbidden them to do. (2 Ki 17:15)

> It is said, 'God stores up a man's punishment for his sons.' Let him repay the man himself, so that he will know it! (Job 21:19)

> You show love to thousands but bring the punishment for the fathers' sins into the laps of their children after them. O great and powerful God, whose name is the LORD Almighty, great are your purposes and mighty are your deeds. Your eyes are open to all the ways of men; you reward everyone according to his conduct and as his deeds deserve. (Jer 32:18-19)

> Our fathers sinned and are no more, and we bear their punishment. (Lam 5:7)

> And after they have been destroyed before you, be careful not to be ensnared by inquiring about their gods, saying, "How do these nations serve their gods? We will do the same." (Deu 12:30)

> So you must obey them and do everything they tell you. But do not do what they do, for they do not practice what they preach. (Mat 23:3)

Thought 2. Note the influence of godly men upon nations.

> You will be for me a kingdom of priests and a holy nation.' These are the words you are to speak to the Israelites." (Exo 19:6)

> As far as the gospel is concerned, they are enemies on your account; but as far as election is concerned, they are loved on account of the patriarchs, (Rom 11:28)
> Because he loved your forefathers and chose their descendants after them, he brought you out of Egypt by his Presence and his great strength, (Deu 4:37)

However, we must always remember that the people of a nation can be restored to God only through repentance, only by turning from sin back to God.

> "'But if they will confess their sins and the sins of their fathers—their treachery against me and their hostility toward me, which made me hostile toward them so that I sent them into the land of their enemies— then when their uncircumcised hearts are humbled and they pay for their sin, I will remember my covenant with Jacob and my covenant with Isaac and my covenant with Abraham, and I will remember the land. (Lev 26:40-42)

	H. The Callous on Israel's Heart is a Warning to Other Nations, 11:17-24	21 For if God did not spare the natural branches, he will not spare you either.	c. God is less likely to spare unnatural branches
1 A parable of the olive tree a. Some branches are broken off: Jews b. Some wild branches are grafted in: Gentiles	17 If some of the branches have been broken off, and you, though a wild olive shoot, have been grafted in among the others and now share in the nourishing sap from the olive root,	22 Consider therefore the kindness and sternness of God: sternness to those who fell, but kindness to you, provided that you continue in his kindness. Otherwise, you also will be cut off.	**4 Warning 3: Take a sharp look at the kindness & sternness of God** a. God was severe to those who fell b. God is kind to the steadfast
2 Warning 1: Do not be arrogant a. Are wild & grafted in b. Are not the root	18 Do not boast over those branches. If you do, consider this: You do not support the root, but the root supports you.	23 And if they do not persist in unbelief, they will be grafted in, for God is able to graft them in again.	**5 Warning 4: The restoration is a probable event** a. If unbelief is removed b. "God is able..." c. The grafting of a natural branch (the Jews) is more likely than the calling of the Gentiles
3 Warning 2: Fear complacency & unbelief a. Israel was not rejected for the Gentiles, but because of unbelief b. The Gentiles stand by faith—not by any merit	19 You will say then, "Branches were broken off so that I could be grafted in." 20 Granted. But they were broken off because of unbelief, and you stand by faith. Do not be arrogant, but be afraid.	24 After all, if you were cut out of an olive tree that is wild by nature, and contrary to nature were grafted into a cultivated olive tree, how much more readily will these, the natural branches, be grafted into their own olive tree!	

DIVISION VII

ISRAEL AND THE GOSPEL OF RIGHTEOUSNESS, 9:1-11:36

H. The Callous on Israel's Heart is a Warning to Other Nations, 11:17-24

(11:17-24) **Introduction**: men can harden their hearts against God. Men can become so callous against God that the conviction of the Holy Spirit is never felt. Hardness of heart can doom men to an eternity of separation from God. The callous on Israel's heart is a warning to all men everywhere, a warning to the nations of the world.

1. A parable of the olive tree (v.17).
2. Warning 1: do not be arrogant (v.18).
3. Warning 2: fear complacency and unbelief (v.19-21).
4. Warning 3: take a sharp look at the kindness and sternness of God (v.22).
5. Warning 4: the restoration is a probable event (v.23-24).

1 (11:17) **Israel vs. Gentiles**: this is a parable of the olive tree. The olive tree was the most useful, productive, and valuable tree in Israel; therefore, it was precious to the economy and welfare of the nation. Because of this, the nation's relationship to God was sometimes pictured as an olive tree (cp. Ps.52:8; Jer.11:16; Hos.14:6).

Now note the exact picture given. The natural branches refer to Israel, and the wild olive branches refer to Gentile believers. The olive tree refers to God and a right relationship with Him.

1. Some natural branches are broken off and rejected. Some Jews did not and do not believe in Christ; therefore, they are not attached to God. They do not have a right relationship with God. But note: only some of the branches were broken off. Some Jews did accept Christ as the Messiah and did maintain a right relationship with God.

> "Therefore I tell you that the kingdom of God will be taken away from you and given to a people who will produce its fruit. (Mat 21:43)
>
> I tell you, not one of those men who were invited will get a taste of my banquet.'" (Luke 14:24)

> He will come and kill those tenants and give the vineyard to others." When the people heard this, they said, "May this never be!" (Luke 20:16)
>
> If some of the branches have been broken off, and you, though a wild olive shoot, have been grafted in among the others and now share in the nourishing sap from the olive root, (Rom 11:17)
>
> My God will reject them because they have not obeyed him; they will be wanderers among the nations. (Hosea 9:17)

2. Some wild olive branches were grafted into the tree. Note that the words "and you" (kai su) are singular. Paul is not speaking to Gentiles as a whole, but to the individual Gentile. Note two things.

   a. The Gentile believer is said to have been a *wild olive branch*. The word "wild" means that the Gentile was not part of the olive tree (God); he was outside and estranged and alienated from the olive tree (God). Therefore, he was...
   * part of the wilderness and desert and uncultivated world.
   * growing loose and uncontrolled.
   * useless and worthless.
   * uncared for and unprotected.
   * insect-infested and sour and inferior.

   b. The Gentile believer is now said to have been grafted into the olive tree. He is now attached to God, that is, in a right relationship with God; therefore, he now partakes of the root and fatness of the olive tree. Very simply, this means that the believer is fed and nourished by God.

Thought 1. The glorious privilege of being nourished by God becomes as much the right of the Gentile as it is of the Jews.

And through your offspring all nations on earth will be blessed, because you have obeyed me." (Gen 22:18)

All the ends of the earth will remember and turn to the LORD, and all the families of the nations will bow down before him, (Psa 22:27)

All the nations you have made will come and worship before you, O Lord; they will bring glory to your name. (Psa 86:9)

The people walking in darkness have seen a great light; on those living in the land of the shadow of death a light has dawned. (Isa 9:2)

He says: "It is too small a thing for you to be my servant to restore the tribes of Jacob and bring back those of Israel I have kept. I will also make you a light for the Gentiles, that you may bring my salvation to the ends of the earth." (Isa 49:6)

Nations will come to your light, and kings to the brightness of your dawn. (Isa 60:3)

He was given authority, glory and sovereign power; all peoples, nations and men of every language worshiped him. His dominion is an everlasting dominion that will not pass away, and his kingdom is one that will never be destroyed. (Dan 7:14)

I will plant her for myself in the land; I will show my love to the one I called 'Not my loved one. ' I will say to those called 'Not my people, ' 'You are my people'; and they will say, 'You are my God.'" (Hosea 2:23)

The apostles and the brothers throughout Judea heard that the Gentiles also had received the word of God. (Acts 11:1)

When the Gentiles heard this, they were glad and honored the word of the Lord; and all who were appointed for eternal life believed. (Acts 13:48)

After much discussion, Peter got up and addressed them: "Brothers, you know that some time ago God made a choice among you that the Gentiles might hear from my lips the message of the gospel and believe. (Acts 15:7)

But when the Jews opposed Paul and became abusive, he shook out his clothes in protest and said to them, "Your blood be on your own heads! I am clear of my responsibility. From now on I will go to the Gentiles." (Acts 18:6)

"Therefore I want you to know that God's salvation has been sent to the Gentiles, and they will listen!" (Acts 28:28)

So that the Gentiles may glorify God for his mercy, as it is written: "Therefore I will praise you among the Gentiles; I will sing hymns to your name." (Rom 15:9)

This mystery is that through the gospel the Gentiles are heirs together with Israel, members together of one body, and sharers together in the promise in Christ Jesus. (Eph 3:6)

The seventh angel sounded his trumpet, and there were loud voices in heaven, which said: "The kingdom of the world has become the kingdom of our Lord and of his Christ, and he will reign for ever and ever." (Rev 11:15)

c. Note the word "sharing." The Gentile believer is grafted into the olive tree *to share with the natural branches*. This is important to note, for it means there is *only* one family of God, not two. Both the natural branches and the wild branches are part of the same olive tree. The only difference is that the natural branches were the first branches that grew on the olive tree. The wild branches had to be brought or grafted into the tree.

Thought 1. Note that some natural branches are broken off because they did not bear fruit.

If anyone does not remain in me, he is like a branch that is thrown away and withers; such branches are picked up, thrown into the fire and burned. (John 15:6)

2 (11:18) **Arrogance—Pride—Gentile vs. Jew**: there is the first warning. The Gentile believer must not be arrogant and prideful over the Jews. The idea is that...

- we must not treat them as inferior beings because they deny Christ.
- we must not insult and ridicule them because they differ from us as Christian believers.
- we must not trample them underfoot because they refuse to believe and be like us.
- we must not boast that we know the truth about the Messiah and they do not.
- we must not glory in our knowledge of Christ, conveying the idea that we are better than the Jews.

The Gentile believer has no right to elevate himself over the Jews nor over anyone else. The reason is clearly seen. We were wild branches, very wild. We did not bear the root (Judaism); the root bore us (Christianity). If it had not been for Judaism, there would be no Christianity. If it had not been for Jewish believers, there would be no Christian believers. If Peter and Paul and the others had not surrendered their lives to preach Christ, then the message of Christ would have never reached us. We must never forget that "salvation is from the Jews" (Jn.4:22).

Thought 1. Every Gentile believer owes a debt to Jewish people. We must carry the gospel to the Jews even as some of the earliest Christian Jews brought the gospel to us.

I am not ashamed of the gospel, because it is the power of God for the salvation of everyone who believes: first for the Jew, then for the Gentile. (Rom 1:16)

Therefore go and make disciples of all nations, baptizing them in the name of the Father and of the Son and of the Holy Spirit, (Mat 28:19)

Thought 2. All boasting and arrogance, pride and conceit against the Jews is wrong. It is wrong to elevate ourselves above others; in fact, it is even wrong to think that we are *better* or *higher* than anyone else.

For by the grace given me I say to every one of you: Do not think of yourself more highly than you ought, but rather think of yourself with sober judgment, in accordance with the measure of faith God has given you. (Rom 12:3)

Live in harmony with one another. Do not be proud, but be willing to associate with people of low position. Do not be conceited. (Rom 12:16)

If you are convinced that you are a guide for the blind, a light for those who are in the dark, (Rom 2:19)

Do nothing out of selfish ambition or vain conceit, but in humility consider others better than yourselves. Each of you should look not only to your own interests, but also to the interests of others. (Phil 2:3-4)

Humble yourselves before the Lord, and he will lift you up. (James 4:10)

Do not be wise in your own eyes; fear the LORD and shun evil. (Prov 3:7)

Better a little with righteousness than much gain with injustice. (Prov 16:8)

Woe to those who are wise in their own eyes and clever in their own sight. (Isa 5:21)

3 (11:19-21) **Unbelief—Complacency—Gentile vs. Jew**: there is the second warning. The Gentile believer must fear complacency and unbelief. (See outline and notes—Heb.3:7-19 for more discussion.) There is the danger of Gentile believers thinking…

- that they are more *acceptable* to God because they have replaced the Jews as the true followers of God.
- that they are safe and secure in Christianity because Christianity is the religion that acknowledges God's Son.

However, we must always remember what this Scripture is saying. Israel was not rejected by God so that we, the Gentiles, might be saved. Israel was rejected by God because of unbelief. God did not and does not reject one people in order to save another people. God reaches out to every nation of people longing for all to be grafted into Him.

God accepts a person because the person believes in His Son Jesus Christ. The Jews did not believe; some Gentiles did believe. A Gentile believer stands attached to the olive tree by faith, not because of any goodness or merit or value within himself.

Now note: the Gentile believer must guard against complacency, against feeling safe and secure and more acceptable because he stands in Christianity, the religion that acknowledges God's Son. The Gentile believer must not be high-minded, but rather fear. He must fear, for God is less likely to spare the unnatural branches than He was the natural branches. The warning is strong: "He will not spare you either" (v.21).

Thought 1. If God did not spare the Jews because of their unbelief, how much more will He not spare us. The Jews were the natural branches; we are the unnatural branches.

⇒ The Jews had the godly heritage; we had the wild, ungodly heritage.
⇒ The Jews had the fathers, the followers of the only living and true God; we had heathen, poly-

theistic fathers, fathers who created humanistic gods to suit their own fancies.

⇒ The Jews had the Word of God and the Savior; we had neither.
⇒ the Jews had the prophets of God; we had the false humanistic priests of the world.

In light of this and of so much more depravity, we must guard against self-complacency and conceit. We must walk in the fear of God and humility, fearing unbelief lest we too be *broken off* (v.17).

Whoever believes in the Son has eternal life, but whoever rejects the Son will not see life, for God's wrath remains on him." (John 3:36)

I told you that you would die in your sins; if you do not believe that I am the one I claim to be, you will indeed die in your sins." (John 8:24)

See to it, brothers, that none of you has a sinful, unbelieving heart that turns away from the living God. (Heb 3:12)

Let us, therefore, make every effort to enter that rest, so that no one will fall by following their example of disobedience. (Heb 4:11)

Since you call on a Father who judges each man's work impartially, live your lives as strangers here in reverent fear. (1 Pet 1:17)

And now, O Israel, what does the LORD your God ask of you but to fear the LORD your God, to walk in all his ways, to love him, to serve the LORD your God with all your heart and with all your soul, (Deu 10:12)

The LORD Almighty is the one you are to regard as holy, he is the one you are to fear, he is the one you are to dread, (Isa 8:13)

4 (11:22) **Judgment—God, Goodness of**: there is the third warning. The Gentile believer must take a sharp look at the kindness and severity or "sternness" of God.

1. The sternness of God is seen in the spiritual fall of Israel. The word "sternness" (apotomia) means abrupt, sharp, rough, cut off. The Jews had committed the very sins the Gentiles are being warned about in this passage. The Jews…

- had developed an attitude of arrogance and boasting toward other people, refusing to carry the Word of God to them.
- had felt high-minded and complacent, feeling safe and secure, thinking themselves to be more acceptable to God than other people.

In addition to these gross sins, the Jews had rejected God's prophets down through the centuries until they eventually killed God's very own Son. In one brief word, their sin was *unbelief*. The vast majority of the Jews never did believe God, not to the point that they loved God supremely. As a result, the judgment and sternness of God fell upon them (see DEEPER STUDY # 2, *Judgment*—Ro.11:7-10 for more discussion).

"You only have I chosen of all the families of the earth; therefore I will punish you for all your sins." (Amos 3:2)

"That servant who knows his master's will and does not get ready or does not do what his master wants will be beaten with many blows. (Luke 12:47)

If anyone does not remain in me, he is like a branch that is thrown away and withers; such branches are picked up, thrown into the fire and burned. (John 15:6)

Why not say—as we are being slanderously reported as saying and as some claim that we say—" Let us do evil that good may result"? Their condemnation is deserved. What shall we conclude then? Are we any better ? Not at all! We have already made the charge that Jews and Gentiles alike are all under sin. (Rom 3:8-9)

How much more severely do you think a man deserves to be punished who has trampled the Son of God under foot, who has treated as an unholy thing the blood of the covenant that sanctified him, and who has insulted the Spirit of grace? (Heb 10:29)

I will punish the world for its evil, the wicked for their sins. I will put an end to the arrogance of the haughty and will humble the pride of the ruthless. (Isa 13:11)

I will punish you as your deeds deserve, declares the LORD. I will kindle a fire in your forests that will consume everything around you.'" (Jer 21:14)

At that time I will search Jerusalem with lamps and punish those who are complacent, who are like wine left on its dregs, who think, 'The LORD will do nothing, either good or bad.' (Zep 1:12)

2. The kindness of God is seen in the grafting in and acceptance of the Gentiles by God. But note the stress of this point: the kindness of God is given only to those who continue in God's kindness. A person who knows about the love of God must walk and live in God's kindness. The word "continue" (epimeno) means to remain, be steadfast, abide, persevere, endure. The idea is both *position* and *relationship*. The believer...

• is positioned in the kindness of God.
• is related to the kindness of God.

It is the picture of a person who is remaining and abiding in the house of God's kindness. A Gentile believer must continue and abide, endure and persevere in the kindness of God, or else he too will be cut off (ekkopesei) just as the Jews were cut off (v.17).

Or do you show contempt for the riches of his kindness, tolerance and patience, not realizing that God's kindness leads you toward repentance? (Rom 2:4)

"For God so loved the world that he gave his one and only Son, that whoever believes in him shall not perish but have eternal life. (John 3:16)

But God demonstrates his own love for us in this: While we were still sinners, Christ died for us. (Rom 5:8)

In him we have redemption through his blood, the forgiveness of sins, in accordance

with the riches of God's grace [goodness] (Eph 1:7)

Anyone who runs ahead and does not continue in the teaching of Christ does not have God; whoever continues in the teaching has both the Father and the Son. (2 John 1:9)

5 (11:23-24) **Israel, Restoration**: there is the fourth warning. The Gentile believer must know that Israel's restoration is a probable event.

1. The restoration of Israel is conditional. Note the word "if"—"if they do not persist in unbelief." Genuine belief is the condition for salvation. A person has to run from his unbelief to belief in order to be grafted in and accepted by God. No person comes to God unless he believes in His Son Jesus Christ.

"For God so loved the world that he gave his one and only Son, that whoever believes in him shall not perish but have eternal life. (John 3:16)

Repent, then, and turn to God, so that your sins may be wiped out, that times of refreshing may come from the Lord, (Acts 3:19)

"Return, faithless people; I will cure you of backsliding." "Yes, we will come to you, for you are the LORD our God. (Jer 3:22)

2. God is able to graft the Jews back into the olive tree. Two things are meant by this.

a. God is able because of His enormous love. God loves everyone and will forgive any person for any thing if that man will turn from his life of sin and unbelief. God will accept any person who approaches Him through His Son Jesus Christ.

Who is a God like you, who pardons sin and forgives the transgression of the remnant of his inheritance? You do not stay angry forever but delight to show mercy. (Micah 7:18)

But when the kindness and love of God our Savior appeared, he saved us, not because of righteous things we had done, but because of his mercy. He saved us through the washing of rebirth and renewal by the Holy Spirit, whom he poured out on us generously through Jesus Christ our Savior, so that, having been justified by his grace, we might become heirs having the hope of eternal life. (Titus 3:4-7)

b. God is able because of His enormous knowledge and power. God is God; therefore, He has unlimited knowledge and power. He knows when a man's heart is subject to Him and moving toward Him. He knows just when to move upon a person's heart, and He can arrange circumstances that will cause the person to turn to Him. Therefore, when the time comes, He has the power to stir Jewish hearts to turn to Him in large numbers. The valley of dry bones can be resurrected by the power of God (Ezk.37:1f).

Now to him who is able to establish you by my gospel and the proclamation of Jesus

Christ, according to the revelation of the mystery hidden for long ages past, (Rom 16:25)

For nothing is impossible with God." (Luke 1:37)

I pray also that the eyes of your heart may be enlightened in order that you may know the hope to which he has called you, the riches of his glorious inheritance in the saints, And his incomparably great power for us who believe. That power is like the working of his mighty strength, which he exerted in Christ when he raised him from the dead and seated him at his right hand in the heavenly realms, (Eph 1:18-20)

As for you, you were dead in your transgressions and sins, (Eph 2:1)

Wealth and honor come from you; you are the ruler of all things. In your hands are strength and power to exalt and give strength to all. (1 Chr 29:12)

3. The grafting in of the natural branches (the Jews) is much more likely than the calling of the Gentiles was. Note the words "much more." Paul is confident that God is not only able, but God will graft the Jews back into the olive tree. Paul proclaims that the Jews will turn to Christ and be restored into a right relationship with God (see notes— Ro.11:16 for discussion).

Isaiah cries out concerning Israel: "Though the number of the Israelites be like the sand by the sea, only the remnant will be saved. (Rom 9:27)
So too, at the present time there is a remnant chosen by grace. (Rom 11:5)

I do not want you to be ignorant of this mystery, brothers, so that you may not be conceited: Israel has experienced a hardening in part until the full number of the Gentiles has come in. And so all Israel will be saved, as it is written: "The deliverer will come from Zion; he will turn godlessness away from Jacob. (Rom 11:25-26)

Then the LORD your God will restore your fortunes and have compassion on you and gather you again from all the nations where he scattered you. (Deu 30:3)

Unless the LORD Almighty had left us some survivors, we would have become like Sodom, we would have been like Gomorrah. (Isa 1:9)

"I myself will gather the remnant of my flock out of all the countries where I have driven them and will bring them back to their pasture, where they will be fruitful and increase in number. (Jer 23:3)

My eyes will watch over them for their good, and I will bring them back to this land. I will build them up and not tear them down; I will plant them and not uproot them. I will give them a heart to know me, that I am the LORD. They will be my people, and I will be their God, for they will return to me with all their heart. (Jer 24:6-7)

This is what the LORD says: "Sing with joy for Jacob; shout for the foremost of the nations. Make your praises heard, and say, 'O LORD, save your people, the remnant of Israel.' See, I will bring them from the land of the north and gather them from the ends of the earth. Among them will be the blind and the lame, expectant mothers and women in labor; a great throng will return. (Jer 31:7-8)

Yet there will be some survivors—sons and daughters who will be brought out of it. They will come to you, and when you see their conduct and their actions, you will be consoled regarding the disaster I have brought upon Jerusalem—every disaster I have brought upon it. (Ezek 14:22)

So I prophesied as he commanded me, and breath entered them; they came to life and stood up on their feet—a vast army. (Ezek 37:10)

"I will surely gather all of you, O Jacob; I will surely bring together the remnant of Israel. I will bring them together like sheep in a pen, like a flock in its pasture; the place will throng with people. (Micah 2:12)

Therefore, as surely as I live," declares the LORD Almighty, the God of Israel, "surely Moab will become like Sodom, the Ammonites like Gomorrah— a place of weeds and salt pits, a wasteland forever. The remnant of my people will plunder them; the survivors of my nation will inherit their land." (Zep 2:9)

	I. The Restoration of Israel and Its Surety, 11:25-36		mercy & witness to the Jews

1 Surety 1: God's great revelation about the Jews[DS1]
a. Was a mystery
b. Israel's blindness is only partial: "In part"
c. Israel's blindness is only temporary
  1) Until the fullness of the Gentiles is come
  2) All Israel will be saved
2 Surety 2: The Promise of Scripture—God's Deliverer, Jesus Christ, shall turn Israel
3 Surety 3: God's pleasure with Israel's forefathers
a. God loves Israel because of the great faith of their forefathers
b. God is unchangeable: He shall fulfill His will for Israel
4 Surety 4:The believer's
	25 I do not want you to be ignorant of this mystery, brothers, so that you may not be conceited: Israel has experienced a hardening in part until the full number of the Gentiles has come in.
	26 And so all Israel will be saved, as it is written: "The deliverer will come from Zion; he will turn godlessness away from Jacob.
	27 And this is my covenant with them when I take away their sins."
	28 As far as the gospel is concerned, they are enemies on your account; but as far as election is concerned, they are loved on account of the patriarchs,
	29 For God's gifts and his call are irrevocable.
	30 Just as you who were at
		one time disobedient to God have now received mercy as a result of their disobedience,
		31 So they too have now become disobedient in order that they too may now receive mercy as a result of God's mercy to you.
		32 For God has bound all men over to disobedience so that he may have mercy on them all.
		33 Oh, the depth of the riches of the wisdom and knowledge of God! How unsearchable his judgments, and his paths beyond tracing out!
		34 "Who has known the mind of the Lord? Or who has been his counselor?"
		35 "Who has ever given to God, that God should repay him?"
		36 For from him and through him and to him are all things. To him be the glory forever! Amen.
			5 Surety 5: God's holiness and mercy
			
			6 Surety 6: God's glorious plan for the world
			a. His plan includes His wisdom & knowledge, His judgments & paths
			b. No man can grasp God's plan
			c. No man can earn God's gift
			
			d. God alone is the source, the channel, & the end of all things

DIVISION VII

ISRAEL AND THE GOSPEL OF RIGHTEOUSNESS, 9:1-11:36

I. The Restoration of Israel and Its Surety, 11:25-36

(11:25-36) **Introduction**: Israel's history is a surety. God loves man with an infinite love, and God's love is unchangeable. Therefore, any person can be restored to God if the person will call upon the name of the Lord Jesus Christ and ask Christ to save him. This is clearly seen in the history of Israel. Israel's restoration is a surety, and as such, Israel stands as a prime example of the unchangeable love of God toward man.

1. Surety 1: God's great revelation about the Jews (v.25-26).
2. Surety 2: the promise of Scripture—God's Deliverer, Jesus Christ, shall turn Israel (v.26-27).
3. Surety 3: God's pleasure with Israel's forefathers (v.28-29).
4. Surety 4: the believer's mercy and witness to the Jews (v.30-31).
5. Surety 5: God's holiness and mercy (v.32).
6. Surety 6: God's glorious plan for the world (v.33-36).

1 (11:25-26) **Israel, Restoration—Blindness**: the first surety is God's great revelation about Israel. The revelation comes from Paul. Note three significant facts.

1. The revelation had been an unknown mystery until Paul. The word "mystery" (musterion) in the Bible is not used as most men use the word, as something mysterious or difficult to understand. *A Biblical mystery means that...*

* something that was unknown is now revealed.
* something that was hidden is now made known.
* something that was a secret is now told.

The future of Israel is now revealed and made known to men. Note exactly why God revealed the future of Israel: that we not be ignorant of Israel's future, and that we not

be wise in our own conceits or imaginations. This last reason can mean two things.

⇒ Gentiles become guilty of looking down upon the Jews because the Jews are so different from the rest of us. They have rejected Jesus Christ and are opposed to Christianity to such a degree that they remain almost exclusively among themselves. Gentiles face the danger of becoming puffed up, of thinking that they are more acceptable to God because they look with favor upon Jesus Christ and are more open in professing Him. There is the danger of being prideful and arrogant, of lording it over the Jews.

⇒ A Gentile, especially a Gentile believer, can begin to think that his idea of Israel's destiny is the correct idea and that he and the followers of his position are the persons who have a full understanding of the truth. All other understandings are incorrect. There is the danger of becoming "conceited."

2. Israel's blindness is only partial, only "in part." There were Jewish believers who followed Christ in His day and there have been Jewish believers who have followed Christ down through the centuries. The blindness and hardness of Israel to the gospel is not total; it is only partial. Granted, just as Scripture says, so many Jews have rejected and still do reject Christ that it is as though *all Israel as a nation* has stumbled and fallen over Him (cp. v.8-9). However, there have been and always will be some Jews who believe. Israel's blindness is only partial.

3. Israel's blindness is only temporary. Two statements clearly show this.

a. Israel's blindness is only "until the full number of the Gentiles has come in." Note a significant point. *It does not matter how a person interprets this clause,* when the full number of the Gentiles is completed, *Israel's blindness will be removed* according to Scripture. Just what "the full number of the Gentiles" means is open to different interpretations, but it does not change what is to happen to Israel. It only affects *when* the blindness is to be removed from Israel. Israel's blindness is to continue *only* until the full number of the Gentiles comes. Now what does this event mean? The full number of the Gentiles can mean...

- a certain number of Gentile converts are to be saved, to fill up the "cut off branches of Israel" (v.17-21).
- the end of the Gentile age, a time when the emphasis of salvation will no longer be upon the Gentiles, but upon the Jews.
- the end of the Gentile age, a time when God will rapture the church (all believers) and cause a revival among the Jews who will then become the primary witnesses for Him.

The point is worth repeating. No matter what the phrase "the full number of the Gentiles" means, it does not change the event of Israel's revival. The blindness of Israel will be removed.

b. "All Israel will be saved." The fact could be stated no clearer:
⇒ Israel's blindness is only temporary.
⇒ The restoration of Israel is a surety.
⇒ Israel shall experience a revival.
⇒ Israel shall turn to God's Son, the Lord Jesus Christ.

Thought 1. There is hope for every person. Note two critical facts:
1) A person's blindness to the Lord Jesus Christ is only partial. As long as a person is alive, he can still turn to Christ.
2) A person's blindness is temporary *only* if the person turns to the Lord Jesus Christ. Unless a person believes and commits his life to Christ, his blindness becomes permanent, and he is lost forever.

This is the verdict: Light has come into the world, but men loved darkness instead of light because their deeds were evil. (John 3:19)

For he has rescued us from the dominion of darkness and brought us into the kingdom of the Son he loves, in whom we have redemption, the forgiveness of sins. (Col 1:13-14)

But it has now been revealed through the appearing of our Savior, Christ Jesus, who has destroyed death and has brought life and immortality to light through the gospel. (2 Tim 1:10)

This is the message we have heard from him and declare to you: God is light; in him there is no darkness at all. If we claim to have fellowship with him yet walk in the darkness, we lie and do not live by the truth. But if we walk in the light, as he is in the light, we have fellowship with one another, and the blood of Jesus, his Son, purifies us from all sin. (1 John 1:5-7)

DEEPER STUDY # 1
(11:25-26) **Israel, Restoration:** there are many reasons for taking this passage at its face value, that is, as a prediction of the Jewish people's conversion as a nation.

1. The whole context favors this view. The conversion of the Jews as a probable event has been described in the plainest and simplest of terms.
2. The nation was rejected, not as individuals but as a community or nation. Therefore, it is only natural to say that when God speaks of a restoration, He is speaking not only of individuals being restored, but of the community or nation as being restored (v.11, 15).
3. Paul speaks of a great event, something that will attract universal attention.
4. Paul says this is a "mystery." The gradual conversion of a few Jews would be no mystery. When speaking of the mystery of the Gentiles (Eph.1:9; 3:4), Paul is speaking of the Gentiles as a community being admitted into the church of God. Therefore, it is only natural to assume that when Paul speaks of the mystery of the Jews, he is speaking of a great event, of a great movement of Jews into Christ.
5. The words "all Israel" (v.26) cannot mean the spiritual Israel. Such an interpretation would do violence to the use of the word "Israel" throughout this whole context. It simply means Israel as a nation, as a community of people. This is also clear from the warnings that are given throughout this passage to both Gentile and Jew.

However, "all Israel" looks at the nation en masse. It does not necessarily have to mean every single individual. Note a very significant fact: when the nation became hardened, Scripture speaks of the nation, that is, of all Israel being rejected. However, not every single person was rejected. There were a few individuals who still believed and who comprised a remnant (cp. Ro.11:1-10). Every single individual was not lost, so the same is probably true when the nation is restored. There will be a large number of Jews who will become open and tender to the gospel, but not necessarily every individual. In one simple statement: Israel will be open to the gospel just as the Gentiles are open to the gospel. Many Jews will begin to be saved just as many Gentiles are now saved.

Then the LORD your God will restore your fortunes and have compassion on you and gather you again from all the nations where he scattered you. (Deu 30:3)

I will restore your judges as in days of old, your counselors as at the beginning. Afterward you will be called the City of Righteousness, the Faithful City." (Isa 1:26)

He will raise a banner for the nations and gather the exiles of Israel; he will assemble the scattered people of Judah from the four quarters of the earth. (Isa 11:12)

And in that day a great trumpet will sound. Those who were perishing in Assyria and those who were exiled in Egypt will come and worship the LORD on the holy mountain in Jerusalem. (Isa 27:13)

Look upon Zion, the city of our festivals; your eyes will see Jerusalem, a peaceful abode, a tent that will not be moved; its stakes will never be pulled up, nor any of its ropes broken. (Isa 33:20)

Speak tenderly to Jerusalem, and proclaim to her that her hard service has been completed, that her sin has been paid for, that she has received from the Lord's hand double for all her sins. (Isa 40:2)

This is what the Sovereign LORD says: "See, I will beckon to the Gentiles, I will lift up my banner to the peoples; they will bring your sons in their arms and carry your daughters on their shoulders. (Isa 49:22)

"Foreigners will rebuild your walls, and their kings will serve you. Though in anger I struck you, in favor I will show you compassion. (Isa 60:10)

"I myself will gather the remnant of my flock out of all the countries where I have driven them and will bring them back to their pasture, where they will be fruitful and increase in number. (Jer 23:3)

My eyes will watch over them for their good, and I will bring them back to this land. I will build them up and not tear them down; I will plant them and not uproot them. I will give them a heart to know me, that I am the LORD. They will be my people, and I will be their God, for they will return to me with all their heart. (Jer 24:6-7; cp. Jer.31:7-8)

Yet there will be some survivors—sons and daughters who will be brought out of it. They will come to you, and when you see their conduct and their actions, you will be consoled regarding the disaster I have brought upon Jerusalem—every disaster I have brought upon it. (Ezek 14:22)

For on my holy mountain, the high mountain of Israel, declares the Sovereign LORD, there in the land the entire house of Israel will serve me, and there I will accept them. There I will require your offerings and your choice gifts, along with all your holy sacrifices. (Ezek 20:40)

"'But you, O mountains of Israel, will produce branches and fruit for my people Israel, for they will soon come home. (Ezek 36:8)

So I prophesied as he commanded me, and breath entered them; they came to life and stood up on their feet—a vast army. (Ezek 37:10)

"I will surely gather all of you, O Jacob; I will surely bring together the remnant of Israel. I will bring them together like sheep in a pen, like a flock in its pasture; the place will throng with people. (Micah 2:12)

Therefore, as surely as I live," declares the LORD Almighty, the God of Israel, "surely Moab will become like Sodom, the Ammonites like Gomorrah— a place of weeds and salt pits, a wasteland forever. The remnant of my people will plunder them; the survivors of my nation will inherit their land." (Zep 2:9)

"Proclaim further: This is what the LORD Almighty says: 'My towns will again overflow with prosperity, and the LORD will again comfort Zion and choose Jerusalem.'" (Zec 1:17)

"I will strengthen the house of Judah and save the house of Joseph. I will restore them because I have compassion on them. They will be as though I had not rejected them, for I am the LORD their God and I will answer them. (Zec 10:6)

It will be inhabited; never again will it be destroyed. Jerusalem will be secure. (Zec 14:11)

And the offerings of Judah and Jerusalem will be acceptable to the LORD, as in days gone by, as in former years. (Mal 3:4)

2 (11:26-27) **Israel, Restoration—Forgiveness of Sin**: the second surety is the promise of Scripture. God's great Deliverer, Jesus Christ Himself, shall turn Israel. Scripture gives a glimpse into the future of Israel's restoration in this verse, but note that it is only a glimpse. Just how Israel will be restored is not discussed in this passage. Only two major things are given.

1. Some great manifestation of Christ the Deliverer will cause Israel to turn to the gospel.

For I tell you, [Israel] you will not see me again until you say, 'Blessed is he who comes in the name of the Lord.'" (Mat 23:39)

Repent, then, and turn to God, so that your sins may be wiped out, that times of refreshing may come from the Lord, and that he may send the Christ, who has been appointed for you [Israel]—even Jesus. He must remain in heaven until the time comes for God to restore everything, as he promised long ago through his holy prophets. (Acts 3:19-21)

I do not want you to be ignorant of this mystery, brothers, so that you may not be conceited: Israel has experienced a hardening in part until the full number of the Gentiles has come in. (Rom 11:25)

But their minds [Israel] were made dull, for to this day the same veil remains when the old covenant is read. It has not been removed, because only in Christ is it taken away. Even to this day when Moses is read, a veil covers their hearts. But whenever anyone turns to the Lord, the veil is taken away. (2 Cor 3:14-16)

Oh, that salvation for Israel would come out of Zion! When the LORD restores the fortunes of his people, let Jacob rejoice and Israel be glad! (Psa 14:7)

"The Redeemer will come to Zion, to those in Jacob who repent of their sins," declares the LORD. "As for me, this is my covenant with them," says the LORD. "My Spirit, who is on you, and my words that I have put in your mouth will not depart from your mouth, or from the mouths of your children, or from the mouths of their descendants from this time on and forever," says the LORD. (Isa 59:20-21)

By this, then, will Jacob's guilt be atoned for, and this will be the full fruitage of the removal of his sin: When he makes all the altar stones to be like chalk stones rushed to pieces, no Asherah poles or incense altars will be left standing. (Isa 27:9)

"For I will forgive their wickedness and will remember their sins no more." (Jer 31:34)

For the Israelites will live many days without king or prince, without sacrifice or sacred stones, without ephod or idol. Afterward the Israelites will return and seek the LORD their God and David their king. They will come trembling to the LORD and to his blessings in the last days. (Hosea 3:4-5)

"And I will pour out on the house of David and the inhabitants of Jerusalem a spirit of grace and supplication. They will look on me, the one they have pierced, and they will mourn for him as one mourns for an only child, and grieve bitterly for him as one grieves for a firstborn son. (Zec 12:10)

2. The great Deliverer, Jesus Christ, will do two things for Israel.
   a. Jesus Christ will turn away godlessness from Israel (cp. Is.27:9).
   b. Jesus Christ will fulfill God's covenant with Israel: He will take away their sins (cp. Is.59:21; 27:9).

Peter replied, "Repent and be baptized, every one of you, in the name of Jesus Christ for the forgiveness of your sins. And you will receive the gift of the Holy Spirit. (Acts 2:38)

God exalted him to his own right hand as Prince and Savior that he might give repentance and forgiveness of sins to Israel. (Acts 5:31)

"Therefore, my brothers, I want you to know that through Jesus the forgiveness of sins is proclaimed to you. (Acts 13:38)

In him we have redemption through his blood, the forgiveness of sins, in accordance with the riches of God's grace (Eph 1:7)

"I, even I, am he who blots out your transgressions, for my own sake, and remembers your sins no more. (Isa 43:25)

I have swept away your offenses like a cloud, your sins like the morning mist. Return to me, for I have redeemed you." (Isa 44:22)

Let the wicked forsake his way and the evil man his thoughts. Let him turn to the LORD, and he will have mercy on him, and to our God, for he will freely pardon. (Isa 55:7)

3 (11:28-29) **Israel, Restoration**: the third surety is God's pleasure with Israel's Patriarchs (Abraham, Isaac, and Jacob).

1. The statement "they [the Jews] are enemies on your account" sounds as though God predestined Israel's rejection. However, God does not cause sin (Jas.1:13-14); God does not cause people to reject His Son and His will. What the statement means is this: the word "enemy" (echthroi) has both an active and passive meaning. It means either hostile or hated by, and it means either hating or being hated. It is possible that in this particular passage it is to be read both ways. The Jews were hostile to God; they had refused the offer of God's righteousness in Jesus Christ, and they had refused to be the missionary force for God's Son.

Therefore, they had aroused God's displeasure. They hated God; consequently, God was displeased with them.

Note that God did what He had to do. He turned to the Gentiles. Israel had refused to be the missionary force for God's Son, so God had to turn to the Gentiles. Among the Gentiles, God found a receptive people. The Gentiles accepted the offer of God's righteousness in Jesus Christ, and they have become the missionary force for Christ to the world. It is critical to remember something, however: this does not mean that every Gentile is saved. Most are not, but a fair number of them have accepted and still do accept Jesus Christ. We must remember this: in this passage God is speaking *nationally, not individually*.

⇒ A few Jews do accept Christ as the Messiah, but the number is small. The number is so small that God can say that Israel as a nation has rejected Christ.

⇒ A far greater number of Gentiles accept Christ as their Savior. However, as is clearly evidenced by the unholy lives of most Gentiles, the majority reject Christ; but the number who do accept Him is fairly large. It is large enough for God to say that the Gentiles as a *community* do accept His offer of salvation in Christ.

Thought 1. The point is that God is speaking *nationally, not individually*. And we must remember this, for it is absolutely essential for everyone to make a *personal decision* to receive Christ and to follow Him by living a pure life.

For the grace of God that brings salvation has appeared to all men. It teaches us to say "No" to ungodliness and worldly passions, and to live self-controlled, upright and godly lives in this present age, while we wait for the blessed hope—the glorious appearing of our great God and Savior, Jesus Christ, who gave himself for us to redeem us from all wickedness and to purify for himself a people that are his very own, eager to do what is good. (Titus 2:11-14)

2. The statement "they [the Jews] are loved on account of the patriarchs" shows that God still loves Israel. As a people they are still very precious to Him. How can this be when they have been so hostile to God's Son, Jesus Christ, and against the missionary force of God's Son? There are two reasons why God still loves Israel.
   a. The forefathers or patriarchs of Israel were a godly people, a people of unusual faith in God. (See note—Ro.11:16; also see DEEPER STUDY # 1, *Abraham*—Ro.4:1-25 for more discussion.) There were people such as Abraham, Isaac, Jacob, Moses, Joshua, Deborah, Ruth, Elijah—the list could go on and on. As Scripture says:

And what more shall I say? I do not have time to tell about Gideon, Barak, Samson, Jephthah, David, Samuel and the prophets, who through faith conquered kingdoms, administered justice, and gained what was promised; who shut the mouths of lions, quenched the fury of the flames, and escaped the edge of the sword; whose weakness was turned to strength; and who became powerful in battle and routed foreign armies. Women received back their dead, raised to life again. Others were tortured and refused to be released, so that they might gain a better resurrection. Some faced jeers and flogging, while still others were chained and put in prison. They were stoned ; they were sawed in two; they were put to death by the sword. They went about in sheepskins and goatskins, destitute, persecuted and mistreated—the world was not worthy of them. They wandered in deserts and mountains, and in caves and holes in the ground. (Heb 11:32-38)

Such godly men and women knew God—knew Him personally and intimately—and God would never forget a people who loved Him so greatly. Keep this in mind as well: godly people are a praying people, a people who pray for their families and neighbors, for their nation and world. And God hears and answers the prayers of His people. God would never turn His back upon Israel for this reason alone.

b. There is a second reason why God still loves Israel: God Himself is *unchangeable in His gifts and calling*. God called and promised some very special gifts to the patriarchs, the forefathers of Israel, and God is unchangeable; therefore...

• every purpose for which God called Israel shall be fulfilled in the lives of many Jews.
• every gift God promised Israel shall be given to many Jews.

The point is striking. God does not change His mind. He is constant, immutable, unchangeable. He shall perfectly fulfill His calling and gifts to Israel.

But the plans of the LORD stand firm forever, the purposes of his heart through all generations. (Psa 33:11)
But you remain the same, and your years will never end. (Psa 102:27)
Your name, O LORD, endures forever, your renown, O LORD, through all generations. (Psa 135:13)
Your kingdom is an everlasting kingdom, and your dominion endures through all generations. The LORD is faithful to all his promises and loving toward all he has made. (Psa 145:13)
"I the LORD do not change. So you, O descendants of Jacob, are not destroyed. (Mal 3:6)
You will roll them up like a robe; like a garment they will be changed. But you remain the same, and your years will never end." (Heb 1:12)
Jesus Christ is the same yesterday and today and forever. (Heb 13:8)
Every good and perfect gift is from above, coming down from the Father of the heavenly lights, who does not change like shifting shadows. (James 1:17)
"I am the Alpha and the Omega," says the Lord God, "who is, and who was, and who is to come, the Almighty." (Rev 1:8)

(11:30-36) **Another Outline**: God's Worldwide Plan for All Men.
1. God had chosen the Jews (v.30).

2. God moved the Gentiles: from unbelief to mercy (v.30).
3. God is to move the Jews again: from unbelief to mercy (v.31).
4. God's purpose is to move all men: from unbelief to mercy (v.32).
5. God's worldwide plan rests in the depth of the richness of His wisdom and knowledge (v.33).
   a. No man can grasp God's plan (v.34).
   b. No man can earn God's gift (v.35).
   c. God is all in all (v.36).

4 (11:30-31) **Israel, Restoration**: the fourth surety is the believer's mercy and witness to the Jews. These two verses are speaking historically. Very simply, history shall be repeated.
⇒ In times past—before Christ ever came—the Gentiles did not know and obey God, but the Jews did.
⇒ Eventually, the Jews rejected God which is ultimately seen in their killing God's Son, Jesus Christ. They, too, failed to believe (obey God).
⇒ Therefore, God turned to the Gentiles.

Now note: if we came to know God through the unbelief of the Jews, how much more shall the Jews be shown mercy through the mercy of the Gentiles! To word the matter another way...
• if mercy resulted from unbelief, how much more shall mercy result from mercy?
• if mercy to the Gentiles came through the unbelief of the Jews, how much more shall mercy to the Jews come through the mercy of the Gentiles?

The point seems to be this: we truly know the mercy of God through Jesus Christ our Lord; therefore, we want the world to experience the same mercy and forgiveness of sins. In particular, we feel indebted to the Jews, the people through whom God gave us His Word, His Son, and His promises. Therefore, Scripture predicts that the evangelistic efforts to reach the Jews will someday bear fruit. The Jews will be reached by the mercy of God; they shall believe and obey Jesus Christ as Lord. The Jews shall be restored into the favor of God.

Thought 1. Every believer who knows the mercy of God should share the mercy of God. God hates exclusiveness, prejudice, partiality. The world desperately needs the gospel, the Jew as well as the Gentile, and God demands that His mercy be shared with the world.

Again Jesus said, "Peace be with you! As the Father has sent me, I am sending you." (John 20:21)
That God was reconciling the world to himself in Christ, not counting men's sins against them. And he has committed to us the message of reconciliation. We are therefore Christ's ambassadors, as though God were making his appeal through us. We implore you on Christ's behalf: Be reconciled to God. (2 Cor 5:19-20)
We proclaim to you what we have seen and heard, so that you also may have fellowship with us. And our fellowship is with the Father and with his Son, Jesus Christ. (1 John 1:3)

5 (11:32) **Israel, Restoration**: the fifth surety is God's holiness and mercy. The word "bound" (sunekleisen) means to shut up in a place, to close up, to lock up. This is an unusual idea: God has taken men, both Jews and Gentiles, and shut them up to disobedience (apeitheian). This is the judicial judgment of God (see DEEPER STUDY # 2—Ro.11:7-10; note—1:24; DEEPER STUDY # 1—Jn.12:39-41). It is the picture of God using sin and events for good. God takes sin and works it out for the good of the world. Man has chosen sin, choosing to go his own way in life, so God allows man to do his own thing. God locks man up in his own world of selfishness, allowing man to roam around in his world of sin. Why? So that man's true nature of sinfulness will be clearly seen, and thereby cause the honest and thinking man to seek God. God wishes and will have mercy upon all, both Jew and Gentile; but before men can come to God, they must confess two things:

⇒ that they are sinful and dying creatures in desperate need of God.
⇒ that God exists and that He will have mercy upon the person who diligently seeks Him.

Now note: all men, both Jew and Gentile, are shut up in their world of sin. Why? That God may have mercy upon both. The holiness and love of God assures that the Jews will be saved and restored to the mercy of God. All that is needed is for the Jews to begin seeking God. God will have mercy upon any who genuinely seek Him.

> **And without faith it is impossible to please God, because anyone who comes to him must believe that he exists and that he rewards those who earnestly seek him. (Heb 11:6)**
>
> **But if from there you seek the LORD your God, you will find him if you look for him with all your heart and with all your soul. (Deu 4:29)**
>
> **If my people, who are called by my name, will humble themselves and pray and seek my face and turn from their wicked ways, then will I hear from heaven and will forgive their sin and will heal their land. (2 Chr 7:14)**
>
> **But from everlasting to everlasting the Lord's love is with those who fear him, and his righteousness with their children's children— (Psa 103:17)**
>
> **My mouth speaks what is true, for my lips detest wickedness. (Prov 8:7)**
>
> **You will seek me and find me when you seek me with all your heart. (Jer 29:13)**
>
> **Because of the Lord's great love we are not consumed, for his compassions never fail. (Lam 3:22)**
>
> **Rend your heart and not your garments. Return to the LORD your God, for he is gracious and compassionate, slow to anger and abounding in love, and he relents from sending calamity. (Joel 2:13)**
>
> **Who is a God like you, who pardons sin and forgives the transgression of the remnant of his inheritance? You do not stay angry forever but delight to show mercy. (Micah 7:18)**

6 (11:33-36) **Israel, Restoration**: the sixth surety is God's glorious plan for the world. Note four points.

1. God's glorious plan for the world involves four great acts of God.
   a. His infinite wisdom and knowledge: knowing how to do everything perfectly; knowing how to create and arrange, order and govern everything so that all things work out perfectly. Note how God's wisdom and knowledge are said to be deep and rich: "Oh the depth of the riches of the wisdom and knowledge of God." God's wisdom and knowledge are so deep and rich...
      • that angels desire to look into them (1 Pt.1:13).
      • that they are infinite (Eph.3:18).
      • that they are too wonderful for man (Ps.139:6. This one verse alone shows just how great God's mercy is toward us.)
      • that they include thoughts more numerous than the grains of sand in the world (Ps.139:17-18).
   b. His infinite judgments and ways: His judgment in planning and deciding everything, and His ways in executing His purposes and decisions. Note that His judgment and ways are said to be unsearchable and past finding out.
      ⇒ Secret things belong to God (Dt.29:29).
      ⇒ God is glorified by His infinite judgments and ways (Pr.25:2).
      ⇒ The great things of God are unsearchable and without number (Job 5:9; 9:10).
      ⇒ Man cannot discover God by searching (Job 11:7).
      ⇒ There is no searching of God's understanding (Is.40:28).
2. No man can grasp God's plan. No man can know the mind of the Lord; no man can be a counselor to God. Note two significant points.
   a. No man can grasp God's plan. Scripture makes this abundantly clear.

> **[Jesus Christ] who alone is immortal and who lives in unapproachable light, whom no one has seen or can see. To him be honor and might forever. Amen. (1 Tim 6:16)**
>
> **"Can you fathom the mysteries of God? Can you probe the limits of the Almighty? (Job 11:7)**
>
> **He has made everything beautiful in its time. He has also set eternity in the hearts of men; yet they cannot fathom what God has done from beginning to end. (Eccl 3:11)**

   b. Believers do, however, have *the mind of Christ*. This does not mean that believers understand God and His ways perfectly, but it does mean that God reveals Himself and the truth to believers—enough of Himself and His ways to save them from sin, death, judgment, and hell.

> **"For who has known the mind of the Lord that he may instruct him?" But we have the mind of Christ. (1 Cor 2:16)**
>
> **We have not received the spirit of the world but the Spirit who is from God, that we may understand what God has freely given us. (1 Cor 2:12)**
>
> **Jesus answered, "My teaching is not my own. It comes from him who sent me.**
>
> **If anyone chooses to do God's will, he will find out whether my teaching comes**

from God or whether I speak on my own. (John 7:16-17)

To the Jews who had believed him, Jesus said, "If you hold to my teaching, you are really my disciples. Then you will know the truth, and the truth will set you free." (John 8:31-32)

Now this is eternal life: that they may know you, the only true God, and Jesus Christ, whom you have sent. (John 17:3)

We have not stopped praying for you...that you may live a life worthy of the Lord and may please him in every way: bearing fruit in every good work, growing in the knowledge of God, (Col 1:9-10)

Let us acknowledge the LORD; let us press on to acknowledge him. As surely as the sun rises, he will appear; he will come to us like the winter rains, like the spring rains that water the earth." (Hosea 6:3)

3. No man can earn God's gift. Note two facts about this verse.

a. No man can put God in debt to him. No man can give anything to God and claim that God owes him something in return. God owes man nothing. Man has rejected and rebelled against following God, choosing to go his own way. Man is committing high treason against God. Man does not deserve nor can he earn any favor from God. If man is to receive a favor from God, God has to freely give the favor.

Many will say to me on that day, 'Lord, Lord, did we not prophesy in your name, and in your name drive out demons and perform many miracles?' Then I will tell them plainly, 'I never knew you. Away from me, you evildoers!' (Mat 7:22-23)

Therefore no one will be declared righteous in his sight by observing the law; rather, through the law we become conscious of sin. (Rom 3:20)

Know that a man is not justified by observing the law, but by faith in Jesus Christ. So we, too, have put our faith in

Christ Jesus that we may be justified by faith in Christ and not by observing the law, because by observing the law no one will be justified. (Gal 2:16)

For it is by grace you have been saved, through faith—and this not from yourselves, it is the gift of God—not by works, so that no one can boast. (Eph 2:8-9)

But when the kindness and love of God our Savior appeared, he saved us, not because of righteous things we had done, but because of his mercy. He saved us through the washing of rebirth and renewal by the Holy Spirit, (Titus 3:4-5)

b. Man's depravity should silence his boasting. It does not, but it should (see note—Ro.3:19-20. Cp. Ro.3:9-20 for discussion.)

4. God alone is the source, the means, and the end of all things. Therefore, God is to be glorified forever and ever.
⇒ All things are *from God*: all things were created by and find their source in God.
⇒ All things are *through God*: all things come through His wisdom and knowledge, His judgments and ways.
⇒ All things are *to God*: all things exist for God, for His goodness and pleasure.

"You are worthy, our Lord and God, to receive glory and honor and power, for you created all things, and by your will they were created and have their being." (Rev 4:11)

You who fear the LORD, praise him! All you descendants of Jacob, honor him! Revere him, all you descendants of Israel! (Psa 22:23)

All you have made will praise you, O LORD; your saints will extol you. (Psa 145:10)

You were bought at a price. Therefore honor God with your body. (1 Cor 6:20)

This is to my Father's glory, that you bear much fruit, showing yourselves to be my disciples. (John 15:8)

CHAPTER 12

VIII. THE BELIEVER AND
HIS DAILY BEHAV-
IOR, 12:1-15:13

A. The Believer and God,
12:1-2

1 **Devotion urged**
2 **Present your bodies to
God**^{DS1}
   a. As a living sacrifice, holy
   b. The reason: Is accept-
      able & spiritual
3 **Do not be conformed to
   this world**
4 **Be transformed**
   a. By the renewing of
      your mind
   b. The reason: To prove
      the will of God

Therefore, I urge you, brothers, in view of God's mercy,
to offer your bodies as living
sacrifices, holy and pleasing
to God—this is your spiritual
act of worship.
2 Do not conform any longer
to the pattern of this world,
but be transformed by the renewing of your mind. Then
you will be able to test and
approve what God's will is—
his good, pleasing and perfect
will.

DIVISION VIII

THE BELIEVER AND HIS DAILY BEHAVIOR, 12:1-15:13

A. The Believer and God, 12:1-2

(12:1-2) **Introduction**: the believer is to be devoted to God. Everything he is and has is to be dedicated to the worship and service of God. Anything less than total devotion is short of God's glory: it is sin. Therefore, when discussing the believer's relationship to God, Scripture is strong in its exhortation. Without equivocation, Scripture urges total devotion.
   1. Devotion urged (v.1).
   2. Present your bodies to God (v.1).
   3. Be not conformed to this world (v.2).
   4. Be transformed (v.2).

1 (12:1) **Dedication—Commitment**: devotion is strongly urged. The word "therefore" launches a new subject for discussion. It connects what is about to be said to what has been said. What has been said is this:
   ⇒ The world desperately needs to get right with God (Ro.1:18-3:20).
   ⇒ The way for the world to get right with God is now clearly revealed through God's Son, the Lord Jesus Christ. The way is *justification*: believing in the Lord Jesus Christ and having God *count* one's faith as righteousness (Ro.3:21-5:21).
   ⇒ The believer in Christ can now be *sanctified*, that is, set apart to God and set free from sin to life eternal by the Lord Jesus Christ and by the Holy Spirit (Ro.6:1-8:39).
   ⇒ The believer or the church, not Israel, is now God's choice to carry the gospel of His Son to the whole world (Ro.9:1-11:36).

This is the glorious message of how much God loves us and of what God has done for us. This is what is meant by "in view of God's mercy." The mercy of God is overflowing; it is beyond anything any person could ever desire. Just think about what God has done for us. God has...
   • met our desperate need to get right with Him.

   • provided the power to be set free from the terrible bondages of this life and to live eternally.
   • given the most glorious purpose to life: that of proclaiming the news of God's Son, of how to be set free from sin and death and to live eternally.

Therefore, in light of God's mercy, of all this that God has done for us, we must devote ourselves to God. We must dedicate and commit ourselves to Him.

Note the words "I urge you" (parakaleo)—implore you, beseech you, beg you—devote yourselves to God. Note a significant point: what is about to be said is not being said to the world, that is, to the lost. It is being directed to *brothers in Christ*: "Therefore, I urge you, brothers." Devotion to God is strongly urged. The believer is to do the things covered in the next three points of the outline.

2 (12:1) **Body—Dedication**: the believer is to present his body to God. The importance of the human body cannot be overstated. The one thing upon earth that is abused more than anything else is man's body. Man abuses, neglects, and ignores his body...
   • by overeating
   • by becoming inactive
   • by being too active
   • by cursing, fighting, and killing
   • by partaking of harmful substances
   • by caring for the external abusing the internal
   • by getting too much or too little rest

The list could go on and on, but just the mention of these few *sins* clearly strikes the point home. If there is an exhortation in Scripture that must be heeded by Christian believers, it is the exhortation of these two verses.
   1. The believer is to present his body as a *living* sacrifice to God. Note three facts.

205

a. God demands the *believer's body*. God is not only interested in man's spirit; He is vitally interested in man's body. His interest could not be any stronger nor made any clearer. This is clearly seen by contrasting the world's view of the body with God's view (see DEEPER STUDY # 1, *Body*—Ro.12:1 for discussion).

b. The believer is to present his body *to God*. The dedication...
  • is not to be made to *self*: living as one wishes; doing one's own thing.
  • is not to be made to *others*: living for family, wife, husband, child, parent, mistress, companion, sexual partner, or employer.
  • is not to be to *something else*: houses, lands, property, money, cars, possessions, profession, recreation, retirement, luxury, power, recognition, fame.

The body is to be offered to God and to God alone. God demands the body, demands that it be presented to Him. God wants the body to be sacrificially living for Him.

c. The believer is to present his body to God as a *living sacrifice*. Note the believer's offering of his body is to be *sacrificial*. This is the picture of Old Testament believers taking animals and offering them to God as sacrifices. The believer is to make the same kind of sacrificial offering to God, but note the profound difference. The believer's offering is not to be the sacrifice of an animal's flesh and blood. The offering and sacrifice of the believer is to be his body: he is to offer his body as a *living sacrifice*. A living sacrifice means at least four things.
  • A *living sacrifice* means a constant, continuous sacrifice, not just an occasional dedication of one's body. A person does not sacrifice his body to God today, and then take his body back into his own hands and do his own thing tomorrow. A *living sacrifice* means that a person dedicates his body *to live for God and to keep on living for God*.
  • A *living sacrifice* means a sacrifice of a person's body wherever the body is. A particular place is not needed. The sacrifice of the body is a living sacrifice; it can be made while the body is living right where it is. And the offering of a living sacrifice is to be made *right now* while the body is living.
  • A *living sacrifice* means that the body sacrifices its own desires and lives for God. The body lives a holy, righteous, pure, clean, and moral life for God. The body does not pollute, dirty, nor contaminate itself with the sins and corruption of the world: not the cravings of sinful man; nor the boasting of what he has or does; not the lust of the flesh, nor the lust of eyes. The believer's body is sacrificed for God and dedicated to live as He commands.
  • A *living sacrifice* means that the body lives for God by serving God. It means that the body sacrifices and gives up its own ambitions and desires, and it serves God while upon this earth. The body gives itself to the work of proclaiming the love of God and of ministering to a world reeling in desperate needs. The body sacrifices itself to serve God and Him alone. The body is dedicated to God as a living sacrifice.

In summary, the believer is to dedicate his body to God as a living sacrifice in the home, church, school, office, plant, field, restaurant, club, plane, car or bus. No matter where the believer's body is, his body is to be sacrificed for God. Sacrificing to God is not something that is transacted in a church. Sacrificing to God is transacted in every act of the human body. The world, that is, the whole universe, is the sanctuary of God; and the believer's body is the temple of God. Therefore, every act of the believer's body is to be an act of service to God.

You were bought at a price. Therefore honor God with your body. (1 Cor 6:20)

2. The reasons why the believer is to present his body to God are twofold.
  a. The dedication of the body to God is *acceptable* or pleasing (euareston) to God. The word means well-pleasing, approving and extremely satisfying to God. God accepts and joys and rejoices over a body that is dedicated and living for Him.

Thought 1. This is the very thing for which believers should seek: to be acceptable and well-pleasing to God. We should seek to cause Him to joy and to rejoice in our bodies. Our bodies should be so dedicated—so pure and holy and clean, and so committed and involved in helping people—that God's heart is just flooded with joy and rejoicing.

Thought 2. Note: the believer's body is either causing God's heart to feel pain and hurt or joy and rejoicing.

So we make it our goal to please him, whether we are at home in the body or away from it. (2 Cor 5:9)

  b. The dedication of the body to God is the believer's spiritual act of worship.
  ⇒ The word "spiritual" (logiken) means rational, intelligent, logical. It is an act of the mind thinking and figuring out what and how to do something.
  ⇒ the "act of worship" (latpeian) means worship, service, ministry.

The idea is that the believer is to use his mind in dedicating his body to the service and worship of God. He is to study the Scriptures, and intelligently think about how to best serve God as he walks through life day by day.

Thought 1. Note how this indicates a worship time in God's Word and in prayer every day. The believer must be constantly seeking to know what is allowed and what is not allowed for his body. The believer's body must know what it can eat, drink, and do; therefore, rational and intelligent study and decisions must be made about what to allow the body to do. (What an enormous difference from the way most of us conduct our lives and treat our bodies in this life!)

DEEPER STUDY # 1

(12:1) **Body**: the world's view of the human body differs radically from God's view. This is clearly seen by contrasting the two views.

1. Some persons treat the body as though it is all that matters in this world. They believe the body—its physical, mental, and social development—is what life is all about. Therefore, they declare that man must take care of his body to the ultimate degree, developing and getting the most out of it. The developing process may range all the way from *body-building through weight-lifting to mental apprehension through concentrated study*. Some just view the body—its development, life, and contribution to society—as the very purpose for the existence of man, as the very reason lying behind the evolutionary process of man's being. (Note: this view is most often held by the humanist, the disciplined, and the stoics of society; however, there are *few persons* who hold to a *pure* view of the human body. Most persons cross this view with the next view so as to live as they choose when they choose.)

2. Other persons treat the body as though it matters little. It is reasonably or moderately important, but not of supreme importance. The supreme significance in life is the *spirit of living* and getting the most out of life. What a person does with the body matters little just so he takes reasonable care of it. *What matters is the enjoyment and pleasure of life, the spirit of living*, of really experiencing the most enjoyment possible. The attitude is "care for the body, yes, but be reasonable about its care. The body is not going to last forever, so do not let its care interfere with the enjoyment and pleasure of life. *Eat, drink, and be merry*—just do not kill yourself. A few hours or months taken off a person's life for over-indulging here and there do not matter that much. Do not take the fun out of life by over-stressing the body." (Note: this view is most often held by the carnal, the undisciplined, and the Epicureans of society. However, remember the statement above: there are few persons who hold to a *pure* view of either position.)

3. God's view of the human body differs radically from man's view. God's view of the body is *higher* and *more supreme* than man's view. Scripture reveals several significant things about the human body.

   a. When God created man, He created him in His own image (Gen.1:27). That image rested in the human body. No matter what the *image* is, or what a person thinks the image is, it rested in the human body. An image is only a shadow. It is like the picture on a stamp: the picture is not the person; it is only an image of the person. However, it is an image, and it is a likeness. Just what is meant by the "image" may be disputed, but the arguments do not matter. Whatever the image is…

     • it was given to man by God.

     • it was a part of man, of his being, of his person, of his body.

     The point is this: man's body is of supreme importance to God. God gave the body the stamp of His very own image.

   b. When God sent His Son into the world, He chose to send Him in a human body.

     Since the children have flesh and blood, he too shared in their humanity so that by his death he might destroy him who holds the power of death—that is, the devil—and free those who all their lives were held in slavery by their fear of death. (Heb 2:14-15)

   c. When God's Son was put to death and His body buried, God raised His body up from the grave and took His resurrected body into the spiritual world.

   d. Scripture teaches that the body is the temple of the Holy Spirit, that the body actually *houses* the presence of God's Spirit.

     Do you not know that your body is a temple of the Holy Spirit, who is in you, whom you have received from God? You are not your own; you were bought at a price. Therefore honor God with your body. (1 Cor 6:19-20)

   e. Scripture teaches that the body has been created to exist eternally and that the body of man will actually be resurrected from the dust of the ground and recreated into a perfect body (1 Cor.15:1-58; 1 Th.4:14-18).

   f. Scripture teaches that the body is to be cared for to the ultimate degree, being developed and disciplined to the fullest.

   ⇒ The ultimate degree of physical discipline.

     Do not offer the parts of your body to sin, as instruments of wickedness, but rather offer yourselves to God, as those who have been brought from death to life; and offer the parts of your body to him as instruments of righteousness. (Rom 6:13)

   ⇒ The ultimate degree of mental discipline.

     We demolish arguments and every pretension that sets itself up against the knowledge of God, and we take captive every thought to make it obedient to Christ. (2 Cor 10:5)

   ⇒ The ultimate degree of social discipline.

     And the second is like it: 'Love your neighbor as yourself.' (Mat 22:39)
     So in everything, do to others what you would have them do to you, for this sums up the Law and the Prophets. (Mat 7:12)

   g. Scripture teaches that the body is to enjoy life to the fullest.

     The thief comes only to steal and kill and destroy; I have come that they may have life, and have it to the full. (John 10:10)
     But the fruit of the Spirit is love, joy, peace, patience, kindness, goodness, faithfulness, gentleness and self-control. Against such things there is no law. (Gal 5:22-23)

     In summary, Scripture teaches that the human body is of supreme importance to God; therefore, man should take care of his body as well as is humanly possible. The body does not exist for this life alone; it has a far more supreme purpose than to just exist for a few years and then cease to be. The body of man has been created by God to be resurrected and to live eternally.

     Therefore, I urge you, brothers, in view of God's mercy, to offer your bodies as living sacrifices, holy and pleasing to God—this is your spiritual act of worship. (Rom 12:1)

3 (12:2) **Conformed—World—Worldliness:** the believer is not to be conformed to this world.

1. The word "conform" (sunschematizo) comes from the root word *schema* which means fashion, the outward form, the appearance of a man. It is the appearance of a person that changes from day to day and year to year. A man dresses differently for work than he does for an evening out. A man looks different as a young man than he does as an older man. His schema, his fashion, his outward appearance differs.

2. The word "world" (aion) in the simplest of terms means the world itself and everything in it, for it is all corruptible. The world, including the heavens and earth and all therein, is aging, deteriorating and dying; and it will pass away. The world is not perfect: not in being, order, morality, or justice.

3. The believer is not to conform to this world. Now note something: the world, the very fashion and appearance of the world...

• seems to be lasting, permanent, and unending.
• seems to offer the very best of everything: pleasure, enjoyment, happiness, fulfillment, satisfaction, completeness.

However, the fashion and appearance of the world is a lie, a mask, a masquerade. Even the very *spirit of the world* has within it the seed of corruption. The seed of corruption is seen in the acts of the world and its nature, in the terrible spirit of...

• selfishness	• conflict
• greed	• ignorance
• anger	• deterioration
• hatred	• death
• bitterness	• sickness
• godlessness	• disease
• savagery	• cursing
• division	• pride
• war	• disorder
• deceitfulness	• decay
• suffering	

Note two significant facts, facts that desperately need to be heeded by the world as well as by believers.

a. The world itself and everything in it shall pass away.

For this world in its present form is passing away. (1 Cor 7:31)

So we fix our eyes not on what is seen, but on what is unseen. For what is seen is temporary, but what is unseen is eternal. (2 Cor 4:18)

But the day of the Lord will come like a thief. The heavens will disappear with a roar; the elements will be destroyed by fire, and the earth and everything in it will be laid bare. Since everything will be destroyed in this way, what kind of people ought you to be? You ought to live holy and godly lives as you look forward to the day of God and speed its coming. That day will bring about the destruction of the heavens by fire, and the elements will melt in the heat. But in keeping with his promise we are looking forward to a new heaven and a new earth, the home of righteousness. So then, dear friends, since you are looking forward to this, make every effort to be found spotless, blameless and at peace with him. (2 Pet 3:10-14; cp. v.3-14)

The world and its desires pass away, but the man who does the will of God lives forever. (1 John 2:17)

Then I saw a new heaven and a new earth, for the first heaven and the first earth had passed away, and there was no longer any sea. (Rev 21:1)

The earth dries up and withers, the world languishes and withers, the exalted of the earth languish. (Isa 24:4)

Just as man is destined to die once, and after that to face judgment, (Heb 9:27)

But the one who is rich should take pride in his low position, because he will pass away like a wild flower. (James 1:10)

Why, you do not even know what will happen tomorrow. What is your life? You are a mist that appears for a little while and then vanishes. (James 4:14)

For, "All men are like grass, and all their glory is like the flowers of the field; the grass withers and the flowers fall, (1 Pet 1:24)

We are aliens and strangers in your sight, as were all our forefathers. Our days on earth are like a shadow, without hope. (1 Chr 29:15)

"My days are swifter than a weaver's shuttle, and they come to an end without hope. (Job 7:6)

"My days are swifter than a runner; they fly away without a glimpse of joy. (Job 9:25)

You have made my days a mere handbreadth; the span of my years is as nothing before you. Each man's life is but a breath. Selah (Psa 39:5)

But man, despite his riches, does not endure; he is like the beasts that perish. (Psa 49:12)

He remembered that they were but flesh, a passing breeze that does not return. (Psa 78:39)

In the beginning you laid the foundations of the earth, and the heavens are the work of your hands. They will perish, but you remain; they will all wear out like a garment. Like clothing you will change them and they will be discarded. (Psa 102:25-26)

For he knows how we are formed, he remembers that we are dust. (Psa 103:14)

As for man, his days are like grass, he flourishes like a flower of the field; the wind blows over it and it is gone, and its place remembers it no more. (Psa 103:15-16)

Stop trusting in man, who has but a breath in his nostrils. Of what account is he? (Isa 2:22)

A voice says, "Cry out." And I said, "What shall I cry?" "All men are like grass, and all their glory is like the flowers of the field. The grass withers and the flowers fall, because the breath of the LORD blows on them. Surely the people are grass. (Isa 40:6-7)

All of us have become like one who is unclean, and all our righteous acts are like filthy rags; we all shrivel up like a leaf, and like the wind our sins sweep us away. (Isa 64:6)

b. The believer is not to conform, that is, fashion himself after the world…
- not to follow the fellowship of the world.

"Therefore come out from them and be separate, says the Lord. Touch no unclean thing, and I will receive you." "I will be a Father to you, and you will be my sons and daughters, says the Lord Almighty." (2 Cor 6:17-18)
You adulterous people, don't you know that friendship with the world is hatred toward God? Anyone who chooses to be a friend of the world becomes an enemy of God. (James 4:4)
Then Simeon blessed them and said to Mary, his mother: "This child is destined to cause the falling and rising of many in Israel, and to be a sign that will be spoken against, (Luke 2:34)

- not to follow the fashion, the evil desires and lusts of the world.

Do not love the world or anything in the world. If anyone loves the world, the love of the Father is not in him. For everything in the world—the cravings of sinful man, the lust of his eyes and the boasting of what he has and does—comes not from the Father but from the world. (1 John 2:15-16)
As obedient children, do not conform to the evil desires you had when you lived in ignorance. (1 Pet 1:14)

- not to follow the ways of this world.

In which you used to live when you followed the ways of this world and of the ruler of the kingdom of the air, the spirit who is now at work in those who are disobedient. (Eph 2:2)

- not to follow the god of this world, Satan.

The god of this age has blinded the minds of unbelievers, so that they cannot see the light of the gospel of the glory of Christ, who is the image of God. (2 Cor 4:4)

- not to follow the leaders of this world.

We do, however, speak a message of wisdom among the mature, but not the wisdom of this age or of the rulers of this age, who are coming to nothing. No, we speak of God's secret wisdom, a wisdom that has been hidden and that God destined for our glory before time began. None of the rulers of this age understood it, for if they had, they would not have crucified the Lord of glory. (1 Cor 2:6-8)

- not to follow the false security of the world.

For in the days before the flood, people were eating and drinking, marrying and giving in marriage, up to the day Noah entered the ark; and they knew nothing about what would happen until the flood came and took them all away. That is how it will be at the coming of the Son of Man. (Mat 24:38-39)
For you know very well that the day of the Lord will come like a thief in the night. While people are saying, "Peace and safety," destruction will come on them suddenly, as labor pains on a pregnant woman, and they will not escape. (1 Th 5:2-3)

- not to follow after the deceitful wealth of this world.

The one who received the seed that fell among the thorns is the man who hears the word, but the worries of this life and the deceitfulness of wealth choke it, making it unfruitful. (Mat 13:22)

- not to live in pleasure on earth.

You have lived on earth in luxury and self-indulgence. You have fattened yourselves in the day of slaughter. (James 5:5)

- not to follow the crowd of the world.

"Do not follow the crowd in doing wrong. (Exo 23:2)

4 (12:2) **Transformed—Mind**: the believer is to be transformed (metamorphousthe). The Greek root of the word is *morphe*. *Morphe* means the real being of a man. It is the very nature and essence, the inseparable part, the unchanging shape of a man. The man in evening clothes looks different than he does in work clothes, but he is still the same man inwardly. The elderly man is the same man inwardly that he was as a young man.
What the Bible is saying is clearly evident: the believer must undergo a radical change within his inner being in order to escape the world and its doom. The believer must be transformed and changed inwardly. His real self—his very nature, essence, personality, inner being, his inner man—must be changed.
1. How is a man transformed within his inner person? The Bible declares as simply as can be stated, "by the renewing of your mind." The believer's mind is to be renewed (anakainosis), which means to be made new, readjusted, changed, turned around, regenerated.
  a. The mind of man has been affected by sin. It desperately needs to be renewed. The mind is far from perfect. It is *basically worldly*, that is…
  - selfish
  - self-centered
  - self-seeking
  - centered on this world
  - centered on the flesh
  - centered on this life

Scripture is clear about the corruption of man's mind. The human mind has been tragically corrupted by man's selfishness and sin.

⇒ Man's mind has become futile in his thinking, *vain*, empty, and futile in its *imaginations*.

> **For although they knew God, they neither glorified him as God nor gave thanks to him, but their thinking became futile and their foolish hearts were darkened. (Rom 1:21)**

⇒ Man's mind has become depraved.

> **Furthermore, since they did not think it worthwhile to retain the knowledge of God, he gave them over to a depraved mind, to do what ought not to be done. (Rom 1:28)**

⇒ Man's mind has become unspiritual, carnal and hostile to God.

> **The sinful mind is hostile to God. It does not submit to God's law, nor can it do so. (Rom 8:7)**

⇒ Man's mind has become blinded by Satan: he cannot see the light of the gospel.

> **The god of this age has blinded the minds of unbelievers, so that they cannot see the light of the gospel of the glory of Christ, who is the image of God. (2 Cor 4:4)**

⇒ Man's mind has become futile in his thinking, empty.

> **So I tell you this, and insist on it in the Lord, that you must no longer live as the Gentiles do, in the futility of their thinking. (Eph 4:17)**

⇒ Man's mind has become focused upon earthly things.

> **For, as I have often told you before and now say again even with tears, many live as enemies of the cross of Christ. Their destiny is destruction, their god is their stomach, and their glory is in their shame. Their mind is on earthly things. (Phil 3:18-19)**

⇒ Man's mind has become alienated from God and an enemy to God.

> **Once you were alienated from God and were enemies in your minds because of your evil behavior. (Col 1:21)**

⇒ Man's mind has become unspiritual, fleshly.

> **Do not let anyone who delights in false humility and the worship of angels disqualify you for the prize. Such a person goes into great detail about what he has seen, and his unspiritual mind puffs him up with idle notions. (Col 2:18)**

⇒ Man's mind has become corrupted, defiled.

> **To the pure, all things are pure, but to those who are corrupted and do not believe, nothing is pure. In fact, both their minds and consciences are corrupted. (Titus 1:15)**

b. The mind is renewed by the *presence and the image* of Christ in the life of the believer. When a person receives the Lord Jesus Christ as His Lord, the man is *spiritually*...
   • born again (Jn.3:3-8; 1 Pt.1:23).
   • made into a new self or new man (Eph.4:24; Col.3:10).
   • made into a new creation (2 Cor.5:17).
   • given the mind of Christ (1 Cor.2:16; cp. v.9-15).
   • changed into the image of Christ (2 Cor.3:18; cp. Ro.8:29; 1 Cor.15:49; Col.3:10; 1 Jn.3:2).

What this means is a most wonderful truth, and it is easily seen. When a person receives Jesus Christ into his life, he receives the *mind and the image* of Christ as well. Christ places His mind into the believer's mind; that is, Christ changes the believer's mind to focus upon God. In addition, He stamps His image upon the person. Whereas the believer's mind and image used to be centered upon the world, they are now centered upon spiritual matters. The believer's mind and image are renewed, changed, turned around, and regenerated to focus upon God. However, it is critical to remember that only Christ can renew the human mind and image. Only Christ can implant *the mind and image of Christ* within a person. Only Christ can give His thoughts and the spirit to *live out* His thoughts to a person.

c. The believer is to live a transformed life; that is, he is to walk day by day *renewing his mind more and more*. He is to allow the Spirit of Christ (the Holy Spirit) to focus his mind more and more upon God and spiritual things.

⇒ The believer is to love the Lord with all his mind.

> **Jesus replied: "'Love the Lord your God with all your heart and with all your soul and with all your mind.' (Mat 22:37)**

⇒ The believer is to keep his mind upon spiritual things, not unspiritual, carnal things.

> **Those who live according to the sinful nature have their minds set on what that nature desires; but those who live in accordance with the Spirit have their minds set on what the Spirit desires. The mind of sinful man is death, but the mind controlled by the Spirit is life and peace; (Rom 8:5-6)**

⇒ The believer is to demolish arguments: cast down imaginations and every pretension that interrupts his knowledge of God and to captivate every thought for Christ.

> **For though we live in the world, we do not wage war as the world does. The weapons we fight with are not the weapons of the world. On the contrary,**

they have divine power to demolish strongholds. We demolish arguments and every pretension that sets itself up against the knowledge of God, and we take captive every thought to make it obedient to Christ. (2 Cor 10:3-5)

⇒ The believer is not to let his mind be led astray.

But I am afraid that just as Eve was deceived by the serpent's cunning, your minds may somehow be led astray from your sincere and pure devotion to Christ. (2 Cor 11:3)

⇒ The believer is not to gratify the cravings of his sinful nature, his sinful desires and thoughts.

All of us also lived among them at one time, gratifying the cravings of our sinful nature and following its desires and thoughts. Like the rest, we were by nature objects of wrath. (Eph 2:3)

⇒ The believer is not to live as the world lives, in the futility of their thinking.

So I tell you this, and insist on it in the Lord, that you must no longer live as the Gentiles do, in the futility of their thinking. (Eph 4:17)

⇒ The believer is to be made new in the attitude of his mind.

To be made new in the attitude of your minds; (Eph 4:23)

⇒ The believer is to let the mind of Christ be in him by walking humbly before God and men.

Your attitude should be the same as that of Christ Jesus: (Phil 2:5)

⇒ The believer is to think only upon the things that are excellent or praiseworthy.

Finally, brothers, whatever is true, whatever is noble, whatever is right, whatever is pure, whatever is lovely, whatever is admirable—if anything is excellent or praiseworthy—think about such things. (Phil 4:8)

⇒ The believer is to live by the laws of God which God has put into his mind.

This is the covenant I will make with the house of Israel after that time, declares the Lord. I will put my laws in their minds and write them on their hearts. I will be their God, and they will be my people. (Heb 8:10)

⇒ The believer is to arm himself with the same mind as Christ in bearing suffering.

Therefore, since Christ suffered in his body, arm yourselves also with the same attitude, because he who has suffered in his body is done with sin. (1 Pet 4:1)

2. The reason why the believer is to be transformed is extremely significant. The believer must approve (dokimazo) the will of God. The word "approve" means both to *find* and to *follow* God's will. This is certainly understandable. If a person's mind is not renewed and focused upon God...

• how can the person ever find or discover or know the will of God?
• how can the person ever follow or obey or do the will of God?

The only conceivable way a person can ever *find* and *follow* God's will is to focus and keep his mind upon God and upon the things of God.

Note also how the will of God is described. Meditating upon the threefold description stirs a person to crave after God's will. God's will is said to be...

• good (agathon): beneficial, rich, bountiful, suitable, moral.
• pleasing (euareston): acceptable, satisfactory, welcomed.
• perfect (teleion): without error or mistake, flawless, complete, absolute, free from any need, short of nothing, completely fulfilled.

In summary, victory over the world is gained by the believer renewing his mind more and more. The believer must focus his mind upon God and the things of God. He must...

• focus His mind upon living and moving and having his being in God.
• learn to concentrate upon God and the things of God.
• mentally practice the presence of God.

Very practically, the believer must do exactly what Scripture says. Note the clarity and life-changing instructions in these passages. What an enormous impact is made upon lives when they actually follow the Word of God in these instructions!

Finally, brothers, whatever is true, whatever is noble, whatever is right, whatever is pure, whatever is lovely, whatever is admirable—if anything is excellent or praiseworthy—think about such things. (Phil 4:8)

We demolish arguments and every pretension that sets itself up against the knowledge of God, and we take captive every thought to make it obedient to Christ. (2 Cor 10:5)

I am saying this for your own good, not to restrict you, but that you may live in a right way in undivided devotion to the Lord. (1 Cor 7:35)

You will keep in perfect peace him whose mind is steadfast, because he trusts in you. (Isa 26:3)

The mind of sinful man is death, but the mind controlled by the Spirit is life and peace; (Rom 8:6)

	B. The Believer and Himself, 12:3-8	each member belongs to all the others.	

1 Think highly of oneself, but not too highly
a. Think soberly: Sanely, accurately
b. The reasons
  1) What we have came from God
  2) God gifts every person
  3) We are all one body in Christ
	3 For by the grace given me I say to every one of you: Do not think of yourself more highly than you ought, but rather think of yourself with sober judgment, in accordance with the measure of faith God has given you.
	4 Just as each of us has one body with many members, and these members do not all have the same function,
	5 So in Christ we who are many form one body, and
		6 We have different gifts, according to the grace given us. If a man's gift is prophesying, let him use it in proportion to his faith.
		7 If it is serving, let him serve; if it is teaching, let him teach;
		8 If it is encouraging, let him encourage; if it is contributing to the needs of others, let him give generously; if it is leadership, let him govern diligently; if it is showing mercy, let him do it cheerfully.
			2 Use the gifts God has given
			a. The gift of prophecy
			
			b. The gift of serving
			c. The gift of teaching
			
			d. The gift of encouragement
			e. The gift of giving
			
			f. The gift of leadership
			g. The gift of mercy

DIVISION VIII

THE BELIEVER AND HIS DAILY BEHAVIOR, 12:1-15:13

B. The Believer and Himself, 12:3-8

(12:3-8) **Introduction**: after looking at the subject of the believer and God, the believer needs to look at the subject of himself. He needs to see what the exhortation of God is to him personally. God directs two forceful charges to the believer personally.

1. Think highly of oneself, but not too highly (v.3-5).
2. Use the gifts God has given (v.6-8).

1 (12:3-5) **Humility—Gifts, Spiritual—Church—Body of Christ**: the believer is to think of himself, but not too highly. The exhortation is directed to *"every one of you."* Every believer needs to work at humility. There is a tendency within many persons to think too highly of themselves. Too many become conceited, prideful, and arrogant. They become *puffed up* with their own...

- importance
- looks
- popularity
- position
- ability
- performance
- wealth
- possessions
- opinions
- education
- goodness
- title

There are too many who esteem themselves too highly and who think of themselves as *better* than others. God stands against such *puffed up* attitudes.

1. Think of yourself, but think soberly (sophronein). The word means to be balanced, sane, in one's right mind. Therefore, the exhortation is to think of oneself wisely and accurately, making a sane and well-balanced evaluation of one's person and abilities. An evaluation of oneself should be made, but it should be a sober and sane judgment, not an insane, imbalanced judgment. Note how strong this is: thinking too highly of oneself is an insane thought. Thinking that one is more important than someone else is insane behavior. Every person is important to God; every person is meaningful and significant to God's kingdom, no matter who the person is.

2. The reasons why we are to live humbly before others are clearly spelled out.

    a. What we are and have has come from God. It is God who has given each believer "the measure of faith." The word "faith" in the context of these verses means a *working faith*. It includes both...

- the gifts and abilities God gives to a person.
- the faith and drive or confidence to use the gifts.

Very simply, a *working faith* is the ability and drive within a person to get to it and to serve God, to make his contribution to life and society. Another way to say the same thing is this: the measure of faith (v.3) and the proportion of faith (v.6) mean the spiritual gift and power which God gives to each believer for his special task on earth. Very simply, everything a person is and has comes from God. Nothing comes from man himself. Therefore, no person has reason to think too highly of himself.

> **Every good and perfect gift is from above, coming down from the Father of the heavenly lights, who does not change like shifting shadows. (James 1:17)**
> **For who makes you different from anyone else? What do you have that you did not receive? And if you did receive it, why do you boast as though you did not? (1 Cor 4:7)**

Note another fact as well: what we have received from God is *only a measure*. No person has a full measure of anything. No person is perfected in any area. We all age, deteriorate, and decay. We all have to move aside eventually for others, no matter what our abilities and contributions. We have no reason to think too highly of ourselves.

> **But to each one of us grace has been given as Christ apportioned it. (Eph 4:7)**

    b. God gifts *every person*, not just one person nor just a few persons. Note that God deals to *every person* a measure of faith. No person or persons have a monopoly on any gift or ability. Every single believer has been gifted by God; not a single believer has been omitted by God. One believer is as important to God as any other believer, no matter who the believer may be. There is no room for pride and arrogance in the Kingdom of God, no place for thinking that one is more important than others. Such thoughts are insane.

c. Genuine believers are *one body* in Christ. This is the most beautiful picture of the body of Christ in Scripture, and because of its effectiveness it is often used (cp. 1 Cor.10:17; 12:12f; 12:27; Eph.1:22-23; 2:16; 4:4, 15-16; 5:22f; Col.1:18, 24).

Believers can be compared to the human body. The human body has many parts or members, and no two members have the same function. So it is with believers. Believers are many, yet they are one body *in Christ*. Every single believer has a distinct function to fulfill in the world, yet he is a member of all other believers. It should be noted that the believer's union is not organizational. It is not the same kind of unity that exists in a civic or social club, which is a unity based upon such things as friendship, preference, neighborhood, profession, human need, opinion, or organization. The union between genuine believers is born of the Spirit of God, of a true *spiritual birth and union*. It is a union that is in constant and intimate fellowship with God and that draws its life and purpose and meaning and significance from God. The union between genuine believers is a union that is *quickened and made alive* by a common Spirit, a Spirit that truly lives, the Holy Spirit of God Himself.

The point is clearly stated: all members do not have the same function (praxis). God has set the believer in the world for a specific purpose, and God has gifted the believer with whatever measure of faith is needed to fulfill his function. The believer is a member or a part of the whole body, with each member having his task to perform. There is no room for self-elevation, pride, or arrogance—no room for thinking too highly of oneself. The believer does not stand alone in the world. Every believer has a measure of faith to do his task, and every member is needed to get the task done. Therefore, no believer has the right to think of himself more highly than any other believer. Every single believer is important to the *body of Christ*. Every believer is needed to complete, fulfill, and perfect the body. The body becomes handicapped without the active functioning of every member. Every member is very important.

The point is this: believers are to evaluate and know themselves well. They are to know who they are and the gifts which God has given them. They are to evaluate the measure of faith God has given and they are to be honest and accurate in their evaluation. They are not to over-evaluate nor to under-evaluate. A believer's judgment about himself must be accurate and wise in order to accomplish his task upon earth.

Thought 1. Only as we know ourselves—accurately, honestly, and truthfully—can we make the contribution we should to our families, jobs, society, church, and the world. Only as we serve to our full capacity can we fulfill our task on earth.

⇒ If we think too highly of ourselves, we attempt too much and end up failing.

⇒ If we think too little of ourselves, we never do as much as we could nor make the contributions that we could have made.

> **Do nothing out of selfish ambition or vain conceit, but in humility consider others better than yourselves. Each of you should look not only to your own interests, but also to the interests of others. (Phil 2:3-4)**

> **But when you are invited, take the lowest place, so that when your host comes, he will say to you, 'Friend, move up to a better place.' Then you will be honored in the presence of all your fellow guests. (Luke 14:10)**

> **But you are not to be like that. Instead, the greatest among you should be like the youngest, and the one who rules like the one who serves. (Luke 22:26)**

> **Humble yourselves before the Lord, and he will lift you up. (James 4:10)**

> **Young men, in the same way be submissive to those who are older. All of you, clothe yourselves with humility toward one another, because, "God opposes the proud but gives grace to the humble." (1 Pet 5:5)**

> **Humility and the fear of the LORD bring wealth and honor and life. (Prov 22:4)**

> **A man's pride brings him low, but a man of lowly spirit gains honor. (Prov 29:23)**

Thought 2. God gifts the believer with a certain measure of spiritual gifts; therefore, the believer is to use whatever measure of faith he has to use his gifts for God. However, the believer should always be praying for more and more faith.

> **Lord, "Increase our faith!" (Luke 17:5)**

> **[Lord], "I do believe; help me overcome my unbelief!" (Mark 9:24)**

> **Consequently, faith comes from hearing the message, and the message is heard through the word of Christ. (Rom 10:17)**

2 (12:6-8) **Gifts, Spiritual:** the believer is to use the gifts God has given him. The word "gift" (charisma) means the very special ability given to the believer by God. Note that the gift is from God; it is not a natural talent. The believer could not have attained nor secured the ability himself. It is a spiritual gift; that is, it is given by the Spirit of God for spiritual purposes. It is given to the believer so that he can fulfill his task on earth.

Note also that the gifts are said to be given "according to the grace given us." This means that the gifts are given after we come to know the *grace* of God. This is part of our *heritage in Christ*, the glorious privilege...

- of being given a very special task upon earth.
- of being given purpose and meaning and significance in life.
- of being given a very special gift or gifts to fulfill our task on earth.

Now, what are the gifts? Several are singled out in this passage (see outline and notes—1 Cor.12:4-11; 12:12-31; 13:1-13; Eph.4:7-16 for more discussion).

1. There is the *gift of prophecy*. In the Old Testament the gift of prophecy was the gift to proclaim and explain the will of God. The proclamation dealt with past, present,

and future events. However, in the New Testament, the gift of prophecy changes dramatically. The prophet is seldom seen predicting the future. Instead, he is seen proclaiming what has taken place in the Lord Jesus Christ and what has been *revealed by Christ* concerning future events. His function is to edify, exhort, and comfort. The Scripture is clear about this.

> **But everyone who prophesies speaks to men for their strengthening, encouragement and comfort. (1 Cor 14:3)**

The prophet is the man who proclaims and explains the Word of God...

- the living Word, the Lord Jesus Christ Himself.
- the written Word, the Holy Scripture.

Having said this, it should be noted that prophecy is the gift of speaking under the inspiration of God's Spirit. It includes both prediction and proclamation, and neither one should be minimized despite the abuse of the gift.

There is no question, the gift to predict events has been abused to the point of the ridiculous. However, the abuse of a gift does not eliminate the gift: the Spirit of God does sometimes give believers a glimpse into coming events in order to prepare and strengthen them to face the events.

However, the major function of prophecy is clearly stated by Scripture, and the fact should be learned by all believers:

> **But everyone who prophesies speaks to men for their strengthening, encouragement and comfort. (1 Cor 14:3)**

Thought 1. Note a crucial point. A prophet of the Lord Jesus Christ must first know Jesus Christ before he can proclaim the good news about Jesus Christ. How can a man tell the world about Someone when he does not know the person himself?

2. There is the *gift of serving* (diakonia). The word is often used of a servant or of a person who serves and ministers to others in the most practical ways. Therefore, the meaning would be the very special ability to serve, minister, aid, help and assist others—to assist them in such a way that they are *built up* and truly helped. It is the most practical of gifts. Most of us know a few people who are always willing and who are unusually gifted to help others when help is needed. All of us can help, and all of us can develop our willingness and ability to help, but there are some believers who are unusually gifted with the very special gift of serving.

> **And if anyone gives even a cup of cold water to one of these little ones because he is my disciple, I tell you the truth, he will certainly not lose his reward." (Mat 10:42)**
> **Therefore, as we have opportunity, let us do good to all people, especially to those who belong to the family of believers. (Gal 6:10)**
> **Your attitude should be the same as that of Christ Jesus: Who, being in very nature God, did not consider equality with God something to be grasped, But made himself nothing, taking the very nature of a servant, being made in human likeness. (Phil 2:5-7)**

> **Religion that God our Father accepts as pure and faultless is this: to look after orphans and widows in their distress and to keep oneself from being polluted by the world. (James 1:27)**

3. There is the *gift of teaching* (didaskon). Teaching is the ability to explain, root, and ground people in the truth. The Word of God not only needs to be proclaimed by the prophet, but it must also be explained by the teacher. People must be guided and rooted in all the truths of the Word day by day, week by week, and year by year. This is the teacher's task.

Thought 1. How desperately the church needs good, solid teaching. People are walking out the back door of the church almost as fast as they are coming in the front door, all because they are not rooted and grounded in Christ.

> **And in the church God has appointed first of all apostles, second prophets, third teachers, then workers of miracles, also those having gifts of healing, those able to help others, those with gifts of administration, and those speaking in different kinds of tongues. (1 Cor 12:28)**
> **It was he who gave some to be apostles, some to be prophets, some to be evangelists, and some to be pastors and teachers, (Eph 4:11)**
> **And teaching them to obey everything I have commanded you. And surely I am with you always, to the very end of the age." (Mat 28:20)**

4. There is the gift of encouragement (parakalesei). This is the very special ability to excite, motivate, advise, exhort, comfort, and warn people. The dominant factor would be the motivation and encouragement of people, the ability to stir people to make a decision for Christ and to grow in Him. It is the gift that arouses people to get up and get busy fulfilling their task for the Lord.

> **Preach the Word; be prepared in season and out of season; correct, rebuke and encourage—with great patience and careful instruction. (2 Tim 4:2)**
> **He must hold firmly to the trustworthy message as it has been taught, so that he can encourage others by sound doctrine and refute those who oppose it. (Titus 1:9)**
> **For the grace of God that brings salvation has appeared to all men. It teaches us to say "No" to ungodliness and worldly passions, and to live self-controlled, upright and godly lives in this present age, while we wait for the blessed hope—the glorious appearing of our great God and Savior, Jesus Christ, who gave himself for us to redeem us from all wickedness and to purify for himself a people that are his very own, eager to do what is good. These, then, are the things you should teach. Encourage and rebuke with all authority. Do not let anyone despise you. (Titus 2:11-15)**

5. There is the *gift of giving* (metadidomi). This simply means the giving of one's earthly possessions such as

money, clothing, and food. Note that in listing this particular gift, Scripture adds a point: it tells how the person is to give. He is to give "generously" (haplotetes). The word has several ideas. It means...

- to give with sincerity and in simplicity.
- to give with singleness of heart and without show.
- to give liberally and generously.

The point is this: God gives some persons the special gift to make money in order to have plenty to help others and to spread the gospel around the world. These persons...

- must give and give generously. God gave them the gift of making money in order to have enough to fulfill the will of God for the world. Therefore, they must give liberally.
- must not hoard and bank and misuse their gift of wealth.
- must not give grudgingly and complainingly about having to give.
- must not give to attract attention or to heap honor upon themselves.
- must not give to boost their own egos and pride.

> **But when you give to the needy, do not let your left hand know what your right hand is doing, (Mat 6:3)**
> **On the first day of every week, each one of you should set aside a sum of money in keeping with his income, saving it up, so that when I come no collections will have to be made. (1 Cor 16:2)**
> **Each man should give what he has decided in his heart to give, not reluctantly or under compulsion, for God loves a cheerful giver. (2 Cor 9:7)**

6. There is the gift of leadership (proistemi). This means the ability of leadership, authority, administration, government. Note that this person is to lead with diligence (spoude): with haste, zeal, desire, and concentrated attention. There is no room for laziness, complacency, and irresponsibility in the Kingdom of God and His church. The leaders are the ones who are to blaze the path for the flock of God, and they are to do it with zeal, hard work, and iron determination.

> **Never be lacking in zeal, but keep your spiritual fervor, serving the Lord. (Rom 12:11)**
> **Be shepherds of God's flock that is under your care, serving as overseers—not because you must, but because you are willing, as God wants you to be; not greedy for money, but eager to serve; Not lording it over those entrusted to you, but being examples to the flock. (1 Pet 5:2-3)**

7. There is the *gift of mercy* (eleon). This is a person who is full of forgiveness and compassion, pity and kindness toward others. Note that the merciful person is to show mercy with a cheerful (hilarotes) heart. The word means kind, cheerful, joyful. The person with the gift of mercy...

- is not to forgive grudgingly.
- is not to hesitate in forgiving others.
- is not to show mercy in an annoyed spirit.
- is not to show mercy in a spirit of criticism and rebuke toward the person who needs help. (This often happens when the person is down and out because of unemployment, lack of education, or some other unfortunate circumstance.)

The believer who has the spirit of mercy is to show mercy with a cheerful and joyful heart, doing all he can to lift up the person needing mercy.

> **Blessed are the merciful, for they will be shown mercy. (Mat 5:7)**
> **Be merciful, just as your Father is merciful. (Luke 6:36)**
> **But you must return to your God; maintain love and justice, and wait for your God always. (Hosea 12:6)**
> **He has showed you, O man, what is good. And what does the LORD require of you? To act justly and to love mercy and to walk humbly with your God. (Micah 6:8)**

	C. The Believer & Other Believers, 12:9-13
1 Love sincerely-without hypocrisy a. By hating evil b. By clinging to good c. By loving as brothers d. By giving preference	9 Love must be sincere. Hate what is evil; cling to what is good. 10 Be devoted to one another in brotherly love. Honor one another above yourselves.
2 Serve the Lord a. Do not lag in zeal b. Be on fire—spiritualy	11 Never be lacking in zeal, but keep your spiritual fervor, serving the Lord.
3 Conquer trials a. By rejoicing in hope b. By praying constantly	12 Be joyful in hope, patient in affliction, faithful in prayer.
4 Meet needs unselfishly a. By giving generously b. By being hospitable	13 Share with God's people who are in need. Practice hospitality.

DIVISION VIII

THE BELIEVER AND HIS DAILY BEHAVIOR, 12:1-15:13

C. The Believer and Other Believers, 12:9-13

(12:9-13) **Introduction**: How should the believer relate to other believers? How should he treat believers and behave toward them? This subject is of vital concern to Christ.

1. Love sincerely—without hypocrisy (v.9-10).
2. Serve the Lord (v.11).
3. Conquer trials (v.12).
4. Meet needs unselfishly (v.13).

1 (12:9-10) **Brotherhood—Love**: the believer is to love sincerely without hypocrisy. The word "sincere" (anupokritos) means without hypocrisy, without play-acting. It means that a person does not just say "I love you," but he actually loves. He sincerely loves; he honestly and truthfully loves. The love being spoken about is love for all men and not only for believers. The believer must never pretend, be hypocritical, play-act, or have an ulterior motive when dealing with others. He must show love and respect, interest and attention, care and concern; but he must not show it from an impure motive:

⇒ to seek gain
⇒ to gain an advantage
⇒ to gain position
⇒ to gain attention
⇒ to fulfill a duty
⇒ to push self forward
⇒ to court favor
⇒ to boost self

The believer must love others with a pure and sincere love, being completely free of selfish motives. He must love others for themselves because they are fellow human beings who have the same emotional and spiritual needs which he has, needs which can only find their fulfillment in Christ. He must love them because God loves them and because they desperately need to know that Jesus Christ has come to earth to reveal God's love to all men. The believer's dealings with all men must be in love: a sincere love, a love without hypocrisy and double-dealing.

> We put no stumbling block in anyone's path...in sincere love; (2 Cor 6:3, 6)

> Test the sincerity of your love. (2 Cor 8:8)

> Dear children, let us not love with words or tongue but with actions and in truth. (1 John 3:18)

There are four very practical ways the believer is to demonstrate his love for other men. Remember that the love being commanded is love for all men, for the lost as well as for other believers.

1. The believer is to love by hating evil. The word "hate" (apostugountes) is extremely strong. It means to despise with intense feeling, to loathe, to look upon with horror. Love desires the very best for people; therefore, love hates evil, for evil destroys human life. The believer stands against evil, doing all he can to fight...

- hunger and poverty
- hurt and pain
- drunkenness and drugs
- cursing and bitterness
- suggestive and enticing dress
- unjust and improper
- hoarding and divisiveness
- disease and suffering
- ignorance and godless education
- family divisiveness and divorce
- off-colored and dirty talk
- immorality and destructive sex
- selfishness and greed
- corruption and death

The list could go on and on. The point is that the believer must love, and he shows his love by hating and fighting against that which is evil.

> Love must be sincere. (Rom 12:9)
> Now these things occurred as examples to keep us from setting our hearts on evil things as they did. (1 Cor 10:6)
> Avoid every kind of evil. (1 Th 5:22)
> Anyone, then, who knows the good he ought to do and doesn't do it, sins. (James 4:17)

216

He must turn from evil and do good; he must seek peace and pursue it. (1 Pet 3:11)

And he said to man, 'The fear of the Lord—that is wisdom, and to shun evil is understanding.'" (Job 28:28)

Turn from evil and do good; seek peace and pursue it. (Psa 34:14)

Let those who love the LORD hate evil, for he guards the lives of his faithful ones and delivers them from the hand of the wicked. (Psa 97:10)

Do not swerve to the right or the left; keep your foot from evil. (Prov 4:27)

A wise man fears the LORD and shuns evil, but a fool is hotheaded and reckless. (Prov 14:16)

"This is what the LORD Almighty says: 'Administer true justice; show mercy and compassion to one another. Do not oppress the widow or the fatherless, the alien or the poor. In your hearts do not think evil of each other.' (Zec 7:9-10)

2. The believer is to love by clinging to that which is good. The word "cling" (kollomenoi) means to join or fasten together, to attach, to cement or glue together. The believer is to desire only the very best—all the good possible—for people. He is to cling to the good and to work for everyone to know and experience the good. The believer shows that he truly loves people by holding fast and working for the good.

But love your enemies, do good to them, and lend to them without expecting to get anything back. Then your reward will be great, and you will be sons of the Most High, because he is kind to the ungrateful and wicked. (Luke 6:35)

Love must be sincere. Hate what is evil; cling to what is good. (Rom 12:9)

Therefore, as we have opportunity, let us do good to all people, especially to those who belong to the family of believers. (Gal 6:10)

Command them to do good, to be rich in good deeds, and to be generous and willing to share. (1 Tim 6:18)

And do not forget to do good and to share with others, for with such sacrifices God is pleased. (Heb 13:16)

For it is God's will that by doing good you should silence the ignorant talk of foolish men. (1 Pet 2:15)

3. The believer is to love by loving his brothers in Christ, by being kind and devoted toward them. The word "devoted" (philostorgoi) means the love existing between family members. This charge is dealing with the Christian family, the brothers and sisters within the church. We are to love each other by being kind and devoted. We are a family of children who have actually been adopted by God as His sons and daughters (2 Cor.6:17-18; Gal.4:4-6; Ro.8:16-17). Therefore, the believer is to live as a family member with his brothers and sisters; he is to live being both kind and devoted. Note: there is no dissension or divisiveness in love. The church is to live in love, and living in love is peace.

"A new command I give you: Love one another. As I have loved you, so you must love one another. By this all men will know that you are my disciples, if you love one another." (John 13:34-35)

Be devoted to one another in brotherly love. Honor one another above yourselves. (Rom 12:10)

Love is patient, love is kind. It does not envy, it does not boast, it is not proud. (1 Cor 13:4)

Be kind and compassionate to one another, forgiving each other, just as in Christ God forgave you. (Eph 4:32)

If you have any encouragement from being united with Christ, if any comfort from his love, if any fellowship with the Spirit, if any tenderness and compassion, then make my joy complete by being like-minded, having the same love, being one in spirit and purpose. (Phil 2:1-2)

Therefore, as God's chosen people, holy and dearly loved, clothe yourselves with compassion, kindness, humility, gentleness and patience. (Col 3:12)

For this very reason, make every effort to add to your faith goodness; and to goodness, knowledge; and to knowledge, self-control; and to self-control, perseverance; and to perseverance, godliness; and to godliness, brotherly kindness; and to brotherly kindness, love. (2 Pet 1:5-7)

We know that we have passed from death to life, because we love our brothers. Anyone who does not love remains in death. (1 John 3:14)

4. The believer is to love by giving preference to other believers. The word "honor" (time) means to reverence, respect, esteem. The charge is clear: the believer is to take the lead in esteeming and expressing respect for others. Imagine a church full of believers with each taking the lead in esteeming and honoring the other. What a picture of true love and care, of real warmth and tenderness, of great strength and manliness.

Thought 1. How needed this exhortation is in the church and among believers! How many are hurt—how many have launched out to stir up trouble—how much divisiveness has been caused because a brother or sister was...

- overlooked
- not honored
- not esteemed
- not thanked
- not recognized
- not given a position
- not given a right
- not given a place
- not shown appreciation

For by the grace given me I say to every one of you: Do not think of yourself more highly than you ought, but rather think of yourself with sober judgment, in accordance with the measure of faith God has given you. (Rom 12:3)

Be devoted to one another in brotherly love. Honor one another above yourselves. (Rom 12:10)

Do nothing out of selfish ambition or vain conceit, but in humility consider others better than yourselves. Each of you should

217

look not only to your own interests, but also to the interests of others. (Phil 2:3-4)

Even as I try to please everybody in every way. For I am not seeking my own good but the good of many, so that they may be saved. (1 Cor 10:33)

Nobody should seek his own good, but the good of others. (1 Cor 10:24)

2 (12:11) **Service—Ministry**: the believer is to serve the Lord. The charge is twofold.

1. Do not lag in zeal; do not be lacking in zeal. The word "lacking" (okneros) means to be lazy, slow-moving, sluggish, lethargic, complacent, hesitating, delaying. The word "zeal" (spoude) means diligence, earnestness. The exhortation is clear: the believer must...

- not be lazy or slow-moving in zeal.
- not be sluggish or lethargic in diligence.
- not be hesitating or delaying in earnestness.

The believer just cannot approach life in a lackadaisical, easy-going, slow-moving fashion. The world is reeling in pain, with millions starving and suffering due to man's selfishness and sin, hoarding, disease, war, death—and the list could go on and on. The believer must not give in to sluggishness and complacency. He must serve the Lord with all diligence and zeal and earnestness. He must be enthusiastic in his service.

Never be lacking in zeal. (Rom 12:11)

He who has been stealing must steal no longer, but must work, doing something useful with his own hands, that he may have something to share with those in need. (Eph 4:28)

For even when we were with you, we gave you this rule: "If a man will not work, he shall not eat." We hear that some among you are idle. They are not busy; they are busybodies. Such people we command and urge in the Lord Jesus Christ to settle down and earn the bread they eat. (2 Th 3:10-12)

We do not want you to become lazy, but to imitate those who through faith and patience inherit what has been promised. (Heb 6:12)

All hard work brings a profit, but mere talk leads only to poverty. (Prov 14:23) Laziness brings on deep sleep, and the shiftless man goes hungry. (Prov 19:15)

Do not love sleep or you will grow poor; stay awake and you will have food to spare. (Prov 20:13)

Whatever your hand finds to do, do it with all your might, for in the grave, where you are going, there is neither working nor planning nor knowledge nor wisdom. (Eccl 9:10)

2. Be on fire—spiritually. The word "fervor" (zeo) means to be hot, to boil, to set aflame. The believer's spirit is to be hot, that is, boiling and flaming for Christ. The believer must have a holy zeal for Christ. He must be aflame in his service for Christ. Why? The world is reeling under the weight of desperate need and dying without Christ and being doomed to an eternity separated from God.

Never be lacking in zeal, but keep your spiritual fervor, serving the Lord. (Rom 12:11)

So it is with you. Since you are eager to have spiritual gifts, try to excel in gifts that build up the church. (1 Cor 14:12)

For this reason I remind you to fan into flame the gift of God, which is in you through the laying on of my hands. (2 Tim 1:6)

We have much to say about this, but it is hard to explain because you are slow to learn. In fact, though by this time you ought to be teachers, you need someone to teach you the elementary truths of God's word all over again. You need milk, not solid food! (Heb 5:11-12)

Therefore, my brothers, be all the more eager to make your calling and election sure. For if you do these things, you will never fall, (2 Pet 1:10)

I think it is right to refresh your memory as long as I live in the tent of this body, (2 Pet 1:13)

So then, dear friends, since you are looking forward to this, make every effort to be found spotless, blameless and at peace with him. (2 Pet 3:14)

3. Serve the Lord. The idea is that we are to be focusing upon the Lord in all we do. It is Him whom we serve. We live in order to serve Him; that is, our very purpose for being on earth is to minister for Him and His kingdom.

Serving the Lord. (Rom 12:11)

Whatever you do, work at it with all your heart, as working for the Lord, not for men, since you know that you will receive an inheritance from the Lord as a reward. It is the Lord Christ you are serving. (Col 3:23-24)

Therefore, since we are receiving a kingdom that cannot be shaken, let us be thankful, and so worship God acceptably with reverence and awe, (Heb 12:28)

Slaves [employees], obey your earthly masters [employers] with respect and fear, and with sincerity of heart, just as you would obey Christ. Obey them not only to win their favor when their eye is on you, but like slaves of Christ, doing the will of God from your heart. Serve wholeheartedly, as if you were serving the Lord, not men, (Eph 6:5-7)

But he said to me, "My grace is sufficient for you, for my power is made perfect in weakness." Therefore I will boast all the more gladly about my weaknesses, so that Christ's power may rest on me. That is why, for Christ's sake, I delight in weaknesses, in insults, in hardships, in persecutions, in difficulties. For when I am weak, then I am strong. (2 Cor 12:9-10)

And now, O Israel, what does the LORD your God ask of you but to fear the LORD your God, to walk in all his ways, to love him, to serve the LORD your God with all your heart and with all your soul, (Deu 10:12)

Serve the LORD with fear and rejoice with trembling. (Psa 2:11)

3 (12:12) **Trials—Hope—Prayer:** the believer is to conquer trials. While on earth the believer will face problems, difficulties, troubles, trials, tests, tribulations, traumas, ordeals, sufferings and pain. Nevertheless, the believer has an *overcoming resource.* He can conquer the trials of life by doing three critical things.

1. The believer is to rejoice in hope. His hope is God—God's presence, concern, and care. The believer knows that God will do one of two things: either *remove* the trial or deliver him *through* the trial. The believer knows he does not have to face trials alone, that no situation is hopeless. The believer is the eternal optimist: his hope is in the eternal God. Therefore, he not only hopes in the delivering power of God, he joys and rejoices in the hope God has given him.

Be joyful in hope. (Rom 12:12)
It teaches us to say "No" to ungodliness and worldly passions, and to live self-controlled, upright and godly lives in this present age, while we wait for the blessed hope—the glorious appearing of our great God and Savior, Jesus Christ, (Titus 2:12-13)
Praise be to the God and Father of our Lord Jesus Christ! In his great mercy he has given us new birth into a living hope through the resurrection of Jesus Christ from the dead, and into an inheritance that can never perish, spoil or fade—kept in heaven for you, (1 Pet 1:3-4)
In this you greatly rejoice, though now for a little while you may have had to suffer grief in all kinds of trials. These have come so that your faith—of greater worth than gold, which perishes even though refined by fire—may be proved genuine and may result in praise, glory and honor when Jesus Christ is revealed. Though you have not seen him, you love him; and even though you do not see him now, you believe in him and are filled with an inexpressible and glorious joy, for you are receiving the goal of your faith, the salvation of your souls. (1 Pet 1:6-9)
Dear friends, do not be surprised at the painful trial you are suffering, as though something strange were happening to you. But rejoice that you participate in the sufferings of Christ, so that you may be overjoyed when his glory is revealed. (1 Pet 4:12-13)
Sorrowful, yet always rejoicing; poor, yet making many rich; having nothing, and yet possessing everything. (2 Cor 6:10)
You sympathized with those in prison and joyfully accepted the confiscation of your property, because you knew that you yourselves had better and lasting possessions. (Heb 10:34; cp. Acts 5:41; 16:23-25)

2. The believer is to endure trials. The word "patient" (hupomenontes) means to endure, remain, persevere, abide, bear up bravely. The believer actually experiences a surge of fortitude from Christ when trials confront him.

Be joyful in hope, patient in affliction, faithful in prayer. (Rom 12:12)
I can do everything through him who gives me strength. (Phil 4:13)
I pray that out of his glorious riches he may strengthen you with power through his Spirit in your inner being, (Eph 3:16)
Now to him who is able to do immeasurably more than all we ask or imagine, according to his power that is at work within us, (Eph 3:20)
So do not fear, for I am with you; do not be dismayed, for I am your God. I will strengthen you and help you; I will uphold you with my righteous right hand. (Isa 41:10)

3. The believer is to continue in prayer. The phrase "faithful in" (proskartereo) means to give constant attention to; to be devoted and attentive to; to give unceasing care to; to wait steadfastly upon, to persevere. Very simply, the believer overcomes trials by giving constant attention to God and waiting upon His delivering power. The believer stays in constant communion with his Lord, depending upon Him to supply the strength to walk through the trials of daily living.

Patient in affliction. (Rom 12:12)
"Ask and it will be given to you; seek and you will find; knock and the door will be opened to you. For everyone who asks receives; he who seeks finds; and to him who knocks, the door will be opened. (Mat 7:7-8; cp. v.9-11)
"Watch and pray so that you will not fall into temptation. The spirit is willing, but the body is weak." (Mat 26:41)
Then Jesus told his disciples a parable to show them that they should always pray and not give up. (Luke 18:1)
Until now you have not asked for anything in my name. Ask and you will receive, and your joy will be complete. (John 16:24)
And pray in the Spirit on all occasions with all kinds of prayers and requests. With this in mind, be alert and always keep on praying for all the saints. (Eph 6:18)
Pray continually; (1 Th 5:17)
Look to the LORD and his strength; seek his face always. (1 Chr 16:11)

4 (12:13) **Stewardship—Ministry:** the believer is to meet the needs of people unselfishly. Two very simple demands are made of believers.

1. The believer is to give generously, to share with those in need. He is to "share" (koinoneo), that is, to give and distribute in order to meet their needs.

Share with God's people who are in need. (Rom 12:13)
Now, however, I am on my way to Jerusalem in the service of the saints there. For Macedonia and Achaia were pleased to make a contribution for the poor among the saints in Jerusalem. They were pleased to do it, and indeed they owe it to them. For if the Gentiles have shared in the Jews'

spiritual blessings, they owe it to the Jews to share with them their material blessings. (Rom 15:25-27)

I commend to you our sister Phoebe, a servant of the church in Cenchrea. I ask you to receive her in the Lord in a way worthy of the saints and to give her any help she may need from you, for she has been a great help to many people, including me. (Rom 16:1-2)

There were no needy persons among them. For from time to time those who owned lands or houses sold them, brought the money from the sales and put it at the apostles' feet, and it was distributed to anyone as he had need. (Acts 4:34-35)

The disciples, each according to his ability, decided to provide help for the brothers living in Judea. This they did, sending their gift to the elders by Barnabas and Saul. (Acts 11:29-30)

And now, brothers, we want you to know about the grace that God has given the Macedonian churches. Out of the most severe trial, their overflowing joy and their extreme poverty welled up in rich generosity. For I testify that they gave as much as they were able, and even beyond their ability. Entirely on their own, they urgently pleaded with us for the privilege of sharing in this service to the saints. (2 Cor 8:1-4)

There is no need for me to write to you about this service to the saints. For I know your eagerness to help, and I have been boasting about it to the Macedonians, telling them that since last year you in Achaia were ready to give; and your enthusiasm has stirred most of them to action. (2 Cor 9:1-2)

2. The believer is to practice hospitality. He is to open the door of his home to believers who are in need.

⇒ The overseer or minister must practice hospitality.

Now the overseer must be above reproach, the husband of but one wife, temperate, self-controlled, respectable, hospitable, able to teach, (1 Tim 3:2)
Rather he must be hospitable, one who loves what is good, who is self-controlled, upright, holy and disciplined. (Titus 1:8)

⇒ All believers must open their door—even to strangers in need.

Do not forget to entertain strangers, for by so doing some people have entertained angels without knowing it. (Heb 13:2)

⇒ All believers must use hospitality as a means to minister and use it without grumbling.

Practice hospitality. (Rom 12:13)
Offer hospitality to one another without grumbling. (1 Pet 4:9)

⇒ Widows in particular are to use hospitality as a means to minister.

And is well known for her good deeds, such as bringing up children, showing hospitality, washing the feet of the saints, helping those in trouble and devoting herself to all kinds of good deeds. (1 Tim 5:10)

	D. The Believer and Unbelievers, 12:14-21	18 If it is possible, as far as it depends on you, live at peace with everyone.	5 Live at peace with all a. If possible b. As far as possible
1 Bless those who persecute you 2 Show genuine interest in the experiences of men	14 Bless those who persecute you; bless and do not curse. 15 Rejoice with those who rejoice; mourn with those who mourn.	19 Do not take revenge, my friends, but leave room for God's wrath, for it is written: "It is mine to avenge; I will repay," says the Lord.	6 Give no place to revenge a. Because vengeance belongs to God
3 Seek harmony & associate with the lowly a. By living in harmony b. By not being snobbish c. By avoiding conceit	16 Live in harmony with one another. Do not be proud, but be willing to associate with people of low position. Do not be conceited.	20 On the contrary: "If your enemy is hungry, feed him; if he is thirsty, give him something to drink. In doing this, you will heap burning coals on his head."	b. Because treating an enemy with kindness will shame & store up wrath against him
4 Live above reproach a. By not reacting b. By showing good behavior	17 Do not repay anyone evil for evil. Be careful to do what is right in the eyes of everybody.	21 Do not be overcome by evil, but overcome evil with good.	c. Because vengeance makes evil victorious

DIVISION VIII

THE BELIEVER AND HIS DAILY BEHAVIOR, 12:1-15:13

D. The Believer and Unbelievers, 12:14-21

(12:14-21) **Introduction**: the believer is expected to conduct himself in the most *noble fashion* when dealing with the world of unbelievers. God expects His follower to control himself and to gain complete victory over his sinful nature. He expects the believer to give a strong testimony to the love of God, to demonstrate the love and forgiveness of God for all men.

1. Bless those who persecute you (v.14).
2. Show genuine interest in the experiences of men (v.15).
3. Seek harmony and associate with the lowly (v.16).
4. Live above reproach (v.17).
5. Live at peace with all (v.18).
6. Give no place to revenge (v.19-21).

1 (12:14) **Persecution**: the believer is to bless those who persecute him. The word "bless" (eulogeo) means to *speak well of*. Therefore, the believer is charged to do something that could be most difficult: to speak well of those who persecute him. Picture how difficult this is when you are verbally or physically attacked: mistreated, insulted, bypassed, overlooked, slandered, cursed, abused, injured. You are to bless the person who attacks you; you are to bless your persecutor whether he is your…

- next door neighbor
- family member
- fellow worker
- classmate
- employee
- employer
- friend
- fellow committee member
- fellow church member

What does it mean to bless and to speak well of?

1. It means to *speak well to our persecutors*. We do not react against them by cursing, speaking harshly, or striking out at them. We do not try to hurt them either verbally or physically. On the contrary, we seek to find something that is commendable about them and we commend them for it.

> Do not repay evil with evil or insult with insult, but with blessing, because to this you were called so that you may inherit a blessing. (1 Pet 3:9)
>
> Get rid of all bitterness, rage and anger, brawling and slander, along with every form of malice. Be kind and compassionate to one another, forgiving each other, just as in Christ God forgave you. (Eph 4:31-32)

2. It means to *speak well about our persecutors*. When speaking to others, we do not down the persecutor, but we mention some commendable trait. We praise some "good thing" about the person; we do not tear him down.

3. It means to *pray for our persecutors*. We must do as Jesus said and did.

> But I tell you: Love your enemies and pray for those who persecute you, (Mat 5:44)
>
> Jesus said, "Father, forgive them, for they do not know what they are doing." And they divided up his clothes by casting lots. (Luke 23:34)

Thought 1. Think of the impact upon persecutors when an attitude of love and blessing is demonstrated toward them. Every persecutor is not won to Christ, but every persecutor does have a strong witness, a strong witness that can be used by the Holy Spirit in the persecutor's quiet and thoughtful moments. And some persecutors are won to Christ. This is what God is after.

> "For God so loved the world that he gave his one and only Son, that whoever believes in him shall not perish but have eternal life. (John 3:16)

4. It means to do good to our persecutors.

> "But I tell you who hear me: Love your enemies, do good to those who hate you, (Luke 6:27)
>
> But love your enemies, do good to them, and lend to them without expecting to get anything back. Then your reward will be great, and you will be sons of the Most High, because he is kind to the ungrateful and wicked. (Luke 6:35)
>
> On the contrary: "If your enemy is hungry, feed him; if he is thirsty, give him

221

something to drink. In doing this, you will heap burning coals on his head." (Rom 12:20)

Make sure that nobody pays back wrong for wrong, but always try to be kind to each other and to everyone else. (1 Th 5:15)

If you see the donkey of someone who hates you fallen down under its load, do not leave it there; be sure you help him with it. (Exo 23:5)

If your enemy is hungry, give him food to eat; if he is thirsty, give him water to drink. (Prov 25:21)

2 (12:15) **Service**: the believer is to show genuine interest in the experiences of men. Two particular acts are mentioned.

1. We are to rejoice with those who rejoice. This does not mean that we are to participate in what the world calls its *joyful moments and affairs*, that is, in the *partying affairs* of the world. Far from it, God calls the believer to separation (2 Cor.6:17-18). What it means is that we are to rejoice with our neighbors and friends and acquaintances when something good happens to them. We are to join them in their moment of joy:

⇒ a new baby
⇒ some achievement
⇒ some promotion
⇒ some new purchase
⇒ some recognition
⇒ some honor

Whatever the moment of joy is, we are to rejoice with them. However, this charge is not as easy as it sounds on the surface, for it often goes against the grain of human nature. Too often it is human nature…

• to envy a person's success
• to feel disappointment
• to act indifferent

Sometimes we have a difficult time in rejoicing over another person's success. This is the reason for this charge to the believer. The believer is to *feel and act* differently than the world. The believer is to conquer his nature: he is to feel joy over the success of others and to show his joy by congratulating and joining them in their moment of joy.

Thought 1. Note that this is the very behavior of God. God rejoices in the prosperity of His people.

May those who delight in my vindication shout for joy and gladness; may they always say, "The LORD be exalted, who delights in the well-being of his servant." (Psa 35:27)

Be devoted to one another in brotherly love. Honor one another above yourselves. (Rom 12:10)

Be kind and compassionate to one another, forgiving each other, just as in Christ God forgave you. (Eph 4:32)

Therefore, as God's chosen people, holy and dearly loved, clothe yourselves with compassion, kindness, humility, gentleness and patience. (Col 3:12)

2. We are to mourn with those who mourn. This, of course, refers to our friends and fellow men who are facing some trial or loss, some moment of suffering. It may be some personal pain or business loss, some family hurt or sorrow or suffering. No matter what it is that causes the weeping, the Christian believer is to draw near the person and *feel with* him. The noteworthy trait of the believer is empathy, the fact that he is touched by the weaknesses of men.

Thought 1. Note that this, too, is a trait of God.

In all their distress he too was distressed, and the angel of his presence saved them. In his love and mercy he redeemed them; he lifted them up and carried them all the days of old. (Isa 63:9)

For we do not have a high priest who is unable to sympathize with our weaknesses, but we have one who has been tempted in every way, just as we are—yet was without sin. Let us then approach the throne of grace with confidence, so that we may receive mercy and find grace to help us in our time of need. (Heb 4:15-16)

In everything I did, I showed you that by this kind of hard work we must help the weak, remembering the words the Lord Jesus himself said: 'It is more blessed to give than to receive.'" (Acts 20:35)

We who are strong ought to bear with the failings of the weak and not to please ourselves. (Rom 15:1)

Carry each other's burdens, and in this way you will fulfill the law of Christ. (Gal 6:2)

Remember those in prison as if you were their fellow prisoners, and those who are mistreated as if you yourselves were suffering. (Heb 13:3)

Religion that God our Father accepts as pure and faultless is this: to look after orphans and widows in their distress and to keep oneself from being polluted by the world. (James 1:27)

Is it not to share your food with the hungry and to provide the poor wanderer with shelter— when you see the naked, to clothe him, and not to turn away from your own flesh and blood? (Isa 58:7)

3 (12:16) **Unity—Brotherhood**: the believer is to seek harmony and to associate with the lowly. Three very specific instructions are given.

1. The believer is to "live in harmony" with others. This refers primarily to our attitude and behavior toward others and their lot in life. The believer is to strive to *get into the very mind* of other men and to understand them. He is to strive to understand their lives:

⇒ their person and being
⇒ their lot and condition in life
⇒ their status and position
⇒ their needs and feelings

The believer is to understand the other person to such a degree that he can completely identify and feel with the person. It is to be said that the believer is to "live in harmony" with the other person. Just think of the enormous impact such love and empathy would have upon the world in bringing peace and unity and in meeting the desperate needs of so many. How can the believer demonstrate such love and empathy? The next two points clearly answer the question.

> I appeal to you, brothers, in the name of our Lord Jesus Christ, that all of you agree with one another so that there may be no divisions among you and that you may be perfectly united in mind and thought. (1 Cor 1:10)
>
> Finally, brothers, good-by. Aim for perfection, listen to my appeal, be of one mind, live in peace. And the God of love and peace will be with you. (2 Cor 13:11)
>
> Make every effort to keep the unity of the Spirit through the bond of peace. (Eph 4:3)
>
> Whatever happens, conduct yourselves in a manner worthy of the gospel of Christ. Then, whether I come and see you or only hear about you in my absence, I will know that you stand firm in one spirit, contending as one man for the faith of the gospel (Phil 1:27)
>
> Finally, all of you, live in harmony with one another; be sympathetic, love as brothers, be compassionate and humble. (1 Pet 3:8)

2. The believer is not to be proud, but be willing to associate with people of low position. "Proud" refers to seeking the things of preeminence, honor, prestige, and recognition. It means keeping one's mind upon...

- high society
- high positions
- affluence

The believer is not to be snobbish, not to allow his mind to roam around in the *prideful* things of this world. On the contrary, he is to associate with people of low position. He is to look upon the poor and lowly and to give his life to meeting their needs. The believer is not to be *above* the lowly of this world. He is not to neglect, ignore, separate, criticize, or despise the lowly. He is to associate and give himself to walking among them and helping them. He is to be friendly and kind, loving and gracious in helping to meet the needs of a desperate world.

> But you are not to be like that. Instead, the greatest among you should be like the youngest, and the one who rules like the one who serves. (Luke 22:26)
>
> For by the grace given me I say to every one of you: Do not think of yourself more highly than you ought, but rather think of yourself with sober judgment, in accordance with the measure of faith God has given you. (Rom 12:3)
>
> My brothers, as believers in our glorious Lord Jesus Christ, don't show favoritism. Suppose a man comes into your meeting wearing a gold ring and fine clothes, and a poor man in shabby clothes also comes in. If you show special attention to the man wearing fine clothes and say, "Here's a good seat for you," but say to the poor man, "You stand there" or "Sit on the floor by my feet," have you not dis-

criminated among yourselves and become judges with evil thoughts? (James 2:1-4)

> Humble yourselves before the Lord, and he will lift you up. (James 4:10)
>
> Young men, in the same way be submissive to those who are older. All of you, clothe yourselves with humility toward one another, because, "God opposes the proud but gives grace to the humble." (1 Pet 5:5)
>
> He has showed you, O man, what is good. And what does the LORD require of you? To act justly and to love mercy and to walk humbly with your God. (Micah 6:8)

3. The believer is not to be conceited. He is not to have too high an opinion of himself, as though he is above and better than the lowly. Of course, many do feel above and better than others, and they choose the most foolish of things to give them superior feelings, for example, clothes.

What is it that makes people conceited, that makes them feel above or better than others? While we stir our thoughts, just note how weak and shabby these things are (and yet people base their lives upon such weak things). People feel above and better than others because of...

- clothes
- social group
- position
- cars
- job
- recognition
- school
- honor
- wealth

The list could go on and on, but note how weak a foundation each of these provides to *human life*. Not just any one of them, but all of them could disappear or collapse overnight. The believer is not to walk through life as a *conceited fool*, thinking himself above and better than other persons. He is to walk humbly, knowing that he is a man just like all other men. He is of inestimable value, yes, but of no more value than any other man—even those who have little of this world's vanishing possessions.

Note another fact that needs to be considered. The pride of intellect or fancied superiority is probably the worst pride there is. It is more insidious and more injurious than any other pride. It leads to a contempt of the opinions of others and an extreme reliance on self (Col.1:18; 3 Jn.9).

The attitude which the gospel requires is that of a little child: simple, trusting, and humble (Pr.3:7; Is.5:21; Ro.11:25).

> For by the grace given me I say to every one of you: Do not think of yourself more highly than you ought, but rather think of yourself with sober judgment, in accordance with the measure of faith God has given you. (Rom 12:3)
>
> The man who thinks he knows something does not yet know as he ought to know. (1 Cor 8:2)
>
> If anyone thinks he is something when he is nothing, he deceives himself. (Gal 6:3)
>
> Do not be wise in your own eyes; fear the LORD and shun evil. (Prov 3:7)
>
> Woe to those who are wise in their own eyes and clever in their own sight. (Isa 5:21)

4 (12:17) **Believer, Life and Walk:** the believer is to live above reproach in the sight of all men. Two behaviors in particular are mentioned.

1. The believer is not to react; he is not to repay evil for evil to anyone. In the world and in the course of behavior between men, everyone is mistreated and reacted against at one time or another. Therefore, the believer suffers evil and mistreatment just as everyone else does—just in the course of behavior as a man. However, the genuine believer also suffers evil and mistreatment because he is a follower of Jesus Christ. As a follower of Christ...

- the believer is living a life of righteousness and purity, honesty and truthfulness; and such behavior is often opposed by the world. Therefore, the worldly person often opposes and abuses the believer.
- the believer is bearing testimony to the corruption of the world and to man's need to escape the corruption by turning to Jesus Christ and His righteousness. Again, the worldly person often opposes the message of Jesus Christ and His righteousness.

The point is this: the believer is not to react against a person who mistreats and does evil against him. There are at least two reasons why he is not to react.

a. Reaction will most likely lose the friendship of the person and lose all hope of ever reaching the person for Jesus Christ. The evil doer will be able to say, "A Christian did that to me." The believer will have made Christ an *unappealing* Savior. On the other hand, if the believer returns good for evil, he opens the door for eventual friendship and bears testimony to the love of God for all men, even for those who do evil.

b. Reaction is not the way of God or of Christ.

> **But I tell you, Do not resist an evil person. If someone strikes you on the right cheek, turn to him the other also. that you may be sons of your Father in heaven. He causes his sun to rise on the evil and the good, and sends rain on the righteous and the unrighteous. (Mat 5:39, 45)**
>
> **Do not repay evil with evil or insult with insult, but with blessing, because to this you were called so that you may inherit a blessing. (1 Pet 3:9)**
>
> **Make sure that nobody pays back wrong for wrong, but always try to be kind to each other and to everyone else. (1 Th 5:15)**
>
> **"'Do not seek revenge or bear a grudge against one of your people, but love your neighbor as yourself. I am the LORD. (Lev 19:18)**
>
> **Do not say, "I'll pay you back for this wrong!" Wait for the LORD, and he will deliver you. (Prov 20:22)**
>
> **Do not say, "I'll do to him as he has done to me; I'll pay that man back for what he did." (Prov 24:29)**

2. The believer is to demonstrate good behavior in the sight of all men. The word "careful" (pronooumenoi) means to think before acting. The idea is this: when someone does evil against the believer, the believer is to think before he acts. He is to think and pray through his behavior. Why? So that he can respond in the right and proper way. The believer needs to do what is right and noble, and the only way to do it is to think the situation through.

Note another point, a critical point. Scripture clearly tells the believer why he is to respond this way: so that his honest and noble response is seen by men. In essence, the believer is to love by turning the other cheek to the evil doer in "eyes of everybody." A strong testimony of God's love will then be seen by men.

> **Let no debt remain outstanding, except the continuing debt to love one another, for he who loves his fellowman has fulfilled the law. (Rom 13:8)**
>
> **For we are taking pains to do what is right, not only in the eyes of the Lord but also in the eyes of men. (2 Cor 8:21)**
>
> **Let love and faithfulness never leave you; bind them around your neck, write them on the tablet of your heart. Then you will win favor and a good name in the sight of God and man. (Prov 3:3-4)**

5 (12:18) **Peace—Brotherhood—War—Divisiveness**: the believer is to live at peace with everyone. However, peace is not always possible. There are two qualifications.

⇒ *If it is possible*, the believer is to live at peace with everyone. However, it is *not always possible*. Some persons are troublemakers: grumblers, complainers, dissenters, splitters, fighters, ego-hunters, self-centered leaders, image-seekers, power-builders, warmongers. Some persons have no interest in living at peace with the believer.

⇒ *As much as possible*, the believer is to live at peace with everyone. The believer is to work for as much peace as possible. Some level of harmony and concord can be achieved at least some of the time. The believer is never to give up, not as long as there is hope for some degree of peace. He is to achieve as much peace as possible. However remember, peace is not always possible—not with everyone.

Now note two significant points that need to be carefully considered and thought through by every believer.

1. The cause of conflict must not arise from a believer. He is to try everything possible to bring about peace and to keep peace (Ro.12:20; cp. Mt.5:39-41). However, this may be impossible because of the wickedness of others or because the control of peace is not within his hands. It is possible that some will not live peaceably. They continue to indulge every whim and live a life of repugnant license. Such living often threatens the peace and security, preservation and life of oneself and family and friends.

2. What is it that determines whether a believer is to turn the "other cheek" or to defend himself? For example, Jesus spent His life combating evil and wrong, and He did not always turn the other cheek (Jn.18:22-23); neither did Paul (Acts 23:2-3). Paul encouraged the believer not to give license to anyone, and he was strict in the command. For example, he said that if a man did not work because of laziness, he should not eat (2 Th.3:7, 10).

The governing principle for the believer is clear: "do not be overcome by evil, but overcome evil with good" (Ro.12:21). There are times when an attacker, if allowed to continue in his attack, is encouraged in his evil nature of indulgence and license. If allowed to continue, his evil overcomes the believer—either *within* through bitterness and revenge, or *without* through domination. Thus, a believer is not to sacrifice truth in order to preserve peace. Evil is not to be allowed to overcome truth.

> If a ruler's anger rises against you, do not leave your post; calmness can lay great errors to rest. (Eccl 10:4)
> If it is possible, as far as it depends on you, live at peace with everyone. (Rom 12:18)
> Let us therefore make every effort to do what leads to peace and to mutual edification. (Rom 14:19)
> Make every effort to live in peace with all men and to be holy; without holiness no one will see the Lord. (Heb 12:14)

6 (12:19-21) **Vengeance—Revenge—Retaliation**: the believer is to give no place to revenge. There are three reasons for this charge.

1. Vengeance belongs to God. Note the words, "My friends." The exhortation is definitely directed to believers. It would be a wonderful thing if *all men* practiced and lived by this rule, but the world never has and never will live free of vengeance. However, the *beloved* of God are given no choice. Any person who follows God is to leave vengeance up to God. Vengeance belongs to God, not to man. No man has the right to judge others, not in a private judgment nor in a personal vengeance. The right to judge and to execute vengeance is God's and God's alone. However, Scripture is clear: God will repay—God will execute vengeance. The day of His wrath is coming and it will be inescapable.

> Do not take revenge, my friends, but leave room for God's wrath, for it is written: "It is mine to avenge; I will repay," says the Lord. (Rom 12:19)
> And give relief to you who are troubled, and to us as well. This will happen when the Lord Jesus is revealed from heaven in blazing fire with his powerful angels. He will punish those who do not know God and do not obey the gospel of our Lord Jesus. (2 Th 1:7-8)
> For we know him who said, "It is mine to avenge; I will repay," and again, "The Lord will judge his people." (Heb 10:30)
> It is mine to avenge; I will repay. In due time their foot will slip; their day of disaster is near and their doom rushes upon them." (Deu 32:35)
> O LORD, the God who avenges, O God who avenges, shine forth. (Psa 94:1)

2. Treating an enemy with kindness will affect him greatly. By doing good the believer heaps "burning coals" on his enemy's head. This means at least two things.

a. Kindness will shame and cause anguish for an enemy. In his lonely moments, his thoughts will focus upon his evil treatment of believers and cause him to think and wonder about God. There is some chance the enemy might repent and be converted.

> On the contrary: "If your enemy is hungry, feed him; if he is thirsty, give him something to drink. In doing this, you will heap burning coals on his head." (Rom 12:20)
> If your enemy is hungry, give him food to eat; if he is thirsty, give him water to drink. In doing this, you will heap burning coals on his head, and the LORD will reward you. (Prov 25:21-22)

b. Kindness will store up wrath against the evil doer in the day of judgment. If an evil doer represses his thoughts of God and hardens himself more and more and continues in his wicked treatment of God's people, then he stores up more and more wrath against himself in the terrible day of judgment.

> But because of your stubbornness and your unrepentant heart, you are storing up wrath against yourself for the day of God's wrath, when his righteous judgment will be revealed. (Rom 2:5)

3. Vengeance makes evil victorious. If the believer takes vengeance, then he allows evil to conquer him, and this he must never do. The believer is to conquer evil, never allowing evil to conquer him. Note how he conquers evil: by doing good. He overcomes evil by doing what he should do, in particular by doing good toward those who mistreat and abuse him.

> But I tell you, Do not resist an evil person. If someone strikes you on the right cheek, turn to him the other also. And if someone wants to sue you and take your tunic, let him have your cloak as well. If someone forces you to go one mile, go with him two miles. (Mat 5:39-41)
> But I tell you: Love your enemies and pray for those who persecute you, (Mat 5:44)
> "In your anger do not sin" : Do not let the sun go down while you are still angry, and do not give the devil a foothold. (Eph 4:26-27)
> Make sure that nobody pays back wrong for wrong, but always try to be kind to each other and to everyone else. (1 Th 5:15)

CHAPTER 13

E. The Believer and the State, 13:1-7

1 Government is to be obeyed
2 Government is established by God
	Everyone must submit himself to the governing authorities, for there is no authority except that which God has established. The authorities that exist have been established by God.	what is right and he will commend you.
		4 For he is God's servant to do you good. But if you do wrong, be afraid, for he does not bear the sword for nothing. He is God's servant, an agent of wrath to bring punishment on the wrongdoer.
			good, but upon evil
			  b. Rulers are the servants of God for good:
			    To maintain the welfare of the citizens
			    1) They bear the sword against evil
			    2) They execute justice
			  c. The believer is to obey the state for conscience sake

a. Resistance equals resisting God's institution b. Resistance shall be condemned	2 Consequently, he who rebels against the authority is rebelling against what God has instituted, and those who do so will bring judgment on themselves.	5 Therefore, it is necessary to submit to the authorities, not only because of possible punishment but also because of conscience.	

3 Government is established to promote good & restrain evil
  a. Rulers are not established to be a restraint upon the
	3 For rulers hold no terror for those who do right, but for those who do wrong. Do you want to be free from fear of the one in authority? Then do	6 This is also why you pay taxes, for the authorities are God's servants, who give their full time to governing.
		7 Give everyone what you owe him: If you owe taxes, pay taxes; if revenue, then revenue; if respect, then respect; if honor, then honor.
			4 Government is established to provide benefits through taxesDS1
			  a. Rulers are to provide benefits
			  b. Believers are to pay taxes
			  c. Believers are to pay whatever is due: Money or respect

DIVISION VIII

THE BELIEVER AND HIS DAILY BEHAVIOR, 12:1-15:13

E. The Believer and the State, 13:1-7

(13:1-7) Introduction: What is the relationship between the believer and the state? The question has been debated down through the centuries. Which is supreme, the church or the state? God pulls no punches in dealing with the issue, and what He has to say to the genuine believer is startling to some persons. Simply stated, God expects the genuine believer to live as a testimony of righteousness (doing what is right) while a citizen of this earth.

1. God is to be obeyed (v.1).
2. Government is established by God (v.1-2).
3. Government is established to promote good and restrain evil (v.3-5).
4. Government is established to provide benefits through taxes (v.6-7).

1 (13:1) **Government—State—Civil Authorities**: Government is to be obeyed, believers are to obey civil authorities. It does not matter how the civil authorities were appointed or by whom. It may have been by a senate, an army, or the people. The authority, whether just or unjust, whether legitimate or illegitimate, is to be obeyed.

However, the sphere of authority is to be noted. The government has authority only within the *civil realm*. The authority of the government does not extend beyond its position. For example, when Paul commands wives to obey their husbands, they are required to obey them as *husbands*, not as masters or as kings. Children are to obey their parents as *parents*, not as sovereigns. So it is in the case of government leaders.

When the laws of civil government conflict with the explicit commandments of God, then Christians must say, "we ought to obey God rather than men" (Acts 5:29). When a ruler claims divine rights, Christian believers must answer "no," for the ruler is going beyond the civil authority delegated to him by God. The ruler is trespassing on territory which is not his (see note—Ro.12:18). But the

Christian believer is to say "yes" to all civil matters not conflicting with the commandments of God. Scripture gives several reasons for this. (See outline and notes—1 Tim.2:2; Tit.3:1; 1 Pt.2:13-17 for more discussion.)

2 (13:1-2) **Government**: government is established by God; that is, the existence, the authority, the position, the offices of government are established by God. It is God's will that government exist and that persons have the authority to rule within the state. There are three institutions established by God: the family, the church, and the government. All three exist because God set them up as the means by which men are to relate to each other and to Him as God. God has established...

- that the family exist as the means by which family members share together, and that the office of parents rule within the family.
- that the church exist as the means by which people share with God, and that the office of church leaders exercise authority within the church.
- that the government exist as the means by which citizens relate to each other, and that the office of government officials exercise authority within the state.

The institutions and their authority are established by God, and men are responsible for how they carry out their functions. Each of the three institutions has leaders who are faithful and do an excellent job, and each has leaders who are totally disobedient to God and do a terrible job. This includes the men who hold authority within various levels of government as well as men serving on various levels in the other two institutions. The fact to remember is that government is established by God, and rulers are answerable to Him: they shall give an account to God.

Everyone must submit himself to the governing authorities, for there is no authority except that which God has established. The authorities that exist have been established by God. (Rom 13:1)

Kings detest wrongdoing, for a throne is established through righteousness. (Prov 16:12)

In love a throne will be established; in faithfulness a man will sit on it. (Isa 16:5)

However, the *thrust* of this passage is not the rulers of government; the *thrust* is the believer and his duty to the state. Usually the believer can do little about how the authorities in government conduct their affairs, but the believer can do a great deal about his behavior as a citizen within the state; and God is very, very clear about the believer's behavior. Keep in mind that the infamous Nero was ruling as the emperor when God led Paul to give these instructions.

1. The believer is not to resist the government because resistance equals resisting the institution of God. Note three points.

a. Christianity must not become confused with a political movement nor with a national government. Christ has nothing to do with insurrection, rebellion, or civil disobedience. Christians are not to be identified with murder and assassination; nor are they to be known as terrorists. They are not to cause havoc upon people nor wreck communities.

b. There is one exception to resisting government that is allowed the believer. When rulers begin to exercise personal and immoral mastery over human life, then the believer is to obey God and not man. The believer is always to follow after righteousness, that is, morality and justice. However, note a crucial point: the morality and justice pursued must be the morality and justice of Scripture and not of man's making. (See note—Ro.13:1 for more discussion).

c. World leaders are in the hands of God and are playing their part under His sovereign administration. This is a great comfort to the heart of the Christian believer (although it may not be to the unbeliever), for it means that God is working in the affairs of world leaders. He holds the world in His hands. He is taking the failure and evil of nations and leaders and working "all things...for the good of those who love him who have been called according to His purpose" (Ro.8:28).

2. The believer who resists the authorities will be condemned. The word "judged" *krima* means judgment. The idea is that the disobedient believer will have to face the judgment of God if he disobeys the just laws of government. Some commentators think this refers to the judgment of the civil authorities. There is no question, if the believer is caught breaking the laws of the state, he will be punished. However, the civil authorities may never catch the believer; but God knows every law broken by the believer, and by resisting the laws of the state the believer has broken the law of God. Therefore, the believer stands guilty before God, and he shall be judged by God.

Submit yourselves for the Lord's sake to every authority instituted among men: whether to the king, as the supreme authority, or to governors, who are sent by him to punish those who do wrong and to commend those who do right. (1 Pet 2:13-14)

Whoever does not obey the law of your God and the law of the king must surely be punished by death, banishment, confiscation of property, or imprisonment. (Ezra 7:26)

Fear the LORD and the king, my son, and do not join with the rebellious, for those two will send sudden destruction upon them, and who knows what calamities they can bring? (Prov 24:21-22)

3 (13:3-5) **Government**: government is established to promote good and to restrain evil. Note three points.

1. Rulers are not established to be a restraint upon good works, but upon evil. Civil authorities and laws exist to restrain evil; therefore, any believer who breaks the law can expect to be punished by the state. For this reason, the believer should...

- fear the state enough to obey its laws.
- do that which is good and lawful.

By fearing and doing that which is good and lawful, the believer has the *praise* of the state. The idea is that the believer contributes to the good and to the praise of the state. He helps to build up righteousness and truth within the state, and thereby he is able to be the citizen of a good and praiseworthy state. The believer has the praise of the state; he is allowed to live in peace as a citizen of the state.

"Do not blaspheme God or curse the ruler of your people. (Exo 22:28)

Obey the king's command, I say, because you took an oath before God. (Eccl 8:2)

"Caesar's," they replied. Then he said to them, "Give to Caesar what is Caesar's, and to God what is God's." (Mat 22:21)

Paul replied, "Brothers, I did not realize that he was the high priest; for it is written: 'Do not speak evil about the ruler of your people.'" (Acts 23:5)

Everyone must submit himself to the governing authorities, for there is no authority except that which God has established. The authorities that exist have been established by God. (Rom 13:1)

Remind the people to be subject to rulers and authorities, to be obedient, to be ready to do whatever is good, (Titus 3:1)

Submit yourselves for the Lord's sake to every authority instituted among men: (1 Pet 2:13)

Show proper respect to everyone: Love the brotherhood of believers, fear God, honor the king. (1 Pet 2:17)

Thought 1. Note that civil government and law are a *restraint* upon evil. The power of evil and corruption is so strong that when men are without law, they go on a rampage of selfishness and sin. History and the breakdown of law within communities, cities, societies, and even families provide ample evidence. When law does not exist or when law is not enforced, evil runs rampant. Society desperately needs to heed this fact.

We also know that law is made not for the righteous but for lawbreakers and rebels, the ungodly and sinful, the unholy and irreligious; for those who kill their fathers or mothers, for murderers, for adulterers and perverts, for slave traders and liars and perjurers—and for whatever else is contrary to the sound doctrine (1 Tim 1:9-10)

2. Rulers are the servants of God for good: to maintain the welfare of its citizens. Note that the civil authority rules for the citizens' good. This verse is merely reviewing what has already been said in the preceding three verses.

   a. The office of ruler is established by God for good; it is for the welfare and the good of the citizens.

> The God of Israel spoke, the Rock of Israel said to me: 'When one rules over men in righteousness, when he rules in the fear of God, (2 Sam 23:3)
> He told them, "Consider carefully what you do, because you are not judging for man but for the LORD, who is with you whenever you give a verdict. (2 Chr 19:6)
> Therefore, you kings, be wise; be warned, you rulers of the earth. Serve the LORD with fear and rejoice with trembling. (Psa 2:10-11)
> Love and faithfulness keep a king safe; through love his throne is made secure. (Prov 20:28)
> By justice a king gives a country stability, but one who is greedy for bribes tears it down. (Prov 29:4)
> If a king judges the poor with fairness, his throne will always be secure. (Prov 29:14)

   b. The believer is to fear breaking the laws of the state because the civil authority exists to maintain order by punishing evil-doers or lawbreakers.

> Submit yourselves for the Lord's sake to every authority instituted among men: whether to the king, as the supreme authority, or to governors, who are sent by him to punish those who do wrong and to commend those who do right. (1 Pet 2:13-14)

3. The believer is to obey the state for conscience' sake as well as out of fear of punishment. There are two reasons for obeying civil laws:
⇒ For wrath's sake, that is, fearing the punishment of the state.
⇒ For conscience's sake, that is, fearing the punishment of God.

There are two ways in which conscience is involved. First, the Christian believer is told that God establishes government and that to resist government equals resisting God's institution. Therefore, the believer has a principle to govern his conscience: to abuse his citizenship is to resist God's will and to violate his conscience.
Second, conscience determines a man's state of being. A restful conscience brings peace to a man; a disturbed conscience brings restlessness and pain. The man in rebellion against his government disturbs his conscience and lives under the restless fear of being caught and punished.

> So I strive always to keep my conscience clear before God and man. (Acts 24:16)
> Now this is our boast: Our conscience testifies that we have conducted ourselves in the world, and especially in our relations with you, in the holiness and sincerity that are from God. We have done so not according to worldly wisdom but according to God's grace. (2 Cor 1:12)
> The goal of this command is love, which comes from a pure heart and a good conscience and a sincere faith. (1 Tim 1:5)
> Holding on to faith and a good conscience. Some have rejected these and so have shipwrecked their faith. (1 Tim 1:19)
> They must keep hold of the deep truths of the faith with a clear conscience. (1 Tim 3:9)
> Pray for us. We are sure that we have a clear conscience and desire to live honorably in every way. (Heb 13:18)
> For it is commendable if a man bears up under the pain of unjust suffering because he is conscious of God. (1 Pet 2:19)
> Keeping a clear conscience, so that those who speak maliciously against your good behavior in Christ may be ashamed of their slander. (1 Pet 3:16)

4 (13:6-7) **Government**: government is established to provide benefits *through taxes*. Note three points.
  1. Rulers are God's ministers who are appointed for "governing;" that is, *God appoints rulers as ministers to serve to the people*. The rulers are to serve by providing certain benefits for the citizens.
   a. The government provides justice, protection, and services for its citizens. It is the agreement between the law and the people to live by the law that keeps the strong from dominating the weak. It keeps life from becoming the law of the jungle. It is also the state that often provides services such as roads, public transportation, and electricity.
   b. The government keeps the world from diving into chaos. Whatever peace is known within a country, it is known through the government that exists. It is not perfect peace, but usually within its boundaries there is a semblance of peace. Therefore, man is to work for worldwide peace through the framework of government.
  2. The believer is, therefore, to pay taxes. Every citizen is obligated to the government for the benefits which he receives from the state. Certain benefits come from the cooperative effort of people within a state. A man could not receive these benefits acting as an individual. These benefits and privileges are his because the government has brought them about. Therefore, the man is obligated to the state to pay his share.

> After Jesus and his disciples arrived in Capernaum, the collectors of the two-drachma tax came to Peter and asked, "Doesn't your teacher pay the temple tax?" "But so that we may not offend them, go to the lake and throw out your line. Take the first fish you catch; open its mouth and you will find a four-drachma coin. Take it and give it to them for my tax and yours." (Mat 17:24, 27)

"Caesar's," they replied. Then he said to them, "Give to Caesar what is Caesar's, and to God what is God's." (Mat 22:21)

This is also why you pay taxes, for the authorities are God's servants, who give their full time to governing. (Rom 13:6)

3. The believer is not only to pay taxes, but he is to pay whatever is due to *every man*. The word "pay" (teleo) means to fulfill or to complete. The believer is to fulfill his obligations no matter what they are.

⇒ If a nation is due taxes, he is to pay his taxes.
⇒ If a civil authority is due revenue (taxes), he is to pay his revenue.
⇒ If an authority or person is due respect, he is to reverence the authority or person.
⇒ If an authority or person is due honor, he is to honor the authority or person.

Very simply, the believer is to live above reproach before all men, and this includes being a *good citizen* of his government.

Through the blessing of the upright a city is exalted, but by the mouth of the wicked it is destroyed. (Prov 11:11)

Righteousness exalts a nation, but sin is a disgrace to any people. (Prov 14:34)

Remove the wicked from the king's presence, and his throne will be established through righteousness. (Prov 25:5)

When a country is rebellious, it has many rulers, but a man of understanding and knowledge maintains order. (Prov 28:2)

In righteousness you will be established: (Isa 54:14)

DEEPER STUDY # 1

(13:6) **Revenue—Taxes**: this was a difficult command. For most believers, the command caused anything but pleasure, for the taxes levied by the Roman government against its conquered nations were heavy to bear (see note—Mt.9:9).

1. There was the income tax: one percent of a man's income.

2. There was the ground tax: a man had to pay one-tenth or one-fifth of the crops produced by his ground. He could make payment in money or in the actual crops harvested.

3. There was a poll tax: paid by everyone between the ages of twelve or fourteen and sixty-five. It amounted to about one day's wage. (See DEEPER STUDY # 3—Mt.22:17.)

There were also local taxes that had to be paid. There were import and export taxes, and there were custom duties including taxes for using main roads, crossing bridges, entering markets and harbors, transferring animals, and driving carts or wagons.

	F. The Believer and His Fellow Citizens, 13:8-10	not murder," "Do not steal," "Do not covet," and whatever other commandment there may be, are summed up in this one rule: "Love your neighbor as yourself."	3 Love forbids murder
			4 Love forbids stealing
1 The basic law			5 Love forbids covetousness
a. Owe no man anything	8 Let no debt remain outstanding, except the continuing debt to love one another, for he who loves his fellowman has fulfilled the law.		
b. Owe no man anything *but love*		10 Love does no harm to its neighbor. Therefore love is the fulfillment of the law.	6 Love sums up all the commandments
2 Love forbids adultery	9 The commandments, "Do not commit adultery," "Do		7 Love does no harm to a neighbor

DIVISION VIII

THE BELIEVER AND HIS DAILY BEHAVIOR, 12:1-15:13

F. The Believer and His Fellow Citizens, 13:1-7

(13:8-10) **Introduction**: the commandments of God to believers are clear and forceful—especially when dealing with their neighbors, that is, with the fellow-citizens of the world. God's laws are few, but they are striking.

1. The basic law (v.8).
2. Love forbids adultery (v.9).
3. Love forbids killing (v.9).
4. Love forbids stealing (v.9).
5. Love forbids covetousness (v.9).
6. Love sums up all the commandments (v.9).
7. Love does no harm to a neighbor (v.10).

1 (13:8) **Love—Debts**: there is one very basic law that sums up all the other laws of men. It is amazing to think that all the laws of human life can be summed up into one law, yet they can. The one law that embraces all others is *love*. Scripture clearly declares: "Let no debt remain outstanding, except the continuing debt to love one another, for he who loves his fellowman has fulfilled the law" (v.8). Note two significant points.

1. The believer is to owe no man anything. At first glance, the verse seems to be saying that the believer is not to borrow and become indebted to any man. In light of what has just been taught this is true, and it is both God's will and a *must* for Christian believers to practice. A believer is to *set the example* in paying men honor when honor is due as well as in paying debts when debts are due (v.7).

How does this commandment work out in day to day practice? Does this commandment mean that a believer should never borrow money or purchase things on an installment plan, for example, a house or a car? There are, of course, different interpretations as to how this commandment should be related to various societies and monetary practices. Three things can be clearly said and should be diligently practiced by all believers.

a. Nothing should ever be purchased by a believer that is not really needed. The money should be used to meet the needs of a world that is reeling under the weight of starving, diseased, and dying masses every day.

b. Nothing should ever be purchased unless a believer can meet the obligation of paying for it.

c. If the believer *has to purchase* an expensive item such as a car or house and make periodic payments, he *must be able to make his payments* or else not purchase the item. In reality, he does not owe the money until the payment is due, but he does owe it *when it is due*. If he does not pay when it is due, he is definitely disobeying God.

The point is this: a believer is to owe no one anything. The reason is clearly seen. The people of the world live for the world and its money and possessions. It is all they have; therefore, they judge men by how much they have. It does not matter who the person is, Christian or non-Christian, he is judged by how well off he is financially. If a believer is not prompt in paying what he owes and in meeting his obligations, he is considered unethical and dishonest, a crook and a thief. And he is, for he has taken something that belongs to someone else. Moreover, he has deceived and lied to the man from whom he bought the item. He convinced the man that he could and would pay, and now he is not paying what he owes.

Very simply, a Christian believer *must* always pay his debts and fulfill his obligations. He must never owe any man anything lest he damage the name of Christ, and push men farther away from the Kingdom of God because of a negative view of Christian believers. The believer must live above reproach, and one of the most significant ways to live above reproach is to owe no man anything—to pay his debts and fulfill his obligations promptly.

> **"Woe to you, teachers of the law and Pharisees, you hypocrites! You clean the outside of the cup and dish, but inside they are full of greed and self-indulgence. (Mat 23:25)**
>
> **Give everyone what you owe him: If you owe taxes, pay taxes; if revenue, then revenue; if respect, then respect; if honor, then honor. (Rom 13:7)**
>
> **Look! The wages you failed to pay the workmen who mowed your fields are crying out against you. The cries of the harvesters have reached the ears of the Lord Almighty. (James 5:4)**
>
> **She went and told the man of God, and he said, "Go, sell the oil and pay your debts. You and your sons can live on what is left." (2 Ki 4:7)**
>
> **Better a little with righteousness than much gain with injustice. (Prov 16:8)**
>
> **A fortune made by a lying tongue is a fleeting vapor and a deadly snare. (Prov 21:6)**
>
> **Like a partridge that hatches eggs it did not lay is the man who gains riches by unjust means. When his life is half gone, they will desert him, and in the end he will prove to be a fool. (Jer 17:11)**
>
> **"Woe to him who builds his palace by unrighteousness, his upper rooms by injustice, making his countrymen work for nothing, not paying them for their labor. (Jer 22:13)**

"'I will surely strike my hands together at the unjust gain you have made and at the blood you have shed in your midst. (Ezek 22:13)

2. The believer is to owe no man anything *but love*. Love will do more to win men to Jesus Christ and to bring about the ideal society than any other virtue. As this verse says, love fulfills the law. Therefore, if everyone will love one another, then everyone will be fulfilling the law; and the ideal society and life for which we all long will become a reality. This is clearly seen in this passage; in fact, it is the major thrust of these verses. God is telling believers to love one another in order to demonstrate what society *can* be. The world and society can live in love if they will turn to Him. However, if believers continue to live owing debts and committing the sins about to be discussed, then believers are no different from the world. They prove to be men of false profession. Believers become nothing more than hypocrites. For this reason believers *must* obey God: "Let no debt remain outstanding, except the continuing debt to love one another, for he who loves his fellowman has fulfilled the law" (v.8).

Just how love fulfills the law is the subject of the following points. Note that the laws mentioned are the laws dealing with man's behavior toward his neighbor, all of which are taken from the ten commandments. Love fulfills the commandments of God.

2 (13:9) **Adultery—Love**: love forbids adultery. "You shall not commit adultery" (Ex.20:14; Dt.5:18; see note and DEEPER STUDY # 1—Mt.5:27-30 for more discussion). Note two significant points.

1. In the context of the ten commandments, adultery refers to all forms of sexual immorality. This would include sex before marriage, homosexuality, and all other sexual deviations.

2. Love forbids adultery, that is, any sex outside the marriage bond. How can love forbid a loving act? Is not sex an act of love, an act of mutual sharing that enriches life? Scripture says:

⇒ Yes, if it is experienced within a true marriage, that is, a marriage that is truly spiritually united by God.
⇒ No, if it is experienced outside a true marriage, outside a couple who have been truly bound together by God.

Scripture is pointed and clear about this fact. Note closely what Scripture says:

Flee from sexual immorality. All other sins a man commits are outside his body, but he who sins sexually sins against his own body. (1 Cor 6:18)

How is sexual immorality a sin against the human body? How is a person's body affected by immorality? There are five ways that the body is affected by sexual immorality.

1. Sexual immorality destroys a person's rationality and intelligence. This is a critical point that is clearly seen by the honest and thinking person. Men and women are rational creatures; therefore, they can look at themselves and their world, and study and learn and know what is happening when a man and woman have sex. Sex is the means of procreation, that is, of having children and carrying on the human race. Now note: it is through the act of sex that a person's innermost being, his or her genes and nature, flow into another person and produce another life. That is, sex involves the most private and intimate part of a person—a

person's very genes and nature. Therefore, *by its very nature*, sex is the most private and intimate act of a person. From this fact alone, a rational creature knows that sex is bound to require some privacy, some limitation. But there is much more to think about that tells us just how private and limited sex should be.

Consider having and bearing children. By nature a woman cannot have a child by herself. It requires a man as well as a woman. One man and one woman have a child, and to have the child requires...

- the most private parts of their *two bodies*.
- the most intimate act of their *two bodies*.

Therefore while rearing the child, rational and moral creatures know that the *two are meant* to be each other's. Why? The man and woman have put their very *nature and genes* into the child, and the child has their nature and genes; therefore...

- they are the ones who should *rear* the child.
- they are bound together, their genes and nature, *within the body* of the child.

No closer bond and relationship, no greater love or trust or hope exists than the union of the three. The man has given the woman his very nature, and the woman has willingly received his nature and given both his and her nature to the child. The three are bound together in a most unique relationship, no matter how much it may be ignored, denied and abused. The husband and wife and their sexual relationship is a very unique relationship. But note this: men and women are set off from other animals by their rationality. This is one of the features that makes man's sexual relationship different from the relationship between animals. They can know who they are and what is happening to them when other animals do not. Men and women can know that their relationship is not just *animalistic*. Therefore when they have immoral relationships, they ignore, neglect, violate, abuse, and damage their minds. They do what they know should not be done. As God says:

The wrath of God is being revealed from heaven against all the godlessness and wickedness of men who suppress the truth by their wickedness, since what may be known about God is plain to them, because God has made it plain to them. (Rom 1:18-19)
(Indeed, when Gentiles, who do not have the law, do by nature things required by the law, they are a law for themselves, even though they do not have the law, since they show that the requirements of the law are written on their hearts, their consciences also bearing witness, and their thoughts now accusing, now even defending them.) (Rom 2:14-15)

2. Sexual immorality destroys a person's body in that it lowers his body to the level of an animal. It is simply the wrong view of a man. It views man as a beast, ignoring man's spirit. It declares that life is to be lived on the level of passion and instinct, ignoring the life of the spirit. (See DEEPER STUDY # 1, *Immorality*—1 Cor.6:18 for more detailed discussion of this point.)

3. Sexual immorality destroys a person's body in that it corrupts the most intimate temple of the Holy Spirit. Scripture declares that the human body was made to be the temple of the Holy Spirit. God created man to be His child. Man is spirit as well as body, and when a man truly believes in Christ, Christ is said to enter and to dwell *within*

the man's body. Therefore, when a man commits sexual immorality, he destroys his body; that is, he violates, misuses, and abuses the temple of God.

4. Sexual immorality destroys a person's body in that it uses the human body only as an object or tool to satisfy urges and passions. It keeps a human body from reaching its fullest potential. It ignores the *satisfaction and peace and fulfillment and development* of both the spirit and mind that comes from a union wrought by God.

5. Sexual immorality destroys a person's body in that it creates all sorts of emotional and spiritual problems for the persons involved. Having sex outside marriage creates guilt and negative thoughts within a person whether admitted or not. After an illicit act, when the person is alone with his thoughts, he thinks about his life and senses lack and need. No matter who the person is and no matter how long the person has been engaged in sexual misbehavior, there are times when the person thinks about his or her life and the need for something more meaningful. God sees that we all have these thoughts. They are a safeguard to try and turn us back to Him. Sexual misconduct eats away at our emotions and thoughts and spirits until we are destroyed, unless we repent and turn to God.

Now, the thrust of the point is this: love forbids sexual immorality. A person who really loves someone would never destroy the body of his loved one. Anyone who honestly loves a person could never cause such problems for the one loved.

> "You have heard that it was said, 'Do not commit adultery.' But I tell you that anyone who looks at a woman lustfully has already committed adultery with her in his heart. (Mat 5:27-28)
>
> Because of this, God gave them over to shameful lusts. Even their women exchanged natural relations for unnatural ones. In the same way the men also abandoned natural relations with women and were inflamed with lust for one another. Men committed indecent acts with other men, and received in themselves the due penalty for their perversion. Furthermore, since they did not think it worthwhile to retain the knowledge of God, he gave them over to a depraved mind, to do what ought not to be done. They have become filled with every kind of wickedness, evil, greed and depravity. They are full of envy, murder, strife, deceit and malice. They are gossips, (Rom 1:26-29)
>
> Do you not know that the wicked will not inherit the kingdom of God? Do not be deceived: Neither the sexually immoral nor idolaters nor adulterers nor male prostitutes nor homosexual offenders (1 Cor 6:9)
>
> The acts of the sinful nature are obvious: sexual immorality, impurity and debauchery; and envy; drunkenness, orgies, and the like. I warn you, as I did before, that those who live like this will not inherit the kingdom of God. (Gal 5:19, 21)
>
> They will be paid back with harm for the harm they have done. Their idea of pleasure is to carouse in broad daylight. They are blots and blemishes, reveling in their pleasures while they feast with you. With eyes full of adultery, they never stop sinning; they seduce the unstable; they are

> experts in greed—an accursed brood! They have left the straight way and wandered off to follow the way of Balaam son of Beor, who loved the wages of wickedness. (2 Pet 2:13-15)

3 (13:9) **Murder**: love forbids murders. "You shall not murder." The law against murder is the sixth commandment (Ex.20:13; Dt.5:17). God gave the commandment to protect human life. Life is to be respected and cherished; no life is to be taken—not one's own life nor the life of anyone else. Civilized societies have always considered murder to be a serious crime and worthy of judgment. However, note what Scripture says:

> "You have heard that it was said to the people long ago, 'Do not murder, and anyone who murders will be subject to judgment.' But I tell you that anyone who is angry with his brother will be subject to judgment. Again, anyone who says to his brother, 'Raca, ' is answerable to the Sanhedrin. But anyone who says, 'You fool!' will be in danger of the fire of hell. (Mat 5:21-22)
>
> Anyone who hates his brother is a murderer, and you know that no murderer has eternal life in him. (1 John 3:15)
>
> "Which ones?" the man inquired. Jesus replied, "'Do not murder, do not commit adultery, do not steal, do not give false testimony, (Mat 19:18)
>
> If you suffer, it should not be as a murderer or thief or any other kind of criminal, or even as a meddler. (1 Pet 4:15)

Christ says that anger and hate are equal to murder. Therefore, the answer to solving the problem of murder and killing is to get rid of anger and hate. How? Scripture has the answer. Look at...

- verse 8: "He who loves his fellowman has fulfilled the law."
- verse 9: "Love your neighbor as yourself."
- verse 10: "Love does no harm to its neighbor."
- verse 10: "*Love* is the fulfillment of the law."

Love is the answer to anger, hate, and killing. It is the duty of men to love one another: God expects and demands it. But how? It is not enough to simply say that men must love each other. Words alone will not get rid of the anger, hate, and killing in the world. How can men be turned from their anger and hate to love? The answer is found in God's people, in those who follow God and are already loving others.

⇒ God's people must *demonstrate love* before the world more clearly and forcefully than ever before.
⇒ God's people must proclaim love to the world more than ever before—explaining just how a man can have his heart changed from hate to love.

Very simply stated, Christian believers must demonstrate what it is to love and proclaim how a person can have his heart changed from anger and hate to love. There are four steps in *securing* a changed heart and in *learning* how to love.

1. A person must come to know God and be born of God through His Son, Jesus Christ. The Bible clearly says that true love is possible *only* if a person is born of God.

Dear friends, let us love one another, for love comes from God. Everyone who loves has been born of God and knows God. Whoever does not love does not know God, because God is love. This is how God showed his love among us: He sent his one and only Son into the world that we might live through him. This is love: not that we loved God, but that he loved us and sent his Son as an atoning sacrifice for our sins. Dear friends, since God so loved us, we also ought to love one another. (1 John 4:7-11)

2. A person must think upon and understand the love of God. When a person truly comes to know the love of God, he will then love others. In fact, if he does not love others, the Bible says that he does not know the love of God. Therefore, the answer to changing a person's heart from anger and hate is to share the love of God with him.

This is how we know what love is: Jesus Christ laid down his life for us. And we ought to lay down our lives for our brothers. (1 John 3:16)

3. A person must seek the *gift of love* from the Holy Spirit. The Holy Spirit of God can stir men to love one another if they will seek Him.

Follow the way of love and eagerly desire spiritual gifts, especially the gift of prophecy. (1 Cor 14:1; cp. 1 Cor.13:1-13)
And hope does not disappoint us, because God has poured out his love into our hearts by the Holy Spirit, whom he has given us. (Rom 5:5)
But the fruit of the Spirit is love, joy, peace, patience, kindness, goodness, faithfulness, (Gal 5:22)

4. A person must diligently seek to obey the very special commandment of the Lord Jesus.

"A new command I give you: Love one another. As I have loved you, so you must love one another. By this all men will know that you are my disciples, if you love one another." (John 13:34-35)

4 (13:9) **Stealing—Ministering—World, Needs of**: love forbids stealing. "You shall not steal" (Ex.20:15; Dt.5:19). In the Bible the word "steal" (*klepheis*) means to cheat, to take wrongfully from another person, *either legally or illegally*. Note that the laws of men are not the determining rule governing whether a person is stealing or not. This is what is so often misunderstood about stealing.

⇒ Men can sometimes use the law to steal.
⇒ Men can take from others without ever breaking a law.
⇒ Men can secure too much of something, well beyond what they need—something that rightfully belongs to others.

Very simply stated, the Bible teaches that stealing is the taking of anything that *rightfully* belongs to others. There are at least three forms of stealing.

1. A person steals by taking something which is *actually possessed or personally owned* by another person. If he owns it and we take it, then we are guilty of stealing. It may be something as simple as a pencil from the office or an answer to a test from a fellow student, or it may be something as complex as embezzlement of funds through bookkeeping procedures. If we take it, we have broken God's commandment and stand guilty as thieves.

And not to steal from them, but to show that they can be fully trusted, so that in every way they will make the teaching about God our Savior attractive. (Titus 2:10)
If you suffer, it should not be as a murderer or thief or any other kind of criminal, or even as a meddler. (1 Pet 4:15)
The LORD abhors dishonest scales, but accurate weights are his delight. (Prov 11:1)
"It's no good, it's no good!" says the buyer; then off he goes and boasts about his purchase. (Prov 20:14)
A fortune made by a lying tongue is a fleeting vapor and a deadly snare. (Prov 21:6)
The merchant uses dishonest scales; he loves to defraud. (Hosea 12:7)

2. A person steals by hoarding and banking more than he needs. *Keeping back* is stealing. It is...
• keeping what is not needed for one's own needs.
• keeping back what is desperately needed by others.
• taking away what nature and the earth have provided to meet the needs of the human population.
• hoarding the knowledge and gifts and blessings God gave to be used for the welfare of a desperate world filled with so many who are less privileged and gifted.

We may call it by whatever name we wish, but to God it is stealing. God has put within the earth enough resources to meet the needs of His people, and He has given men both the *ability and command to subdue and have dominion over the earth*. Look closely at His command:

God blessed them and said to them, "Be fruitful and increase in number; fill the earth and subdue it. Rule over the fish of the sea and the birds of the air and over every living creature that moves on the ground." (Gen 1:28)

The earth is to be subdued and taken dominion over by men. Men are commanded by God to develop the technology to explore the universe and to control nature, and to feed, clothe, house and give health to people. Note what God is saying. He is not saying this: only some are to have the benefits and blessings of the earth. God is saying this: men are to love each other and *share* the blessings of the earth together. When men use their God-given ability to make money and produce goods, and then begin to keep back and hoard, they are stealing; they are keeping for themselves what rightfully belongs to others. Therefore, they will suffer catastrophic loss in the next world. They will suffer total devastation (Lk.12:20; 16:22-23). Why? Because they did not *love enough* to do what they and their particular talents were put on earth to do: provide for those who were less gifted and less fortunate.

"Do not store up for yourselves treasures on earth, where moth and rust destroy, and where thieves break in and steal. But store up for yourselves treasures in heaven, where moth and rust do not destroy, and where thieves do not break in and steal. For where your treasure is, there your heart will be also. (Mat 6:19-21)

"Don't collect any more than you are required to," he told them. (Luke 3:13)

He who has been stealing must steal no longer, but must work, doing something useful with his own hands, that he may have something to share with those in need. (Eph 4:28)

People who want to get rich fall into temptation and a trap and into many foolish and harmful desires that plunge men into ruin and destruction. (1 Tim 6:9)

Command those who are rich in this present world not to be arrogant nor to put their hope in wealth, which is so uncertain, but to put their hope in God, who richly provides us with everything for our enjoyment. Command them to do good, to be rich in good deeds, and to be generous and willing to share. In this way they will lay up treasure for themselves as a firm foundation for the coming age, so that they may take hold of the life that is truly life. (1 Tim 6:17-19)

In you men accept bribes to shed blood; you take usury and excessive interest and make unjust gain from your neighbors by extortion. And you have forgotten me, declares the Sovereign LORD. (Ezek 22:12)

3. A person steals by living extravagantly, beyond what he needs. There are some who give to meet the crying needs of the world, yet they do not live sacrificially. They *keep plenty* for themselves, indulging their flesh...

- in clothing
- in food
- in jewelry
- in housing
- in transportation
- in recreation
- in possessions
- in property

Many within industrialized nations are guilty of *selfishness* despite a tenderness and concern for the needy in the world. However, *concern and some giving* are not enough to fulfill the demand of God that we share and meet the needs throughout the world. Every day that we awaken and arise out of bed, the world is reeling under the weight of *masses*...

- who are hungry and starving to death.
- who are without drinking water.
- who are without adequate clothing.
- who are diseased and without medicine.
- who have no roof over their heads.
- who have no one to teach them.

There is no question, the means to help meet the needs of the world exist today. The lack is not manpower and resources; the lack is *sacrificial commitment* to give the resources and to go and become personally involved. The extravagant and indulgent are stealing from the needy, and the gifted are not meeting the needs of the less gifted. The scene is tragic, for God put the gifted upon earth to *sacrificially* meet the needs of the less gifted. But instead of meeting their needs, the gifted are living in excessive comfort and pleasure, indulging the whims of their flesh.

Jesus answered, "If you want to be perfect, go, sell your possessions and give to the poor, and you will have treasure in heaven. Then come, follow me." (Mat 19:21)

"Woe to you, teachers of the law and Pharisees, you hypocrites! You clean the outside of the cup and dish, but inside they are full of greed and self-indulgence. (Mat 23:25)

But the worries of this life, the deceitfulness of wealth and the desires for other things come in and choke the word, making it unfruitful. (Mark 4:19)

Sell your possessions and give to the poor. Provide purses for yourselves that will not wear out, a treasure in heaven that will not be exhausted, where no thief comes near and no moth destroys. (Luke 12:33)

You trample on the poor and force him to give you grain. Therefore, though you have built stone mansions, you will not live in them; though you have planted lush vineyards, you will not drink their wine. (Amos 5:11)

What is the answer? Love—loving people enough to stop stealing from them. However, we *must always remember* that words alone are not enough. Just *telling* a person not to steal will not keep him from stealing. Some very practical steps must be taken.

a. A person must follow Christ by giving all he is and has to the poor. This is unequivocally proclaimed by Christ time and again (see outline and notes—Lk.18:18-30).

In the same way, any of you who does not give up everything he has cannot be my disciple. (Luke 14:33)

When Jesus heard this, he said to him, "You still lack one thing. Sell everything you have and give to the poor, and you will have treasure in heaven. Then come, follow me." When he heard this, he became very sad, because he was a man of great wealth. Jesus looked at him and said, "How hard it is for the rich to enter the kingdom of God! Indeed, it is easier for a camel to go through the eye of a needle than for a rich man to enter the kingdom of God." (Luke 18:22-25)

Whoever loves money never has money enough; whoever loves wealth is never satisfied with his income. This too is meaningless. (Eccl 5:10)

b. A person must stop playing the fool and storing up treasure in heaven; he must remember that his soul can be required of him this very night.

"Then he said, 'This is what I'll do. I will tear down my barns and build bigger ones, and there I will store all my grain and my goods. And I'll say to myself, "You have plenty of good things laid up for many years. Take life easy; eat, drink and be merry."' "But God said to him, 'You fool! This very night your life will be demanded from you. Then who will get what you have prepared for yourself?' "This is how it will be with anyone who stores up things for himself but is not rich toward God." (Luke 12:18-21)

c. A person must keep the truth before his mind: a selfish indulgent life that neglects and ignores the poor will send him to hell.

"There was a rich man who was dressed in purple and fine linen and lived in luxury every day. At his gate was laid a beggar named Lazarus, covered with sores And longing to eat what fell from the rich man's table. Even the dogs came and licked his sores. "The time came when the beggar died and the angels carried him to Abraham's side. The rich man also died and was buried. In hell, where he was in torment, he looked up and saw Abraham far away, with Lazarus by his side. (Luke 16:19-23)

d. A person must give all that he has and not try to cheat God.

Now a man named Ananias, together with his wife Sapphira, also sold a piece of property. With his wife's full knowledge he kept back part of the money for himself, but brought the rest and put it at the apostles' feet. Then Peter said, "Ananias, how is it that Satan has so filled your heart that you have lied to the Holy Spirit and have kept for yourself some of the money you received for the land? Didn't it belong to you before it was sold? And after it was sold, wasn't the money at your disposal? What made you think of doing such a thing? You have not lied to men but to God." When Ananias heard this, he fell down and died. And great fear seized all who heard what had happened. (Acts 5:1-5)

e. A person must work at his job as though he serves the Lord Jesus. In fact, the Bible says that he is working for the Lord Jesus.

Slaves [employees], obey your earthly masters in everything; and do it, not only when their eye is on you and to win their favor, but with sincerity of heart and reverence for the Lord. Whatever you do, work at it with all your heart, as working for the Lord, not for men, since you know that you will receive an inheritance from the Lord as a reward. It is the Lord Christ you are serving. (Col 3:22-24)
Slaves [employees], obey your earthly masters [employers] with respect and fear, and with sincerity of heart, just as you would obey Christ. Obey them not only to win their favor when their eye is on you, but like slaves of Christ, doing the will of God from your heart. Serve wholeheartedly, as if you were serving the Lord, not men, (Eph 6:5-7)

f. A person must work to make more than he needs so that he can earn enough to help others.

He who has been stealing must steal no longer, but must work, doing something useful with his own hands, that he may have something to share with those in need. (Eph 4:28)

5 (13:9) **Covetousness**: love forbids covetousness. "You shall not covet" (Ex.20:17; Dt.5:21). The word "covet" (epithumeseis) means to crave and desire. A person can desire both good and bad things; the word can be used in both a good and bad sense (cp. 1 Cor.14:1 for the good sense). In the present context the believer is not to covet in an evil sense. If he loves his neighbors and fellow citizens he will not covet. (See DEEPER STUDY # 4, Covetousness—Ro.1:29 for the full meaning of the word.) Note two points.

1. The commandment condemns not only the act of sin, but the *desire* to sin. The *desire* is what covetousness is; craving or desiring something is what covetousness means. It precedes the act. Therefore, this commandment strikes at the very heart of what a man is *deep within* himself. It exposes the innermost being of man, showing him that the cravings of his heart are evil. Why do we say this? Because desiring and craving are *natural*. It is a fact of human nature that we crave the thing which others have. We might not crave what they have; that is, we might not wish to steal their possessions, but we crave to have possessions like they have. As said, such desire is natural, but note: God is saying that we are not to covet what our neighbors have. To covet is evil. Why? Because it causes us to focus our attention, energy, and efforts—our lives—upon securing more and more. We neglect God and the needs of a world reeling under the weight of starving and dying masses. *Love* focuses upon sharing and helping *people*, not upon craving *things*. There is a world of difference between centering one's life upon *people* instead of *things*.

The point is this: the commandment "You shall not covet" exposes the human heart. It shows us that we are depraved, basically sinful, and that we need a Savior. We desperately need *Someone* who can change our hearts and turn them toward God and the needs of our fellow citizens—the lost and dying masses of the world.

2. Note the kinds of things we are forbidden to covet. The tenth commandment is clear: "You shall not covet your neighbor's...
   - house: personal provisions.
   - wife: companion and love.
   - manservant or maidservant: employee, position, employment, authority.
   - ox and donkey: possessions, property, wealth.

And, if this list does not include all that our neighbors have, God adds: "You shall not covet...*anything* that is your neighbor's." Look at the commandment as a whole.

"You shall not covet your neighbor's house. You shall not covet your neighbor's wife, or his manservant or maidservant, his ox or donkey, or anything that belongs to your neighbor." (Exo 20:17)

A believer who loves his neighbor and fellow citizens will not covet what they have. Instead of desiring their possessions, he will be focusing upon blessing them and building them up. He will encourage them to know the Lord and to surrender their lives to the great task of meeting the needs of a lost and dying world.

Then he said to them, "Watch out! Be on your guard against all kinds of greed; a man's life does not consist in the abundance of his possessions." (Luke 12:15)

But among you there must not be even a hint of sexual immorality, or of any kind of impurity, or of greed, because these are improper for God's holy people. (Eph 5:3)

Put to death, therefore, whatever belongs to your earthly nature: sexual immorality, impurity, lust, evil desires and greed, which is idolatry. (Col 3:5)

For, as I have often told you before and now say again even with tears, many live as enemies of the cross of Christ. Their destiny is destruction, their god is their stomach, and their glory is in their shame. Their mind is on earthly things. (Phil 3:18-19)

People who want to get rich fall into temptation and a trap and into many foolish and harmful desires that plunge men into ruin and destruction. For the love of money is a root of all kinds of evil. Some people, eager for money, have wandered from the faith and pierced themselves with many griefs. (1 Tim 6:9-10)

But mark this: There will be terrible times in the last days. People will be lovers of themselves, lovers of money, boastful, proud, abusive, disobedient to their parents, ungrateful, unholy, (2 Tim 3:1-2)

Keep your lives free from the love of money and be content with what you have, because God has said, "Never will I leave you; never will I forsake you." (Heb 13:5)

"From the least to the greatest, all are greedy for gain; prophets and priests alike, all practice deceit. (Jer 6:13)

My people come to you, as they usually do, and sit before you to listen to your words, but they do not put them into practice. With their mouths they express devotion, but their hearts are greedy for unjust gain. (Ezek 33:31)

They covet fields and seize them, and houses, and take them. They defraud a man of his home, a fellowman of his inheritance. (Micah 2:2)

6 (13:9) **Love**: love sums up all the commandments, no matter what the commandment is. The royal commandment is "Love your neighbor as yourself." We *are* supposed to love ourselves, but we are not to love *only* ourselves. God expects us to love our neighbors *as ourselves*. (See note and DEEPER STUDY # 7, *Love*—Mt.22:39 for more discussion).

7 (13:10) **Love—Neighbor—Brotherhood**: love does no harm or evil to a neighbor. To *do harm* or *evil* against a person does not mean just the doing or the carrying out of harm against a person. Doing harm means…
- thinking evil
- wishing and hoping evil
- planning and devising evil
- practicing and doing evil
- withholding good

Note the last fact, for it is often overlooked, but Scripture clearly states that withholding good from a person is plotting harm.

Do not withhold good from those who deserve it, when it is in your power to act. Do not say to your neighbor, "Come back later; I'll give it tomorrow"— when you now have it with you. Do not plot harm against your neighbor, who lives trustfully near you. (Prov 3:27-29)

A person who loves will not do harm or evil against a neighbor, but on the contrary, he will do good. He will love his fellow citizens, the neighbors of his world. What does it mean to love? Scripture spells out some very practical acts which are involved in love.
⇒ Love is patient.
⇒ Love is kind.
⇒ Love does not envy (is not jealous).
⇒ Love does not boast (does not brag).
⇒ Love is not proud (is not vainglorious, arrogant).
⇒ Love is not rude (unbecoming, indecent, unmannerly).
⇒ Love is not self-seeking (is not selfish, insisting on one's rights and way).
⇒ Love is not easily angered (is not touchy, angry, fretful, resentful).
⇒ Love keeps no records of wrongs.
⇒ Love does not delight in evil (in wrong, sin, injustice), but rejoices with the truth (with justice, in righteousness).
⇒ Love always protects.
⇒ Love always trusts (exercises faith in everything, under all circumstances).
⇒ Love always hopes (never gives up).
⇒ Love always perseveres (never weakens; has the power to endure).

The call of believers is to love their neighbors—all the citizens of the world. God's love is to be demonstrated to the world through us. The world is to be given the opportunity of seeing God's love in action so that they, too, will become worshippers of Him through His Son, the Lord Jesus Christ. The commandment is clear:

Let no debt remain outstanding, except the continuing debt to love one another, for he who loves his fellowman has fulfilled the law. The commandments, "Do not commit adultery," "Do not murder," "Do not steal," "Do not covet," and whatever other commandment there may be, are summed up in this one rule: "Love your neighbor as yourself." (Rom 13:8-9)

We who are strong ought to bear with the failings of the weak and not to please ourselves. Each of us should please his neighbor for his good, to build him up. (Rom 15:1-2)

The entire law is summed up in a single command: "Love your neighbor as yourself." (Gal 5:14)

If you really keep the royal law found in Scripture, "Love your neighbor as yourself," you are doing right. (James 2:8)

		darkness and put on the armor of light.	
1 The believer is to know the time	**G. The Believer and the Threat of Time, 13:11-14**	13 Let us behave decently, as in the daytime, not in orgies and drunkenness, not in sexual immorality and debauchery, not in dissension and jealousy.	**4 It is time to behave properly** a. To live in the light b. Not to live in the sins done in the dark
2 It is time to wake up[DS1] a. Salvation is nearer than when we first believed b. Judgment is almost here	11 And do this, understanding the present time. The hour has come for you to wake up from your slumber, because our salvation is nearer now than when we first believed. 12 The night is nearly over; the day is almost here. So let us put aside the deeds of	14 Rather, clothe yourselves with the Lord Jesus Christ, and do not think about how to gratify the desires of the sinful nature.	**5 It is time to put on the Lord Jesus Christ & to make no provision for the sinful nature or flesh**[DS2]
3 It is time to put aside the deeds of darkness & to put on the armor of light			

DIVISION VIII

THE BELIEVER AND HIS DAILY BEHAVIOR, 12:1-15:13

G. The Believer and the Threat of Time, 13:11-14

(13:11-14) **Introduction**: time is important, very important, to most people. Without time, man is not living; he *is* no more. The one thing he does not want is to run out of time. Therefore, it is critical for every man to know the threat of time.

1. The believer is to know the time (v.11).
2. It is time to wake up (v.11-12).
3. It is time to put aside the deeds of darkness and to put on the armor of light (v.12).
4. It is time to behave properly to live in the light and not to live in the sins done in the dark. (v.13).
5. It is time to put on the Lord Jesus Christ and to make no provision for the sinful nature or flesh (v.14).

(13:11-14) **Another Outline**: four pictures are also given in this passage.

1. Picture 1: Sleeping vs. awakening (v.11).
2. Picture 2: Darkness vs. light (v.12).
3. Picture 3: Walking straight vs. walking crooked (v.13).
4. Picture 4: Clothing—putting on Christ vs. putting on the sinful nature or flesh (v.14).

1 (13:11) **Time—History, Pivotal Points**: the believer is to know the time. The word "knowing" or "understanding" (eridotes) means to make sure that you know or understand; do not dare miss knowing or understanding. The phrase "present time" (ton kairon) means the critical period; the strategic or special period of time.

What strategic or critical period of time is meant? What is the period of human history that we must not overlook?

⇒ The day of "our salvation," the day which is nearer than when we first believed.
⇒ The day is almost here, the day when we shall meet the Lord Jesus Christ face to face.

2 (13:11-12) **Time—Dedication—Sleep, Spiritual**: it is time to awaken out of sleep. (See DEEPER STUDY # 1, *Spiritual Darkness*—Ro.13:11 for more discussion.) Too many believers are *slumbering* and paying no attention to what is going on in the world; too many are not watching; too many are not observing the signs of the time. Too many are *complacent and slothful*, lazily passing through life with *little commitment* to serving Christ. Too few are meeting the needs of the suffering and dying masses of the world. It is time "to wake up" (egerthenai) out of sleep: time to wake up, to be aroused and stirred. It is time to get up and to move and act—*now*—before it is too late. The

exhortation is strong, and there are two reasons for its forcefulness.

1. Our salvation is nearer than when we first believed. The word "salvation" is being used in a future sense, referring to the glorious day when we shall be fully saved. It is the day when our salvation will be consummated, and we will be delivered from this present evil world and perfected forever to live in the presence of God. The point is dramatic: the day is *nearer* than when we first believed. Awaken out of sleep—arouse yourself—get up—pay attention:

- Look at the world situation
- Look at yourself
- Look at life, its uncertainty
- Look at the signs
- Look at your body, its condition
- Look at the time

The day of salvation, the day of our redemption, is nearer than when we first believed.

> **When these things begin to take place, stand up and lift up your heads, because your redemption is drawing near." (Luke 21:28)**
>
> **But in these last days he has spoken to us by his Son, whom he appointed heir of all things, and through whom he made the universe. (Heb 1:2)**
>
> **Who through faith are shielded by God's power until the coming of the salvation that is ready to be revealed in the last time. In this you greatly rejoice, though now for a little while you may have had to suffer grief in all kinds of trials. (1 Pet 1:5-6)**
>
> **Dear children, this is the last hour; and as you have heard that the antichrist is coming, even now many antichrists have come. This is how we know it is the last hour. (1 John 2:18; cp. 2 Tim.3:1; 2 Pt.3:3; Jude 18)**

2. Judgment is almost here. The night is nearly over; the day is almost here. What day? The day when we will meet God face to face, either through death or through the return of the Lord Jesus. Time is fleeting, passing ever so rapidly—so prepare.

> **"Prepare to meet your God, O Israel." (Amos 4:12)**

ROMANS 13:11-14

'Prepare the way for the Lord, make straight paths for him.'" (Mat 3:3)

It's like a man going away: He leaves his house and puts his servants in charge, each with his assigned task, and tells the one at the door to keep watch. "Therefore keep watch because you do not know when the owner of the house will come back—whether in the evening, or at midnight, or when the rooster crows, or at dawn. If he comes suddenly, do not let him find you sleeping. What I say to you, I say to everyone: 'Watch!'" (Mark 13:34-37)

Come back to your senses as you ought, and stop sinning; for there are some who are ignorant of God—I say this to your shame. (1 Cor 15:34)

For it is light that makes everything visible. This is why it is said: "Wake up, O sleeper, rise from the dead, and Christ will shine on you." (Eph 5:14)

So then, let us not be like others, who are asleep, but let us be alert and self-controlled. (1 Th 5:6)

DEEPER STUDY # 1
(13:11) Spiritual Darkness—Carnal—Unspiritual: there is the sleep of false security; the sleep of slothfulness, complacency and neglect; and the sleep of indifference.

3 (13:12) **Darkness—Light**: it is time to put aside the deeds of darkness and to put on the armor of light.

1. The deeds of darkness are the deeds which men do *under the cover* of darkness and want to keep secret. They are sins...

- which men want to keep secret
- which men know are unacceptable
- which men know would cause hurt
- which men are ashamed of
- which men fear the results of
- which men know would do great damage

This is the verdict: Light has come into the world, but men loved darkness instead of light because their deeds were evil. Everyone who does evil hates the light, and will not come into the light for fear that his deeds will be exposed. (John 3:19-20)

The night is nearly over; the day is almost here. So let us put aside the deeds of darkness and put on the armor of light. (Rom 13:12)

Have nothing to do with the fruitless deeds of darkness, but rather expose them. For it is shameful even to mention what the disobedient do in secret. (Eph 5:11-12)

For those who sleep, sleep at night, and those who get drunk, get drunk at night. (1 Th 5:7)

Then the man and his wife heard the sound of the LORD God as he was walking in the garden in the cool of the day, and they hid from the LORD God among the trees of the garden. (Gen 3:8)

In the dark, men break into houses, but by day they shut themselves in; they want nothing to do with the light. (Job 24:16)

He who conceals his sins does not prosper, but whoever confesses and renounces them finds mercy. (Prov 28:13)

Woe to those who go to great depths to hide their plans from the LORD, who do their work in darkness and think, "Who sees us? Who will know?" (Isa 29:15)

"Woe to the obstinate children," declares the LORD, "to those who carry out plans that are not mine, forming an alliance, but not by my Spirit, heaping sin upon sin; (Isa 30:1)

He said to me, "Son of man, have you seen what the elders of the house of Israel are doing in the darkness, each at the shrine of his own idol? They say, 'The LORD does not see us; the LORD has forsaken the land.'" (Ezek 8:12)

2. The armor of light differs entirely from the clothing of darkness. Note: the picture is that of clothing oneself. The believer is to strip off whatever dark sins and works he has wrapped around himself, and he is to cast them away. Once he has stripped himself, the question arises: What is the believer to put on? What he puts on is striking: he is not exhorted to just put on the clothes of light; he is told to put on the *armor of light*. The believer is to be clothed with the heavy shield and protective armor of light—a shield and protection so full of splendor and glory and brilliance that it cannot be penetrated by the works of darkness. What is this armor of light?

a. It is the weapons of righteousness (2 Cor.6:7).

Rather, as servants of God we commend ourselves in every way: in great endurance; in troubles, hardships and distresses; in truthful speech and in the power of God; with weapons of righteousness in the right hand and in the left; (2 Cor 6:4, 7)

b. It is the armor of God (see outline and notes—Eph.6:10-20).
⇒ the belt of *truth*
⇒ the breastplate of *righteousness*
⇒ the sandals of the *gospel*
⇒ the shield of *faith*
⇒ the helmet of *salvation*
⇒ the sword of the Spirit, *the Word of God*
⇒ the supernatural resource of the soldier: *prayer*

Finally, be strong in the Lord and in his mighty power. Put on the full armor of God so that you can take your stand against the devil's schemes. (Eph 6:10-11)

But since we belong to the day, let us be self-controlled, putting on faith and love as a breastplate, and the hope of salvation as a helmet. (1 Th 5:8)

4 (13:13) **Sin**: it is time to walk straight. The word "decently" (euschemonos) means proper, honorable, decent, noble. The believer is to walk in honesty before God. He is to live a life of honesty, decency, and nobility. He is to live a life of honor and honesty before God. He is to walk in the day, not hiding nor trying to hide anything. Scripture gives six sins in particular which the believer is to cast off and turn from—forever.

238

1. Orgies (komois): reveling, carousing, partying, feasting, intemperance, debauchery, unrestrained revelry and indulgence, giving license to basic urges.

> The acts of the sinful nature are obvious: sexual immorality, impurity and debauchery; and envy; drunkenness, orgies, and the like. I warn you, as I did before, that those who live like this will not inherit the kingdom of God. (Gal 5:19, 21)
>
> For you have spent enough time in the past doing what pagans choose to do—living in debauchery, lust, drunkenness, orgies, carousing and detestable idolatry. They think it strange that you do not plunge with them into the same flood of dissipation, and they heap abuse on you. But they will have to give account to him who is ready to judge the living and the dead. (1 Pet 4:3-5)

2. *Drunkenness* (methais): to take intoxicating drink or drugs to affect the senses and faculties; to become intoxicated for the purpose of lust or pleasure; to seek to be tipsy or intoxicated; to seek to loosen moral restraint for the sake of bodily pleasure.

> "Be careful, or your hearts will be weighed down with dissipation, drunkenness and the anxieties of life, and that day will close on you unexpectedly like a trap. (Luke 21:34)
>
> Nor thieves nor the greedy nor drunkards nor slanderers nor swindlers will inherit the kingdom of God. And that is what some of you were. But you were washed, you were sanctified, you were justified in the name of the Lord Jesus Christ and by the Spirit of our God. (1 Cor 6:10-11)
>
> "Woe to him who gives drink to his neighbors, pouring it from the wineskin till they are drunk, so that he can gaze on their naked bodies. (Hab 2:15)

3. Sexual immorality (koitais):, adultery, fornication (pre-marital sex).

> In the same way the men also abandoned natural relations with women and were inflamed with lust for one another. Men committed indecent acts with other men, and received in themselves the due penalty for their perversion. (Rom 1:27)

4. Debauchery (aselgeiais): sensuality, running wild, licentiousness,; homosexuality, lasciviousness, living a wild, partying, and immoral life. It is excess lust, unbridled lust that consumes one's thoughts and behavior through...
- looks and dress
- films and pictures
- dances and parties
- suggestions and gestures
- books and pamphlets
- songs and music
- talk and jokes
- touch and behavior

> You [the rich] have lived on earth in luxury and self-indulgence. You have fattened yourselves in the day of slaughter. (James 5:5)

> For they mouth empty, boastful words and, by appealing to the lustful desires of sinful human nature, they entice people who are just escaping from those who live in error. (2 Pet 2:18)

5. Dissension (eridi): contention, quarreling, arguing, striving. It is the craving deep within a person that wants recognition, honor, position, and authority. It is a spirit that is in constant competition with others, that will push one forward...
- by putting others down
- by bypassing others
- by ignoring others
- by holding others back
- by blaming others
- by neglecting others

> Do nothing out of selfish ambition or vain conceit, but in humility consider others better than yourselves. (Phil 2:3)
>
> Keep reminding them of these things. Warn them before God against quarreling about words; it is of no value, and only ruins those who listen. (2 Tim 2:14)
>
> And the Lord's servant must not quarrel; instead, he must be kind to everyone, able to teach, not resentful. (2 Tim 2:24)
>
> Like one who seizes a dog by the ears is a passer-by who meddles in a quarrel not his own. (Prov 26:17)

6. Jealousy (zeloi): that begrudges others. It looks upon the position, recognition, and success of others with a jealous eye. It regrets the success of others.

> Love is patient, love is kind. It does not envy, it does not boast, it is not proud. (1 Cor 13:4)
>
> Let us not become conceited, provoking and envying each other. (Gal 5:26)
>
> But if you harbor bitter envy and selfish ambition in your hearts, do not boast about it or deny the truth. (James 3:14)
>
> A heart at peace gives life to the body, but envy rots the bones. (Prov 14:30)
>
> Do not let your heart envy sinners, but always be zealous for the fear of the LORD. (Prov 23:17)
>
> Do not envy wicked men, do not desire their company; (Prov 24:1)

5 (13:14) **Believer—Clothing, Spiritual**: it is time to put on the Lord Jesus Christ and to make no provision for the sinful nature or flesh. Note two points.

1. We are to put on the Lord Jesus Christ. Again, the picture is that of clothing ourselves. We are to clothe ourselves with Jesus Christ and His righteousness. We are to be as closely bound to Him and His righteousness as we are to our clothes. This means two things.
   a. Jesus Christ becomes our clothing. As our clothing He...
   - touches us
   - protects us
   - warms us
   - covers us
   - hides us

   b. We are wrapped up in Jesus Christ. Being in Him means that we live, move, and have our being in

Him: in His life and thoughts and behavior. Therefore, we must...

- look only at that upon which He would look.
- listen only to that to which He would listen.
- talk only as He would talk.
- touch only what He would touch.
- eat and drink only what He would eat and drink.
- think only that upon which He would think.

And to put on the new self, created to be like God in true righteousness and holiness. (Eph 4:24)

Your attitude should be the same as that of Christ Jesus: (Phil 2:5)

Since, then, you have been raised with Christ, set your hearts on things above, where Christ is seated at the right hand of God. Set your minds on things above, not on earthly things. For you died, and your life is now hidden with Christ in God. (Col 3:1-3)

And have put on the new self, which is being renewed in knowledge in the image of its Creator. Therefore, as God's chosen people, holy and dearly loved, clothe yourselves with compassion, kindness, humility, gentleness and patience. (Col 3:10, 12)

Then he said to them all: "If anyone would come after me, he must deny himself and take up his cross daily and follow me. (Luke 9:23)

2. We must not make provision for the flesh or the sinful nature. The idea is that we do not give in to the sinful nature or flesh and its lusts; we do not indulge or give license to the flesh. We do not fulfill the lusts of the flesh.

If your right eye causes you to sin, gouge it out and throw it away. It is better for you to lose one part of your body than for your whole body to be thrown into hell. (Mat 5:29)

For we know that our old self was crucified with him so that the body of sin might be done away with, that we should no longer be slaves to sin— (Rom 6:6)

Rather, clothe yourselves with the Lord Jesus Christ, and do not think about how to gratify the desires of the sinful nature. (Rom 13:14)

So I say, live by the Spirit, and you will not gratify the desires of the sinful nature. (Gal 5:16)

Put to death, therefore, whatever belongs to your earthly nature: sexual immorality, impurity, lust, evil desires and greed, which is idolatry. (Col 3:5)

Dear friends, I urge you, as aliens and strangers in the world, to abstain from sinful desires, which war against your soul. (1 Pet 2:11)

As a result, he does not live the rest of his earthly life for evil human desires, but rather for the will of God. (1 Pet 4:2)

DEEPER STUDY # 2
(13:14) **Believer—Clothing, Spiritual—Put on**: Scripture lists seven things that the believer is to put on or with which he is to clothe himself.
1. The believer is to put on and be clothed (endusesthe), with the *Holy Spirit* (Lk.24:49).
2. The believer is to put on and be clothed with the *Lord Jesus Christ* (Ro.13:14; Gal.3:27).
3. The believer is to put on and be clothed with *immortality* (1 Cor.15:53-54; 2 Cor.5:3).
4. The believer is to put on and be clothed with the *new self or new man* (Eph.4:24; Col.3:10).
5. The believer is to put on and be clothed with the *nature of God* (Col.3:12).
6. The believer is to put on and be clothed with the *armor of light and of God* (Ro.13:14; Eph.6:11f).
7. The believer is to put on and be clothed with *love* (Col.3:14).

240

CHAPTER 14

H. The Strong Believer and the Weak Believer: Questionable Functions & Behavior—Christian Liberty, 14:1-23

1 **Accept the weak brother**
   a. Without arguing, without criticizing
   b. Simply because there is a difference[DS1]

2 **Do not look down on & judge (criticize) others**
   a. God has accepted the strong
   b. No one has the right to judge the Lord's servant
   c. Because God will hold him up

3 **Be fully convinced of right & wrong behavior**
   a. In your own mind, not violating your conscience: Be careful to do no wrong
   b. A man is to live as he sees & understands God's will

4 **Watch out—watch what you do**
   a. You are under the watchful eye of Christ
   b. You belong to Christ—in life and death
   c. You have been purchased by the Lord's death & resurrection

5 **Leave the judgment up to God**
   a. Because everyone will be judged by Christ

Accept him whose faith is weak, without passing judgment on disputable matters. 2 One man's faith allows him to eat everything, but another man, whose faith is weak, eats only vegetables. 3 The man who eats everything must not look down on him who does not, and the man who does not eat everything must not condemn the man who does, for God has accepted him. 4 Who are you to judge someone else's servant? To his own master he stands or falls. And he will stand, for the Lord is able to make him stand. 5 One man considers one day more sacred than another; another man considers every day alike. Each one should be fully convinced in his own mind. 6 He who regards one day as special, does so to the Lord. He who eats meat, eats to the Lord, for he gives thanks to God; and he who abstains, does so to the Lord and gives thanks to God. 7 For none of us lives to himself alone and none of us dies to himself alone. 8 If we live, we live to the Lord; and if we die, we die to the Lord. So, whether we live or die, we belong to the Lord. 9 For this very reason, Christ died and returned to life so that he might be the Lord of both the dead and the living. 10 You, then, why do you judge your brother? Or why do you look down on your brother? For we will all stand before God's judgment seat. 11 It is written: "'As surely as I live,' says the Lord,

'every knee will bow before me; every tongue will confess to God.'" 12 So then, each of us will give an account of himself to God. 13 Therefore let us stop passing judgment on one another. Instead, make up your mind not to put any stumbling block or obstacle in your brother's way. 14 As one who is in the Lord Jesus, I am fully convinced that no food is unclean in itself. But if anyone regards something as unclean, then for him it is unclean. 15 If your brother is distressed because of what you eat, you are no longer acting in love. Do not by your eating destroy your brother for whom Christ died. 16 Do not allow what you consider good to be spoken of as evil. 17 For the kingdom of God is not a matter of eating and drinking, but of righteousness, peace and joy in the Holy Spirit, 18 Because anyone who serves Christ in this way is pleasing to God and approved by men. 19 Let us therefore make every effort to do what leads to peace and to mutual edification. 20 Do not destroy the work of God for the sake of food. All food is clean, but it is wrong for a man to eat anything that causes someone else to stumble. 21 It is better not to eat meat or drink wine or to do anything else that will cause your brother to fall. 22 So whatever you believe about these things keep between yourself and God. Blessed is the man who does not condemn himself by what he approves. 23 But the man who has doubts is condemned if he eats, because his eating is not from faith; and everything that does not come from faith is sin.

b. Because every knee will bow & confess: Christ alone is God
c. Because everyone will give an account of himself to God

6 **Judge only one thing: Stumbling blocks**

   a. By watching the things which men think are unclean

   b. By acting in love: Not hurting, wounding, ruining

7 **Give no occasion for criticism**
   a. Because the Kingdom of God is the believer's concern, not pleasure

   b. Because serving Christ & the Kingdom of God pleases God & men

8 **Pursue things that bring peace & edification**

9 **Do not destroy or ruin the work of God in another person's life: It is sin to do so**

10 **Do nothing to cause a brother to fall**

11 **Watch & do not condemn yourself**
   a. By keeping your faith
   b. By not going against conscience

   c. By acting on faith, from a conviction that God approves your behavior

DIVISION VIII

THE BELIEVER AND HIS DAILY BEHAVIOR, 12:1-15:13

H. The Strong Believer and the Weak Believer: Questionable Functions and Behavior—Christian Liberty, 14:1-23

(14:1-23) **Introduction**: the issue of Christian liberty vs. license is always confronting the believer and the church who wish to please their Lord. What can a believer *do and not do* socially and personally? Can he…

- drink socially?
- attend films, and if so, are any unacceptable?
- watch television, and if so, are all programs acceptable?
- gamble, and what is considered gambling?
- dance, and is there any form of dance unacceptable?
- listen to loud and suggestive music or lyrics?
- attend athletic contests on Sunday?

There are a host of social and recreational functions that are sometimes questioned by the believer who is truly seeking to please his Lord in *all that he does*. This passage deals with the principles which are to guide the believer as he faces these issues.

1. Accept the weak brother (v.1-2).
2. Do not look down on and judge (criticize) others (v.3-4).
3. Be fully convinced of right and wrong behavior (v.5-6).
4. Watch out—watch what you do (v.7-9).
5. Leave the judgment up to God (v.10-12).
6. Judge only one thing: stumbling blocks (v.13-15).
7. Give no occasion for criticism (v.16-18).
8. Pursue things that bring peace and edification (v.19).
9. Do not destroy or ruin the work of God in another person's life: it is sin to do so (v.20).
10. Do nothing to cause a brother to fall (v.21).
11. Watch and do not condemn yourself (v.22-23).

1 (14:1-2) **Believers, Duty—Brotherhood—Ministry—Weakness, Spiritual—Receive**: accept the weak brother. The word "accept" (proslambano) means to welcome, to accept, to take to oneself. However, there is a significant fact about the word that must be noted. It means…

- to accept a weak person just as *God graciously receives* men.
- to take a weak person to oneself just as God graciously takes men to Himself.

The believer is to "accept" the weak brother just as God accepts him. The exhortation is both forceful and tender, demanding and hopeful. It is forceful and demanding in that it gives the believer the opportunity to act as God acts, and it gives the weak believer great hope in being cared for and looked after. Now, note two instructions about accepting the weak brother.

1. The weak brother is to be received without criticism and argument over his weaknesses. There is to be no passing judgment in accepting him. He is to be accepted with open arms just as God receives men.

> **We who are strong ought to bear with the failings of the weak and not to please ourselves. (Rom 15:1)**
>
> **To the weak I became weak, to win the weak. I have become all things to all men so that by all possible means I might save some. (1 Cor 9:22)**

2. There are differences between Christians as to how they should live—about what is and is not allowed by God. For example, one Christian believes he can eat anything, whereas another Christian believes he must be a vegetarian.

The Roman church was apparently dealing with this very problem. The Jews from their earliest history had a long list of laws governing food (cp. Lev.11:1f), so there was probably some division within the church between the Jewish and Gentile converts as to just how closely these laws should be observed, if indeed at all. The point, however, is not limited to rules governing food. The Scripture is applicable to all the rules, scruples, taboos, and restrictions of behavior which some believers and churches say should regulate our lives. However, having said this, it is absolutely critical to note two facts.

a. This passage is *not dealing with the clear commandments of God*; it is dealing with those behaviors about which there are *clear differences of opinions* among men. *There is no dispute about the commandments of God in Scripture: they are to be obeyed*. In fact, Christian maturity is measured by our obedience to Christ (see note—Mt.5:17-18 for more discussion).

> **Whoever has my commands and obeys them, he is the one who loves me. He who loves me will be loved by my Father, and I too will love him and show myself to him." (John 14:21)**
>
> **If you obey my commands, you will remain in my love, just as I have obeyed my Father's commands and remain in his love. You are my friends if you do what I command. (John 15:10, 14)**
>
> **But Samuel replied: "Does the LORD delight in burnt offerings and sacrifices as much as in obeying the voice of the LORD? To obey is better than sacrifice, and to heed is better than the fat of rams. (1 Sam 15:22)**

b. The person who is a vegetarian, that is, who governs his life by *strict rules*, is called the "*weak*" brother. Why would the keeping of strict rules cause a believer to be called a "weak" Christian? (see DEEPER STUDY #1, *Christian Liberty*—Ro.14:2 for discussion).

DEEPER STUDY # 1

(14:2) **Christian Liberty**: both the weak Christian believer and the strong Christian believer thought the other was weak. This is important to see, for both are subject to criticizing and condemning the other (v.3f).

Paul faced the issue of Christian liberty often; therefore, he is an excellent example to consider in discussing this issue. Paul was willing to become all things to all men when principle *was not at stake*, but when principle *was at stake*, he would concede nothing.

For example, Paul had Timothy circumcised, conforming to the law of Moses; however, here in Romans he exhorts believers to ignore outward observances and to resist them to the utmost. In another instance, he *would not allow* Titus to be circumcised—under any circumstance (Gal.2:3-5); and he warned the Galatians that if they were circumcised, Christ would profit them nothing. They would be renouncing their salvation. What is the difference?

When rules and observance are made the *means of salvation*, they become a fatal heresy, and in the case of Titus and the Galatians this is what was happening. Rules and observances are contrary to God's method of saving men.

There is all the difference in the world between a man who approaches God *by means of rules* and the man who approaches God *by means of Christ*. The first man believes he is saved by his works, that is, by the morality of keeping rules; whereas the second man believes he is saved by Christ and Christ alone.

The problem of the weak brother is that he is just a little bit mixed up as to how day to day cleanliness comes. He feels a tinge of conscience to observe some rule in order to keep his life clean. He feels that he keeps the favor of God by doing *extra* works. He just has not matured to the point of understanding that even his day to day cleanliness comes from the *righteousness of Christ*.

There are essentially two reasons why the strict or judgmental man is weak in the faith.

1. He still believes in the necessity of works. Down deep within his heart he still believes that he can gain *some favor* from God by doing certain things and abstaining from others—things that are not taught in the Bible, that are reasoned out by himself and others as commendable and beneficial. To some degree he is still trying to gain and to maintain a right relationship with God by his own works. He has not fully accepted the way of God's grace and love. He has not yet understood that he is accepted *in* the righteousness of Christ and in His righteousness alone. He has not yet understood—not fully—that he is short and always will be short of God's glory, unable to do any work or act perfectly. He has not grasped that he must trust the love of God to count him righteous in Christ *every day*. He is not completely liberated from a belief in works and self-righteousness.

2. He does not know the meaning of Christian liberty. He sees Christianity as a thing of rules and regulations, and he governs his life by these rules and observances. In many cases even the thought of Christian liberty *frightens* him.

Now, having said this, it is of *utmost importance* that a believer keep in mind his duty as a Christian (see notes—Ro.6:1-2; 6:14-15). There are *commands and prohibitions* given in the Bible about which there are no questions. A believer must unquestionably obey them (see notes—Ro.14:13-15; 15:1-3; cp. Ex.20:1f; Ro.1:29f; Gal.5:19f; Eph.4:17f).

2 (14:3-4) **Judging Others—Criticizing**: do not look down on or criticize and judge others. As the strong believer and the weak believer associate together, both are subject to serious sin.

⇒ The believer who understands his liberty in Christ is subject to *look down on* the weaker brother. The words looking down on, condemn, despise (exoutheneito) mean to hold in contempt, to treat as meaningless and utterly wrong.

⇒ The weak believer, the believer who feels he must observe some *extra* rules, is subject to judging (krineto), to criticizing, to censoring.

Three reasons are given for not looking down on, despising and judging one another, three reasons that stand as a warning to believers.

1. God Himself has accepted the strong believer. The believer who walks in the liberty of Christ and does not live a strict life has been accepted by God, no matter what the more legalistic believer may think. There may be some man-made religious rules which he does not observe, but he has trusted Christ, and he obeys the Word of God. Therefore, he is not to be criticized and judged, but he is to be accepted into the fellowship of the more legalistic believer.

2. No one has the *right* to judge the Lord's servant. Note: both believers belong to the Lord; both are the servants of the Lord. Therefore, the Lord alone has the right to judge them. Believers do not have the *right to play God* and to judge each other. They have no right to condemn and pass judgment upon each other's behavior and works, for they do not belong to each other. They each belong to Christ; therefore, He alone determines whether or not they stand or fall and are accepted or rejected.

3. God *will hold* the believer up. There is no question about the matter: the believer will be held up, for God is able to make him stand.

> **Being confident of this, that he who began a good work in you will carry it on to completion until the day of Christ Jesus. (Phil 1:6)**
>
> **That is why I am suffering as I am. Yet I am not ashamed, because I know whom I have believed, and am convinced that he is able to guard what I have entrusted to him for that day. (2 Tim 1:12)**
>
> **The Lord will rescue me from every evil attack and will bring me safely to his heavenly kingdom. To him be glory for ever and ever. Amen. (2 Tim 4:18)**
>
> **[You] who through faith are shielded by God's power until the coming of the salvation that is ready to be revealed in the last time. (1 Pet 1:5)**
>
> **I am with you and will watch over you wherever you go, and I will bring you back to this land. I will not leave you until I have done what I have promised you." (Gen 28:15)**
>
> **For the LORD loves the just and will not forsake his faithful ones. They will be protected forever, but the offspring of the wicked will be cut off; (Psa 37:28)**
>
> **For he guards the course of the just and protects the way of his faithful ones. (Prov 2:8)**

3 (14:5-6) **Believers, Behavior**: be fully convinced of right and wrong behavior. The Jews had made a maze of rules governing the Sabbath and special holy days.

> **But now that you know God—or rather are known by God—how is it that you are turning back to those weak and miserable principles? Do you wish to be enslaved by them all over again? You are observing special days and months and seasons and years! (Gal 4:9-10)**
>
> **Therefore do not let anyone judge you by what you eat or drink, or with regard to a religious festival, a New Moon celebration or a Sabbath day. These are a shadow of the things that were to come; the reality, however, is found in Christ. (Col 2:16-17)**

Again, this issue was apparently a hotly debated issue between the Jewish and Gentile believers in the Roman church. But again, the issue is much broader than the mere observances of *holy days*; it involves all the man-made restrictions laid upon men by legalistic believers and churches. In saying this, however, it bears repeating:

Scripture is not talking about the commandments found throughout the Bible. The commandments and instructions of Scripture are to be kept. The present passage is dealing with the legalistic tendencies of men, the rules and regulations which some men put forth as commendable and beneficial to practice.

Another fact needs to be mentioned as well. Paul is not suggesting that the Lord's Day is not important. He is not suggesting that it is all right to ignore, neglect, or abuse the Lord's Day. Far from it. What he is attacking is an attitude that substitutes a Christian day for Christianity. The Lord's Day is very important to God, for it is the day set aside for the worship of His Son and for the rest and relaxation of His followers. However, the believer is not to worship the day, but worship the Lord of all days.

The point is this. Whatever the believer does, he must be fully convinced that it is right and not wrong. Note two points.

1. The believer is to be fully convinced in his own mind when dealing with questionable matters. The believer is to make the decision for himself; no one else is to decide for him. But note:

⇒ He must make sure the matter *is questionable*, that it is not covered by some command in the Scripture.
⇒ He must be honest and intelligent in deciding if the behavior is right.
⇒ He must not violate his conscience *at all*, not in the least.
⇒ He must be absolutely sure to do no wrong.

2. The believer is to live as he sees and understands God's will. The point is very simply stated: one man dedicates every day to the Lord and sees every day as the Lord's; the other man dedicates every day to the Lord, but he believes Sunday and holy days are more special and meaningful and should be especially set aside for God. Note that the same attitudes prevail toward food: one man *gives thanks* to God and eats everything; another man *gives thanks* and eats only vegetation. The point to note is that...

• both men dedicate and worship the Lord every day. They differ only in that one man sets aside some days for an extended celebration to God.
• both men thank God for their food. They differ only in what they are eating.

Now note the crucial factor: the hearts of both men are focused upon God. Both men are dedicating their lives to worship and serve God and both are thanking God for what they have. Their hearts are right with God. The differences between them are external and concern material things: days and food. Therefore, both are acceptable to God. Both are fully convinced that what they are doing is right before God.

4 (14:7-9) **Dedication—Purchased—Possession—Surrender**: watch out—watch what you do. There are two *supreme reasons* why the believer must watch what he does.

1. The believer belongs to Christ in both life and death.

⇒ He does not live to himself alone: he does not do as he wills, follow his own desires, do his own thing, give in to his urges and passions.
⇒ He does not die to himself alone: take his death into his own hands or expect to handle death by himself.

The believer does not live for himself; he lives for Christ. He has committed both his life and his death into the hands of Christ, surrendering all he is to Christ. While he lives He is the Lord's, and when he dies he is the Lord's. The Lord's dominion does not extend only to this life, but in the other life as well. No matter where the believer is or what he is doing, he is the Lord's. The Lord is his Lord, for the believer has placed his life and death under the care and keeping of the Lord. The Lord is the Master and God of his life; therefore, the believer watches closely what he does: he makes sure that what he does pleases his Lord, *for the welfare of his life and death is under the Lord's care.*

> **He is not the God of the dead, but of the living, for to him all are alive." (Luke 20:38)**
>
> **If we live, we live to the Lord; and if we die, we die to the Lord. So, whether we live or die, we belong to the Lord. (Rom 14:8)**

2. The believer has been purchased by the Lord's death and resurrection. Christ died, bearing the sin of the believer upon Himself, so that the believer could be freed from the coming judgment upon sin. The believer has faith in the death of Christ. He believes that...

• when Christ died, he *symbolically died* with Christ.
• when Christ hung upon the cross, he *symbolically hung* upon the cross with Christ. How? By faith. God loves man so much that when a man truly believes in the death of Christ for his sins, God will take that man's *faith* and count it as the death of Christ, as the believer having died with Christ. It is the same with the resurrection of Christ. When a man truly believes in Christ, God counts the man's belief as the resurrection of Christ. The man is identified with Christ in the resurrection of Christ, and he is given a new life that is both abundant and eternal.

The point is this: it was for this purpose that Christ died and arose—that He might be the Lord both of the living and the dead. He is the Lord of all believers whether they are living on this earth or deceased and passed on into heaven. The true believer has been purchased by the death and resurrection of the Lord Jesus. The believer does not belong to himself: he cannot act selfishly and sinfully in making decisions about behavior. He must obey and please the Lord, for the Lord has purchased the right to the believer's life and death.

> **The death he died, he died to sin once for all; but the life he lives, he lives to God. In the same way, count yourselves dead to sin but alive to God in Christ Jesus. (Rom 6:10-11)**
>
> **For Christ's love compels us, because we are convinced that one died for all, and therefore all died. And he died for all, that those who live should no longer live for themselves but for him who died for them and was raised again. (2 Cor 5:14-15)**
>
> **I have been crucified with Christ and I no longer live, but Christ lives in me. The life I live in the body, I live by faith in the Son of God, who loved me and gave himself for me. (Gal 2:20)**

5 (14:10-12) **Judgment**: leave the judgment up to God.
⇒ Why do you judge and criticize your brother?
⇒ Why do you despise and look down upon your brother?

The questions are forceful and disturbing because so many believers stand guilty before God.

Note the word "brother." The person being criticized and judged is a brother, and what he is doing is coming from a sincere conviction that it is either God's will or acceptable to God (v.5-6). Why then do you set yourself up as God and criticize and judge him? Watch out! For "we will all stand before God's judgment seat" (v.10). Everyone of us will be judged *by Christ, not by each other*.

a. Every knee will bow *to Christ*, not to each other. Every tongue will confess *to God*, not to each other. None of us are God; therefore, we absolutely have no right to be judging and criticizing each other. God alone is the judge of men.

> It is written: "'As surely as I live,' says the Lord, 'every knee will bow before me; every tongue will confess to God.'" (Rom 14:11)
>
> Therefore God exalted him to the highest place and gave him the name that is above every name, that at the name of Jesus every knee should bow, in heaven and on earth and under the earth, and every tongue confess that Jesus Christ is Lord, to the glory of God the Father. (Phil 2:9-11)
>
> Who will not fear you, O Lord, and bring glory to your name? For you alone are holy. All nations will come and worship before you, for your righteous acts have been revealed." (Rev 15:4)
>
> "Turn to me and be saved, all you ends of the earth; for I am God, and there is no other. By myself I have sworn, my mouth has uttered in all integrity a word that will not be revoked: Before me every knee will bow; by me every tongue will swear. (Isa 45:22-23)

b. Everyone will give an account of himself to God. We are not going to be called to give an account of others before God. We are going to give an account of ourselves. Each one shall be held accountable *for himself only*. God is not going to be asking us what we think or know about Stephen or Ruth. Each one will stand alone before God and give an account for his own behavior only.

> All the nations will be gathered before him, and he will separate the people one from another as a shepherd separates the sheep from the goats. (Mat 25:32)
>
> Moreover, the Father judges no one, but has entrusted all judgment to the Son, (John 5:22)
>
> He commanded us to preach to the people and to testify that he is the one whom God appointed as judge of the living and the dead. (Acts 10:42)
>
> For he has set a day when he will judge the world with justice by the man he has appointed. He has given proof of this to all men by raising him from the dead." (Acts 17:31)

> This will take place on the day when God will judge men's secrets through Jesus Christ, as my gospel declares. (Rom 2:16)
>
> You, then, why do you judge your brother? Or why do you look down on your brother? For we will all stand before God's judgment seat. (Rom 14:10)
>
> Therefore judge nothing before the appointed time; wait till the Lord comes. He will bring to light what is hidden in darkness and will expose the motives of men's hearts. At that time each will receive his praise from God. (1 Cor 4:5)
>
> In the presence of God and of Christ Jesus, who will judge the living and the dead, and in view of his appearing and his kingdom, I give you this charge: (2 Tim 4:1)

6 (14:13-15) **Stumbling Block—Judging—Criticism—Socials, Questionable**: judge but one thing—if you are a stumbling block to a brother. The word "stumbling block" (proskamma) means an obstacle placed in the way of someone. The word "obstacle" (skandalon) means to trap, to snare, to do something that causes a person to stumble and fall. It has reference in particular to leading or causing someone to sin. The exhortation is strong: believers are not to be criticizing and judging each other; they are to be judging themselves. Every single believer is to be constantly looking at his own life making sure…

• that he is not putting a stumbling block in his brother's path to God, not even a single obstacle or hindrance of any kind.

• that he is not doing a single thing that will cause his brother to stumble or fall into sin.

If a believer is constantly looking at his own life and guarding against becoming a stumbling block, he does not have time to judge and talk about his brother. There are three very practical behaviors that will keep us from putting stumbling blocks in our brother's walk toward God.

1. First, we must watch for the things which our brothers think are unclean. And, very simply, if some behavior or activity is thought to be unclean, we are not to do it. Scripture gives us a great principle in these three verses, a principle that could revolutionize the behavior of believers and much of society if we would just do what God says.

Note the words, "no food is unclean in itself." The immediate situation of the early church was dealing with eating certain foods and keeping special holy days. However, the fact is applicable to the questionable functions faced by every generation of believers. In its pure and natural form, all of God's creation is acceptable to God. It is what man does with things that make them impure.

⇒ The grape is pure, but man takes it and makes an intoxicating drink out of it that damages the human body and leads to immoral behavior.

⇒ Fellowship is pure; but man takes it and turns it into a loose, partying atmosphere that leads to exposure of the human body, suggestive thoughts and conversation, and immoral behavior.

⇒ Vegetation and forest plants are pure, but man takes them and makes all kinds of harmful and intoxicating drugs, drinks, and foods that harm the human body and lead to immoral and unjust behavior.

The point is this: because of what man does with the things and activities of the earth, believers must watch the things which men make unclean and the things which other believers think are unclean. We must not do anything that would cause a brother to stumble.

> **Therefore let us stop passing judgment on one another. Instead, make up your mind not to put any stumbling block or obstacle in your brother's way. (Rom 14:13)**
>
> **If your brother is distressed because of what you eat, you are no longer acting in love. Do not by your eating destroy your brother for whom Christ died. (Rom 14:15)**
>
> **Be careful, however, that the exercise of your freedom does not become a stumbling block to the weak. (1 Cor 8:9)**
>
> **"A little yeast works through the whole batch of dough." (Gal 5:9)**
>
> **Whoever loves his brother lives in the light, and there is nothing in him to make him stumble. (1 John 2:10)**

2. Second, we must walk in love toward our brother. Note:

⇒ We are to do nothing that would distress a brother. Imagine! We are not to cause "distress" for him—not to cause any kind of *misery or disturbance* whatsoever for him. (What an impact this would make upon churches and the world if we would live out this commandment!)

⇒ We are to do nothing that would destroy a brother. This is a forceful command: "Do not destroy him [me apollue]." The words mean to hurt and wound to the point of ruining. Such behavior is absolutely forbidden of the Christian believer. We are to do absolutely nothing that would destroy or ruin our brother.

Thought 1. Imagine the judgment coming upon some because of their judging and criticizing, grumbling and divisiveness, habits and behavior, drinking and partying. Just look at the very nature of some who are constantly causing problems and being a stumbling block for both young and old alike.

> **Therefore, if what I eat causes my brother to fall into sin, I will never eat meat again, so that I will not cause him to fall. (1 Cor 8:13)**
>
> **Nobody should seek his own good, but the good of others. (1 Cor 10:24)**
>
> **Love does no harm to its neighbor. Therefore love is the fulfillment of the law. (Rom 13:10)**
>
> **We who are strong ought to bear with the failings of the weak and not to please ourselves. Each of us should please his neighbor for his good, to build him up. (Rom 15:1-2)**
>
> **The entire law is summed up in a single command: "Love your neighbor as yourself." (Gal 5:14)**
>
> **If you really keep the royal law found in Scripture, "Love your neighbor as yourself," you are doing right. (James 2:8)**

3. Third, we must keep in mind that Christ died for our brother. This is the clear reason we must not distress, much less destroy, our brother: Christ died for him. The argument is forceful: if Christ loved him enough to die for him, then we must love him enough to give up a few desires and activities.

> **So this weak brother, for whom Christ died, is destroyed by your knowledge. (1 Cor 8:11)**
>
> **And he died for all, that those who live should no longer live for themselves but for him who died for them and was raised again. (2 Cor 5:15)**
>
> **Once you were alienated from God and were enemies in your minds because of your evil behavior. But now he has reconciled you by Christ's physical body through death to present you holy in his sight, without blemish and free from accusation— (Col 1:21-22)**

7 (14:16-18) **Criticism—Christian Liberty vs. License:** give no occasion for criticism. Christian liberty can be abused. A believer may be free to eat and drink some things and be free to go and participate in certain activities, but he *should not* do either. Why? Because his behavior would be considered evil. Two facts are to be kept in mind by believers when they are considering questionable things.

1. The Kingdom of God is the believer's concern, not pleasure. Note: the Kingdom of God is not eating and drinking; that is, it is not concerned with external matters but with the heart. It is not a sin to abstain from food and drink and questionable activities; therefore, the believer must readily stay away from anything that will distress or cause others to stumble. The Kingdom of God is...

- righteousness: being and doing what is right; establishing and maintaining the highest possible good with God and man.
- peace: being in a right relationship with both God and man and maintaining that relationship; working for the highest possible good between God and man.
- joy: experiencing the fulfillment and happiness of a right relationship with God and man; bearing the fruit of being right with God and man.

The point is this: the believer is to be concerned with people and their relationships with God and with himself, not with the right to eat, drink and socialize. His primary purpose in life is to reach and build men up, not to distress and cause them to stumble.

2. The believer who puts the spiritual welfare of people before his own desires pleases both God and men. Note a crucial point: this is the person who is *acceptable* to Christ, the person who is a *genuine believer*. A man who professes to know God makes a questionable profession...

- if he does not love God enough to do what He says.
- if he does not love his brother and fellow man enough to keep from grieving and causing him to stumble.

> **"Not everyone who says to me, 'Lord, Lord,' will enter the kingdom of heaven, but only he who does the will of my Father who is in heaven. (Mat 7:21)**
>
> **He replied, "Isaiah was right when he prophesied about you hypocrites; as it is written: "'These people honor me with**

their lips, but their hearts are far from me. (Mark 7:6)

Whoever has my commands and obeys them, he is the one who loves me. He who loves me will be loved by my Father, and I too will love him and show myself to him." (John 14:21)

They claim to know God, but by their actions they deny him. They are detestable, disobedient and unfit for doing anything good. (Titus 1:16)

Note another fact: the believer who seeks the welfare of his brothers will be acceptable to men.

For it is not the one who commends himself who is approved, but the one whom the Lord commends. (2 Cor 10:18)

Don't let anyone look down on you because you are young, but set an example for the believers in speech, in life, in love, in faith and in purity. (1 Tim 4:12)

A good name is more desirable than great riches; to be esteemed is better than silver or gold. (Prov 22:1)

A good name is better than fine perfume. (Eccl 7:1)

8 (14:19) **Purpose, of Believers**: pursue things that bring peace and edification. This is the very purpose for believers being on earth: to bring peace to men and to build them up. Men must secure peace with God and with each other and they must be built up in Christ. Believers have both the message of peace and of growth; therefore, they must *follow only* those things which will make peace and edify men.

If it is possible, as far as it depends on you, live at peace with everyone. (Rom 12:18)

Make every effort to live in peace with all men and to be holy; without holiness no one will see the Lord. (Heb 12:14)

Each of us should please his neighbor for his good, to build him up. (Rom 15:2)

Now about food sacrificed to idols: We know that we all possess knowledge. Knowledge puffs up, but love builds up. (1 Cor 8:1)

All of these must be done for the strengthening of the church. (1 Cor 14:26)

Have you been thinking all along that we have been defending ourselves to you? We have been speaking in the sight of God as those in Christ; and everything we do, dear friends, is for your strengthening. (2 Cor 12:19)

Do not let any unwholesome talk come out of your mouths, but only what is helpful for building others up according to their needs, that it may benefit those who listen. (Eph 4:29)

9 (14:20) **Liberty vs. License**: do not destroy or ruin the work of God in another person's life—it is sin to do so. A person, child or adult, is far more important than having the right to eat and drink certain things and to attend and participate in certain social and recreational activities.

But if anyone causes one of these little ones who believe in me to sin, it would be better for him to have a large millstone hung around his neck and to be drowned in the depths of the sea. (Mat 18:6)

Therefore, if what I eat causes my brother to fall into sin, I will never eat meat again, so that I will not cause him to fall. (1 Cor 8:13)

You, my brothers, were called to be free. But do not use your freedom to indulge the sinful nature ; rather, serve one another in love. (Gal 5:13)

Each of you should look not only to your own interests, but also to the interests of others. (Phil 2:4)

Live as free men, but do not use your freedom as a cover-up for evil; live as servants of God. (1 Pet 2:16)

10 (14:21) **Liberty vs. License; Influence—Testimony**: do nothing to cause a brother to fall. Note how clearly Scripture speaks: food, wine—nothing—is worth causing a brother, child or adult, to fall. What is right for one may be the downfall of another, for men do influence children and other adults, and the fact is not debatable. The weak person, whether child or adult, may do something...

- because everyone else is doing it.
- because he does not wish to go against the crowd.
- because he simply does not wish to be different.
- because he does not wish to be criticized or ridiculed or unpopular.
- because he is weaker in stamina.
- because he looks up to and idolizes his friends (parents).

In everything I did, I showed you that by this kind of hard work we must help the weak, remembering the words the Lord Jesus himself said: 'It is more blessed to give than to receive.'" (Acts 20:35)

Accept him whose faith is weak, without passing judgment on disputable matters. (Rom 14:1)

We who are strong ought to bear with the failings of the weak and not to please ourselves. (Rom 15:1)

Be careful, however, that the exercise of your freedom does not become a stumbling block to the weak. (1 Cor 8:9)

So this weak brother, for whom Christ died, is destroyed by your knowledge. (1 Cor 8:11)

To the weak I became weak, to win the weak. I have become all things to all men so that by all possible means I might save some. (1 Cor 9:22)

Nobody should seek his own good, but the good of others. (1 Cor 10:24)

Each of you should look not only to your own interests, but also to the interests of others. (Phil 2:4)

11 (14:22-23) **Liberty vs. License—Condemnation, Self**: watch—do not condemn yourself. There are three ways a believer can keep from condemning himself.

1. By keeping his faith. *Faith* means the belief that a person can do a certain thing and that it is acceptable to God. If a believer feels free to do a certain thing, then he can do it, but it is to be done in *private before God*. It is not to be paraded publicly and done before men. It is to be eaten and drunk and done only in private. Doing the thing privately and *offering it up to God with thanksgiving* are the only ways it is acceptable. *If* it cannot be offered up to God with thanksgiving, then *it should not be done*.

2. By not going against his conscience. The believer must not condemn himself in what he does and allows in his life and home. (Remember: the children and the wife or husband are being influenced by what the believer does.)

3. By acting on faith, from a conviction that God approves the activity. If there is any question, note how clearly and forcibly Scripture speaks: "Everything that does not come from faith is sin." If a believer cannot eat, drink, and do the thing *in faith*—knowing it is acceptable to God—then *doing it is sin*.

> **And without faith it is impossible to please God, because anyone who comes to him must believe that he exists and that he rewards those who earnestly seek him. (Heb 11:6)**

> **Anyone, then, who knows the good he ought to do and doesn't do it, sins. (James 4:17)**

> **He who despises his neighbor sins, but blessed is he who is kind to the needy. (Prov 14:21)**

> **The schemes of folly are sin. (Prov 24:9)**

	CHAPTER 15	Jesus Christ.	**4** **Mark 4: Everyone accepts one another without discrimination**
	I. The Marks of a Strong Fellowship Within the Church, 15:1-13	7 Accept one another, then, just as Christ accepted you, in order to bring praise to God. 8 For I tell you that Christ has become a servant of the Jews on behalf of God's truth, to confirm the promises made to the patriarchs	a. The pattern: Christ, who accepted us all 1) Christ accepted the Jews & ministered to them
1 **Mark 1: The strong bear the weaknesses of the weak**	We who are strong ought to bear with the failings of the weak and not to please ourselves.	9 So that the Gentiles may glorify God for his mercy, as it is written: "Therefore I will	2) Christ accepted the Gentiles & ministered to them
a. How: By not pleasing self, but one's neighbor—focusing on his good and edification b. The pattern: Christ	2 Each of us should please his neighbor for his good, to build him up. 3 For even Christ did not please himself but, as it is written: "The insults of those who insult you have fallen on me."	praise you among the Gentiles; I will sing hymns to your name." 10 Again, it says, "Rejoice, O Gentiles, with his people." 11 And again, "Praise the Lord, all you Gentiles, and	b. The Scriptures prove the point
2 **Mark 2: Everyone studies the Scriptures**	4 For everything that was written in the past was written to teach us, so that through endurance and the encouragement of the Scriptures we might have hope.	sing praises to him, all you peoples." 12 And again, Isaiah says, "The Root of Jesse will spring up, one who will arise to rule over the nations; the Gentiles will hope in him."	
3 **Mark 3: Everyone works for harmony** a. How: By prayer & relying upon God b. The pattern: Christ c. Purpose: To glorify God with one heart & one mouth	5 May the God who gives endurance and encouragement give you a spirit of unity among yourselves as you follow Christ Jesus, 6 So that with one heart and mouth you may glorify the God and Father of our Lord	13 May the God of hope fill you with all joy and peace as you trust in him, so that you may overflow with hope by the power of the Holy Spirit.	**5** **Mark 5: Everyone is filled by the God of hope** a. Not with division & malice b. With joy, peace, hope c. Source: The Holy Spirit

DIVISION VIII

THE BELIEVER AND HIS DAILY BEHAVIOR, 12:1-15:13

I. The Marks of a Strong Fellowship Within the Church, 15:1-13

(15:1-13) **Introduction**: this passage is a continuation of the former chapter. It clearly pinpoints the marks of a strong church. Once studying this passage, a believer can never claim he did not know his duty within the church. Every believer's part in building and making the church strong is clearly spelled out.

1. Mark 1: the strong bear the weaknesses of the weak (v.1-3).
2. Mark 2: everyone studies the Scriptures (v.4).
3. Mark 3: everyone works for harmony (v.5-6).
4. Mark 4: everyone accepts one another without discrimination (v.7-12).
5. Mark 5: everyone is filled by the God of hope (v.13).

1 (15:1-3) **Brotherhood—Ministry—Weak—Weak-nesses**: in a strong church, the strong bear the weaknesses of the weak. The *weak* believers are described in Chapter 14. They are...

- those who judge, grumble, complain, murmur, and criticize (cp. Ro.14:2-3, 10, 13).
- those who still trust in a legalistic behavior, a do and don't behavior (Ro.14:1, 14-15).
- those who disobey God's Word and go against the explicit commands of God (Ro.14:10-12, 16-23).

The word "bear" (bastazein) does not mean to bear in the sense of putting up with and forbearing with an attitude of begrudging. It means to *bear the weak along*, to support them, to carry them along as a father or mother would

carry a child—in love and tenderness, understanding and care.

1. How can such an attitude ever prevail in the church? Scripture clearly gives the answer: "Each *of us* should please his neighbor." It is that simple: let us not please ourselves, but let us please our neighbor—let us live for his good and edification. No matter what we may wish...
   - the place we may want to go,
   - the drink we may want to drink,
   - the food we may want to eat,
   - the film we may want to see,
   - the thing we may want to buy,

...if it is going to be a stumbling block to our brother—we do not do it. We please, help, support, and live for the good of our brothers and sisters so that they might be edified and built up in the faith.

2. The believer has the greatest pattern in all the world for denying self and living for his neighbor: Jesus Christ Himself. "For *even* Christ did not please himself."
   ⇒ The insults that were cast against God—the cursing, dishonor, unbelief, denial, hostility, all the shame and rebellion against God—cut the heart of Christ. Therefore, Christ set out to bear the insults against God: He came to earth and bore the sin of the insults and made it possible for all persons to praise God instead of insulting His glorious name. The zeal to remove all the dishonor cast against God consumed Christ and fell upon Him. (Cp. Ps.69:19-20.)

Note the point: Christ did not live to please Himself. He did not pray "Father, remove this cup of sacrifice and denial from me—no matter what." He prayed: "My Father, if it is possible, may this cup be taken from me: yet not as I will, but as you will" (Mt.26:39). Jesus Christ is the believer's pattern for pleasing others instead of self.

> **Your attitude should be the same as that of Christ Jesus: Who, being in very nature God, did not consider equality with God something to be grasped, but made himself nothing, taking the very nature of a servant, being made in human likeness. And being found in appearance as a man, he humbled himself and became obedient to death— even death on a cross! (Phil 2:5-8)**

> **To this you were called, because Christ suffered for you, leaving you an example, that you should follow in his steps. (1 Pet 2:21)**

> **For Christ died for sins once for all, the righteous for the unrighteous, to bring you to God. He was put to death in the body but made alive by the Spirit, (1 Pet 3:18)**

> **But he was pierced for our transgressions, he was crushed for our iniquities; the punishment that brought us peace was upon him, and by his wounds we are healed. (Isa 53:5)**

Thought 1. What a glorious spirit would prevail in the church if this was really practiced as Scripture says: by "each *of us*."

> **In everything I did, I showed you that by this kind of hard work we must help the weak, remembering the words the Lord Jesus himself said: 'It is more blessed to give than to receive.'" (Acts 20:35)**

> **Carry each other's burdens, and in this way you will fulfill the law of Christ. (Gal 6:2)**

> **Remember those in prison as if you were their fellow prisoners, and those who are mistreated as if you yourselves were suffering. (Heb 13:3)**

> **Religion that God our Father accepts as pure and faultless is this: to look after orphans and widows in their distress and to keep oneself from being polluted by the world. (James 1:27)**

Thought 2. Note how *life-changing* this point really is. The serious believer no longer asks if questionable behavior is right and moral, but if is it good for his brother. Will this thing edify and build up his brother?

> **Love the Lord your God with all your heart and with all your soul and with all your mind and with all your strength.' The second is this: 'Love your neighbor as yourself.' There is no commandment greater than these." (Mark 12:30-31)**

> **"A new command I give you: Love one another. As I have loved you, so you must love one another. By this all men will know that you are my disciples, if you love one another." (John 13:34-35)**

> **Love does no harm to its neighbor. Therefore love is the fulfillment of the law. (Rom 13:10)**

> **Let us therefore make every effort to do what leads to peace and to mutual edification. (Rom 14:19)**

> **We are glad whenever we are weak but you are strong; and our prayer is for your perfection. (2 Cor 13:9)**

> **The entire law is summed up in a single command: "Love your neighbor as yourself." (Gal 5:14)**

> **Do not let any unwholesome talk come out of your mouths, but only what is helpful for building others up according to their needs, that it may benefit those who listen. (Eph 4:29)**

> **If you really keep the royal law found in Scripture, "Love your neighbor as yourself," you are doing right. (James 2:8)**

2 (15:4) **Scripture—Study**: in a strong church, everyone studies the Scripture. This is a great verse on the purpose of the Holy Scriptures. In very simple terms it tells us why God gave us the Bible.

1. The Scriptures were written to teach us (didaskalian): to instruct, direct, and guide us.

> **But these are written that you may believe that Jesus is the Christ, the Son of God, and that by believing you may have life in his name. (John 20:31)**

> **Now the Bereans were of more noble character than the Thessalonians, for they received the message with great eagerness and examined the Scriptures every day to see if what Paul said was true. (Acts 17:11)**

> **For everything that was written in the past was written to teach us, so that through endurance and the encouragement of the Scriptures we might have hope. (Rom 15:4)**

> **These things happened to them as examples and were written down as warnings for us, on whom the fulfillment of the ages has come. (1 Cor 10:11)**

> **Do your best to present yourself to God as one approved, a workman who does not need to be ashamed and who correctly handles the word of truth. (2 Tim 2:15)**

> **All Scripture is God-breathed and is useful for teaching, rebuking, correcting and training in righteousness, (2 Tim 3:16)**

> **I write these things to you who believe in the name of the Son of God so that you may know that you have eternal life. (1 John 5:13)**

2. The Scriptures were written to stir three things within believers.
   a. Endurance (see note—Ro.5:3-5 for discussion).
   b. Encouragement (parakleseos): consolation, solace, help, exhortation, supplication. Whatever is needed to comfort the believer, the Scripture gives him.

I tell you the truth, if anyone keeps my word, he will never see death." (John 8:51)

"If you love me, you will obey what I command. (John 14:15)

And I will ask the Father, and he will give you another Counselor to be with you forever— (John 14:16)

Jesus replied, "If anyone loves me, he will obey my teaching. My Father will love him, and we will come to him and make our home with him. (John 14:23)

"I have told you these things, so that in me you may have peace. In this world you will have trouble. But take heart! I have overcome the world." (John 16:33)

c. Hope (see note—Ro.5:3-5 for discussion).

For everything that was written in the past was written to teach us, so that through endurance and the encouragement of the Scriptures we might have hope. (Rom 15:4)

I am not ashamed of the gospel, because it is the power of God for the salvation of everyone who believes: first for the Jew, then for the Gentile. (Rom 1:16)

He was chosen before the creation of the world, but was revealed in these last times for your sake. Through him you believe in God, who raised him from the dead and glorified him, and so your faith and hope are in God. Now that you have purified yourselves by obeying the truth so that you have sincere love for your brothers, love one another deeply, from the heart. For you have been born again, not of perishable seed, but of imperishable, through the living and enduring word of God. (1 Pet 1:20-23)

3 (15:5-6) **Unity—Brotherhood**: in a strong church, everyone works for harmony. When there are so many differences and different ideas among people, believers must be constantly striving to be of one heart.

1. How can a church—a church with so many diverse personalities—achieve harmonious feelings and one mind? Note: these two verses are a prayer of Paul. He has just said that the endurance and comfort necessary to live for God comes from the Scriptures. Now he says they come from God. In fact, he says that God is the God of endurance (endurance) and encouragement. Therefore, the believer secures his strength or endurance and comfort from both the Scriptures and God. If he wishes to stick—to endure to the end—he must study the Scriptures and pray, asking God to give him...

- the strength and endurance.
- the comfort and encouragement.

Now, note the point. If we know the endurance and comfort of God, then we are bearing the weaknesses of each other; we are constantly supporting and helping and caring for each other. We are living in harmony and being of one heart.

2. The pattern of endurance and encouragement and of harmonious feelings with God and man was Christ Jesus.

⇒ He was faithful to God, sticking ever so close to God and fulfilling His ministry to the ultimate degree.

⇒ He experienced the comfort and the encouragement of God, possessing an unbroken relationship with God.

⇒ He never held any ill feelings toward God or God's people. He was of one heart with God and was always working to bring every person into harmony with God.

The believer could have no greater pattern than the pattern of Christ Himself. Christ was always working to bring men together with God so that they could have the endurance and comfort to live through all the trials and sufferings of life.

3. The purpose for unity between believers and within the church is striking: that we might *glorify God*—all of us together—with one heart and one mouth. God longs for our worship and praise. It is the very reason He created us and saved us. Note a significant point: a divided church cannot worship God. This is exactly what is being said. A church has to be of one heart and mouth to worship God. If a people are not of one heart and mouth, God is not glorified; He is not worshipped.

The point is clear. Every one of us must work for the unity of the church so that we may be of one heart and fulfill the very purpose for our existence: to glorify God.

I appeal to you, brothers, in the name of our Lord Jesus Christ, that all of you agree with one another so that there may be no divisions among you and that you may be perfectly united in mind and thought. (1 Cor 1:10)

Finally, brothers, good-by. Aim for perfection, listen to my appeal, be of one mind, live in peace. And the God of love and peace will be with you. (2 Cor 13:11)

Make every effort to keep the unity of the Spirit through the bond of peace. (Eph 4:3)

Whatever happens, conduct yourselves in a manner worthy of the gospel of Christ. Then, whether I come and see you or only hear about you in my absence, I will know that you stand firm in one spirit, contending as one man for the faith of the gospel (Phil 1:27)

Finally, all of you, live in harmony with one another; be sympathetic, love as brothers, be compassionate and humble. (1 Pet 3:8)

4 (15:7-12) **Unity**: in a strong church everyone accepts one another. There is no discrimination whatsoever in a strong church. The word "accept" (proslambanesthe) means to take to oneself; to accept a person as a friend; to treat as the closest of friends with the most caring kindness. Believers are to accept one another in the closest of bonds.

1. The believer has the greatest pattern imaginable: Christ Himself. Christ accepted us, and note why: that God may be glorified. Therefore, believers must accept each other so that God may be glorified through their lives and church. Just look at how far Christ went.

a. Christ accepted the Jews and ministered to them. He did it for the truth of God: to confirm and fulfill the promises made to the Jewish nation. Think how discriminating, prejudicial, and judgmental the Jews were; yet Christ came to them and received and ministered to them. Why? For the truth of God—to fulfill the Word and praise of God.

b. Christ accepted the Gentiles and ministered to them. He came to bring them the mercy of God, that they might praise God for His mercy. Remember He received and ministered to the Gentiles when they were living the most licentious and indulgent life-style imaginable (cp. Ro.1:18-32).

2. The Scripture proves the point. Scripture foretold...
- that the Gentiles would have the gospel preached to them (v.9; cp. Ps.18:49).
- that the Gentiles would rejoice with God's people (v.10; cp. Dt.32:43).
- that the Gentiles would praise God and trust Christ as their Savior and Lord (v.11; cp. Is.11:1, 10).

Believers are to accept one another even as Christ has accepted us. No person is too prejudicial or critical, too weak or base for us to accept. The point is that Christ received and ministered to the most prejudicial and judgmental (the Jews), sinful and base (the Gentiles) people in the world; therefore, believers can accept one another. No one is too far gone to be rejected and thrown aside.

⇒ We are to accept each other, as Christ also accepted us.

> When the apostles in Jerusalem heard that Samaria had accepted the word of God, they sent Peter and John to them. (Acts 8:14)
> "Can anyone keep these people [Gentiles] from being baptized with water? They have received the Holy Spirit just as we have." (Acts 10:47)
> When they heard this, they had no further objections and praised God, saying, "So then, God has granted even the Gentiles repentance unto life." (Acts 11:18)
> "It is my judgment, therefore, that we should not make it difficult for the Gentiles who are turning to God. (Acts 15:19)
> There is neither Jew nor Greek, slave nor free, male nor female, for you are all one in Christ Jesus. (Gal 3:28)
> But now in Christ Jesus you who once were far away have been brought near through the blood of Christ. For he himself is our peace, who has made the two one and has destroyed the barrier, the dividing wall of hostility, (Eph 2:13-14)

⇒ We are to accept each other for *the glory of God*.

> So that with one heart and mouth you may glorify the God and Father of our Lord Jesus Christ. (Rom 15:6)
> You were bought at a price. Therefore honor God with your body. (1 Cor 6:20)
> We pray this so that the name of our Lord Jesus may be glorified in you, and you in him, according to the grace of our God and the Lord Jesus Christ. (2 Th 1:12)

5 (15:13) **Church—Hope**: in a strong church everyone is filled by the God of hope. God is the "God of hope"...
- the Author of our hope.
- the Foundation of our hope.
- the Builder of our hope.
- the Finisher of our hope.

Note that this is a prayer. The things mentioned cannot be possessed apart from God, and we can possess them only as He gives them to us.

1. There is joy (charas): an inner gladness; a deep seated pleasure. It is a depth of assurance and confidence that ignites a cheerful heart. It is a cheerful heart that leads to cheerful behavior.

> "I am coming to you now, but I say these things while I am still in the world, so that they may have the full measure of my joy within them. (John 17:13)
> Though you have not seen him, you love him; and even though you do not see him now, you believe in him and are filled with an inexpressible and glorious joy, (1 Pet 1:8)
> I delight greatly in the LORD; my soul rejoices in my God. For he has clothed me with garments of salvation and arrayed me in a robe of righteousness, as a bridegroom adorns his head like a priest, and as a bride adorns herself with her jewels. (Isa 61:10)

2. There is peace (see note, *Peace*—Ro.5:1 for discussion). Note that peace comes through believing. No man has peace apart from God.

> Peace I leave with you; my peace I give you. I do not give to you as the world gives. Do not let your hearts be troubled and do not be afraid. (John 14:27)
> "I have told you these things, so that in me you may have peace. In this world you will have trouble. But take heart! I have overcome the world." (John 16:33)
> Do not be anxious about anything, but in everything, by prayer and petition, with thanksgiving, present your requests to God. And the peace of God, which transcends all understanding, will guard your hearts and your minds in Christ Jesus. (Phil 4:6-7)
> The LORD gives strength to his people; the LORD blesses his people with peace. (Psa 29:11)
> Do good to your servant according to your word, O LORD. (Psa 119:65)
> You will keep in perfect peace him whose mind is steadfast, because he trusts in you. (Isa 26:3)

3. There is hope (see note—Ro.5:3-5 for discussion).

> And I have the same hope in God as these men, that there will be a resurrection of both the righteous and the wicked. (Acts 24:15)
> For in this hope we were saved. But hope that is seen is no hope at all. Who hopes for what he already has? (Rom 8:24)

The faith and love that spring from the hope that is stored up for you in heaven and that you have already heard about in the word of truth, the gospel (Col 1:5)

It teaches us to say "No" to ungodliness and worldly passions, and to live self-controlled, upright and godly lives in this present age, While we wait for the blessed hope—the glorious appearing of our great God and Savior, Jesus Christ, (Titus 2:12-13)

God did this so that, by two unchangeable things in which it is impossible for God to lie, we who have fled to take hold of the hope offered to us may be greatly encouraged. We have this hope as an anchor for the soul, firm and secure. It enters the inner sanctuary behind the curtain, (Heb 6:18-19)

How great is the love the Father has lavished on us, that we should be called children of God! And that is what we are! The reason the world does not know us is that it did not know him. Dear friends, now we are children of God, and what we will be has not yet been made known. But we know that when he appears, we shall be like him, for we shall see him as he is. Everyone who has this hope in him purifies himself, just as he is pure. (1 John 3:1-3)

When calamity comes, the wicked are brought down, but even in death the righteous have a refuge. (Prov 14:32)

Again note: these great qualities come only through the power of the Holy Spirit. God and God alone is the source of the things that give life (cp. Gal.5:22-23. See note, *Justification*—Ro.5:1).

	IX. THE MESSENGER OF GOD AND HIS PLANS 15:14-16:27 A. The Messenger or Minister of God, 15:14-21	17 Therefore I glory in Christ Jesus in my service to God. 18 I will not venture to speak of anything except what Christ has accomplished through me in leading the Gentiles to obey God by what I have said and done— 19 By the power of signs and miracles, through the power of the Spirit. So from Jerusalem all the way around to Illyricum, I have fully proclaimed the gospel of Christ. 20 It has always been my ambition to preach the gospel where Christ was not known, so that I would not be building on someone else's foundation. 21 Rather, as it is written: "Those who were not told about him will see, and those who have not heard will understand."	4 He gloried & talked about Jesus Christ a. Gloried through Jesus Christ b. Gloried in the obedience of converts—accomplished by Christ c. Gloried in the mighty signs and miracles accomplished by the Spirit d. Gloried in the fact that he had been able to preach the gospel of Christ all around 5 He strived to preach for Christ in pioneer areas a. To reach those who had never heard b. To fulfill God's call for his life: To reach the pioneer areas of the world
1 He was gracious in dealing with people a. Called them brothers b. Acknowledged their commendable qualities 2 He was bold in reminding people 3 He was called to minister the gospel of God	14 I myself am convinced, my brothers, that you yourselves are full of goodness, complete in knowledge and competent to instruct one another. 15 I have written you quite boldly on some points, as if to remind you of them again, because of the grace God gave me 16 To be a minister of Christ Jesus to the Gentiles with the priestly duty of proclaiming the gospel of God, so that the Gentiles might become an offering acceptable to God, sanctified by the Holy Spirit.		

DIVISION IX

THE MESSENGER OF GOD AND HIS PLANS, 15:14-16:27

A. The Messenger or Minister of God, 15:14-21

(15:14-21) **Introduction**: this is one of the most descriptive passages dealing with the minister of God. It forcefully reveals what it was that made Paul such a great minister of God.

1. He was gracious in dealing with people (v.14).
2. He was bold in reminding people (v.15).
3. He was called to minister the gospel of God (v.16).
4. He gloried and talked about Jesus Christ (v.17-19).
5. He strived to preach for Christ in pioneer areas (v.20-21).

1 (15:14) **Minister**: the minister of God is gracious in dealing with people. Note two significant points.

1. Paul called the members of the Roman congregation brothers (v.15, 16). Paul did not look upon himself as being superior to the Roman congregation. He did not see himself...

 • as being better
 • as being more spiritual
 • as being more intellectual
 • as being more educated

Paul never looked upon himself as being superior to other believers in any sense of the word. Note also: Paul was not nagging, harping, or badgering the Roman congregation. On the contrary, he was addressing the congregation in the most gracious of spirits, treating them as his equal before God. Paul called the members *brothers*, not *sons* and *daughters*.

2. Paul acknowledged the commendable qualities of the Roman congregation. He mentioned three qualities or traits in particular.

 a. The believers were "complete in knowledge" (mestoi agathosunes): full of kindness and helpfulness, of virtue and excellence, of peace and conciliation, of inner depth and richness.

> And to know this love that surpasses knowledge—that you may be filled to the measure of all the fullness of God. (Eph 3:19)
>
> The LORD loves righteousness and justice; the earth is full of his unfailing love. (Psa 33:5)
>
> Taste and see that the LORD is good; blessed is the man who takes refuge in him. (Psa 34:8)
>
> I will tell of the kindnesses of the LORD, the deeds for which he is to be praised, according to all the LORD has done for us— yes, the many good things he has done for the house of Israel, according to his compassion and many kindnesses. (Isa 63:7)

 b. The believers were filled "complete in knowledge" (pases gnoseos): spiritual insight and perception; knowledge of Christ, God, and the Holy Spirit, and of the spiritual need of man and his world; spiritual truth.

> Jesus answered, "My teaching is not my own. It comes from him who sent me. If anyone chooses to do God's will, he will find out whether my teaching comes from God or whether I speak on my own. (John 7:16-17)
>
> To the Jews who had believed him, Jesus said, "If you hold to my teaching, you are really my disciples. Then you will know the truth, and the truth will set you free." (John 8:31-32)
>
> Now this is eternal life: that they may know you, the only true God, and Jesus Christ, whom you have sent. (John 17:3)

254

I want to know Christ and the power of his resurrection and the fellowship of sharing in his sufferings, becoming like him in his death, (Phil 3:10)

And we pray this in order that you may live a life worthy of the Lord and may please him in every way: bearing fruit in every good work, growing in the knowledge of God, (Col 1:10)

For this very reason, make every effort to add to your faith goodness; and to goodness, knowledge; (2 Pet 1:5)

Many will follow their shameful ways and will bring the way of truth into disrepute. In their greed these teachers will exploit you with stories they have made up. Their condemnation has long been hanging over them, and their destruction has not been sleeping. (2 Pet 2:2-3)

c. The believers were able "able to instruct" (nouthetein) one another: to put in mind, to implant the truth into the mind, to guide and correct and instruct.

Let the word of Christ dwell in you richly as you teach and admonish one another with all wisdom, and as you sing psalms, hymns and spiritual songs with gratitude in your hearts to God. (Col 3:16)

And we urge you, brothers, warn those who are idle, encourage the timid, help the weak, be patient with everyone. (1 Th 5:14)

Yet do not regard him as an enemy, but warn him as a brother. (2 Th 3:15)

Thought 1. Remember that Paul had never visited the Roman church. He had only met a few of the Roman believers in his travels over the Mediterranean world. What he knew about the Roman believers was only what he had heard about them. Therefore, his writing to them is comparable to a visiting preacher. Note his gracious spirit and attitude toward other believers and congregations. Every minister can learn from this soft, tender spirit of Paul.

Therefore, whoever humbles himself like this child is the greatest in the kingdom of heaven. (Mat 18:4)

But you are not to be like that. Instead, the greatest among you should be like the youngest, and the one who rules like the one who serves. (Luke 22:26)

For by the grace given me I say to every one of you: Do not think of yourself more highly than you ought, but rather think of yourself with sober judgment, in accordance with the measure of faith God has given you. (Rom 12:3)

Do nothing out of selfish ambition or vain conceit, but in humility consider others better than yourselves. Each of you should look not only to your own interests, but also to the interests of others. (Phil 2:3-4)

Here is a trustworthy saying that deserves full acceptance: Christ Jesus came into the world to save sinners—of whom I am the worst. (1 Tim 1:15)

Young men, in the same way be submissive to those who are older. All of you,

clothe yourselves with humility toward one another, because, "God opposes the proud but gives grace to the humble." (1 Pet 5:5)

2 (15:15) **Minister, Duty of**: the minister of God is bold in reminding people of the great truths of the gospel. Glance at the overall outline of Romans, and you quickly see how Paul has covered the great truths of the Christian faith. This is the task of the minister of God. The minister must proclaim the truths of the gospel—to preach the gospel is the very reason for his call. He exists for no other purpose.

I thank Christ Jesus our Lord, who has given me strength, that he considered me faithful, appointing me to his service. (1 Tim 1:12)

We are therefore Christ's ambassadors, as though God were making his appeal through us. We implore you on Christ's behalf: Be reconciled to God. (2 Cor 5:20)

All this is from God, who reconciled us to himself through Christ and gave us the ministry of reconciliation: (2 Cor 5:18)

Therefore, since through God's mercy we have this ministry, we do not lose heart. Rather, we have renounced secret and shameful ways; we do not use deception, nor do we distort the word of God. On the contrary, by setting forth the truth plainly we commend ourselves to every man's conscience in the sight of God. (2 Cor 4:1-2)

But to each one of us grace has been given as Christ apportioned it. This is why it says: "When he ascended on high, he led captives in his train and gave gifts to men." (Eph 4:7-8)

And of this gospel I was appointed a herald and an apostle and a teacher. (2 Tim 1:11)

3 (15:16) **Minister, Duty**: the minister of God is called to minister the gospel of God. When Paul called himself a minister (leitourgon), the Greek word was often used to refer to the priests of the Old Testament. This is a beautiful passage describing the nature of the Christian ministry. The Christian ministry is seen as a priestly ministry. However, we must always remember that the ministry is not an office to make atonement for sin, nor to offer an atoning, a propitiatory sacrifice to God. It is a ministry of preaching the gospel under the influence of the Holy Spirit. The purpose of the ministry is this: to bring men to the point where they will offer themselves as living sacrifices, holy, pleasing to God (cp. Ro.12:1-2). A minister's only priesthood is the preaching of the gospel, and his only offering is the offering of redeemed and sanctified men to God. He is not a mediator between God and men; he does not offer atoning sacrifices. He is only an instrument which God uses to share the gospel of salvation with men. He is a priest only in the sense that he serves the gospel of God *to men* and brings men to God through the gospel of God.

Note what the "offering" was that God wanted Paul to make: the offering of the Gentiles, of human lives. God wanted Paul to bring people to Him. This is the task of ministers: to offer the lives of men, women, boys, and girls to God.

> You did not choose me, but I chose you and appointed you to go and bear fruit—fruit that will last. Then the Father will give you whatever you ask in my name. (John 15:16)
>
> Therefore, I urge you, brothers, in view of God's mercy, to offer your bodies as living sacrifices, holy and pleasing to God—this is your spiritual act of worship. (Rom 12:1)
>
> You also, like living stones, are being built into a spiritual house to be a holy priesthood, offering spiritual sacrifices acceptable to God through Jesus Christ. (1 Pet 2:5)

Note: the offering that God wants from ministers, the only offering that is "acceptable," is the offering of human lives. The word *"acceptable"* is significant. If ministers bring any other offering, it is unacceptable. God is not after buildings, programs, money, equipment, or anything else. God is after the lives of people.

The word acceptable means something else as well. It means that the offering of a human life is acceptable only if the person is brought…

- by "the gospel of God" and is "sanctified [set apart to God] by the Holy Spirit."

The good news of God's Son, Jesus Christ, has to be proclaimed and accepted for a person to be acceptable to God. The only person set apart to God by the Holy Spirit is the person who comes to God in the name of His Son, Jesus Christ.

> Jesus answered, "I am the way and the truth and the life. No one comes to the Father except through me. (John 14:6)
>
> Salvation is found in no one else, for there is no other name under heaven given to men by which we must be saved." (Acts 4:12)
>
> For there is one God and one mediator between God and men, the man Christ Jesus, who gave himself as a ransom for all men—the testimony given in its proper time. (1 Tim 2:5-6)

4 (15:17-19) **Minister—Boasting—Glorying**: the minister of God talks about Jesus Christ. Note four facts.

1. Paul talked about and gloried in Jesus Christ alone. There is a legitimate boasting, a justified glorying for the minister. However, it is critical to note where. The minister's boasting…

- is not in material things such as buildings, programs, membership, and numbers.
- is not in fleshly things such as position, charisma, fluency of speech, education, and titles.

Paul demonstrated this fact clearly, for he did not talk about himself nor about what he had done. He talked only about the things that pertained to God, only about the things wrought through Jesus Christ.

> Therefore, as it is written: "Let him who boasts boast in the Lord." (1 Cor 1:31)
>
> My soul will boast in the LORD; let the afflicted hear and rejoice. (Psa 34:2)
>
> In God we make our boast all day long, and we will praise your name forever. Selah (Psa 44:8)

> But in the LORD all the descendants of Israel will be found righteous and will exult. (Isa 45:25)
>
> But let him who boasts boast about this: that he understands and knows me, that I am the LORD, who exercises kindness, justice and righteousness on earth, for in these I delight," declares the LORD. (Jer 9:24)

2. Paul talked about and gloried in the obedience of converts. Note that the Gentile converts were *accomplished through Christ*, not by Paul. Christ used what Paul said and did to reach the converts, but it was Christ who worked in their hearts to convict and convert them.

The point is this: Paul talked about and shared the glorious news of converts, but he was careful…

- to give all the credit to Christ.
- to make no claims that were not true ("I will not venture to speak of anything except what Christ has accomplished").

> For by the grace given me I say to every one of you: Do not think of yourself more highly than you ought, but rather think of yourself with sober judgment, in accordance with the measure of faith God has given you. (Rom 12:3)
>
> Humble yourselves before the Lord, and he will lift you up. (James 4:10)
>
> He has showed you, O man, what is good. And what does the LORD require of you? To act justly and to love mercy and to walk humbly with your God. (Micah 6:8)
>
> When pride comes, then comes disgrace, but with humility comes wisdom. (Prov 11:2)
>
> Pride goes before destruction, a haughty spirit before a fall. (Prov 16:18)
>
> Like clouds and wind without rain is a man who boasts of gifts he does not give. (Prov 25:14)
>
> As it is, you boast and brag. All such boasting is evil. (James 4:16)
>
> For everything in the world—the cravings of sinful man, the lust of his eyes and the boasting of what he has and does—comes not from the Father but from the world. (1 John 2:16)

3. Paul talked about and gloried in the mighty signs and miracles accomplished by the Holy Spirit. This is a term used in Scripture to refer to the wonderful miracles accomplished by God—miracles which could be accomplished by God. Apparently, Paul had an extensive ministry of both evangelism and healing among people. But note the emphasis: it was all accomplished through the "power of the Spirit [of God]." It was the Holy Spirit who did the miracles (cp. Acts 13:11; 14:3, 10; 16:18; 19:11; 20:10; 28:5, 8).

> But you will receive power when the Holy Spirit comes on you; and you will be my witnesses in Jerusalem, and in all Judea and Samaria, and to the ends of the earth." (Acts 1:8)
>
> With great power the apostles continued to testify to the resurrection of the Lord Jesus, and much grace was upon them all. (Acts 4:33)

God did extraordinary miracles through Paul, so that even handkerchiefs and aprons that had touched him were taken to the sick, and their illnesses were cured and the evil spirits left them. (Acts 19:11-12)

My message and my preaching were not with wise and persuasive words, but with a demonstration of the Spirit's power, (1 Cor 2:4)

I pray that out of his glorious riches he may strengthen you with power through his Spirit in your inner being, (Eph 3:16)

For to which of the angels did God ever say, "You are my Son; today I have become your Father?" Or again, "I will be his Father, and he will be my Son?" (Heb 1:5)

For God did not give us a spirit of timidity, but a spirit of power, of love and of self-discipline. (2 Tim 1:7)

4. Paul talked about and gloried in the fact that he had been given the privilege to *preach the gospel* all around: "from Jerusalem all the way around to Illyricum" (present day Yugoslavia or Serbia). Note that God had used Paul to preach throughout the world, but note the emphasis: "I have fully proclaimed the gospel of Christ." It was the gospel of Christ that God wanted the world to hear and receive, not the gospel of Paul. Paul was only the instrument that God used. Paul talked about *the gospel of Christ penetrating and reaching the world*.

At once he began to preach in the synagogues that Jesus is the Son of God. (Acts 9:20)

But we preach Christ crucified: a stumbling block to Jews and foolishness to Gentiles, (1 Cor 1:23)

Yet when I preach the gospel, I cannot boast, for I am compelled to preach. Woe to me if I do not preach the gospel! (1 Cor 9:16)

For we do not preach ourselves, but Jesus Christ as Lord, and ourselves as your servants for Jesus' sake. (2 Cor 4:5)

5 (15:20-21) **Minister**: the minister of God strives to preach in pioneer areas for Christ. Note two striking points.

1. Paul strived to reach those who had never heard about Christ. His one ambition was to carry the gospel to those to whom no other preacher had gone. God had called him to be an apostle, a missionary evangelist, not to pastor and to build upon the ministry of other men.

⇒ Too many in the world had never heard about Christ.
⇒ Too many were still doomed to die without ever having heard.
⇒ Too many were to spend eternity apart from God.

Why? Simply because they had never heard. There were not enough ministers going into the pioneer areas and staying with the people long enough to root and grow them in the Lord.

2. Paul strived to fulfill God's call to him by reaching the Gentiles, for God had called him to reach the pioneer areas (Acts 9:15; 22:14-15; 26:15-18). Note: Scripture predicts that the gospel is to be carried to those who "have not heard" (Is.52:15).

Thought 1. Paul was the first of God's chosen vessels to carry the message to those who had never heard. Tragically, there are still multitudes who have not heard the gospel of Christ and who are dying and will spend eternity apart from God—all because we have not carried the gospel to them.

⇒ Who will be the "Pauls" of today?
⇒ Who has the courage to go to the pioneer areas today?
⇒ Who will reach those who have never even had the opportunity to hear?

Therefore go and make disciples of all nations, baptizing them in the name of the Father and of the Son and of the Holy Spirit, (Mat 28:19)

He said to them, "Go into all the world and preach the good news to all creation. (Mark 16:15)

And repentance and forgiveness of sins will be preached in his name to all nations, beginning at Jerusalem. (Luke 24:47)

During the night Paul had a vision of a man of Macedonia standing and begging him, "Come over to Macedonia and help us." (Acts 16:9)

You will be his witness to all men of what you have seen and heard. (Acts 22:15)

Ask of me, and I will make the nations your inheritance, the ends of the earth your possession. (Psa 2:8)

Declare his glory among the nations, his marvelous deeds among all peoples. (Psa 96:3)

	B. The Messenger & His Ministry, 15:22-33	shared in the Jews' spiritual blessings, they owe it to the Jews to share with them their material blessings.	
1 He did a thorough job where he was	22 This is why I have often been hindered from coming to you.	28 So after I have completed this task and have made sure that they have received this fruit, I will go to Spain and visit you on the way.	**4 He served in the gospel of Christ—in the full measure of the blessing of Christ**
a. He stayed & handled problems, but wanted to go elsewhere	23 But now that there is no more place for me to work in these regions, and since I have been longing for many years to see you,	29 I know that when I come to you, I will come in the full measure of the blessing of Christ.	a. He maintained a worldwide vision
b. He completed his ministry—fully	24 I plan to do so when I go to Spain. I hope to visit you while passing through and to have you assist me on my journey there, after I have enjoyed your company for a while.	30 I urge you, brothers, by our Lord Jesus Christ and by the love of the Spirit, to join me in my struggle by praying to God for me.	b. He served the gospel of Christ & nothing else
2 He had a worldwide vision			**5 He begged for much prayer in behalf of his ministry**
a. His vision: To reach the limits of the world (Spain)			
b. His expectation: To have the help & support of believers	25 Now, however, I am on my way to Jerusalem in the service of the saints there.	31 Pray that I may be rescued from the unbelievers in Judea and that my service in Jerusalem may be acceptable to the saints there,	a. That he might be rescued from unbelievers
3 He did not forget immediate needs as he made worldwide plans	26 For Macedonia and Achaia were pleased to make a contribution for the poor among the saints in Jerusalem.	32 So that by God's will I may come to you with joy and together with you be refreshed.	b. That his service might be acceptable
	27 They were pleased to do it, and indeed they owe it to them. For if the Gentiles have	33 The God of peace be with you all. Amen.	c. That he might carry out his worldwide vision & be refreshed by believers
			6 He set the example of intercessory prayer

DIVISION IX

THE MESSENGER OF GOD AND HIS PLANS, 15:14-16:27

B. The Messenger & His Ministry, 15:22-33

(15:22-33) **Introduction**: this passage is a remarkable description of the ministry of God's messenger. The messenger may be a preacher, a teacher, or a witnessing believer—it matters not—the principles of ministry are the same for all.

1. He did a thorough job where he was (v.22-23).
2. He had a worldwide vision (v.24).
3. He did not forget immediate needs as he made worldwide plans (v.25-27).
4. He served in the gospel of Christ—in the full measure of the blessing of Christ (v.28-29).
5. He begged for much prayer in behalf of his ministry (v.30-32).
6. He set the example of intercessory prayer (v.33).

1 (15:22-23) **Ministry**: the minister of God does a thorough job where he is. Paul set a dynamic example for every minister and teacher of the gospel to stay where he is and complete the job God called him to do—despite the enormity of the task and great difficulties.

Paul stayed where he was and completed his ministry despite the desire to move on. God had called him to evangelize and minister throughout the region from Jerusalem to Illyricum, the country formerly known as Yugoslavia. Note how Paul longed to reach Spain and Rome for Christ, but he stayed in his present ministry because of the enormous problems and needs of the churches. (A quick glance at the overall outlines of the Epistles Paul wrote will give a review of some of the problems.) In addition to the problems within the churches, think of the opposition and personal attacks against Paul himself. Yet Paul stuck to the task at hand, working ever so diligently trying to straighten

out the problems within the churches, and to meet their desperate need to grow in Christ. Note the words "there is no more place for me to work in these regions." Paul was saying that he had now completed his task and finished his work. He had fought a good fight and finished his course. He had "fully proclaimed the gospel of Christ" (v.19). Therefore, he could now move on.

Thought 1. What a convicting example Paul is to so many ministers who long to flee instead of facing the problems and meeting the needs of God's people.

> **Are they servants of Christ? (I am out of my mind to talk like this.) I am more. I have worked much harder, been in prison more frequently, been flogged more severely, and been exposed to death again and again. Five times I received from the Jews the forty lashes minus one. Three times I was beaten with rods, once I was stoned, three times I was shipwrecked, I spent a night and a day in the open sea, I have been constantly on the move. I have been in danger from rivers, in danger from bandits, in danger from my own countrymen, in danger from Gentiles; in danger in the city, in danger in the country, in danger at sea; and in danger from false brothers. I have labored and toiled and have often gone without sleep; I have known hunger and thirst and have often gone without food; I have been cold and naked. Besides everything else, I face daily the pressure of my concern for all the churches. (2 Cor 11:23-28)**

2 (15:24) **Minister—Stewardship**: the minister of God has a worldwide vision.

1. Paul had a worldwide vision. He longed and ached to reach the outer limits of the world. In the days of Paul, the western borders of Spain were considered the outposts of the civilized world. Paul knew that if he could *personally evangelize* the outposts of western Europe, the gospel would spread out into the uncivilized world.

> **Thought 1.** He was consumed with the passion to reach every man, woman, and child with the gospel of the Lord Jesus Christ who had died for them.

> > **We proclaim him [Christ], admonishing and teaching everyone with all wisdom, so that we may present everyone perfect in Christ. To this end I labor, struggling with all his energy, which so powerfully works in me. (Col 1:28-29)**

2. Paul had a strong expectation: to have the help and fellowship and support of other believers in his attempt to reach the world. When he visited the Roman church, he expected…
- to be filled with the company and fellowship and help of the believers.
- to be financially supported in his mission to Spain ("Assist me on my journey there").

Thought 1. In the great task of reaching the world for Christ, there are those who go forth to preach the gospel, and there are those who prayerfully and financially support the preachers. Both are *absolutely* essential.

> > **For, "Everyone who calls on the name of the Lord will be saved." How, then, can they call on the one they have not believed in? And how can they believe in the one of whom they have not heard? And how can they hear without someone preaching to them? And how can they preach unless they are sent? As it is written, "How beautiful are the feet of those who bring good news!" (Rom 10:13-15)**
> > **We have different gifts, according to the grace given us. If a man's gift is prophesying, let him use it in proportion to his faith. If it is serving, let him serve; if it is teaching, let him teach; If it is encouraging, let him encourage; if it is contributing to the needs of others, let him give generously; if it is leadership, let him govern diligently; if it is showing mercy, let him do it cheerfully. (Rom 12:6-8)**
> > **The disciples, each according to his ability, decided to provide help for the brothers living in Judea. (Acts 11:29)**

3 (15:25-27) **Ministering**: the minister of God does not forget immediate needs as he makes future or worldwide plans. As much as Paul longed to preach the gospel in Rome and Spain, there was a more immediate need pressing in upon him—a need of enormous proportion. Saints of God all throughout Judaea were suffering from deep poverty. No doubt some of them had lost their jobs because of their witness for Christ, and the land had apparently suf-

fered a famine of some sort. Whatever the cause, many of God's people were hungry, unclothed, and unsheltered. They needed help, and it was the minister's (Paul's) task to help them. For this reason, Paul had taken a special offering from all the churches in Macedonia and Achaia to help the poor saints in Jerusalem. Note how strongly Paul felt about saints helping one another when they were in need. He said that the Gentile churches were debtors to the poor saints at Jerusalem. Why? Because it was from the Jerusalem believers that the gospel had spread. Since they had ministered the spiritual gift of salvation to the Gentile churches, the Gentile churches were now in debt to help the Jerusalem believers in their physical need.

Our task is to always meet the needs (true needs) of local saints before we move out to meet the needs of those in other nations. If we do not meet the needs of our brothers who live next door, how can we expect God to bless us in trying to meet the needs of those in other countries?

> > **In everything I did, I showed you that by this kind of hard work we must help the weak, remembering the words the Lord Jesus himself said: 'It is more blessed to give than to receive.'" (Acts 20:35)**
> > **Share with God's people who are in need. Practice hospitality. (Rom 12:13)**
> > **Therefore, as we have opportunity, let us do good to all people, especially to those who belong to the family of believers. (Gal 6:10)**
> > **Command those who are rich in this present world not to be arrogant nor to put their hope in wealth, which is so uncertain, but to put their hope in God, who richly provides us with everything for our enjoyment. Command them to do good, to be rich in good deeds, and to be generous and willing to share. (1 Tim 6:17-18)**
> > **And do not forget to do good and to share with others, for with such sacrifices God is pleased. (Heb 13:16)**
> > **This is how we know what love is: Jesus Christ laid down his life for us. And we ought to lay down our lives for our brothers. (1 John 3:16)**

Thought 1. Believers are debtors to help other believers throughout the world when they face critical needs. Why? Because genuine believers are ministering to each other through their daily prayers and other spiritual gifts. Genuine believers are the recipients of each other's prayers and gifts as they minister to each other daily through the presence and power of God's Spirit.

4 (15:28-29) **Gospel—Minister**: the minister of God serves in the full measure of the blessing of Christ. Note two significant points.

1. Paul kept his worldwide vision even in the face of the pressing needs of the Jerusalem believers. He intended to evangelize Rome and Spain, and he would not let the desperate plight of the present need—as desperate as it was—deter his worldwide vision.

Thought 1. What a lesson for most of us! How long ago would the world have been reached for Christ if we had *kept* the world before our face despite the pressing needs of our present situations?

Therefore go and make disciples of all nations, baptizing them in the name of the Father and of the Son and of the Holy Spirit, and teaching them to obey everything I have commanded you. And surely I am with you always, to the very end of the age." (Mat 28:19-20)

He said to them, "Go into all the world and preach the good news to all creation. (Mark 16:15)

But you will receive power when the Holy Spirit comes on you; and you will be my witnesses in Jerusalem, and in all Judea and Samaria, and to the ends of the earth." (Acts 1:8)

As surely as I live, declares the Sovereign LORD, because my flock lacks a shepherd and so has been plundered and has become food for all the wild animals, and because my shepherds did not search for my flock but cared for themselves rather than for my flock, (Ezek 34:8)

2. It is the *gospel* or "blessing of Christ" that Paul served. There is no other message or truth that can meet the desperate need of man for life—life that is both abundant and eternal. Paul knew this; therefore, he was gripped with the burning zeal to proclaim Christ.

I am obligated both to Greeks and non-Greeks, both to the wise and the foolish. That is why I am so eager to preach the gospel also to you who are at Rome. (Rom 1:14-15)

Yet when I preach the gospel, I cannot boast, for I am compelled to preach. Woe to me if I do not preach the gospel! (1 Cor 9:16)

"For God so loved the world that he gave his one and only Son, that whoever believes in him shall not perish but have eternal life. (John 3:16)

"I tell you the truth, whoever hears my word and believes him who sent me has eternal life and will not be condemned; he has crossed over from death to life. (John 5:24)

Jesus said to her, "I am the resurrection and the life. He who believes in me will live, even though he dies; and whoever lives and believes in me will never die. Do you believe this?" (John 11:25-26)

He himself bore our sins in his body on the tree, so that we might die to sins and live for righteousness; by his wounds you have been healed. (1 Pet 2:24)

For Christ died for sins once for all, the righteous for the unrighteous, to bring you to God. He was put to death in the body but made alive by the Spirit, (1 Pet 3:18)

5 (15:30-32) **Prayer**: the minister of God begs for much prayer. Note: he does not request prayer for selfish reasons, but for the sake of the Lord Jesus Christ. Paul's one

ambition in life was for Jesus Christ to be praised, worshipped, and served by all men. It was for Christ's sake—for the cause of Christ and His kingdom—that Paul wanted people praying for him. Paul needed prayer in three areas in particular.

1. He needed deliverance, to be rescued from unbelievers. Unbelievers were constantly rejecting, ridiculing, mocking, abusing, threatening, and persecuting him—even while he was sharing the glorious news of eternal life with them.

Thought 1. The fact that men reject the glorious truth of eternal life is shocking to some people. However, we must keep in mind why men react against the gospel. They are unwilling to give their lives to Jesus Christ as Lord: to sacrifice all they are and have to serve Him and to meet the desperate needs of a world reeling under the weight of starvation, disease, sin, and suffering.

2. He needed prayer that his ministry would be accepted by the saints. Unfortunately and tragically, too many believers do not accept the ministry of all of God's servants. The servant may be a lay teacher or a professional preacher—it does not matter—too many ministers are opposed and rejected by believers for selfish and sinful reasons. Paul was constantly being opposed by carnal believers. He desperately needed prayer: prayer that the believers to whom he ministered would understand his call and ministry and understand why God had placed him with them. The churches to whom he ministered needed to receive his spiritual gifts and to grow under his ministry.

3. He needed prayer that he might be allowed to carry out his worldwide vision and be refreshed by believers where he was called to go.

And pray in the Spirit on all occasions with all kinds of prayers and requests. With this in mind, be alert and always keep on praying for all the saints. (Eph 6:18)

Devote yourselves to prayer, being watchful and thankful. (Col 4:2)

Pray continually; (1 Th 5:17)

6 (15:33) **Prayer**: the minister of God sets the example of intercessory prayer. This is striking: while in the midst of requesting prayer, Paul broke out into prayer for the Roman believers. The prayer was only one request, but it was forceful and meaningful: "The God of peace be with you all. Amen." Note these facts:

⇒ What every man needs is peace: peace within and peace without.

⇒ Peace comes from God: if men want true peace, they must seek it in God.

⇒ God is the God of peace: peace is of His very nature.

⇒ If man could make only one request in life, the request should be to receive the God of peace. This is the one request Paul made for the Roman believers. Peace does not come from a genie in a bottle nor from the sorceries and sciences of this world. Peace comes only from the Creator of the world, from the God of peace Himself.

	CHAPTER 16 **C. The Messenger's Commendations: One of God's Halls of Fame, 16:1-16**	apostles, and they were in Christ before I was. 8 Greet Ampliatus, whom I love in the Lord. 9 Greet Urbanus, our fellow worker in Christ, and my dear friend Stachys.	**6 Ampliatus: One loved** **7 Urbanus: A fellow-worker** **8 Stachys: A dear friend**
1 Phoebe: A Christian sister who deserved to be welcomed & befriended	I commend to you our sister Phoebe, a servant of the church in Cenchrea. 2 I ask you to receive her in the Lord in a way worthy of the saints and to give her any help she may need from you, for she has been a great help to many people, including me. 3 Greet Priscilla and Aquila, my fellow workers in Christ Jesus. 4 They risked their lives for me. Not only I but all the churches of the Gentiles are grateful to them. 5 Greet also the church that meets at their house. Greet my dear friend Epenetus, who was the first convert to Christ in the province of Asia. 6 Greet Mary, who worked very hard for you. 7 Greet Andronicus and Junias, my relatives who have been in prison with me. They are outstanding among the	10 Greet Apelles, tested and approved in Christ. Greet those who belong to the household of Aristobulus. 11 Greet Herodion, my relative. Greet those in the household of Narcissus who are in the Lord. 12 Greet Tryphena and Tryphosa, those women who work hard in the Lord. Greet my dear friend Persis, another woman who has worked very hard in the Lord. 13 Greet Rufus, chosen in the Lord, and his mother, who has been a mother to me, too. 14 Greet Asyncritus, Phlegon, Hermes, Patrobas, Hermas and the brothers with them. 15 Greet Philologus, Julia, Nereus and his sister, and Olympas and all the saints with them. 16 Greet one another with a holy kiss. All the churches of Christ send greetings.	**9 Apelles: Tested & approved** **10 Aristobulus' household: Slaves serving a true Master** **11 Herodion: A relative of Paul** **12 Narcissus' household: Enslaved "in the Lord"** **13 Tryphena & Tryphosa: Two ladies who labored much & worked hard** **14 Persis: A beloved believer who worked hard** **15 Rufus: A saintly man** **16 Rufus' mother: A mother to God's servants** **17 The unknown servants: Unknown but faithful in the fellowship of the church**
2 Priscilla & Aquila: A hospitable couple, who opened their hearts & home—even at the risk of death			
3 Epenetus: A courageous first convert			
4 Mary: A lady who labored much & worked hard			
5 Andronicus & Junias: Early converts imprisoned with Paul			

DIVISION IX

THE MESSENGER OF GOD AND HIS PLANS, 15:14-16:27

C. The Messenger's Commendations: One of God's Halls of Fame, 16:1-16

(16:1-16) **Introduction—Church—Christian Brotherhood**: this is one of God's Halls of Fame. It gives a list of some of the believers in the Roman church and their outstanding Christian traits. Each name stands as a challenge to every believer to follow the Lord more closely than ever before. Throughout the passage note the emphasis upon a warm, tender heart. A local church should be a friendly, welcoming church—an open, gracious church. There should be no strangers in the Lord's church. The church should *guard against becoming a closed society*, a body of *cliques*, shut up only *to themselves*.

1. Phoebe: a Christian sister who deserved to be welcomed and befriended (v.1-2).
2. Priscilla and Aquila: a hospitable couple, who opened their hearts and home—even at the risk of death (v.3-4).
3. Epenetus: a courageous first convert (v.5).
4. Mary: a lady who labored much and worked hard (v.6).
5. Andronicus and Junias: early converts imprisoned with Paul (v.7).
6. Ampliatus: one loved (v.8).
7. Urbanus: a fellow-worker (v.9).
8. Stachys: A dear friend (v.9).
9. Apelles: tested and approved (v.10).

10. Aristobulus' household: slaves serving a true Master (v.10).
11. Herodion: a relative of Paul (v.11).
12. Narcissus' household: enslaved "in the Lord" (v.11).
13. Tryphena and Tryphosa: two ladies who labored and worked hard (v.12).
14. Persis: a beloved believer who worked hard (v.12).
15. Rufus: a saintly man (v.13).
16. Rufus' mother: a mother to God's servants (v.13).
17. The unknown servants: unknown but faithful in the fellowship of the church (v.14-16).

1 (16:1-2) **Phoebe—Deaconess**: there was Phoebe, a Christian sister who deserved to be welcomed and befriended. Note these facts about her.

1. The name Phoebe is one of the names of the goddess Diana; therefore, Phoebe was probably a convert from a heathen religion.

2. Paul calls her "our sister," meaning a sister in the faith of Christ. She was a woman loved by Paul and the believers of her church, highly esteemed as a genuine sister of the faith.

3. Phoebe was a *servant* of the church at Cenchrea, which was the seaport of Corinth (see DEEPER STUDY # 1, *Cenchrea*—Acts 18:18). Note the word "servant"

(diakonon). It is the word deacon or deaconess. Does this mean that Phoebe held the official office of a deacon in the early church? Note closely what the Scripture says and it seems to be saying that she did: "Our sister Phoebe, a servant (deaconess) *of the church.*" The words "of the church" (tes ekklesias) modify servant or deaconess. Phoebe was a servant or a deaconess *of the church which is at Cenchrea.* Paul is not saying she is a servant of the Lord to all of God's people in general. She was, of course, just as all believers are. But this is not what Paul is saying. He is very clear about the matter: she is an official "servant [deaconess] of the church in Cenchrea."

The separation of the sexes in that day would almost necessitate some official office of women to minister to the women of the church. This would be especially true in the area of ministry where women would be alone, for example, in visiting and caring for the sick and in distributing food and clothing among the needful.

4. Phoebe deserved to be welcomed and befriended in the Lord. There are two reasons for this.

    a. Believers are always to welcome and befriend other believers. The church is not an exclusive club nor a society of cliques. It is to be a welcoming center for all strangers and neighbors, whether saint or sinner.

    b. Phoebe had been a "great help" (prostatis) to many, including Paul himself. The words *great help* mean that she protected, looked after, and provided for people. Phoebe was a woman who ministered to the needs of many. Apparently she helped and looked after the welfare of any who had need.

Thought 1. The great lessons to be learned from Phoebe are twofold:

    ⇒ We should be servants of the church.
    ⇒ We should be constantly ministering to all who are in need.

> **I was eyes to the blind and feet to the lame. (Job 29:15)**

> **She opens her arms to the poor and extends her hands to the needy. (Prov 31:20)**

> **The Sovereign LORD has given me an instructed tongue, to know the word that sustains the weary. He wakens me morning by morning, wakens my ear to listen like one being taught. (Isa 50:4)**

> **"Then the King will say to those on his right, 'Come, you who are blessed by my Father; take your inheritance, the kingdom prepared for you since the creation of the world. For I was hungry and you gave me something to eat, I was thirsty and you gave me something to drink, I was a stranger and you invited me in, I needed clothes and you clothed me, I was sick and you looked after me, I was in prison and you came to visit me.' (Mat 25:34-36)**

> **And also some women who had been cured of evil spirits and diseases: Mary (called Magdalene) from whom seven demons had come out; Joanna the wife of Cuza, the manager of Herod's household; Susanna; and many others. These women were helping to support them out of their own means. (Luke 8:2-3)**

> **And is well known for her good deeds, such as bringing up children, showing hospitality, washing the feet of the saints, helping those in trouble and devoting herself to all kinds of good deeds. (1 Tim 5:10)**

2 (16:3-4) **Priscilla—Aquila—Hospitality—Church, in Homes**: there was Priscilla and Aquila, a hospitable couple who opened their hearts and home even at the risk of death. Priscilla and Aquila were close companions of Paul. They were originally residents of Rome. But the Roman emperor, Claudius, had the Jews banished from Rome in A.D. 52. Priscilla and Aquila moved to Corinth. They were the couple who opened their home to Paul when he first entered Corinth. They were also the couple who went into business with Paul as tent-makers. They later traveled with Paul to Ephesus where they settled (Acts 18:18). The chief characteristic of this couple was an open heart and an open house. Wherever we find them, we find that their home was the center for Christian worship and fellowship. (See note and Deeper Study # 2—Acts 18:2.)

1. They received the young preacher, Apollos, into their home to instruct him in the faith (Acts 18:24-26).

2. They had a church meeting in their home in Ephesus (1 Cor.16:19).

3. They had another church meeting in their home in Rome (Ro.16:13).

4. Paul called them "*my* fellow workers in Christ Jesus" (Ro.16:3), and he explained what he meant. They risked their lives in order to save him. This probably refers to the attacks made upon Paul and the church in Corinth (Acts 18:6, 12-17), or to some other severe persecution that took place in Ephesus (1 Cor.15:32; cp. 2 Cor.1:8). In either case, this godly couple, Priscilla and Aquila, risked their lives in order to save the life of one of God's dear servants, Paul himself.

Thought 1. Note several lessons.
1) A believer should have an open home and show forth a testimony of hospitality. (See Deeper Study # 1, *Church in Houses*—Lk.9:4 for more discussion.)

> **Share with God's people who are in need. Practice hospitality. (Rom 12:13)**
> **Rather he must be hospitable, one who loves what is good, who is self-controlled, upright, holy and disciplined. (Titus 1:8)**
> **Do not forget to entertain strangers, for by so doing some people have entertained angels without knowing it. (Heb 13:2)**
> **Offer hospitality to one another without grumbling. (1 Pet 4:9)**

2) A believer should be a helper or a fellow-worker and laborer in the ministry of Christ Jesus.

> **Then he said to his disciples, "The harvest is plentiful but the workers are few. Ask the Lord of the harvest, therefore, to send out workers into his harvest field." (Mat 9:37-38)**
> **Do you not say, 'Four months more and then the harvest'? I tell you, open your**

eyes and look at the fields! They are ripe for harvest. Even now the reaper draws his wages, even now he harvests the crop for eternal life, so that the sower and the reaper may be glad together. (John 4:35-36)

Therefore, as we have opportunity, let us do good to all people, especially to those who belong to the family of believers. (Gal 6:10)

So we say with confidence, "The Lord is my helper; I will not be afraid. What can man do to me?" (Heb 13:6)

Remember this: Whoever turns a sinner from the error of his way will save him from death and cover over a multitude of sins. (James 5:20)

The fruit of the righteous is a tree of life, and he who wins souls is wise. (Prov 11:30)

3) A believer should humble and sacrifice himself for the sake of other believers.

For whoever wants to save his life will lose it, but whoever loses his life for me will find it. (Mat 16:25)

Nobody should seek his own good, but the good of others. (1 Cor 10:24)

Each of you should look not only to your own interests, but also to the interests of others. (Phil 2:4)

3 (16:5) **Epenetus—Courage:** there was Epenetus, a courageous first convert. He was probably a member of the *household of Stephanas* whose house is said to have been the first fruits of Achaia (1 Cor.16:15). It took raw courage to be the first convert to Christ in the midst of a pagan society. Just imagine the changed life, the surrendering of himself to Jesus as Lord, and the giving of all he was and had to the Lord's cause. Just imagine the attitude and reactions of his neighbors, friends and fellow workers: the possible questioning, misunderstanding, ridicule, mockery, withdrawal, isolation. Epenetus was unquestionably a man of remarkable courage.

"Whoever acknowledges me before men, I will also acknowledge him before my Father in heaven. But whoever disowns me before men, I will disown him before my Father in heaven. (Mat 10:32-33)

If anyone is ashamed of me and my words in this adulterous and sinful generation, the Son of Man will be ashamed of him when he comes in his Father's glory with the holy angels." (Mark 8:38)

Then he said to them all: "If anyone would come after me, he must deny himself and take up his cross daily and follow me. (Luke 9:23)

Without being frightened in any way by those who oppose you. This is a sign to them that they will be destroyed, but that you will be saved—and that by God. (Phil 1:28)

4 (16:6) **Mary:** there was Mary, a lady who labored much and worked hard. Note that Mary was a member of the Roman church. Paul had never been to the Roman church; therefore, Mary had ministered to him and his fellow-

workers someplace else. In fact, she had ministered so *much* to his corps of workers that Paul commends her for this labor rather than for her ministry to the church. We have no idea what she did for *Paul's team*, but whatever it was, it was an effective ministry that required *much* diligent labor.

Therefore, my dear brothers, stand firm. Let nothing move you. Always give yourselves fully to the work of the Lord, because you know that your labor in the Lord is not in vain. (1 Cor 15:58)

Serve wholeheartedly, as if you were serving the Lord, not men, (Eph 6:7)

Therefore, since we are receiving a kingdom that cannot be shaken, let us be thankful, and so worship God acceptably with reverence and awe, (Heb 12:28)

5 (16:7) **Andronicus—Junias:** these two believers were early converts who were imprisoned with Paul. They were perhaps man and wife. The facts given about them are interesting, for they reveal that Paul had some relatives who were also believers.

1. They were relatives of Paul.
2. They were imprisoned with Paul at some point in his ministry. This indicates…
   - that they were genuine believers willing to stand up for their faith.
   - that they were a part of Paul's mission team, at least for some time.
3. They were known and highly esteemed by the apostles of Christ.
4. They were believers before Paul. This means they were among the very earliest believers, having been converted before Stephen's martyrdom (Acts 7:54-60).

Thought 1. Did these relatives of Paul have an impact upon Paul's conversion? Were they witnessing to him during his days of soul-searching and reaction against the early church? Was the fact that some of his family were becoming Christians arousing bitterness in Paul? Was this part of the reason for his flaming vengeance against Christianity? (See notes—Acts 8:1-4; 9:1-2 for more discussion.) Whatever the case, we should always be witnessing to our family and relatives.

And the things you have heard me say in the presence of many witnesses entrust to reliable men who will also be qualified to teach others. (2 Tim 2:2)

But in your hearts set apart Christ as Lord. Always be prepared to give an answer to everyone who asks you to give the reason for the hope that you have. But do this with gentleness and respect, (1 Pet 3:15)

We proclaim to you what we have seen and heard, so that you also may have fellowship with us. And our fellowship is with the Father and with his Son, Jesus Christ. (1 John 1:3)

Thought 2. We must be willing to stand up for Christ and to bear testimony for Him, even if it means imprisonment and death.

Reflect on what I am saying, for the Lord will give you insight into all this. Remember Jesus Christ, raised from the dead, descended from David. This is my gospel, (2 Tim 2:7-8)

6 (16:8) **Ampliatus**: this believer simply has the testimony of being loved. But note, he is "loved" by a minister of the gospel; and he is greatly loved, for he is called "whom I love." The fact that God has his name recorded as "loved" in the Holy Scripture indicates that he was a man of remarkable love, a man who greatly loved others and who was greatly loved by others.

"A new command I give you: Love one another. As I have loved you, so you must love one another. By this all men will know that you are my disciples, if you love one another." (John 13:34-35)

Love must be sincere. Hate what is evil; cling to what is good. (Rom 12:9)

May the Lord make your love increase and overflow for each other and for everyone else, just as ours does for you. (1 Th 3:12)

Now that you have purified yourselves by obeying the truth so that you have sincere love for your brothers, love one another deeply, from the heart. (1 Pet 1:22)

7 (16:9) **Urbanus**: this believer was a helper, that is, a fellow-worker in the ministry. Three things in particular are noteworthy.

1. Urbanus was a person who worked side by side with God's minister, Paul.

2. Urbanus was a person of unusual diligence. The very fact that he would be laboring with Paul and would be mentioned as a fellow-worker by Paul indicates this.

3. Urbanus was a person of unusual faithfulness who was loyal to Christ wherever he traveled. Remember: he met Paul while on a trip away from Rome. He could have been a tradesman or a salesman; nevertheless, whatever his reason for traveling, he did not become entangled again with the world, joining the crowd in its worldliness. He was faithful in serving and witnessing for his Lord wherever he was.

"Therefore come out from them and be separate, says the Lord. Touch no unclean thing, and I will receive you." "I will be a Father to you, and you will be my sons and daughters, says the Lord Almighty." (2 Cor 6:17-18)

It is for freedom that Christ has set us free. Stand firm, then, and do not let yourselves be burdened again by a yoke of slavery [of sin]. (Gal 5:1)

Whatever happens, conduct yourselves in a manner worthy of the gospel of Christ. Then, whether I come and see you or only hear about you in my absence, I will know that you stand firm in one spirit, contending as one man for the faith of the gospel (Phil 1:27)

Endure hardship with us like a good soldier of Christ Jesus. No one serving as a soldier gets involved in civilian affairs—he wants to please his commanding officer. (2 Tim 2:3-4)

Therefore, dear friends, since you already know this, be on your guard so that you may not be carried away by the error of lawless men and fall from your secure position. (2 Pet 3:17)

Do not love the world or anything in the world. If anyone loves the world, the love of the Father is not in him. For everything in the world—the cravings of sinful man, the lust of his eyes and the boasting of what he has and does—comes not from the Father but from the world. (1 John 2:15-16)

8 (16:9) **Stachys**: this believer is called "my dear friend" by Paul. He was a believer who was characterized by the greatest of all traits and qualities: love founded upon a deep friendship.

Thought 1. Just imagine the strength of a man whose character is said to be so strong that his dominant feature is *love*.

Love is patient, love is kind. It does not envy, it does not boast, it is not proud. It is not rude, it is not self-seeking, it is not easily angered, it keeps no record of wrongs. Love does not delight in evil but rejoices with the truth. It always protects, always trusts, always hopes, always perseveres. (1 Cor 13:4-7)

9 (16:10) **Apelles**: this was a believer who had been tested and approved as faithful. Apparently, Apelles had undergone some extreme suffering and had stood against it, proving his loyalty beyond question. Note: the trial and suffering had been so severe that it had made a lasting impression upon Paul and is mentioned in Scripture.

Thought 1. So far as we know Apelles was a lay believer. The fact that he was tested so fiercely shows that God will meet our need in the midst of suffering—if we will do but one thing: be faithful and loyal. We are to stand fast against suffering, trusting the presence of God's Spirit to carry us through the trial.

No temptation [trial] has seized you except what is common to man. And God is faithful; he will not let you be tempted beyond what you can bear. But when you are tempted, he will also provide a way out so that you can stand up under it. (1 Cor 10:13)

Praise be to the God and Father of our Lord Jesus Christ, the Father of compassion and the God of all comfort, who comforts us in all our troubles, so that we can comfort those in any trouble with the comfort we ourselves have received from God. (2 Cor 1:3-4)

But we have this treasure in jars of clay to show that this all-surpassing power is from God and not from us. (2 Cor 4:7)

Blessed is the man who perseveres under trial, because when he has stood the test, he will receive the crown of life that

God has promised to those who love him. (James 1:12)

In this you greatly rejoice, though now for a little while you may have had to suffer grief in all kinds of trials. These have come so that your faith—of greater worth than gold, which perishes even though refined by fire—may be proved genuine and may result in praise, glory and honor when Jesus Christ is revealed. (1 Pet 1:6-7)

Dear friends, do not be surprised at the painful trial you are suffering, as though something strange were happening to you. But rejoice that you participate in the sufferings of Christ, so that you may be overjoyed when his glory is revealed. (1 Pet 4:12-13)

10 (16:10) **Aristobulus**: the believers being greeted in this statement were slaves who were now serving the true Master, the Lord Jesus Christ. Aristobulus was the name of *Herod the Great's grandson*. This could possibly be a reference to his slaves. The two names surrounding Aristobulus' name would indicate this. Apelles is the Greek name that a Jewish slave would take when enslaved, and Herodion is a name that would be commonly used by a person of Herod's household. At any rate, the charge is to the slaves of some master, probably of royal rank. Since coming to know Christ, they were first and foremost enslaved by Christ, the true Royal Master.

Serve wholeheartedly, as if you were serving the Lord, not men, because you know that the Lord will reward everyone for whatever good he does, whether he is slave or free. (Eph 6:7-8)

Whatever you do, work at it with all your heart, as working for the Lord, not for men, since you know that you will receive an inheritance from the Lord as a reward. It is the Lord Christ you are serving. (Col 3:23-24)

11 (16:11) **Herodion**: this man was another relative of Paul who was a believer (cp. v.7). Others who are mentioned were *Jews*, but are not called relatives by Paul. What effect did this relative have upon Paul's conversion? Again the answer is unknown, but the fact that we should be witnessing to our relatives is driven home to our hearts and minds.

For we cannot help speaking about what we have seen and heard." (Acts 4:20)

It is written: "I believed; therefore I have spoken." With that same spirit of faith we also believe and therefore speak, (2 Cor 4:13)

12 (16:11) **Narcissus**: the believers in this household were the enslaved "in the Lord." Note: not all of the household were believers. Paul greets only those who were believers. The phrase "in the Lord" is in contrast to the phrase "in the world" (cp. 1 Jn.2:15-16). It is probably a deliberate wording to contrast the difference between the laboring slaves and their wealthy master. *Narcissus was probably the wealthy secretary to the Emperor Claudius.*

He determined the appointments of the Emperor and amassed a great fortune from kickbacks. (William Barclay. *The Letter to the Romans*, p.233.)

The fact to note is this: these believers were so enslaved by Christ that they stood up for Him even in the midst of a divided household. Nothing can pose any more of a temptation and threat to one's faith than one's own household when it is filled with unbelievers. The indication is that these believers within this household were faithful to Christ, so loyal that their commitment to Christ merited being recorded in Scripture.

Then Jesus said to his disciples, "If anyone would come after me, he must deny himself and take up his cross and follow me. (Mat 16:24)

"If anyone comes to me and does not hate his father and mother, his wife and children, his brothers and sisters—yes, even his own life—he cannot be my disciple. And anyone who does not carry his cross and follow me cannot be my disciple. (Luke 14:26-27)

In the same way, any of you who does not give up everything he has cannot be my disciple. (Luke 14:33)

What is more, I consider everything a loss compared to the surpassing greatness of knowing Christ Jesus my Lord, for whose sake I have lost all things. I consider them rubbish, that I may gain Christ (Phil 3:8)

Do not love the world or anything in the world. If anyone loves the world, the love of the Father is not in him. For everything in the world—the cravings of sinful man, the lust of his eyes and the boasting of what he has and does—comes not from the Father but from the world. (1 John 2:15-16)

13 (16:12) **Tryphena—Tryphosa**: these two dear ladies worked hard: and labored much in the Lord. The name Tryphena means *dainty* and the name Tryphosa means *delicate*. The word "work" or "labor" means to work to the *point of exhaustion*, toiling to the point of collapse. The point is that the two dainty and delicate ladies were working like horses for the Lord and His church (cp. vs.6, 12b).

In the same way, let your light shine before men, that they may see your good deeds and praise your Father in heaven. (Mat 5:16)

And let us consider how we may spur one another on toward love and good deeds. (Heb 10:24)

14 (16:12) **Persis**: this was a beloved believer who worked hard in the Lord. Note that two traits are recorded in God's Hall of Fame about her:

⇒ She was a dear friend: a woman of such love and ministry that the believers looked upon her as the "beloved Persis."

⇒ She labored and worked ever so diligently for her Lord: witnessing, ministering, and helping in every way she could.

Command them to do good, to be rich in good deeds, and to be generous and willing to share. (1 Tim 6:18)

In everything set them an example by doing what is good. In your teaching show integrity, seriousness and soundness of speech that cannot be condemned, so that those who oppose you may be ashamed because they have nothing bad to say about us. (Titus 2:7-8)

We continually remember before our God and Father your work produced by faith, your labor prompted by love, and your endurance inspired by hope in our Lord Jesus Christ. (1 Th 1:3)

Turn from evil and do good; seek peace and pursue it. (Psa 34:14)

15 (16:13) **Rufus**: this believer is said to be a *saintly man*. Note the word *chosen*. Paul does not say that Rufus was chosen *by the Lord*, but *in the Lord*. The emphasis is not election, but tenderness, preciousness, warmth—an intimate relationship. Rufus was a man who lived ever so close to Christ. He had an intimate, personal relationship and communion with Christ. He was known as a saintly man—a man who was totally set apart unto the Lord. Note that Rufus was probably the son of Simon the Cyrenian who carried the cross for Jesus (see note—Mk.15:21). Our imaginations can easily picture the family of Simon along side the road watching their husband and father carry the cross for Jesus up the hill of Calvary. The impact of the crucifixion would forever change their lives by leading to their conversion.

And we, who with unveiled faces all reflect the Lord's glory, are being transformed into his likeness with ever-increasing glory, which comes from the Lord, who is the Spirit. (2 Cor 3:18)

Since we have these promises, dear friends, let us purify ourselves from everything that contaminates body and spirit, perfecting holiness out [being saintly, sanctified] of reverence for God. (2 Cor 7:1)

Make every effort to live in peace with all men and to be holy; without holiness no one will see the Lord. (Heb 12:14)

For it is written: "Be holy, because I am holy." (1 Pet 1:16)

16 (16:13) **Rufus' Mother**: this dear lady was a mother to God's servants. Note: Paul calls her his *mother*, not literally, but *in the Lord*. On several occasions, perhaps many occasions, she had cared for Paul just as a mother cares for her son. When Paul needed a mother's comfort and care, presence and love, sharing and advice—he went to the mother of Rufus if she was close by.

Thought 1. How many mothers live so close to the Lord that Paul would go to them for a mother's comfort and love and advice?

For whoever does the will of my Father in heaven is my brother and sister and mother." (Mat 12:50)

Then they can train the younger women to love their husbands and children, (Titus 2:4)

Both the one who makes men holy and those who are made holy are of the same family. So Jesus is not ashamed to call them brothers. (Heb 2:11)

17 (16:14-16) **Believers—Hall of Fame**: there are the unknown servants of God—believers who are unknown, but faithful in the fellowship of the church.

⇒ Note the words: "the brothers with them" (v.14).
⇒ Note also the words: "and all the saints with them" (v.15).

Apparently two different groups or congregations are being greeted. The stress is upon the unity and faithfulness and fellowship of the believers. Not all believers are leaders, nor would all believers be counted worthy of a Hall of Fame while on this earth. But in heaven the situation will be different. God will look upon the heart, and every person will be written in the Book of Life, God's eternal Hall of Fame. Only two conditions exist for a person to be written therein:

⇒ Receiving Jesus Christ as Savior and Lord.

Yet to all who received him, to those who believed in his name, he gave the right to become children of God— (John 1:12)

Here I am! I stand at the door and knock. If anyone hears my voice and opens the door, I will come in and eat with him, and he with me. (Rev 3:20)

⇒ Being faithful to the Lord and to the fellowship of His people (His true church).

Let us not give up meeting together, as some are in the habit of doing, but let us encourage one another—and all the more as you see the Day approaching. (Heb 10:25)

If anyone's name was not found written in the book of life, he was thrown into the lake of fire. (Rev 20:15)

Then I saw a new heaven and a new earth, for the first heaven and the first earth had passed away, and there was no longer any sea. Nothing impure will ever enter it, nor will anyone who does what is shameful or deceitful, but only those whose names are written in the Lamb's book of life. (Rev 21:1, 27)

	D. The Messenger's Final Warning: Mark Divisive People, 16:17-20	their own appetites. By smooth talk and flattery they deceive the minds of naive people.	own desires c. Because they use smooth talk & flattering words to deceive
1 Mark divisive people & avoid them a. Because they cause division & are stumbling blocks	17 I urge you, brothers, to watch out for those who cause divisions and put obstacles in your way that are contrary to the teaching you have learned. Keep away from them.	19 Everyone has heard about your obedience, so I am full of joy over you; but I want you to be wise about what is good, and innocent about what is evil.	**2 Mark what is good, & untainted with evil** a. Because you have been obedient until now b. Because you must be wise to know what is good
b. Because they do not serve Christ, but their	18 For such people are not serving our Lord Christ, but	20 The God of peace will soon crush Satan under your feet. The grace of our Lord Jesus be with you.	c. Because God shall soon give victory over Satan

DIVISION IX

THE MESSENGER OF GOD AND HIS PLANS, 15:14-16:27

D. The Messenger's Final Warning: Mark Divisive People, 16:17-20

(16:17-20) **Introduction**: divisiveness and evil are always a threat to the local church. The reason can be simply stated: people have problems, even believers. The fact that we live in a corrupt and depraved world means that people become disgruntled, disappointed, unhappy, selfish, sinful, and in some cases evil. Even the strongest believers become contaminated with corruption by having to live in the very air of a sinful world. It is because of this that Paul warns the church and its believers: mark divisive people, for they are a constant threat to the church.

1. Mark divisive people and avoid them (v.17-18).
2. Mark what is good, and untainted with evil (v.19-20).

1 (16:17-18) **Teachers, False—Division—Stumbling Block**: mark divisive people and avoid them. Note: this warning abruptly cuts into Paul's greeting to the Roman church. Paul is greeting various believers in the church whom he has met on his travels throughout the world. All of a sudden, he interrupts his greeting and issues a severe warning. The abrupt interruption *is not an afterthought*; it is the final exhortation needed by a strong church—an exhortation against an event that is bound to happen: the seeping in of divisive people. A divisive person is a person who...

- grumbles
- complains
- criticizes
- murmurs
- gossips
- is argumentative
- causes strife
- acts out of pride, ambition, or selfishness
- is unloving
- teaches a different doctrine

The most effective way for Satan to get a foothold into a strong church is to quietly and insidiously move a divisive person into some teaching or leadership position where he can influence immature believers. Paul knew this, so he left the warning until the end of his letter. It is a warning that must be heeded by a strong church if it is to keep its witness for the Lord.

There are three reasons why a divisive person must be marked and avoided.

1. A divisive person causes division and lays stumbling blocks in the way of growth. Note exactly what is said: a divisive person acts "contrary to the doctrine which [believers] have learned." He causes "divisions and obstacles."

⇒ The word "division" (dichostasias) means standing apart, being separate, causing cleavage.
⇒ The word "obstacles" (skandala) means laying a stumbling block in someone's way or causing someone to fall.

a. The divisive person acts "contrary to the teaching you [believers] have learned." The teaching of God and of Christ is simply stated:

And this is his command: to believe in the name of his Son, Jesus Christ, and to love one another as he commanded us. (1 John 3:23)

Genuine believers have trusted God's Son. They have accepted Christ as their Lord, giving all they are and have to Him; and they do love one another, having committed their lives to carry the teaching of Christ to the world.

However, this is not true with a divisive person. He acts *contrary* to the teaching of God and of Christ. He opposes...

- the Lordship of Christ.
- the teaching of Christ.
- the love of believers.
- the mission of reaching the world with the gospel: the glorious news of life in Christ, life that is both abundant and eternal.

b. Avoid them because of the terrible devastation that a divisive person can do to the strength of a church. The term "keep away" (ekklinate) means to shun, to turn away from, to remove oneself from. Get away from them and have absolutely nothing to do with them.

c. Watch the divisive person. The word "watch" (skopeite) means to keep one's eye on, to look at, to observe, to focus upon, to contemplate, to scrutinize. Note: it is the divisive person himself who is to be *avoided and turned* away from, not just his sin. We are not to have anything to do with a divisive person...

- for we give the appearance of approving what he is doing.
- for we run the risk of being influenced and stumbling over what he says and does.

267

"Woe to the world because of the things that cause people to sin! Such things must come, but woe to the man through whom they come! (Mat 18:7)

"And if anyone causes one of these little ones who believe in me to sin, it would be better for him to be thrown into the sea with a large millstone tied around his neck. (Mark 9:42)

Jesus knew their thoughts and said to them: "Any kingdom divided against itself will be ruined, and a house divided against itself will fall. (Luke 11:17)

I appeal to you, brothers, in the name of our Lord Jesus Christ, that all of you agree with one another so that there may be no divisions among you and that you may be perfectly united in mind and thought. (1 Cor 1:10)

You are still worldly. For since there is jealousy and quarreling among you, are you not worldly? Are you not acting like mere men? (1 Cor 3:3)

So whether you eat or drink or whatever you do, do it all for the glory of God. Do not cause anyone to stumble, whether Jews, Greeks or the church of God— (1 Cor 10:31-32)

We put no stumbling block in anyone's path, so that our ministry will not be discredited. (2 Cor 6:3)

Whatever happens, conduct yourselves in a manner worthy of the gospel of Christ. Then, whether I come and see you or only hear about you in my absence, I will know that you stand firm in one spirit, contending as one man for the faith of the gospel (Phil 1:27)

2. A divisive person does not serve Christ, but his own desires. The word "appetites" (koiliai) means the stomach and its physical appetites. A divisive person is gripped by...

- selfish desires
- base ambition
- personal urges
- physical appetites
- wanting his own way
- getting what he wants

Note: Scripture clearly says that divisive persons do not serve Christ. They call themselves *Christians*, but their Lord is not Christ. They are not committed to His honor and glory and mission, but to themselves—to getting and doing what they want. The divisive person is still given over to the things of this, unspiritual, carnal, sensual, and secular world.

For, as I have often told you before and now say again even with tears, many live as enemies of the cross of Christ. Their destiny is destruction, their god is their stomach, and their glory is in their shame. Their mind is on earthly things. (Phil 3:18-19)

3. A divisive person uses talk and flatter to deceive. He uses smooth, persuasive, and plausible words to lead peo-

ple to take sides with him. He talks and acts godly, and he shows interest and concern for those whom he wants to convince. But note what Scripture says: the motive of the divisive person is to deceive. He wants others...

- to think as he thinks
- to believe as he believes
- to walk as he walks
- to live as he lives
- to follow as he follows
- to talk as he talks

The result of his divisiveness is tragic: he deceives the naive, that is, the unsuspecting, the innocent, the immature, the carnal, the unspiritual, the new-born believers.

For there are many rebellious people, mere talkers and deceivers, especially those of the circumcision group [religionists]. They must be silenced, because they are ruining whole households by teaching things they ought not to teach—and that for the sake of dishonest gain. (Titus 1:10-11)

[Men] Having a form of godliness but denying its power. Have nothing to do with them. They are the kind who worm their way into homes and gain control over weak-willed women, who are loaded down with sins and are swayed by all kinds of evil desires, always learning [the latest philosophy, theology or novelty] but never able to acknowledge the truth. (2 Tim 3:5-7)

2 (16:19-20) **Church, Strong**: mark what is good, and untainted with evil. A strong church, such as the Roman church, must constantly be marking and focusing upon *what is good and untainted with evil.* If a strong church fails to know and do good, it will be penetrated by evil (divisiveness) and it will become a weak church. Therefore, a strong church must always, with the utmost diligence, be looking for what is good and untainted with evil. Three reasons are given for this charge.

1. A strong church such as the Roman church is obedient to the Lord Jesus Christ. This is the very reason for its strength: the church has been obedient to the Lord, doing exactly as He commands. The believers have been...

a. Living soberly, righteously, and godly in this present world.

It teaches us to say "No" to ungodliness and worldly passions, and to live self-controlled, upright and godly lives in this present age, while we wait for the blessed hope—the glorious appearing of our great God and Savior, Jesus Christ, (Titus 2:12-13)

b. Ministering to the needs of people even as He ministered.

Just as the Son of Man did not come to be served, but to serve, and to give his life as a ransom for many." (Mat 20:28)
Again Jesus said, "Peace be with you! As the Father has sent me, I am sending you." (John 20:21)

c. Witnessing to all far and wide, fulfilling His mission.

Therefore go and make disciples of all nations, baptizing them in the name of the Father and of the Son and of the Holy Spirit, and teaching them to obey everything I have commanded you. And surely I am with you always, to the very end of the age." (Mat 28:19-20)

He said to them, "Go into all the world and preach the good news to all creation. (Mark 16:15)

But you will receive power when the Holy Spirit comes on you; and you will be my witnesses in Jerusalem, and in all Judea and Samaria, and to the ends of the earth." (Acts 1:8)

The result of such a dynamic obedience is a strong testimony that is spread among all men. People know where to go when they need help: they know where the obedient believers are who are truly following the Lord.

2. A strong church must be wise to know what is good. Its people must grow more and more in *goodness*—in knowing what is good and what is evil. Believers must be *wise*...

- to *search* for what is good and untainted with evil.
- to *know* what is good and untainted with evil.

The word "innocent" (akerios) means unmixed, unadulterated, pure, without any mixture of evil. The idea is that the believers of a strong church must constantly mark, focus, and concentrate upon what is good in order to keep the bad out of its fellowship. The way to keep evil out of a church is to focus upon the good. The way to demonstrate spiritual wisdom is to concentrate upon the good; then evil will be recognized for what it is, and it will be rejected.

The point is this: a strong church must not only avoid evil (v.17); it must not allow evil to penetrate its fellowship. It must not allow a divisive person to stir up the "naive" (unsuspecting) believers of the church. A church must be wise: it must mark and focus upon what is good and untainted with evil. It must be wise enough to spot evil and to stop its penetration into the fellowship.

3. God will soon give victory over Satan. The meaning of "soon" does not mean shortly, but *quickly* or *swiftly*. The idea *is not* that God is coming soon to destroy Satan, but when God acts to deliver His people from evil and divisiveness, Satan will be quickly defeated. His work against God's consecrated people (a strong church) will last only for a moment. The "God of Peace" will restore peace swiftly and quickly to the fellowship of a strong people. But note: the defeat of Satan and divisive persons is conditional. A strong church must do what has been said: mark and focus upon what is good and untainted with evil. God will bless a church that is obedient and concentrating upon Christ and His mission (cp. point 1 of this note).

Note another fact: God is going to bruise Satan under the *believers' feet*. It is the *feet of the believers* that God uses to bruise Satan. When genuine believers of a strong church do what God says, then God will act to deliver His people from evil and divisiveness.

I have given you authority to trample on snakes and scorpions and to overcome all the power of the enemy; nothing will harm you. (Luke 10:19)

The God of peace will soon crush Satan under your feet. The grace of our Lord Jesus be with you. (Rom 16:20)

No temptation has seized you except what is common to man. And God is faithful; he will not let you be tempted beyond what you can bear. But when you are tempted, he will also provide a way out so that you can stand up under it. (1 Cor 10:13)

Submit yourselves, then, to God. Resist the devil, and he will flee from you. (James 4:7)

You, dear children, are from God and have overcome them, because the one who is in you is greater than the one who is in the world. (1 John 4:4)

		Lord.	
	E. The Messenger's Companions, 16:21-23	23 Gaius, whose hospitality I and the whole church here enjoy, sends you his greetings. Erastus, who is the city's director of public works, and our brother Quartus send you their greetings.	**4 Gaius: A man of hospitality** **5 Erastus: A civil servant, the city director of public works** **6 Quartus: A Christian brother**
1 Timothy: A right-hand man, a fellow worker **2 Lucius, Jason, Sosipater: Relatives who were bels.** **3 Tertius: A humble helper**	21 Timothy, my fellow worker, sends his greetings to you, as do Lucius, Jason and Sosipater, my relatives. 22 Tertius, who wrote down this letter, greet you in the		

DIVISION IX

THE MESSENGER OF GOD AND HIS PLANS, 15:14-16:27

E. The Messenger's Companions, 16:21-23

(16:21-24) **Introduction**: it is important for every minister and believer to have close associates who know and are faithful to the Lord. The strength of the associates greatly affects the witness of the minister. This passage gives a glimpse into the lives of a few of Paul's associates.

1. Timothy: a right-hand man, a fellow worker (v.21).
2. Lucius, Jason, Sosipater: relatives who were believers (v.21).
3. Tertius: a humble helper (v.22).
4. Gaius: a man of hospitality (v.23).
5. Erastus: a civil servant, the city director of public works (v.23).
6. Quartus: a Christian brother (v.23).

1 (16:21) **Timothy**: Paul calls Timothy his right hand man, his fellow worker. There is a great deal of information on Timothy throughout the New Testament. There are even two letters which bear his name included in the New Testament. The letters were written to Timothy by Paul himself (1 and 2 Timothy. Also see DEEPER STUDY # 1—Acts 16:1-3; notes—Ph.1:1; 1 Tim.1:18 for more discussion.) Note two facts mentioned about Timothy, facts which should speak to our hearts.

1. His name, "Timothy," means *one who honors God.* Both his mother and grandmother were faithful believers who reared Timothy in the Scriptures (2 Tim.1:5; 3:15). Apparently when Timothy was born, his mother had dedicated him to the Lord after the pattern of the Old Testament believers. She gave him his name knowing perfectly well what it meant. Her hope and prayer was that Christ would take her child and use him to *bring honor* to God's name.

> **Thought 1.** What a dynamic example for parents! We should all commit our children to Christ, rearing them in the Scriptures and constantly praying for Christ to use them to bring honor to God's name.

> **The goal of this command is love, which comes from a pure heart and a good conscience and a sincere faith. (1 Tim 1:5)**
> **If I am delayed, you will know how people ought to conduct themselves in God's household, which is the church of the living God, the pillar and foundation of the truth. (1 Tim 3:15)**
> **Impress them [God's word] on your children. Talk about them when you sit at home and when you walk along the road,**

> **when you lie down and when you get up. (Deu 6:7)**
> **Train a child in the way he should go, and when he is old he will not turn from it. (Prov 22:6)**

2. Timothy is called Paul's "fellow worker." Paul places Timothy on an equal *par* with himself. Paul sees Timothy's call and ministry as being as important as his own. This says several significant things.

  a. Timothy's mind—his thoughts, imaginations, concepts, ideas, purposes, plans, concerns—was consumed with the very same things as Paul's mind: Christ and His mission and the reaching and caring for people.

> **I have no one else like him, who takes a genuine interest in your welfare. (Phil 2:20)**
> **We demolish arguments and every pretension that sets itself up against the knowledge of God, and we take captive every thought to make it obedient to Christ. (2 Cor 10:5)**
> **Finally, brothers, whatever is true, whatever is noble, whatever is right, whatever is pure, whatever is lovely, whatever is admirable—if anything is excellent or praiseworthy—think about such things. Whatever you have learned or received or heard from me, or seen in me—put it into practice. And the God of peace will be with you. (Phil 4:8-9)**

  b. Timothy was faithful in ministering right along with other ministers of the gospel, doing exactly what God had called him to do. Note that he was second to Paul, that is, Paul's assistant. However, this did not bother Timothy, for Timothy knew something: it was God, not man, who had called him to be second and to serve as the assistant. Therefore, he was *faithful*, always serving his Lord and helping the chief minister.

> **For this reason I am sending to you Timothy, my son whom I love, who is faithful in the Lord. He will remind you of my way of life in Christ Jesus, which agrees with what I teach everywhere in every church. (1 Cor 4:17)**

---

24 May the grace of our Lord Jesus Christ be with all of you. Amen.

Paul and Timothy, servants of Christ Jesus, To all the saints in Christ Jesus at Philippi, together with the overseers and deacons: (Phil 1:1)

But you know that Timothy has proved himself, because as a son with his father he has served with me in the work of the gospel. I hope, therefore, to send him as soon as I see how things go with me. (Phil 2:22-23)

I want you to know that our brother Timothy has been released. If he arrives soon, I will come with him to see you. (Heb 13:23)

Therefore, my dear brothers, stand firm. Let nothing move you. Always give yourselves fully to the work of the Lord, because you know that your labor in the Lord is not in vain. (1 Cor 15:58)

2 (16:21) **Lucius—Jason—Sosipater**: these men were apparently relatives of Paul. It should be noted, however, that the word "relatives" is thought by some to mean fellow-countrymen. This is unlikely, for Paul often mentions others who are fellow Jews and he does not refer to them as relatives. Apparently, Paul had a family tree just like most of us have: branches that just keep on running out from our aunts and uncles and their children who are our cousins. Just who these men were we cannot be sure, but note what is said in this passage.

1. They were relatives of Paul who had trusted Christ as their Savior and surrendered to His Lordship. Who was converted first, Paul or his three relatives? We do not know; but this much is known. Genuine believers pray, and they diligently pray for relatives, believing that it is their responsibility to reach their own families first. For this reason, Paul's family saw quite a few of its members give their lives to Christ (cp. Ro.16:7).

In the same way, let your light shine before men, that they may see your good deeds and praise your Father in heaven. (Mat 5:16)

But so that you may know that the Son of Man has authority on earth to forgive sins." Then he said to the paralytic, "Get up, take your mat and go home." And the man got up and went home. (Mat 9:6-7)

"Return home and tell how much God has done for you." So the man went away and told all over town how much Jesus had done for him. (Luke 8:39)

The first thing Andrew did was to find his brother Simon and tell him, "We have found the Messiah" (that is, the Christ). (John 1:41)

Then the father realized that this was the exact time at which Jesus had said to him, "Your son will live." So he and all his household believed. (John 4:53)

When she and the members of her household were baptized, she invited us to her home. "If you consider me a believer in the Lord," she said, "come and stay at my house." And she persuaded us. (Acts 16:15)

He then brought them out and asked, "Sirs, what must I do to be saved?" They replied, "Believe in the Lord Jesus, and you will be saved—you and your household." (Acts 16:30-31)

But if a widow has children or grandchildren, these should learn first of all to put their religion into practice by caring for their own family and so repaying their parents and grandparents, for this is pleasing to God. (1 Tim 5:4)

2. They were serving the Lord with Paul. Any person serving with Paul was bound to be committed to Christ and to be fully committed, for if any man has ever been committed to Christ, it was Paul. Without question, these three men had given all they were and had to the Lord. They were bound to be gripped with the needs of masses suffering under the weight of starvation, disease, poverty, sin, and death, and with the urgent need to get the gospel of salvation to them. The very fact that they were serving with Paul tells us that this was the heartbeat of their lives.

Then he said to them all: "If anyone would come after me, he must deny himself and take up his cross daily and follow me. (Luke 9:23)

Just as the Son of Man did not come to be served, but to serve, and to give his life as a ransom for many." (Mat 20:28)

Again Jesus said, "Peace be with you! As the Father has sent me, I am sending you." (John 20:21)

3 (16:22) **Tertius**: this believer was a humble helper. Note two significant facts about Tertius.

1. He helped Paul in a most significant but humble way. Apparently he was not a preacher, but he served as the personal secretary to Paul, writing this letter to the Romans for Paul.

Thought 1. The need for dedicated people who are gifted to handle details is desperately needed in the service of Christ! Very little if anything can be done effectively without what may be called the *Service Ministries*. May God stir and arouse men and women to give their lives as Tertius did: to reach out in the *service ministries* of the Lord.

2. He personally knew the Lord and was bold in proclaiming his testimony. Glance at the verse again: "I Tertius, who wrote down this letter, greet you *in the Lord*" (v.22) Paul does not send the greeting for Tertius; Tertius takes it upon himself to send his own greeting. He is a fellow-believer with the Roman Christians, and he wants to greet them in the name of Christ, proclaiming his own faith and his own ministry in the Lord. Men of the world may consider him and his work as secretary of little importance. But he does not: his faith and ministry are the most important things in the world to him. Therefore, he proclaims that he too is "in the Lord" and that he is the secretary who wrote the letter for Paul.

Thought 1. Just imagine how few letters, books, articles, and papers would be written for Christ without the dear saintly servants who labor ever so diligently as the secretaries for God's ministers. Think about all the *service ministries* and how much would never get done without the commitment of God's *detail servants*.

But you are not to be like that. Instead, the greatest among you should be like the

271

youngest, and the one who rules like the one who serves. (Luke 22:26)

For by the grace given me I say to every one of you: Do not think of yourself more highly than you ought, but rather think of yourself with sober judgment, in accordance with the measure of faith God has given you. (Rom 12:3)

Be devoted to one another in brotherly love. Honor one another above yourselves. Never be lacking in zeal, but keep your spiritual fervor, serving the Lord. (Rom 12:10-11)

Your attitude should be the same as that of Christ Jesus: Who, being in very nature God, did not consider equality with God something to be grasped, but made himself nothing, taking the very nature of a servant, being made in human likeness. (Phil 2:5-7)

Thought 2. Something we must always remember and proclaim: no work and no service done for God is small. Men may rank work and labor, but God does not. God ranks and judges only faithfulness.

"Whoever can be trusted with very little can also be trusted with much, and whoever is dishonest with very little will also be dishonest with much. (Luke 16:10)

"'Well done, my good servant!' his master replied. 'Because you have been trustworthy in a very small matter, take charge of ten cities.' (Luke 19:17)

4 (16:23) **Gaius:** this believer was a man of unusual hospitality. Apparently Gaius was a wealthy man who had a home large enough to entertain the whole church and to house God's servants over a long period of time. The point to note is this: he was faithful in using his money, wealth, and estate for the Lord.

"Do not store up for yourselves treasures on earth, where moth and rust destroy, and where thieves break in and steal. But store up for yourselves treasures in heaven, where moth and rust do not destroy, and where thieves do not break in and steal. (Mat 6:19-20)

Share with God's people who are in need. Practice hospitality. (Rom 12:13)

Command those who are rich in this present world not to be arrogant nor to put their hope in wealth, which is so uncertain, but to put their hope in God, who richly provides us with everything for our enjoyment. Command them to do good, to be rich in good deeds, and to be generous and willing to share. In this way they will lay up treasure for themselves as a firm foundation for the coming age, so that they may take hold of the life that is truly life. (1 Tim 6:17-19)

Rather he must be hospitable, one who loves what is good, who is self-controlled, upright, holy and disciplined. (Titus 1:8)

Do not forget to entertain strangers, for by so doing some people have entertained angels without knowing it. (Heb 13:2)

Offer hospitality to one another without grumbling. (1 Pet 4:9)

5 (16:23) **Erastus:** this believer was a civil servant, the city director of public works for the great city of Corinth. This tells us that he was...

- a man highly respected both among believers and the world.
- a man of extreme responsibility who could be greatly trusted to look after his responsibility.
- a man of courage who stood up for his convictions and did not let political office nor friends and associates in high places keep him from confessing Christ.

It is interesting to note that Erastus was apparently called to *preach* the gospel, and eventually he resigned or was removed from political office. He is seen on a mission tour with Timothy (Acts 19:22) and is mentioned as still being faithful in the latter months of Paul's life (2 Tim.4:20).

"Whoever acknowledges me before men, I will also acknowledge him before my Father in heaven. But whoever disowns me before men, I will disown him before my Father in heaven. (Mat 10:32-33)

"I tell you, whoever acknowledges me before men, the Son of Man will also acknowledge him before the angels of God. (Luke 12:8)

Do not love the world or anything in the world. If anyone loves the world, the love of the Father is not in him. For everything in the world—the cravings of sinful man, the lust of his eyes and the boasting of what he has and does—comes not from the Father but from the world. (1 John 2:15-16)

6 (16:23) **Quartus:** this believer is very simply called "our brother." This is significant, for it means...

- that he had made a genuine commitment to Christ and that he was serving mankind as a servant of the Lord Jesus Christ.
- that he had a brotherly heart and love, helping and standing with other believers as a brother in the Lord.

"A new command I give you: Love one another. As I have loved you, so you must love one another. By this all men will know that you are my disciples, if you love one another." (John 13:34-35)

My command is this: Love each other as I have loved you. (John 15:12)

Love must be sincere. Hate what is evil; cling to what is good. (Rom 12:9)

Now that you have purified yourselves by obeying the truth so that you have sincere love for your brothers, love one another deeply, from the heart. (1 Pet 1:22)

	F. The Messenger's Benediction: God is Able to Establish You, 16:25-27	hidden for long ages past, 26 But now revealed and made known through the prophetic writings by the command of the eternal God, so that all nations might believe and obey him— 27 To the only wise God be glory forever through Jesus Christ! Amen.	a. It was a secret b. It is now revealed in the Scriptures c. It is revealed for one purpose: To lead all to be obedient to Christ
1 Established by the gospel 2 Established by the proclamation of Christ 3 Established by God's revelation of the mystery	25 Now to him who is able to establish you by my gospel and the proclamation of Jesus Christ, according to the revelation of the mystery		4 The benediction

DIVISION IX.

THE MESSENGER OF GOD AND HIS PLANS, 15:14-16:27

F. The Messenger's Benediction: God is Able to Establish You, 16:25-27

(16:25-27) **Introduction**: God is able to establish the believer. The word "establish" (sterixai) means to strengthen, secure, make stable, set fast, and make firm. The one thing men long for is to be secure, strong, and firmly established in life. God is able to fulfill this longing. God is able to establish and strengthen man and to give him a strong life.

1. Established by the gospel (v.25).
2. Established by the proclamation of Christ (v.25).
3. Established by God's revelation of the mystery (v.25-26).
4. The benediction (v.27).

1 (16:25) **Spiritual Growth—Stability—Steadfastness—Security**: believers are established and made strong by the gospel. Note a significant point.

Paul calls the gospel "my gospel." He does not mean that he possesses the gospel, nor that he is the author and creator of it. He does not mean that he has formulated a man-made gospel that men are to follow. He simply means that he is a preacher of God's gospel, and God uses the gospel which he and other preachers proclaim to strengthen believers. God is the Sovereign Majesty of the universe who possesses the message of the glorious gospel. God is the Author and Creator of the message, not Paul nor any other preacher. But note: Paul and other preachers are ambassadors; they are the representatives of God who carry forth the gospel of God. The preacher of the gospel stands before the world with *God's message*. He has the right and the authority to proclaim the gospel, and the gospel proclaimed comes forth from his voice. In this sense it is his message—his gospel—that God uses to establish and strengthen believers.

> We are therefore Christ's ambassadors, as though God were making his appeal through us. We implore you on Christ's behalf: Be reconciled to God. (2 Cor 5:20)
> You did not choose me, but I chose you and appointed you to go and bear fruit—fruit that will last. Then the Father will give you whatever you ask in my name. (John 15:16)
> "My prayer is not for them alone. I pray also for those who will believe in me through their message [the word of the gospel given by God] (John 17:20)
> 'Now get up and stand on your feet. I have appeared to you to appoint you as a servant and as a witness of what you have

seen of me and what I will show you. (Acts 26:16)
> "Now I commit you to God and to the word of his grace, which can build you up and give you an inheritance among all those who are sanctified. (Acts 20:32)
> Like newborn babies, crave pure spiritual milk, so that by it you may grow up in your salvation, now that you have tasted that the Lord is good. (1 Pet 2:2-3)

2 (16:25) **Jesus Christ, Preaching of**: believers are established and made strong by the proclamation of Jesus Christ. The preaching of Jesus Christ can mean either the message preached by Jesus Christ Himself or the message about Jesus Christ which is preached by others. Both meanings make sense, and both are certainly true, for the message of salvation preached by Christ and by His followers is the same.

> How shall we escape if we ignore such a great salvation? This salvation, which was first announced by the Lord, was confirmed to us by those who heard him. (Heb 2:3)
> Just as Moses lifted up the snake in the desert, so the Son of Man must be lifted up, that everyone who believes in him may have eternal life. (John 3:14-15)
> "For God so loved the world that he gave his one and only Son, that whoever believes in him shall not perish but have eternal life. (John 3:16)
> "I tell you the truth, whoever hears my word and believes him who sent me has eternal life and will not be condemned; he has crossed over from death to life. (John 5:24)
> I tell you the truth, if anyone keeps my word, he will never see death." (John 8:51)
> Jesus said to her, "I am the resurrection and the life. He who believes in me will live, even though he dies; and whoever lives and believes in me will never die. Do you believe this?" (John 11:25-26)
> For God did not send his Son into the world to condemn the world, but to save the world through him. Whoever believes in him is not condemned, but whoever does not believe stands condemned already be-

273

cause he has not believed in the name of God's one and only Son. (John 3:17-18)

Whoever believes in the Son has eternal life, but whoever rejects the Son will not see life, for God's wrath remains on him." (John 3:36)

3 (16:25-26) **Mystery—Gospel**: believers are established and made strong by God's revelation of the mystery of the gospel. Note three points.

1. The mystery of the gospel had been a secret since the world began. The word "mystery" (musteriou) does not mean something obscure and difficult to understand nor something that has to be searched out and solved by men. It simply means…

- some truth that was not previously known.
- some truth that *could not* be discovered by human reason.
- some truth that had to be *revealed by God* if it was ever to be known.

The gospel could never have been known by man. It is not a creation of man's mind, of his rationalizations, concepts, thoughts, and ideas as to how man is to become reconciled to God. Man could never and can never figure out how to become acceptable to God. No man in this physical world could ever penetrate the spiritual world, no matter what some have claimed. Jesus said so:

No one has ever gone into heaven except the one who came from heaven—the Son of Man. (John 3:13)

The spiritual world and the message of the spiritual world have always been a mystery, and they would have remained a mystery if God had not acted and revealed the spiritual world and dimension to man.

2. The mystery of the gospel is now revealed by the commandment of God in the prophetic Scriptures. God wants the world to know the gospel; therefore, He has commanded that it be revealed and proclaimed to the world. But note the crucial point: it is revealed by the prophetic Scriptures (dia graphon prophetikon). This is extremely important, for it tells us exactly where we are to find out about God and His message to the world. We do not discover God by natural reasoning: God reveals Himself to us.

Thought 1. There are two questions that desperately need to be studied by everyone.

1) Since God has revealed how men are to become acceptable to Him, why do men continue to create their own ideas about how to reach God? Why do men continue to think they will be acceptable to God if they can just do enough good to pacify God? Why do most men continue to think that God will never reject them, that they are not evil enough to be unacceptable to God?

2) Since God has revealed the gospel in the prophetic Scriptures, why do men not rush to the Scriptures to find the truth? Why do men not search the Scriptures daily to find out what God has revealed?

The gospel he promised beforehand through his prophets in the Holy Scriptures regarding his Son, who as to his human nature was a descendant of David, and who through the Spirit of holiness was declared with power to be the Son of God by his resurrection from the dead: Jesus Christ our Lord. (Rom 1:2-4)

But now a righteousness from God, apart from law, has been made known, to which the Law and the Prophets testify. This righteousness from God comes through faith in Jesus Christ to all who believe. There is no difference, (Rom 3:21-22)

3. The mystery of the gospel is revealed for a purpose: to lead all nations to be obedient to Christ. Very simply, God wants from us what any person wants from others: love and trust. We all want others…

- to love us and to care about us.
- to trust us and have confidence in us.

Then they asked him, "What must we do to do the works God requires?" Jesus answered, "The work of God is this: to believe in the one he has sent." (John 6:28-29)

If you obey my commands, you will remain in my love, just as I have obeyed my Father's commands and remain in his love. (John 15:10)

Therefore, since we have been justified through faith, we have peace with God through our Lord Jesus Christ, (Rom 5:1)

Consider Abraham: "He believed God, and it was credited to him as righteousness." (Gal 3:6)

For in Christ Jesus neither circumcision [religious ritual] nor uncircumcision has any value. The only thing that counts is faith expressing itself through love. (Gal 5:6)

And without faith it is impossible to please God, because anyone who comes to him must believe that he exists and that he rewards those who earnestly seek him. (Heb 11:6)

And this is his command: to believe in the name of his Son, Jesus Christ, and to love one another as he commanded us. (1 John 3:23)

4 (16:27) **Benediction**: the benediction is a glorious declaration of praise.

⇒ God is the God of the gospel; therefore, He is the only wise God. As the only wise God and as the Author of the gospel, He is due praise and glory forever.

⇒ But note the simple and clear fact that is proclaimed again and again by Romans: God can be approached and praised only through Jesus Christ.

They said to the woman, "We no longer believe just because of what you said; now we have heard for ourselves, and we know that this man really is the Savior of the world." (John 4:42)

Jesus answered, "I am the way and the truth and the life. No one comes to the Father except through me. (John 14:6)

Salvation is found in no one else, for there is no other name under heaven given to men by which we must be saved." (Acts 4:12)

God exalted him to his own right hand as Prince and Savior that he might give repentance and forgiveness of sins to Israel. (Acts 5:31)

Here is a trustworthy saying that deserves full acceptance: Christ Jesus came into the world to save sinners—of whom I am the worst. (1 Tim 1:15)

For there is one God and one mediator between God and men, the man Christ Jesus, (1 Tim 2:5)

But when the kindness and love of God our Savior appeared, he saved us, not because of righteous things we had done, but because of his mercy. He saved us through the washing of rebirth and renewal by the Holy Spirit, whom he poured out on us generously through Jesus Christ our Savior, so that, having been justified by his grace, we might become heirs having the hope of eternal life. (Titus 3:4-7)

Therefore he is able to save completely those who come to God through him, because he always lives to intercede for them. (Heb 7:25)

But the ministry Jesus has received is as superior to theirs as the covenant of which he is mediator is superior to the old one, and it is founded on better promises. (Heb 8:6)

For this reason Christ is the mediator of a new covenant, that those who are called may receive the promised eternal inheritance—now that he has died as a ransom to set them free from the sins committed under the first covenant. (Heb 9:15)

For Christ did not enter a man-made sanctuary that was only a copy of the true one; he entered heaven itself, now to appear for us in God's presence. (Heb 9:24)

To Jesus the mediator of a new covenant. (Heb 12:24)

My dear children, I write this to you so that you will not sin. But if anybody does sin, we have one who speaks to the Father in our defense—Jesus Christ, the Righteous One. (1 John 2:1)

And we have seen and testify that the Father has sent his Son to be the Savior of the world. (1 John 4:14)

THE

OUTLINE & SUBJECT INDEX

REMEMBER: When you look up a subject and turn to the Scripture reference, you have not only the Scripture, you have *an outline and a discussion* (commentary) of the Scripture and subject.

This is one of the *GREAT VALUES* of **The Preacher's Outline & Sermon Bible**™. Once you have all the volumes, you will have not only what all other Bible indexes give you, that is, a list of all the subjects and their Scripture references, *BUT* you will also have…

- An outline of *every* Scripture and subject in the Bible.
- A discussion (commentary) on every Scripture and subject.
- Every subject supported by other Scriptures or cross references.

DISCOVER THE GREAT VALUE for yourself. Quickly glance below to the very first subject of the Index of Romans. It is:

ABIDE - ABIDING
Meaning. "In" Christ. Ro.8:1

Turn to the reference. Glance at the Scripture and outline of the Scripture, then read the commentary. You will immediately see the *GREAT VALUE* of the *INDEX* of **The Preacher's Outline & Sermon Bible**™.

OUTLINE AND SUBJECT INDEX

ABIDE - ABIDING
Meaning. "In" Christ. 8:1

ABRAHAM
And history. Representative man of human race. 4:11-12
Discussed. 4:1-25
Example.
Of faith over works. Justification & righteousness. 4:1-25
Of great faith. Pivotal point in history. 4:1-25
Of justification by faith. 4:9; 4:17-25
Place in Jewish history.
Father of believers. 4:11-12
Founder of Jewish nation. 4:1-25
Promises to. Discussed. 4:1-25
Seed of.
Christ. 4:1-25
Nations of people. 4:11-12; 4:13; 4:17

ABUNDANCE
Spiritual. Of grace & salvation. Six things. 5:15-18

ACCEPTABLE
How one becomes **a**. 2:25-27

ACCESS
Into the grace, the presence of God. 5:2; 8:15
Verses. 5:2

ADAM
And Christ. Discussed. 5:12-21
And history. Focal point of **h**. 5:12-21
And men.
Caused sin and death. 5:12-14; 5:12
Passes earthly nature to **m**. 5:12-14; 5:12
Representative man for all **m**. 5:12-14; 5:12
Choice of. Vs. choice of men today. Clearer, more positive **c**. today. 5:12-14
Discussed. 5:12-21
Type of Christ. Discussed. 5:12-14

ADMONISH (See INSTRUCT)

ADOPTED - ADOPTION
Fact of. Glorious privilege of believers. 9:4
How one is **a**. By the Holy Spirit. 8:15
Of believer. Discussed. 8:15

ADULTERY
Commandment forbidding. Discussed. 13:9
Discussed. 2:21-24; 13:9
Results. Destroys the human body. Five ways. 13:9

AFFECTION - AFFECTIONS (See HEARTLESS)

ALIENATION
Of men from God. Discussed. 5:1

ANGUISH (See DISTRESS)

APOSTLE
Discussed. 1:1

RIGHT TIME (See FULLNESS OF TIME)

AQUILA & PRISCILLA
Discussed. 16:3-4
Had a church in their home. 16:3-4

ARISTOBULUS
Household of. Were believers. 16:10

ARMOR
Of light. To put on **a**. 13:12

ARROGANCE (See PRIDE)

ARROGANT
Meaning. 1:30

ASHAMED
Of what. Of the gospel. 1:16

ASSISTANTS
Call of. To serve in second place. 16:21; 16:22

ASSURANCE
Needed. In knowing that all things God works for the good. 8:28
Source.
Holy Spirit. Bears witness with our **s**. 8:16-17
Lord Jesus Christ. 8:34

ATONEMENT
Meaning. 3:25
Source. Christ. Died as our **a**. 5:6-7

AUTHORITIES, CIVIL
Discussed. 13:1-7

BACKBITERS (See SLANDERERS)

BACKSLIDING
Examples of. Four **e**. 9:5

BAPTISM
Compared with circumcision. 4:11
Compared with ritual. 4:11
Discussed. 6:3-5
Error. Thinking **b**. saves. 2:25-27; 2:28-29; 6:3-5
Kinds of.
Spiritual. 6:3-5
Water. 6:3-5
Views of. Discussed. 6:3-5

BEAR - BEARING
Meaning. 15:1-3

BELIEVE - BELIEVING - BELIEF
Discussed. 10:16-17
Meaning. To obey. 10:16
Results. Righteousness. 4:22; 4:23-25; 5:1
Steps involved in **b**. Threefold. 10:16-17
Verses. List of. 10:16-17

BELIEVERS (See SPIRITUAL STRUGGLE - WARFARE; VICTORIOUS LIVING)
Blessings of. Fourfold. Called; beloved; made saints; grace & peace. 1:6-7
Character (See **BELIEVERS**, Life - Walk - Behavior)

Described as.
  Children of God. 9:6-13
  Children of the promise. 9:6-13
  False vs. real **b.** 2:17-29
  One body. 12:3-5
  Strong vs. weak **b.** 14:1-23
  Weak. 14:1-2; 15:1-3
Discussed.
  Marks of strong **b.** 15:1-13
  Some **b.**'s of the early church. 16:1-16
  Strong **b.** vs. weak **b.** 14:1-23
Duty - Work.
  Must not elevate self over others. 11:18
  Not to be conceited. 12:16
  Not to be lacking in zeal. 12:11
  Not to continue in sin. Position in Christ forbids. 6:1-10
  Not to repay evil for evil. 12:17
  Not to take vengeance. Reasons. 12:18
  Not to think too highly of self. 12:6-8
  To associate with the lowly. 12:16
  To awaken out of sleep. 13:11-14
  To be enslaved to Christ. 1:1-7; 1:6-7
  To be hospitable. 12:13
  To be led by the Spirit. Meaning. 8:14
  To be on fire spiritually. 12:11
  To bless persecutors. 12:14
  To bruise Satan under our feet. 16:20
  To cling to the good. 12:9-10
  To conquer trials. 12:12
  To constantly pray. 12:12
  To give generously. 12:13
  To hate evil. 12:9-10
  To identify with, show interest in men. 12:15
  To know the power of the Spirit. 8:1-17
  To live above reproach. 12:17
  To live at peace with all. Two qualifications. 12:18
  To meet needs. 12:13
  To rejoice in hope. 12:12
  To serve the Lord with fervor. 6:19-20; 12:11
  To use one's gifts. 12:6-8
  To use one's time wisely. 13:11-14
  To walk humbly. 12:3-5; 12:9-10
Indwelling presence of Christ. (See **IN-DWELLING PRESENCE**)
Life - Walk - Behavior. (See **BELIEVERS**, Duty - Work)
  Not having license to sin. 6:14-23
  Not to be a stumbling block. 14:1-23
  Not to continue in sin. 6:11-13
  Three great traits. 15:1-3
  To be established by God. 16:25-27
  To count one's self dead to sin. 6:1-10
  To dedicate one's body. 12:1-2
  To struggle for deliverance. 8:23-27
  To walk in the Spirit, not in the sinful nature. 8:2-4
  Toward fellow citizens. 13:8-10
  Toward God. 12:1-3
  Toward himself. Discussed. 12:3-8
  Toward other believers. 12:9-13
  Toward the state. 13:1-7
  Toward unbelievers. 12:14-21
  Verses. List of. 8:2-4
Names - Titles - Identity.
  A predestined race of people. 9:6-13
  Body of Christ. 12:3-8
  Children of Abraham. 4:11-12
  Children of God. 9:6-13
  Heirs of God. 8:16-17
  Seed of Abraham. 4:13-16; 4:17-25

  Six points. 9:25-33
  The chosen. 9:25-33
  The true children of God. 2:28-29; 9:6-13
  The true Israel. 9:6-13
Nature.
  Identified with Christ. 6:1-10
  Indwelling presence. Mutual **i.** 8:9-10
  Struggle for deliverance. 8:23-27
Position.
  Baptized, immersed in Christ's death. 6:2-5
  Crucified with Christ. 6:6-7
  Dead to sin & alive to God. 6:1-10
  Discussed. 6:1-10
  Freed from condemnation. 8:1-17
  Freed from sin. 6:1-23
  Freed from the law. 7:1-25
  "In" Christ. Discussed. 6:3-5; 8:1
  Lives by the Spirit. 8:1-17
  Lives with Christ now & forever. 6:1-10; 6:2-5
  Old person "was crucified" in Christ. 6:2-5
Purpose. (See **PURPOSE**)
Spiritual struggle. (See **SPIRITUAL STRUGGLE - WARFARE**)

BIBLE (See **SCRIPTURE; WORD OF GOD**)

BLESSED, THE
Discussed. 4:6-8

BLESSINGS
Fourfold. 1:6-7
Spiritual. Promised to the world in the end time at Israel's conversion. 11:13-15

BLINDNESS, SPIRITUAL (See **SPIRITUAL BLINDNESS**)

BOAST - BOASTING
Answer to - Eliminated by.
  By law & Scripture. 3:19-20
  Faith. 3:27
Caused by.
  Living by a law of works. 3:27; 4:1-3
  Pride. Elevating self over others. Who **b.** 11:18
  Religionists. 2:17-20
  Self-centeredness. 3:27
  Works of righteousness. 3:19-20; 4:1-3
Discussed. 3:27
Duty. Not to boast in self, but in Christ. 15:14; 15:17-19
In men. Discussed. 3:27; 3:28
In self. Cause. Self-centeredness. 3:27
Meaning. 1:30
What to **b.** in. Discussed. 15:14; 15:17-19

BODY, HUMAN
Deeds of. Evil **d.** To put to death. 8:13
Discussed. 12:1
Duty.
  Not to let sin control one's **b.** 6:12
  To be a living sacrifice. 12:1

BONDAGE, SPIRITUAL (See **ENSLAVEMENT, SPIRITUAL**)
Things that hold men in **b.**
  Fear. 8:15
  Law. 8:3
  Sin. 6:14-23; 6:16; 6:19-20

BORROW - BORROWING
Money. (See **MONEY**, Borrowing)

BRAG - BRAGGING
Meaning. 1:30

BROTHERHOOD
Duty.
  Not to be a stumbling block. 14:1-23
  To accept without partiality or favoritism. 15:7-12
  To bear weaknesses of the weak. 15:1-3
  To live at peace if possible. 12:18
  To love sincerely without hypocrisy. 12:9-13
  To seek harmony & to associate with the lowly. 12:16
  To welcome & be tender & gracious. 15:14; 16:1-2
  To work for a strong fellowship. Six things. 15:1-13
  Toward fellow citizens. 13:8-10
  Toward other believers. 12:9-13
  Toward the state. 13:1-7
  Toward unbelievers. 12:14-21
Essential. Must have patience & endurance to maintain brotherhood. 15:5-6
Problem - Difficulty with. **B.** not always possible. 12:18

CALL - CALLING
Purpose. 1:1
  Twofold. 8:28
Source. God. 8:30
To what. To ministry. Discussed. 1:1
Universal **c.** 10:13

CARE - CARING
Duty. To show genuine interest in men's experiences. 12:15
Of God. For man. Verses. List of. 8:34

CARNAL - CARNALITY (See **SINFUL NATURE**)
Caused by. Living after the sinful nature. 8:12-13
Deliverance from **c.** By the power of the Spirit. 8:1-17; 8:12-13
Described as.
  A struggling soul. 7:14-25
  False security. 13:11-14
  Weak. 15:1-3
Discussed. 7:14-17
Meaning. 7:14-17
Mind of.
  Discussed. 8:5-8
  Fate. 8:5-8
  Focus of. 8:5-8
  Meaning. 8:5-8
Result.
  A struggling soul. 7:14-25
  Death. 6:23; 8:5-8; 8:12-13
Vs. the spiritual man. 8:1-17

CEREMONY - CEREMONIAL LAW
Facts about. Do not save. 2:25-27

CHAMBERING (See **SEXUAL IMMORALITY**)

CHARACTER
Growth of. Developed through trials. 5:3-5
Meaning. 5:3-5

CHILDREN
Saved - Salvation of. Benefit from godly parents. 11:16

INDEX

CHILDREN OF GOD (See **BELIEVERS**)
Who they are. Not a race, nation, institution, heritage, etc. 9:6-13

CHOSEN, THE (See **BELIEVERS; ELECTION**)
Who they are. Six points. 9:25-33

CHRISTIANITY
Message of. Discussed. 1:1-7
Philosophy of. Greatest **p.** in the world. To serve & bear fruit. 1:1

CHURCH
Described. As a body. 12:3-5
Duty.
To keep a **c.** strong. 16:17-20
To receive others. 16:1
To use the spiritual gifts. 12:3-8
Marks - Characteristics.
A great **c.** 1:8
A strong **c.** 16:17-20
A strong fellowship. 15:1-13
Location. In home.
Of Aquila & Priscilla. 16:3-5
Of Gaius. 16:23
Names - Titles.
Body of Christ. 12:3-8
C. of Christ. 16:16
C. of the Gentiles. 16:4
Nature. Body of Christ. 12:3-8
Traits. Of a great **c.** The **c.** at Rome. 1:8

CHURCH MEMBERSHIP
Error. Thinking church membership saves. 2:25-27; 2:28-29
Services. To be warm & welcoming. 16:1-2

CIRCUMCISION (See **RITUAL**)
Advantages of. Discussed. 3:1-2
Compared with baptism. Discussed. 4:11
Discussed. 2:25-27; 4:11; 4:9-12
Physical **c.**
A sign of a covenant relationship. 4:9-12
A sign only of an inward work. 2:25-29; 4:9-12
Symbol only. 4:11
Thinking **c.** or a ritual saves. 2:25-27; 2:28-29
Spiritual **c.** Is of the heart; not by the written code. 2:28-29

CITIZEN - CITIZENSHIP
Discussed. 13:1-7
Duty.
Discussed. 13:1-7
Of believers toward fellow **c.** 13:8-10
Rebellion - Resistance. Discussed. 13:1-2

CIVIL AUTHORITIES
Discussed. 13:1-7

CLOTHE - CLOTHING, SPIRITUAL
Duty. To put on, clothe oneself with Christ. 10:11; 13:14

COMFORT (See **ENCOURAGEMENT**)

COMMISSION, GREAT
Zeal for. By Paul. For Israel, his own people. 9:1-3

COMPASSION
Of Paul. For Israel, his own people. 9:1-3

COMPLACENCY (See **SLOTHFUL**)
Described. As arrogance. 11:18; 11:19-21
Discussed. 13:11-14
Duty. To awaken out of sleep. 13:11-12

CONCEIT - CONCEITED (See **PRIDE**)
Discussed. 12:16
Duty. Not to be **c.** 12:16
Results. Elevating self over others. 11:18

CONDEMNED - CONDEMNATION
Caused by.
Adam's sin. 5:12-21
Judging others. 2:1
World's need to get right with God. 1:18-3:20
Deliverance from. Discussed. 8:1-17
Who can condemn.
Only Christ can **c.**, not man. 8:34
Only God can charge man, not other men. 8:31-33

CONFESS - CONFESSION
Duty. To **c.** Christ as Lord. 10:8-10
Results. Determines a person's destiny. 9:5
Source - Stirred by.
A struggling soul. 7:14-25
Sensing need, ungodliness. 4:4-5

CONFORMED
Meaning. 8:29; 12:2
To Christ's image. Is predestined. 8:29
To the world. Is forbidden. 12:2

CONSCIENCE
Defined.
Inner witness to God & righteousness. 2:11-15
Instinctive knowledge of right & wrong. 2:11-15
Thoughts - accusing or approving. 2:11-15
Duty. Obedience demanded. 13:5
Function - Purpose - Work. To correct. 2:11-15
Guilty. Disturbed by disobedience to authority. 13:5
How not to offend.
By being persuaded an act is right. 14:1-23
By subjecting to the state. 13:1-7
Proves. God's existence. 1:19

CONTENTIOUS (See **SELF-SEEKING; CRITICISM; DIVISION**)

CORRUPTION
Caused by - Source.
Adam's sinful nature. 5:12-14
Sin; being carnally minded. 8:5-8; 8:12-13
Deliverance - Escape. Of creation itself. 8:19-22
Problems. Causes pain & infirmities. 8:18; 8:19-22

COVENANT
C. with Israel. Listed. 9:4-5
Meaning. 9:4

COVENANTBREAKERS
Meaning. 1:31

COVET - COVETOUSNESS (See **GREED**)
Discussed. 13:9
Verses. List of. 13:9

CREATION
Deliverance of. All **c.** shall be delivered from struggle. 8:18-27
Nature of.
Corruptible & perishing 8:19-22
Interrelated & interconnected with man. 8:19-22
Suffers & struggles for deliverance. 8:19-22
Of world. By God.
Re-creation of. Discussed. 8:19-22
Rejected by man. 1:20
Ways all men are related to God. 10:12
Reveals.
God exists. His power & Deity. 1:19
Much more than God exists. Several other things. 1:19
State - Condition of.
Corruptible, struggling, suffering. 8:19-22
Cursed by God. Discussed. 8:19-22

CREDIT
Meaning. 4:6-8; 4:22; 6:11

CREDITED
Meaning. 4:6-8; 4:9; 4:22; 6:11

CRITICIZING - CRITICISM
Duty. Not to **c.** or judge. Reasons. 14:3-4
Error of. Sets oneself up as God with the right to judge. 14:3-4

CROOKED
Cause. Sinful nature. 3:10-12

CROSS
Essential. Must be crucified with Christ. 6:3-5; 6:6-7

CURSING
Discussed. 3:13-14

DARKNESS
Described. As sleep. 13:11-12
Of heart.
Unable to know God. 1:21
Verses. List of. 1:21
Works of.
Discussed. 13:12
Verses. List of. 13:12

DAVID
Example of. Justification by faith. 4:6-8

DEATH
Caused by.
Is **d.** too severe a punishment for sin? 5:12
Sin. 6:23
Through Adam. Described. 5:12-21
Deliverance from.
By the Holy Spirit. 8:1-17
Counteracted by Christ. 5:12-21
Described.
As a spirit. 8:2
As spiritual **d.** 6:23
Verses. List of. 5:12
Kinds.
Physical. Verses. List of. 5:12-14
Spiritual **d.**
Described. 6:23
Verses. List of. 1:32
Rule & reign of.
Destroyed by Christ's death. 6:8-10
Fact. Is universal. 5:12

DEATH, SPIRITUAL
Caused by. Carnal mind. 8:5-8
Verses. List of. 1:32

DEBATE (See **STRIFE**)

DEBAUCHERY
Meaning. 13:13

DEBTOR, SPIRITUAL
Duty. To preach. Obligated, indebted to
p. 14:15

DEBTS (See **MONEY**)
Discussed. 13:8
Duty. To owe no man anything. 13:8

DECEIT - DECEPTION
Discussed. 3:13-14
Meaning. 1:29

DECISION
Call to. More clear & positive today than
call to Adam. 5:12-14
Essential. Man determines his own fate.
8:12-13

DEDICATION - COMMITMENT
Discussed. 12:1-3
Duty.
In midst of immoral, cesspool society.
1:8
To be enslaved to Christ. 1:1-7
To be enslaved to the gospel. 1:8-15
To serve God and not sin. 6:16
To serve God with the same fervor as
you served sin. 6:19-20
Steps to **d**. Present bodies as a living sac-
rifice. 12:1-2
Why one should be **d**.
Belongs to Christ in life & death.
14:7-9
Has been purchased by the Lord.
14:7-9

DELIVERANCE
From what. Most severe circumstances.
8:35-37

DENIAL
Of Christ. Determines a person's destiny.
9:5

DEPRAVITY (See **MAN**, Depravity)
Discussed. 3:9-20
Meaning. 1:29
Result. Should not be despair, but salva-
tion. 3:9-20

DEPRESSION
Verses. List of. 5:6

DESPITE - DESPITEFUL (See **INSO-
LENT**)

DESTRUCTION
Sin of. Great sin of man. 3:15-18

DILIGENCE
Duty.
Not to lag behind in **d**. 12:11
To keep your spiritual fervor. 12:11

DISCOURAGEMENT
Verses. List of. 5:6-7

DISCRIMINATION
Discussed. 12:16

DISOBEDIENCE
Discussed. 2:6-10
To parents. Meaning. 1:30

DISSENSION
Meaning. 13:13

DISTRESS
Meaning. 2:9

DIVISION - DIVISIVENESS
Answer to **d**. Marking those who cause **d**.
16:17-20
Described as. Judging others. 2:1
Duty.
Discussed. 16:17-20
To live in peace if possible. 12:18
To mark divisive people. 16:17-20
Results. Judgment. Are to be judged.
2:1-16

DOERS (See **OBEDIENCE**)

DOUBLE-MINDED
Described. Mental assent. 10:16-17

DRUNKENNESS
Meaning. 13:13

DULLNESS
Describes. Depraved nature. 3:10-12

ELECTION
Discussed. 9:7-13; 9:14-24
Fact. God puts up with evil men in order
to share glory with believers. 9:22-24
Proof of. Jacob & Esau. 9:7-13; 9:10-13
Who is elected. Six points. 9:25-33

ELIJAH
Prophecy. Foresaw remnant of Israel.
11:2-4

ENCOURAGEMENT
Gift of. Discussed. 12:6-8
Meaning. 15:4
Source. Scriptures. 15:4

ENDURANCE
Duty. To **e**. trials. 12:12
Meaning. 12:12

ENEMY - ENEMIES (See **PERSECU-
TION**)
Duty. Discussed. 12:14-21
How to treat. Reasons. 12:19-21

ENSLAVEMENT, SPIRITUAL
E. by what. Fear. 8:15

ENVY
Meaning. 1:29; 13:13

ERASTUS
Believer who was the city treasurer for
Corinth. 16:23

ESAU
Rejected by God. As the heir of the
promises. 9:7-13

ESTABLISHED (See **STRONG**)

ETERNAL LIFE
Meaning. 2:6-10
Reward.
Of a fruitful, holy life. 6:21-22
Verses. List of. 2:7; 6:21-22
Source. Is Jesus Christ. 5:19-21

ETHICS
God's case against the moralist. 2:1-16

EVANGELISM (See **MISSIONS**)
Basis of. Discussed. 10:14-15
Duty. To have a world-wide vision.
15:22-33
Message of. Is for everyone, for the
whole world. 4:9
Zeal for. By Paul. For Israel, his own
people. 9:1-3

EVIL
Duty. To shun; to abhor **e**. 12:9-10
Law of. Meaning. 7:21-23
Source. A depraved nature. 3:10-12

EVIL FOR EVIL
Duty. Not to repay evil for evil. 12:17

EVIL, INVENT WAYS OF DOING
Meaning. 1:30

EXALTATION
Of believer. Discussed. 2:6-10

EXHORTATION (See **ENCOURAGE-
MENT**)

EXPOSED
Fact. Sin is **e**., known by God. 2:2-5; 2:16

FAITH
Described as.
A law - a principle. 3:27
Logical. 4:4-5
Discussed. 4:1-8
The way for the world to get right with
God. 3:21-5:21
Example. Of Abraham. 4:1-25
Just shall live by **f**. Meaning. 1:17
Law of. Discussed. 3:27
Results.
Secures the righteousness of God.
1:17; 4:4-5
Threefold **r**. 4:16
Source of.
Belief in God who raised Jesus. 4:23-25
God & God alone. 4:17
Word of God. 10:16-17
Strength of. God's Word & God's Word
alone. 4:18-21
Vs. law. Discussed. 4:13-16
Vs. works.
Discussed. 4:11
Illust. in Abraham. 4:1-3
Stages of. Discussed. 10:16-17
Work of - What **f**. does.
Discussed. 3:27-31; 4:1-25; 4:13-16
Establishes, upholds the law. 3:31
Justifies.
Faith alone **j**. 4:1-25
Proven by logic. 4:1-25; 1-8
Puts an end to boasting. 3:27-31

FAITHFULNESS
Need for **f**. In midst of immoral, cesspool
society. 1:8

INDEX

GOSPEL
Duty toward.
To be enslaved to the **g**. 1:8-15
To be taken to the world. 10:14-15
To be unashamed of the **g**. 1:16-17
Facts. Some are ashamed of **g**. 1:16
Message of.
Outline of. 1:2
Reveals the righteousness of God. 1:16-17
Universal. 10:13; 10:12-21; 10:14-15
Verses. List of. 10:11

GOSSIPS
Meaning. 1:29

GOVERNMENT
And the believer. 13:1-7
Discussed. When **g**. is to be obeyed & when it is not. 13:1-7
Purpose of. Discussed. 13:1-7
Rebellion - Resistance. Discussed. 13:1-7

GRACE
Discussed. 5:2; 6:14-15
Meaning. 4:16; 5:2
Misconceptions about. Grace gives the right to sin. 6:1
Purpose. To share riches of God's glory with believers. 9:22-24
Source. God. Has the right to show **g**. & justice as He wills. 9:14-33
Under **g**. Meaning. 6:14-15
Vs. law.
Believer is under **g**. not law. Meaning. 6:14-15
God is not a hovering judge. 6:14-15
Two problems with **g**. alone. 6:1

GREED (See **COVET - COVETOUS-NESS**)
Meaning. 1:29

HAGAR
Type of flesh, the sinful nature. 9:7-13

HALL OF FAME
Believers of the early church. 16:1-16

HARD - HARDNESS (See **HEART**, Hard)

HATE - HATING
God haters. 1:30

HEAR - HEARER - HEARING
Duty.
To be obedient and not a **h**. of the Word. 2:11-15
To **h**. the message of Christ. 10:16-17

HEART
Hard - Harden.
Israel's close-mindedness. 10:18-21
To guard against. 9:15-18
Known, exposed by God. 2:2-5
State of - Kinds of. Darkened. Cannot see. 1:21

HEARTLESS
Discussed. 1:31

HEATHEN
Basis of judgment. Discussed. 2:11-15
What happens to the **h**. who never hear of Christ. 2:11-15

HEIRS (See **INHERITANCE**)

HELPLESS - HELPLESSNESS
Of man. Cannot save himself. 5:6-7

HERITAGE
Of Israel. 9:5
Weaknesses of. Not saved by **h**. 9:7

HISTORY
Christ & history. Adam & Christ, two representatives of mankind. 5:12-21
Pivotal point of **h**.
Abraham. 4:11-12
Adam. 5:12-21
Believers. 8:29

HOLY - HOLINESS
Duty. To bear fruit of **h**. 6:21-22
Results. Frees believers from sin. 6:1-21
Verses. List of. 6:21-22

HOLY SPIRIT
Law of Spirit of Life. Meaning. 8:2-4
Names - Titles.
Spirit of Adoption. 8:15
Spirit of Life. 8:2
Power of. Discussed. 8:1-17
Work of.
Frees from sin & death. 8:2
In life of believer. Eight **w**. 8:1-17
Indwells the believer. Discussed. 8:9
Justifies. 4:25
Pours out His love into our hearts. 5:5
Proves Christ is the Son of God. 1:4
Saves. 5:10
Seals, guarantees believer. 5:5
To intercede for man. 8:34

HOMOSEXUAL - HOMOSEXUALITY
Discussed. 1:26-27

HONOR
Meaning. 2:7
Of believer. To be rewarded in eternity. 2:6-10
Verses. List of. 2:7

HOPE
Believer's hope. The glory of God. 5:2
Comes through.
Experience through trials. 5:3-5
Scriptures. 15:4
Discussed. 5:2; 8:24-25
Verses. List of. 8:24-25
Duty. To rejoice in **h**. 12:12
For whom. Depraved man. 3:9-20
Meaning. 5:2; 8:24-25
Nature. A redeemed body. 8:23-27
Results. Salvation. 8:24
Verses. List of. 5:2; 8:24-25

HOPELESS - HOPELESSNESS
Caused by. Seeking God by keeping the law. 6:14-15
State - Condition.
Cannot save self. 5:6-7
Discussed. 6:14-15
Verses. List of. 5:6-7

HOSPITALITY
Duty. To practice **h**. 12:13

HUMANISM
Discussed. 1:22-23; 1:24-25

HUMILITY
Duty.
Not to think too highly of self. 12:3-5
To associate with the lowly. 12:16
To give preference to others. 12:9-10
To prefer one another. 12:9-10
To walk in **h**. before other believers. 15:14

HYPOCRITE
Discussed. 2:17-29
Mistakes of. 2:17-29

IDOLS - IDOLATRY
Discussed. 1:22-23; 1:24-25; 2:21-24
Effects. Causes God to give man up to **i**. 1:24-32
Source.
Man. Creates own "gods" in mind & imaginations. 1:22-23; 1:24-25
Pride. Man's claim to be "wise." 1:22-23; 1:24-25

IGNORANT - IGNORANCE
Of God. Cause. Depraved nature. 3:10-12

IMAGE (See **LIKENESS**)

IMAGINATION (See **THINKING**)

IMMORALITY
Discussed. 13:9
Results. Causes God to give man over to **i**. 1:26-27
Verses. List of. 13:9

IMMORTALITY
Meaning. 2:7
Verses. List of. 2:7

IMPARTIAL (See **PARTIALITY**)

IMPUTE (See **CREDIT**)

IN CHRIST
Meaning. 8:1

INDIFFERENT - INDIFFERENCE
Describes. Sinful nature. 3:10-12

INDIGNATION (See **WRATH**)

INDULGE - INDULGENCE
Sin of. Is not love. 3:5-8

INDWELLING PRESENCE
Of Christ. Discussed. 8:9
Of Holy Spirit. Discussed. 8:9
Of the Spirit of Christ. 8:9
Verses. List of. 8:9

INHERITANCE
Of Abraham. Promised that he would **i**. the world. 4:13
Of the believer.
A joint heir with Christ. 8:16-17; 8:17
An heir of God. 8:16-17
Discussed. 8:17
To **i**. whole world. 4:13
Verses. List of. 8:17
Surety of. Is not by law, but by faith. 4:13-16

INDEX

How to escape **j**. Discussed. 2:6-10
Misconceptions of - reactions against.
    Men scoff at. Think God is too good to
    j. 2:2-5; 3:5-8
    Most men think they will escape. 2:2-5
Of believers. Shall stand before the **j**. seat
    of Christ. 14:10-12
Of heathen.
    Basis of. 2:11-15
    What happens to **h**. who never hear of
    Christ. 2:11-15
Reason.
    God's case against all men. 3:9-20
    God's case against all godlessness.
    1:18-32
    God's case against the Jew or religion-
    ist. 2:17-29
    God's case against the moralist. 2:1-16
Results. Severe punishments. Four **p**.
    2:6-10
Surety of.
    Discussed. 2:6-10
    Man is without excuse. 1:18-23
    Verses. List of. 1:18; 2:6-20; 2:16;
    3:5-8
Why God **j**.
    Because love requires **j**. 3:5-8
    Discussed. 1:18-23; 2:6-10; 2:11-15
      World's need to get right with God.
      1:18-3:20
    God has a case against all men. 3:9-20
    God has a case against godlessness
    and wickedness. 1:18-32
    God has a case against the moralist,
    the self-righteous. 2:1-16
    God has a case against the religionists.
    2:17-29
    Men love evil. 1:18-32

JUDICIAL BLINDNESS & JUDGMENT
Discussed. 1:24; 11:7-10

JUST - JUSTICE
Misconception - Error of. Thinking God
    is love & not **j**. 3:5-8
Promise of. At the final judgment. 2:2-5

JUSTIFICATION
Depth of. Discussed. 5:6-11
Discussed. 1:17
Example of.
    Abraham. 4:9; 4:17-25
    David. 4:6-8
How man is **j**.
    By faith & not ritual. 4:9-12
    By faith. Proven by logic. 4:1-8
    By God & God alone. 3:24; 3:25
    By the death of Christ. 5:6-11
    By the Spirit of God. 8:2-4
Meaning. 4:22; 5:1
    Seen in Abraham. 4:1-25; 4:1-3; 4:9-12
Need for. World needs to get right with
    God. 3:21-5:21
Proves. God's righteousness & justice.
    3:25-26
Results of.
    Five **r**. 5:1-5
    Frees from the law. 7:4
Wrong way to seek **j**.
    By law or works. 3:27-31; 4:1-8;
    4:13-16
    By ritual. 4:9-12
Verses. List of. 5:1

KILLING (See **MURDER**)
Discussed. 13:9

KIND - KINDNESS
Duty. To be **k**. 12:9-10

KINGDOM OF GOD
Duty. To be the concern of believers.
    14:16-18
Nature of. Righteousness, peace, & joy.
    14:16-18

KNOWLEDGE
Meaning. 15:14
Of man. Without understanding of God &
    reality. 3:10-12

LAW
Deliverance from.
    By Christ's death. 7:4
    By faith & justification. 4:13-16
Described as.
    Law of faith. Discussed. 3:27
    Of evil. Meaning. 7:21-23
    Of "inward man." 7:21-23
    Of righteousness. Christ ended the
    law. Three ways. 10:4
    Of sin. Meaning. 7:21-23; 7:25
    Of "Spirit & Life." Meaning. 8:2-4
    Of "the mind." 7:21-23
    Of works. Discussed. 3:27
    "Oldness of the letter." 7:6
Duty. To be obedient, not a hearer of the
    l. 2:11-15
Fulfilled by Christ. 3:31; 8:3
Nature.
    Holy, just, & good. 7:12
    Is established, upheld by faith. 3:31
    Is spiritual. 4:14
Purpose of.
    Discussed. 7:7-13
    Fivefold. 3:19-20
    Reveals sin. 7:7
    To arouse sin. 7:5; 7:8
    To bring or work wrath. 4:14-15
    To point out sin, transgression. 4:14-15;
    5:19-21; 5:20; 7:5
    To reveal man's depravity. 3:9-20
    To stop boasting. 3:19-20
Relation to believers.
    Believers are free from the law. 7:1-25
    "Dead" to believers. 7:1-6
Relation to man.
    Not charged when there is no law.
    5:13
    Two positions of **l**. to man. 7:1-6
Results. Voids faith; brings wrath; points
    out sin. 4:14-15
Vs. faith. Discussed. 4:13-16
Vs. grace.
    Believer is under grace, not **l**. Mean-
    ing. 6:14-15
    Christ ended the law. Three ways.
    10:4
Weakness & powerlessness of the **l**.
    Arouses sin. 7:5; 7:8
    Being "under **l**." Pressure, tension,
    discouraged, defeated. 6:14-15
    Cannot give the reward nor fulfill the
    promise of God. 4:13
    Causes sin to dominate a person. 6:14-15
    Discussed. Eleven points. 7:7-13
    Does not produce righteousness. 3:21-22
    Does not receive an inheritance. 4:13-16

Is against man. 3:19-20
Is "alive" or "active" to the unbeliever.
    7:1-6
Is excluded, voided by faith. 3:27-31
Is overcome by the Spirit. 8:2-4
Threefold **w**. 4:14-15
Two positions of **l**. to man. 7:1-6
Wrong way to seek justification. 4:13-16

LEADERSHIP
Gift of. Discussed. 12:6-8

LEGALISM
Discussed. Questionable social activities.
    14:1-23

LIBERTY, CHRISTIAN
Believers.
    Are freed from condemnation. 8:1-17
    Are freed from sin. 6:1-23
    Are freed from the law. 7:1-25
    Discussed. 6:14-15; 14:1-23
    Shall be freed from struggling & suf-
    fering. 8:1-39
Creation. Shall be set free from bondage.
    8:18-27
Questionable social activities. Discussed.
    14:1-12
Vs. license. 6:1

LICENSE
Meaning. Is not love. 3:5-8
To sin. Discussed. 6:1; 6:14-23

LIE - LYING
Discussed. 13:9
Kinds of. Six **k**. 13:9

LIFE
Described as.
    A law. 8:2-4
    Abundant life. Of grace & salvation.
    5:15-18
Duty. To live by the power of the Spirit.
    8:1-17
Kinds of.
    A new life. 6:3-5
    Spiritual. 8:5-8
Nature. Opposite of sin & death. 8:2-4
Source. Holy Spirit & His power. 8:1-17
Victorious. By the power of Spirit. 8:1-17

LIGHT
Armor of. Discussed. 13:12

LIKENESS
Meaning. 8:29

LOGIC
Proves that faith alone justifies a man.
    4:1-8

LOST, THE
Duty toward. Blood of the **l**. are upon the
    hands of believers. 10:14-15

LOVE
Acts of. Listed. Works no ill to one's
    neighbor. 13:10
Duty.
    To love neighbor as self. 13:8-10
    To love with kindness. 12:9-10
    To love without hypocrisy. 12:9-10
    To owe nothing to anyone but love.
    13:8

INDEX

Importance of.
Embraces all the commandments.
13:8-10
Fulfills all the law. 13:8-10
Misconceptions - Errors of. Thinking
God is l. & not just. 2:2-5; 3:5-8
Nature. Requires justice & judgment.
2:2-5; 3:5-8

LUCIUS
Relative of Paul. 16:21

LUSTS (See **HOMOSEXUAL**)
Discussed. 1:24-25; 1:26-27
Meaning. 1:24-25

MALICE
Meaning. 1:29

MALICIOUSNESS (See **DEPRAVITY**)

MALIGNITY (See **MALICE**)

MAN
Achievements of. Discussed. 3:27; 3:28
Case against.
All men. 3:9-20
Godlessness and wickedness of **m.**
1:18-23; 1:24-32
The moralist. 2:1-16
The religionist. 2:17-29
Deliverance.
By faith & justification. 4:1-25
By not continuing in sin. 6:11-13
What God has done for man. 5:6-11
Depravity.
Abandoned by God. 1:24-32
Proven by nature & law. 3:9-20
Rejects the evidence within & without.
1:19; 1:20
Sinful. Utterly s. 3:9-20; cp. 1:18-3:8
Under sin. 1:18-3:20
Duty. Determines his own fate. 8:12-13
Errors.
Creates own gods. 1:22-23; 1:24-25
Deceived. 3:1-8
Objects. Several objections. 3:1-8
Rejects the evidence of God. 1:19;
1:20
Misconception of. Thinks man is basi-
cally good. 2:2-5
Nature.
Are sinners, ungodly & enemies of
God. 5:6-11
Depraved. 3:9-20
Inner witness to God & righteousness.
Threefold. 2:11-15
Interrelated & interconnected with his
world. 8:19-22
Is "sold as a slave to sin." 7:14-17
Is unspiritual, carnal. 7:14-17
Misconception of. Thinks man is basi-
cally good. 2:2-5
Outward vs. inward form. 12:2
Short of God's glory. 7:14-17; 7:18-20
Sinful, depraved. Discussed. 7:14-17;
7:18-20
Slave to sin. 3:9
Struggles for deliverance. 8:28-39
Need of. How to be right with God.
3:21-26
Problem.
Human nature cannot solve sin prob-
lem. 7:14-17

Human will cannot solve sin problem.
7:18-20
Relationship with God. Ways all men are
r. to God. 10:12
Spirit of. Can live forever. 8:10-11
State of.
A reprobate, depraved mind. 1:18-31
Abandoned by God. 1:24-32
Depraved. 1:24-32
Enemy of God. 5:10-11
Enslaved by sin. 1:24-32
Sinner. 5:8-9
Under wrath of God. 1:18; 2:8; 5:9
Without strength, ungodly. 5:6-7

MERCY
Duty. To seek God for **m.** 9:15-18
Gift of. Discussed. 12:6-8

MIND
Discussed. 12:2
How to control. Discussed. 12:2
Law of. Meaning. 7:21-23
New **m.** Renewed by Jesus Christ. Dis-
cussed. 7:25
Of believer.
Duties. Listed with references. 12:2
Pulled to spiritual things by Holy
Spirit. 8:5-8
Renewed. 8:5-8
Of natural man. Vain, empty, unable to
know God. 1:21
Proves. God's existence. 1:19
Verses. List of. 8:5-8
Vs. carnal **m.**
Discussed. 8:5-8
Verses. List of. 12:2

MINISTERS (See **BELIEVERS; DISCI-
PLES**)
Call - Called.
Discussed. 1:1
To offer people up to God. 15:16
To serve as priests of the gospel.
15:16
Commission - Mission.
Is important in God's plans. 10:14-15
To be enslaved by the gospel. 8:15
To be enslaved to Christ. 1:1-7
Discussed. The messenger or minister of
God. 15:14-21
Duty.
Discussed. 15:14-21; 15:22-33
Not to boast in self, but in Christ.
15:17-19
To be an instrument in God's hands.
15:17-19
To be unashamed of the gospel. 1:16-17
To serve & minister. Verses. List of. 1:1
To talk about Christ, not self-
achievements. 15:14
To treat one's congregation gra-
ciously. 15:14
To walk before one's congregation in
humility. 15:14

MINISTRY - MINISTERING
Call to. Discussed. 1:1
Discussed. 15:22-23
Duty.
To bear the weaknesses of the weak.
15:1-3
To identify with, show interest. 12:15
To minister, not judge & criticize. 2:1
To meet the needs of the world. 13:9

To practice hospitality. 12:13
To receive & help weak brother. 14:1-2
Gift of. Discussed. 12:6-8

MISERY
Cause.
Seeking God by law. 6:14-15
Sin, oppression, war. 3:15-18

MISSION - MISSIONS (See **EVANGEL-
ISM**)
Duty.
Are saved to obey & to lead others to
obey. 1:5
To have a world-wide vision. 15:22-33
To reach city-dwellers & religionists.
10:14-15
To reach pioneer areas. 15:20-21
Essentials. Fourfold. 10:14-15

MONEY
Borrowing. Discussed. 13:8

MORALIST, THE
Discussed. 2:1-16
Judgment of. 2:1-16
Misconception of.
Thinks God is too good to judge.
2:20-5
Thinks man is basically good. 2:2-5

MORALITY
Need for. In midst of immoral, cesspool
society. 1:8

MORTIFY (See **PUT TO DEATH**)

MURDER
Discussed. 13:9
Is nature of man. 3:15-18
Meaning. 1:29

MYSTERY OF CHRIST
Discussed. 16:26

NATURE
Deliverance from. Shall be delivered
from corruption. 8:19-22
Discussed. 8:19-22
State of. Is corruptible; suffering under
corruption. 8:19-22
What **n.** reveals & shows. Reveals God.
1:20

NEEDS - NECESSITIES
Duty. To meet **n.** as world missions go
forth. 15:22-33
Verses. List of. 8:34

NEGLECT
Of duty. Knowing, but not doing. 9:4

NEW CREATION
Meaning. Seen in Abraham. 4:1-25

NEW LIFE (See **NEW MAN**)
How to receive. By the resurrection of
Christ. 6:3-5
Results.
Changes masters. 6:17-18
Frees from the law. 7:4

NEW MAN (See **NEW PERSON**)

Deliverance from sin. 6:17-18; 7:14-17
  Fivefold. 1:16
  Swaps sin for God. 6:17-18
  Steps involved in s. 10:16-17
  Who is s. Everyone who calls on the name of the Lord. 10:13

SANCTIFICATION
Discussed. 7:14-25
Of believers.
  Strong vs. weak **b.** 14:1-23
  Struggle for **s.** 7:14-25
  Way for **b.** to be free from sin. 6:1-23
Principles of. Discussed. 14:23
Questionable functions. Discussed. 14:1-23

SATAN
Defeat of. By believer. God uses feet to crush Satan. 16:20

SCRIPTURES (See **WORD OF GOD**)
Duty. To study. 15:4
Inspiration of. Discussed. 1:1-4
Message of. Discussed. 1:1-4
Purpose of - Why God gave the Scriptures. For our learning & to stir us. 15:4
Results. A strong fellowship--if study the Scriptures. 15:4
View of. Paul's **v.** 1:1-7

SEAL
Of Holy Spirit. Guarantees, assures the believer's hope. 5:3-5; 5:5

SECOND COMING (See **JESUS CHRIST**, Return)

SECOND PLACE
Called to serve in second place. 16:21; 16:22

SECURITY
False **s.** Caused by. Stumbling & sleeping. 11:6-10
Of believer. Discussed. 8:28-39
Source. Jesus Christ. 8:34

SEED, THE
Promised to Abraham. 4:1-25

SEEK - SEEKING
Of God. None **s.** God. 3:10-12
Of what. Utopia; life; a deliverer. 10:6-7

SELF-CENTERED - SELF-CENTEREDNESS
Discussed. 3:27; 3:28

SELF-CONFIDENCE (See **SELF-SUFFICIENCY; SELF-RIGHTEOUSNESS**)

SELF-DENIAL
Duty. To count self dead to sin. 6:1-10; 6:11-13; 6:14-23

SELF-GLORYING (See **BOASTING**)

SELF-RIGHTEOUS - SELF-RIGHTEOUSNESS
Discussed. 2:1; 2:2-5; 3:27; 3:28
Judgment of. Four facts. 2:1-16
Misconception of.
  Thinks God is too good to judge. 2:2-5; 3:5-8
  Thinks man is basically good. 2:2-5; 3:5-8

SELF-SEEKING
Meaning. 2:8
Verses. List of. 2:8

SELF-SUFFICIENCY (See **SELF-RIGHTEOUSNESS**)
Discussed. 2:1-16

SELFISH - SELFISHNESS
Describes. Sinful nature. 3:10-12

SENSELESS
Without **s.** Meaning. 1:31; 3:10-12

SEPARATION
Principles to govern. Discussed. 14:1-23
Questionable functions. Discussed. 14:1-23

SERVANT
Discussed. 1:1

SERVE - SERVICE (See **MINISTRY - MINISTERING**)
Call. To serve in second place. 16:21; 16:22
Described. As *service ministries.* 16:22
Discussed. 1:1; 1:9
Duty.
  To **s.** God & not sin. 6:16-23
  To **s.** the Lord diligently. 12:11
Meaning. 1:9
Stirred - Motivated by.
  Jesus Christ. 1:1-7
  The gospel. 1:8-15

SERVICE MINISTRIES
Described. 12:6-8

SEXUAL IMMORALITY
Meaning. 13:13

SEXUAL IMPURITY
Meaning. 1:24-25

SHAMEFUL LUSTS
Meaning. 1:26-27

SHEKINAH GLORY
Discussed. 9:4
History of. 9:4
Meaning. 9:4

SIN
Acts - Behavior of.
  Abandoning God. 1:24
  Arrogance. 1:30
  Boastful. 1:30
  Choosing **s.** over God. 1:24
  Debauchery. 13:13
  Depravity. 1:24-32
  Discussed. 1:18-32; 3:9-20
    The moralists. 2:1-16
    The religionists. 2:17-29
  Disobedient to parents. 1:30
  Dissension. 13:13
  Faithless. 1:30
  God haters. 1:30
  Heartless. 1:31
  Homosexuality, unnatural affection. 1:26-27
  Insolent. 1:30
  Invent evil. 1:30
  Lusts. 1:24-25
  Rebellion against God. 1:18; 2:8; 5:1; 5:10-11
  Reprobate, depraved mind. 1:28-31

Ruthless. 1:31
  Senseless. 1:31
  Sexual impurity. 1:24-25
  Slanderers. 1:30
  Thoughts, not just acts. 2:1; 8:6-7
  Wickedness. 1:29
Caused by.
  Adam, his sin. 5:12-21
  Breaking the law. 7:7-13
  Depravity. Corruptible nature inherited from Adam & parents. 5:12-21
Deliverance from.
  By Jesus Christ. 6:2-5; 7:25
  By grace, not by law. Discussed. 6:14-15
  By putting to death the **s.** of the body. 8:12-13
  By power of Spirit. 8:1-17
  Condemned by Christ. 8:3
  Counteracted by Christ. 5:12-21
  How to conquer **s.** & live victoriously. 6:1-10; 6:11-13; 6:14-23
Described.
  As a disease & a master. 6:13
  As a principle. 7:17, 20
  As body of **s.** Meaning. 6:6-7
  As the "law of sin." 7:21-23
  As universal. Discussed. 3:22-23; 5:12-14
  License. 6:1-2
  Ultimate act against God. Insurrection & high treason. 5:12; 8:34
Discussed. 3:19-20
Exposed.
  By the law. 7:7-13
  Known to God. 2:2-5; 2:16
  The moralist. 2:1-16
  The religionists. 2:17-29
License to. (See **LICENSE**)
Lists of. 1:29-31; 3:9-20
Results - Penalty.
  A helpless, unceasing struggle. 7:14-17
  Abandoned by God. 1:24-32
  Condemnation. World's need to get right with God. 1:18-3:20
  Death. 5:12-21; 7:9-10; 7:13
    Is **d.** too great a penalty for sin? 5:12
  Deceives. Three ways. 7:11
  Despair, misery, hopelessness. 6:14-15
  Enslaves. 6:14-23; 6:16; 6:19-20
  Guilty of sin. 3:9-20
Vs. liberty. 6:1-2

SINFUL NATURE
Discussed. 7:14-17; 7:18-20
Duty.
  To control by struggling against. 8:23-27
  To mortify, put to death. 8:12-13
Meaning. 7:5; 7:14-17; 7:18-20; 8:5-8
Vs. the Spirit. Discussed. 8:1-17

SLANDERERS
Meaning. 1:30

SLEEP, SPIRITUAL (See **SLUMBER, SPIRITUAL**)

SLOTHFUL - SLOTHFULNESS (See **ZEAL, LACKING**)

SLUMBER, SPIRITUAL
Duty. To awaken out of **s.** 13:11-14

SOCIAL ACTIVITIES
Questionable functions. Discussed. 14:1-23

INDEX

INDEX

VENGEANCE
Duty. Not to take **v.** Three reasons.
12:19-21

VICTORIOUS LIVING
By power of Spirit. 8:1-17

VILE AFFECTIONS (See **SHAMEFUL LUSTS**)

VISION
Duty. To have a world-wide vision. 1:10-13
Need for. World-wide vision. 15:22-33

WALK, BELIEVERS (See **BELIEVER, WALK**)

WANTONNESS (See **DEBAUCHERY**)

WANDERERS
Describes. Depraved nation. 3:10-12

WAR (See **MURDER**)
Caused by. Nature of man. 3:15-18
Duty.
Not to allow license & injustice. 12:18
To live in peace if possible. 12:18
Sin of. Great **s.** of man. 3:15-18

WEAK - WEAKNESS
Of man. Cannot save himself. 5:6-7

WHISPERERS (See **GOSSIPS**)

WICKED - WICKEDNESS
Judgment of. (See **JUDGMENT; PUNISHMENT**)
Meaning. 1:29

WICKEDNESS
Meaning. 1:18; 1:29; 2:8
Warning. God's case against. 1:18-23

WISDOM, WORLDLY
Claimed - Professed. By men. 1:22-23
Results. Idolatry. 1:22-23

WITHOUT STRENGTH (See **POWERLESS**)

WITNESS - WITNESSING
Duty.
Are obligated, indebted to **w.** 1:14-15
To be zealous. 10:1-3
Example. Paul's **e.** 10:1-3
Fact. Blood of all the lost is upon our hands. 9:1-3
Fear of. Reasons. Intellectual shame & social shame. 1:16

WITNESS, FALSE (See **LYING**)
Commandment against. 13:9
Discussed. 13:9

WORD OF GOD (See **SCRIPTURES**)
Privilege of. Great **p.** to have access to the Word. 3:1-2
Surety of. Never voided, broken. 3:3-5; 9:6

WORKS
Nature of **w.** Is a law, a principle. 3:27
Vs. faith.
Discussed. 4:1-8; 4:9-12
Illust. in Abraham. 4:1-3
Weakness - powerlessness - insufficiency of. Cannot make a person acceptable to God. 4:1-8

WORLD
Case against.
God's **c.** against all men. 3:9-20
God's **c.** against all ungodliness & wickedness. 1:18-23; 1:24-32
God's **c.** against the moralist. 2:1-16
God's **c.** against the religionists. 2:17-29
Objection of religionist. 3:1-8
Deliverance from.
God's glorious **p.** for world. 11:33-36
How the **w.** is saved. 10:12-17
To be recreated. 8:19-22
W. needs to get right with God. 1:18-3:20
W. shall be delivered from struggle. 8:18-27
Way for **w.** to be right with God. 3:21-5:21
Nature of.
Interrelated & interconnected with man. 8:19-22
Reveals God. 1:20
State - Condition of.
Corruptible - struggling & suffering. 8:19-22
Discussed. 12:2
Need to get right with God. 1:18-3:20
Passes away. Discussed. 12:2
The way for the **w.** to be right with God. 3:21-5:21
Verses. List of. 12:2

WORLDLINESS
Deliverance from. By not being conformed to. 12:2
Discussed. 12:2

WORSHIP
True. Discussed. 9:4

WRATH
How God shows **w.** 1:24-32
Meaning. 2:8
Subjects of **w.** 1:18
Verses. List of. 1:18
Why God shows **w.** 1:18-23

ZEAL
Duty.
Not to lag in **z.** 12:11
To keep your spiritual fervor. 12:11
To be willing to suffer to reach people. 9:1-3
To preach the gospel. 1:14-15

ZEAL, LACKING
Discussed. 13:11-14
Duty.
Not to lack **z.** 12:11
To awaken out of sleep. 13:11-12
Meaning. 12:11

PURPOSE STATEMENT

LEADERSHIP MINISTRIES WORLDWIDE

exists to equip ministers, teachers, and laymen in their
understanding, preaching, and teaching of God's Word
by publishing and distributing worldwide
The Preacher's Outline & Sermon Bible®
and related *Outline* Bible materials,
to reach & disciple men, women, boys, and girls for Jesus Christ.

•MISSION STATEMENT•

1. To make the Bible so understandable - its truth so clear and plain - that men and women everywhere, whether teacher or student, preacher or hearer, can grasp its Message and receive Jesus Christ as Savior; and…

2. To place the Bible in the hands of all who will preach and teach God's Holy Word, verse by verse, precept by precept, regardless of the individual's ability to purchase it.

The *Outline* Bible materials have been given to LMW for printing and especially distribution worldwide at/below cost, by those who remain anonymous. One fact, however, is as true today as it was in the time of Christ:

• The Gospel is free, but the cost of taking it is not •

LMW depends on the generous gifts of Believers with a heart for Him and a love and burden for the lost. They help pay for the printing, translating, and placing *Outline* Bible materials in the hands and hearts of those worldwide who will present God's message with clarity, authority and understanding beyond their own.

LMW was incorporated in the state of Tennessee in July 1992 and received IRS 501(c) 3 non-profit status in March 1994. LMW is an international, nondenominational mission organization. All proceeds from USA sales, along with donations from donor partners, go 100% into under-writing our translation and distribution projects of *Outline* Bible materials to preachers, church & lay leaders, and Bible students around the world.

Box 21310 - Chattanooga, TN 37424 • (423) 855-2181 • FAX (423) 855-8616
• E-Mail - outlinebible@compuserve.com — www.outlinebible.org •

Equipping God's Servants Worldwide

1. **PAYMENT PLANS.** Convenient and affordable ways to get/use your FullSet with easy payments.

2. **NEW TESTAMENT.** In 14 volumes. Deluxe version 3-ring binders. Also: SoftBound Set, 3 volume set, and NIV edition. All on 1 CD-ROM disc.

3. **OLD TESTAMENT.** In process; 1 volume releases about every 6-8 months, in sequence.

4. **THE MINISTERS HANDBOOK.** Acclaimed as a "must-have" for every minister or Christian worker. Outlines more than 400 verses into topics like Power, Victory, Encouragement, Security, Restoration, etc. Discount for quantities.

5. **THE TEACHER'S OUTLINE & STUDY BIBLE™.** Verse-by-verse study & teaching; 45 minute lesson or session. Ideal for study, small groups, classes, even home schooling. Each book also offers a STUDENT JOURNAL for study members.

6. **OUTLINE BIBLE CD-ROM.** Includes all current volumes and books; Preacher, Teacher, and Minister Handbook. 1 disc. WORDsearch STEP format. Also 50+ Bible study tools unlockable on same disc. **FREE Downloads - www.outlinebible.org**

7. THE **OUTLINE.** Quarterly newsletter to all users and owners of *POSB*. Complimentary.

8. **LMW AGENT PLAN.** An exciting way any user sells *OUTLINE* materials & earns a second income.

9. **DISTRIBUTION.** Our ultimate mission is to provide *POSB* volumes & materials to preachers, pastors, national church leaders around the world. This is especially for those unable to purchase at U.S. price. USA sales gain goes 100% to provide volumes at affordable prices within the local economy.

10. **TRANSLATIONS.** Korean, Russian, & Spanish are shipping first volumes — Others in-process: Hindi, Tamil, Telugu, Chinese, French, German, Finnish.

11. **FUNDING PARTNERS.** To cover the cost of all the translations, plus print, publish, and distribute around the world is a multi million dollar project.

    Church-to-Church Partners send *Outline* Bible books to their missionaries, overseas church leaders, Bible Institues and seminaries...at special prices.

12. **REFERRALS.** Literally thousands (perhaps even you!) first heard of *POSB* from a friend. Now Referral Credit pays $16.00 for each new person who orders from a customer's Referral.

13. **CURRICULUM & COPYRIGHT.** Permission may be given to copy specific portions of *POSB* for special group situations. Write/FAX for details.

9/98

For Information about any of the above, kindly FAX, E-Mail, Call, or Write

Please PRAY 1 Minute/Day for LMW!

PO Box 21310, Chattanooga, TN 37424 • (423) 855-2181 • FAX (423) 855-8616
• E-Mail - outlinebible@compuserve.com — www.outlinebible.org •

Sharing

The
OUTLINED
BIBLE

With the World!